Contents

10   Ports of Call   334

Maps & Illustrations

An Invitation to the Reader

Please tell us about your cruising experiences so we can share the information with your fellow travelers in upcoming editions. If you were disappointed or pleased with a recommendation, let us know. Please write to:

Darwin Porter & Danforth Prince
Frommer's Caribbean Cruises '97
Macmillan Travel
1633 Broadway
New York, NY 10019

An Additional Note

Please be advised that travel information is subject to change at any time—and this is especially true of prices. We therefore suggest that you write or call ahead for confirmation when making your travel plans. The authors, editors, and publisher cannot be held responsible for the experiences of readers while traveling. Your safety is important to us, however, so we encourage you to stay alert and be aware of your surroundings. Keep a close eye on cameras, purses, and wallets, all favorite targets of thieves and pickpockets.

WHAT THE STAR MEANS

✪ Frommer's Favorites

Restaurants, attractions, and entertainment you shouldn't miss.

What's New in Sailing

The good news for 1998 and 1999 is that new ships are being launched in the Caribbean at an unprecedented rate, a development that's led to increased competition and, consequently, the lowest cruise fares in decades. Imagine it: Not only do you get the warm weather, the sunshine, the sea breezes, and the colorful and exotic Caribbean ports of call at an amazingly low price, but you get to experience all of this aboard the newest, most remarkable and innovative cruise ships ever built.

As if this weren't reason enough for a winter visit, cruise lines aren't stopping there. They're seeking new ports of call, such as the Grenadines (administered by the island nation of St. Vincent), and even pouring millions into developing private islands for their passengers, as Disney is currently doing.

We know what you're feeling after reading that: You want to grab your hat, run to the nearest travel agent, and book a cruise *now*. Hold on for a minute. If you're looking for the best value, you'll want to consult a cruise specialist instead of a regular travel agent. The industry today is so intricate and the market so complex that only the specialists know all the deals, and even they have difficulty keeping up. A regular travel agent who's busy sending people to Europe, Asia, or Disney World can't give full attention to the fast-changing developments, offers, discounts, and deals in the cruise industry. And there are deals: The main ones continue to be free airfares, twofers, and free passage for kids. They aren't always available, but they're popping up with greater frequency as more and more berths become available.

The number of passengers taking cruises has increased four-fold since the early '80s, but how long that trend will continue is anybody's guess. Even the experts disagree, but there's no denying that the cruise lines are taking those statistics to heart, and building new ships to meet demand. Between December 1996 and spring 1997, seven new ships with a total weekly capacity of 13,500 double-occupancy berths sailed the Caribbean for the first time, and by 1998 and 1999, a record number of ships will have set their compasses for the region, among them the biggest megaships ever. Some people maintain that there are too many ships currently afloat, and that any more would be superfluous, but whether the market is becoming glutted or not remains to be seen. Obviously, cruise lines such as Disney and Celebrity don't think so—with the billions they're putting into development, they must be pretty confident. Still, all this new competition means that cruise lines will have to increase their patronage by some 20% to fill all the new berths they've created and will soon create, which means adding another million or more passengers annually—a daunting challenge no matter how you look at it.

Today's cruiser is faced with an almost overwhelming selection of ships, and deciding which one is for you can be harder than ever before. Add the plethora of deals that are being offered and you have quite a complex puzzle indeed. With this in mind, we've made the reviews in this guide particularly candid, and provided lots of guidance to help you make your vacation decisions. It's like being given a dessert menu that lists 50 equally tasty treats; sometimes you have to ask a friend, "What do *you* think I should have?"

In 1996, the typical cost of a Caribbean cruise ranged from $710 to $800 per person. Many fares, of course, were lower than these, and others much higher, especially if a passenger sailed aboard a luxury vessel such as *Seabourn Pride.* If fares remain approximately at this level in 1998 and 1999, give or take $50 or $100 here or there, it will mean that cruise ships are filling their berths. However, if there is a dramatic drop in fares—say, if the typical cruise to the West Indies costs $500 to $600 per person—it means that ships are sailing at only partial capacity, and that cruise lines are having to scramble to fill berths and cover the mounting costs of doing business. This could be a disaster in the making for the Caribbean cruise industry.

If the Caribbean Sea in the lifetime of this edition proves too crowded, we predict a major repositioning of cruise ships to other areas where the competition isn't as intense. That would mean the Pacific and South America, as well as Mexico and the Panama Canal.

NEW DECKS TO TREAD

The industry buzz right now is centered on the exciting new ships plying the Caribbean's waters, including **Carnival's** *Fascination,* launched in 1995, and *Imagination,* launched in 1996. *Imagination* is praised for its use of mythical or classical themes in its decor. (Its library, for example, contains copies of the columns Bernini added to St. Peter's Basilica in Rome.) *Fascination,* on the other hand, borrows heavily from Broadway and Hollywood movie-star legends for its ambience.

Even bigger excitement in 1996 was the launching of the 3,400-passenger Carnival *Destiny,* the first cruise ship to top the 100,000-ton mark. Carnival fervently believes in carrying a winning ticket as far as it will go, and already has two other Fantasy-Class vessels under commission from the Kvaerner Masa shipyard in Helsinki, Finland, birthplace of each of the half-dozen Fantasy-Class ships previously launched by the line. After much insider speculation, Carnival, like any other proud parent, announced the new ships' names and weights: *Elation* and *Paradise,* two bouncing baby cruise liners, both with a birth weight of 70,000 tons (the equivalent of the line's other Fantasy-Class vessels) and both scheduled for launching in 1998. Specifics about their decorative themes have not been announced, but you can be sure they'll toe the line of fantasy-inducing whimsy so prevalent aboard Carnival's other ships.

What about a mate for the 100,000-ton Carnival *Destiny?* At this writing, at a massive shipyard called Fincantieri, near Trieste, Italy, Carnival is bolting together the *Carnival Triumph,* a huge vessel that will eventually be designated as the twin of the *Destiny.* It will be the largest passenger liner ever built, breaking all molds, towering 14 decks with a passenger load of 3,400. The 450 staterooms that boast private balconies will be an industry first.

In 1995, **Celebrity** garnered praise for its *Century,* which it planned to keep in the Caribbean year-round. It was the largest vessel ever built by Chandris—70,000 tons and carrying 1,750 passengers—and its art collection has been called a "museum at sea." But *Century*'s sibling ship, *Galaxy,* launched in 1996, goes it one better. Celebrity's CEO has claimed—and justifiably so, we think—that this is not a ship for the '90s but for the year 2000 and beyond. Among its special features are a main atrium with a cascading waterfall and an AquaSpa that's one of the best and most spacious afloat.

Holland America has signaled its intention to remain competitive by launching the 1996 *Veendam,* weighing in at 55,451 tons and carrying 1,264 passengers, but even more industry excitement was created by the announcement that the line's circa-1958 flagship, *Rotterdam V,* will be replaced in the autumn of 1997 with *Rotterdam VI,* which will become the largest, fastest, and most glamorous of the HAL fleet.

In 1997, **Princess** launched its *Dawn Princess,* a 77,000-ton ship accommodating 1,950 passengers, as part of its Grand Class series. *Dawn Princess* is the line's most exciting ship to date, with soaring double atriums and more than the usual amount of space devoted to public interiors. Intimacy is enhanced by there being two separate, smaller dining rooms instead of a single massive one, and the meals display greater culinary finesse than is evident on other Princess vessels. It's a similar vessel to *Sun Princess,* launched in 1995.

But even this grand ship will be dwarfed in early 1998 with the launching of the 105,000-ton *Grand Princess,* costing $400 million and boasting six decks, with a passenger capacity of 2,600. Instead of a ship, it'll be more like a floating resort, with new and innovative features including a "Blue-Screen Room," where passengers can be filmed and then merged into pre-existing footage, using the technology popularized by the movie *Forrest Gump.*

In the summer of 1996, **Costa Cruises** made a big splash with the launching of its 76,000-ton *CostaVictoria,* built for $300 million and able to carry 1,950 passengers. The even bigger *CostaOlympia,* at 78,000 tons, is slated for launching late in 1998.

More big news is coming out of **Royal Caribbean Cruises** with the launching in 1997 and 1998 of its *Enchantment of the Seas, Rhapsody of the Seas,* and *Vision of the Seas,* all look-alikes. These ships are the last of the line's "Project Vision" series, which also includes the beautiful *Splendour of the Seas* and *Grandeur of the Seas,* each launched in 1996. Splendor even offers a top-deck, 18-hole miniature golf course.

In 1996, **Disney Cruise Line** began accepting bookings for two ships that will shake up the family cruise industry: *Disney Magic* and *Disney Wonder,* both to be launched in 1998. We offer you a preview of what to expect in this edition of *Caribbean Cruises;* stay tuned for further developments in the next edition.

MEGA, MORE MEGA & THE MAGRODOME

More and more verandas are appearing on the new ships, along with enlarged staterooms and more cabins accessible to persons with disabilities. Suites (which generally get booked up way in advance) have received more attention on the newer vessels, becoming even more opulent than before. Public areas are more lavish, too. "Theaters at sea," with revolving stages and hydraulic orchestra pits, are now commonplace, along with retractable "magrodomes" over swimming pools, shutting out rain and fog but leaving views of the sea unimpeded. Nightclubs set 15 floors above sea level (and accessible via glass-enclosed walkways) have made decors fanciful and fantastic. Some ships have floating 18-hole golf courses, complete with water hazards, tropical foliage, and windmills. Interior decors are less garish and more subtle. For example, Princess is using granite, etched glass, leather, and varnished hardwoods in its newest megaships, instead of neon and chrome.

As a drawback, many of these megaships are so very mega that they're generally locked into the major ports of call that most experienced cruisers have already seen, including San Juan, Dutch St. Maarten, and St. Thomas. They often can't go to the smaller and more remote islands, including the Grenadines and the British Virgin Islands. Likewise, many of them are too wide to pass through the Panama Canal, which for our purposes is just fine, as it will keep them in the Caribbean.

THE LITTLE SHIPS VS. THE BEHEMOTHS

In all this industry excitement of more "mega," it would appear that the smaller ships have been drowned at sea by the behemoths. Not so. To assure their survival, smaller lines such as Windstar are fighting back and reaching younger markets less interested in glitter and glitz and more in ecosensitive tours and "authentic" sailing. This places them at polar opposites to the megaships. **Windstar's** two ships, *Wind Star* and *Wind Spirit,* combine the best of 19th-century clipper design with the best of modern yacht engineering. The **Star Clipper** line, with its *Star Clipper* and *Star Flyer,* offers old-fashioned sailing that's undeniably romantic. This is sailing at its best, with only 170 passengers aboard.

Windjammer Barefoot Cruises, although not for everybody, is also a T-shirt-and-shorts adventure in real sailing. On these boats you'll sail to parts of the Caribbean where the megas dare not go, including Montserrat, Les Iles des Saintes, and Dominica.

Finally, **Tall Ship Adventures,** with its *Sir Francis Drake,* is unique in the industry, with its carefully restored sailing craft that cruises some of the Caribbean's most remote ports, including Barbuda (near Antigua) and Norman Cay in the British Virgin Islands.

As 1997 proved, the cruise industry is the most growth-oriented in the world.

Big changes and even grander surprises are on the way. "What surprises?" you ask. Let's say mind-boggling megaships with skyscraper hotels built on the top deck. We've already spied on the plans for such astounding vessels.

LIFE ON A PRIVATE ISLAND (FOR A DAY)

The hottest new land-based idea in the industry involves cruise lines developing their own private islands where passengers can more or less run wild without having to compete with the tourist hordes. The cruise lines either own these islands outright, almost like sovereign states, or else lease from local governments. Their beaches are invariably spectacular and some have wharves that allow megaships to debark passengers even during rough seas; others feature sheltered deepwater coves and tenders that ferry passengers ashore. Millions of dollars have been spent on these miniports of call, whose names tend toward the romantic or evocative: Blue Lagoon Island, Labadee, Great Stirrup Cay, Mayreau Island, Treasure Island, Palm Island, and even Princess Cays. (Can you guess who owns that one?) These emerging ports have been called "recreation dreamlands," and with land and water sports, pristine beaches, and palm-covered shacks serving first-rate food and drink, that's not all cruise-line hype. To keep everything unspoiled, vast sums have been spent on environmentally sensitive waste-disposal systems, and on security as well. Right now, Disney's island in The Bahamas, Castaway Cay, is being readied at a cost of $25 million. It's the biggest of the private islands, and will be open for business when the company launches its three- to four-day cruises from Port Canaveral in 1998.

Before you go building up too much of a Robinson Crusoe fantasy about these islands, a word of temperance: While they're quieter than Magens Beach in

St. Thomas, you'll hardly be alone. Some of these islands, especially those in The Bahamas, might be called "semiprivate," as they're used by more than one shipping line; that is, the island might be private for one ship only on one particular day, or else an island might be divided up with one ship's passengers being dropped off on one side of the island and another ship's cruisers using the other side.

SPRUCING UP THE PORTS OF CALL

All the news isn't being generated at sea or on the private islands; ports of call are also being developed at rates greater than before. Recognizing how lucrative cruise-ship arrivals are, many island nations in the Caribbean are greeting passengers with new and improved port facilities, and businesses by the score are relocating or opening branches near the docks for the convenience of passengers.

The most dramatic change on land is occurring at the port of Miami, which is the largest and busiest cruise-ship port in the world. It's going ahead with its proposed $250 million Maritime Park on a tract of downtown waterfront land on Biscayne Bay. Construction began late in 1996, and the facility should be operating by 1998. When completed, the park will increase Miami's cruise-ship capacity by 40%. Plans call for four more cruise-ship berths plus a three-tier, 250,000-square-foot underground entertainment complex on a 22-acre site abutting Bayside Marketplace, a dining and shopping enclave.

SPRUCING UP THIS BOOK

As a new feature in this year's edition of *Frommer's Caribbean Cruises,* we've included **sample menus** and **sample daily activities calendars** from nearly every line we've profiled. (Some lines, usually the smaller, adventure-oriented ones, don't publish daily calendars.) Paired with our reviews, these should give you some idea of the kind of days and the kind of meals you can expect aboard the various ships. Also, we've expanded our list of cruise-line and cruise-related **Websites** to help you navigate through cyber-waters for even more info. Both of these features can be found in the appendix.

LATE-BREAKING NEWS

Throughout this book you'll find various "Late-Breaking News" features, which we've included to keep you abreast of the newest developments in the cruise industry, updated right to the minute this book went to press. It's a measure of the vitality of the cruise industry in the 90s: New ships come, old ships go, company buys company, and itineraries shift. Generally speaking, though, change is good—it usually means greater competition, and greater competition means you get more for your cruise buck.

So, check out the news, check the cruise Websites in the appendix for headlines from the cruise lines, and pester your travel agent or cruise-booking specialist for any new doings.

Happy hunting, good sailing, and see you next year.

Read This Box! Major Late-Breaking News

Premier, Dolphin & Seawind Merge

Just as this book was going to press (and we mean just as—we had to snatch the thing back from the printer to get this notice in), Cruise Holdings, the company that owns Premier, Dolphin, and Seawind cruise lines, announced that it would be merging the three lines into one, henceforth to sail under a new, unified name—though nobody could yet tell us what that name will be, no matter how much we kicked and screamed. (We think they just haven't thought of one yet—they're not being mean to us, personally.)

The deal is reportedly due to take effect during the fall of 1997, so if you're reading this after that, the ink should be dry and the merger made. Details were not available as to what changes we can expect from the transition, but the buzz seems to be that the new line will attempt to make itself into the "classic cruise ship" alternative to megaship cruising, running a fleet of older, smaller, more "teakwood-and-porthole" style ships and hoping to snag cruisers who want a more human-sized cruising experience than they'd get aboard today's gargantuan vessels.

We tend to think that few if any of these corporate machinations will effect the prospective cruiser in the short term, though it's amusing to imagine a surreal scene in which Dolphin's Hanna-Barbera cartoon characters have to fight it out for shipboard supremacy with Premier's Warner Brothers characters. For those of you who are leaning toward a cruise aboard one of the affected vessels, then, the reviews in this edition of *Caribbean Cruises* will still provide the information you need, and your travel agent or cruise agent can fill in any new info. You can also call the new line at ☎ **800/327-7113.** Tell 'em Frommer's sent you.

Celebrity Has a Suitor

As we go to press, Celebrity Cruises has become a hot property on the cruise line auction block. Rumors flew for several weeks that the line was being courted by several major players, but Royal Caribbean soon emerged as the top dog and issued a statement on July 20th that the two lines had entered into a "definitive agreement" to merge. The deal is reportedly worth $1.3 billion, and, by the year 2000, will create a fleet of twenty ships with a passenger capacity of 38,000. Big. Very big.

We can pretty easily predict the effects of this rampant capitalism for Celebrity's owners (they'll need bigger wallets), but what does it mean to the average prospective Celebrity passenger? Apparently not a heck of a lot: Sources report that the intention of the merger is that Celebrity remain a separate entity under RCCL's corporate banner, much as Holland America is within Carnival.

Majesty also on the Block

Rumor has it that Majesty Cruise Lines may be purchased lock, stock, and barrel by Norwegian Cruise Line and assimilated into the Norwegian fleet. Talks between the two lines were not complete at press time, and so details and final word are not available. However, NCL executive vice president Bruce Nierrenberg did go out of his way to calm prospective Majesty cruisers who might be scared off by the wheeling and dealing. He stressed that, if the deal goes through, his line is "committed to making the operational transition between Majesty and NCL a seamless process to avoid any inconveniences to travel agents or the passengers. There will be no disruption of service whatsoever." Check with your travel agent or cruise agent for up-to-the-minute details on this story.

The Ratings 2

To give you a quick and handy reference to some features of the various cruise ships, and a basis for quick comparison, we present these two very different charts.

The **Frommer's/Cruises, Inc. Annual Passenger Survey** gives you the honest opinions of the best experts around: the passengers who've sailed the vessels. The survey was conducted by Cruises, Inc., of East Syracuse, New York, the second-largest cruise-only travel agency in the United States, and includes the ratings of both first-time and experienced cruisers. The present survey was culled during the first 10 months of 1996.

Here's how it works. A week after Cruises, Inc., passengers return home, they receive a questionnaire asking for feedback on their experience. The questionnaire evaluates the cruise on factors such as onboard service, food, cabin cleanliness and amenities, activities, ship maintenance (interior and exterior), performance of the cabin stewards, and lounge areas.

Based as they are on a limited number of replies from the company's clients, the ratings are entirely subjective and nothing like an official, scientifically conducted poll. But what they do reflect, industry experts say, is whether or not the passenger was successfully matched with the appropriate ship—the all-important ingredient to a successful cruising experience.

We've also compiled the **Ships at a Glance** chart, which should help you locate the ship of your dreams more quickly. This chart summarizes each ship's features and assigns it an overall Frommer's rating based on our evaluation of all the variables. In chapter 9, "The Cruise Lines & Ships," you'll find detailed reviews and rating charts regarding service, dining, cabins, itineraries, recreation and fitness facilities, shopping, the pros and cons of each line, a passenger profile, and more.

Frommer's/Cruises, Inc. Annual Passenger Survey

Ship's Name	Score Given by by First-Time Cruisers	Score Given by Experienced Cruisers	Average Score as Submitted by First-Time & Experienced Cruisers
Amazing Grace	n/a	n/a	n/a
Celebration	84	81	83
Century	96	90	93
Club Med 1 & 2	n/a	n/a	n/a
CostaRomantica	93	88	91
CostaVictoria	n/a	n/a	n/a
Crown Princess	100	86	88
Dawn Princess	n/a	n/a	n/a
Destiny	n/a	n/a	n/a
Dolphin IV	n/a	n/a	n/a
Dreamward	88	85	87
Ecstasy	80	80	80
Enchanted Isle	100	78	89
Fantasy	86	78	82
Fantôme	n/a	n/a	n/a
Fascination	86	82	84
Flying Cloud	n/a	n/a	n/a
Galaxy	n/a	n/a	n/a
Grandeur of the Seas	n/a	n/a	n/a
Horizon	99	89	94
Imagination	89	86	88
Inspiration	n/a	n/a	n/a
IslandBreeze	82	53	68
Leeward	84	84	84
Legend of the Seas	94	95	95
Maasdam	n/a	91	n/a
Majesty of the Seas	90	89	n/a
Mandalay	n/a	n/a	n/a
Mayan Prince	n/a	n/a	n/a
Monarch of the Seas	93	92	n/a
Nantucket Clipper	n/a	n/a	n/a
Niagara Prince	n/a	n/a	n/a
Nieuw Amsterdam	88	81	85
Noordam	89	90	90

Ship's Name	Score Given by First-Time Cruisers	Score Given by Experienced Cruisers	Average Score as Submitted by First-Time & Experienced Cruisers
Nordic Empress	89	88	89
Norway	92	83	88
Norwegian Crown	80	79	80
OceanBreeze	73	76	75
Polynesia	n/a	n/a	n/a
Radisson Diamond	n/a	93	n/a
Regal Empress	n/a	n/a	n/a
Regal Princess	88	90	n/a
Royal Majesty	n/a	92	n/a
Ryndam	92	94	n/a
Sea Goddess I	n/a	n/a	n/a
Sea Goddess II	n/a	n/a	n/a
Seabourn Pride	n/a	75	n/a
SeaBreeze	98	89	n/a
Seaward	86	84	n/a
Seawind Crown	n/a	75	n/a
Sensation	81	84	83
Sir Francis Drake	n/a	n/a	n/a
Sovereign of the Seas	93	95	n/a
Splendour of the Seas	n/a	98	n/a
Star Clipper	n/a	n/a	n/a
Star/Ship Oceanic	90	89	90
Statendam	91	96	94
Stella Solaris	n/a	87	n/a
Sun Princess	95	88	93
Veendam	n/a	n/a	n/a
Westerdam	98	94	96
Wind Spirit	n/a	n/a	n/a
Wind Star	n/a	n/a	n/a
Windward	90	88	89
Yankee Clipper	n/a	n/a	n/a
Yorktown Clipper	n/a	n/a	n/a
Zenith	91	88	90

| The Ships at a Glance | | | | | |
Cruise Ship	Cruise Line	Type of Ship	Gross Tonnage	Type of Cruise	Duration of Cruise (days)
Amazing Grace	Windjammer	Freighter	1,526	Casual	13
Celebration	Carnival	Cruise Liner	47,262	Casual	7
Century	Celebrity	Megaship	70,000	Semiformal	7
Club Med 1 & 2	Club Med	Motor-sail	14,000	Casual	7
CostaRomantica	Costa	Cruise Liner	54,000	Semiformal	7
CostaVictoria	Costa	Megaship	76,000	Semiformal	7
Crown Princess	Princess	Megaship	70,000	Semiformal	10
Dawn Princess	Princess	Megaship	77,000	Semiformal	7
Destiny	Carnival	Supermegaship	101,000	Casual	7
Dolphin IV	Cape Canaveral	Cruise Liner	13,007	Casual	3–4
Dreamward	Norwegian	Cruise Liner	41,000	Casual	7
Ecstacy	Carnival	Megaship	70,367	Casual	3–4
Enchanted Isle	Commodore	Cruise Liner	23,395	Casual	7
Enchantment of the Seas (preview)	Royal Caribbean	Megaship	70,000–75,000	Casual	7
Fantasy	Carnival	Megaship	70,367	Casual	3–4
Fantôme	Windjammer	Schooner	676	Casual	6
Fascination	Carnival	Megaship	70,367	Casual	7
Flying Cloud	Windjammer	Schooner	400	Casual	6
Galaxy	Celebrity	Megaship	77,713	Semiformal	7–17
Grande Caribe (preview)	American Canadian	Coastal Cruiser	99	Casual	12
Grandeur of the Seas	Royal Caribbean	Megaship	74,000	Casual	7
Grand Princess (preview)	Princess	Supermegaship	105,000	Semiformal	n/a
Horizon	Celebrity	Cruise Liner	46,811	Semiformal	7
Imagination	Carnival	Megaship	70,367	Casual	7
Inspiration	Carnival	Megaship	70,367	Casual	7
IslandBreeze	Dolphin	Cruise Liner	38,125	Casual	7
Leeward	Norwegian	Cruise Liner	25,000	Casual	3–4
Legacy (preview)	Windjammer	Schooner	1,121	Casual	n/a
Legend of the Seas	Royal Caribbean	Megaship	69,130	Casual	10–11
Maasdam	Holland America	Cruise Liner	55,451	Semiformal	10–14
Majesty of the Seas	Royal Caribbean	Megaship	73,941	Casual	7
Mandalay	Windjammer	Schooner	420	Casual	6

Passenger Capacity	Passenger/Crew Ratio	Swimming Pools	Casino	Child Care	Fitness Center	Jogging Track	Library	Sauna/Whirlpool	Nightclub/Disco	Shops/Boutiques	Theater/Cinema	Video Arcade	Wheelchair Access (p=partial)	CDC Sanitation Rating	Frommer's Rating
96	2	0					√	√						n/a	6.4
1,486	2.2	2	√	√	√	√	√	√	√	√	√	√	√	87	7.3
1,750	2	2	√	√	√	√	√	√	√	√	√	√	√	90	8.5
386	2.1	2	√		√	√	√	√	√	√	√		p	93/na	8.1
1,356	2	2	√	√	√	√	√	√	√	√	√	√	√	86	8.4
1,950	2.4	2	√	√	√	√	√	√	√	√	√	√	√	94	8.5
1,590	2.3	2	√		√	√	√	√	√	√	√		√	91	7.9
1,950	2.2	3	√	√	√	√	√	√	√	√	√	√	√	n/a	8.6
2,642	2.6	4	√	√	√	√	√	√	√	√	√	√	√	n/a	8.5
692	2.4	1	√	√		√			√	√	√	√	p	95	6.1
1,246	2.6	2	√	√	√	√	√	√	√	√	√	√	√	90	8.4
2,040	2.9	2	√	√	√	√	√	√	√	√	√	√	√	91	7.9
731	2.1	1	√	√	√		√	√	√	√	√	√	p	93	7.8
1,804	2.5	2	√	√	√	√	√	√	√	√	√	√	√	n/a	n/a
2,044	2.9	2	√	√	√	√	√	√	√	√	√	√	√	91	7.9
128	2.3	0						√	√					n/a	6.3
2,040	2.9	2	√	√	√	√	√	√	√	√	√	√	√	88	7.9
74	3.1	0							√					n/a	6.3
1,870	2	2	√	√	√	√	√	√	√	√	√	√	√	n/a	8.5
96	5	0				√								n/a	n/a
1,950	2.5	2	√	√	√	√	√	√	√	√	√	√	√	n/a	8.0
2,600	2.2	5	√	√	√	√	√	√	√	√	√	√	√	n/a	n/a
1,354	2.1	2	√	√	√	√	√	√	√	√	√	√	√	94	8.4
2,040	2.9	2	√	√	√	√	√	√	√	√	√	√	√	95	7.9
2,040	2.9	2	√	√	√	√	√	√	√	√	√	√	√	97	7.9
1,146	1.9	2	√	√	√		√	√	√	√			√	93	6.9
950	2.4	1	√	√	√	√	√	√	√	√	√		√	96	8.0
n/a	n/a				√			√	√					n/a	n/a
1,804	2.5	2	√	√	√	√	√	√	√	√	√	√	√	98	8.0
1,264	2.1	2	√	√	√	√	√	√	√	√	√	√	√	94	7.9
2,354	2.9	2	√	√	√	√	√	√	√	√	√	√	√	91	7.8
72	2.2	0												n/a	6.3

The Ships at a Glance (continued)					
Cruise Ship	Cruise Line	Type of Ship	Gross Tonnage	Type of Cruise	Duration of Cruise (days)
Mayan Prince	American Canadian	Coastal Cruiser	92	Casual	12
Mercury (preview)	Celebrity	Megaship	73,000	Semiformal	n/a
Monarch of the Seas	Royal Caribbean	Megaship	73,941	Casual	7
Nantucket Clipper	Clipper	Coastal Cruiser	95	Casual	7
Niagara Prince	American Canadian	Coastal Cruiser	99	Casual	12–15
Nieuw Amsterdam	Holland America	Cruise Liner	33,930	Semiformal	7–10
Noordam	Holland America	Cruise Liner	33,930	Semiformal	7–19
Nordic Empress	Royal Caribbean	Cruise Liner	48,563	Casual	3–4
Norway	Norwegian	Cruise Liner	76,049	Semiformal	7
Norwegian Crown	Norwegian	Cruise Liner	34,250	Semiformal	7
OceanBreeze	Dolphin	Cruise Liner	21,486	Casual	7
Polynesia	Windjammer	Schooner	450	Casual	6
Radisson Diamond	Radisson Seven Seas	Cruise Liner	20,295	Semiformal	8–14
Regal Empress	Regal	Cruise Liner	22,979	Casual	4–8
Regal Princess	Princess	Megaship	70,000	Semiformal	10–15
Rhapsody of the Seas (preview)	Royal Caribbean	Megaship	70,000–75,000	Casual	7
Rotterdam VI (preview)	Holland America	Megaship	62,000	Semiformal	7–14
Royal Majesty	Majesty	Cruise Liner	32,396	Semiformal	3–7
Ryndam	Holland America	Cruise Liner	55,451	Semiformal	10
Sea Goddess I	Cunard	Cruise Liner	4,250	Formal	7
Sea Goddess II	Cunard	Cruise Liner	4,250	Formal	7
Sea Princess (preview)	Princess	Megaship	77,000	Semiformal	n/a
Seabourn Pride	Seabourn	Cruise Yacht	10,000	Formal	14–16
SeaBreeze	Dolphin	Cruise Liner	21,010	Casual	7
Seaward	Norwegian	Cruise Liner	42,276	Casual	3–7
Seawind Crown	Seawind	Cruise Liner	24,000	Semiformal	7
Sensation	Carnival	Megaship	70,367	Casual	7
Sir Francis Drake	Tall Ship	Schooner	450	Casual	3–7
Sovereign of the Seas	Royal Caribbean	Megaship	73,192	Casual	3–4
Splendour of the Seas	Royal Caribbean	Megaship	69,130	Casual	10–11
Star Clipper	Star Clippers	Motor-sail	2,298	Casual	7
Star/Ship Oceanic	Premier	Cruise Liner	39,241	Casual	3–4

Passenger Capacity	Passenger/Crew Ratio	Swimming Pools	Casino	Child Care	Fitness Center	Jogging Track	Library	Sauna/Whirlpool	Nightclub/Disco	Shops/Boutiques	Theater/Cinema	Video Arcade	Wheelchair Access (p=partial)	CDC Sanitation Rating	Frommer's Rating
92	5	0			√									91	6.4
1,870	2	2	√	√	√	√	√	√	√	√	√		√	n/a	n/a
2,354	2.9	2	√	√	√	√	√	√	√	√	√	√	√	82	7.8
102	3.2	0			√	√								91	6.6
84	5	0			√	√							√	92	6.7
1,210	2.2	2	√	√	√	√	√	√	√	√	√	√	√	88	7.4
1,210	2.2	2	√	√	√	√	√	√	√	√	√	√	√	88	7.4
1,600	2.4	1	√	√	√	√		√	√	√	√	√	√	92	7.6
2,044	2.3	3	√	√	√	√	√	√	√	√	√	√	√	93	8.3
1,050	2.2	2	√		√	√	√	√	√	√	√	√	√	90	7.9
776	2.5	1	√	√	√	√	√	√	√	√	√	√	p	95	6.8
126	2.4	0					√							n/a	6.3
354	1.8	1	√		√	√	√	√	√	√	√		√	96	8.7
875	2.5	1	√	√	√	√	√	√	√	√	√		√	93	6.0
1,590	2.3	2	√		√	√	√	√	√	√	√		√	91	7.9
1,804	2.5	2	√	√	√	√	√	√	√	√	√	√		n/a	n/a
1,320	2.2	2	√	√	√	√	√	√	√	√	√		√	n/a	n/a
1,056	2.1	1	√	√	√	√	√	√	√	√	√		√	95	7.7
1,264	2.1	2	√	√	√	√	√	√	√	√	√	√	√	93	7.9
116	1.3	1	√	√	√	√	√	√		√	√			95	8.9
116	1.3	1	√	√	√	√	√	√						96	8.9
1,950	2.1	3	√	√	√	√	√	√	√	√	√	√	√	n/a	n/a
204	1.5	1	√	√	√	√			√	√			√	90	8.9
840	2.1	1	√	√	√	√	√	√	√	√	√		p	94	6.8
1,504	2.4	2	√	√	√		√	√	√	√			√	88	8.0
728	2.3	2	√	√	√	√	√	√	√	√			√	n/a	7.5
2,040	2.9	2	√	√	√	√	√	√	√	√	√	√	√	93	7.9
28	2	0												n/a	5.5
2,276	2.8	2	√	√	√	√	√	√	√	√	√	√	p	91	7.7
1,804	2.5	2	√	√	√	√	√	√	√	√	√	√	√	n/a	8.0
170	2.4	2				√				√				80	7.1
1,180	2.3	2	√	√	√	√		√	√	√	√	√	p	96	7.1

Cruise Ship	Cruise Line	Type of Ship	Gross Tonnage	Type of Cruise	Duration of Cruise (days)
The Ships at a Glance (continued)					
Statendam	Holland America	Cruise Liner	55,451	Semiformal	10–21
Stella Solaris	Sun Line	Cruise Liner	17,832	Semiformal	7–30
Sun Princess	Princess	Megaship	77,000	Semiformal	7
Veendam	Holland America	Cruise Liner	55,541	Semiformal	7
Vision of the Seas (preview)	Royal Caribbean	Megaship	70,000-75,000	Casual	n/a
Westerdam	Holland America	Cruise Liner	53,872	Semiformal	7
Wind Spirit	Windstar	Motor-sail	5,703	Casual	7
Wind Star	Windstar	Motor-sail	5,703	Casual	7–12
Windward	Norwegian	Cruise Liner	41,000	Casual	7–11
Yankee Clipper	Windjammer	Schooner	327	Casual	6
Yorktown Clipper	Clipper	Coastal Cruiser	97	Casual	7
Zenith	Celebrity	Cruise Liner	47,225	Semiformal	7

[1] U.S. Department of Health & Human Services (Centers for Disease Control) Sanitation Ratings as of October 4, 1996,

Passenger Capacity	Passenger/Crew Ratio	Swimming Pools	Casino	Child Care	Fitness Center	Jogging Track	Library	Sauna/Whirlpool	Nightclub/Disco	Shops/Boutiques	Theater/Cinema	Video Arcade	Wheelchair Access (p=partial)	CDC Sanitation Rating	Frommer's Rating
1,264	2.2	2	√	√	√	√	√	√	√	√	√	√	√	97	7.9
620	2	1	√	√	√	√	√	√	√	√	√		p	91	7.6
1,950	2.1	3	√	√	√	√	√	√	√	√	√	√	√	91	8.6
1,264	2.1	2	√	√	√	√	√	√	√	√	√	√	√	94	7.9
n/a	n/a	2	√	√	√	√	√	√	√	√	√	√	√	n/a	n/a
1,494	2.3	2	√	√	√	√	√	√	√	√	√	√	√	92	7.2
148	1.6	1	√		√	√	√	√	√					99	8.6
148	1.6	1	√		√	√	√	√	√					n/a	8.6
1,246	2.6	2	√	√	√	√	√	√	√	√	√	√	√	96	8.4
64	2.4	0												n/a	6.3
138	3.5	0				√	√							97	6.6
1,374	2.1	2	√	√	√	√	√	√	√	√	√	√	√	96	8.4

3 Frommer's Favorites

To make it easier for you to select a ship, we've compiled these "Frommer's Favorites," our picks of the best ships for different types of cruises.

1 Best Luxury Cruises

Here's the very best for the Caribbean cruiser who's used to traveling deluxe, and who doesn't mind paying for the privilege.

- **Seabourn:** Our vote goes to Seabourn for overall style, impeccable service, luxurious accommodations, and first-class cuisine unequaled by any other line. On the *Seabourn Pride,* you'll sail with well-heeled, discriminating, and experienced travelers. Lottery winners are welcome as well.
- **Cunard:** Cunard's *Sea Goddess I* and *Sea Goddess II* stand out for their divine decadence. Launched in 1984, *Sea Goddess I* introduced the all-suite concept to cruise ships. The concept (and the ship) was so successful it begat a "daughter," *Sea Goddess II.* Cruises are sophisticated and stylish, yet decidedly unsnobbish.
- **Celebrity Cruises:** Celebrity made a major splash in 1995 by launching the *Century,* and an even bigger splash in 1996 with its *Galaxy.* These vessels, larger than their fleet-mates, feature panoramic vistas, sumptuous decors, and top-of-the-line staffs hand-picked from the other ships in the fleet. Passengers enjoy master chef Michel Roux's famous cuisine. The true luxury seeker will want to book the Penthouse, Royal, or Sky suites aboard either vessel.
- **Windstar Cruises:** For a 19th-century clipper ship sailing adventure with great style, Windstar is without parallel in the industry. The *Wind Star* and *Wind Spirit* are where the elite meet to retreat, getting excellent food, first-class service, and, if they want it, a chance to be alone. Most Windstar passengers don't need canned entertainment—they amuse themselves.

2 Best Cruises for First-Timers

Short jaunts are good for first-time cruisers and families.

- **Carnival Cruise Lines:** *Ecstasy,* sailing from Miami to Nassau on three-day cruises, is the winner in short-term cruises from that port. This is one of Carnival's newest superliners, weighing in at around 70,000 tons. While cabins are usually small on short cruises, the ones aboard *Ecstasy* are about 50% larger than those on most competitive ships.

- **Cape Canaveral Cruise Line:** This line is charting a new market for short-term cruises with its ***Dolphin IV,*** which sails from Port Canaveral. This low-key cruise is moderately priced and attracts a varied passenger list that ranges from retirees to first-time cruisers and even honeymooners on a budget.
- **Premier Cruise Lines:** The **"Big Red Boat"** leaving from Port Canaveral is the best ship for families who want to sample a cruising experience. With all the entertainment, food, and games, children usually enjoy the experience, and will soon be begging you to take them on another cruise. Parents have fun, too.
- **Dolphin Cruise Line:** Many first-time cruisers are drawn by the low prices Dolphin charges for its aging fleet, ***IslandBreeze, OceanBreeze,*** and ***SeaBreeze.*** Kids like the Hanna-Barbera characters who sail along as well. The ships' friendly staffs and crews, along with fun activities and entertainment, turn most first-timers into second-timers.
- **Norwegian Cruise Line:** The line's theme cruises have attracted a horde of first-time cruisers drawn from among a pool of special-interest groups. The company aggressively promotes its costume evenings, sports programs, theme cruises, and general entertainment/activities agenda to attract the skeptical passenger who might be wondering what to do with all that time at sea.
- **Radisson Seven Seas Cruises:** ***Radisson Diamond*** wins our vote for the first-timer who want to splurge a bit and cruise in style. Because of its twin-hull design, it's also the best ship afloat for those who suffer from motion sickness. In addition to stability, the *Diamond* offers excellent itineraries, one of the grandest dining rooms afloat (with superb service),

all outside cabins, and first-class amenities.

- **Royal Caribbean Cruise Line:** *Nordic Empress* is a good choice for the cruiser on a moderate budget. This smooth-running vessel features a good activities program and top-notch facilities, even though its cabins tend to be small.

3 The Most Romantic Cruises

Nearly three-quarters of all cruising passengers today are couples, romantic or otherwise. And more of those romantic couples than ever are renewing their vows on board. For how to get married on board, see question no. 28 in chapter 4.

- **Carnival Cruise Lines:** Any line that names its vessels after moments of high passion has to take romance seriously, though one cruiser complained that the names reminded him of something he'd seen in a high-priced Vegas bordello. Regardless, Carnival sells romance on the high seas, and does so rather aggressively. If you want charmed interludes and quiet times with your loved one, sail on Windstar Cruises. But if you believe love is a fiesta à la Carmen Miranda, make it your *Destiny* to have a sybaritic *Celebration* aboard a *Sensation* where you might opt for a night of *Ecstasy* if you have the *Imagination* to explore your *Fantasy* or *Fascination*.
- **Windstar Cruises:** Pure romance. Spend the day with your loved one on a private cove with the four-masted ***Wind Star*** or ***Wind Spirit*** anchored offshore, bobbing calmly on the waves. Later, with sails billowed by gentle trade winds from off the Grenadines, sail into the setting sun, the only sound that of waves lapping against the hull. Sounds nice, huh?
- **Holland America Line:** This line is the leader of cruise ships offering married couples the opportunity to

The Crystal & Silversea Gold-Dust Twins

They're luxurious, they're in the news, and they've managed to infiltrate the dreams of every potential cruise passenger who wants to live like the sultan of Brunei on the high seas. Oft-feted, oft-envied, highly competitive, and ranked just a nudge behind the intensely upscale Seabourn Cruise Line (which we review in chapter 9), they're the gold-dust twins of the cruise industry.

Don't look for venerable pedigrees or formidable genealogies here. Despite their sense of chic, they're relative upstarts on the cruise-going marketplace. Much, much younger than Cunard, which dredges up its 19th-century pedigree whenever sales begin to flag, Crystal and Silversea manage to be both brash and highly civilized at the same time, and are continually engaged in a high-stakes, up-market cruise duel.

Recognizing that many affluent and frequent cruisers long ago grew jaded with waters near the U.S. mainland, both Silversea and Crystal concentrate their cruises on the more exotic waters off the coasts of Brazil, Argentina, Chile, East Africa, and Southeast Asia. In brief, if you've had a fantasy about exotic ports of call, either of these lines will make your dreams come true.

Where don't they tend to go? The Caribbean. In the words of one company's marketing executives, the Caribbean is already "overpopulated" with less elegant competitors whose ships are filled with clients less well heeled than the typical Silversea or Crystal passenger. True, *Crystal Harmony,* a glitteringly upscale ship, occasionally pulls into San Juan or Cozumel on some (but not all) of its trips through the Panama Canal, and at rare intervals might visit Grand Cayman or St. Barts for a half-day of sailing en route between Acapulco and either Fort Lauderdale or New Orleans. Overall, though, Crystal is focused away from the Caribbean, presuming that to its worldly clientele the Antilles are simply old hat.

The same holds true for Silversea. This glittering prestigious line recently announced that in 1998 its ships would spend less than a week within Caribbean waters—and even that brief foray is designed as an eight-day transit between Nassau and Barbados, as a stage of a long cruise between New York and Rio de Janeiro.

Crystal has set a goal for itself, and in the main it meets its own challenge: to provide the best and most elegant large-ship luxury cruise experience. Superb food, first-rate entertainment, generous onboard facilities, service among the finest in the industry, and overall ambience have pushed Crystal to the front rank of world cruisers.

Occasionally following in the sea-lanes of Vasco de Gama, Crystal sails the world, traveling the eastern coast of Africa or tracing the route of 15th-century gold traders as its vessels journey south to Cape Town, South Africa, or visit

renew their vows at sea. (Shipboard clergy can't actually marry couples, but they can lead either group or individual exchanges of vows. For an actual marriage, certain restrictions apply. See question no. 28 in chapter 4. One of the best ships on the line to put you in the mood is the **Westerdam,** which cruises the eastern Caribbean in winter. Its Veranda Res-taurant offers live music at lunch, and the pool area has a sliding glass dome that lets you take a dip even in nippy weather. Some itineraries call for two full but lazy days at sea, allowing you and your loved one plenty of quality time together. *Two full days.* Think of the possibilities.

• **Cunard:** If you've already found your true love, the **Sea Goddess I** and **II** are the Mediterranean to see the treasures of Italy, Spain, or Greece. In the Western Hemisphere, Crystal concentrates on the Panama Canal, Mexico, Alaska, and the coasts of South America.

Exceptionally sleek and sophisticated, *Crystal Harmony* was launched in 1990. With its dazzling white walls, glass stairways and railings, it is tastefully decorated, weighs in at 49,400 tons, and provides 480 spacious cabins (96% of which are outside) reserved for 960 passengers. Crystal's *Symphony* was launched in 1995. Weighing 50,000 tons, it's one of the biggest ships ever built with all outside cabins. It too carries 960 passengers. The *Harmony* has a crew of 545, the *Symphony* 530. On both ships, crews are mainly Europeans intensely trained in European (formal) modes of service.

Silversea sails the *Silver Cloud* and *Silver Wind,* small boats (weighing a mere 16,800 tons each) that are among the most luxurious, intensely social, and stress-free afloat. Launched in 1994 and 1995, respectively, they contain no cabins whatsoever, only outside suites with panoramic views of the sea, 75% of which have private teakwood verandas (the remainder have large picture windows). Aboard either vessel, 196 crew members—professionals trained in the finest European hotels—serve only 296 passengers. Silversea's chefs emphasize fresh natural foods, using the best ingredients possible, such as wild salmon from Scotland or culatello ham from Parma. Even though small, both ships have first-rate entertainment in their multi-tiered show lounges, and, as you'd expect on such well-monied ships, fine casinos. Usually, they're lively, though not nearly as animated and boisterous as those aboard many of the industry's megaships.

Both Silversea vessels have larger swimming pools and more deck space than other cruise yachts. Water sports are heavily emphasized. Both *Silver Cloud* and *Silver Wind* sail the eastern North American seaboard, South America, and the Panama Canal, with somewhat infrequent visits to the Caribbean.

Since the routing of both Crystal and Silversea lines is always changing, it's best to check with a travel agent or the lines themselves for their latest offerings. Contact **Crystal Cruises** at 2121 Avenue of the Stars, Los Angeles, CA 90067 (☎ **800/ 446-6620**), and **Silversea** at 110 E. Broward Blvd., Fort Lauderdale, FL 33301 (☎ **800/722-6655** or 305/522-4477).

So what's an upscale passenger with a yen for both unmitigated luxury and azure Caribbean waters to do? Call **Seabourn,** whose vessels make more calls in the Antilles than either of the other two. And it couldn't hurt to keep a weather eye on Crystal and Silversea. Access to the world's most exotic destinations is always changing, and who's to say that the wind might not blow either or both of these lines back Caribbean-ways someday?

good choices for a romantic sea holiday. The line promises the elegance and intimacy of a private club, and for the most part lives up to that claim. It's not hard to imagine you're on your own private yacht in the best tradition of Jackie and Ari. Even the itineraries are romantic: the Mediterranean in summer, the Caribbean in winter.

4 Best Cruises for Singles

The solo traveler at sea is claiming an increasing share of the market, representing one of every four of today's cruisers. Here are the best possibilities for the single cruiser (chosen with various ages in mind):

- **Windjammer Barefoot Cruises:** If you're under 30, believe in equality between the sexes, and don't mind getting together for some fun at sea, these cruises are your best romantic bet. The shorter the cruise, the more singles on board, so if you like to mix and mingle, try a three- or four-day excursion. Windjammer Cruises attract many young singles, and, strangely enough, the gender division is usually about equal.
- **Club Med:** The *Club Med 1* and *2* are good boats for singles, but single passengers don't necessarily find love among the passenger list; usually they're more attracted to the lovely young women or handsome men serving as GOs (*gentiles organisateurs*), the social hosts who coordinate the many onboard activities.
- **Carnival Cruise Lines:** Single women under 30 seek out Carnival's ships, in part because they attract more young men under 30 than any other cruise line. Who knows who you might meet in that aerobics class, on that shore excursion, or even at your dining table? Nothing is very formal here, just people getting together and letting nature take its course.
- **Premier Cruise Lines:** The line makes a special effort to attract single parents with their children. Cartoon characters like Bugs Bunny and Sylvester can entertain the offspring while mom or dad enjoys the company of another single parent.
- **Royal Caribbean Cruise Line:** This line is best for single travelers who are 35 to 50 years old, and who have perhaps been married before. Their ships draw a good cross section of men and women from all walks of life.

5 Best Cruises for Families

Family cruises are now one of the most important money-makers in the cruise industry, so much so that we've devoted a whole section of chapter 5 to the matter. Plus, the cruise-line reviews in chapter 9 describe children's activities in detail. Here's our list of the most family-friendly lines:

- **Premier Cruise Lines:** Premier's **"Big Red Boat"** reigns supreme as the best for families, at least until Disney launches in 1998. Your kids will sail with cartoon characters such as Tweety, Sylvester, Bugs Bunny, and the Tasmanian Devil. Premier's three- to four-day cruises to The Bahamas are particularly good for families on their first cruise. Best of all, the line can book you on a full-week holiday at Disney World before or after your cruise.
- **Celebrity Cruises:** Not only does this line offer an activity-filled agenda for families, but a tie-in with the Sony Corporation means a wonderland of electronic bliss for the kids. The computerized games, especially those aboard Celebrity's newest ships, the *Century* and *Galaxy,* are the best in the industry. Even some adults can't keep away from the fun.
- **Norwegian Cruise Line:** The line offers excellent children's programs, especially on the *Norway,* and both parents and kids enjoy the line's theme cruises, especially those featuring famous sports personalities. The theme cruises based on music and popular television game shows also make for fine family entertainment.
- **Carnival Cruise Lines:** Carnival, as its name implies, goes out of its way to amuse people of all ages, and does a particularly fine job with kids 3 to 17 years old. The line carries more family groups than any other, and hires the largest staff of trained counselors in the cruise industry. Children's activities are amusing and sometimes educational.
- **Costa Cruises:** From the warm and attentive supervision to the inevitable

pizza parlor, Costa ships cater to family groups. Its programs turn kid sailors into one very big and happy Italian family.

- **Princess Cruises:** Well-trained counselors both aboard ship and at the cruise line's private Pleasure Island work closely with children, and activities are kept separate from the main passenger areas and adult pursuits—a policy that probably suits the kids just as well as it does their parents.

6 Best Party Cruises

With the right passengers, every night aboard ship can be a party. Some passengers like to pick their own, which could mean choosing a theme cruise featuring square dancing or perhaps one of the *Norway*'s jazz cruises. Others like to book shorter three- or four-day cruises, finding that the party starts to wear thin by the fifth day.

- **Princess Cruises:** There's a constant party aboard the *Dawn Princess* and *Sun Princess,* and the very similar *Crown Princess* and *Regal Princess.* Passengers can enjoy everything from gala buffets to pajama parties, "Karaoke Madness," or country-western parties complete with line dancing. Even the afternoons are lively aboard Princess vessels, with water Olympics, *Jeopardy* game shows, and "midday melodies."
- **Club Med:** On the *Club Med 1* and *Club Med 2,* the social hosts (GOs) keep the ships rocking. This free-wheeling abandon makes the line popular with honeymooners, singles, and loving couples. The ships are informal and very, very social. The GOs display their talents every evening in song and dance, but the biggest blast occurs one night a week on every cruise: Carnival Night, when anything goes!
- **Carnival Cruise Lines:** Carnival's ships truly live up to their names—

you'll find a *Celebration* to please your *Imagination.* You may find your *Ecstasy* or *Fantasy,* even your *Destiny.* These are called "fun ships" for good reason. The staff is always organizing events for all ages, and the fun keeps going after the sun goes down, with some of the best entertainment afloat. Usually three different live bands and orchestras play aboard a Carnival ship, and the discos rock until the early morning hours. Casino action is big on Carnival ships, as are Las Vegas–style revues. All the ships offer gala midnight buffets, except on three-day cruises.

- **Norwegian Cruise Line:** This line is a heavy contender in the party and entertainment sweepstakes, particularly aboard the *Dreamward, Leeward, Norway, Seaward,* and *Windward.* Everything from a giant jackpot bingo to a galley raid at midnight is designed to amuse passengers. The ships also provide the best theme cruises in the industry, with options such as big bands, country music, jazz, blues, and sports. And when the sun goes down, NCL's ships shine with outstanding entertainment. Fully equipped theaters have stages big enough to put on Broadway hits, or you could opt for NCL's own extravagant production, *Sea Legs Review.*
- **Royal Caribbean Cruise Line:** You'll definitely find a party on *Grandeur of the Seas, Legend of the Seas, Majesty of the Seas, Monarch of the Seas, Nordic Empress, Splendour of the Seas,* and *Sovereign of the Seas.* From dancing to singing to comedy to elaborately costumed revues, RCCL's got it all. The line actually pioneered bringing entertainment aboard cruises. Once each cruise, waiters and bartenders take the stage and dance to island music while balancing drinks, candles, and full trays on their heads. In some ports of call, local acts are brought on board. The best disco is aboard *Sovereign of the Seas.*

7 Best Adventure Cruises

If you want to explore more remote areas of the Caribbean where the megaships can't venture, or be aboard a vessel that recalls the sailing days of yore, here are your best bets:

- **Royal Olympic Cruises:** *Stella Solaris* is one of several ships that stop at Caribbean ports before heading up the Amazon River to Manaus, Brazil, but no other ship has Capt. Loren McIntyre aboard as a guide; he's the explorer, author, and photographer who discovered the most distant source of the Amazon, and he's also the best in the business. You'll stop at Tobago, of Robinson Crusoe fame, and perhaps St. Lucia, where cone-shaped twin peaks rule over the lush landscape. Some of these jaunts explore Curuá Una, a black-water Amazon tributary where you can fish for piranha.
- **American Canadian Caribbean Line:** *Mayan Prince* heads for the remote waters of the Caribbean, especially off-shore Belize and Honduras. This fascinating and relatively untouched part of Central America opens onto one of the world's greatest barrier reefs, which you may glimpse on a ride in the glass-bottomed boats ACCL carries aboard ship. More boat than ship, the *Mayan Prince* is far from a floating hotel, but this is your vessel if you want to visit parts of the Caribbean that few other travelers see.
- **Windstar Cruises:** *Wind Star* makes some of the most intriguing stopovers in the Caribbean, such as Dominica or Bequia, one of the jewels of the Grenadines but a place where the megaships can't go. *Wind Star* stops at Carriacou, that remote, little-visited island owned by Grenada, and even explores the Tobago Cays. It doesn't just "do" Guadeloupe, but takes you to the even more exotic offshore Isle des Saintes.

- **Tall Ship Adventures:** Being aboard the *Sir Francis Drake* is one of the great sailing adventures still left in the Caribbean. This authentic 1917 three-masted schooner originally transported copper around Cape Horn between the western Chilean coast and Europe. Today, this vessel makes seven-day voyages in the British Virgin Islands, the old sailing grounds of Sir Francis Drake himself, as well as other parts of the Caribbean. The ship doesn't have many of the standard cruise-ship comforts, but if you choose this ship you probably aren't looking for those anyway. Instead, you'll experience the true adventure of Caribbean sailing.
- **Clipper Cruise Line:** The *Nantucket Clipper* and *Yorktown Clipper* retain the spirit of adventure now lost on all the megaships. These twin clippers can tie up in remote, out-of-the-way ports that most other ships have to avoid. They're almost yachtlike. Some cruises will introduce you to history and culture, but others are oriented toward pure adventure, concentrating on ports of call with rugged scenic beauty and opportunities for wildlife viewing, including spotting the elusive whale. Clipper ships call at remote islands in the British Virgins such as Jost Van Dyke, Salt Island, and Norman Island, which, according to legend, inspired Robert Louis Stevenson's *Treasure Island*. The line sails the Caribbean in the winter months and is a worthy rival of American Canadian Caribbean.

8 Best Theme Cruises

Theme cruises abound, from solar eclipse viewing to an Oktoberfest, from a jazz festival to golfing. Check with a travel agent or cruise specialist for the current offerings.

- **Norwegian Cruise Line:** When it comes to theme cruises, the Norwegian Cruise Line, which pioneered the concept of theme cruises in the early

1980s, is the tops. Its annual floating jazz festival has been so successful that it's now a two-week-long extravaganza, with back-to-back cruises to both the eastern and the western Caribbean. Jazz and blues cruises feature a bring-your-own-instrument passenger jam session, so get those chops honed before boarding. Country music cruises bring out such stars as George Jones and Tammy Wynette, and the 1950s and 1960s rock-and-roll cruises book such acts as Bobby Vee and the Shirelles. The big band cruises, featuring classic, indestructible bands like the Duke Ellington and Jimmy Dorsey orchestras, are among the most heavily booked. The line's newest ships offer cruises with popular sports themes in which professional football, basketball, baseball, and hockey players are celebrity guests.

- **Majesty Cruise Line:** *Royal Majesty* is making a name for itself in theme cruises, although its program doesn't come close to equaling that of Norwegian Cruise Line. Majesty has major success with its yearly Elvis-themed three-night cruises to The Bahamas and Key West, which feature an Elvis impersonator (of course), along with rock-and-roll dance contests, a 1950s drag contest, trivia questions, and other music and entertainment to draw Elvis devotees, many of whom claim to have recently seen the King. Other theme cruises might include a Greek or Irish festival or one catering to fans of professional sports.

- **Dolphin Cruise Line:** The line has entered the fray for music-themed voyages on its three-, four-, and seven-night cruises to The Bahamas and the Caribbean. If you like the music of the 1950s and 1960s, the *IslandBreeze,* the *OceanBreeze,* and the *SeaBreeze* rock and roll to the sounds of groups such as the Platters, the Drifters, and the Coasters. Other theme cruises include an Irish festival and an Oktoberfest cruise.

- **Royal Olympic Cruises:** Believing that cruising can be both fun and educational, this line has offered special cruises to view Halley's Comet, the May Equinox at Chichén Itzá, and the Perseid meteor shower, and brought guest lecturers aboard its *Stella Solaris* that are the best in the industry. After visiting major ports in the Caribbean, Sun Line often heads for the Amazon on its "Sail with the Stars" program, which celebrates theater at sea with theatrical icons such as Anne Jackson and Eli Wallach.

9 Best Shipboard Cuisine

Here's where you'll find the best floating restaurants:

- **Seabourn Cruise Line:** *Seabourn Pride* tops them all, spending more on food per passenger than any other ship in the business. The sophisticated and contemporary cuisine is prepared to order using only the freshest ingredients available. Dishes are flavorful and artfully presented, and if there's anything you want specially prepared, just ask. Your wish is their command, and we're not kidding: The dining room service is the finest of any vessel afloat.

- **Windstar Cruises:** While the fare aboard the *Wind Spirit* and *Wind Star* doesn't equal that aboard Seabourn, it's still an attraction all to itself. In 1995, this fleet upgraded its cuisine by hiring renowned Los Angeles–based restaurateur Joachim Splichal as consultant, and increased the amount it spends per passenger for food. The decision paid off, as the food is vastly improved.

- **Radisson Seven Seas Cruises:** *Radisson Diamond's* award-winning chefs produce artful culinary presentations that compare favorably to those of New York or San Francisco's top restaurants. It's amazing how a ship at sea manages to secure such fresh-tasting produce, but this one does. Salt cod it's not! The waiters, many of whom have trained aboard the *Seabourn Pride* and *Sea Goddess I,* are some of the industry's best, and they certainly enhance your dining experience. An excellent selection of vintage wines is also available.

- **Cunard Line:** On the *Sea Goddess I* and *II,* fine dining is always the evening's highlight. You'll enjoy food comparable to that served in the top two dining rooms of Cunard's flagship, *QE2.* The chefs prepare a concise menu that is highlighted daily with different specialties, flavors, and tastes. That way, you don't feel you're eating the same meal twice, as you do on some of the less-expensive lines, such as Dolphin or American Canadian Caribbean.

- **Celebrity Cruise Line:** The floating deluxe restaurants aboard the *Century* and *Galaxy* have won praise for their cuisine, which was designed by Michel Roux, Britain's most famous and celebrated chef, who sometimes cooks for Queen Elizabeth when she "drops in" to his place on the Thames. Under Roux's tutelage, the *Century* and *Galaxy* chefs have learned to prepare seagoing menus that are to die for. You'll feel like royalty. As if that weren't enough, service is white-glove and professional, topped only by that of Seabourn.

10 Best Cruises for Island Hoppers

If you want to see as much of the Caribbean as possible in the shortest amount of time, consider one of the following cruises for their packed itineraries—you'll see it all fast. Many lines offer discounts if you book back-to-back cruises.

- **American Canadian Caribbean Line:** *Niagara Prince* has no equal or competition in the remote Caribbean and Central American hinterlands it visits. You'll visit all the cays and islets you've never have heard of, including Laughingbird Cay, Ambergris Cay, and Man-of-War Cay, plus Mayan ruins and even remote territories in Honduras.

- **Commodore Cruises:** *Enchanted Isle* offers alternating week-long cruises from New Orleans to Key West, one stopping at Cozumel and Playa del Carmen on Mexico's eastern coast, the other at Cozumel, Playa del Carmen, and Grand Cayman before arriving at Montego Bay. There's enough to do at Cozumel to make two visits in two weeks—a day-long trip to Chichén Itzá for the Mayan ruins and a day at the resort of Cozumel itself.

- **Norwegian Cruise Line:** *Seaward* has alternating weekly schedules from San Juan, the Caribbean's most interesting port for sightseeing: One week it visits Barbados, Santo Domingo, Dominica, Antigua, and St. Thomas; the second week its stops include Santo Domingo, St. Lucia, St. Kitts, St. Maarten, and St. Thomas.

- **Seawind Cruises:** *Seawind Crown* wins our vote for the most interesting stopovers at ports of call in the southern Caribbean. It has two different weekly itineraries, with Sunday departures from Aruba: One seven-night cruise sails to Curaçao, Grenada, Barbados, and St. Lucia, and the other visits Trinidad and Tobago, Barbados, and Martinique. Some cruises stop at Dominica, a remote, rather primitive, yet lush island.

- **Windjammer Cruises:** *Amazing Grace* is the supply ship for the Windjammer sailing ships, so it leaves for 13-day cruises from Freeport to Trinidad and vice versa. It's the ultimate island hopper! The roster of ports includes St. Kitts, Nevis, Montserrat, Isle de Saintes, Guadeloupe, Dominica, Jost Van Dyke, Beef Island, Virgin Gorda, Norman Island, and Peter Island—and possibly others.

11 Best Cruises for Beach Lovers

If time logged on the beach is just as important to you as days spent at sea, you'll want to consider the following cruises:

- **Seawind Cruises:** *Seawind Crown* is a beach buff's favorite because it sails in and out of Aruba, where sunshine is virtually guaranteed and you'll find some of the Caribbean's finest beaches, about 7 miles of uninterrupted sugar-white sand, including the truly wonderful Palm Beach and Eagle Beach. If you book a cruise in one of *Seawind Crown*'s top four categories, you receive a complimentary week-long stay at La Cabana All Suite Beach Resort and Casino, where you can get in all the beach time you've ever needed.

- **Star Clippers:** The line's twin vessels, *Star Clipper* and *Star Flyer,* can take you to some uncrowded and remote white-sand beaches that the big cruise ships can't reach, including Norman Island, Jost Van Dyke, and Isle des Saintes off the coast of Guadeloupe—some of the Caribbean's best. Clipper's vessels also stop at the more popular and crowded beaches of Antigua, St. Croix, and Anguilla.

- **Royal Caribbean Cruise Line:** If you sail aboard *Splendour of the Seas, Majesty of the Seas, Sovereign of the Seas,* or the newly launched *Grandeur of the Seas,* you'll stop for a day at a private peninsula called Labadee on Haiti's northwestern tip. This dream island has good security and is safe to visit. It's the best of the private cruise-ship resorts, better than similar properties in The Bahamas. Ships anchor in a calm lagoon, and passengers flock to the white sandy shores.

- **Commodore Cruise Line:** *Enchanted Isle* makes frequent calls at Grand Cayman, whose Seven Mile Beach (actually it's 5½ miles) is one of the Caribbean's finest. Australian pines and plush resorts surround the area,

which is known for translucent aquamarine waters with an average winter water temperature of 80°F, powdery white sand, and many water sports. *Enchanted Isle* also calls at Playa del Carmen, with some of the best beachfront along the fabled eastern strip of Mexico's Riviera.

- **Norwegian Cruise Line:** *Norway* sails to some of the finest beaches in the eastern Caribbean, including the island of two nations, Dutch St. Maarten and French St. Martin, both known for their excellent beaches. The ship also goes to St. Thomas, where Magens Beach isn't as good as it used to be, and nearby St. John, where Trunk Bay remains a gem. Protected by the U.S. National Park Service, Trunk Bay is known for its underwater trail, where markers guide beachcombers along the reef lying just off the white sandy beach. The *Norway* also calls at Great Stirrup Cay, the line's private island in The Bahamas, which is also known for its great beaches.

12 Best Cruises for Divers & Snorkelers

Tie on your tanks and slip into your flippers; these ships stop at the best scuba diving and snorkeling spots in the Caribbean:

- **American Canadian Caribbean Line:** This line is unbeatable. Few major cruise lines ever call at Bélize, which has the world's second-largest barrier reef, but ACCL's *Niagara Prince* cruises here from early December to mid-April. Excursions of between 7 and 12 days always take in the offshore waters of Honduras and Guatemala, and stopovers tend to be in ports known for their superb snorkeling and wealth of marine life. On the other hand, if you want to dive The Bahamas and Turks and Caicos, the *Mayan Prince* visits these waters from late November to mid-December.

- **Commodore Cruise Line:** *Enchanted Isle,* departing from Orleans for seven-day western Caribbean loops, calls at Grand Cayman, the Caribbean's largest single island for dive tourism. Coral reefs and formations filled with marine life encircle the island, and dedicated scuba divers rate the waters here among the very best in the West Indies.
- **Royal Caribbean Cruise Line:** *Grandeur of the Seas* is a snorkeler's delight, departing from Miami and stopping off at private islands including Labadee, Haiti, and CocoCay in The Bahamas, where the waters are pristine and clear, and offer astonishing visibility. Diving here, you'll be one of the privileged few to explore these specially guarded enclaves, which are reserved for the passengers of select cruise ships.
- **Seawind Cruise Line:** Both certified and noncertified divers can take advantage of the "Reef Roamer" diving programs offered by Seawind's onboard dive contractor, Aqua Fun Adventures, which arranges dives in such lesser-known sites as Barbados (with dives both day and night), St. Lucia, Grenada, and Curaçao. Temporary PADI certification, valid for the course of the cruise, is granted to noncertified divers who can demonstrate reasonable swimming skills.
- **Princess Cruises:** Princess features "New Waves," a PADI-certified diving program available aboard ships sailing the Caribbean on seven-day itineraries. Endorsed by Scuba Schools International, this program offers introductory scuba tours, dive trips, and demonstrations, and employs fully certified instructors that are some of the best in the business.
- **Windjammer Barefoot Cruises:** Windjammer has always numbered divers among some of its most valued passengers. Its schooners and barquentines offer year-round diving possibilities on 6- to 13-day cruises to some 50 ports of call in the Caribbean

and The Bahamas. Even the rarely visited Grenadines are featured. For divers, the best ship in this fleet is the *Flying Cloud,* which departs from Tortola, capital of the British Virgin Islands.
- **Star Clippers:** This line is not to be ignored. Its owner, Mikael Krafft, is a dedicated scuba diver, and he selects his ship's itineraries through the Caribbean based in part on the accessibility of superior, intriguing, and often offbeat dive sites, including small ports that many big cruise ships can't even approach. The line's *Star Clipper* is the largest sailing vessel to feature onboard PADI dive centers.
- **Majesty Cruise Line:** *Royal Majesty* takes you on three- and four-day cruises that depart from Miami and visit Nassau, Key West, Cozumel, and Royal Isle, the cruise line's own private island, which is ideal for snorkeling. There are certified instructors aboard.

13 Best Cruises for Golfers

Only on a few ships can you practice putting on board; on the rest, you'll have to wait until your ship calls at a port. Many lines will arrange tee times for you.

- **Royal Caribbean Cruise Line:** This line is the golfer's favorite, as its ships feature a nine-hole putting course that can be covered with a sliding glass roof during inclement weather. Ships are so huge and well stabilized that golfers are seldom bothered by motion. The Professional Golf Association has officially sanctioned RCCL as its official cruise line, and RCCL tries to have tie-ins with golf courses at various ports of call and make special greens fees available to cruisers. *Monarch of the Seas* also departs from San Juan, and stops at ports of call where you can play some of the finest courses in the West Indies, including Antigua with its Cedar Valley Golf Club, Barbados with its Sandy

Lane Club and its even better Royal Westmoreland, Martinique's *Golf de l'Impératrice-Joséphine,* St. Maarten's Mullet Bay Resort, and St. Thomas with its Mahogany Run, one of the Caribbean's most beautiful courses.

- **Carnival Cruise Line:** *Fascination* and *Inspiration* leave from San Juan, the golf capital of the Caribbean, where serious golfers might want to stay on a pre- or postcruise package to take advantage of the island's many courses, which include the Hyatt Resorts Puerto Rico with its 72 holes. Other courses are at the Hyatt Regency Cerromar and the Hyatt Dorado Beach, and match the finest anywhere.

- **Dolphin Cruise Line:** *SeaBreeze* will almost guarantee you get in a good round of golf wherever the vessel stops. It departs year-round from Miami, and since South Florida is a golfer's dream, you may want to consider booking in on a pre- and postcruise package. In Nassau, you can play golf at the 18-hole Paradise Island Golf Course, a championship course designed by Dick Wilson. The ship stops in San Juan, the Caribbean capital of golf, and St. Thomas, where you can play the beautiful course at Mahogany Run. At Montego Bay, you can play some of the Caribbean's finest courses, especially at Tryall and Half Moon. In Grand Cayman you can play the Britannia Golf Course at the Hyatt Regency Grand Cayman Hotel, one of the Caribbean's most unusual courses. Jack Nicklaus designed a special golf ball that only goes half of the regular distance to accommodate this very short nine-hole course, which becomes 18 holes by employing separate tees.

- **Seawind Cruise Line:** *Seawind Crown* is hardly thought of as a golfer's favorite, yet it does take you to some of the best golf courses in the southern Caribbean, beginning with its point of embarkation, Aruba, and stopping at such islands as Grenada,

Curaçao, Barbados, St. Lucia, and even Martinique.

14 Best Cruises for Serious Shoppers

Our comparison shopping aboard vessels has revealed that most merchandise sold on board sells for a third less than shoreside prices—and items sold while a ship is at sea are tax free. Ships also hold special sales to move certain merchandise and make way for newer wares.

If you want to shop on shore, Charlotte Amalie in St. Thomas still ranks as the numero uno port of call among shoppers, but it's rapidly going downhill. Meanwhile, in a veritable war of the saints, St. Maarten is rapidly moving up to become a challenger, as are Aruba and even St. Lucia.

- **Royal Caribbean Cruise Line:** This line, more than any other, caters to dedicated shoppers, both on board and ashore. Their ship shops sell some excellent and discounted merchandise, including jewelry and perfumes; some onboard prices are even better than those found ashore. Plus, RCCL staffers will recommend the best shops in the various ports of call, merchants the line has found to be consistently reliable.

- **Carnival Cruise Lines:** These ships call at more major shopping destinations in The Bahamas and the Caribbean than any other line. Florida residents particularly appreciate its three-day trips to The Bahamas, departing from Miami. At times, the *Ecstasy* seems packed to the rafters with shoppers eager to sample Nassau's discounted merchandise. *Fantasy* also makes these three-day loops, departing from Port Canaveral, so if you can't find what you're looking for in Nassau, you might find it in Freeport/Lucaya. Carnival ships such as *Fascination* call at the virtual island bazaars that are St. Thomas, San Juan, and Aruba.

- **Norwegian Cruise Line:** Its mammoth *Norway* is a shopper's delight, in part because its gargantuan size confines it to big ports, which is just where dedicated shoppers want to be. On its seven-day eastern Caribbean loops, *Norway* calls at the shopping meccas of St. Maarten/St. Martin, as well as St. Thomas and the smaller neighboring island of St. John. The ship itself is a bazaar, a souk, a shopper's dream, a vast department store at sea.
- **Princess Cruises:** The itineraries of the *Dawn Princess* make the vessel a favorite of serious shoppers. A recent trip, departing from Fort Lauderdale, called at all the big names in Caribbean shopping, including St. Thomas, Aruba, Barbados, and St. Maarten. It also sailed into Martinique, where high-quality French merchandise is sold, and Dominica, one of the Caribbean's forgotten islands, which specializes in native crafts.
- **Dolphin Cruise Line:** This line is included for short-term cruisers because the *OceanBreeze* departs from either Miami or Fort Lauderdale, the great shopping meccas of Florida, dwarfing anything you'll find in the Caribbean or The Bahamas—and there are bargains galore. Cruises stop in Nassau, which is a world-class shopping mecca, and on the four-day cruises you not only stop at such Mexican ports as Cozumel or Playa del Carmen, but you get to shop till you drop at Key West, America's southernmost mainland port, unique among East Coast shopping scenes.

15 Best Cruises for Gamblers

Most cruise ships, except for the Clipper, Windjammer, Tall Ship, and American Canadian Caribbean fleets, have casinos. Some casinos emulate those of Las Vegas, whereas others are small and cozy, such as those aboard *Seabourn Pride*. Most have slot machines, blackjack tables, roulette wheels, crap tables, and Caribbean stud poker (the latter a sucker's game if ever we saw one). Some blackjack tables are nonsmoking.

If that isn't enough gambling for you, you may consider visiting one or more of the many casinos that dot the islands and are quite active in the afternoon, when the cruise ships are in port. Puerto Rico has the most glittering array of casinos, but other major stops are St. Maarten, the Dominican Republic, and Aruba, which is considered the gambling capital of the southern Caribbean.

- **Carnival Cruise Lines:** If you like all the glitter and glitz of Vegas, try the "Rainbow Club" casino aboard *Celebration,* with its brassy art, vibrant colors, neon lights, and entertainment lounges of steel and marble. For sheer flash at sea, this casino is hard to match. Yes, some people have actually won money here—enough to pay for their cruise and still have change to spare—but they're the lucky few.
- **Royal Caribbean Cruise Line:** The Casino Royale in the *Sovereign of the Seas,* a glittering "palace" with table games, was an industry leader when first launched in 1988, and it's still going strong. You can place your wagers at blackjack, poker, roulette, or slots in this pulsating casino. One woman exclaimed that this casino "glistens, gleams, clatters, and tempts until the witching hour and beyond."
- **Princess Cruises:** The line attracts gamblers to all its ships, especially the *Crown Princess* and *Regal Princess.* Casinos aboard these vessels have been called a "mini Las Vegas," where you can play horse racing or the tamer bingo, or roulette, blackjack, poker, "Let It Ride," and Caribbean stud poker. Each vessel also has about 160 slot machines. Blackjack tournaments are staged occasionally.
- **Holland America Line:** This line has some of the best casinos afloat, more low-key and less flashy and garish than

those on Carnival Cruises. **Westerdam** is the line's best ship for gambling, both on board and at some of the best casinos in the Caribbean and The Bahamas, especially at St. Maarten and Nassau. At the latter, you can hop over to adjoining Paradise Island to meet Lady Luck.

- **Celebrity Cruises:** Some of the Caribbean's best casinos are aboard Celebrity ships, but if we had to narrow it down we'd say our favorites are those aboard the new *Century* and the recently launched *Galaxy.* These 7,460-square-foot casinos are both larger and more low-key than most. Croupiers offer blackjack, craps, roulette, and slots, and the staffs are among the industry's best. *Century* and *Galaxy* both call at San Juan, where the major hotels all have glittering casinos.

16 Best Fitness Facilities & Spas

If you're concerned about keeping fit while on your cruise, most ships now have excellent fitness facilities and spas where you can work out to your heart's content. Or, you can walk around the deck—again and again and again.

- **Celebrity Cruises:** *Century* and *Galaxy* recently inaugurated "The Spas of the Century," 10,000-square-foot AquaSpas that are the latest and greatest in the industry. With a design inspired by Japanese gardens and bathhouses, the spas are meant to be a tranquil retreat. Facilities include whirlpools, a golf simulator, saunas, mud baths, massage rooms, Turkish baths, a gym, an aerobics room, and a beauty salon. There's even a Thalassotherapy pool, along with aqua-meditation and hydrotherapy baths. *Century* and *Galaxy* exclusively offer the Rasul, an Oriental therapy that includes a medicinal mud pack, seaweed soap shower, herbal steam bath and massage, and a Thalassotherapy pool. Special features include deep-cleansing

La Therapie facials and the revolutionary slimming treatment ionithermie.

- **Princess Cruises:** The line aggressively caters to fitness-oriented passengers aboard all its vessels, offering daily "Cruisercise" classes, including walk-a-mile, stretch-and-tone, high- or low-impact aerobic workouts, and, on some ships, aquacise. One of the best in the fleet is the *Sun Princess,* on which the gym equipment is housed in a glass-walled health center with an open-air pool and two whirlpool spas. There are six swimming pools aboard, including a 50-foot lap pool. The sports deck features basketball, volleyball, badminton, and table tennis.
- **Norwegian Cruise Line:** The *Norway* features the only full-service European spa at sea. Deep in the heart of this great megaship you'll find eight massage rooms, an aquacise pool, steam rooms, a Jacuzzi, showers, and saunas, plus state-of-the-art exercise equipment. A team of European-trained specialists administers many treatments, such as a thermal body wrap that uses aromatherapy oils to detoxify your body as they stimulate your circulation. Five different spa packages are available.
- **Carnival Cruise Lines:** All Carnival ships have Nautica Spas, the best being the 12,000-square-foot incarnations on its 2,040-passenger superliners *Ecstasy, Fantasy, Fascination, Imagination,* and *Sensation.* In the *Ecstasy*'s spa, you can relax in an oval-shaped chamber, surrounded by soothing smells and sounds. The ships also have full gyms complete with free weights and state-of-the-art Keiser progressive resistance exercise machines. Passengers will find low-impact and hour-long advanced aerobics classes, three swimming pools, organized walks on the ships' upper decks, and weight circuit classes. Ships also feature saunas and steam rooms, plus whirlpools, aqua calisthenics and, on some ships, $1/8$-mile-long jogging tracks.

4

The 30 Most Frequently Asked Questions About Cruising

1. **Q: How do I know if I booked the right cruise?**
   A: Frankly, you can never be sure. It's a little like going to a party with strangers—you have no idea whether you're going to have a good time until you get there. However, you can reduce your chances of disappointment by deciding in advance what you're looking for—a wild party scene, say, or peace and quiet—and then reading the detailed ship reviews in chapter 9 and soliciting the advice of a cruise specialist who understands your needs.

2. **Q: How much time is enough at sea?**
   A: First-timers are often best off with a cruise of seven days or less. For families in particular, we recommend a three- to four-day cruise to start, usually from a Florida port to The Bahamas. More than 10 days is not recommended unless you're familiar with the shortcomings of life at sea and accept them with grace and humor.

3. **Q: When should I go?**
   A: You'll find the greatest selection of Caribbean cruise options between November and April, with the peak season during December, January, and February. Fall cruises run the risk of changed itineraries, cancellation, or postponement due to hurricanes. Lower-priced cruises are an off-season lure from June to late September.

4. **Q: Exactly what is a theme cruise?**
   A: More and more travelers are choosing a theme cruise tailor-made to their interests: sports, gardening, golf, wine, jazz, country-and-western music, gay, lesbian, or whatever. Some of the best theme cruises, generally attracting an over-40 crowd, focus on the golden oldies of the 1950s and 1960s, bring aboard some of the aging legends of that era, and put a distinct premium on Elvis impersonators.

   Many ships choose a topic and cruise with world-renowned experts in that field, who give seminars, answer questions, and make themselves available for discussions. A "Gala Society Cruise" might recreate the glamour of the Golden Age of the 1930s, with Hollywood celebrities, classic films, and big bands. Other entertaining themes include theater-at-sea cruises, musical cruises, and murder mystery cruises.

   To choose a theme cruise, contact a cruise specialist or travel agent. Various themes are announced every season. Among the lines, Norwegian Cruise Line is a leader in theme cruises.

5. Q: Aren't all ships basically alike?
A: Only to the extent that they all float. The experience of cruising can be as different depending on your ship as visits to New Jersey and France, an overnight stay in a Days Inn or in a Ritz-Carlton. Some ships offer elegant dining rooms with gourmet cuisine, others have summer camp–style buffets. Service can range from nonexistent to breakfast in bed, cabin sizes from shack to palace, and itineraries from well structured to nonstructured. Weigh what's important to you, and choose wisely.

6. Q: Is cruising a good value for the money?
A: Because the cruise price is relatively all-inclusive, it can offer great value. But don't forget to add in some serious extras, like tipping, shore excursions, shopping, and gambling. We've outlined how to get the best price on a cruise in chapter 6.

7. Q: Will a single person feel lost at sea?
A: Cruise ships are ideal for singles, unless they deliberately choose to be alone. Cruises are generally divided evenly between men and women. Industry trends indicate that somewhere around 30% of passengers are single.

8. Q: Are brochure prices realistic?
A: No. Use them only for general guidelines and comparison shopping. For more information, refer to chapter 6.

9. Q: What extra charges can I expect?
A: Airfare, port taxes, tipping, incidentals such as liquor and suntan lotion, laundry, shore excursions, and shopping. For many passengers, the biggest expense is gambling, which can run into the thousands if you're not careful.

10. Q: What exactly are port taxes or charges?
A: Port taxes—actually port charges in today's terminology—are a subject of controversy and even a major lawsuit that may take years to resolve. Once "port tax" was the actual fee a ship line had to pay at a port of call. Today, they are called port charges, and for a seven-day Caribbean cruise they average $120 in addition to the price of your ticket. Cruise lines claim they are not making money on port charges, but use the fee to settle with the port tax collectors and to cover dockage fees, extra security costs, trash disposals, tugboats, or whatever.

11. Q: How do you go about booking a cruise when there are so many to choose from?
A: First, narrow down your destination; certain ports of embarkation tend to lead you to certain ports of call. For instance, departures from New Orleans explore the western Caribbean, while cruise ships departing from Miami, Fort Lauderdale, and Tampa sail to both the eastern and western Caribbean: The Bahamas, Key West, the Cayman Islands, Jamaica, and the Yucatán peninsula. If you want to combine a cruise with a stateside vacation, you can easily hit Disney World from Port Canaveral.

If you want to explore the eastern or southern Caribbean, San Juan is the best port of embarkation. It's within easy sailing distance of the U.S. and British Virgin Islands, as well as all the Leeward Islands, such as St. Kitts, and all the Windward Islands, including the French West Indies and Barbados. Some cruises leave from St. Maarten, Barbados, Martinique, and even Aruba.

The Caribbean Islands

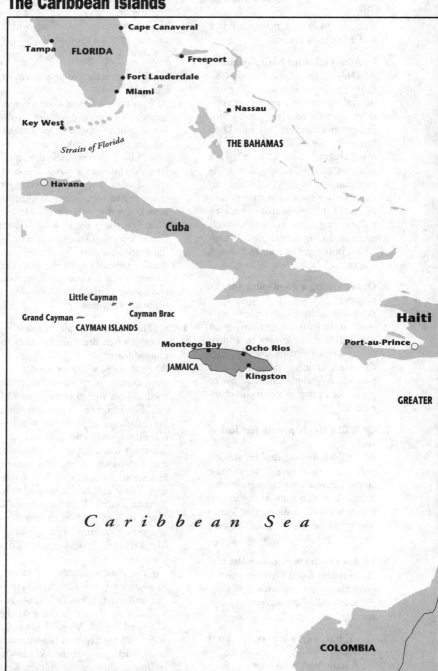

Cape Canaveral

Tampa

FLORIDA

Freeport

Fort Lauderdale

Miami

Nassau

Key West

Straits of Florida

THE BAHAMAS

Havana

Cuba

Little Cayman

Cayman Brac

Grand Cayman

CAYMAN ISLANDS

Haiti

Port-au-Prince

Montego Bay

Ocho Rios

JAMAICA

Kingston

GREATER

Caribbean Sea

COLOMBIA

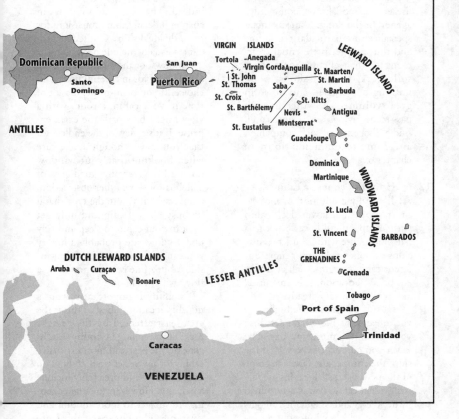

0 | 200 mi
320 km

Atlantic

Ocean

TURKS AND CAICOS ISLANDS

Dominican Republic

Santo
Domingo

San Juan

Puerto Rico

VIRGIN ISLANDS

Tortola Anegada

Virgin Gorda Anguilla

St. John

St. Thomas

St. Croix

St. Barthélemy

St. Eustatius

Saba

St. Maarten/
St. Martin

Barbuda

St. Kitts

Nevis

Montserrat

Antigua

ANTILLES

LEEWARD ISLANDS

Guadeloupe

Dominica

Martinique

WINDWARD ISLANDS

St. Lucia

St. Vincent

THE
GRENADINES

BARBADOS

Grenada

DUTCH LEEWARD ISLANDS

Aruba Curaçao

Bonaire

LESSER ANTILLES

Tobago

Port of Spain

Trinidad

Caracas

VENEZUELA

But, you ask, how do I decide what destinations are for me? Well, what's your idea of a perfect vacation? A sun-drenched beach fronting crystal-clear ocean and a cool drink in your hand? Perhaps an all-night casino with a floor show that'll knock your socks off? Or maybe a thousand little shops all spread out before you like a buffet? If it's beaches and/or gambling you're after, the western Caribbean is for you, but if shopping's your bag, try the eastern Caribbean. For more detailed info, refer to chapter 10, "Ports of Call," where we give you the low-down on each port.

Price is obviously a major factor. To get the best deal, we suggest you use a cruise specialist or "cruise-only" agency for booking. Some agencies specialize in a particular cruise line and thus can get preferential treatment for their clients. Some "consolidators" (bucket shops) book nothing but cruises, and do so in great volume, allowing them to pass some savings on to you. You'll find a discussion of such companies, and some recommendations, in chapter 6.

12. Q: How do I choose a cabin?
A: It's really a question of money. From an inside, lower-deck cabin with an upper and lower bunk to a balconied suite with a butler, cruise ships can offer a dozen or more different cabin categories, all at different prices. Location, size, amenities, and service can vary greatly.

As a rule of thumb, the higher up you are and the more light gets into your cabin, the more you pay. The lower you go into the bowels of the ship, the cheaper the fare. On some of the newer ships, all cabins are virtually identical, so cost is determined by deck level and whether it's an outside cabin with a window or an inside cabin without. There's pros and

cons for both. For instance, cabins on the promenade deck are often costly and sound just grand, but you may be distracted by passengers walking or talking outside, particularly those who decide to peek inside your stateroom to catch the "view."

Potential cruisers have been known to pace off their cabin space on the floor at home, because cabin size measurements advertised in brochures don't mean a lot in the abstract. Know, however, that 120 square feet means 10 feet by 12 feet. This is small and cramped for most passengers. If you want more room, book the medium-size 180-square-foot cabin. Some suites give you 250 to 300 square feet, which is roomy indeed. The cruise ship reviews in chapter 9 detail cabin dimensions for the individual ships. Cruise line brochures usually include deck plans.

Windows, or the lack of them, are also a big factor in determining cabin choice. If you plan to spend a lot of time in your cabin, a room with a view might be worth the extra expense. If it's a view of the endless sea that you crave, though, make sure when booking that your window doesn't just give you a good view of a lifeboat or some other obstruction. Conversely, if you're the type that'll be busy aboard ship and only get back to your cabin to sleep and tidy up, windows are probably a luxury you can do without, making an inside cabin a fine bet and providing a tidy savings to boot.

If stability is important to you, a midship location is best as this is the area least affected by the vessel's rocking and rolling in stormy seas. In general, the best and most expensive cabins on any vessel are both high up and midship, and preferably include a balcony. However, the higher cabins are subject to more motion and swaying. The cheaper cabins are down below in the bow and stern;

those toward the stern may suffer from engine vibrations.

Once you've determined cabin location, check for proximity to elevators. Again, there's pros and cons: An elevator close by is convenient, but it can also be noisy. Also check if there are any public rooms, such as the disco, above or below a chosen cabin. An experienced travel agent can tell you how good the soundproofing is.

Within the cabin itself, your preference for a twin or queen-size bed is another factor. Most twin-bedded cabins can be converted, but some, such as those with upper and lower berths, cannot. Some ship cabins will accommodate as many as five passengers. Not all cabins have television sets or VCR capabilities. If these amenities are important to you, always determine their availability in advance (they're listed in our ship reviews in chapter 9). Most cabins have showers only; only the most luxurious staterooms have tubs.

Final word of advice: You'll have a better choice of cabins the earlier you book.

13. **Q: How can I be protected if a cruise line unexpectedly goes bankrupt, as Regency Cruises did?**
A: For most cruises, you'll make two payments: the initial deposit and then the final payment, usually due 70 days before departure. You can be partially protected by making the last payment by credit card, because the credit card company might help you through any mess that arises. By federal law, cruise lines have to post indemnity bonds, but they apply only to passengers who leave from American ports. Airfare to the port is not covered.

14. **Q: Can I arrange my own air transportation?**
A: Absolutely. Many people use frequent-flier mileage, and Floridians often drive to the ports. Cruise lines contract with airlines far in advance, without consideration of any special deal the airline may run, so you may get a better deal booking on your own, particularly if there's a price war going on. In any case, it's always a good idea to compare prices. All cruise lines will sell you the sea portion of a cruise without airfare, if that's what you want. See chapter 6 for details.

15. **Q: What happens if a flight delay causes me to miss the sailing or my luggage is missing?**
A: Cruise lines handle each flight delay case separately, so there's no standard answer. The lines are not responsible for airline delays, even if your flight was included in your air/sea package, and the airlines are not liable for you missing your sailing, so it's a no-win situation unless the cruise line and/or airline makes some voluntary arrangement. You can buy trip cancellation or interruption insurance that covers these possibilities.

If your luggage is missing, don't leave the airport until you've made a claim. In most cases, your ship will work with the airline to get your bags forwarded to one of the first ports of call.

16. **Q: Are the days numbered for older cruise ships?**
A: The mysterious acronym SOLAS is said to have sealed the doom of older liners such as the *QE2*. SOLAS stands for "Safety of Life at Sea," and it's administered by the London-based International Maritime Organization (IMO), which sets safety standards for all but a small percentage of the world's ships. New regulations came into being after 158 people died in a 1990 fire at sea on the *Scandinavia Star* sailing between Denmark and Norway. These new regulations have forced a shift away from wood to less combustible

Model Deck Plan

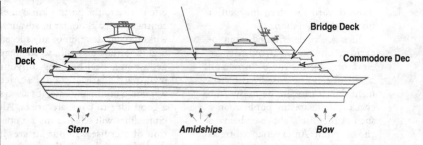

Mariner Deck

Bridge Deck

Commodore Dec

Stern   Amidships   Bow

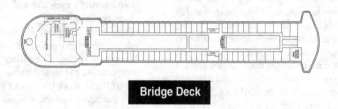

Bridge Deck

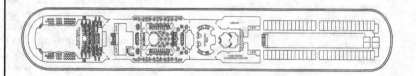

Promenade Deck

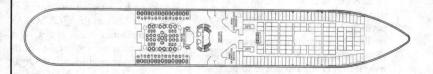

Main Deck

Typical Outside Cabin Configurations

- Twin beds (can often be pushed together)
- Upper berths for extra passengers fold into walls
- Bathrooms usually have showers only (no tub)
- Usually (but not always) have TVs and radios
- May have portholes or picture windows

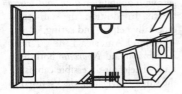 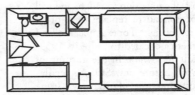

Typical Suite Configurations

- Queen-size or double beds
- Sitting areas (sometimes with sofa beds for extra passengers)
- Large bathrooms, usually with tub
- Refrigerators (sometimes stocked, sometimes not)
- Stereos and TVs with VCRs are common
- Large closets
- Large windows or outside verandas

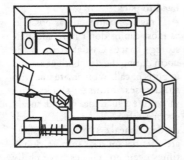 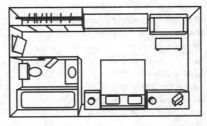

materials and mandated safer stairwells, more smoke detectors and sprinklers, and emergency lighting leading to exits. Not even older vessels are exempt from the latest SOLAS requirements, though the expense of retrofitting them can be horrendous. By 2005, all ships must have met such requirements as the installation of sprinkler systems, and by 2010 all vessels, including those built before 1980, will be forced to use only noncombustible materials. Some ship lines have deemed the cost of conversion too high, and will opt instead to replace their older ships outright. For example, Holland America decided to retire its 1959-built *Rotterdam* in the autumn of 1997, before new SOLAS regulations become mandatory. Some ships, such as Fantasy cruises' 1932-constructed *Britanis,* have already bowed out. Estimates are that about one-fourth of the North American fleet will require major retrofitting. That means a lot of ships, including many now sailing in Caribbean waters, will be for sale.

It may indeed be the sunset years of the classic liners so beloved by the likes of the Astors and Rockefellers, so if your dream cruise is more teakwood than titanium, the time to sail is now.

17. **Q: Which ships are best for passengers with disabilities?**
A: Certain ships have a few cabins specially designed and equipped for passengers with disabilities. However, many cruise lines require that a passenger with disabilities travel with an able-bodied companion. You might consider Norwegian Cruise Line's *Dreamward* and *Windward,* which are more accessible to persons with disabilities than most ships. All decks and most activities are wheelchair accessible, except for the Sky Deck and public toilets. Special cabins are also available for passengers

with hearing impairments. Other cruise lines supply special headsets in their theaters for those with hearing difficulties.

Celebrity Cruises' *Century* and its twin, *Galaxy,* have eight wheelchair-accessible cabins. Passengers must bring their own collapsible wheelchairs.

Costa Cruise Lines' *CostaAllegra* and *CostaClassica* both have wheelchair-accessible elevators and public toilets. The *CostaAllegra* has eight cabins designated for passengers with disabilities; the *CostaClassica* has six. In addition, the staff seems especially helpful and caring.

Holland America Line's *Nieuw Amsterdam* and *Noordam* both have four wheelchair-accessible cabins on the ships' Navigation decks, listed as Category B deluxe outside double rooms. All elevators aboard can accommodate wheelchairs.

Majesty Cruise Line's *Royal Majesty* has "wheelchair-friendly" decks, with four elevators. Public toilets can also accommodate wheelchairs. Four cabins were specially equipped for passengers with disabilities. Both the ship and its helpful staff get high marks.

Ships that aren't suitable for passengers with disabilities include the *Club Med 1, Sir Francis Drake,* and Star Clippers' or Wind Stars' ships.

18. **Q: What type of clothing do I need to pack?**
A: Travel as compactly as possible, as most cabins don't have adequate storage space. Casual attire is the norm during the day, both at sea and in ports of call. Women are fine with sundresses, blouses, slacks, and shorts. It's a good idea to pack sneakers or rubber-soled sandals to wear on deck; sneakers or walking shoes are essential for days in port. Sometimes even hot climes have chilly evenings, so it's handy to have a jacket, sweater, or scarf.

A typical three- or four-day cruise includes one formal evening; a seven-day cruise has two. If men don't have formal wear or don't want to pay the cost of a rental, a dark suit is generally acceptable. (A few large cruise ships have tuxedos for rent.) Nonformal evenings aboard such lines as Carnival see men wearing sports shirts and women wearing slacks. However, aboard such up-market ships as Seabourn, men and women tend to dress up every night; for men, jacket and tie are de rigueur.

19. Q: Should I take a shore excursion or not?
A: It depends on the port. (We make recommendations for each in chapter 10.) As a general rule, it's best not to go on organized shore excursions unless you're worried about getting around on your own, or would rather leave the logistics to others. In virtually every Caribbean port of call you can find a taxi to take you just where you want to go, and at your own pace. Splitting a cab with three or four passengers may be cheaper and more fun than rubbing elbows with a busload of strangers. We've not met anyone who thinks waiting for 50 or more people to come ashore and climb on and off a bus is fun; it's a waste of time that can be better spent sightseeing or shopping.

A shore excursion may make sense if it's otherwise difficult and expensive to reach a remote or hard-to-find sight. In Dominica, for example, you may not want to venture into the jungle on your own. Most shore excursions cost $25 to $50 per person, although some elaborate ones could cost as much as $300 if "flightseeing packages" are included.

Sightseeing on your own can sometimes cost less than a group tour, so it pays to compare prices. In St.

Thomas, for instance, the dives on the submarine *Atlantis* cost less if you buy them at a booth in the downtown area of Charlotte Amalie than they do if you go as part of an excursion.

20. Q: What are the rules for tipping?
A: Mass-market cruise lines pay their stewards as little as $45 per month, expecting passengers to make up the difference in tips. The amount you tip is merely suggested; the actual amount is up to you. Cruise Lines International Association (CLIA), the industry authority, recommends tipping both your room steward and your dining room waiter $2.50 to $3 per day, and half that per day for your busboy. (We're a little more generous; we suggest at least $4.50 per day for your steward and waiter, and half that for your busboy.)

On some ships you're asked to pay a single sum, which is distributed to everyone; on others, you're given a list of people to reward individually, which generally costs more than a blanket tip. Tipping waiters, busboys, and stewards is expected, but tipping a full salaried maître d' or housekeeper is not really necessary, although it's quite common. Most ships now include a 15% tip in their drink prices, so tipping bartenders may not be necessary. For more advice on tipping, see chapter 7.

21. Q: What is duty-free shopping and is it a good deal?
A: Duty-free means a traveler can make purchases free of duty or tax when leaving a country, on the assumption that those goods will be used or consumed after departure. Once tobacco, liquor, and perfumes dominated duty-free purchases, but now virtually all premium luxury goods are sold duty-free, including jewelry and electronics. In a Caribbean port of call, the savings on duty-free merchandise can range from as

little as 5% to as much as 50% on a particular item.

It pays to check out prices on goods you may want to buy before you leave home. Unless there's a special sale being offered, many products will carry comparable price tags from island to island.

22. Q: How can I avoid dining with people I don't like?
A: Maître d's will go to great lengths to make table reassignments; just ask. Our cruise line reviews in chapter 9 discuss seating arrangements and table configurations; also see "The Politics of Dining" in chapter 7.

23. Q: What about special diets?
A: Almost any imaginable diet can be handled by cruise-ship chefs— vegetarian, low fat, low cholesterol, salt-free, Kosher, and on and on. But it's absolutely necessary to let cruise lines know your dietary restrictions at least two weeks before you sail. See the individual cruise line reviews in chapter 9 for details.

24. Q: What about the dreaded *mal de mer?*
A: Seasickness is the curse of cruising. Some people succumb to it even on ships that are well stabilized and even when the seas aren't rough; others don't ever seem to be bothered.

Many antiseasickness medicines are sold over the counter or by prescription. One of the best known is Dramamine. Most physicians recommend and prescribe the Transderm patch, which is applied behind the ear and left on for three days. This patch may lead to complications, however, such as dilation of the pupils, disorientation, restlessness, blurred vision, and dry mouth.

Many cruise specialists have for years been recommending ginger, which can be taken in capsules available at health food stores. We've tried them several times and found them effective; others, however, have

found them no help at all. You might also try a canned drink called "Smooth Sailing," which its manufacturer claims was specifically designed to help beat the queasy feeling of mal de mer. It contains a blend of papaya, passion fruit, and pineapple juices, plus ginger and a combination of other, all-natural, herbal extracts, is lightly sweetened with fructose, and carries only 90 calories to a 12-ounce can. If your local health food store doesn't sell it, you can contact **Smooth Sailing,** 851 Coho Way, Suite 203, Bellingham, WA 98225 (☎ **800/ 570-1188**) to place an order.

There are also wristbands available that apply acupressure via a small embedded plastic button, and some people swear they keep the seasickness beast at bay. You can find them in travel supply shops and catalogs and in some onboard shops as well.

25. Q: What should I do if I miss the boat?
A: A potential nightmare but it happens frequently. If you get delayed in a port of call and your ship sails without you, appeal to the line's port agent. Aping an episode of *I Love Lucy,* the port agent can send a passenger out by chartered boat or tug, or even on a ship that goes out to reclaim the harbor pilot that guides a vessel out of port. If the ship has gone too far to sea, authorization can be obtained from the ship's captain to provide funds for a room, food, and airfare to the next port of call— necessary services if you're caught in Martinique, for example, with only a bikini and no toothbrush or credit card. (Don't think the lines do this out of the goodness of their hearts, though—you will be billed later.) Cruise lines don't advertise this service, because they don't want you to think you can miss their ships with impunity. You'll usually find the name of the port agent and his

phone number listed obscurely in a daily activities calendar. Make a note of it. You might be glad you did.

26. Q: What recourse do I have if a ship changes its itinerary and doesn't call at a port I was looking forward to?
A: None. The fine print on a cruise contract carefully explains that captains and/or cruise lines can do whatever they feel is necessary to ensure the safety of the ship and its passengers. There may be reasons certain ports have to be avoided, the most obvious being the threat of storms or hurricanes.

27. Q: Should I be worried about the June 1 to November 1 hurricane season in the Caribbean?
A: Thanks to satellite surveillance, it's extremely unlikely that a cruise ship will be caught in a hurricane. Moreover, ships can travel at 20 or more knots, which is faster than most storms. To avoid a hit by a hurricane, ships can head south to islands such as Aruba, Bonaire, and Curaçao, which lie outside the hurricane belt. If a storm should strike suddenly, modern ships are well constructed to withstand heavy seas.

28. Q: Can I get married aboard ship?
A: Yes, but not at sea by the captain, as you may have thought. In port, you can invite your own priest, rabbi, or minister aboard, plus friends and family to attend the ceremony and reception, but they must all disembark before sailing or else pay the full fare.

Many cruise lines will offer to help you tie the knot with your beloved. Because of its massive volume of bookings, Carnival is the market leader in walking couples down the aisle. Legally binding weddings, properly officiated and accessorized with enough grace notes to soften most wedding-day jitters, are a common sight aboard Carnival ships when they're anchored at any continental U.S. port (particularly Miami) or within the harbors of either St. Thomas or Grand Cayman. (Wedding ashore on other islands requires a period of advance residency and some legal restrictions that don't usually coincide with most cruise lines' itineraries.) You'll have to pay a fee to bring your officiant aboard, but Carnival will sell you a package to help celebrate the event. A Carnival basic wedding costs $490 and a "deluxe romance" wedding goes for $1,100. The cost of an on-island wedding (such as on St. Thomas or Grand Cayman) is $675 per couple. For more information, you can always elicit the advice of such outfits as **The Cruise Line, Inc.,** 150 NW 168th St., N. Miami, FL 33169 (☎ **800/777-0707**).

29. Q: What are sanitation ratings?
A: Every six months, inspectors from the Centers for Disease Control (CDC) check any ship sailing between a U.S. port and a foreign destination; the U.S. Food and Drug Administration inspects ships that remain solely in U.S. waters.

Cruise ships are rated on general cleanliness, storage, and repair; potential for contamination of food; food preparation and handling; and purity of fresh-water supplies. Ships that score below 86 on the agency's scale of 1 to 100 must make corrective repairs and be reinspected within 30 to 60 days.

See "The Ships at a Glance" chart in chapter 2 for CDC ratings on the individual vessels. You can receive a more detailed individual vessel report—or order the free "Green Sheet" (document no. 510051), which lists the score of every ship inspected within the previous six months—by writing to **The Chief of the Vessel Sanitation Program,** National Center for Environmental Health, 1015 North America Way,

Room 107, Miami, FL 33132 (☎ **305/536-4307**). You can also fax your request and get a fax back (fax 404/332-4565).

30. Q: Since the cruise industry is constantly changing, where can I get the latest industry information?
A: We've made every effort to make this book as up-to-date as it could be right up until the minute it went to press, but for last-minute updates, check out the bimonthly *Porthole Magazine* (☎ **954/746-5554**), *Cruise Travel Magazine* (☎ **800/ 877-5893**), or the monthly *Ocean*

and Cruise News (☎ and fax **203/ 329-2787**).

You can also contact **Cruise Lines International Association** (CLIA), 500 Fifth Ave., Suite 1407, New York, NY 10110 (☎ **212/921- 0066**), for reliable and impartial cruise industry data.

Finally, those of you who have Internet access should check out **Cruise News** at **http://www. travelpage.com/cruise/c_news.htm** for up-to-the-minute news. (Look for other informative pages in the "Websites" section at the back of this book.)

Family Cruising 5

Not long ago, one of every five couples took their children to sea with them; today, that figure has almost doubled. Why the increase? In the 1980s, cruise-line strategists turned the decline in summer camps to their own personal advantage. Many lines announced a new roster of activities for young children and teens, backed by a staff of professional counselors and baby-sitters. In addition, special children's rates or discounted family fares were introduced. Suddenly there was an armada of jumbo ships waiting to float children away with their parents for a round of nonstop activity. Lines such as Premier, with its "Big Red Boat," Carnival, and even Celebrity actively court the family market, but even their efforts will be eclipsed by those of Disney when it enters the cruise competition in 1998.

Cruise lines offer various arrangements for families. Sometimes children sharing a cabin with their parents get to travel free and eat free meals; other times, they're granted a substantial discount. Policies change seasonally, so it always pays to check with a cruise specialist.

So how do you engineer a successful waterborne adventure with your children? Any family cruise vacation will have its share of frustrations and stresses, so it pays to plan carefully before you plunge into the deep. Among the variables to consider is cruise duration: If this is your first family cruise, we strongly recommend choosing an itinerary of three or four days, certainly no more than seven. Imagine that last long drive, where the kids wanted out of the car after the first couple of hours—now extrapolate to what would happen after the first few days at sea if the kids didn't take to it. We think you get the idea.

1 Cruising with Kids

Even with all the family discounts and incentives, a cruise will still cost more than a basic land vacation at the nearest beach or pool. But there are ways of cutting costs. Most cruise lines stipulate that any child under 18 who shares a cabin with two adults is charged only 50% of the rate, *if* the family agrees to hole up in the least desirable accommodations. The discount decreases the better the cabin a family books. Some lines let very young children, usually under two years, sail for free in a shared stateroom with their parents. Children under 18 will never have to pay more than the discounted third- or fourth-passenger rate that cruise lines grant to all passengers, which could be a rate of $70 to $150 per day, depending on the ship.

What children's programs can you expect to find? Some ships offer everything from pin-the-tail-on-the-donkey games and scavenger hunts to teen disco nights and versions of the *Dating Game* that might raise eyebrows among more puritanical parents. At the opposite extreme, some lines bring along a lineup of popular cartoon characters and clowns: Premier Cruise Lines gives you Daffy Duck, the Road Runner, and Bugs Bunny; Dolphin Cruise Lines gives you the Flintstones and the Jetsons; Disney, when it starts up, will give you Disney.

Activities aren't always as corny as you or your bright teenager might think. Many emphasize arts and crafts; computer knowledge; tours of unusual parts of the ship, such as the galley and navigation areas; kite-flying contests off the stern; discussions of the colonial histories of each port of call; and, in some of the best of the children's programs, rehearsals for a show that will be performed near the end of the cruise for parents and well-wishers. Teenagers will also enjoy disco parties, Sadie Hawkins dances (where shy girls can ask even more bashful boys to dance), cooking classes, and macramé-weaving contests. Your child might develop an interest in such activities as trap-shooting, aerobics, dance, golf, or maybe even reading.

And don't worry about interviewing baby-sitters on board. Any cruise line geared to children has a bevy of them. You can arrange for baby-sitting in-cabin or in an activities center designed just for kids. Each line's offerings are described in chapter 9.

2 Choosing a Family-Friendly Ship

It's not difficult to determine which ships welcome families and which ships don't. Our reviews make this distinction clear. You can also check brochures, because a cruise line that likes kids will lavishly publicize it, emphasizing rates, menus, games, lectures, and lessons for children.

Family Travel Times, published quarterly by Travel with Your Children (TWYCH), is a valuable source of information, rich with tips and insights into the intricacies of traveling with children. Subscriptions cost $40 a year, and include a weekly call-in service for subscribers. TWYCH also publishes a nitty-gritty guide called *Great Cruise Vacations with Your Kids,* third in a series of child-friendly guidebooks edited by company founder Dorothy Jordan. The price is $11.95 plus postage and handling. For a subscription, a purchase, or a free information packet that includes a sample issue of the newsletter, write **TWYCH,** 40 Fifth Ave., New York, NY 10011 (☎ **212/ 477-5524**).

3 The Best Cruise Lines for Kids

We've picked the top cruise lines for families in chapter 3, but can't resist talking about it again here (and mentioning a few more good picks). Keep in mind that even certain adult-only cruise lines cater to young travelers at certain times of the year, particularly in the summer.

All of the following lines offer top-rated children's programs, which are described in detail in the chapter 9 ship reviews. Here we compare what each cruise line offers in the way of such kid-related factors as baby-sitting, children's menus, and children's discounts.

- **Carnival Cruise Lines:** This line is the market leader in family cruises, hosting a record 100,000 kids annually aboard its "Fun Ships." Its counselors run a wide variety of fun-filled activities year-round, and private baby-sitters can be arranged through the purser's office.

  Most ships have cabins designed to accommodate families, with twin beds as well as one or two upper berths. Roll-aways are available to provide a fifth berth, as are cribs for the little ones. Onboard restaurants are ready with children's menus, and elsewhere on board are facilities for the hot-dog-and-ice-cream fast-food fare that sets kids' hearts aflutter.

Families can take advantage of heavily discounted rates for third and fourth occupants of double cabins.

- **Celebrity Cruises:** During summer and in certain seasonal periods when its family cruising program is in effect, this line takes good care of children, with an imaginative program for three age groups. Group baby-sitting is available from 10pm to 1am every evening for children ages three and up, and you can also arrange for private baby-sitting.

  Many cabins, even those of standard dimensions, are suitable for three to four people, and cribs are available for toddlers. For breakfast, kids can keep their own company at a special Celebrity Breakfast Club. At dinner, a special children's menu is available.

  Children under two travel free, and those ages 3 to 11 occupying the cabin of two full-fare adults are charged special rates. Special single-parent discounts are offered, although not during peak periods at Christmas and during January and February.

- **Costa Cruise Line:** This line has one of the best youth programs afloat, known as "The Kids Club" for children ages 5 to 12 and as "The Costa Teens Club" for teenagers 13 to 17. On most cruises, group baby-sitting is available for children ages three and up.

  Some ship cabins are outfitted for berthing up to two additional passengers. There's no special children's menu, but the line is ever-ready with pizzas served throughout the day and Italian ice cream that kids can't get enough of.

  Children under two travel free, and those over two are granted substantial reductions at a third- or fourth-person rate in a shared room with their parents.

- **Dolphin Cruise Line:** Dolphin's three- and four-night cruises are good for families on their first cruise. The line's Camp Jellystone children's program is supervised by trained counselors and, as you might have guessed, is heavy on Hanna-Barbera cartoon themes. Baby-sitting is generally available during the day and in the evening, as well as when the ship is in port.

  Many inside cabins have four berths, but a family of four might find this arrangement cramped. Special children's menus, with a Hanna-Barbera theme, include Puppy Power Pizza or Spacey Steak Surprise. Kids must eat with their families.

  Children under two sail free, and children over two are granted substantial discounts at third- or fourth-passenger rates in shared cabins with their parents.

- **Holland America Line:** Each ship has a year-round children's program, with at least one counselor aboard. The line features three-night packages to Orlando either pre- or postcruise.

  Some cabins can accommodate a third and fourth passenger on a sofa bed that folds away when not in use. A children's menu is offered, and families must eat together.

  Traveling with two adults, children ages 2 to 12 are granted substantial reductions as the third or fourth passenger listed in a cabin. Cribs must be reserved when you book your tickets.

- **Norwegian Cruise Line:** The "Kids Crew" program is offered year-round for children ages six and seven, and during the summer months or major holidays for children ages three to five. Norwegian offers guaranteed baby-sitting from noon to 2am.

  Lower category cabins, not the more upscale staterooms, can accommodate a third or fourth passenger. Aboard *Dreamward* and *Windward,* deluxe suites can house four people, and some U-shaped suites can accommodate a family of six. Children's menus are available, and kids enjoy the Chocoholic Bar dessert buffets. They can even order chocolate pizzas. Ice cream is served every afternoon.

Children under two sail for free, and substantial discounts are granted children over two at third- or fourth-passenger rates in a shared room with their parents.

- **Premier Cruise Lines:** This is America's number-one family cruise and vacation line. (We'll have to wait and see if Disney knocks them off that pedestal.) Because their embarkation point at Port Canaveral is close to Walt Disney World, Premier has successfully marketed holidays with time at sea and time spent on land in the magic of Walt's kingdom. A typical land/sea package would include a three- or four-night cruise to The Bahamas, combined with a three- or four-night stay at a Walt Disney World Resort Hotel such as the Yacht and Beach Club.

Premier continues to be the industry leader with innovative onboard programming and amenities for children. Private baby-sitting isn't available, but children ages 2 to 12 can spend a few hours or even stay overnight (from 10pm to 9am) in an accessory-packed recreation area called Pluto's Playhouse.

Cabins sleep between two and five occupants, with upper berths and sofas that convert to beds. Children's menus are available, and many families request the early seating at dinner.

Children under two sail free, and children ages two to seven who share rooms with parents get major discounts at third- and fourth-passenger rates. A fifth passenger in the same cabin also receives substantial discounts.

- **Princess Cruises:** Aboard the *Star Princess, Sky Princess,* and *Sun Princess,* children and teenagers will enjoy their own youth facility and a full schedule of entertainment and counselor-supervised activities. The other ships in Princess's fleet run a full youth program when at least 15 youngsters are aboard, but those ships don't have formal children's areas. Group baby-sitting is available only on some ships (determine which ones when you're booking).

Many cabins have third or fourth berths, although they might feel cramped. Ships have poolside pizzerias, and children enjoy lunch buffets of hot dogs, hamburgers, and barbecued chicken. Families must eat together.

Children from 18 months to 17 years pay half the minimum fare in a shared cabin with their parents.

- **Royal Caribbean Cruise Line:** The Kids/Tweens/Teens Program, available for children ages 5 to 17, is offered year-round on such ships as *Majesty of the Seas, Monarch of the Seas,* and *Sovereign of the Seas.* During vacation periods and holidays, programs are featured on all the vessels. Royal Caribbean vessels feature some of the most extensive children's facilities afloat, including a teen disco and a children's playroom on certain ships. Baby-sitting is usually available in the evenings, and sometimes during the day and in port.

Some cabins can hold third or fourth passengers in upper berths, and there are also some six-person family suites. Special children's menus are available, and kids eat with their families except when participating in group meals.

The best values are the third- and fourth-person rates for children with two adults; babies sail free.

4 Cruising Tips for Families

Here are some suggestions for better sailing and smoother seas on your family cruise.

- Check in advance with the cruise line to make sure the ship you're sailing offers everything your child might need. Are cribs or bottle warmers available?

Will the kitchen prepare special food for your child?

- Sometimes too much family togetherness in cramped cabins can lead to conflicts. Did you know that your teenager spent that much time in the bathroom, or that he or she could ever be that messy in closed quarters? If your budget allows, consider booking a separate cabin for your children. Some enforced separation can be an excellent investment. It may even be possible to book interconnecting cabins.
- Pack a thermometer, basic first-aid supplies, and any medications your doctor may suggest. Cruise lines have limited supplies of these items, and can quickly run out if the ship has many families aboard. If an accident should happen aboard, virtually every ship afloat has its own infirmary staffed by doctors and nurses. First aid can usually be summoned more readily aboard ship than on land.
- No one needs to tell you: Warn younger children about the danger of falling overboard and make sure they know not to play on the railings.
- This might be the time to buy your young children their first wristwatches. Although oceangoing schedules may seem relaxed, shipboard life is rigorously timed, with arrivals and departures, activities, meals, and entertainment beginning and ending promptly. Life aboard ship might cure chronic tardiness because your child might miss meals, meetings with friends—or the boat.
- Whenever a ship is in port, establish a meeting spot (such as your cabin or a corner of a public lounge), and meet there after boarding to make sure no one is still ashore.
- For shore excursions, you may want to pack beach accessories—toys, water wings, sandals, and so on.
- No matter how much money you spend on your family's cabin or suite, it will invariably be smaller (often *much* smaller) than your home. Your children will size up the cabin's limitations in about three seconds and probably want to explore the ship. Before they do, make sure they know their cabin's number, what deck it's on, and when and where you expect to see them again.
- Prepare kids for the sad news that not every cabin has a TV, and that those that do offer a narrow range of programs. On the brighter side, your ship is likely to have nightly movies, a video arcade, and nonstop activities.
- Some children take to cruising like ducks to water; others are more intimidated by the experience. To make the transition easier, consider packing a security blanket for your young child, and favorite toys and books.
- Yes, you and your partner can go on a date, even with kids in tow. All you have to do is take them to the early dinner seating or let them get room service in the cabin.

6 Booking a Cruise for the Best Price

Except for peak-season cruises between Christmas and New Year's, forget the prices listed in the cruise-line brochures. Overcapacity and fierce competition have ushered in the age of the discounted fare. There are great bargains out there, enough at times to baffle even the most experienced cruise-line travel specialists. In this chapter, we'll show you how to find them.

1 Calculating the Cost

The cost of your cruise adds up to a great value—an all-inclusive vacation package. Included are accommodations, stops at ports of call, as many as eight meals a day, a packed schedule of activities, and free use of resort-quality facilities, as well as cabaret, jazz performances, dance bands, and discos. For the most part, there are no hidden costs, except for your bar tab and gambling bill.

Cruises typically cost less than comparable land-based vacations. The key word, of course, is *comparable*. If you stay at a Motel 6 and eat only at the local burger joint, you'll do better on land.

The following chart illustrates what kind of vacation values can be found on the high seas. Prices are based on travel agent estimates for a mid-range vacation to typical Caribbean destinations. According to the Cruise Lines International Association (CLIA), passengers spend on average $175 to $225 per person per day.

	Bahamas Resort—7 Nights	Cruise—7 Nights (Eastern Caribbean, 3 Ports/From Miami)
Brochure Price	$680	$1,475
Airfare	$400	Included
Transfers	Included	Included
Meals	$350	Included
Service Charges (15% Food/Beverage)	$93	n/a
Tips	n/a	$60
Taxes	$76	$89
Sightseeing	$35	$40
Entertainment	$55	Included
Beverages	$150	$100
TOTAL	**$1,839**	**$1,764**
PER DIEM COST	**$263**	**$252**

Average Cost of Onboard Extras

Remember, its not *all* free. Just so you're not shocked when your shipboard account is settled at the end of your trip, here are some prices of onboard extras.

Cost of a cummerbund or cuff links	$20–$250
Dry cleaning a dress	$3.50–$8.50
Dry cleaning a tuxedo or men's two-piece suit	$5–$8.50
Massage (30-minute session)	$30–$45
Men's shampoo and haircut	$18–$22
Women's shampoo and haircut	$20–$32
Photograph purchased from ship's photographer	$5–$8.50
Scotch and soda at an onboard bar	$2.50–$4.50
Ship-to-shore phone call or fax	$9–$15/minute
Shore excursions	$0–$250
Wine to accompany dinner	$5.50–$500
Shipboard souvenirs, logo T-shirts, etc.	$3–$35
Spa treatments	$12–$85

To calculate the per diem cost of your cruise vacation, simply divide the cruise cost, plus the airfare from your place of residence to and from the ports of embarkation and disembarkation, by the number of nights contained within the cruise package. You can use this number to see what kind of cabin you can get on comparable ships. Children occupying a cabin with their parents sail for a lower rate than adults, which will bring down the per diem rate of all persons traveling in your party.

Beware of "superlow" rates when you calculate the per diem. If the price is incredibly lower than that of most competitors, there's probably a reason. Perhaps more charges than usual are tacked on as additional costs.

MORE COSTS TO CONSIDER

Almost everything is included in the cruise price. But you'll have to pay extra for your bar and wine tabs, port taxes, shore excursions, gambling losses, tips, the exorbitant cost of any ship-to-shore phone calls or faxes, any special pampering (hairdressers, manicurists/pedicurists, massages, skin treatments), purchases in the shipboard boutiques and at the ports of call, and medical treatments in the ship's infirmary.

According to the latest survey conducted by Price Waterhouse for the Florida-based Caribbean Cruise Association, the typical cruise passenger spends an average of $124 per island visited in the Caribbean and The Bahamas. The table on the next page breaks down the average passenger's per port expenditure for seven of the most frequently visited ports. Shopping, as you'll see, takes the biggest bite out of most people's wallets.

Pretrip incidentals that could add to your trip cost might include boarding your pets, hiring someone to check on your house, airport or port parking fees, trip or flight insurance, car rentals, and pre- or postcruise hotel packages.

2 How to Find the Best Deals

Pricing in the cruise industry is all about time. As the sailing date approaches, the pressure to fill every unsold cabin increases. Sales and ticketing strategies are adjusted on a weekly basis.

The economics of the cruise industry usually work in your favor. Larry Fishkin, president of The Cruise Line, a Miami-based discount cruise agency, says that "Unlike the airline industry, the economics of the cruise industry demand 100% or

Average Cruise Passenger Expenses										
Port	Average Expenditure Per Person	Food	Shopping	Gambling	Attractions	Entertainment	Taxi	Phone	Tips	Other*
Aruba	$65	8%	64%	8%	8%	1%	6%	0%	1%	4%
Bahamas	$83	19%	51%	10%	7%	2%	3%	1%	2%	5%
Barbados	$61	11%	57%	0%	11%	2%	8%	1%	3%	7%
Curaçao	$63	5%	72%	7%	8%	0%	3%	0%	0%	5%
Key West	$41	17%	64%	1%	9%	1%	2%	1%	2%	3%
Montego Bay	$57	6%	61%	0%	24%	0%	1%	0%	6%	2%
Ochos Rios	$101	3%	75%	9%	4%	0%	3%	1%	3%	2%
San Juan	$158	20%	41%	20%	4%	2%	4%	1%	4%	4%
St. Kitts	$47	10%	42%	2%	18%	1%	20%	1%	3%	3%
St. Thomas	$255	3%	88%	0%	2%	1%	2%	0%	1%	3%
Overall Average	**$124**	**13%**	**61%**	**7%**	**7%**	**1%**	**4%**	**1%**	**2%**	**4%**

* "Other" might include long-distance phone calls, postage for mailing gifts, cash outlays for medical or dental emergencies, etc.

as close to 100% occupancy as possible. It's not economical to operate a ship at 90% occupancy. That extra 10% could represent a large majority of a cruise line's profit." The result: low last-minute fares for travelers with the flexibility to take advantage of them.

Many cruise lines that were once regarded as pricey have become affordable because of all the discounts. Some lines, such as Seabourn, still remain beyond the financial reach of the average cruiser, but nearly all the major lines, including Cunard, Royal Caribbean, and most definitely Carnival, now have deals afloat that put their cabins within the reach of the lower-middle-income cruiser.

DISCOUNT CRUISE LINES

The lines listed below have the lowest per diem rates in the industry:

- **Dolphin Cruise Line** has a fleet of older vessels that attracts many budget and first-time cruisers. Its low prices and helpful, concerned staff have given it a large repeat business.
- **Commodore Cruise Line,** Dolphin's major competitor, operates a 1950s-vintage vessel, *The Enchanted Isle,* which has made a name for itself in the budget cruise market. Although the ship hasn't aged gracefully, it's still a classic old-time liner, and the combination of nostalgia and low prices have added up to continued business for Commodore.

- **American Canadian Caribbean Line** also draws tremendous repeat business, not only for its low prices, but because it offers some of the most exotic itineraries in the Caribbean. Its vessels aren't old, but are far less glamorous than most of the other liners and don't have a huge list of facilities. In other words, they're boats more than floating hotels. With this line, the destination is more important than the way you get there.

DISCOUNTED AIRFARE ADD-ONS

By booking your airfare simultaneously with your cruise, you can often, but not always, get considerable savings. Airfares purchased from the cruise line separately from the cruise price are called "airfare add-ons." To offer a low airfare, the cruise line prepurchases a bulk number of passenger seats on an airline, then absorbs the differences in airfare between points near and far and passes along the discount to you. However, if a price war breaks out between airlines (as is so frequent these days), you'll save even more by booking your own flight. This is a tricky situation and involves a lot of phoning on your part, unless you have the assistance of a good travel agent who's willing to spend a lot of time hunting down the best deal for you.

These airfare packages sometimes include transfers from the airport to the ship and/or a night's hotel stay (sometimes at a hotel the cruise line partially owns). Any changes from the preapproved airline route will be subject to a supplemental fee.

You might not want to add an airline ticket to your cruise package if you've accumulated enough points on a frequent-flier program to fly free; if you live close enough to the port of embarkation to make driving there a realistic option; or if your airline add-on would require a circuitous routing before finally arriving at your port of embarkation.

If you end up arranging your own air transportation, ask whether airfare is part of your cruise contract. If it is, you're often granted a deduction (usually around $250 per person) off the cruise fare.

When the price of a cabin is more than you really want to pay, but the cruise line is standing firm, you can try agreeing to the cabin price but asking for a reduction in airfare. This tactic doesn't always work, but it's paid off for us many times.

SHOULD YOU BOOK YOUR CRUISE EARLY OR AT THE LAST MINUTE?

Once upon a time you'd secure your best cruise deals by booking at the last minute. Though this can still be a good strategy, cruise lines have lately begun to reward those who book early, giving as much as a 15% or greater discount if you pay your passage in full between four and six months in advance of a sailing.

On the down side, discounts almost never apply to peak-season cruises from December through February, and if you've got your eye on an upper-tier suite you'll likely be disappointed, as they often sell out well in advance and are therefore seldom offered at a discount. There are no steadfast rules about this, however; policies differ from line to line, and from week to week. Some cruise lines start out cutting cabin costs for early bookings by up to $500 per person, double occupancy, then reduce the discount radically as the ship fills up.

Of course, you may still get a good deal on a last-minute booking if you have the flexibility essential for the waiting game. These last-minute negotiations are a gamble and they aren't for everyone, particularly not for families who need to plan trips around school holidays. First, you have to be willing to settle for whatever is available, with regard to cabins and ships. Second, savings are not offered on every ship, or every sailing, so you may have to settle for something that isn't the cruise of your dreams. Third, if you have to fly to the port of embarkation, you may have to pay an airfare so high that it cancels out your savings on the cruise. If you were planning to use frequent-flier miles, you'll likely discover that frequent-flier seats are all taken on the flights you need. Moreover, most last-minute deals are completely nonrefundable.

You'll find last-minute deals advertised in the travel section of your Sunday newspaper, particularly those papers circulated within a day's drive of the cruise ship capitals of Fort Lauderdale, Miami, and New Orleans. You should also check with a travel agent or, better yet, an agency that specializes in cruises.

Incidentally, no matter how intrepid you are, don't think you can just walk, suitcase and passport in hand, into a cruise-ship terminal an hour before embarkation and negotiate the killer cruise deal of a lifetime. Most cruise lines protect their pricing policies by rejecting last-minute, pier-side attempts at discounting.

Sure, try it if you want—there's no rule that hasn't been broken by someone out to make a buck—but you'll almost always pay the brochure rate rather than a discounted one.

3 More Ways to Cut Cruise Costs

Here are some more suggestions to save money when you're negotiating your cruise package.

REPOSITIONING CRUISES

You can get good deals on "repositioning cruises," which occur when ships leave one cruise area and sail to another; for instance, when a ship summers in Alaska or New England and migrates to the Caribbean for the winter months. These cruises tend to have lower costs per mile traversed than those solely in the Caribbean, but there will be fewer stops at ports of call, and your cruise will include long stretches of time exclusively at sea.

BACK-TO-BACK CRUISES

When you can't decide where in the Caribbean you want to cruise, consider taking a "back-to-back" cruise: two cruises, one right after another. You'll be on the same boat, but you'll be visiting different ports on the second phase of your journey, and you'll sail with a different set of passengers.

Cruise lines offer big discounts to passengers who book what is in essence a double cruise. Some offer a third week free if you're already combining two weeks together, whereas others grant a flat discount of up to 50% on your second cruise. Carnival, for example, offers back-to-back discounts combining four-day cruises to Cozumel and Key West with three-day cruises to The Bahamas, while Seabourn combines cruises of the southern Caribbean with cruises through the Panama Canal. Your back-to-back scheduling can combine an almost

unlimited number of cruises of long or short duration.

SAIL-AND-STAY PROMOTIONS

These days, cruises are departing from ports that are tourist attractions in their own right. You might want to explore Miami before you sail, drive to Disney World from Port Canaveral, or spend a few days in San Juan.

Many cruise lines negotiate group discounts at hotels for passengers interested in prolonging their vacation. These packages usually include transportation from the hotel to the ship (before the cruise) or from the docks to the hotel (after a cruise). Carnival, for instance, owns a major hotel in Miami and will cut prices significantly for passengers opting to stay there before or after a cruise.

UNADVERTISED SPECIALS

Most passengers don't know that cruise lines often advertise different prices for the same cruise in different American cities. Fares advertised in Atlanta, for example, might not be promoted or advertised in New York. These lower-priced fares are known in the business as "unadvertised regional specials."

How can you, a New Yorker or Chicagoan, get the same discount available to a passenger from Los Angeles or Atlanta? Contact **Cruises of Distinction,** 2750 South Woodward, Bloomfield Hills, MI 48304 (☎ **800/634-3445** or 810/332-2020). A discount broker that stays on top of unadvertised and underpublicized specials, Cruises of Distinction can book a cruise on virtually any ship anywhere in the world. Established clients receive a roster of mailings sent out to the agency by the cruise lines, but if you're a neophyte and tell a phone representative there what some of your preferences are regarding lines and destinations, chances are you'll be added to one or another of the firm's mailing lists for future sales promoted by one or another of the Caribbean's cruise lines.

TWOFERS

Promotions called "twofers" are two-for-one deals that let you bring a companion free. They come and go like hurricane winds, so if you see one, it's worth considering. A cruise specialist should know if some cut-rate discount for two is being offered at the time you plan to sail. (Don't expect to find any of these deals during the Caribbean's peak winter season, though.)

You'll have to negotiate these twofers carefully, and compare them with various air/sea packages to see if you are indeed getting a discounted deal. If airfare is included for both of you, then go for it. But if airfare has to be booked separately, compare the cost of a twofer without airfare to an air/sea package for two to see which one is the better deal.

DISCOUNTS FOR A THIRD OR FOURTH PASSENGER

Many lines still offer cabins that can house a total of three or four passengers, so if you have some very good friends you'd like to cruise with and are willing to be a bit crowded, you can save money by sharing your cabin. Depending on the season and their special promotions, many lines will offer a massively discounted rate for the third and/or fourth passenger sharing a cabin with two passengers paying a "regular" fare. This is especially true for lines with older ships that struggle to compete with the new crop of megaships being launched. For example, sailings aboard three of Norwegian Cruise Line's ships (*Norway, Dreamward,* and *Windward*) offer accommodation in "deluxe inside cabins" on November and early December sailings at a per person per diem rate of $57 for the first two occupants and an almost embarrassingly low $14.30 daily rate for third or fourth occupants. Port taxes and airfare, naturally, are additional, but at these rates, it's more expensive to stay at home. Per diem rates on somewhat more prestigious, better-accessorized ships, such

as Princess Cruises' *Star Princess,* are also worth a second look. If four occupants share a communal inside cabin, the per person per diem on some November sailings goes as low as $108 for each of the four occupants, not including airfare and port charges.

GROUP BOOKINGS

Many cruise lines offer reduced rates to groups of 10 passengers or more, making cruise ships a good bet for family reunions and the like. (Also, travel agents are especially good at coordinating widely scattered members of a group that plans to travel together, which could save you significant time and frustration.) Discounts for this type of group travel can be significant, but are wholly determined by the cruise line and seasonal demand at the time you're booking.

Some high-volume cruise agencies may be able to team you up with a "group" of their own devising that they're booking aboard a certain ship; ask about the possibility. Unlike group travel on land, shipboard groups are not herded about as a community and, of course, have individual cabins.

AVOIDING THE SINGLE PENALTY

When it comes to booking a cabin, cruise lines are a lot like a confirmed bachelor's mother: They make you pay for being single. Most ships impose a supplement of between 125% and 200% of the per person price for single occupancy of a double cabin.

To avoid this penalty, you could let the cruise line match you with a (same-sex) stranger in a shared cabin. Some devoted party lines like Carnival will put up to four single cruisers in a quad cabin at bargain-basement prices. You'll lose your privacy, but you'll love the price: around $275 per person for three days, $395 for four days, and $650 for a week.

You could also tap into the "singles" and "senior singles" phone network run by

The Cruise Line, Inc., 150 NW 168th St., North Miami Beach, FL 33169 (☎ **800/777-0707**). When you call this number, you'll hear information geared to general passenger needs before you get to information pertinent to the single traveler. Be patient.

SENIOR CITIZEN DISCOUNTS

The cruise industry offers more discounts to seniors (usually defined as anyone 55 years or older) than almost any targeted group, so don't keep your age a secret. Membership in AAA, AARP, and dozens of other seniors' clubs can net you discounts ranging from 5% to 50%. Always ask when you're booking.

The nonprofit **National Council of Senior Citizens,** 1331 F St., NW, Washington, DC 20004 (☎ **202/347-8800**), charges $12 per person or couple, for which you receive 11 issues annually of a newsletter that is devoted partly to travel tips, including cruises. Membership benefits include discounts on hotels, motels, and auto rentals.

Tour operators, many of whom are experienced in selling cruise packages to senior citizens, are alert to cruise industry discounts, and in some cases configure blocks of cabins aboard selected cruise ships that are marketed directly to established, mature clients. **Grand Circle Travel** (☎ **800/221-2610** or 617/350-7500) offers experiences aboard such ships as Celebrity's *Meridien* where most of the clients will be like-minded seniors looking for competitive prices and a special understanding of their priorities and needs. For a free booklet entitled *101 Tips for the Mature Traveler,* write to Grand Circle Travel, 347 Congress St., Boston, MA 02110. Grand Circle's sibling company, **Overseas Adventure Co.,** 625 Mount Auburn St., Cambridge, MA 02138 (☎ **800/221-0814**), is an outfit geared to more adventurous, small-group forms of travel: Groups almost never exceed 16 participants.

REPEAT PASSENGER PROGRAMS

If you've cruised before and are considering booking on the same line, be sure to ask what discounts might be available for repeat passengers. Cruise lines try to hold on to passengers by coddling them with perks—maybe champagne and flowers in the cabin, cabin upgrades, price incentives, or cocktail receptions with the ship's officers. Some lines, including Cunard, offer a frequent flier–type program with "sailing miles" that are redeemable for cabin upgrades or discounted cruises. Other lines, such as Seabourn, offer free medical and trip-cancellation insurance.

SAILING AS A GENTLEMEN HOST OR GUEST LECTURER

About a decade ago, the now-defunct Royal Cruise Line recognized that sophisticated and courteous gentlemen were needed aboard to be escorts and dining and dancing partners for widows, divorced women, and females whose male companions didn't know how to dance. Since then, the concept has caught on like wildfire.

So, if you're male and at least 45 years old, and are reasonably charming and articulate, you might be considered appropriate as a male escort/dance partner/gentleman host aboard a cruise ship. And you'll sail practically for free.

Lauretta Blake runs **The Working Vacation,** 610 Pine Grove Court, New Lenox, IL 60451 (☎ **815/484-8307**), an agency that matches suitable candidates with such Caribbean cruise operators as Holland America Line and Cunard. An information packet outlines what the company considers appropriate comportment for a professional beau.

Blake's agency also looks for guest lecturers. Cruise lines like to have celebs, semicelebs, and scholars or media types on board, and will pay for their cruises. Blake always has a weather eye out for historians, astronomers, oceanographers, geographers, marine biologists, naturalists, and even gemologists, as well as celebrity chefs, golfers, and tennis pros.

Some cruise lines are also discreetly in the market for suitable gents or guest lecturers, so you could send a resumé directly to the line's personnel department.

IT NEVER HURTS TO ASK

It's amazing what can happen if you imply that you can't book a cruise unless the deal is sweetened. So just ask for a complimentary cabin upgrade, free shore excursions, free wine with dinner on your anniversary, or free or discounted lodging at a company-owned hotel before or after your cruise. It never hurts to ask.

4 If You're Paying the Brochure Price, You're Paying Too Much

Should you brave the shark-infested waters of cruise booking alone or seek help from a professional travel agent or cruise specialist? In the United States, 95% of all cruise bookings are arranged through travel agents. You can try to do all the homework yourself, and you might even be successful at landing a good deal, but an agent will know more about what discounts and special promotions are currently available.

You may want to find a travel agent who is a member of the National Association of Cruise Only Agents (NACOA). Many NACOA members are also accredited by the Cruise Line International Association (CLIA).

CRUISE BROKERS & DISCOUNT BROKERS

Cruise brokers and discount brokers are relatively new on the scene. They tap into unsold inventories of cruise-ship cabins that are available and offer them at rates significantly less than the published rates offered by the line itself.

If you don't have your heart set on a specific ship sailing for specific ports on specific dates, you can save money using a cruise or discount broker. Note, though, that the discounter may not be able to sell you airfare to reach the port of embarkation, provide the category of cabin you want, or secure the dinner seating you prefer.

Recommended below are reputable cruise brokers with impressive buying clout. These cruise brokers are known for taking a bit more time and expending a bit more effort to match potential passengers with a suitable cruise line.

- **Ambassador Tours,** 120 Montgomery St., Suite 400, San Francisco, CA 94104 (☎ **800/989-9000** or 415/981-5678), devotes part of its business to the cruise industry. With nearly every vacation, it offers an amenities package that usually includes a "booking bonus": a check presented with travel documents, prepaid gratuities, and gifts such as T-shirts or an inexpensive camera. Even more worthwhile is its travel catalog, which details cost-saving information and promotions and is updated three times a year.
- **Cruises, Inc.,** 5000 Campuswood Dr. East, Syracuse, NY 13057 (☎ **800/854-0500** or 315/463-9695; fax 315/434-9175), is the oldest and second-largest cruises-only travel agent in the United States, booking in the neighborhood of 15,000 shipboard cabins yearly. Some 175 cruise agents, each of whom has cruised at least three times, are on hand to help advise you on the many choices available within the cruise market. The company's efforts are supplemented by those of **Premier Travel** (same address and phone), a full-service travel agency that helps a cruise passenger with land or sea bookings.
- **Cruises of Distinction,** 2750 South Woodward Ave., Bloomfield Hills, MI

48304 (☎ **800/634-3445** or 810/
332-3030), maintains one of the largest inventories of unsold shipboard
cabins in the world, often with com-
mensurate savings to clients who aren't
overly fussy about the exact where and
when of their cruise holiday.

- **Cruise Fairs Of America,** Century
Plaza Towers, 2029 Century Park
East, Suite 950, Los Angeles, CA
90067 (☎ **800/456-4FUN** or 310/
556-2925). Because of its role as one
of the largest West Coast travel agencies specializing in cruises (especially
those offered by Carnival and Royal
Caribbean), Cruise Fairs' discounts
can be as much as 45% or 50% less
than the official brochure price. Its
specialty is pre- and postcruise
hotel packages that include airfare,
transfers, and, in some cases, even
porterage.

- **Cruise Headquarters,** P.O. Box
12288, La Jolla, CA 92039 (☎ **800/
424-6111** or 619/453-1201), is a one-
woman operation that specializes in
personalized attention for well-heeled
clients wishing to sail aboard such upscale lines as Windstar, Crystal
Cruises, Seabourn, and Silversea.
Owner Barbara Farrell is knowledgeable and experienced in matching clients to whatever degree of formality
they prefer, often at rates that are less
than those publicized in the cruise
lines' official brochures.

- **The Cruise Line,** 150 NW 168th St.,
North Miami Beach, FL 33169
(☎ **800/777-0707**), is a cruise-only
specialist that's closely linked to the
goings-on around the ports of Florida.
The company's greatest bargaining
power, and consequently some of its
best deals, involve cruises aboard the
megaliners operated by Carnival, Princess, Royal Caribbean, and Holland
America Line.

- **Don Ton Cruise Tours,** 3151 Airway
Ave., Costa Mesa, CA 92626 (☎ **800/
318-1818** or 714/545-3737), is one of
the nation's leaders in booking cabins,

often at reduced rates, aboard such
lines as Cunard, Holland America, and
Princess. Many of their packages include such pleasant benefits as prepaid
gratuities, cruise gifts, and shipboard
credits.

- **Hartford Holidays Travel,** 626 Willis
Ave., Williston Park, NY 11596
(☎ **800/828-4813**), publishes a
monthly newsletter and catalog that
lists seasonal bargains and short-term
discounts on selected cruises from
Crystal, Dolphin, Princess, Carnival,
Celebrity, Cunard, Holland America,
and Norwegian Cruise Line, among
others. Most of the company's offerings are promoted without airfare, although a nearby associated full-service
travel agent can take care of this for
you.

- **Kelly Cruises,** 1315 W. 22nd St.,
Suite 105, Oak Brook, IL 60521
(☎ **800/837-7447** or 708/990-1111),
offers discounts for bookings made six
months in advance, and seems especially good at serving groups.

- **Time To Travel,** 582 Market St.,
San Francisco, CA 94104 (☎ **800/
524-3300** or 415/421-3333). This
full-service travel agent has been in
business since 1935 and is able to
book any aspect of a client's holiday. It
has shown considerable finesse in
matching clients with an appropriate
cruise, so much so that it's one of the
top-five cruise-booking agencies on the
West Coast. Most of the company's
bookings take advantage of seasonal or
temporary promotions offered by such
competitive lines as Princess Cruises,
Holland America, Royal Caribbean,
and Crystal Cruises.

BARGAIN HUNTER SPECIALISTS

Few people have the time to go sleuthing
around to track down the cheapest and
best deals in the cruise industry. Fortunately, it's no longer necessary. A number
of specialists are now in business that will

help you locate last-minute cruise bargains. The best are listed below.

- **Cruises of Distinction** (☎ 800/634-3445) is the nation's leading cruise broker and publishes the best cruise-shopping guide around, an annually updated treasure-trove of information that divides the world into various watery regions and includes itineraries, prices, and details about each ship. There's no membership fee, but a $39 payment is required for receipt of the 80-page catalog plus inclusion of your name and address on the company's frequent mailers and special price promotion advertisements.

- **Vacations to Go,** 1502 Augusta Drive, Suite 415, Houston, TX 77057 (☎ **800/338-4962**), is a cruise-only sales agent whose frequently changing roster of discounts and special promotions is mailed out twice a month. Subscriptions to the service cost only $5.95 annually, which is a small price to pay for the savings you might potentially realize.

- **Moment's Notice,** 7301 New Utrecht Ave., Brooklyn, NY 11204 (☎ **718/234-6295**), is an outfit geared to the last-minute sale and distribution of special travel deals, usually package tours or cabin space on international (often Caribbean) cruises. Annual membership dues of $25 allow members access to a recorded message that outlines the deals and special discounts, which often exceed 20% on selected cruises.

- **Spur of the Moment Cruises,** 411 North Harbor Blvd., Suite 302, San Pedro, CA 90731 (☎ **800/343-1991**). Founded in 1983, this California-based outfit has made a name for itself by maintaining a discreet, low-key relationship with cruise-ship operators, who release blocks of unsold cabins to them for sale at discounts that can run as high as 70% off brochure rates. Despite the company's name, don't think you'll have to wait till the day before departure to snag a favorable deal: Some bargains are available between 14 days and several months before departure. You won't find the outfit's best deals advertised in any newspaper; instead, a call to a prerecorded message on the company's hotline (☎ **310/521-1060**) will inform you of their most worthwhile offers. For more information, send a self-addressed stamped envelope to the company to receive its free 14-page circular, which is updated monthly.

- **Cruises Only,** 1011 East Colonial Drive, Orlando, FL 32803 (☎ **800/683-7447**), is a large-volume cruise discounter whose proximity to Florida's ports allows it quick and ready access to late-breaking discounts. The company publishes bulletins of last-minute specials every few weeks.

TRAVEL CLUBS

Travel clubs handle an unsold inventory of air tickets and cruise-ship bookings, offering discounts in the usual range of 20% to 60%. After you pay an annual fee, you're given a "hotline" number that lists available discounts, some of which become available a few days in advance of actual departure, some a week in advance, and some as much as a month. Of course, you're limited to what's available, so you have to be flexible.

Two of the best travel clubs are **Moment's Notice** (☎ 718/234-6295), with a $25 yearly membership fee for hotline access, and **Sears Discount Travel Club** (☎ 800/255-1487 in the U.S.), which issues a quarterly, magazine-like catalog that lists discounted cruises. Membership costs $49.95 annually or $1 for a three-month trial membership.

REBATORS

Rebators also compete in the discount cruise market, offering services roughly similar to standard travel agents, with the difference that these outfits pass along part of their commission to the passenger (although many assess a fee for their services). Most rebators offer discounts averaging anywhere from 10% to 25% off published fares, but this varies greatly. There's usually a handling charge, usually in the neighborhood of $25.

Travel Avenue, 10 South Riverside Plaza, Suite 1404, Chicago, IL 60606 (☎ **800/333-3335** in the U.S. or 312/876-6866), offers what amounts to an average rebate of 7% on cruises booked through their services, and rebates of between 5% and 12% for tickets booked to international (i.e., non-domestic) destinations. Although Travel Avenue handles clients throughout North America, most of its clients come from the Middle West. **The Smart Traveler,** P.O. Box 330010, Miami, FL 33133 (☎ **800/448-3338** or 305/448-3338), is a full-service travel agent that books hundreds of cruises every month and consequently is able to offer favorable rates, promotional discounts, and a cash rebate of around 6% on the value of most of its cruise packages.

GROUP TRAVEL FOR GAY MEN & LESBIANS

Gay libbers remember fondly the Cole Porter song "Anything Goes" as an ode to the relaxed mores aboard a cruise ship. This abandonment of society's strictures has sometimes implied greater sympathy for same-sex unions on the high seas, a phenomenon that has been widely acknowledged but handled in widely different ways in different periods of human history.

So whereas gay activities on the high seas are anything but a new development, a gay person's ability to meld and mingle with an otherwise mainstream cruise-ship clientele can sometimes be iffy if not fraught with potential social pitfalls.

You may be gay and eager to feel the swell of the blue main beneath your feet, but you fear your particular brand of joie de vivre might not be fully appreciated in

the general hoopla encouraged among the predominantly straight majority aboard most big ships. What to do?

The answer is to get specialized and contact any of a variety of organizations formulated to compete for your holiday dollar. Gay or gay-friendly, many of them are remarkably savvy about both marketing and gay politics.

Foremost among them is **RSVP Cruises,** 2800 University Ave., SE, Minneapolis, MN 55414 (☎ **800/328-7787** or 617/379-4697), established in 1985 by the late Kevin Mossier, who was active in raising gay consciousness within the U.S. travel industry and who co-founded the International Gay Travel Association (IGTA). The company charters every berth aboard about a half-dozen Caribbean sailings every year. Vessels ranging in size from the *Star Clipper,* with 170 passengers, to Carnival's *Jubilee,* with 1,600 passengers, are booked solidly several months in advance by a clientele that consists of 80% to 95% gay men and 5% to 20% lesbians.

Although entertainment is lively and communal bonding among cruise participants is encouraged, every effort is made to avoid the "floating bath house" motif that RSVP's detractors sometimes imply. Entertainment, though gay-specific, is deliberately tasteful and well conceived. The long-term staff aboard each vessel chartered tends to be cooperative and helpful beyond most passengers' expectations. That's true even for such vessels as Holland America Line's *Noordam,* which is usually the venue for much older and more conservative clients. Onboard lecturers include such gay celebrities as Harvey Fierstein and spokespersons for the Human Rights Commission.

Since the company's establishment, more than 50,000 vacations have been booked. RSVP estimates that about half of its passengers book as members of same-sex couples, with the remainder being single and unattached, at least when they come aboard.

RSVP is not alone in filling the travel needs of the gay traveler. **Pied Piper Travel,** 330 West 42nd St., Suite 1804, New York, NY 10036 (☎ **800/TRIP-312** or 212/239-2412), is one of the country's leading specialists in gay and gay-friendly group cruises, booking community holidays aboard Holland America, Crystal, and Cunard vessels, including the *QE2.* Participation in Pied Piper's group cruises brings extra services and benefits, including special cocktail parties, shore excursions, and so on. The real incentive here is the prices, which, thanks to the agency's buying clout and its membership in CLIA, tend to be less, and sometimes a lot less, than if clients had booked their cruises independently.

Advance-Damron Vacations, 1 Greenway Plaza, Suite 890, Houston, TX 77046 (☎ **800/695-0880**), is known for its all-male Caribbean jaunts aboard such sail-driven vessels as the *Star Clipper* or any of the Windjammer ships. The outfit is committed to chartering an entire vessel for groups of 68 to 170 men, and is unwilling to ghettoize a subgroup of extroverted gay passengers within a potentially family-values crowd aboard a larger vessel. Look for an expansion of this outfit's itineraries from its usual roster of southern Caribbean venues: In 1998, it will be branching into the western Caribbean, including the coast of Mexico and Central America.

Women usually feel extremely comfortable contacting **Mariah Wilderness Expeditions,** P.O. Box 248, Point Richmond, CA 94807 (☎ **800/462-7424** or 510/233-2303), a company that earned its reputation by arranging adventure tours (especially sea-kayaking and white-water rafting tours) to Guatemala, Costa Rica, Baja California, and Vietnam. Although a few of their tours are co-ed, most are designated specifically for women, often with gay women in mind. Founded in 1982, the company attracts special attention with one or two cruises a year aboard the *Belize Temptress* that are open only to women, many of whom are gay. All-women cruises are offered every spring, usually in March or April, with special emphasis on respect and appreciation for the unusual ecosystems of the western Caribbean coast.

A roster of all-women cruises is offered, usually in May, by a California-based outfit that developed in 1990 from the core of a music-recording company that expanded into lesbian travel. **Olivia Cruises and Resorts,** 4400 Market St., Oakland, CA 94608 (☎ **800/631-6277** or 510/655-0364), offers a week-long cruise every April through both sides of the Caribbean aboard the *Dolphin,* all of whose cabins are booked exclusively to women.

Another cruise-only agency that derives about 25% of its revenue from booking cruises from gay men and lesbians is **Cruise World,** 901 Fairview Ave. N, Suite A150, Seattle, WA 98109 (☎ **800/340-0221** or 206/343-0221). Its specialty involves placing cohesive groups of gay men and women among the "general population" of ships that have included the *Radisson Diamond,* Norwegian Cruise Line's *Dreamward,* and Celebrity's *Horizon* and *Meridien.*

5 Cancellations & Insurance

What should you do if the cruise you've booked is canceled before it departs? A cruise could be canceled due to threat of impending hurricane, acts of war, outbreak of an infectious disease, or mechanical breakdowns such as nonfunctioning air-conditioning. (Would you like to be trapped in a hermetically sealed cabin without ventilation during a trip to the tropics?)

In the event of a cancellation, cruise lines have usually made extraordinary efforts to appease disappointed passengers, including offering big discounts on future cruises. It's hard to predict exactly what a cruise line will do, however, most

Beware of Scams

If you're uneasy about the agent you're working with, call your state consumer protection agency, the Better Business Bureau, or the cruise line to check on the agent's credentials.

If you're told that a widely advertised special is sold out and the salesperson tries to switch you onto a more expensive product, beware. If you ever fail to receive a voucher or ticket on the date it's been promised, place an inquiry immediately. If you're told that your cruise reservation was canceled because of overbooking, and that you must pay extra for a confirmed and rescheduled sailing, demand a full refund.

If in doubt about the ethics or reliability of a particular agency, you can contact the **American Society of Travel Agents (ASTA),** 1101 King St., Suite 200, Alexandria, VA 22314 (☎ **703/739-2782**), or the **National Association of Cruise Only Agents (NACOA),** 7600 Red Rd., Suite 128, South Miami, FL 33143 (☎ **305/663-5626**).

passengers are usually satisfied with the compensation they're offered.

Travel insurance, like all insurance, comes with many optional riders that protect you against eventualities you hope you'll never encounter. Two possibilities are of major concern. The first is the potential expense of an emergency medical evacuation from the Caribbean and, if your regular insurance doesn't cover it, the potential cost of major medical treatment while away from home. The second concern is the loss of your prepaid fare if your cruise is interrupted or if you must cancel because of a death in the family, a medical emergency, or if you missed the boat at the pier because of a flight delay.

Most companies charge between $10 and $15 for every $100 worth of coverage, which is usually "bundled" up into a cluster of benefits that will reimburse you for bona fide trip interruptions, trip cancellations, and emergency medical costs incurred by you (or, under most policies, your traveling companion) during the duration of the policy. If you cancel your cruise before ever leaving home, your insurance will usually replace the funds you paid, less any refund you receive from the cruise line. Most lines provide a full refund if you cancel two months prior to your departure date, although details vary from line to line. Most insurance policies reimburse you when your trip is affected by unexpected events, such as airplane crashes or dockworkers' strikes, but not by "acts of God" such as hurricanes and earthquakes.

Additional insurance to protect your jewelry and valuables on a cruise usually falls under the riders attached to your homeowners policy. If you're in any doubt as to whether they're covered, though, either leave your baubles at home, guard them carefully (confining them to your in-cabin safe or the purser's safe when not in use), or check the fine print of your policy.

The best policy tailor-made for cruise-line passengers is sold by **Mutual of Omaha,** P.O. Box 31716, Omaha, NE 68131 (☎ **800/228-9792**). It's a well-orchestrated "bundle" whose benefits include reimbursement of losses caused by trip cancellations, interruptions, or delays; medical expenses up to $5,000; medical evacuation or repatriation up to $25,000; benefits for accidental death and dismemberment up to $50,000; reimbursement for bona fide loss of baggage and personal effects up to a combined maximum of $500; and reimbursement of up to $100 for delayed arrival of luggage. The policy will even reimburse you for part of the cost of arranging additional transport to the ship if flight delays or cancellations cause you to miss your ship's departure. You can call for information or even buy the policy directly over the phone with a valid credit card.

The cost of the insurance, per person, depends on the price you paid for your cruise. Insurance for cruises of $2,000 to $3,000 per person goes for $145; insurance for cruises priced from $4,001 to $5,000 per person costs $305. In view of the benefits you receive in the event of mishap, the policy is worth every nickel, if only for the coverage of medical evacuation alone. If you have a serious medical condition that existed before your cruise's departure, it's advisable to buy additional insurance (a waiver) that will cover treatment for medical problems caused by that pre-existing condition.

Warning: This policy, like some of its competitors (but not all), reimburses its owners for losses caused by the bankruptcy of an airline or cruise line. It does not, however, reimburse its owners for bankruptcy of the travel agent who arranged for your cruise-ship tickets. It's a very good idea, when buying large-ticket items through a travel agency, to insist on writing your check out to the cruise line, and not to the travel agency who sold it to you. Likewise, when paying by credit card, try to insist that the card be run through the machine of the cruise-line operator rather than through the machine of the individual travel agency. This is sometimes tricky, and the need for precaution is really minimal, but for clients who invest in travel policies like the one recommended above, the bankruptcy of a travel agency poses greater risks than the bankruptcy of a cruise line.

6 Putting Down a Deposit & Reviewing Tickets

You've booked your cruise and now have to send the cruise line a deposit. Depending on the policies of the line you selected, the amount will either be fixed at a predetermined amount or will represent a percentage of the ticket's total cost. A receipt for your deposit will be mailed to you from the cruise line.

Carefully review your ticket, invoice, and/or vouchers to confirm that it accurately reflects the departure date, ship, and cabin category you negotiated. The printout will usually list a specific cabin number; if it doesn't, it will designate a cabin category whose exact location will be assigned at the time of embarkation.

The ticket also represents a legal agreement established between you and the cruise line. The fine print should explain what happens if the cruise is canceled or you fail to show up at the pier on time. You might also check what happens if you're faced with a personal emergency and can't take the cruise or if you abandon ship before cruises' end and fly back home on your own.

7 The Cruising Experience

You've bought your ticket and you're getting ready to cruise. Here's a few nuts and bolts, odds and ends, FYIs, and helpful hints to smooth your path to shipboard life.

1 Getting Ready to Go

PASSPORTS & VISAS

Even though the Caribbean islands are for the most part independent nations and thereby classified as international destinations, passports are not generally required. You do, however, need identity documents, and for that you can't do better than the tried and true passport, which will also speed your way through Customs and Immigration. Other acceptable forms of ID include an ongoing or return ticket, plus a current voter registration card or an original birth certificate (or a copy that has been certified by the U.S. Department of Health). If you use one of these other documents, you will also need some photo identification, such as a driver's license or an expired passport. Be aware, however, that a driver's license is not acceptable as a sole form of identification. Visas are usually not required, but some countries may ask you to fill out a tourist card.

Before leaving home, make two photocopies each of your documents, including your driver's license, the information pages of your passport, your airline ticket, and any hotel vouchers. If you're on medication, you should also make copies of prescriptions.

Technically, a "valid" passport is one that isn't scheduled to expire for six months. For more information, call the **Department of State Office of Passport Services** information line at ☎ 202/647-0518.

Never pack your passport in your luggage while traveling. Once on board, you should carry it with you or leave it locked in the safe inside your cabin or at the purser's office. Each particular port has its own passport ritual—sometimes you'll be asked to turn your passport over to cruise-line officials, who will facilitate the procedures for group or individual port clearances and immigration formalities.

Aliens residing in the United States need to have valid passports and alien registration cards. All non-U.S. and non-Canadian citizens must have valid passports and the requisite visas when boarding any cruise ship or aircraft departing from and/or returning to American soil. Non-citizens also need to present an ongoing or return ticket for an airline or cruise ship as proof that you intend to remain on local shores only for a brief stay.

Very few islands require inoculations against tropical diseases, but should this situation change, your cruise line will inform you.

Canadians need an identity card for entry and re-entry into the United States. It's better, however, to travel with a passport, available at 28 regional offices in Canada as well as certain travel agencies or post offices. For further information call ☎ **800/567-6868** (in Canada only) or 819/994-3500. The cost is $60 Canadian or $48 U.S. Application by mail will take about three weeks; application in person at any of the bureau's regional offices can take as little as five working days.

MONEY MATTERS

The safest way to carry large amounts of money is to have traveler's checks, although credit cards are accepted virtually everywhere in the Caribbean, on water or land. The U.S. dollar is widely accepted on many of the islands, and is the legal currency of the U.S. Virgin Islands, the British Virgin Islands, and Puerto Rico. Specific currency information is included in chapter 10, "Ports of Call."

Three major traveler's check issuers are **American Express** (☎ **800/221-7282** in the U.S. and Canada, with many regional representatives around the world); **Citicorp** (☎ **800/645-6556** in the U.S. and Canada, or **813/623-1709,** collect, from other parts of the world); and **Thomas Cook** (☎ **800/223-7373** in the U.S. and Canada, or **609/987-7300,** collect, from other parts of the world).

Cirrus, Plus, and other automated teller machine (ATM) networks operate in the Caribbean. For locations of **Cirrus** abroad, call ☎ **800/424-7787;** for **Plus** usage abroad, dial ☎ **800/843-7587.** All Carnival ships have ATMs aboard, and other lines are following in their footsteps.

Most cruise lines operate on a cashless system; you just sign for your shore excursions, purchases from onboard shops and boutiques, and bar tabs. Shortly before or after embarkation, a purser will request the imprint of one of your credit cards. On the last day of your cruise, a tally sheet itemizing each charge you've authorized will be slipped beneath your cabin door. If you agree with the charges, they will be debited from your credit card account. If you dispute the charges, you'll have to wait in line at the ship's cashier or purser's office to clarify the bill.

Larger ships request that you present the identification card you were issued at embarkation every time you sign for something. Smaller ships are less stringent, at least after the second day, when the staff begins to recognize you.

Some onboard casinos will extend credit for a limited amount, rarely more than $5,000.

TIPS FOR PACKING

Your wardrobe, and its extent, will depend on the season, the climate, the formality of the cruise, and the number of formal evenings the line has scheduled during your time aboard. A bit of advice: Decide what you want to take, then try to discard at least a third of it before leaving home. Storage space is extremely limited within cabins, and remember that whatever you bring will likely be augmented along the way by whatever you buy in the various ports of call. (And while we're on that subject, you might want to pack an extra bag or folding suitcase to carry whatever Caribbean loot you acquire along the way.) Whatever luggage you use, make sure it's sturdy enough to withstand being hauled around the docks and corridors of cruise ships.

DRESS CODES   If an occasion is defined as **formal,** it means that tuxedos for men and evening garb for women are appropriate and desirable (though some men opt for a dark business suit). Most seven-day cruises feature two formal nights.

For **informal** occasions, men are requested to wear jackets and in many cases neckties; women are expected to dress up a bit. An *informal* evening does not mean a *casual* evening. Depending on the cruise line, **casual** can mean anything from a bedsheet toga to stylish sportswear.

What if your luggage arrives late and doesn't make it aboard until the second day of sailing? Don't worry. Almost no cruise line schedules black-tie soirees for the first or last nights afloat. On a cruise's first night, passengers are presumably exhausted from travel; on a cruise's final night, suitcases are already packed and waiting in the hallways for disembarkation the following morning.

LAUNDRY & CLEANING SERVICES ON BOARD   Salt air and humidity wreak havoc with garments, so whatever clothes you pack should ideally be of the low-maintenance variety. Try to bring clothes that don't require ironing; if that's not possible and something does need pressing, most lines have onboard laundry and dry-cleaning facilities (listed in chapter 9 cruise-ship reviews). A few of the largest ships have coin-operated washing machines. Maintaining high-maintenance clothing will definitely be pricier than it is back home.

GENERAL PACKING TIPS

Some jaded frequent cruisers recommend one basic outfit—not counting accessories or the formal outfits you only want to be seen in once—for every 2 or 2½ days at sea. Plan on dressing in layers when the weather looks dicey. For shoes, opt for natural (nonsynthetic) and well-ventilated fabrics and fibers, such as canvas sneakers or espadrilles. Rubber soles definitely get the nod over leather, as they slip less on teakwood or metal decks, and of course, high heels are out during rough weather, when even the most elegant, not-a-hair-out-of-place woman would be sorely challenged to remain balanced.

Don't forget an extra pair of eyeglasses and that book you've wanted to read for the past year but haven't found the time to start. Sunscreen and other sundries are available aboard the ship or at a port of call, but it's cheaper to bring them yourself.

We also suggest packing a lightweight raincoat (showers are frequent in many areas of the Caribbean); a lightweight sweater for overenthusiastic air-conditioning; and a simple all-purpose shirt, blouse, or sweater for moments when modest daytime attire is appropriate, such as when visiting a church in a Latin country like the Dominican Republic.

If you're into fitness, bring along your workout shoes and gear. Bird-watchers will want their binoculars and manuals, golfers their clubs, and tennis buffs their rackets. Hiking boots, riding jodhpurs, snorkeling or scuba-diving gear, and bungee-jumping cords will depend entirely on your interests, the nature of your cruise, and how much luggage you're willing to lug.

It's important to keep the following items with you, and *not* leave them in your checked luggage: passport, traveler's checks, credit cards, life-saving medication, eyeglasses or contact lenses, house and car keys, claim checks for parking garages or checked luggage, and cruise and/or airline tickets.

Finally, if you're single, romantically inclined, and look forward to meeting someone and sharing some starlit moments (and more), don't forget to pack a supply of condoms and/or contraceptives.

PACKING TIPS FOR MEN   Onboard necessities for a seven-day cruise will include a tuxedo. (This can be optional, but isn't always. Check the policy aboard your cruise line.) We prefer to bring our own on board, but if need be, a few of the largest cruise ships maintain an inventory of rentals. Other components of a man's wardrobe should include two sports jackets, a selection of tropical-weight pants, Bermuda shorts, both knit and button-down sports shirts, and a bathing suit.

PACKING TIPS FOR WOMEN   If in doubt, opt for the simple solution. Even for the most formal of evenings, you could wear a long skirt with a dressy blouse and jewelry. Your best bet might be to carry a selection of blouses, shorts, pants, and skirts that are mix and matchable.

To bejewel oneself or not? No gemstone glitter is worth the risk to your person if someone attacks you to steal it. Plus, you may have some explaining to do to a Customs agent upon your return home. If the piece is truly expensive, don't forget to carry a copy of the original receipt, so you don't get stuck paying duty on it. We think it's wise to leave the truly valuable gemstones home in the bank vault.

2 Boarding & Disembarking

You're ready to go, packed, at the port, and even on the right pier. Do you remember the name of the ship on which you're sailing? We don't mean to be insulting, but cruise industry officials claim that hundreds of people forget the name of the ship they intend to board. Those names can sound alike, you know.

As a safety precaution against emergencies at home, distribute your ship's satellite phone and fax number to persons in charge of your affairs back home, but advise them only to contact you in an emergency. If they lose the ship's number, AT&T offers a service (albeit an expensive one) that will connect them with the ship's operator, who will in turn connect the call to the phone in your cabin or take a message for you. The number is ☎ 800/SEA-CALL.

ARRIVING AT THE DOCKS

After you arrive at the docks, find a porter and tip at least $1 for every bag he carries for you. Luggage should be clearly identified with your name and address, your cruise line and ship, and (if you know it) your cabin number. In many cases, your luggage will disappear for a time, but will then be delivered directly to your cabin. At least one hopes it will.

Rituals at the pier vary according to the ship's size and the formality of the cruise.

You might have to line up alphabetically behind signs posted with letters of the alphabet. These lines can move slowly, and the wait during the crush of embarkation can extend for up to two hours. To mitigate the tedium, efforts are made to transform the warehouse-style appearance of most cruise-ship terminals with streamers, balloons, happy smiles, a briskly professional staff, and a hint of the partying and pleasures to come.

It doesn't pay to arrive too early at the pier. Even if your ship has been berthed at port since early in the morning, new passengers are often not allowed on board until about three hours before sailing. The cruise lines enforce this policy stringently to allow enough time for luggage and supplies to be unloaded and loaded, cabins to be vacated by former occupants and cleaned, and paperwork and customs documents to be properly completed.

For security reasons, very few cruise lines allow temporary visitors on board ship. You'll have to say your good-byes on land.

STEPPING ABOARD

Shipboard staffs tend to put on their best and most efficient faces as new passengers are boarding. Every effort is made to ensure that luggage, people, and supplies are safely secured, comfortable, and "stowed away." Cruise line employees will be around to point you in the right direction as you navigate the ship for the first time.

Despite the fray when arriving on board, the ship's photographer will be waiting to snap your picture, whether you want this memento or not. These pictures, which sell for $5 to $8 each depending on the line, will be posted behind glass in a public corridor later during the cruise.

After you find your cabin, your cabin steward will stop by to introduce him/herself, inquire if the configuration of beds is appropriate, and explain how to summon him or her back when needed (usually by pressing a buzzer or calling a central telephone number). The brochures and daily programs in your cabin will answer many questions pertinent to your ship's social and safety rituals.

PREPARING TO LEAVE THE SHIP AT THE END OF YOUR CRUISE

It's a good idea to begin packing before dinner of the final night aboard. During dinner, or perhaps late on the cruise's final night, a crew of deckhands will pick up your luggage, which you will have left outside your cabin door. Fill out the luggage tags, which might be color-coded, and attach them securely to each piece. The luggage will be assembled into a communal cluster on rolling carts somewhere below deck. At disembarkation, you'll find your baggage waiting for you at the terminal. If you've neglected to place any baggage outside your door before the designated deadline, you'll have to lug it off the ship yourself.

If you leave something behind, the cruise line might eventually return it to you, but not without a prolonged hassle. (And even that doesn't always work.)

DISEMBARKING

Ships normally arrive in port on the final day of the cruise between 6 and 8am, and need at least 90 minutes to unload baggage and complete dockage formalities. That means that no one disembarks before around 9am.

When disembarkation is announced, hold onto your hats. Departures just aren't graceful. Some passengers find the disembarkation process a blunt return to reality and the staff distracted, but that's because another group of passengers will begin boarding very soon, and the crew has only about five hours to reconfigure the ship for the next departure.

Disembarking through the cruise ship terminal is the equivalent of departing from an international flight. In the portside end of the terminal, there might not be porters to carry your luggage. Alternately, you should be able to use or rent

wheeled carts (for no more than $1.50 each) to help you push your possessions out the door. En route, you'll have to pass through customs.

CUSTOMS

Customs officers are most interested in expensive, big-ticket items like cameras, jewelry, china, or silverware. They don't care much about your souvenir items unless you've bought so many that they couldn't possibly be intended for your personal use, or they're concealing illegal substances.

U.S. CUSTOMS The U.S. government generously allows U.S. citizens $1,200 worth of duty-free imports every 30 days from the U.S. Virgin Islands; those who exceed their exemption are taxed at a 5% rate, rather than 10%. The limit is $400 for international destinations such as the French islands of Guadeloupe and Martinique, and $600 for many other islands, including Jamaica. If you visit only Puerto Rico, you don't have to go through Customs at all, since it's an American commonwealth.

U.S. citizens or returning residents 21 years of age who are traveling directly or indirectly from the U.S. Virgin Islands are allowed to bring in free of duty 1,000 cigarettes, five liters of alcohol, and 100 cigars (so long as they're not Cuban). Duty-free limitations on articles from other countries are generally one liter of alcohol, 200 cigarettes, and 200 cigars. Unsolicited gifts can be mailed to friends and relatives on the U.S. mainland at the rate of $100 per day from the U.S. Virgin Islands or $50 per day from other islands. Unsolicited gifts of any value can be mailed from Puerto Rico. Most meat or meat products, fruit, plants, vegetables, or plant-derived products will be seized by U.S. Customs agents unless they're accompanied by an import license from a U.S. government agency.

Joint Customs declarations are possible for members of a family traveling together. For instance, if you're a husband

and wife with two children, your exemptions in the U.S. Virgin Islands become duty-free up to $4,800!

Collect receipts for all purchases made abroad. Sometimes merchants suggest making up a false receipt to undervalue your purchase, but be aware that you could be involved in a "sting" operation—the merchant might be an informer to U.S. Customs. You must also declare on your Customs form all gifts received during your stay abroad. It's prudent to carry proof that you purchased expensive cameras or jewelry on the U.S. mainland. If you purchased such an item during an earlier trip abroad, you should carry proof that you have previously paid customs duty on the item.

If you use any medication containing controlled substances or requiring injection, carry an original prescription or note from your doctor.

For more specifics, request the free *Know Before You Go* pamphlet from the **U.S. Customs Service,** P.O. Box 7407, Washington, DC 20044 (☎ **202/927-6724**).

CANADIAN CUSTOMS Canada allows its citizens a $300 exemption, and they are permitted to bring back duty-free 200 cigarettes, 2.2 pounds of tobacco, 40 Imperial ounces of liquor, and 50 cigars. In addition, they are allowed to mail gifts to Canada from abroad at the rate of $60 (Canadian) a day, provided the gifts are unsolicited and aren't alcohol or tobacco. (Write on the package: "Unsolicited gift, under $60 value.") All valuables, such as expensive cameras you already own, should be declared with their serial numbers on the Y-38 Form before departure from Canada. *Note:* The $300 exemption can be used only once a year and only after you've been out of the country for at least seven days. For more information, write for the *I Declare* booklet, issued by **Revenue Canada,** 2265 St. Laurent Blvd., Ottawa, ON, KIG 4K3 (☎ **800/461-9999** or 613/993-0534).

BRITISH CUSTOMS If you return from the Caribbean either directly to the United Kingdom or arrive via a port in another European Community (EC) country where you and your baggage did not pass through Customs controls, you must go through U.K. Customs and declare any goods in excess of the allowances. These are: 200 cigarettes, 100 cigarillos, 50 cigars, or 250 grams of tobacco; two liters of still table wine and one liter of spirits or strong liqueurs (over 22% alcohol by volume), or two liters of fortified or sparkling wine or other liqueurs, or two liters of additional still table wine; 60cc/ml of perfume; 250cc/ml of toilet water; and £136 worth of all other goods, including gifts and souvenirs. (No one under 17 years of age is entitled to a tobacco or alcohol allowance.) Only go through the green "nothing to declare" line if you're sure you have no more than the Customs allowances and no prohibited or restricted goods. For further information, contact **HM Customs and Excise Office,** Dorset House, Stamford St., London SE1 9NG (☎ **0171/202-4510**).

3 Life on Board

Here's a breakdown of the lingo you're likely to hear and the options you face:

WHO'S WHO

No matter what ship you're aboard, it won't be the *Bounty* and it won't be the *Pequod,* so nobody's going to be asking you to hoist the topsail or trim the mizzen—aboard today's cruise ships, more useful words to know might be *spa* or *trattoria*. With that in mind, a short course in cruise-ship nomenclature might be in order.

The **purser** is the ship's accountant, banker, and money-changer. He or she also prepares the dozens of forms and affidavits that allow ships to dock at various ports of call. Unless you have a safe within your cabin, the purser also administers access to safety-deposit boxes.

The shipboard **hotel manager** administers all details related to passengers and their comfort, including all aspects of a ship's restaurants, bars, and sleeping accommodations. Especially on larger ships, the hotel manager usually supervises the people responsible for cabin maintenance **(the head housekeeper)** and food and beverage facilities (this might include a **head steward**).

Kitchens (galleys) are likely to be the domain of a cruise's **head chef,** usually a seasoned veteran not prone to outbursts of temper, even when frantically preparing meals for a thousand diners in rough seas.

The **cruise director** is the highly visible coordinator of passenger activities. This is the consummate "people person," skilled at soothing ruffled feathers and infusing shipboard life with a sense of excitement and whimsical fun.

Two other important staff members who will influence your experience include the **shore excursion director,** who's often pressed into duty as a lecturer to promote tours through ports of call or to sites of historic, cultural, or natural interest; and the **entertainment director,** who's usually occupied even before breakfast with rehearsals for whatever cabaret show or dance band is scheduled to perform later that evening. All of their activities are made possible through the diligence of an additional (usually unseen) army, including **chief engineers** and **engineers, ship's doctors** and **nurses, navigators,** and a hardworking crew of workers who labor, often below decks and for not very much money, to keep the wheels of your vacation turning.

CABIN AMENITIES

In your cabin, the beds should be configured as you requested; if they aren't, alert your steward promptly. Cabins have air-conditioning and heating, usually controlled individually; hot and cold running water (be careful the first time you use it—the hot water is sometimes scalding); life preservers for the number of people occupying the cabin (a legal requirement and essential to your safety at sea—check that they're there); extra blankets and pillows; and a safe for storing your valuables, operated either with a key or combination lock.

Most ships sailing the Caribbean have North American–style electrical outlets (twin flat prongs, 110 AC current), although some ships have outlets for both European (220 AC) current and North American. Reviews in chapter 9 note which ships have European current.

With a few notable exceptions, cruise liners have telephones in cabins, along with instructions on how to use them, informing you who to contact in the event of an emergency or if you want room service or a steward. Most cabins contain telephone directories identifying the phone numbers of the various departments or services on board; you can either use this direct-dial method or have the onboard operator connect you. From most cabin phones you can call, via satellite beams, anywhere in the world, but this is extremely expensive. Charges begin at around $15 a minute, and it's only a little less expensive if someone wants to call you. It's cheaper to call home from a public telephone at any port of call.

Lastly, if you're baffled by how to work your cabin's TV set and VCR, you're not alone. There's usually an instruction book, but you may have to ask your steward.

CASINOS & GAME ROOMS

Onboard casinos are a fixture in the cruise industry, with many sporting all the glitz of Vegas and the glamour of Monte Carlo. Depending on the ship, you'll usually find baccarat, blackjack, craps, poker, roulette, and an ever-present array of (sometimes overly loud) slot machines. Stakes aboard most ships are usually relatively low, with maximum bets rarely exceeding $200, and even when they're higher, they're allowed only at carefully designated tables. The cruise line rarely acts as a financier to extend credit.

Gambling is legal once a ship has sailed 12 miles from American shores, but local laws require onboard casinos to close down whenever a ship is in port. Children are not allowed in onboard casinos, but some occasionally get away with playing the slots during slow periods when supervision is relaxed.

An annex to every shipboard casino is the game room, or card room, which is usually filled with serious bridge or poker players and sometimes supervised by a full-time attendant/instructor. Most ships furnish cards for free, although some charge $1 per deck.

MEDICAL CARE

Ships carrying more than 12 passengers are legally required to carry a doctor, who works in an infirmary, usually with the help of a nurse or two. However, if a ship remains within a "convenient" distance from a coastline, an onboard doctor and infirmary are not necessary. This situation may occur on the Clipper Cruise Line or American Canadian Caribbean Line.

4 The Politics of Dining

Aboard some ships, usually the smaller and more expensive ones, you can eat when, where, and with whom you want. Meal hours are maintained over an extended period (say, from 7 to 10pm), during which an open seating plan allows you to dine alone, with a spouse or companion at a table for two, or with whatever group of six or eight you find compatible. Under this arrangement, no one cares if you're the first person in the dining room, or if you linger over drinks in the bar, then arrive fashionably late.

On most ships, however, dining and its scheduling are more complicated. Meal-time arrangements depend on the ship's configuration, how crowded the ship is on that particular cruise, the cruise line's policy, and how the staff accommodates hordes of passengers all clamoring to be treated with a reasonable degree of personalized service.

Most medium, large, and megaships compensate for larger passenger rosters by having smaller dining areas, with the saved space devoted to cabins. As a result, passengers are fed in two shifts, known as the first seating (with breakfast at 7 or 7:30am, lunch at noon, and dinner at 6 or 6:30pm) and the second seating (with breakfast at 8:30am, lunch at 1:30pm, and dinner at 8 or 8:30pm).

First seatings are for those who prefer dining early and are ready to leave the dining room once the dishes are cleared. Elderly passengers and families with children tend to choose this seating. First seating advantages include a less crowded dining room and a staff that is more alert, better rested, and less busy than those working later. Plus, all menu items will be a bit fresher. There's less emphasis on alcohol and drinking at the early seating.

First-seaters consider it an advantage to be released early from dinner, free to retire exhausted to their cabins or, conversely, attend an early show and then move on to whatever entertainment suits their fancy. Many are ready to eat again when the midnight buffet opens.

Advantages of the second seating include sleeping longer in the morning, since breakfast is later. For dinner, you won't have to rush through predinner showering and dressing rituals after an active day at a port of call. And the meal is more leisurely, allowing you to linger over coffee and after-dinner drinks.

Regardless of your scheduled seating, you'll have no trouble finding a tasty treat at any time, should hunger strike. Cruise lines want passengers to feel like they're receiving lots of gastronomic bang for their buck, so in addition to regular meals you'll have the option of round-the-clock pizzas and hot dogs, bouillon tastings, afternoon teas, and midnight buffets, plus the occasional ice cream sundae–making contest, all held in various places aboard ship.

If you strongly prefer a certain seating, request that time when you book your cruise or soon after you board. Your scheduled dining time might be confirmed at the pier during check-in or soon after within your cabin. If you don't get the seating you want, tell your maître d'hôtel, who will probably be at or near his or her station in the dining room during your initial embarkation. Most will be able to accommodate your wishes, if not on the first night of sailing, then on the second night.

If the entire setup isn't to your liking, some lines maintain additional dining areas (called "specialty restaurants") for passengers who want a change of pace. Compared to the main dining area, these venues are smaller and less formal, and serve cuisine that's geared to specific culinary themes. Currently, this often means Italian, though we predict more Japanese and/or Thai specialty dining aboard megaships in the not-too-distant future. You can dine in these restaurants for any or all nights of your cruise.

Whichever dining time you choose, don't ever worry that you'll miss a cabaret revue or a planned activity: Cruise directors juggle the starting times of onboard entertainment and activities to accommodate different dining schedules.

TABLES FOR TWO OR TEN?

Many cruisers claim their dining companions either made or ruined their cruise. We suggest you request a certain kind of table and a specific seating when you book your ticket, no matter what the line's policy. All lines will try to meet your request, although few will guarantee you a specific seating arrangement. In some cases, you may learn about your table arrangements only at the last possible moment, often after embarkation. That's part of the surprise, and, truly, part of the fun. If you absolutely hate your assignment, you'll probably be able to change it later.

If you want to dine alone or as a couple, select a cruise ship where such an option is viable; not every floating dining room has tables for two (or one) readily available. Conversely, if you're amenable to companionship you can throw yourself on the mercy of the maître d'hôtel, within whom—if our experiences are any indication—lies the interpersonal genius of an old-world matchmaker. Many deep and lasting friendships have developed among cruise diners as a result of using this technique.

If you're willing to sit at a table with strangers, we'd recommend trying for one that seats between six and eight passengers. It's the perfect balance between too few companions and too many. You'll be more likely to meet likable dining companions and it won't be as potentially boring as a smaller grouping of four. (Tables for four almost always consist of two couples who haven't previously met.) Also, if you decide to ditch your table, it's easier to move from a larger table. It's harder to converse at tables seating 10 or 12, but if you end up at one you can keep it lively by rotating seats every once in a while.

DINING TABLE DIVORCES

Many cruise-ship table groupings are unsuccessful from the first moment. If the chemistry is just not right for you, don't suffer in silence. It's best to explain to the maître d' as courteously and as soon as possible that your table assignment simply won't do, and request a change. Shipboard staffs have dealt with this thousands of times before, and can alter a seating chart like Bobby Fisher moving pieces in a chess match. And rest assured that you won't be the only person (or party) asking for a different table. In fact, adding your name to the roster will make a new grouping that much easier. A tip might make your table change happen more quickly, but it won't guarantee that you'll be happy with grouping number two.

Also, bear in mind that as much as the maître d' may want to please you, you may not get what you want if the ship is packed and everyone else is pleased with his or her dining companions.

THE CAPTAIN'S TABLE

Few other rituals manage to inspire as much social maneuvering (and envy) as an invitation to dine at the captain's table. Captains are masters at the art of social dining, and use their table both to preen the feathers of those atop the onboard pecking order and to chat with passengers and gain insight into how the cruise line can adapt its product to suit their needs and wants.

Seating between 8 and 10 people, the captain's table is usually positioned prominently in the dining room. Who sits with the captain? Among the fortunate few some are the captain's personal friends, some are cruisers picked from the passenger list, and others might include any executives of the cruise line who happen to be aboard. If the ship's dining room has two seatings, the captain might attend the second seating one night, the first seating another night, or miss dinner altogether if circumstances call him away. To some extent, the captain's social duties are shared by some senior officers, who sometimes host dinner tables of their own, either with a semipermanent gathering of tablemates or with a changing roster of passengers, depending on the ship's policy.

How great a prize is an invitation to the captain's table? That depends on you. Some passengers aggressively lobby for the honored invitation, while others couldn't give a hoot. If you want to be there, make your wishes known, preferably at the time of booking. You might want to compile a short professional biography (not exceeding two paragraphs) and discreetly submit it to your travel agent or directly to the ship's maître d'.

Invitees usually include frequent passengers on the cruise line or occupants of the ship's larger suites. But any first-time cruisers, honeymooners, or single travelers housed in run-of-the-mill cabins might find themselves on the list, because a passenger's oft-repeated story about his or her dinner with the captain is the best advertising a cruise line can get.

If you are invited, dress up, not down. Even if the evening is designated as casual, men should wear a jacket and tie. And there are certain rituals to be observed: For instance, women should not invite the captain to dance, since that is his prerogative. Also, the captain almost always provides wine for his dinner companions. Since this is a social ritual, it's not the time to badmouth the line or its staff unless something is absolutely, horrendously wrong with your cruise experience.

SPECIAL DIETS

If medical concerns or religious beliefs require you to follow a special diet, inform the cruise line as early as possible. Vegetarian dishes and kosher food are commonly available, and almost all cruise lines now feature low-salt, low-fat, heart-healthy choices as a matter of course. Our chapter 9 cruise line reviews discuss which ships' dining rooms will best accommodate your dietary needs.

Trying to please all parties is the hallmark of a successful chef, but what if you develop a hankering for something special—say, sweetbreads in Grand Marnier sauce—and only make this wish clear after embarkation? In that case, it's a matter of luck; many floating restaurants will do their best to meet your request, but even the best chefs are limited by what's already been socked away in the ship's larders. At sea, many dishes are simply not possible without advance notification.

On all but the most cost-conscious cruise lines, the kitchen usually tries to satisfy reasonable culinary requests, and we've observed that relatively simple dishes can usually be prepared the way a passenger wants. Remember that it's appropriate to tip a maître d' for efforts in adapting the ship's menu to your culinary whims.

5 Tipping

The cruise industry pays its staff low wages, with the understanding that the bulk of their salaries will be won through tips. Only some upscale lines, including Seabourn and some vessels maintained by Cunard, forbid tipping altogether, since their high cruise prices include respectable staff salaries.

Remember, when it comes to tipping, the price you paid for your cabin is less important than the nature and number of additional services you requested while on board. Tipping is so formally integrated into the cruise experience that it's almost ritualistic, and if you need help finding your way through the litanies, the cruise line and its directors won't be shy about guiding you. Each line has clear guidelines for gratuities, which they often announce during the end-of-cruise closing remarks. Some lines seem downright pushy when it comes to who and how much a passenger should tip. Cabin stewards may leave prestamped sheaths of envelopes (designated for cabin attendants, dining stewards, and waiters) along with suggested tipping percentages and amounts. Other lines, including most Greek-registered vessels and lines specializing in off-the-beaten-track "adventure" travel, prefer that a single tip be delivered to a central source, from whence these funds are then evenly distributed to the staff and crew.

Most lines, however, publish polite guidelines, then back away as guests scramble to find plain white envelopes to hold their gratuities. Amounts vary with the line and its degree of luxury. As a rule of thumb, however, expect to tip between $8 and $15 per day, per person, of which about 70% should be distributed among your cabin steward, dining steward, and, to a somewhat lesser degree, your dining room busperson. You should distribute the remainder among whatever attendants made your life particularly pleasant during your time on board. This might include a croupier in the casino, a hairdresser or manicurist, an attendant at the health club/spa, or the attendant at the card games where you developed your bridge-playing skills.

Wine stewards and bartenders have probably already been rewarded with a 15% surcharge that's usually added onto a bill every time you sign it. If they've been particularly helpful, however, you should probably reward them with something extra, say $15 to $30. Tip masseurs

and masseuses immediately after they work on you, or arrange to tip them before signing up for the next massage. Maître d's always appreciate a discreet tip at either the crucial moment of assigning your table the first night out, midway through the cruise, or at dinner on the final night out. This is the optimal time to do your Cary Grant impersonation, suavely palming a bill into the maître d's hand as he guides you to the perfect table.

We suggest tipping your waiter and your cabin steward each between $4.50 and $7, minimum, per person, per day. Give the busperson an additional, but lesser, bonus.

When do you distribute your tips? It's good form to tip your table stewards during the cruise's final dinner, rather than waiting until breakfast the next morning, when stewards might be assigned other stations or be unavailable.

On one cruise, we sat at a dining table whose members were matched more successfully than any we'd ever experienced before or since. All members, generous folk indeed, agreed to pool tips for the dining staff into an anonymous pot, only to face the scowls of the waiter after the envelope was opened. Closer investigation revealed that a Madame X had contributed nothing, yet sheltered her stinginess within the communal format. So, our advice is that even if you're getting along wonderfully with other members of your table, refrain from pooling your tips collectively. It's best to distribute gratuities individually and privately.

Tipping the captain or one of the captain's officers is gauche and embarrassing for all involved. In their official capacity, the captain and officers are expected to be above such matters.

If you found someone among the staff to be outstandingly able and helpful, you can also write a brief letter praising this person's performance and send it to the cruise line's director of passenger services. This act of generosity might have far-reaching consequences for that person's career and salary level.

Ports of Embarkation

T he main port of embarkation for the Caribbean is Miami, followed by Port Everglades in Fort Lauderdale and Port Canaveral at Cape Canaveral. Tampa, on Florida's west coast, is becoming a major port, especially for cruise ships visiting the eastern coast of Mexico, and New Orleans is also a popular port for ships sailing to Mexico. In the Caribbean Basin itself, San Juan is the major port of embarkation as well as a major port of call. (We've also covered San Juan in chapter 10, "Ports of Call.")

All of these ports are tourist destinations themselves, so cruise lines now offer special deals to extend all Caribbean or Bahamian cruise vacations either pre- or postcruise, sometimes in a line-owned hotel. These packages, for two, three, or four days, often offer major hotel and car-rental discounts. Have your travel agent or cruise specialist check so you won't have to pay a hotel's rack (published) rates.

In this chapter, we describe each port of embarkation, tell you how to get there, and suggest things to see and do in the city, whether hitting the beach, sightseeing, or shopping. We also recommend restaurants and places to stay, as well as bars, clubs, and other evening entertainment. You'll find more detailed information about each destination in *Frommer's Florida '98; Frommer's Miami and the Keys, 4th edition; Frommer's New Orleans '98;* and *Frommer's Puerto Rico, 3rd edition.*

1 Miami & the Port of Miami

Miami is the cruise capital of the world, boasting the world's busiest cruise harbor, which is home to more than 15 different vessels operated by eight cruise lines. Some three million passengers currently pass through the port, and that total is expected to climb to four million by 1999.

Five of the world's largest oceangoing vessels berth at Miami, including Carnival Cruise Line's 2,600-passenger superliner *Ecstasy* and its sibling ship, the *Sensation,* as well as Royal Caribbean Cruise Line's 2,355-passenger *Majesty of the Seas* and the 2,276-passenger *Sovereign of the Seas.* Norwegian Cruise Line's 2,044-passenger *Norway* also pulls into the port.

In the not-quite-megaship category, Carnival's 1,486-passenger *Celebration* also sails from Miami, as does Royal Caribbean Cruise Line's 1,600-passenger *Nordic Empress* and Norwegian Cruise Line's 1,534-passenger *Seaward* and 1,400-passenger *Leeward.* Many other smaller lines also use the port.

Miami not only has the port facilities to welcome such superliners, but also has the people-moving capacity to get passengers on and off such ships. The Port of Miami is only 8 miles from Miami International Airport, and is served by a variety of ground transportation. Its dozen bilevel passenger terminals offer duty-free shopping, customs clearance, and easy car access.

The port plans to increase its cruise-ship capacity by 40% with its maritime expansion program, adding four new passenger terminals as part of a waterfront park. The 53-acre park will be a combined cruise facility and entertainment village with shops, restaurants, museums, and theme parks. Already just across the bridge from the Port of Miami is Bayside Marketplace, downtown Miami's waterfront and restaurant shopping complex, which can be reached via regular shuttle service between each cruise terminal and Bayside's main entrance.

The **Port of Miami** is at 1015 North America Way, in central Miami. It lies on Dodge Island, reached via a five-lane bridge from the downtown district. For information, call ☎ **305/371-PORT.**

GETTING TO MIAMI & THE PORT

BY AIR   Miami International Airport is about 8 miles west of downtown Miami and its port. The fare from the airport to the Port of Miami is about $17. The meter must read $1.10 at the start of your trip, and one fare pays for all passengers in the cab. Tolls are extra. Some leading taxi companies include **Central Taxicab Service** (☎ 305/532-5555), **Diamond Cab Company** (☎ 305/545-5555), or **Metro Taxicab Company** (☎ 305/888-8888).

Metrobus no longer provides service to the Port of Miami.

You can go by van on **SuperShuttle** (☎ 305/871-2000), which charges $7 per person for a ride within Dade County, including the Port of Miami. Their vans operate 24 hours a day.

BY CAR   The Florida Turnpike, a toll road, and **I-95** are the main arteries for those arriving from the north. Ongoing road construction on I-95 virtually guarantees slow-moving traffic. Coming in from the northwest, take **I-75** or **U.S. 27** to reach the center of Miami.

Avis (☎ 800/831-2847), **Budget** (☎ 800/527-0700), **Dollar** (☎ 800/800-4000), **Hertz** (☎ 800/654-3131), **National** (☎ 800/227-7368), and **Value** (☎ 800/468-2583) can all be found on Miami International Airport's lower level near the baggage-claim area.

Parking at the Port   Parking lots right at street level face the cruise terminals. Parking runs $8 per day. Porters can carry your luggage to the terminals.

BY TRAIN   Amtrak (☎ 800/872-7245) offers twice-daily service between New York and Miami and service three times a week between Los Angeles and Miami. You'll pull into Amtrak's Miami terminal at 8303 NW 37th Ave. (☎ 305/835-1205).

EXPLORING MIAMI

Miami is no longer just a beach vacation—you'll also find high-quality hotels, distinctive restaurants serving exotic and delectable food, unusual attractions, and top shopping, and you can complement relaxing days on the water with evenings that include theater or opera, a hopping club scene, and a lively cafe culture.

ESSENTIALS
VISITOR INFORMATION   The best up-to-date information is provided by the **Greater Miami Convention and Visitors Bureau,** 701 Brickell Ave., Miami, FL 33131 (☎ **800/283-2707** or 305/539-3063).

GETTING AROUND   For a taxi, call **Metro** (☎ 305/888-8888) or **Yellow** (☎ 305/444-4444); on Miami Beach, try **Central** (☎ 305/532-5555). The meter starts at $1.10, and ticks up another $1.75 each mile and 25¢ for each additional minute, with standard flat-rate charges for frequently traveled routes.

Miami's suburban layout is not conducive to getting around by bus. Call ☎ **305/638-6700** for public transit information. Fare is $1.25, and transfers are 25¢.

Metromover, a 4.4-mile elevated line, circles downtown, stopping at important attractions and shopping and business districts. It runs daily from about 6am to midnight, and the fare is 25¢.

HITTING THE BEACH

A 300-foot-wide sand beach runs for about 10 miles from the south of Miami Beach to Haulover Beach Park in the north. Hotels line the beach, but you're free to frolic along the entire strip. There are toilet facilities, concession stands, and metered parking (bring quarters). A wooden boardwalk runs along the hotel side of the beach from 21st to 46th streets—about 1 1/2 miles.

Lifeguard-protected public beaches include **21st Street,** at the beginning of the boardwalk; **35th Street,** popular with an older crowd; **46th Street,** next to the Fontainebleau Hilton; **53rd Street,** a narrower, more sedate beach; **64th Street,** one of the quietest strips around; and **72nd Street,** a local old-timers spot. On the southern tip of the beach is family favorite **South Pointe Park,** where you can watch the cruise ships. **Lummus Park,** in the center of the Art Deco district, is the place to head if you have the body of a model. (Though families also like the beaches here.) If you're gay, head for the beach lying between 11th and 13th streets; if you're a senior, the beach from 1st to 15th Street is a popular spot.

You can escape the crowds at the 40-acre **North Shore State Recreation Area,** Collins Avenue between 79th and 87th streets (☎ **305/673-7730**). Parking is metered.

In Key Biscayne, **Crandon Park,** 4000 Crandon Blvd. (☎ **305/361-5421**), is one of metropolitan Miami's finest white-sand beaches, stretching for some 3 1/2

miles and patrolled by lifeguards. Saturdays and Sundays the beach can be especially crowded. Parking is $3.50 per vehicle.

SOUTH BEACH & THE ART DECO DISTRICT

Miami's best sight is a part of the city itself. Located at the southern end of Miami Beach, the **Art Deco District** is a whole community of outrageous and fanciful 1920s and 1930s architecture.

Thanks to the efforts of the Miami Design Preservation League, the district has put the brakes on urban decay and made a spectacular comeback. In 1979, approximately 1 square mile of South Beach was granted a listing on the National Register of Historic Places. This treasure trove features more than 900 buildings in the art deco and Spanish Mediterranean Revival style, stretching from 6th to 23rd streets and from the Atlantic Ocean to Lennox Court. Ocean Drive, with more sidewalk cafes than you'd care to try counting, boasts many of the premier art deco hotels.

Lummus Park Beach, which runs along Ocean Drive from about 6th to 14th streets in South Beach, is the place to people-watch, as models and other fashion-world denizens spread out their towels and tan.

Also in South Beach is the **Bass Museum of Art,** 2121 Park Ave. (☎ **305/673-7533**), which hosts a permanent collection of Old Masters along with textiles, period furnishings, objets d'art, ecclesiastical artifacts, and sculpture.

CORAL GABLES & COCONUT GROVE

These two Miami neighborhoods are fun to visit for their architecture and ambience. In **Coral Gables,** the old world meets the new as curving boulevards, sidewalks, plazas, fountains, and arched entrances will make you imagine you're in Seville. Today the area is home to the **University of Miami** and a retail mecca known as the **Miracle Mile** (though it's actually half a mile), which runs from Douglas Road (37th Avenue) to Le Jeune Road (42nd Avenue). If you're interested in the history of the area, you can visit the boyhood home of George Merrick, the man who originally developed Coral Gables. Located at 907 Coral Way (☎ 305/460-5361), the **Coral Gables Merrick House and Gardens** has been restored to its 1920s look and is filled with Merrick memorabilia.

Coconut Grove, South Florida's oldest settlement, remains a village surrounded by the urban sprawl of Miami. It dates back to the early 1800s when Bahamian seamen first sought to salvage treasure from the wrecked vessels stranded along the Great Florida Reef. Attractions include the **Vizcaya Museum and Gardens,** 3251 South Miami Ave. (☎ 305/250-9133), a spectacular 70-room Italian Renaissance–style villa. Thirty-four rooms are open to the public, but people mostly come here to shop, drink, dine, or simply to walk around and explore.

ANIMAL PARKS

Just minutes from the Port of Miami in Key Biscayne, the **Miami Seaquarium,** 4400 Rickenbacker Causeway (☎ 305/361-5705), holds enough aqueous fascination for all with its six daily shows. Dolphins perform with "Lolita the Killer Whale," TV's superstar Flipper goes through a routine, and there's a shark feeding that's downright gruesome. You can also see endangered manatees, feed the sea lions, and take in the sights at tropical-theme aquariums.

At **Monkey Jungle,** 14805 SW 216th St., Homestead (☎ 305/235-1611), the gimmick is that the visitors are caged and the nearly 500 resident monkeys frolic freely and make fun of them, with the most talented of these free-roaming primates performing shows for the amusement of their "guests." The site also contains one of the richest fossil deposits in South Florida, having yielded some 5,000 specimens.

In South Miami, **Parrot Jungle and Gardens,** 11000 SW 57th Ave. (☎ 305/666-7834), is actually a botanical garden, wildlife habitat, and bird sanctuary all rolled into one. Children can enjoy a petting zoo and a playground.

ORGANIZED TOURS

BY BOAT   Heritage Tours of *Miami II* features jaunts aboard an 85-foot topsail two-masted schooner. Tours depart from the Bayside Marketplace at 401 Biscayne Blvd. (☎ 305/442-9697). A one-hour tour past movie-star mansions and Vizcaya costs $12 for adults, $6 for children under 12.

ON FOOT   An **Art Deco District Walking Tour** is sponsored by the Miami Design Preservation League (☎ 305/672-2014) on Saturdays at 10:30am and Thursdays at 6:30pm. The 90-minute tour, which costs $6, leaves from the Art Deco Welcome Center at 1001 Ocean Dr., South Beach.

SHOPPING

Most cruise-ship passengers shop right near the Port of Miami at **Bayside Marketplace,** 401 Biscayne Blvd., a mall with 150 specialty shops, street performers doing their thing, and boat tours for when you're shopped out. Some 20 eateries serve everything from Nicaraguan to Italian food; there's even a Hard Rock Cafe.

You can catch a free shuttle from the Hotel Inter-Continental in downtown Miami to the **Bal Harbour Shops** at 9700 Collins Ave., a lavishly landscaped mall wherein you'll find big-name stores such as Chanel and LaCoste, as well as Florida's largest Saks Fifth Avenue and Neiman-Marcus.

In South Beach, **Lincoln Road,** an eight-block pedestrian mall, runs between Washington Avenue and Alton Road, near the northern tier of the art deco district. It's filled with antique shops, interior design stores, art galleries, and even vintage clothing outlets, as well as coffeehouses, restaurants, and cafes.

Centered around Main Highway and Grand Avenue, **Coconut Grove** is the heart of the city's boutique district. **Coco Walk,** 3015 Grand Ave., between Main

Highway and Virginia Street (☎ 305/ 444-0777), is more for novelties, movies, a late-night rendezvous, or a bookstore browse. For swanky shopping, go to **Mayfair Shops in the Grove,** 2911 Grand Ave. (☎ 305/448-1700), just east of Commodore Plaza.

In Coral Gables, **Miracle Mile,** a stretch of SW 22nd Street between Douglas and Le Jeune roads, features more than 150 shops.

For offbeat shopping, make yourself look glitzy and hop over to **Babalú,** 432 Española Way (☎ 305/538-0679), a few blocks off South Beach's Ocean Drive. At this Havana-style haven, Herb Sosa capitalizes off the current nostalgia craze for Cuba. Try the Cuban coffee, the hand-rolled Babalú brand cigars, and the tropical-flavored ice cream that only needs Carmen Miranda to serve it, all while shopping for such memorabilia as vintage magazine covers, Cuban flags, linen guayaberas, and Batista-era cigar-box labels.

ACCOMMODATIONS

Thanks to the network of highways that cuts through town, you can stay virtually anywhere in Greater Miami and still be within 10 to 20 minutes of your cruise ship. However, if you want to stay really close by, the following hotels are closest to the port.

If you're embarking for a cruise, or disembarking, you won't be without company at the **Crowne Plaza Miami Hotel,** 1601 Biscayne Blvd. (☎ 800/2-CROWNE or 305/374-0000), located above the Omni International Shopping Mall. Carnival Cruise Lines radically renovated the hotel in 1994, and it now hosts more pre- and postcruise bookings than any other Miami hotel, about 35,000 room nights a year. Rooms here are large and comfortable.

The **Sheraton Biscayne Bay Hotel,** 495 Brickell Ave. (☎ 800/284-2000 or 305/ 373-6000), is in a parklike area flanking the riverside. All rooms offer both city and

water views, but we've found that the best rooms are on floors 17 and 18.

Set across the bay from the cruise-ship piers and designed on a bold scale, the **Miami Inter-Continental Hotel,** 100 Chopin Plaza (☎ 800/327-0200 or 305/577-1000), is a triangular tower soaring 34 stories. Bedrooms are big and bathrooms comfortably proportioned.

In trendy South Beach, the stylish, art deco, coral-pink **Astor,** 956 Washington Ave. (☎ 800/270-4981 or 305/531-8081), was originally built in 1936 and reopened in 1995 after a massive renovation. Standard bedrooms are small but elegantly decorated, with French-milled cabinetry and large, user-friendly bathrooms. Backed by a waterfall, the hotel bar is a chic rendezvous spot, as is the hot new restaurant, the **Astor Place Bar and Grill.** The Astor is only two blocks from the beach, but if even that's too far for you, try the **Ocean Front Hotel,** 1230-38 Ocean Dr. (☎ 305/672-2579), a place that lives up to its name.

A $20 million facelift turned the landmark 1947 **Delano,** at 1685 Collins Ave. (☎ 800/555-5001 or 305/672-2000), into the "seductive" space sought by world-renowned hotelier Ian Schrager and designer Philippe Starck. The investment has paid off. The Delano is a celebrity hot spot that's sleek, postmodern, and self-consciously hip. Superstar Madonna co-owns the hotel restaurant, whose clientele has been described as "material girls and boy toys."

Publicity about the Astor and Delano has cooled somewhat these days, making room for the latest shrine of chic, trend-setting Chris Blackwell's little hotel **The Kent,** 1131 Collins Ave., Miami Beach (☎ 800/688-7678 or 305/531-6771). It's designed for those seeking seclusion and/or those who look like (or are) fashion models.

Inland in Miami Beach is the **Indian Creek Hotel,** 2727 Indian Creek Dr. at 28th St. (☎ 305/531-2727). Each room is a meticulously restored homage to the art deco age.

Further north in Miami Beach, you can stay at popular updated 1950s resorts including the **Eden Roc,** 4525 Collins Ave. (☎ **800/327-8337** or 305/531-0000), or the **Fontainebleau Hilton Resort and Towers,** next door at 4441 Collins Ave. (☎ **800/548-8886** or 305/538-2000). Both hotels have spas, health clubs, outdoor swimming pools, and beach access.

A good anchor in Bal Harbour is the **Sheraton Bal Harbour,** 9701 Collins Ave. (☎ **800/325-3535** or 305/865-7511), with 655 newly renovated rooms and 53 sumptuous suites. Some $52 million has made it tonier than ever. The lagoon-style pools and waterfalls and the lush tropical foliage may all be faux, but you'll enjoy it so much you'll overlook that.

In Coconut Grove, near Miami's City Hall and the Coconut Grove Marina, the **Grand Bay Hotel,** 2669 South Bayshore Dr. (☎ **800/327-2788** or 305/858-9600), overlooks Biscayne Bay. It's the most glamorous European-style hotel in the Greater Miami area.

In Coral Gables, the famous **Biltmore Hotel,** 1200 Anastasia Ave. (☎ **800/727-1926** or 305/445-1926), was recently restored. Everything is monumental except the rooms. There's also the **Hotel Place St. Michel,** 162 Alcazar Ave. (☎ **800/848-HOTEL** or 305/444-1666), a three-story establishment that has the feel of an inn in provincial France.

In Key Biscayne, many cruise-ship passengers appreciate the **Sonesta Beach Resort Key Biscayne,** 350 Ocean Dr. (☎ **800/SONESTA** or 305/361-2021), for its relative isolation from the rest of congested Miami. This eight-story structure is set on 10 landscaped acres with a white-sand beach.

DINING

In Bayside Marketplace is **Lombardi's** (☎ **305/381-9580**), a moderately priced Italian restaurant. Try the lobster *fra diavolo,* one of the best items on the menu. Other good picks include one of the dozen zesty risottos and pastas; veal, fish, beef, and chicken dishes cooked according to one of those fabled "old Italian recipes"; and freshly prepared salads.

East Coast Fisheries and Restaurant, 360 West Flagler at South River Drive (☎ **305/372-1300**), is a no-nonsense retail market and restaurant offering a tremendous variety of the freshest fish available. The huge menu features every fish imaginable, cooked just the way you want it.

Only a five-minute taxi ride from the cruise docks, **The Fish Market,** on the fourth floor of the Crowne Plaza Hotel, 1601 Biscayne Blvd. (☎ **305/374-0000**), is one of Miami's finest and most elegant restaurants, and their fixed-price lunch is one of the city's best bargains. There are few fish dishes in Miami that can equal such Fish Market favorites as herb-seared salmon burgers with boursin cheese or sesame-flavored snapper with oriental vinaigrette.

In the lobby of the elegant Hotel Inter-Continental Miami, **Le Pavilion,** 100 Chopin Plaza (☎ **305/577-1000**), is one of the most artful and European restaurants in town. The menu blends Continental and Floridian cuisine in dishes like a mélange of Florida seafood simmered in a light saffron broth; panfried, corn-fed squab; and roast fillet of milk-fed veal with wild mushrooms and an herb compote.

The large windows and minimalist decor at **Mercury,** 764 Washington Ave. (☎ **305/532-0070**), create a heady atmosphere for celebrity chef Kerry Simon's delectable menu. The roasted red and yellow pepper soup, served with grilled radicchio and smoked mozzarella, is a tantalizing appetizer before a filling main course of roast loin of venison or pistachio-crusted grouper. Critics have called the food here "true Miami vice."

Take time to stroll down the pedestrian mall on Lincoln Road, which offers art galleries, specialty shops, and one of the area's most promising new dining establishments, **South Beach Brasserie,** 910

Lincoln Rd. (☎ 305/534-5511), the creation of actor-cum-restaurateur Michael Caine. Housed in a beautifully renovated 1929 Mediterranean-style landmark building, this place redefines urban cool, with a relaxing, tropical atmosphere and a menu that features such delectable choices as pan-seared lemongrass red snapper and wild-rice-and-apple-stuffed quail.

At **Joe's Stone Crab,** 227 Biscayne St., between Washington and Collins avenues (☎ **305/673-0365**), about a ton of stone-crab claws are served daily when in season. The place is a hot spot, so unless you go very early, you'll have to wait in line.

Even if Gloria Estefan weren't part-owner of **Larios on the Beach,** 820 Ocean Dr. (☎ **305/532-9577**), the crowds would still flock to this Cuban bistro for old-fashioned Cuban dishes such as *masitas de puerco* (fried pork chunks), and for the live Cubano jazz that's performed on Friday and Saturday nights.

Some of the best fresh fish dishes in town are served at **South Pointe Seafood House,** 1 Washington Ave. (☎ **305/673-1708**). We particularly like the teriyaki tuna, blackened swordfish, and grilled mahimahi with caramelized pineapple-papaya salsa and rum-coconut butter. Take note: There's also a brew pub on the premises.

If you're strolling along Ocean Drive, stop by **The News Café,** 800 Ocean Dr. (☎ **305/538-6397**), at any time of the day or night for drinks, ice cream, sandwiches, and more. This is one hip joint.

In Coconut Grove, **Café Sci-Sci,** 3043 Grand Ave. at McFarlane Road (☎ **305/446-5104**), is red, glitzy, and Italian. This expensive restaurant serves surprisingly good food, with fresh oysters, a perfectly cooked salmon with chives, an excellent carpaccio of lamb with fresh artichokes and balsamic vinegar, and a choice of pastas.

The Chart House, 51 Chart House Dr., off South Bayshore Drive (☎ **305/856-9741**), overlooks an upscale marina. Steaks, chicken, pork, and fish are thick and appropriately juicy, and lobsters

are fresh from the tank and never overcooked. Be warned: There can be a long wait.

In the Grand Bay Hotel, **Grand Café,** 2669 South Bayshore Dr. (☎ **305/858-9600**), lives up to its name. Culinary-star-of-the-minute Pascal Oudin serves "fussed over" dishes such as seared rare yellowfin tuna crusted with black beans. There's a lavish luncheon buffet, and ever more elaborate dinners.

In Coconut Grove, it's fun to people-watch from **Kaleidoscope,** 3112 Commodore Plaza, off Main Highway (☎ **305/446-5010**), located one floor above street level. Straightforward and well-prepared dishes include steak au poivre, shrimp Creole, oven-roasted lamb shanks, and an array of fattening desserts.

The surf and turf is routine at the **Rusty Pelican,** 3201 Rickenbacker Causeway (☎ **305/361-3818**) in Key Biscayne, but it's worth coming for a drink and the spectacular sunset view.

MIAMI AFTER DARK

Miami nightlife is as varied as its population. On any night, you'll find world-class opera or dance as well as grinding rock and salsa. Restaurants and bars are open late and many clubs, especially on South Beach, stay open past dawn.

The Miami Herald lists major cultural events, and you can buy tickets to most major events through **TicketMaster** (☎ **305/358-5885**).

The 2,500-seat **Dade County Auditorium,** 2901 W. Flagler St. in downtown Miami (☎ **305/547-5414**), is home to the city's Greater Miami Opera and also to productions of the Concert Association of Florida and the Miami Ballet Company.

Broadway shows, opera, and dance performances are often held at the **Jackie Gleason Theater of the Performing Arts,** 1700 Washington Ave., South Beach (☎ **305/673-7300**). You can often catch the **Miami City Ballet** (☎ **305/532-4880**), directed by Edward Villella, performing here, or you can watch them in practice at their Lincoln Road studio (no. 905).

The **Greater Miami Opera,** 1200 Coral Way, Miami (☎ **305/854-1643**), performs from November through April (excluding December) at the Dade County Auditorium.

THE CLUB & MUSIC SCENE

Whether you're looking for a cool beachfront bar, a hot jazz club, or something in between, South Beach has the nighttime diversion for you. In a word, the place is hopping.

Amnesia, 136 Collins Ave. (☎ **305/ 531-5535**), is one of the leading straight discos at the beach, with Top 40, reggae, jazz, and blues to shake your booty to. It's open to the air in a kind of semitropical amphitheater layout, and the crowd has been known to break into crazed singing and dancing when showers pass over.

The jazz is hot and the audience cool at **MoJazz Café,** 928 71st St. (☎ **305/865- 2636**), in the Normandy Isle section. Since 1993, South Beach jazz aficionados have made their way to this hangout cafe known for taking its jazz straight, no chaser. Big-name players appear here occasionally, and before the live music begins at 9pm you can catch some good jazz on film—when we were there the *artiste du jour* was Count Basie. A neighborhood favorite as well, MoJazz is known for its nightly happy hour and good, hearty country cookery.

At **Rosa's Bar and Music Lounge,** 754 Washington Ave. (☎ **305/532-0228**), new talent is showcased every Monday as the stage clears for an open-mike night.

You can dance to a 10-piece orchestra and enjoy a Las Vegas–style floor show at the **Club Tropigala at La Ronde,** in the Fontainebleau Hilton Resort and Towers, 4441 Collins Ave. (☎ **305/672-7469**). You'll spot more than your share of tourists making their way through the club's tropical jungle aura, but you may also spot such hip stars as Elton John, Madonna, or Sylvester Stallone.

Opened in 1912, landmark **Tobacco Road,** 626 South Miami Ave. (☎ **305/ 374-1198**), has hosted practically all the big names who ever visited Miami. Local and national blues bands perform at night, and you can also hear funk, R&B, and jazz.

Coco Loco's, in the Sheraton Biscayne Bay Hotel, 495 Brickell Ave. (☎ **305/ 373-6000**), has the area's best happy hour buffet. You might not need dinner! Happy hour is Monday through Friday from 5 to 7pm.

The lavish and glitzy **Les Violins Supper Club,** 1751 Biscayne Blvd. (☎ **305/ 371-8668**), re-creates nightlife in pre-Castro Cuba. Its floor shows are among the best in Miami, its live band will make you want to take a turn around the dance floor, and who can resist tipping those strolling violinists?

In Coconut Grove, **The Hungry Sailor,** 3064^1/$_2$ Grand Ave. (☎ **305/444-9359**), is the closest southern Florida gets to a British pub. Entertainment is live or via DJ Tuesday through Saturday. For a lively happy hour, stop by **Monty's Raw Bar,** 2550 South Bayshore Dr. (☎ **305/858- 1431**), perched atop a pier and featuring panoramic views, live music, and fresh oysters and chowders. Finally, the **Taurus Steak House,** 3540 Main Hwy. (☎ **305/ 448-0633**), is one of the most frequented night-time rendezvous spots in the Grove, drawing a mainly 35-and-over crowd with its live music.

In Coral Gables, head for happy hour at **Alcazaba,** in the Hyatt Regency Hotel, 50 Alhambra Plaza (☎ **305/441-1234**), which has the best tapas and tropical drinks around.

2 Fort Lauderdale & Port Everglades

Anchor to more four- and five-star ships than any seaport in the world, Port Everglades is the home port of many cruise lines, including Cunard, Holland America, Princess, and Seabourn. With Florida's deepest harbor, Port Everglades, just next door, it's the second busiest cruise-ship base in Florida (after Miami) and one of the top five in the world. The port on State Road 84, east of U.S. 1, lies about a five-minute drive from the airport. It's some 40 miles north of Miami center.

Many of the ships operating from here are decidedly upscale, including Seabourn's *Seabourn Pride,* Cunard's *QE2,* and other ships making Cunard's Caribbean runs. Princess Cruises is also a heavy port user—its *Crown Princess, Regal Princess,* and *Sky Princess* sometimes depart from here—as is Holland America, whose *Maasdam, Noordam, Statendam,* and *Westerdam* sail from here as well.

Celebrity Cruises launched its 1,740-passenger, 70,000-ton *Century* from Port Everglades for the 1995–96 cruise season, and its *Zenith* also departs from here.

Other lines leaving from Port Everglades include Radisson Seven Seas, with its distinctive *Radisson Diamond.* Sun Line Cruises also occasionally operates *Stella Solaris* from here on trips to the Caribbean.

The port itself is fairly congestion free. Nine modern cruise terminals offer covered loading zones, drop-off/pick-up staging, and curbside baggage handlers. Terminals are comfortable and safe. If you're waiting between ships, you'll find covered hydraulic-loading bridges, comfortable seating areas, snack bars, clean rest rooms, and plenty of pay phones.

If you need more information about the port, call **Port Everglades** at ☎ **954/523-3404.**

GETTING TO FORT LAUDERDALE & THE PORT

BY AIR   The **Fort Lauderdale/Hollywood International Airport** (☎ **954/359-6100**) is small, extremely user-friendly, and less than 2 miles from Port Everglades. **Carnival** (☎ **954/925-1386**) flies into Fort Lauderdale.

Cruise-ship buses meet incoming flights when they know transfer passengers are on board, so you'll need to make arrangements for pickup when you book your cruise. Taking a taxi to the port costs $5 to $10 per person.

BY CAR   The port has a trio of passenger entrances: **Spangler Boulevard,** an extension of State Road 84 East; **Eisenhower Boulevard,** running south from the 17th Street Causeway (A1A); and **Eller Drive,** connecting directly with Interstate 595. Interstate 595 runs east/west, with connections to the Fort Lauderdale/Hollywood Airport, Interstate I-95, State Road 7 (441), Florida's Turnpike, Sawgrass Expressway, and I-75.

The following car-rental firms provide shuttle service from the port to their rental terminal sites: **Avis** (☎ **800/331-1212** or 954/359-3255); **Budget/Sears Rent-a-Car** (☎ **800/527-0700** or 954/359-4700); **National** (☎ **800/227-7368** or 954/359-8303); and **Dollar** (☎ **800/800-4000** or 954/359-7800).

Parking at the Port   Convenient parking is available at two large garages. The 2,500-space Northport Parking Garage, next to the Greater Fort Lauderdale/Broward County Convention Center, serves terminals 1, 2, and 4. The 1,000-space Midport Parking Garage serves terminals 18, 19, 21, 22, 24, 25, and 26. Garages are well lit, security-patrolled, and designed to accommodate RVs and buses. The 24-hour parking fee is $7.

BY TRAIN   Amtrak (☎ **800/USA-RAIL**) trains from New York to Miami make various stops along the way, including Fort Lauderdale. The local station is at 200 SW 21st Terrace (☎ **305/587-6692**). Taxis are available to deliver you to Port Everglades for a $10 to $15 per person fare.

EXPLORING FORT LAUDERDALE

Fort Lauderdale Beach, a 2-mile strip along Florida A1A, gained fame in the 1950s and 1960s as a spring-break playground, popularized by the movie *Where* *the Boys Are.* But by the 1980s, the party-ing college kids, who brought the city more mayhem than money, were no longer welcome. Fort Lauderdale tried to attract a more mainstream, affluent crowd and transform itself into the "Venice of the Americas." And it's been relatively successful.

In addition to miles of beautiful wide beaches, Fort Lauderdale includes more than 300 miles of navigable waterways, plus innumerable artificial canals that per-mit thousands of residents to anchor boats in their backyards. Visitors can easily get on the water, too, by renting a boat or hailing a private, moderately priced water taxi.

ESSENTIALS

VISITOR INFORMATION The **Greater Fort Lauderdale Convention and Visitors Bureau,** 1850 Eller Drive, Suite 303, Fort Lauderdale, FL 33316 (☎ **954/765-4466**), is an excellent re-source, distributing a comprehensive guide about events and sightseeing in Broward County.

GETTING AROUND   For a taxi, call **Yellow Cab** (☎ **954/565-5400**), radio-dispatched right to your door, with rates that start at $2.45 for the first mile and $1.75 for each additional mile.

Broward County Mass Transit (☎ **954/357-8400**) runs bus service throughout the county. Each ride costs $1. An additional transfer fee of 15¢ is expected along with the base cost if you plan to take a second bus.

HITTING THE BEACH

The Fort Lauderdale Beach Promenade recently underwent a $20 million renova-tion, and it looks marvelous. This beach is still backed by an endless row of hotels and is popular with visitors and locals alike. On weekends, parking at the ocean-side meters is difficult to find. Try biking or blading to the beach instead. It's lo-cated along Atlantic Boulevard (Fla. A1A), between SE 17th Street and Sunrise Bou-levard. The fabled strip from *Where the*

Boys Are is Ocean Boulevard, between Las Olas Boulevard and Sunrise Boulevard.

Ft. Lauderdale Beach at the **Howard Johnson** is a perennial favorite with locals and those who stay at this oceanfront ho-tel. A jetty bounds the beach on the south side, making it rather private, and the water here gets a little choppy, making it rather exciting. High school and college students share this area with an older crowd. The beach is located at 4660 North Ocean Dr. in Lauderdale by the Sea.

SEEING THE SIGHTS

The **Museum of Discovery and Science,** 401 SW Second St. (☎ **954/467-6637**), is an excellent interactive science museum that includes an IMAX theater. The 52-foot-tall "Great Gravity Clock," located in the museum's atrium, is the largest kinetic energy sculpture in Florida.

The **Museum of Art,** 1 Las Olas Blvd. (☎ **954/763-6464**), is a gem of a small modern and contemporary art museum.

A guided tour of the **Bonnet House,** 900 N. Birch Rd. (☎ **954/563-5393**), offers a glimpse into the lives of the pio-neers of the Fort Lauderdale area. This unique 35-acre plantation home and es-tate survives in the middle of an otherwise highly developed beachfront condo-minium area. Tours are offered Wednes-day through Friday from 10am to 2pm and Saturday and Sunday from noon to 3pm.

Butterfly World, Tradewinds Park South, 3600 W. Sample Rd., Coconut Creek, west of the Florida Turnpike (☎ **954/977-4400**), cultivates more than 150 species of these colorful and delicate insects. In the park's walk-through, screened-in aviary, visitors can watch newborn butterflies emerge from their cocoons and flutter around as they learn to fly.

ORGANIZED TOURS

BY BOAT   The Mississippi River–style steamer *Jungle Queen,* Bahia Mar Yacht Center, Fla. A1A (☎ **954/462-5596**), is one of Fort Lauderdale's best-known attractions. Dinner cruises and three-hour sightseeing tours take visitors up the New River past Millionaires' Row, Old Fort Lauderdale, the new downtown, and the Port Everglades cruise-ship port. Call for prices and departure times.

Water Taxi of Fort Lauderdale, 651 Seabreeze Blvd. (☎ **954/467-6677**), is a fleet of old-port boats that navigate this city of canals, operating taxi service on demand and carrying up to 48 passengers. You can be picked up at your hotel and then be shuttled among dozens of restaurants and bars for the rest of the night. The service operates daily from 10am to midnight or 2am. The cost is $7 per person per trip, $12 round-trip, $15 for a full day. Opt for the all-day pass—it's worth it. **Water Taxi** also offers a 90-minute guided tour of the Historic New River, departing Saturday mornings at 10:30am from the Doubletree Guest Suites Hotel at 2670 East Sunrise Blvd. The tour costs $16 per person.

BY TROLLEY BUS   South Florida Trolley Tours (☎ **954/429-3100**) reveals Fort Lauderdale's entire history during a 90-minute open-air trolley tour that costs $12 for adults and is free for children under 12. The trolleys pick up passengers from most major hotels beginning at 9am. Departures vary according to your hotel's location; call for exact times.

BY FOOT   A Historical Society Walking Tour, 219 SW Second Ave. (☎ **954/463-4431**), sponsored by the Historical Society Museum, offers the best walking tours of the city's historic center. Guided tours are given periodically throughout the year and cost $10 per person.

You can also walk along **Riverwalk,** a 10-mile linear park along the New River that connects the cultural heart of Fort Lauderdale with its historic district.

SHOPPING

Not counting the number of discount "fashion" stores on Hallandale Beach Boulevard's "Schmatta Row," there are

three places every visitor to Broward County should know about.

The first is **Antique Row,** a strip of U.S. 1 around North Dania Beach Boulevard (in Dania, about 1 mile south of Fort Lauderdale/Hollywood International Airport) that holds about 200 antique shops. Some are a bit overpriced, but if you're persistent you'll find some good buys in furniture, silver, china, glass, linens, and more. Most shops are closed Sundays.

The **Fort Lauderdale Swap Shop,** 3291 W. Sunrise Blvd. (☎ **954/791-SWAP**), is one of the world's largest flea markets. In addition to endless acres of vendors, there's a mini–amusement park, a 12-screen drive-in movie theater, weekend concerts, and even a free circus complete with elephants, horse shows, high-wire acts, and clowns. It's open daily.

Sawgrass Mills, 12801 W. Sunrise Blvd., Sunrise (☎ **954/846-2300**), a behemoth mall shaped like a Florida alligator, is nearly 2.5 million square feet of effervescent capitalism covering 50 acres of ground. Strap on comfortable walking shoes to trek around the more than 300 shops and kiosks, which include Donna Karan, Saks Fifth Avenue, Levi's, Ann Taylor, Cache, Waterford Crystal, and hundreds more claiming to sell at 30% to 80% below retail. A spot check revealed that some stores offered prices that are 20% to 60% less than in many places in the Caribbean. Take I-95 North to 595 West until Flamingo Road, where you'll exit and turn right. Drive 2 miles until Sunrise Boulevard. It's the monster you'll see on the left. You can't miss it. Parking is free.

Las Olas Boulevard is the swank Fifth Avenue of Fort Lauderdale, and is not the place to go if you're looking for bargains. Close to Fort Lauderdale Beach, the **Galleria** mall, 2414 East Sunrise Blvd., between NE 26th Avenue and Middle River Drive (☎ **954/564-1015**), has Neiman-Marcus, Saks, Macy's, Cartier, Brooks Brothers, Lord and Taylor, and many other stores.

ACCOMMODATIONS

Fort Lauderdale beach has a hotel or motel on nearly every block, and the selection ranges from rundown to luxurious. A number of chains operate here, including **Best Western** (☎ 800 528-1234), **Days Inn** (☎ 800/866-6501), **Doubletree Hotels** (☎ 800/222-8733), and **Holiday Inn** (☎ 800/465-4329). Call the **Fort Lauderdale Convention and Visitors Bureau** (☎ 954/765-4466) for its "Superior Small Lodgings" guide to the area.

There are also two Marriotts: **The Fort Lauderdale Marina Marriott,** 1881 SE 17th St. (☎ 800/433-2254 or 954/463-4000), and the far superior **Marriott in Harbor Beach** at 3030 Holiday Dr. (☎ 800/222-6543 or 954/525-4000). The resort in Harbor Beach is the only hotel set directly on the beach. Its modest-sized rooms have water views.

Hyatt Regency Fort Lauderdale, at Pier 66 Marina, 2301 SE 17th St. Causeway (☎ 800/233-1234 or 954/525-6666), is a circular landmark that recently received a much-needed facelift. Its famous Piertop Lounge, a revolving bar perched on the hotel's roof, is often filled with cruise-ship transients. Bedrooms are 30% larger than those of some equivalently priced hotels in town.

Sheraton Yankee Clipper Beach Resort, 1140 Seabreeze Blvd. (☎ 800/325-3535 or 954/524-5551), is a long-time favorite for cruise-ship passengers who like to continue the party scene even after leaving ship. A gargantuan sprawl with more than 500 rooms scattered over several buildings, it attracts beachgoers and goes frantic at spring break time. This clipper shares facilities with its nearby sibling, the **Sheraton Yankee Trader Resort,** 321 N. Atlantic Blvd. (☎ 800/325-3535 or 954/467-1111), which consists of two high-rise towers opposite the beach between Las Olas Boulevard and Sunrise Boulevard. Rooms are standardized in both hotels and share vague tropical motifs.

The Pillars Waterfront Inn, 111 North Birch Rd. (☎ 800/763-7666 or 954/467-9639), is the best inn of its size in the region. The clean and simple accommodations have very comfortable beds.

Radisson Bahia Mar Beach Resort, 801 Seabreeze Blvd. (☎ 800/327-8154 or 954/764-2233), is scattered over 42 acres of seacoast. A four-story row of units is adjacent to Florida's largest marina.

The **Riverside Hotel,** 620 East Las Olas Blvd. (☎ 800/325-3280 or 954/467-0671), opened in 1936, is a local favorite. Try for one of the ground floor rooms, which have higher ceilings and more space.

DINING

The only restaurant at Port Everglades, **Burt and Jacks,** at Berth 23 (☎ 954/522-2878), is an elegant collaboration between actor Burt Reynolds and restaurateur Jack Jackson. From your table you can watch the cruise ships and other boats pass by. A waiter will arrive with raw steaks, lobster, veal, pork chops, or other fare; you choose your cut and the dish will soon arrive back at your table, perfectly cooked.

Bahia Cabana Beach Resort, 3001 Harbor Dr. (☎ 954/524-1555), offers American-style meals in hearty portions three times a day. The hotel's bar, known for its Frozen Rumrunner, is without equal as the most charming and laid-back in town.

In the Quarry Shopping Center, **Bimini Boat Yard,** 1555 SE 17th Causeway (☎ 954/525-7400), serves the best burgers around, salads, pizzas, and a selection of sandwiches that includes grilled grouper and roast beef foccacia, all available at any hour you want.

In the shadow of the Hyatt Pier 66 Hotel, **California Café,** Pier 66, 2301 SE 17th Causeway (☎ 954/728-8255), is known for its zesty, flavorful, and affordably priced avant-garde modern cuisine. Try the pepper-grilled tuna with jasmine-flavored rice or the potato-crusted salmon with lemongrass butter.

The famous old-time seafood joint **Cap's Place,** 2765 NE 28th Court, in Lighthouse Point (☎ **954/941-0418**), offers good food at affordable prices. The restaurant floats on a barge; you get a ferry ride over. Dolphin and grouper are popular, and like all the fish, beef, chicken, or pasta served here, can be prepared any way you want.

Evangeline, 213 South Atlantic Blvd. off of Hwy. A1A (☎ **954/522-7001**), is like a restaurant in Arcadian Louisiana. At lunch, enjoy an oyster or catfish po' boy or rabbit gumbo at dinner. Or try the alligator.

Il Tartufo, 2400 East Las Olas Blvd. (☎ **954/767-9190**), is the most charming and fun Italian restaurant in Fort Lauderdale, serving pizzas, oven-roasted specialties, Italian standards, and a selection of fish baked in rock salt.

Mark's Las Olas, 1032 East Las Olas Blvd. (☎ **954/463-1000**), is the showcase of Miami restaurant mogul Mark Militello. The food is as carefully prepared as you'd expect, but the place is a lot less fun than it should be. The daily changing menu might include Jamaican jerk chicken with fresh coconut salad or a superb sushi-quality tuna crusted in peppercorns and served with root vegetable mash, foie gras, and veal drippings.

Set across the highway from the beach on "the strip" is the very hip **Mistral,** 201 Hwy. A1A near Las Olas Boulevard (☎ **954/463-4900**). Portions are generous, dishes flavorful, and prices moderate. The varied menu includes baby artichoke lasagna, pan-seared dolphin, and designer pizzas that are larger than you'd expect. The pizza with seafood and herbs is worth the trip.

Paesano, 1301 East Las Olas Blvd. (☎ **954/467-3266**), is chic and elegant with good, albeit old-fashioned, food. The 16-ounce T-bone steak is usually grilled to perfection, or you may prefer one of the numerous pasta dishes.

Garlic crabs are the specialty at the **Rustic Inn Crabhouse,** 4331 Ravenswood Rd. (☎ **954/584-1637**), located west of the airport. This riverside dining choice has an open deck over the water.

One of the city's two four-star restaurants is **Sheffield's,** in the Marriott's Harbor Beach Resort, 3030 Holiday Dr. (☎ **954/525-4000**). The menu appears simpler than it actually is; dishes are original, and, if slow to arrive, are at least worth the wait.

FORT LAUDERDALE AFTER DARK

With the 1991 completion of the **Broward Center for the Performing Arts,** 201 SW Fifth Ave. (☎ **954/462-0222**), Fort Lauderdale finally got itself a venue worthy of the kind of talent the community craved. This stunning $55 million complex contains both a 2,700-seat auditorium and a smaller 590-seat theater, and attracts top opera, symphony, dance, and Broadway productions, as well as more modest-sized shows.

The region has some superb theater groups whose seasons run roughly from October through May. **Hollywood Boulevard Theatre,** 1938 Hollywood Blvd., Hollywood (☎ **954/929-5400**), is the newest addition, and there's also the **Vinnette Carroll Repertory Company,** 503 SE 6th St., Fort Lauderdale (☎ **954/462-2424**). **Brian C. Smith's Off-Broadway Theater,** NE 26th St., between Federal Highway and Dixie Highway, Fort Lauderdale (☎ **954/566-0554**), specializes in smaller, independent, and sometimes offbeat productions of contemporary plays, while a landmark in the Fort Lauderdale theater community is the **Parker Playhouse,** 707 NE Eighth St. (☎ **954/763-2444**), which offers a popular series of touring Broadway shows.

Another long-time local tradition is the **Opera Guild** (☎ **954/462-0222**), a society of music lovers that stages a wide-ranging series of shows. Good classical music is performed in season by the **Florida Philharmonic** (☎ **954/561-2997**) and the **Symphony of the Americas** (☎ **954/561-5882**). Look for listings in the *Sun-Sentinel* or *The Miami Herald* for schedules and performers or call the 24-hour **Arts and Entertainment Hotline** (☎ 954/357-5700).

THE BAR & CLUB SCENE

You'll get a 360° panoramic view of Fort Lauderdale from the area's most famous bar, the **Piertop Lounge,** in the Hyatt Regency at Pier 66 (☎ 954/525-6666). The bar revolves every 66 minutes, has no cover or drink minimum, and there's a dance floor and floor shows five nights a week (Tuesday through Saturday).

Inspired by the TV series of the same name, **Cheers,** 941 East Cypress Creek Rd. (☎ 954/771-6337), has two bars and a dance floor. Its specialty is "Acoustic Blues" Sunday through Tuesday, with rock and roll the rest of the week.

On weekends it's hard to get in **Club M,** 2037 Hollywood Blvd. (☎ 954/925-8396), one of the area's busiest music bars. Although the small club is primarily a local blues showcase, both electric and acoustic jazz bands also perform.

O'Hara Pub and Sidewalk Café, 722 East Las Olas Blvd. (☎ 954/524-1764), is often packed with a trendy crowd that comes here to be entertained by live blues and jazz. Call their jazz hotline (☎ 954/524-2801) to hear the lineup.

If you want to dance, try the **Baja Beach Club,** 3200 North Federal Hwy. (☎ 954/561-2432), perhaps the only dance club in the world that anchors an entire shopping mall. Kids just want to have fun, and the club delivers with a great sound system and crowd-pleasing promotions.

Desperado, 2520 South Miami Rd. (☎ 954/463-2855), is the area's best country-western club, offering free line-dance lessons. Live entertainment starts nightly at 9:30pm and lasts until closing.

3 Cape Canaveral & Port Canaveral

Port Canaveral is Florida's most unusual and multifaceted port, and also the most underrated. Its facilities for pleasure cruising are the most up-to-date, stylish, and least congested of any port in Florida. Yet as you head for your cruise ship you might see shrimp and fish nets drying in the sun, a touch of the old that reflects Canaveral's status as the home base of the region's fishing industry. It's a coexistence you're not likely to find in any other Florida port.

Port Canaveral also has bars and restaurants, facilities noticeably absent at many other Florida harbors. The best ones are positioned adjacent to the frequently dredged deepwater access channels used by most ships, which pass so close you'll feel you could reach up from your seat and shake hands with one of the passengers on deck.

Cruise lines appreciate the port's proximity to both Disney World, an hour's drive away, and the Kennedy Space Center, which lies on the opposite side of a marshy, low-lying wildlife refuge. Many lines offer pre- or postcruise packages to these places. Some one million cruise-ship passengers embark or disembark here annually, making the port the second busiest for passengers taking three- or four-day cruises.

Sailing from this port is Premier Cruise Line's *Star/Ship Oceanic,* which specializes in three- and four-night tours to Nassau and Freeport. Cape Canaveral Cruise Line's *Dolphin* leaves here for frequent sun-and-sand runs to Freeport. The biggest fish calling Port Canaveral home is Carnival Cruise Lines' megaship *Fantasy.* Several Europe-based lines sometimes dock their ships here, and Port Canaveral has been designated as home base for the *Disney Magic,* the megaship coming from Disney Cruise Line in April 1998.

The 3,300-acre port covers an area larger than the Port of Miami. Terminal no. 10, a $24 million structure completed in 1995, was built in a modern and dramatic style, and is nicknamed the Bahnhof since it resembles a high-tech, futuristic German railway station. Terminal no. 5, built in 1991, looks a bit like a glossy downtown hotel. Both these facilities supplement the older terminals 2, 3, and 4, which look more industrial, like oversized Quonset huts. The port's facilities were designed to allow ships to moor parallel to the shore, partly a function of the muddy geology of the region, partly as a means of saving costs.

For information about the port, call the **Canaveral Port Authority** at **407/783-7831.**

GETTING TO CAPE CANAVERAL & THE PORT

BY AIR   The nearest airport is the **Orlando International Airport** (☎ **407/825-2001**), a 45-mile drive from Port Canaveral via Highway 528 (the Bee Line Expressway).

There's no public bus service between Orlando and the port, so many passengers arrange chartered vans or take buses organized by the cruise lines. The **Cocoa Beach Shuttle** (☎ **800/633-0427** or 407/784-3831) offers shuttle service between Orlando's airport and Port Canaveral; the trip costs $20 per person each way.

BY CAR   Port Canaveral and Cocoa Beach are accessible from virtually every interstate highway along the east coast. Most visitors arrive via Route 1, I-95, or Highway 528 (the Bee Line Expressway from Orlando).

You can rent a car at the Orlando airport, which has branches of many car-rental companies, or in Cocoa Beach through **Budget** (☎ **800/527-7000** or 407/784-0622) or **Americar** (☎ **800/743-7483** or 407/868-1800).

Parking at the Port   Parking lots include the North Lots for north terminals 5 and 10. The South Lots service southern terminals 2, 3, and 4. Parking costs $7 a day.

BY TRAIN   Amtrak (☎ **800/USA-RAIL**) trains make stops at Kissimmee, Sanford, and Orlando, the closest points to the port, but still 55 miles away. You'll

have to rent a car or take a taxi to the port. The Kissimmee railway station is at 111 Dakin St. The Orlando station is at 1400 Sligh Blvd., between Columbia and Miller streets.

EXPLORING CAPE CANAVERAL

Most passengers spend only a night or two in Cocoa Beach, visiting the Kennedy Space Center and going to the beach before rushing to nearby Orlando and Walt Disney World.

ESSENTIALS
VISITOR INFORMATION   Contact the **Cocoa Beach Chamber of Commerce,** 400 Fortenberry Rd., Merritt Island, FL 32952 (☎ **407/459-2200**).

GETTING AROUND   When cruise ships arrive in port, you can count on every cab in town coming to greet them; at other times you can try to flag one down, but it's better to call for service. Local operators include **Cocoa Beach Cab Co.** (☎ **407/783-7200**) and **Yellow Top Taxi Service** (☎ 407/636-7017), which also operates under the name Brevard Yellow Cab Company and Banana River Yellow Cab.

Buses are run by the **Space Coast Area Transit Authority (SCAT)** (☎ **407/633-1878** for information and schedules). A ticket costs $1 for adults age 18 to 60; 50¢ for students, senior citizens, and persons with disabilities; and is free for children under six. No buses pass close to the port.

KENNEDY SPACE CENTER
NASA's **Kennedy Space Center,** located on State Road 405 E, Titusville (☎ **407/452-2121**), has been the launch site for all U.S. manned space missions since 1968, including the most famous "small step" in history: man's first voyage to the moon.

A massive renovation in visitor facilities scheduled for completion in 1998 has and will continue to dramatically alter the experience of a trip here, making it more of an interactive adventure. At the **Visitor Center,** the past, present, and future of space exploration are explored on bus tours of the facility, in movie presentations, and in numerous exhibits. It takes at least a full day to see and do everything. Arrive early and make your first stop at Information Central (it opens at 9am) to pick up a map and a schedule of events.

For now, visitors take the two-hour **Red Tour,** boarding a double-decker bus to explore the complex. At the first stop, in a simulated launch-control firing room, visitors view a film about the Apollo 8 mission. The tour continues to Complex 39 Space Shuttle launch pads and the massive Vehicle Assembly Building where Space Shuttles are assembled. You'll get a close-up look at an actual Apollo/Saturn V moon rocket, America's largest and most powerful launch vehicle. Also on view are massive six-million-pound Crawler Transporters that carry Space Shuttles to their launch pads. Tours depart at regular intervals beginning at 9:45am, with the last tour leaving late in the afternoon (call for details). Purchase tickets at the Ticket Pavilion as soon as you arrive.

Note: Itinerary variations may occur subject to launch schedules.

A second two-hour **Blue Tour** (same hours) visits Cape Canaveral Air Station. You'll see where America's first satellites and astronauts were launched in the Mercury and Gemini programs, view launch pads currently being used for unmanned launches, visit the original site of Mission Control, and stop at the Air Force Space Museum.

"Satellites and You" is a 45-minute voyage through a simulated future space station. In Disneyesque fashion, the attraction combines audio-animatronic characters with innovative audiovisual techniques to explain satellites and their uses.

In the **Galaxy Center** building, three spectacular IMAX films projected on 5$^1/_2$-story screens are shown continually throughout the day. The Galaxy Center also houses a NASA art exhibit and a

walk-through replica of a future Space Station. You can also visit the "Spinoffs from Space" exhibit that displays some of the 30,000 spin-offs resulting from space program research, including improved consumer products ranging from football helmets to cordless tools.

The large **Gallery of Manned Spaceflight** houses hardware and models relating to significant space projects and offers interesting exhibits on lunar exploration and geology.

Spaceport Theater presents films and live demonstrations on a variety of topical space-related subjects. The **Astronauts Memorial,** a 42$^1/_2$-by-50-foot black granite "Space Mirror" dedicated May 9, 1991, honors the 16 American astronauts who have lost their lives in the line of duty. Aboard *Explorer,* a full-size replica of a Space Shuttle orbiter, visitors can experience the working environment of NASA astronauts. And the **Rocket Garden** displays eight actual U.S. rockets.

ANOTHER SPACE-RELATED ATTRACTION

Six miles west of the Kennedy Space Center is the **U.S. Astronaut Hall of Fame,** State Road 405, 6225 Vectorspace Blvd., Titusville (☎ **407/269-6100**), a satellite attraction founded by the astronauts who flew the first Mercury and Gemini missions into outer space. It contains memorabilia from the Space Age, displayed with a decidedly human and anecdotal touch. Open daily 9am to 5pm.

HITTING THE BEACH

Cocoa Beach, Merritt Island, and the surrounding landscapes are known as "the Space Coast," and on the Space Coast most all municipal parks have the Atlantic Ocean for a swimming pool. Here are our favorite spots.

Cruise-ship passengers prefer **Jetty Park,** 400 E. Jetty Rd. (☎ **407/783-7111**), near the port. It's more like a Florida version of Coney Island than the other beachside parks mentioned. A massive stone jetty, topped with asphalt, juts seaward as protection for the mouth of Port Canaveral. You'll see dozens of anglers waiting for a bite. Parking costs $1 per car.

On the border between Cocoa Beach and Cape Canaveral, **Cherie Down Park,** 8492 Ridgewood Ave. (☎ 407/455-1380), is a relatively tranquil sunning and swimming area, with lifeguards on duty in summer. You'll find a boardwalk, as well as showers, picnic shelters, and a public restroom. Parking is $1 per car.

Set in the heart of Cocoa Beach, **Lori Wilson Park,** 1500 N. Atlantic Ave. (☎ 407/455-1380), has children's playgrounds and a boardwalk that extends through about five acres of protected grasslands. Parking is $1 per car. Next to it is **Fischer Park** (☎ 407/868-3274), with public restrooms and a seasonal scattering of food kiosks. Parking is $3 per car.

The region's best surfing is at **Robert P. Murkshe Memorial Park,** SR A1A and 16th Street, Cocoa Beach (☎ 407/455-1380), which also has a boardwalk and public restrooms.

SHOPPING

Cocoa Beach offers a wide array of shopping, but for a unique shopping experience visit the **Ron Jon Surf Shop,** 4151 North Atlantic Ave., Cocoa Beach (☎ 407/799-8888), a veritable shrine to wave culture. You can't miss it as you're driving down Florida A1A. The building is more interesting than the merchandise, but if you're looking for a surfing souvenir, you'll find it here. The store also rents beach bikes, boogie boards, surfboards, in-line skates, and other fun stuff by the hour, day, or week.

ACCOMMODATIONS

Chain hotels in the area include the **Cocoa Beach Hilton,** 1550 North Atlantic Ave. (A1A) (☎ 800/HILTONS or 407/799-0003); **the Holiday Inn Cocoa Beach Resort,** 1300 North Atlantic Ave. (☎ 800/2BOOKUS or 407/783-2271),

which is more upscale and better designed than the average Holiday Inn; and the **Howard Johnson Plaza Hotel / Cocoa Beach,** 2080 North Atlantic Ave. (☎ 800/654-2000 or 407/783-9222).

Between the sea and route SR-520, and behind Ron Jon's Surf Shop, **The Inn at Cocoa Beach,** 4300 Ocean Beach Blvd. (☎ 800/343-5307 or 407/799-3460), is our preferred roost. It's actually more of an upscale, personalized inn than a traditional hotel (it even defines itself as an oversized bed-and-breakfast).

Closest to the port and the Kennedy Space Center is the **Radisson Resort at the Port,** 8701 Astronaut Blvd. (☎ 800/333-3333 or 407/784-0000). The bedrooms are comfortable, but not as appealing as those at the Inn at Cocoa Beach. The hotel's only drawback is that it lies on a river—the beach is a 20-minute drive away.

Typical taxi fares from Port Canaveral to a midbeach hotel such as the Inn at Cocoa Beach will run $12 to $13 from the North Terminal and $15 to $16 from the South Terminal.

DINING

Flamingo's, in the Radisson Resort at the Port, 8701 Astronaut Blvd. (☎ 407/784-0000), lies near the port and is the only five-star restaurant in town. Lunches seem fairly typical, but dinners are fabulous, with a menu that changes daily. The fish dishes are the best around the port, made with top-notch ingredients and deftly prepared by the kitchen staff.

Set amid the port area's densest concentration of commercial activity, **Lloyd's Canaveral Feast,** 610 Glen Cheek Dr. (☎ 407/784-8899), is the waterfront's best-designed seafood restaurant. Outdoor tables are set on pier-like terraces over the water, and you can watch the cruise ships sail from their berths to the sea. (The best viewing times are Thursday to Monday at 5:30pm.) The luncheon buffet, served 11am to 2pm, is an amazing value. The cooking is a bit slapdash, but satisfying if you're not too demanding.

The Mango Tree, 118 North Atlantic Ave. (☎ 407/799-0513), is the most beautiful and sophisticated restaurant in Cocoa Beach. Indian River crab cakes are perfectly flavored, and we especially like the sesame-seed-crusted grouper with a tropical fruit salsa, and almost any of the veal dishes. Pastas are always reliable, including the pasta primavera, which is the best you'll find on the Space Coast.

PORT CANAVERAL AFTER DARK

The Pier, 401 Meade Ave. (☎ 407/783-7549), is the largest and busiest entertainment complex in Cocoa Beach, crowded every afternoon and evening with diners, drinkers, and sunset-watchers. Two open-air cafes, four bars, and a pair of restaurants jut 800 feet beyond the shoreline into the waves and surf. The more upscale restaurant is **Pier House,** open for dinner only, daily from 5pm to 10pm, but we prefer **Marlin's Sports Bar,** where you'll enjoy fish platters, drinks, or sandwiches and a view of the sea that practically engulfs you. One or sometimes two bands play live six nights a week.

Cocoa Beach's Heidelberg-style restaurant, the smoky and noisy **Heidi's Jazz Club,** 7 North Orlando Ave. (☎ 407/783-6806), offers just what its name says: jazz, along with a good helping of classic blues, played live Tuesday through Saturday from 5 to 8pm and 9pm to around midnight, and Monday from 5 to 8pm.

4 Tampa & the Port of Tampa

The Port of Tampa is set amid a complicated network of channels and harbors near the historic Cuban enclave of Ybor City and its deepwater Ybor Channel. It's a true safe port in a storm, having kept ships secure during tropical storms that have devastated others berthed nearby. It's also a hub of waterfront activity and entertainment, supporting on its 30-acre site the Florida Aquarium; the Deuteron Entertainment Complex, a $30 million music theater; and the Garrison Seaport Center, a massive complex of restaurants and shops inspired by Baltimore's Inner Harbor complex.

The port's position on the western (Gulf) side of Florida makes it the logical departure point for ships headed for westerly ports of call, including the beaches and Mayan ruins of the Yucatán, the reefs of Central America, and the ports of Venezuela. Ships of several cruise lines currently dock here, including Holland America Line's *Noordam* and Carnival Cruise Line's *Celebration.*

The port is busy already, and is rife with possibilities. Today, the bulk of the port's 300,000 annual passengers make their way through the modern terminal no. 2, also known as the Seaport Street Terminal. Terminal 202, an older terminal on the less attractive eastern edge of the port, is being used for cargo and is eyed for future cruise expansion. What expansion? Ferryboat service, for instance, could easily run across the Bay of Mexico between the Yucatán and the U.S. mainland (the newer of the port's two terminals, no. 6, could be adapted into a ferryboat terminal); and if U.S.-Cuba relations ever thaw, the sailing link between Havana and Tampa could be re-established.

The Port of Tampa is located at 811 Wynkoop Rd. For information, call ☎ 813/272-0555.

GETTING TO TAMPA & THE PORT

BY AIR   Tampa International Airport (☎ 813/870-8700) lies 5 miles northwest of downtown Tampa, near the junction of Florida 60 and Memorial Highway.

The port is an easy 15-minute taxi ride away; the fare is $10 to $15. **Central Florida Limo** (☎ 813/396-3730) also runs a minivan service, which costs $7.50 per person from the airport to Pier 202 and Garrison Terminal.

BY CAR   Tampa lies 200 miles southwest of Jacksonville, 63 miles north of

Sarasota, and 254 miles northwest of Miami. It's easily accessible from I-275, I-75, I-4, U.S. 41, U.S. 92, U.S. 301, and many state roads.

The following car-rental companies have kiosks in the airport as well as offices downtown: **Avis** (☎ 800/331-2112); **Dollar** (☎ 800/800-4000); **National** (☎ 800/328-4567); **Budget** (☎ 800/472-3325); **Hertz** (☎ 800/654-3131); **Alamo** (☎ 800/327-9633); **Thrifty** (☎ 800/367-2277); and **Value** (☎ 800/327-2501).

Parking at the Port   The port has ample parking with good security. Parking costs $6 per day.

BY TRAIN   Amtrak (☎ 800/USA-RAIL) trains arrive at the Tampa Amtrak Station, 601 Nebraska Ave. N, Tampa. Taxi fare to the port costs $5 to $7.

EXPLORING TAMPA

Tampa is best explored by car, as only the commercial district can be covered on foot. If you want to go to the beach, you'll have to head to neighboring St. Petersburg.

ESSENTIALS

VISITOR INFORMATION   Contact the **Tampa/Hillsborough Convention and Visitors Association (THCVA),** 400 N. Tampa St., Suite 1010, Tampa, FL 33602 (☎ 800/44-TAMPA or 813/223-2752).

You can also stop by the **Tampa Bay Visitor Information Center,** 3601 E. Busch Blvd. (☎ 813/985-3601), north of downtown in the Busch Gardens area. The office books organized tours of Tampa and the rest of Florida.

GETTING AROUND   Taxis in Tampa do not normally cruise the streets for fares, but they do line up at public loading places. You can also call **Tampa Bay Cab** (☎ 813/251-5555), **Yellow Cab** (☎ 813/253-0121), or **United Cab** (☎ 813/253-2424).

The **Hillsborough Area Regional Transit/HARTline** (☎ 813/254-HART)

provides regularly scheduled bus service between downtown Tampa and the suburbs. Fares are $1.15 for local service and $1.50 for express routes; rates for local service are discounted to 55¢ for senior citizens, Medicare recipients, persons with disabilities, and students age 5 to 17 with proper identification. Correct change is required.

The **People Mover,** a motorized tram on elevated tracks, connects downtown Tampa with Harbour Island. It operates from the third level of the Fort Brooke Parking Garage, on Whiting Street between Franklin Avenue and Florida Street. Travel time is 90 seconds, and service is continuous Monday through Saturday from 7am to 2am, and Sunday from 8am to 11pm. The fare is 25¢ each way.

The **Tampa-Ybor Trolley** connects the city's sites in one 15-mile loop. You can board at any of 17 stops (each clearly marked with orange and green signs), including Harbour Island, downtown Tampa, the Florida Aquarium, and the Garrison Cruise Ship Terminal. Service is provided daily from 7:30am to 5:30pm. The fare is 25¢.

Tampa Town Ferry, 801 Channel Side Drive (☎ 813/223-1522), provides several transportation and sightseeing services. Its taxi service runs on a call-in basis; a round-trip fare is $6 for adults, $5 for senior citizens, and $4 for students.

BUSCH GARDENS

Yes, admission prices are high, but Busch Gardens remains Tampa Bay's most popular attraction. The 335-acre family entertainment park, at 3000 E. Busch Blvd. (☎ 813/987-5171), features thrill rides, animal habitats in naturalistic environments, live entertainment, shops, restaurants, and games. Capturing the spirit (or at least the perception) of turn-of-the-century Africa, the park ranks among the top zoos in the country, with nearly 3,400 animals.

The world's longest and tallest inverted roller coaster, Montu, is the newest addition to **Egypt,** the ninth themed area of the park. The area also includes a replica of King Tutankhamen's tomb, plus a sand-dig area for kids.

Timbuktu is a recreation of that ancient desert trading center, with African craftspeople at work, a sandstorm-style ride, a boat-swing ride, a roller coaster, and an electronic games arcade. **Morocco,** a walled city with exotic architecture, has Moroccan craft demonstrations, a sultan's tent with snake charmers, and the Marrakech Theaters. The **Serengeti Plain** is an open area with more than 500 African animals roaming freely in herds. This 80-acre natural grassy veldt may be viewed from the monorail, Trans-Veldt Railway, or skyride.

Nairobi is home to a baby animal nursery and a natural habitat for various species of gorillas and chimpanzees, as well as a petting zoo, reptile displays, and Nocturnal Mountain, where visitors can observe animals that are active at night. **Stanleyville,** a prototype African village, has a shopping bazaar and live entertainment, as well as two water rides: the Tanganyika Tidal Wave and Stanley Falls. **The Congo** features Kumba, the largest steel roller coaster in the southeastern United States; Claw Island, a display of rare white Bengal tigers in a natural setting; and white-water raft rides.

Bird Gardens, the original core of Busch Gardens, offers rich foliage, lagoons, and a free-flight aviary for hundreds of exotic birds, including golden and American bald eagles, hawks, owls, and falcons. This area also offers Land of the Dragons, a new children's adventure area.

Crown Colony is the home of a team of Clydesdale horses, as well as the Anheuser-Busch hospitality center. Questor, a flight simulator adventure ride, is also located here.

A one-day ticket costs $36.15 for adults, $29.75 for children ages three to nine, and kids under three are free. The park is open daily from 9:30am to 6pm, with extended hours in summer and during holiday periods. To get here, take I-275 northeast of downtown to Busch Boulevard (Exit 33), and go east 2 miles to the entrance on 40th Street (McKinley Drive). Parking is $4.

MORE ATTRACTIONS

Adjacent to the Garrison Seaport Center, the **Florida Aquarium** (☎ 813/273-4000) celebrates the role of water in the development and maintenance of Florida's topography and ecosystems, with saltwater exhibits and more than 4,350 specimens in all. One intriguing exhibit follows a drop of water as it bubbles through Florida limestone, wending its way to the sea.

Thirteen silver minarets and distinctive Moorish architecture make the **Henry B. Plant Museum,** 401 West Kennedy Blvd. (☎ 813/254-1891), the focal point of the Tampa skyline. Modeled after the Alhambra in Spain, this National Historic Landmark, built in 1891 as the 511-room Tampa Bay Hotel, is filled with European and Oriental art and furnishings.

The **Museum of African-American Art,** 1305 North Florida Ave. (☎ 813/272-2466), features visual art by and about people of African descent. The collection, covering the 19th and 20th centuries, represents more than 80 artists.

The permanent collection of the **Tampa Museum of Art,** 600 North Ashley Dr. (☎ 813/274-8130), is especially strong in ancient Greek, Etruscan, and Roman artifacts and 20th-century art. The museum grounds, fronting the Hillsborough River, contain a sculpture garden and a reflecting pool.

In St. Petersburg, the **Salvador Dali Museum,** 1000 Third St. S. (☎ 813/823-3767), contains the largest assemblage of works by the flamboyant artist outside Spain. The building that contains this widely divergent collection is a one-time marine warehouse, as starkly modern and surreal as the works of art displayed within.

ORGANIZED TOURS

BY BUS   Swiss Chalet Tours, 3601 E. Busch Blvd. (☎ 813/985-3601), operates guided tours of Tampa, Ybor City, and the surrounding region. Four-hour tours (10am to 2pm) run on Monday and Thursday and cost $35 for adults, $25 for children. Eight-hour tours run on Tuesday and Friday, and cost $70 for adults, $50 for children. You can also book full-day tours to most Orlando theme parks, including MGM Studios, Epcot/Walt Disney World, and Sea World, as well as to the Kennedy Space Center and Cypress Gardens.

HITTING THE BEACH

You have to go across the bay to St. Petersburg for a north-south string of interconnected white sandy shores.

St. Petersburg Municipal Beach lies on Treasure Island. **Clearwater Beach,** with its silky sands, is the place for beach volleyball. Water sports rentals, lifeguards, restrooms, showers, and concessions are available. The swimming is excellent and there's a pier for fishing. Parking is $7 a day in gated lots.

If you want to shop as well as suntan, consider **Madeira Beach,** midway between St. Petersburg and Clearwater, where you'll find St. John's Pass, a little bit of Coney Island plunked down on the Florida sands. It's got a boardwalk, ice cream parlors, and emporiums that sell T-shirts and other casual items.

Most beaches have restrooms, refreshment stands, and picnic areas. You can park either on the street at meters (which will usually run you 25¢ per half hour) or at one of the four major parking lots, located from north to south at **Sand Key Park,** beside Gulf Boulevard, just south of the Clearwater Pass Bridge; **Redington Shores Beach Park,** beside Gulf Boulevard at 182nd Street; **Treasure Island Park,** on Gulf Boulevard just north of 108th Avenue; and **St. Pete Beach Park,** beside Gulf Boulevard at 46th Street.

Honeymoon Island isn't great for swimming, but it has its own rugged beauty and a fascinating nature trail. From here, you can catch a ferry to **Caladesi Island State Park,** a 3¹/₂-mile stretch of sand that has a no-cars policy. It's located

at no. 3 Causeway Blvd. in Dunendin (☎ 813/469-5918 for information).

You can also go south to **Fort Desoto Park,** 3500 Pinellas Bayway S. (☎ 813/866-2484), comprising about 900 acres and 7 miles of waterfront exposed to both the Gulf of Mexico and a brackish channel. There are fishing piers, shaded picnic areas, a bird and animal sanctuary, campsites, and a partially ruined fort near the park's southwestern tip. Take I-275 south to the Pinellas Bayway (Exit 4) and follow the signs.

SHOPPING

In **Ybor Square,** 1901 13th St. (☎ 813/247-4497), nearly 40 shops are housed in three brick buildings from 1886 that once housed the world's largest cigar factory. Shops sell everything, including, of course, cigars. More upscale stores are located in **Old Hide Park Village,** Swann and Dakota avenues near Bayshore Boulevard (☎ 813/251-3500).

Malls include the **Brandon Town Center,** at the intersection of State Road 60 and I-75; **Eastlake Square Mall,** 56th Street at Hillsborough Avenue; and the city's largest mall, **Tampa Bay Center,** at Himes Avenue and Martin Luther King, Jr., Boulevard. You find substantial discounts at the **Gulf Coast Factory Shops,** 5461 Factory Shops Blvd., off of I-75 on the corner of Highway 301 and 60th Avenue (☎ 941/723-1150).

ACCOMMODATIONS

The **Doubletree Guest Suites,** 11310 North 30th St. (☎ 800/222-TREE or 813/971-7690), feels like a friendly college dormitory. Each handsomely furnished accommodation contains two separate rooms, one with a wet bar and small refrigerator.

There are two Tampa Hyatts: the **Hyatt Regency Tampa,** Two Tampa City Center (☎ 800/233-1234 or 813/225-1234), which towers over the city's commercial center; and the **Hyatt Regency Westshore,** 6200 Courtney Campbell

Causeway (☎ **800/233-1234** or 813/ 874-1234), at the Tampa end of the long causeway traversing Tampa Bay. A number of Spanish-style town houses/villas are set about $1/2$ mile away, separated from the main hotel building by a forested bird sanctuary. These enjoy access to a seafood restaurant maintained by the hotel.

Sheraton Grand Hotel Tampa Westshore, 4860 West Kennedy Blvd. (☎ **800/866-7177** or 813/286-4400), is Tampa's most stylish modern hotel. Its 11-story floor plan is inspired by the form of a butterfly.

Wyndham Harbour Island, 725 South Harbour Island Blvd. (☎ **813/229-5000**), sits on one of Tampa Bay's most elegant residential islands.

In St. Petersburg, **The Don CeSar,** 3400 Gulf Blvd. (☎ **800/282-1116** or 813/360-1881), is the most famous landmark in town. This pink-sided Moorish/ Mediterranean fantasy, on the National Register of Historic Places, sits on $7^1/2$ acres of beachfront. Guest rooms are first-rate, and usually have water views.

Also in St. Pete, **Stouffer Renaissance Vinoy Resort,** 501 Fifth Ave. NE (☎ **800/HOTELS1** or 813/894-1000), reigns as the grande dame of the region's hotels. Accommodations in the new wing ("The Tower") are slightly larger than those in the hotel's original core.

DINING

On the 14th floor of the Hyatt Regency Westshore Hotel, **Armani's,** 6200 Courtney Campbell Causeway (☎ **813/874-1234**), is a northern Italian restaurant with flair. Dishes are all prepared with deluxe ingredients.

The steaks at **Bern's Steak House,** 1208 South Howard Ave. (☎ **813/251-2421**), are close to perfect. You order according to thickness and weight. All main courses come with onion soup, salad, baked potato, garlic toast, and onion rings. Dessert is served in an upstairs warren of cubbyholes crafted from wine casks.

Le Bordeaux, 1502 South Howard Ave. (☎ **813/254-4387**), presents competent French food at reasonable prices. The changing menu often includes bouillabaisse, pot-au-feu, salmon en croûte, veal with wild mushrooms, and fillet of beef with Roquefort sauce, each impeccably cooked and presented. A jazz club called **The Left Bank** opens off the restaurant and presents live jazz from Thursday through Sunday, beginning at 9pm.

In Ybor City, **Columbia Restaurant,** 2117 Seventh Ave. E., between 21st and 22nd streets (☎ **813/248-4961**), occupies a tile-sheathed building that fills an entire city block about a mile from the cruise docks. The aura is pre-Castro Cuba. We love lunching in the big-windowed cafe and eating dinner in the scarlet-and-mahogany room dominated by a massive crystal chandelier and a dance floor where flamenco shows begin Monday through Saturday at 7:30pm. The more simple your dish is, the better it's likely to be. The filet mignons, *palomillo,* and roasted pork, along with the black beans, yellow rice, and plantains, are flavorful and well prepared.

At lunch, **Mise en Place,** 442 West Kennedy Blvd. (☎ **813/254-5373**), serves an array of well-stuffed sandwiches, as well as savory pastas, risottos, and platters. More formal dinners feature free-range chicken with smoked tomato coulis, sautéed rainbow trout with Swiss chard, and loin of venison with asparagus, tarragon mash, and red-onion balsamic marmalade.

Mojo, 238 East Davis Blvd. (☎ **813/259-9949**), sits on Davis Island, a residential island separated from the commercial heart of Tampa by a narrow channel. It is the most flamboyant and charming restaurant in town, featuring wonderful Caribbean cooking that's all explained on a user-friendly menu. At lunch, try the roast pork sandwich with lime-flavored cumin, onions, and provolone cheese on Cuban bread. For dinner, try the *feijoada* (roasted pork with plantains) or the *ropa vieja* (Cuban beef hash).

The best fish in Tampa is served at **Oystercatchers,** in the Hyatt Regency

Westshore Hotel complex, 6200 Courtney Campbell Causeway (☎ 813/874-1234). Pick the fish you want from a glass-fronted buffet or enjoy mesquite-grilled steaks, chicken rollatini, and shellfish. There's also a short list of sashimi dishes.

Selena's, 1623 Snow Ave., Old Hide Park (☎ 813/251-2116), serves a mix of New Orleans Cajun and northern Italian cuisine. The food is competently prepared, and the portions generous. You can catch some live jazz performed in an upstairs bar/lounge Friday and Saturday.

TAMPA AFTER DARK

When night falls on Ybor City, Tampa's century-old Latin Quarter, the streets are transformed into a hotbed of people seeking and finding a smorgasbord of music, ethnic food, poetry readings, and after-midnight coffee and dessert. Thousands crowd 7th Avenue, one of its main arteries, on Wednesday through Saturday evenings.

The Tampa/Hillsborough Arts Council maintains its **Artsline** (☎ 813/229-ARTS), a 24-hour information service about current and upcoming cultural events. **The Tampa Bay Performing Arts Center,** 1010 North MacInnes Place (☎ 813/229-STAR, or **TicketMaster** at 813/287-8844), contains four theaters and the Museum of African-American Art. **Tampa Theater,** 711 Franklin St. (☎ 813/274-8981), built in 1926 as a movie palace, is now a registered national historic site.

THE CLUB & MUSIC SCENE

The Skipper Dome / Skipper's Smokehouse, 910 Skipper Rd. (☎ 813/971-0666), is our favorite evening spot, featuring an all-purpose restaurant and bar where oysters and fresh shellfish are sold by the dozen and half-dozen. For live music, head out back to the "Skipper Dome," a sprawling deck sheltered by a canopy of oak trees. You'll hear soca, reggae, blues, progressive New Orleans–style jazz, and more.

If you're an urban cowboy (or girl), the place to go on Friday and Sunday nights is the boisterous Texas-style **Dallas Bull,** 8222 N U.S. 301 (☎ **813/985-6877**), where you'll be part of a stomping, line-dancing hoe-down set to the big-hat stomp of the country sound. Wear your jeans and lizard-skin boots.

Set within a 1940s movie palace, **The Masquerade** (formerly The Ritz), 1503 East 7th Ave. (☎ **813/247-3319**), is the first of the many nightclubs that pepper the streets of historic Ybor City. A raucous, high-volume emporium of DJ-powered dance music and electronic lights, it occasionally spices up its mix with live bands. The crowd is young and hip (at least for Tampa), and the revelation of your pierced belly button gets you a free "Fuzzy Navel Shooter." The scene changes nightly, everything from "psycho disco" to retro '80s.

5 New Orleans & the Port of New Orleans

There's power and majesty to this port, located 110 miles upriver from the Gulf of Mexico. By some yardsticks, it's the busiest port in the nation, servicing vessels that dwarf the handful of cruise ships that call New Orleans home.

Some 170,000 cruise-ship passengers pass through here annually, departing from the piers/port on the river's eastern bank, near the commercial heart of town, a five-minute walk from the edge of the French Quarter. This westerly port mainly handles ships whose ports of call lie along the western edge of the Caribbean, including the western "Mexican Riviera" and Cancún and Cozumel.

Your access will be via the Julia Street Cruise Ship Terminal on the Julia Street Wharf, which was originally developed as part of the 1984 Louisiana World's Exposition and converted to serve the needs of cruise-ship passengers in 1993, then doubled in size in 1996. On rare occasions, southbound cruise-ship passengers might board at the Robin Street Wharves (which are usually reserved for paddlewheelers headed on cruises upriver), or, even less likely, at the Mandeville Street Wharves, which are usually reserved for the mooring of barges.

Ships departing from New Orleans include Commodore Cruise Line's *Enchanted Isle,* and, from October through May, Holland America Line's *Nieuw Amsterdam.* Carnival's *Celebration* divides its time between moorings here and in Tampa.

The port is located at 1350 Port of New Orleans Place. For information about the port, call the **Port of New Orleans** at ☎ **504/522-2551.**

GETTING TO NEW ORLEANS & ITS PORT

BY AIR New Orleans International Airport is 10 miles northwest of the port. A taxi to the port costs about $21 and takes about 20 minutes. **Airport Shuttle** (☎ 504/592-0555) runs vans at 10- to 12-minute intervals from outside the airport's baggage claim to the port and other points in town. It costs $10 per passenger each way, and is free for children under 6.

BY CAR Highways I-10, U.S. 90, U.S. 61, and Louisiana 25 (the Lake Pontchartrain causeway) lead directly to New Orleans.

Local car-rental agencies include **Avis** (☎ 800/331-1212); **Budget** (☎ 800/472-3325); **Dollar Rent-a-Car** (☎ 800/800-4000); and **Hertz** (☎ 800/654-3131).

Parking at the Port You can park your car in long-term parking at the port, but only for blocks of one week. Details and reservations for this are arranged directly with your cruise-ship operator, and you must present a boarding pass or ticket before you'll be allowed to park within the port facilities. The price is $42 per week.

BY TRAIN Amtrak (☎ 800/USA-RAIL) trains stop at the **Union Passenger Terminal** at 1001 Loyola Ave. in the central business district. Taxis will be outside the passenger terminal's main entrance; fare to the port is $8.

EXPLORING NEW ORLEANS

In many respects, the French Quarter *is* New Orleans, and many visitors never leave its confines. The French Quarter is where it all began and it's still the city's most popular sightseeing spot, but if you go outside the French Quarter, you'll feel the pulse of the city's commerce, see river activities that keep the city alive, stroll through spacious parks, drive or walk by the impressive homes of the Garden District, and get a firsthand view of the bayou/lake connection that explains why New Orleans grew up here in the first place.

ESSENTIALS

VISITOR INFORMATION Contact the **New Orleans Metropolitan Convention and Visitors Bureau,** 1520 Sugar Bowl Dr., New Orleans, LA 70112 (☎ 504/566-5011), for brochures, pamphlets, and information.

Once you arrive, stop at the **Louisiana Information Center,** 529 St. Ann St. in the French Quarter (☎ 504/566-5031).

GETTING AROUND Taxis are plentiful and can be hailed on the street, found lined up at taxi stands near the bigger hotels, or arranged by phone. Call **United Cabs** (☎ 504/522-9771) and a cab will come within 5 to 10 minutes. The meter begins at $2.10 as soon as it's turned on, and is $1.20 per mile thereafter.

The oldest **streetcar** lines run the length of St. Charles Avenue, and a ride in both directions takes 90 minutes. You can board at the corner of Canal and Carondelet streets in the French Quarter. Trolleys run 24 hours a day and cost $1 per ride (you must have exact change). A transfer from streetcar to bus costs 10¢. A riverfront streetcar line costs $1.25 per ride. A VisiTour Pass, which gives you unlimited rides on all streetcar and bus lines, costs $4 for one day, $8 for three days.

Where the trolleys don't run, a city bus will. For route information call ☎ **504/ 248-3900** or pick up a map at the Visitor Information Center (see address above). Most buses charge $1 (plus 10¢ for a transfer) per ride, although some express buses cost $1.25.

A **Vieux Carré Minibus** takes you to French Quarter sights. The route is posted along Canal and Bourbon streets, and it operates daily between 5am and 6:45pm. The price is $1.

From Jackson Square (at Decatur Street), you can take a 2¹/₄-mile horse-drawn carriage ride through the French Quarter. **The Gay Nineties Carriage Tour Co.** (☎ **504/943-8820**) pulls fringe-topped wagons suitable for up to eight passengers at a time, daily from 9am to midnight. A ride costs $8 per adult and $4 per child.

A free **ferryboat** departs at frequent intervals from the foot of Canal Street, carrying cars and passengers across the river. A round-trip passage takes about 25 minutes.

SEEING THE SIGHTS

The well-designed **Aquarium of the Americas,** 1 Canal St., at the Mississippi River (☎ **504/861-2537**), is a million-gallon tribute to the diversity of life lurking in freshwater lakes and the sea. A 400,000-gallon tank holds a kaleidoscope of species from the deep waters of the nearby Gulf of Mexico.

You'll need at least three hours to visit the **Audubon Zoo,** 6500 Magazine St. (☎ **504/861-2537**), home to 1,500 animals who live within simulations of their natural habitats. In a Louisiana swamp replication, alligators and reptiles slither and hop around clusters of marsh grasses and native birds.

Despite its massive Doric columns and twin staircases, local architects nonetheless refer to **Beauregard-Keyes House,** 1113 Chartres St. (☎ **504/523-7257**), as a "Louisiana raised cottage." Built in 1826,

it's one of the most impressive and socially prestigious structures in town.

Incorporating seven historic buildings connected by a brick courtyard, the **Historic New Orleans Collection,** 533 Royal St. (☎ **504/523-4662**), evokes the New Orleans of 200 years ago. The oldest building in the complex escaped the tragic fire of 1794, and the others hold exhibitions about Louisiana's culture and history.

Housed in a former granary four blocks from the river, the **Louisiana Children's Museum,** 420 Julia St. (☎ **504/523- 1357**), divides its exhibits into activities for children over and under the age of eight. The Lab demonstrates principles of physics and math, motion, and inertia. Younger children play in a simulated supermarket and attend puppet workshops, cooking programs, and storytelling sessions.

The **Musee Conti Wax Museum,** 917 Conti St. (☎ **504/525-2605**), is the bayou equivalent of Madame Tussaud's, featuring characters pivotal in Louisiana history and legend. Look for replicas of jazz master Pete Fountain, Andrew Jackson, Jean Lafitte, and the Kingfish himself, politico Huey Long.

The collections of the **New Orleans Historic Voodoo Museum,** 724 Dumaine St. (☎ **504/523-7685**), celebrate the occult and the curious mixture of African and Catholic rituals whose tenets were first brought to New Orleans by slaves from Hispaniola. An herb shop/ apothecary is stocked with the ingredients any voodoo practitioner would need and staffed by people who can put you in touch with psychics if you have such a need. A guided voodoo walking tour of the French Quarter departs from the museum Monday through Friday at 1pm and Sunday at 10am.

The collections of the **New Orleans Museum of Art (NOMA),** Lelong Ave., 1 Collins Diboll Circle, City Park, (☎ **504/ 488-2631**), span the centuries, with one floor devoted to ethnographic and non-Western art.

The **Old Absinthe House / Tony Moran's Restaurant,** 240 Bourbon St. (☎ **504/523-3181**), is the oldest bar in America, built in 1806 by two Spanish partners. Virtually any drink is available. Upstairs is a restaurant, Tony Moran's, open only for dinner.

The **World Trade Center of New Orleans,** 2 Canal St. (☎ **504/529-1601**), one of the tallest buildings in town, has an observation platform called the Viewpoint on its 31st floor. From here you can check out the freighters, cruise ships, tug boats, submarines, and aircraft carriers that ply the swift-flowing waters of New Orleans's deepwater harbor. A cocktail lounge spins slowly on the 33rd floor.

ORGANIZED TOURS

BY FOOT   Friends of the Cabildo (☎ **504/523-3939**) lead two-hour walking tours of Vieux Carré (the French Quarter) that leave from the Museum Store at 523 St. Ann St. every Tuesday through Sunday at 10am and 1:30pm, and Monday at 1:30pm, except holidays. Donations are expected: $10 per adult, $8 for seniors over 65 and children ages 13 to 20.

Magic Walking Tours (☎ **504/593-9693**) offers theme tours associated with the city's cemeteries, its Garden District, or its traditions of voodoo. Tours cost $10 per person.

You can see historic interiors on a **Hidden Treasures Tour** (☎ **504/529-4507**). The **National Park Service** also conducts free one-mile walking tours through the French Quarter that depart from the Jean Lafitte National Park Service French Quarter Folklife and Visitor Center, 916 N. Peters St. (☎ **504/589-2636**).

BY BUS   A two-hour bus tour from **Gray Line,** 1300 World Trade Center of New Orleans (☎ **800/535-7786** or 504/587-0861), offers a fast overview of the city. Tours cost $18 for adults and $9.50 for children, and require advance booking.

BY BOAT   The paddlewheeler *Creole Queen* (☎ **504/524-0814**) departs from the Poydras Street Wharf, adjacent to

Riverwalk, every day at 10:30am and 2pm for a 2¹/₂-hour waterborne odyssey. There's a buffet restaurant and a cocktail lounge on board. Daytime cruises cost $14 for adults, $7 for children. Evening cruises, with live jazz, cost $39 for adults, $18 for children.

Another steam-powered stern-wheeler is the *Natchez,* departing daily from the Toulouse Street Wharf, next to the French Quarter's Jackson Street Brewery. Cruises begin at 11:30am and 2:30pm and feature live jazz and an optional Creole-style luncheon. The cost is $14.75 for adults, $7.25 for children 6 to 12, free for children under 6 (food is an additional $5.95 per person). Evening jazz cruises, with a buffet dinner, cost $38.75 for adults, $19.25 for children.

The riverboat *John James Audubon* (☎ **504/586-8777**) departs from the Canal Street dock at Riverwalk and travels the Mississippi as far as the Audubon Zoo and the Aquarium. The cruise costs $26.50 for adults and $15.25 for children, including admission to both the zoo and aquarium. The cruise alone sells for $12.50 for adults or $6.25 for children.

The *Queen of New Orleans,* at the New Orleans Hilton Riverside (☎ **504/587-7777**) is a casino paddlewheeler boat with slot machines. The 90-minute cruises run 24 hours a day, departing every three hours. The trip costs $5.

SWAMP/ECO-TOURS   You can tour the Louisiana Bayou with several outfits located about an hour outside the city. **L'il Cajun Swamp Tours,** Highway 301, Lafitte (☎ **800/725-3213** or 504/689-3213), runs a two-hour tour on a shallow-draft boat holding 67 passengers. The tour costs $16 for adults, $14 for seniors, and $12 for children. You can arrange for pickup for about $15 to $20. Tours leave daily at noon in winter, but during the rest of the year there are two daily departures, one at 10am, another at 2pm.

Honey Island Swamp Tours, Inc., Crawford Landing Road, Slidell (☎ **504/242-5877**), operates a flotilla of flat-bottomed motorboats that carry up to 22

passengers. Tours leave daily at 9am, 2pm, and 4pm, by reservation only, and cost $20 per person. Also in Slidell, **Gator Swamp Tours,** off of Highway 90 (☎ **800/875-4287** or 504/484 6100), offers two swamp tours daily. The two-hour excursions depart at 9:30am and 2:30pm, and cost $20 for adults, $10 for children.

SHOPPING

Shopping in New Orleans is fun. Antique stores are especially interesting and gift shops seem to stock more than just a cheap array of T-shirts and souvenir items.

Major shopping venues include the triple-tiered **Canal Place** mall, at the junction where Canal Street meets the Mississippi Wharves. **The Esplanade,** 1401 West Esplanade, boasts a constantly busy food court and more than 150 retailers. The **French Market,** whose main entrance is on Decatur Street across from Jackson Square, is big on nostalgic Louisiana kitsch and cookware. The **Jackson Brewery,** adjacent to Jackson Square, is a transformed suds factory filled with more than 125 retailers. And **Riverwalk,** of course, is a covered mall that runs along the wharves between Poydras Street and the Convention Center. You'll remember it as one of the few malls in history that's ever been rammed by a ship, as it was in 1996. We wouldn't worry: Chances of it happening again are pretty slim.

You'll find a row of art galleries along **Julia Street,** between the Mississippi and Camp Street. A jumble of antiques and flea market–style emporiums sits along a six-block stretch of **Magazine Street,** between Audubon Park and Canal Street, among them **Magazine Arcade Antiques,** 3017 Magazine St. (☎ **504/895-5451**).

For crafts, try the **Idea Factory,** 838 Chartres St. (☎ **504/524-5195**), where woodworkers, both on and off the premises, stay busy shaping and gluing letter boxes, trays, paper-towel holders, and wall brackets. You'll find new and antique silver at **New Orleans Silversmiths,** 600 Chartres St. (☎ **504/522-8333**).

You can see pralines being made at **Aunt Sally's Praline Shops,** 810 Decatur St. (☎ **504/524-5107**). They'll ship anything home for you, and sell you items such as cookbooks, packaged Creole food, and Louisiana memorabilia.

ACCOMMODATIONS

Conveniently located near both the French Quarter and the embarkation piers for cruise-ship passengers, the **Doubletree Hotel,** 300 Canal St. (☎ **504/581-1300**), is at the edge of the city's business district. Rooms are comfortable and clean.

About seven blocks from the cruise-ship terminal is the French Quarter grande dame, the **Monteleone Hotel,** 214 Royal St. (☎ **800/535-9595** or 504/523-3341). Decor and floor layouts are slightly different in each of the 600 rooms. The place provides ample atmosphere.

The **New Orleans Hilton Riverside and Towers Hotel,** 2 Poydras St. (☎ **800/HILTONS** or 504/561-0550), is only about a block away from the Julius Street Wharves. Some travelers prefer the low-rise intimacy of the hotel's newer annex (the Riverside building). This also holds the Riverwalk Marketplace, a waterside emporium of shops, bars, and restaurants.

The **Lafayette Hotel,** 600 St. Charles Ave., at Lafayette Square (☎ **800/733-4754** or 504/524-4441), resembles an upscale, turn-of-the-century hotel in London. Bedrooms have comfortable easy chairs and roomy closets.

Set within the heart of the Garden District is the grand and antique **Pontchartrain Hotel,** 2031 St. Charles Ave. (☎ **800/777-6193** or 504/524-0581), which prides itself on a charmingly idiosyncratic style resulting from decades of tradition, lots of local nostalgia, and a staff of long-term employees well versed in New Orleans lore.

The **Sheraton New Orleans,** 500 Canal St. (☎ **800/253-6156** or 504/525-2500), is huge, splashy, and eclectic. A 1¹/₂-mile taxi ride south of the city's Cruise Ship

Terminal, the Sheraton contains standardized bedrooms that are large and stylish. Rooms on the top floors (42 to 49) are the best accessorized.

DINING

Don't ask what's new at **Antoine's,** 713 St. Louis St. (☎ **504/581-4422**), which was established in 1840 and hasn't substantially changed since. (The most radical alteration occurred in the 1990s, when English translations were added to the French menu.) Oysters Rockefeller, first served here in 1899, are still available, and tournedos of beef, ramekins of crawfish cardinal, and pompano en papillote remain perennial favorites.

The legendary **Arnaud's,** 813 Bienville Rue. (☎ **504/523-5433**), lies within three interconnected, once-private houses from the 1700s, divided among five belle epoque dining rooms lush with Edwardian embellishments. Shrimp Arnaud, snails en casserole, oysters stewed in cream, rack of lamb diablo, roasted duck à l'orange, and classic bananas Foster or crème brûlée are staples here, along with a few modern dishes created by chef Bernard Ibarra. The food is better than it has been in years.

Broussard's, 819 Conti St. (☎ **504/581-3866**), has thrived here since 1920. It's a quieter, more dignified version of Antoine's, less heavily patronized by out-of-towners, and more authentic to the "Nawlins" ethic. Dishes include filets of Pompano Napoleon-style (with scallops and a mustard-caper sauce, served in puff pastry with a side order of shrimp), and the Casserole Broussard, a mix of crab meat and brie cream cheese sauce with a spinach border.

The hot new chef in New Orleans is Devlin Roussel at **Bizou,** 701 St. Charles Ave. (☎ **504/524-4114**), who has virtually rejuvenated the tired old Creole and French traditional cookery. The place is hardly the most glamorous in New Orleans, but its cuisine has the exuberance of a spring day. Even the vinegar potato chips you nibble while waiting for your meal are addictive. Try the crawfish cakes with Creole mustard and baby greens in a Tabasco-infused white butter, or the red snapper with pecans in a green-onion coulis. Try anything, but try something!

In its way, **Galatoire's,** 209 Bourbon St. (☎ **504/525-2021**), feels like a bistro in turn-of-the-century Paris, and still basks in its legendary reputation. Menu items include trout (meunière or amandine), rémoulade of shrimp, oysters en brochette, a savory Creole-style bouillabaisse, and a good-tasting eggplant stuffed with a puree of seafood. If you head here early, you can avoid long waits in line.

Lines often stretch halfway down the block for one of the 116 seats at **K-Paul's Louisiana Kitchen,** 416 Chartres St. (☎ **504/524-7394**), one of Louisiana's most famous simple restaurants. Once seated, expect company: Tables on the street level are communal. Try fiery gumbos, Cajun popcorn shrimp, roasted rabbit, and blackened fish (especially tuna) that's as delicious as it is spicy.

At **Nola,** 534 St. Louis St. (☎ **504/522-6652**), Cajun New Orleans mingles gracefully with Hollywood-style razzle-dazzle and media glitz. Chef Emeril Lagasse uses locally available ingredients to present meals inspired by old Creole recipes, with some well-conceived modern permutations. His plank-fish baked on a cedar plank in a wood-burning oven, piri-piri shrimp with homemade chorizo sausage, and Lafayette boudin baked in beer are some of our zesty favorites.

NEW ORLEANS AFTER DARK

Dixieland and jazz were born in this town, whose nickname, "The Big Easy," is synonymous with partying, the good life, and sometimes raucous entertainment. You can reel from club to club in the neighborhoods around Bourbon and St. Louis streets, where the fun never seems to end, or take in a play in one of the major halls—or do both, depending on your constitution.

The major concert halls for the presentation of opera, ballet, and symphonies include the **Mahalia Jackson Theater of the Performing Arts,** 801 N. Rampart St. (☎ 504/522-0996); the **Contemporary Arts Center,** 900 Camp St. (☎ 504/523-1216); and **Le Petit Théatre,** 616 St. Peter St. (☎ 504/522-2081).

The **Saenger Performing Arts Center,** 143 N. Rampart St. (☎ 504/524-2490), was restored for use by the **Louisiana Philharmonic Orchestra** (☎ 504/523-6530), which also plays at the **Orpheum Theater,** University Place (☎ 504/524-3285), and in parks and gardens throughout the city. The **Southern Repertory Theater,** 3rd Level, Canal Place, 333 Canal St. (☎ 504/861-8163), specializes in plays by local and southern writers. More avant-garde are the productions at the **Theatre Marigny,** 616 Frenchmen St. (☎ 504/944-2653), just outside the borders of the French Quarter.

THE CLUB & MUSIC SCENE

Jazz aficionados consider **Preservation Hall,** 726 St. Peter St. (☎ 504/522-28412 or 504/523-8939), the Holy of Holies, a world-famous monument devoted to the presentation of jazz in its most pure and elemental form. The hall is deliberately shabby, with very few places to sit and no air-conditioning. Despite that, the place is usually packed with bodies swaying and clapping to the music that pours out of great musicians who never believed that the pastures outside New Orleans could possibly be greener than the ones inside.

Dixieland clarinet maestro Pete Fountain is one of the most endearing musical celebrities of New Orleans. After running a Bourbon Street jazz club, he set up shop, with double the space, at **Pete Fountain's** in the plush third-floor interior of the New Orleans Hilton, 2 Poydras St. (☎ 504/523-4374 or 504/561-0500). If he's not on tour, Fountain will usually show up several nights a week to perform.

Jazz, blues, Dixieland, and virtually every other kind of music can be heard at the nostalgia-laden bar and concert hall **Tipitina's,** at 501 Napoleon Ave. (☎ 504/895-8477), while on a small stage in back of **Fritzel's European Bar and Cuisine,** 733 Bourbon St. (☎ 504/561-0432), musicians improvise, blow, boogie, or shake, rattle, and roll. Very late at night, musicians from other clubs might hop onto the stage to jam.

House of Blues, 225 Decatur St. (☎ 504/529-1421), is one of the city's largest live music venues. There's only a limited number of stools and tiny, rather uncomfortable places to sit, but most patrons remain on their feet anyway, kibitzing, flirting, and moving among the several bars. As the name implies, the club offers loud blues and, to a lesser extent, reggae, funky rock, and country-roots rock. There's also a restaurant.

Not to be confused with the Old Absinthe House / Tony Moran's Restaurant, **Old Absinthe House Bar,** 400 Bourbon St. (☎ 504/525-8108), features antique bar fixtures and a rock and blues atmosphere that attracts energetic fans from throughout Louisiana and keeps them there through the night.

Follow the footsteps of Michael Jordan and U2 to the Victorian Lounge at the **Columns Hotel,** 3811 St. Charles Ave. (☎ 504/899-9308), and try one of the staff's justly celebrated made-from-scratch Bloody Marys. On the fringe of the Garden District, the hotel, formerly the mansion of a tobacco warehouser, was the setting for the Louis Malle film *Pretty Baby.* A young local crowd is attracted to this bar, where a jazz trio entertains on Tuesday nights.

At **Palm Court Café,** 1204 Decatur St. (☎ 504/525-0200), you'll find an equal appreciation of jazz and food—the one hot, and the other international.

At **Chris Owens Club,** 500 Bourbon St. (☎ 504/523-6400), mistress of ceremonies Owens performs a one-woman cabaret act, singing along, Las Vegas–style, with whatever band has been brought in that night. Jazz legend Al Hirt performs here between two and four nights a week.

On nights when Ms. Owens is indisposed, it becomes a dance club.

To put a different spin on your ball, check out **Mid-City Lanes Rock and Bowl,** 4133 S. Carrollton Ave. (☎ **504/482-3133**), tucked into a battered strip mall on Carrollton Avenue between Tulane Avenue and Ulloa Street. You can bowl and drink during the day, then continue at night when the bands crank up and the joint starts rockin'.

Established in 1933, and quite touristy, **Pat O'Brien's,** 718 St. Peter St. (☎ **504/525-4823**), is famous for its twin piano players, raucous high jinks, live comedians, outdoor courtyard, and gargantuan Hurricanes: rum-based libations that'll knock your socks off.

Lafitte's Blacksmith Shop, 941 Bourbon St. (☎ **504/523-0066**), is a French Quarter pub housed in an 18th-century Creole house. Tennessee Williams used to hang out here.

6 San Juan & the Port of San Juan

Navigators have recognized the strategic importance of the Isleta de San Juan since the days of the earliest Spanish colonization of the island. The deepwater San Antonio Channel, which separates the southern shore of Old San Juan from the northern coast of Isla Grande, is able to shelter the biggest megaships in the cruise industry from tropical storms thanks to frequent dredgings and a decades-long buildup of the cement wharves and piers on either side.

San Juan is the number-one cruise-ship port in the Caribbean, and its facilities have received a $100 million upgrade. Although it doesn't handle the sheer volume of Miami, it stands at the top among ports in the West Indies. For many cruisers, it will be either their port of embarkation or a port of call. (We've covered San Juan as a port of call in chapter 10.)

Most cruise ships in Puerto Rico dock on the historic south shore of Old San Juan, beside any of eight piers that stretch between the Plaza de la Marina and the Puerto Rican capitol building less than a mile away. Piers 1 and 4 are the newest or most recently remodeled. Along with no. 3, they are the most convenient to the shops and attractions of San Juan's historic core.

For passengers headed for the Old Town, piers 5, 6, 7, and 8 are less than a 10-minute stroll past the fortifications of the Spanish colonial fortress of San Cristóbal. Pier no. 2 is reserved for the dockage of ferryboats that make frequent runs across the San Antonio Channel to Cataño, site of the Bacardi rum distillery, and Hato Rey, Puerto Rico's financial district.

The above-mentioned piers receive the bulk of cruise ships landing in San Juan. During periods of heavy volume, usually Saturday and Sunday in midwinter, when as many as 10 cruise ships might dock in San Juan on the same day, additional, less convenient piers are activated. Foremost among these are the Frontier Pier, at the western edge of the Condado near the Caribe Hilton Hotel, and the Pan American Dock, in Isla Grande, across the San Antonio Channel from Old San Juan. Passengers berthing at either of these docks need some kind of motorized transit (usually a taxi or a van provided by the cruise line as part of the shore excursion program) to get to Old Town.

Near the Plaza de la Marina, adjacent to pier no. 3, stands the nine-story, 242-room Wyndham Old San Juan Hotel and Casino. It's the centerpiece of the Barrio de la Marina, a radical urban renewal project that's transformed a dull and underused (albeit historic) San Juan district into the centerpiece of Puerto Rico's cruise industry.

Cruise lines that sail from San Juan include Costa Cruise Line and Princess.

For information about the port, contact the **Port of San Juan,** P.O. 362829, San Juan, Puerto Rico 00936-2829 (☎ **787/723-2260**).

GETTING TO SAN JUAN & THE PORT

BY AIR Visitors from overseas arrive at **Luis Muñoz Marín International Airport** (☎ 787/791-1014), situated on the city's easternmost side. It's about 7¹/₂ miles from the port.

Taxis will be lined up outside the airport. The fixed fare is $16, and the ride takes about 30 minutes, depending on traffic conditions.

PARKING AT THE PORT Because of severe parking difficulties at the port, we recommend returning your rental car to the site identified in your rental contract, and then taking a taxi to the port.

EXPLORING SAN JUAN

Since San Juan is a major port of call, we've covered it in chapter 10, so turn there for detailed sightseeing, gambling, shopping, and restaurant information. Here we'll suggest where to stay and what to do after dark.

VISITOR INFORMATION

For information before you leave home, contact one of the **Puerto Rico Tourism Company** offices: 575 Fifth Ave., New York, NY 10017 (☎ 800/223-6530 or 212/599-6262); 3575 W. Cahuenga Blvd., Suite 405, Los Angeles, CA 90068 (☎ 800/874-1230 or 213/874-5991); or 901 Ponce de Leon Blvd., Suite 604, Coral Gables, FL 33134 (☎ 800/815-7391 or 305/445-9112). In Canada call 800/667-0394 or 416/368-2680, or write 41-43 Colbourne St., Suite 301, Toronto, ON, M5E 1E3.

ACCOMMODATIONS

In Old San Juan, the most atmospheric place to stay is the **Galería San Juan,** Calle Norzagaray 204–206 (☎ 787/722-1808), set on a hilltop in the old town, with a sweeping view of the sea. One of the oldest private residences in the area, it

has been turned into a whimsically bohemian inn with individually decorated bedrooms, a small gallery, and a working artists' studio.

After falling into disrepair, Puerto Rico's most famous hotel, **El Convento,** 100 Cristo St. (☎ 800/468-2779 or 787/723-9020), has bounced back. A five-minute taxi ride from the cruise piers, it's ideal for a pre- and postcruise holiday. It offers only 57 handsomely furnished bedrooms in a former convent dating from the 17th century.

In Puerto de Tierra, the **Caribe Hilton,** Calle Los Rosales (☎ 800/HILTONS from the U.S. or Canada, or 787/721-0303), stands near the old Fort San Jerónimo, and is close to the walled city of San Juan. You can walk to the 16th-century fort or spend the day on a tour of Old San Juan, then come back and enjoy the swimming cove and beach.

Geared to the upscale business traveler, **Radisson Normandie,** Avenida Muñoz-Rivera at the corner of Calle Los Rosales (☎ 800/333-3333 from the U.S., or 787/729-2929), is built in the shape of the famous French ocean liner *Normandie.* The hotel lies only five minutes from Old San Juan, and its beachside setting adjoins the noted Sixto Escobar Stadium. The elegant and elaborate rooms are well furnished with amenities.

In Condado, an area now filled with high-rise hotels, restaurants, and nightclubs, the **Condado Plaza Hotel and Casino,** 999 Ashford Ave. (☎ 800/468-8588 from the U.S., or 787/721-1000), with more style and flair than the Hilton, is one of Puerto Rico's busiest hotels. It's also most visible, set on a strip of beachfront at the beginning of the Condado. All rooms have private terraces, and deluxe rooms are in the Plaza Club.

Radisson Ambassador Hotel and Casino, 1369 Ashford Ave. (☎ 800/468-8512 from the U.S., or 787/721-7300), is a star-studded hotel with theatrical drama and big-time pizzazz, but no resort amenities. Accommodations are in a pair of high-rise towers, one of which is devoted to suites. Each unit has a balcony.

The 21-story **San Juan Marriott Resort,** 1309 Ashford Ave. (☎ **800/228-9290** or 787/722-7000), is the tallest building on the Condado, with comfortable but bland bedrooms.

Beach-bordering Isla Verde is closer to the airport than the other sections of San Juan. If you don't mind the isolation and want access to the fairly good beaches, then consider staying at the **El San Juan Hotel and Casino,** Isla Verde Ave. (☎ **800/468-2818** or 787/791-1000), the best hotel in Puerto Rico. Its 700-yard beach is the finest in the San Juan area. About 150 of the accommodations are designed as comfortable bungalows in the outer reaches of the garden.

Sands Hotel and Casino Beach Resort, 187 Isla Verde Ave. (☎ **800/443-2009** from the U.S., or 787/791-6100), is a Caribbean version of the Sands Hotel in Atlantic City. Bedrooms are comfortable, with balconies and terraces. The best rooms are in the Plaza Club, a minihotel within the hotel.

The most convenient hotel for cruise-ship passengers, and one of the grandest on the island, **Wyndham Old San Juan Hotel and Casino,** 101 Calle Marina, 00901 San Juan (☎ **800/996-3426** or 787/721-5100), opened in spring 1997. Part of a multimillion-dollar renovation of the dock area, the hotel is luxurious, lush, and the most up-to-date within the old city.

SAN JUAN AFTER DARK

Qué Pasa, the official visitors' guide to Puerto Rico, lists cultural events, including music, dance, theater, film, and art exhibits. It's distributed free by the tourist office.

Major cultural venues include **Centro de Bellas Artes,** avenida Ponce de Léon 22 (☎ **787/724-4747** or 787/725-7334), with 1,883 seats in the Festival Hall, 760 in the Drama Hall, and 210 in the Experimental Theater. Standing across from the Plaza de Colón is **Teatro Tapía,** avenida Ponce de León (☎ **787/722-0407**), built around 1832.

San Juan night life comes in all varieties. From the vibrant performing-arts scene to street-level salsa or the casinos, discos, and bars, there's plenty of entertainment available almost any evening.

Along the beachfront strip, **Copa,** in the Sands Hotel and Casino, Isla Verde Ave. (☎ **787/791-6100**), is one of the major showrooms for Las Vegas–style revues.

Egipto, Avenida Roberto H. Todd 1 (☎ **787/725-4664**), is the area's newest nightclub. The building is styled after an Egyptian temple—there's even a reproduction of King Tutankhamen's tomb. However, the atmosphere is far from ancient; Spanish and American dance music and a young crowd make for a fun night out. No jeans are allowed.

Krash, 1257 Avenue Ponce de León (☎ **787/722-1390**), has some of the best music for dancing in Puerto Rico, and perhaps for that reason attracts a large gay following. With its multiple levels for after dark amusement, **Lazers,** 251 Calle Cruz (☎ **787/721-4479**), is a roof deck with landscaping overlooking the lights of San Juan. Different nights are devoted to different themes, including gay nights on Thursday and Sunday.

If you just want a drink, **Fiesta Bar,** in the Condado Plaza Hotel and Casino, 999 Ashford Ave. (☎ **787/721-1000**), attracts locals and visitors. The margaritas are appropriately salty, and the rhythms are hot and Latin. **Palm Court,** in the El San Juan Hotel and Casino, Isla Verde Avenue (☎ **787/791-1000**), is the most beautiful bar in the Caribbean. After 9pm Thursday through Saturday, live music emanates from an adjoining room, the El Chico Bar.

At **Shannon's Irish Pub,** Calle Bori 496, Rio Piedras (☎ **787/281-8466**), Ireland and its ales get tropicalized with a Latin accent. The pub is a regular watering hole for university students. There are pool tables, and a simple cafe serves inexpensive fare daily from 11:30am to 11pm.

At the popular **Tiffany's Pub,** Calle del Cristo 213 (☎ 787/725-1167), in old San Juan, many young folks have wandered expecting a quick piña colada or daiquiri, only to stay all evening. Tropical drinks and frappés are also popular.

Stylish and comfortable, **Violeta's,** Calle Fortaleza 56 (☎ 787/723-6804), occupies the ground floor of a 200-year-old beamed house two blocks from the landmark Gran Hotel Convento. An open courtyard provides additional seating.

9 The Cruise Lines & Ships

In this chapter, we'll try to help you answer the big question: "Which cruise should I choose?" Choosing a cruise is like choosing a spouse: Pick the wrong one and you'll not only be miserable, but you'll be stuck together for a long time. With this in mind, it's our aim to see that you get on the right ship, and our insider reviews of the major lines sailing the Caribbean today should help you find the cruise that's right for you.

We've been honest. We've tried to give you a real feel for the mood and passengers on each ship, something that's vitally important when choosing a cruise. Think hard about what you want out of your vacation. Are you looking for fun in the sun and partying aboard a mega-ship, or do you want to relax and enjoy peace and quiet on a clipper ship?

Our reviews evaluate the cruise lines themselves and then each ship in the line's fleet. For each line, we provide passenger profiles as well as reasons to sail or not sail with the line. We also review cuisine and dining facilities, entertainment, onboard activities, children's programs, shopping, service, and more.

We've rated everything to make it easy for you to compare the various ships. (Within a line, ships that are similar in structure and amenities are grouped together.) These ratings, on a scale of 1 to 10, judge 14 aspects of shipboard life, from cabins and crew to the ship's cleanliness and decor. In addition, there's detailed information on cabin rates, and which cabins to choose. (Rates do not include such extras as port taxes and airfare to and from your port of embarkation unless specifically stated.) We also give you the lowdown on pools, spas, and other recreation facilities, as well as the ship's public areas, so you'll know where to escape for a quiet drink or where the disco is.

You can use our Frommer's Favorites in chapter 2 to point you to ships and lines you might like, but be sure to read these reviews carefully to narrow the search down and find the cruise of your dreams.

What the Anchors Mean

⚓ ⚓ ⚓ ⚓ ⚓	Best on the seas
⚓ ⚓ ⚓ ⚓	Very good, and often excellent
⚓ ⚓ ⚓	Good, but not exceptional
⚓ ⚓	Only fair
⚓	A tub

American Canadian Caribbean Line

SHIPS   Grande Caribe (Preview) • Mayan Prince • Niagara Prince
461 Water St., Warren, RI 02885. ☎ 800/556-7450 or 401/247-0955; fax 401/247-2350.

Despite their drawbacks, this trio of innovative small ships offers the most unusual cruising experience of any line in the business. These ships' special features allow them to navigate such forgotten hinterlands of the Caribbean as the cays off the coast of Belize and remote out-islands in The Bahamas that regular and larger ships have to avoid.

Luther Blount, founder/builder/captain/president, claims his ships are "destination-oriented," rather than being destinations themselves or floating hotels. He readily admits his ships are different: "We seek out unusual places and then build the ships to take us there." If you sail this line, you'll sail waters normally traveled only by private yachts and be treated to the unique experience of your ship actually nudging its bow up to the shore so you can walk directly onto the pristine beach.

That's the good news. Now for the bad news: These ships are not for every cruiser. While the *Princes* are certainly better and more upscale than the vessel Bogie took Madame Hepburn aboard in *The African Queen,* a few disgruntled passengers have commented that they aren't *much* better. Admittedly, with the sale of the line's least luxurious vessel, the *Caribbean Prince,* in 1996 (to an outfit that plans to sail it under a different name in the waters off Alaska), many of the line's most egregious technical shortcomings have been eliminated. Even so, don't expect luxury or any particular degree of pampering. Instead, expect a more communal, rough-and-ready lifestyle than is usual aboard the typical cruise ship, a fact that the line itself is absolutely forthright about to prospective clients during the sales and reservations process.

In the least charitable terms, one could describe American Canadian Caribbean Line (ACCL) ships (they're more like boats) as cheap motels on a barge with an eatery. That, however, would be a disservice to owner-builder Blount. In the closed world of New England shipyards, his ships' designs, as well as the way they float and maneuver, have been the subject of everything from endless speculative gossip to outright industrial espionage.

These ships are certainly nautically innovative, if not exactly pretty, but they're among the most uncomfortable ships competing within the Caribbean cruise market. Most passengers, however, are repeaters, so Blount must be doing something right. He has tapped into a nonglitzy, unflashy market that would deliberately shun most major cruise lines. His boats are real Americana; not only the vessels themselves, but the officers, passengers, and crew. They are true red, white, and blue.

Of course, the problem with sailing aboard such small ships is that if you don't happen to fit in with the type of conservative, older passengers that tend to sail aboard these vessels, you may feel trapped and eager to return to your point of embarkation. Unlike the big ships, the trio of *Prince* vessels has no places for you to run and hide. You're in close quarters and constant contact, so if you dislike your fellow passengers (or they dislike you), you're stuck. Staff members are generally warm and perky—again, only if you fit in—but there have been some notable exceptions, including a hostile New England captain on occasion.

Whatever its pros and cons, American Canadian isn't standing still. Taking full advantage of its dual role as cruise line operator and boatyard, it will launch an all-new vessel, its biggest and most technically advanced ever, the *Grande Caribe* (see preview that follows), to replace the now-divested *Caribbean Prince* and bring its fleet back to three.

PROS & CONS   If you're looking for a do-it-yourself, roughneck adventure on the high seas or on salty backwaters, hop aboard one of Blount's tiny yet innovative vessels. The itineraries he offers are the most imaginative in the Caribbean winter cruise market, upstaging the standard and often boring jaunts of the megaships, which many passengers have already tried once or twice before.

In addition, ACCL's prices are among the lowest (per diem) in the industry. If you choose one of the minimum cabins, and book in on the right deal, you may get to sail for $99 per person, an industry low.

But keep in mind that this is an adventure. These ships do not have any of the basic amenities generally associated with cruise ships. There is no room service, except for a routine clean-up of the cramped cabins. Towels are changed every other day, and you'd better pack your own beach towels. Cabins are small and spartan, and the lower-deck budget berths (at or below the waterline) are almost unacceptable. Also, don't expect gourmet fare. Meals are served country-style in rituals appropriate for a north woods summer camp.

Don't expect any Las Vegas–style entertainment or casinos aboard these ships, either. The bars serve soft drinks, but no liquor. You can bring your own, however. An employee will mark your bottles with your name and store them on a shelf. Be aware some passengers might not approve of drinking; it's against their religion.

Since the vessels accommodate only between 84 and 96 people, passengers easily become acquainted with one other. This is often cited as one of ACCL's greatest drawing cards, but it can also be a major drawback when passengers don't get along. Once you board the ship, you have no privacy unless you go to your room, and even then the line's accordion-style doors prevent you from locking yourself in, or others out. By the end of the cruise, the passengers—except for a few rare but inevitable misfits—are one big, happy family.

TYPES OF PASSENGERS   This line appeals to a more adventure-oriented, no-frills crowd, people who want to escape the overrun ports of the Caribbean, such as St. Thomas, and flee to isolated beaches and secluded havens. They want to become quietly acquainted with native cultures (or what's left of them) or comb the beaches and pretend to be Gauguin, if only for the afternoon. They also want to snorkel and see unusual Caribbean marine life, either in the water or from a glass-bottom boat. Lastly, they seem to want to do all of this again and again, giving American Canadian the highest percentage of repeat customers in the cruise industry.

Passengers tend to be in their 50s to 70s, well traveled, and looking for something out of the ordinary. Most are couples who seem to have been married forever and a day. Many voted for Eisenhower, though some had misgivings that he might have been too liberal. They tend to be well aware of just exactly what they are buying, and good value is of prime importance.

Although the vessels attract some naturalists, Greenpeacers, and young travelers who want to experience unique water sports in the Caribbean, most passengers are retired professionals or business owners, including school teachers and insurance agents. They're definitely not pretentious, and they don't look too kindly upon those who are. They dress simply; no formal wear is ever seen aboard, even at the captain's dinners. In the words of one of the line's booking agents, "If you've brought your sequins on board, you'll quickly learn that you're with the wrong line."

On one voyage, passengers were asked to evaluate their cruise and they suggested to Blount that he refrain from advertising his cruises in the New York/New Jersey area, claiming it might bring aboard "the wrong element." That element would definitely include what used to be called "swingers" in the 1960s. Swingers should swing it elsewhere, as this is an early-to-bed crowd. It's not unheard of for passengers talking and laughing at the dining tables after 10pm to be denounced by an "early-to-bedder" for disturbing the peace.

Passengers who demand top-rate cuisine and amenities should also book elsewhere, and if your political views are more liberal, you'll find more compatible conversation on other lines. There are no children's facilities, and the ships aren't a good choice for passengers with disabilities.

DINING The food served aboard American Canadian Caribbean ships is about the same as one might find in a decent boarding house: ample and varied. Leftovers are craftily used. Last night's roast beef might appear at lunch tomorrow in the form of a beef and vegetable soup served with cornbread and maybe a canned bean salad. Some wines are available and reasonably priced, but don't expect any great selection. Many passengers prefer iced tea with their evening meals instead of wine, and many forego cocktails altogether.

Sometimes the chef will purchase fresh items in port—the day's catch, for instance—which enlivens the otherwise rather bland fare. High-cholesterol foods are commonly featured, including eggs and pancakes with lots of butter at breakfast and "assemble-your-own" BLTs for lunch. The ship will cater to special diets, but much advance notice should be given. Food is cooked in an open-kitchen galley, so it's easy to determine what's for supper.

The best dinners are presented on the second and final nights of each cruise as part of what are known as the "captain's dinners." Birthdays or anniversaries are honored with cakes, with well-wishing passengers joining in the congratulations. On some occasions, you're invited to make your own sundae. Free set-ups and ice are provided for your drinks.

There is one meal seating, and the crew eats at what might be termed the second

seating. Don't be tempted to linger at the table—you're likely to be bustled off so your place can be occupied by your hungry cabin attendant. Seating is casual at tables for 4, 6, 8, and 10. Like-minded groups quickly pair off and sit where the conversation is suited to their interests.

ACTIVITIES Except for some party games or card games conducted in the much-used dining room after the dishes have been cleared, the activities the line offers don't really happen on board. The most interesting action takes place ashore at various offbeat ports of call—at one of the stopovers scheduled specifically for ecology tours and lectures, at some of the western hemisphere's most superb snorkeling and bird-watching sites, or on visits to historic sites built by the colonial Spaniards or the Mayans.

Blount said he had wanted to view marine life close up, and consequently equipped his ships with small glass-bottom boats, from which you can do just that. Each ship also has a swimming platform in the stern, and hauls along a Sunfish for use during beach breaks.

CHILDREN'S ACTIVITIES The minimum age for children on board is 14 years old, and there are no special facilities aboard even for those who clear that mark. Frankly, unless you have a particularly self-reliant teenager who doesn't chafe under the gaze of too many older passengers, you might find that high school students won't particularly thrill to the communal gatherings that seem so frequent (and sometimes so claustrophobic) on board these ships.

ENTERTAINMENT Amusement is mostly of the do-it-yourself nature, combined with a few marshmallow roasts or fireworks ashore. The BYOB cocktail hour, where set-ups (but not the requisite liquor) are included, is a time for songfests, piano music, announcements, and an occasional lecture about an upcoming sight or experience. The cruise director might arrange some onboard activities, but these will be low key. Sometimes local entertainers (such as Garifuna dancers in Belize) will be invited on board for an evening.

SHOPPING   Forget shopping, at least on board. However, since Blount's ships sail into often uncharted Caribbean frontiers, unique shopping opportunities will likely present themselves; we've had quite a few while ashore, especially in Honduras and Guatemala. You can find such handcrafts as painted doorstops carved into human figures, unusual weavings and crewel-style embroideries, and benches and chairs fashioned from leather and tropical hardwoods that can be easily disassembled, packed into a suitcase, and brought home.

SERVICE   Staff merits a mixed report. Some crew members are so young, friendly, and enthusiastic you want to adopt them and take them home, while others are rather surly and rude. Most come from Luther Blount country (Rhode Island) and probably won't be doing this type of work as a career. In fact, serving aboard an ACCL vessel seems like a summer job, like being a camp counselor in Maine. The crew is versatile by necessity, having to double on many jobs that bigger ships have developed into separate departments. You may see your cabin attendant waiting tables at dinner, or one of the laundry workers clearing dishes. Elderly passengers report that they've been treated with extreme courtesy and politeness by the much younger crew. We've personally found some crew members (not all) far more interesting than the passengers, and they mingle freely with guests, free of the rigidity imposed upon the staffs of many megaships.

ITINERARIES   The company's small size, plus the shallow drafts and legendary navigability of its ships, allow it a greater flexibility of itinerary than virtually any other line afloat. Consequently, each of the routes outlined below is likely to change on short notice. With the addition late in 1997 of an all-new vessel, the *Grande Caribe* (see preview), there's a

possibility, depending on bookings, that one ship will be substituted for another along an already predetermined itinerary. As is the case with any and all ships, storm warnings will quickly scuttle their itineraries and send them scurrying for cover, or take them on alternative routes that avoid the storm's predicted path.

The schedules here are for winter cruises in the Caribbean. As noted below, the *Mayan Prince* might be substituted for the *Grande Caribe* if circumstances warrant it. Like snowbirds, ACCL ships migrate north with the warm weather of summer, usually plying such rarely cruised waterways as the Erie Canal, the St. Lawrence Seaway, and the Intracoastal Waterway.

Niagara Prince—From early December to mid-April, the ship navigates through the offshore waters of Belize, Honduras, and Guatemala on excursions of between 7 and 12 days. Depending on the itinerary, tours begin at either Belize City (Belize) or Roatan (Honduras). Stopovers in waters known for their superb snorkeling and wealth of marine life include, among others, Goff Cay, South Water Cay, Ambergris Cay, Man-o-War Cay, Laughingbird Cay, Placencia, Lime Cay, West Snake Cay, and Punta Gorda (all in Belize); Livingston, Fort San Felipe, Lago de Izabel, Mariemonte, Mariscos, and the Quiriqua Mayan Ruins (all territories of Guatemala); Omoa Beach, Fortaleza de San Fernando de Omoa, and Utila (all territories of Honduras).

Mayan Prince—From late November to mid-December, the ship embarks on 12-day cruises through The Bahamas and the Turks and Caicos. From mid-December to mid-April, 12-day itineraries sail through and around Panama, calling at such ports as Panama City, Colon, the village of El Provenir, Balboa, Punta Alegre, the Spanish colonial fortress of Portobelo, and such offshore sites as the San Blas Islands, the pelican sanctuary on Taboga, the Isla del Rey, and the isolated Pacific islands of Contadora and Le Esmeralda. Included is an expedition by dugout canoe

Grande Caribe (Preview)

The inauguration of ACCL's newest and largest vessel during the autumn cruising season of 1997 will celebrate 30 successful years in which innovative entrepreneur Luther Blount's line has sailed some of the most unusual itineraries in the cruise world. Priced at $7.5 million, the *Grande Caribe* is ACCL's most expensive ship to date, and puts a greater emphasis on style than does any of its predecessors. Designed for cruises along the coasts of North, Central, and South America, it includes 48 cabins, each outfitted with either two twins or a queen-size bed, making its full complement 96 passengers. Its format will add a much-needed improvement to the ACCL design: a lounge-bar on the upper deck that's separate from the rest of the dining room. The lounge doubles as a rendezvous point that can accommodate every passenger on board all at once.

The *Grande Caribe* will include the special features that have helped ACCL carve a niche for itself within the cruise industry, including a shallow draft (only 6 1/2 feet), a bow ramp that permits direct access from the ship onto shore, a retractable pilot house that can be lowered to allow the ship to pass beneath low-slung bridges of America's inland waterways, a stern dock for passenger swimming, and a system of cabin ventilation that's a marked improvement over earlier ACCL vessels.

As with its sibling vessels, the *Grande Caribe* will allow access to remote outposts and waterways that many other adventure-style, expeditionary cruise vessels simply cannot reach. For access to even *more* remote sites, the *Grande Caribe* will carry two 24-passenger launches, one of which features a glass bottom for easy perusals of marine flora and fauna.

The ship will be powered by a 1,400 hp twin-screwed diesel propulsion system that's mounted on flexible connections as a means of achieving the lowest levels of engine noise in the industry. The ship's streamlined design is more stylish and more sleek than any of its corporate predecessors.

The *Grande Caribe* will explore regions of the Caribbean that are considerably less exotic than the Central American routes favored by its siblings, the *Mayan* and the *Niagara Prince*. It will include trips through the Virgin Islands (both U.S. and British) from mid-December to mid-January, with stops at about 10 of the least-visited and most pristine beaches in the archipelago. Beginning in mid-January, it will embark on two 12-day cruises down the length of the Lesser Antilles, with stopovers at such Caribbean ports as Dutch St. Maarten, French St. Martin, Tintamarre, Iie Forche, St. Barts, Saba, St. Kitts, Nevis, and Antigua. During early February, the ship will continue south from Antigua, stopping in Guadeloupe, Dominica, Martinique, St. Lucia, St. Vincent, Bequia, Canouan, Mayreau, Carriacou, and Grenada.

Beginning in February 1998, ACCL plans to run *Grande Caribe* (or, depending on market conditions, one of its sibling ships) on three 12-day jaunts that originate in Trinidad and head up the Macareo and Orinoco rivers of Venezuela, stopping at Cojoida, Barancas, Angel Falls (optional), Corporita, and San Jose Macuro (all in Venezuela), with a final call at Charlottesville, Tobago, before disembarkation on Trinidad. In mid-March, the ship (again, or one of its siblings) will reposition itself between Trinidad and Curaçao, with stops at several offshore islands of Venezuela en route. In mid-April, the ship will begin a 12-day jaunt through The Bahamas, with stops at many of that country's relatively remote cays and islets as well as calls at ports in Turks and Caicos.

up the Samba River into the tangled vegetation of the Darien Jungle.

SPECIAL DISCOUNTS   Christmas and New Year's cruises are discounted by 10%. The same discount is granted when two cruises are booked back-to-back. A 15% discount is granted for each third passenger. The line gives passengers an eleventh cruise for free after their tenth (paid) cruise.

SINGLE SUPPLEMENTS   Solo travelers pay 175% of the per person double-

occupancy rates, but only in a limited number of cabins (numbers 20 through 22 on all vessels). American Canadian waives the supplement if a passenger agrees to share a cabin with another passenger (of the same sex). If the line doesn't find another solo passenger, the supplement is waived and you sail with the cabin all to yourself.

PORT CHARGES   Depending on the itinerary, port charges are $125 to $260.

Mayan Prince

Specifications

Size (in tons)	92	Crew	17 (American)
Number of Cabins	46	Passenger/Crew Ratio	5 to 1
Number of Outside Cabins	39	Year Built	1992
Number of Passengers	92	Last Major Refurbishment	None
Officers	American		

Frommer's Ratings (Scale of 1–10)

Activities	8.5	Public Areas	6.0
Cabins	5.5	Public Comfort/Space	5.0
Cleanliness/Maintenance	6.0	Recreational Facilities/Pool	1.5
Entertainment	4.0	Service	7.0
Food & Beverage	5.0	Ship Crew/Officers	7.0
Interior Decor	5.0	Shore Excursions	10.0
Ports of Call	10.0	Worth the Money	9.5
		Overall Average	**6.4**

Since its construction in 1992, the *Mayan Prince* has functioned as a reliable sea horse in the ACCL fleet. Part of its success derives from the fact that the flaws of its earlier prototype (*Caribbean Prince,* built in 1990) were hammered out and resolved by the time *Mayan Prince* came along. Therefore, although it's the oldest ship in the ACCL flotilla, *Mayan Prince* is not the austere guinea pig that the now-defunct *Caribbean Prince* was, a fact that's a boon to the many clients who have sailed aboard it.

The ship's special features descend directly from the early days of Luther Blount's visionary fervor, among them an extendible bow ramp that, combined with an unusually shallow draft, makes it possible for the ship to cruise directly onto the sands of beaches or silted riverbanks so passengers can disembark directly on shore. The vessel also contains a stern swimming platform, a Blount-designed glass-bottom boat, and Sunfishes that are launched for short sails during Caribbean and Central American beach breaks.

Additionally, the vessel is designed to allow loading forward and aft, port and starboard, on both the Main and Sun decks, both to accommodate virtually any docking configuration in the world and to avoid a crush of passengers and luggage all trying to squeeze through one portal at embarkation.

Cabins & Rates

Cabins	Average per diem	Bathtub	Fridge	Phone	Sitting Area	TV
Inside	$122–$183	No	No	No	No	No
Outside	$184–$225	No	No	No	No	No
Suite	n/a	n/a	n/a	n/a	n/a	n/a

THE CABINS No one who ever sailed aboard an ACCL cruise ever raved about the luxury or spaciousness of his or her cabin. Cramped, austere, and hyperfunctional, they're among the bleakest in the industry, with almost no attention to decor. Some passengers compare the worst of them to an engine crew's quarters aboard a naval vessel. The windowless units on the lowest deck—and amidships on the Main deck, just behind the clatter and noise of the galley—are virtually unacceptable except to *Let's Go* readers on the leanest of budgets. If the highly worthwhile itineraries offered by this line appeal to you, remember that it's worth investing the extra money for one of the line's more expensive cabins. The per diem costs will still be low compared to the rest of the industry, and at least you'll have a picture window and a lounge chair, and even a small table, if you specially request one. Some outside cabins have portholes, but some cabins on the Sun Deck have views that are obstructed by equipment. Cabins aboard the *Grande Caribe* promise to be larger and better accessorized than those aboard the line's other vessels.

The least appealing cabins are numbers 20 through 22 (often booked by singles). These inside bottom-deck cabins have no windows and an "extrawide" bed of only 42 inches. Storage space in all cabins is a meager four drawers plus a small metal cabinet for hanging clothing. Luggage is stored under the beds. Cabins have accordion-style doors that close tight but don't lock. In many cabins, beds can be converted from twin sleepers to double beds.

About 10 of the cabins aboard the *Mayan Prince* open onto the Promenade deck. If one is available and your budget allows, book it; after 12 days aboard one of these ships, you'll welcome the extra convenience.

Cabins on the Main deck are aft of the dining room and kitchen, near the stern, and these draw the most complaints from older passengers who wish they'd booked away from the noise, especially if they like to turn in early. If you suffer from claustrophobia, avoid the lower-deck cabins altogether.

The cramped, functional bathrooms in all cabins are designated very nautically as "heads." The entire bathroom is transformed into the shower cubicle whenever you want to bathe, thanks to a hand-held spray that hangs from a fixture in the wall and shoots water virtually everywhere when activated. Water is evacuated through a small trap in the floor. Unpleasant odors can emerge from the sewer, especially within cabins on the lowest decks, if these bathrooms are not properly used and sanitized at frequent intervals.

None of the cabins is designated as wheelchair-accessible or even wheelchair-friendly.

RECREATION & FITNESS FACILITIES
There are no exercise facilities aboard, which suits many of the older passengers just fine. You can walk around the Sun Deck for fitness, and aerobics classes are offered aboard some cruises. The ships are in port daily for swimming, snorkeling, and enjoying the beaches. There are no swimming pools aboard ship.

PUBLIC AREAS   The public areas are limited, and not at all comparable to what's found on major cruise lines. The one main dining room becomes an all-purpose rendezvous point for group meetings and communal cocktails whenever meals are not being served. Each ship also has a small library-style "den," which, if all the passengers used it, would be wholly inadequate. Reading material consists of a few paperbacks placed on a shelf, so bring your own books if you're contemplating major reading binges between ports of call. Other than the cramped confines of your cabin, don't expect to find any cozily isolated nooks and crannies where you can curl up with your favorite author—there aren't any. The bar is extremely small, no more than a sterile-looking corner of the dining room, so if your idea is to settle in comfortably for a few drinks you might want to carry your bottle and setup to an outdoor chair on the upper deck. As far as shopping goes, there is none to speak of—no formalized display area, that is, but the cruise director will sell you a jacket, a tube of toothpaste, or perhaps a shirt, pulled straight out of a cupboard and sold "over the counter" as a souvenir of your cruise.

The ship has three passenger decks, and ceilings lower than those aboard most vessels. One of the nicest features on this cramped ship is the wraparound promenade on the upper deck. A crowded area at each end of the vessel has chairs placed for passengers to sunbathe, read, or watch the view. Some additional chairs are on the ships' roof.

Niagara Prince

⚓ ⚓

Specifications

Size (in tons)	99	Crew	17 (American)
Number of Cabins	42	Passenger/Crew Ratio	5 to 1
Number of Outside Cabins	40	Year Built	1994
Number of Passengers	84	Last Major Refurbishment	n/a
Officers	American		

Frommer's Ratings (Scale of 1–10)

Activities	8.5	Public Areas	6.5
Cabins	6.5	Public Comfort/Space	5.5
Cleanliness/Maintenance	7.5	Recreational Facilities/Pool	1.5
Entertainment	4.0	Service	7.0
Food & Beverage	5.0	Ship Crew/Officers	7.0
Interior Decor	5.5	Shore Excursions	9.5
Ports of Call	9.5	Worth the Money	9.5
		Overall Average	**6.7**

The new 101,000 gross-register-ton Carnival *Destiny* towers in the sea air at 207 feet. The 99 gross-register-ton *Niagara Prince,* with its funnel dismantled and mast folded to the deck, struggles up to its full height at 16$^1/_2$ feet. The difference is that the *Destiny* can't cruise from Chicago to New Orleans on inland waterways, while the *Niagara* is equally at home on a canal in New York State or an out-island in The Bahamas. It should be noted, though, that many of *Niagara's* remarkable engineering features were designed specifically for northern waters, not for the smooth Bahamian winter waters.

Like its siblings, the *Niagara Prince* is equipped with a unique retractable pilot house, allowing for passages beneath low bridges, which are basically nonexistent in The Bahamas. More effective in this area is the extendible bow ramp, which, combined with a shallow draft, makes it possible to cruise right up to beaches or remote landings not accessible to other cruise ships. Off the stern is a swimming platform that is broader than those on the other two *Prince* vessels. Blount's trademark glass-bottom boat is on board, as is a Sunfish, ready for short sails whenever the winds and setting are appropriate.

In lieu of an elevator, this craft has a stair lift for passengers with difficulty negotiating stairs. The ship's design allows passengers to board forward and aft, at both port and starboard on the main and second decks, making for easy embarkation.

Cabins & Rates

Cabins	Average per diem	Bathtub	Fridge	Phone	Sitting Area	TV
Inside	$122–$172	No	No	No	No	No
Outside	$122–$208	No	No	No	Partial	No
Suite	n/a	n/a	n/a	n/a	n/a	n/a

CABINS   In the Luther Blount tradition, cabins aboard his latest vessel remain rather small and cramped, with a minimum of storage space. However, the drawers for storage and the metal lockers are more generous than those aboard the *Mayan Prince.* Cabins are also more attractively decorated, with bright prints and replicas of treasure maps.

The cabins that include a table and chair are also a welcome addition, as are the individual climate controls. Upon request, a cabin key will be issued. Try for a cabin in the number range of the 50s, 60s, or 70s, which offer sliding picture windows. There are only two inside cabins, which are the least expensive. The 40 outside cabins are generally identical. Beds within three-quarters of the cabins can be made up as two singles or as a queen-size bed, and 10 cabins can be converted into triples, with the third occupant offered a 15% discount off the per-person price for a double.

No cabins are wheelchair accessible.

RECREATION & FITNESS FACILITIES Like the line's other two ships, there are no swimming pools and no exercise facilities aboard. You can walk on the promenade deck, but all other sports will have to wait until you go ashore. At frequent stopovers, you can go hiking and birding, in addition to the usual ocean swimming and snorkeling. If you're athletic you might feel confined aboard ship, but remember that this line is destination-oriented, assuring you of minimal onboard time between landings.

PUBLIC AREAS   This *Prince* has wraparound windows in its main (and only) dining room and a small lounge for daytime sightseeing. Although similar to the dining area aboard the *Mayan Prince,* this one is positioned on a higher deck, the Sun Deck, and accommodates all passengers on board for single-seating dining. Passengers more or less compose the seating charts for their own tables.

Cape Canaveral Cruise Line

SHIPS   Dolphin IV

101 George King Blvd., Suite 6, Cape Canaveral, FL 32920. ☎ 800/910-SHIP or 407/783-4052; fax 407/783-2380.

Although Cape Canaveral Cruise Line is a new contender, its main asset, the *Dolphin IV*, is one of the oldest ships afloat, with its own distinctive personality.

The line offers good value for your cruise dollar, with two-night quickie cruises—from Florida for a one-day outing in The Bahamas—that are an excellent opportunity for the first-time cruiser to get his or her feet wet. The line is also a good choice for passengers with limited time and/or money who want to escape the midwinter doldrums.

If ships, like humans, have personalities, then *Dolphin IV*'s is cynical, scarred, and weathered, a survivor of many corporate battles and stormy seas, and still going strong. This seaworthy and solid ship, with decorative features long ago surpassed by newer entries, has survived ownership by no fewer than six corporate entities, several of which counted the ship as their principal asset and primary income source.

The boat was commissioned in 1955 to be a combination passenger and freight carrier. Originally named *Zion,* it was renamed a decade later by a Portuguese owner as the *Amelia de Mello,* and made frequent cargo and passenger runs between Lisbon and the Canary Islands. After at least two years in mothballs, it was sold in 1972 to a Greek line that reconfigured it into a cruise ship named *Ithaca.* Finally, in 1979, a Greek-French consortium purchased the ship, renamed it *Dolphin IV,* and poured millions into a 1981 refurbishment.

The *Dolphin*'s subsequent owners seem to believe the superstition about never changing a ship's name. In 1984, the ship was purchased by the Miami-based Dolphin Line, which was specifically created to administer the *Dolphin IV.* The company opted to honor the vessel's most

recent moniker. In 1995, after short-term ownership by the Royal Bank of Scotland, the aging vessel changed hands once again, this time moving into the corporate fold of the newly created Canaveral Cruise Line, whose name derived from its principal port of embarkation, Port Canaveral. In March 1996, Canaveral changed its name to Cape Canaveral Cruise Lines to avert a lawsuit with Carnival Cruise Lines, which claimed the names were too similar and could be confused. Technically, Cape Canaveral is a subsidiary of the Kosmas Shipping Group, vacation time-share marketers and operators of a dozen Florida-based resorts. Although the line has worked hard to assert its independence within the niche market it fills, it still maintains some links (albeit increasingly weak) to both the Dolphin and Majesty Lines.

The ship's first cruise under the auspices of its new owners departed early in 1996 after extensive dry-docking and a series of mostly cosmetic refurbishments.

PROS & CONS   Despite its age and a layout that's anything but cutting edge, you can still enjoy a worthwhile cruise aboard the *Dolphin*. The ship is neither luxurious nor plush, its glamour long ago surpassed by newer ships, but it does have a number of things in its favor. It's teakwood decks, scarred and much-used as they might be, are a luxury you won't find on most new ships, whose owners often opt for more economical coverings. Other strengths include a worthwhile children's program and the enthusiasm that the many first-timers bring to the cruises. There's also a kind of insouciance to the fact that your cruise experience is more or less a weekend shuttle service from Florida "across the lake" to the shops, casinos, and beaches of Freeport. The onboard atmosphere is casual,

In case you want to be welcomed there.

We're here to see that you're always welcomed at establishments everywhere. That's why millions of people carry the American Express® Card — for peace of mind, confidence, and security, around the world or just around the corner.

do more®

Cards

In case you're running low.

We're here to help with more than 118,000 Express Cash locations around the world. In order to enroll, just call American Express before you start your vacation.

do more

Express Cash

And just in case.

We're here with American Express® Travelers Cheques and Cheques *for Two*.® They're the safest way to carry money on your vacation and the surest way to get a refund, practically anywhere, anytime.

Another way we help you…

do more

Travelers Cheques

upbeat, and friendly, albeit with a sense that the crew has traveled this itinerary with similar crowds many times before. The daily program is fairly standard, but nonetheless tolerable considering the short duration of each cruise. Drawbacks include small cabins, but since most passengers travel light this is generally not a problem.

The ship isn't good for a sophisticated, romantic sojourn awash with comforts and a sense of privacy, and neither the destination (Freeport) nor the onboard setting will necessarily appeal to seasoned travelers.

TYPES OF PASSENGERS Non-Floridians visiting such Orlando-area attractions as Disney World, Sea World, and Universal Studios comprise a healthy percentage of all bookings, and passengers from the snowbelt often get a worthy package deal when they combine a two-day holiday aboard the *Dolphin* with three days in Disney World. On the other hand, Floridians use the line much like the British use their new Chunnel, as an easy way to escape the country for a weekend of fun and shopping. The cruise line itself does everything to encourage the habit with slogans like "Take a cab over to Port Lucaya."

The short cruises appeal to retirees, first-time cruisers, economy-minded honeymooners, and families who favorably compare the price of a cruise aboard the *Dolphin* to the total expense of a land-based motorized vacation. Ages of travelers range from their late 20s to around 58.

DINING Don't expect culinary luxury. The one dining room, rather glamorously named the Barbizon, is a long, narrow, L-shaped space with a low ceiling. Mirrors and elaborate food displays help make the room appear larger than it really is, and the emphasis is on clean napery and a breezy, clean-lined modernism. A pianist tickles the ivories during the two dinner seatings.

The fare is American with a hint of continental, and would never be considered haute cuisine or even something whipped up by a weekend gourmet. Nevertheless, it's appetizing and tasty, similar to what you'd be served at a competent, middle-bracket Florida country club. Specific theme meals, such as Italian, Mexican, or tropical/Caribbean, appear frequently from a galley that's staffed 24 hours a day with workers baking bread and pastries and boiled down stocks for the next round of meals. Nonethnic dishes are always available for the meat-and-potatoes crowd. The kitchen will accommodate kosher and vegetarian diets.

Additional dining options are offered in the Lido, one of the best-designed casual restaurants afloat. This indoor/outdoor space is divided between a barbecue and a cold buffet, and its physical layout makes access to the buffet easier than at poolside restaurants aboard other ships. Whether you want to get there is another question: The buffets look better than they taste. Midnight buffets are always available, with showy displays that feature food as art.

Children must dine with their families. Children's menus and small portions are offered; the menus change daily to correspond with what's being served to adults. High chairs are readily available in the dining room.

ACTIVITIES Cruises are short enough that by the time many passengers finish exploring the ship and familiarize themselves with the rituals of life at sea, the cruise is over. For this reason, passengers often seem to be dashing from one shipboard venue to another, trying to cram as much activity into their onboard experience as possible. Recognizing this tendency, the line works hard to offer enough razzle-dazzle to distract virtually anyone during the short hop over to Freeport. Activities are likely to include the kind of "fun in the sun" distractions that stimulate participation from as many onlookers as possible. Examples include bingo, ship-styled horse racing, parties for singles and those who want to be, and a

Captain's Welcoming Party. Organized visits to the Bridge draw an enthusiastic response from first-timers and their children.

The center of activity during the day revolves around the small (some say "ornamental") pool of the Lido Deck, which is flanked by a bar and a frequently replenished (and frequently picked-over) buffet. Teenagers favor, and most adults avoid, the clanging and whirring video-game arcade.

After dark, activities revolve around the Barbizon dining room, the Monte Carlo casino, the disco, and the dance floors of the Rendezvous and Miramar Lounges. In at least one of those lounges, live music is presented by a pair of musicians whose instruments are electronically enhanced and computerized for the illusion that the orchestra is larger than it really is.

CHILDREN'S ACTIVITIES   The latest owners of the *Dolphin IV* retained many of the children's programs put in place by the previous owners. Assuming (probably correctly) that children over 12 really don't want to participate in counselor-supervised gatherings, the line offers formalized programs only for children between the ages of 2 and 12. These programs include such interactive, summer-campy pastimes as pizza parties, video presentations, arts and crafts classes, hula contests, tours of the Bridge and lessons in navigation, "Coke-tail" parties, kids-only comedy hours, scavenger hunts, and pool games. There's a supervised playroom on board, and at least one counselor/supervisor with the authority to press additional crew members into supervisory service as needed.

Pending the availability of a cooperative crew member, baby-sitting can be arranged throughout the day and evening for $5.50 per child per hour.

ENTERTAINMENT   Cape Canaveral recognizes that part of the allure of its product involves offering as much glitter and diversion as possible during the brief but high-energy shuttle to Freeport. Consequently, onboard entertainment sometimes

has its own share of verve and spontaneity. Las Vegas it's not, but for the price this line charges, you can't expect Barbra or Liza. The comedy menu is usually competent, featuring comedians who have performed for the HBO comedy hour and at comedy clubs across the country. Comedic references are urban, often themed to the cruise experience or politics, and often presented in one of the metallic-looking lounges with as much input as the performer can elicit from the audience.

Dancing is featured before and after dinner in a pair of onboard lounges, and there's a somewhat oppressive and rather small disco set claustrophobically within the hold of the ship, accessible via a steep flight of metal stairs. The Café Miramar, an all-purpose bar/cafe/lounge/meeting room, is intimate during some times of the day and absolutely jammed whenever the ship is full. The Monte Carlo casino is small and often crowded, but gives a taste of the larger and glossier casinos that await guests after their arrival in Freeport.

SHOPPING   An onboard shopping arcade is stocked with notions and souvenirs, both tasteful and tasteless, and replacements for whatever cotton wear and resort wear you might have forgotten, lost, or ruined since your departure from home. The inventory is affordable rather than esoteric, so your mind and pocketbook will be rested and ready when you arrive in Freeport and encounter one of the world's most unusual, albeit tacky, shopping marts, the International Bazaar.

Covering ten acres, the International Bazaar blends architecture and cultures from some 25 countries. You'll see areas patterned after the Ginza in Tokyo and shopping neighborhoods in Paris and London, all in a somewhat outdated and sun-bleached style of palm-dotted tropical kitsch. You'll find duty-free prices on leather goods, jewelry, lingerie, and gifts from shops with names like *The Love Boutique*.

SERVICE   Service is adequate, if hurried. Despite their occasional inexperience, the staff is friendly and tries to please, but they often work under cramped, over-crowded conditions. It's not a "snap your fingers at the waiter and he'll come running" kind of place, but you'll eventually get whatever it was you thought you needed. Dining room attendants are the best of the lot, usually remaining courteous despite sometimes trying circumstances.

ITINERARIES   *Dolphin IV* sails from Port Canaveral's Terminal 3 at 4pm, arriving in Freeport, on Grand Bahama Island, the following morning at 8am. Check for actual days of departure. Passengers spend the day at Freeport shopping, sunning, cycling, gambling, or whatever, then depart that evening for their return the next morning to Port Canaveral. All cruises are two-day, two-night experiences, with absolutely no variation in the oft-traveled route.

SPECIAL DISCOUNTS   Since this line's marketing policy is evolving rapidly, it's best to ask about available special discounts before booking. Many cabins can accommodate three or four passengers, and these are always discounted when cabins are shared, with a third or fourth passenger paying a per diem rate of $59. If you book far enough in advance, you can also get a discount, sometimes up to $200 per passenger. Sometimes, the third and fourth occupants of a cabin can sail for free. Special discounts, depending on whatever promotion is in effect at the time of your booking, sometimes apply to senior citizens.

SINGLE SUPPLEMENTS   Since there are no single rooms aboard, a solo traveler pays 150% of the double occupancy rate.

PORT CHARGES   Port charges on these short jaunts to The Bahamas are unreasonably high at $79 per passenger.

Dolphin IV

⚓ ⚓

Specifications

Size (in tons)	13,007	Crew	290 (International)
Number of Cabins	286	Passenger/Crew Ratio	2.38 to 1
Number of Outside Cabins	206	Year Built	1955–56
Number of Passengers	692	Last Major Refurbishment	1991, 1993, 1995
Officers	Greek		

Frommer's Ratings (Scale of 1–10)

Activities	6.2	Public Areas	6.5
Cabins	6.3	Public Comfort/Space	6.0
Cleanliness/Maintenance	6.5	Recreational Facilities/Pool	4.0
Entertainment	6.5	Service	6.8
Food & Beverage	6.8	Ship Crew/Officers	8.0
Interior Decor	6.2	Shore Excursions	4.0
Ports of Call	4.0	Worth the Money	7.0
		Overall Average	**6.1**

The *Dolphin IV* has undergone many design changes, and at some point, a terrace was added to the ship's stern, the upper decks were enlarged, and cabins were configured to make more efficient use of space than is the case in many equivalent small ships.

Cabins & Rates

Cabins	Average per diem	Bathtub	Fridge	Phone	Sitting Area	TV
Inside	$70–$90	No	No	Yes	No	No
Outside	$95–$115	No	No	Yes	No	No
Suite	$115–$135	No	No	Yes	Yes	No

CABINS   The bywords are cramped, minuscule, and, if you bring lots of possessions aboard, inadequate. Storage space is minimal, and bathrooms have tiny showers that force you to move gingerly. If you drop the soap either in or out of the shower, be very careful not to bang your head, knees, elbow, or derriere against something as you stoop to pick it up.

Cabins are scattered over five of the ship's six decks, and come in five different price categories and several configurations for sleeping arrangements. Some have double beds, some have twins, others have one or two upper berths, and some come with a double bed and a sofa bed. Each cabin has air-conditioning, wall-to-wall carpeting, and a radio. Decor is what you might expect to find at a roadside motel in central Florida: bland, impersonal, color-coordinated, angular, and minimalist.

If you opt to share your cabin with children or friends, take along a sense of humor and the mind-set of a tinned sardine, and plan to catch up on sleep during daylight hours on a chaise lounge beside the pool. Cabins on lower decks get lots of engine noise and an occasional whiff of fumes from the ship's diesel engines.

If you want or can afford some extra space, consider booking a junior suite. At a generous 250 square feet, they are substantially larger than the barely comfortable cabins, the smallest of which are only 75 cramped square feet. Be warned, however, that five of the ship's nine suites are positioned on the uppermost Boat Deck. Although they're somewhat larger than conventional cabins in other parts of the ship, your view of the sea may be obstructed to a greater or lesser extent by a row of hanging lifeboats, a fact that doesn't seem to matter to most people who book them. Other suites lie two decks below and are positioned beside one of the most heavily traveled pedestrian zones of the ship, adjacent to the purser's office. Some inside cabins offer nominally more room than some outside cabins, a fact that compensates passengers for their lack of a sea view.

Although some cabins are advertised as wheelchair accessible, they still require that the passenger has enough maneuverability to navigate through bathroom doors that are only 20 inches wide. Passengers with limited mobility must be accompanied by an able-bodied helper or traveling companion.

RECREATION & FITNESS FACILITIES
There is plenty of sunning space on the wooden decks surrounding the Lido swimming pool, which is far too small to accommodate all passengers when the ship is fully booked.

This ship doesn't have a gym or exercise equipment, although considering the short length of any cruise, passengers don't usually miss it. The ship contains lots of stairs, so you might consider huffing and puffing your way up and down a set of them as a means of compensating for the lack of a health club. If you're a dedicated jogger, remember that eight laps around the unobstructed expanse of the boat deck equals one mile. Skeet shooting is usually available.

PUBLIC AREAS   When the *Dolphin IV* is full, *everything* on board is crowded, so be forewarned.

The ship's interior decor differs from the glitz and post-modernism of the industry's newest models. You'll see a lot of wood, scarred and frequently revarnished but nonetheless authentic, sometimes looking as retro-nostalgic as the wood trim on an Eisenhower-era station wagon. Many accessories and up-to-date features were added in the late 1980s and early 1990s, including clean modern colors and a steel-and-brass wall sculpture of leaping dolphins at play, one of the first things new arrivals see when they board. The overall effect is human-scaled and cozy, suitable for the short "fun cruises" that are the ship's stock and trade.

There's a card room on board, and a hairdresser. Bars and lounges usually convert to public areas for group meetings of whatever ilk. The library, where the modern decor resembles an airport cocktail lounge, converts to a movie theater. Far below the water line is a disco so isolated from the rest of the ship that virtually no one complains about the dusk-to-dawn noise. Incredibly, there's only one elevator on board, an antique and unpredictable affair that interconnects only four of the six decks used by up to 700 passengers.

Carnival Cruise Lines

SHIPS   Celebration • Destiny • Ecstasy • Fantasy • Fascination • Imagination • Inspiration • Sensation
3655 NW 87th Ave., Miami, FL 33178-2428. ☎ 800/438-6744 or 305/599-2600; fax 305/471-4740.

Carnival Cruise Lines (CCL) is the boldest, brashest, most innovative, most scorned, most feared, most successful, and most begrudgingly respected cruise line in the industry today. Since its establishment by the Arison family in 1972, the line has brought the cruise experience down from Olympian heights to a mass-market middle-American diversion enjoyed by millions, captured 25% of the cruise-ship market, and defined the way fun ships should be decorated. The size of its ships, some of the industry's biggest, and its capacity for high-volume sales are staggering. The number of passengers who have experienced a Carnival Cruise since the company's founding rivals the population of many world-class cities, and more than 25,000 passengers can and sometimes do sail aboard the Carnival fleet during any given week of the year. During some peak seasons, the line boasts a staggering passenger load that can exceed 100%. In those instances, every Carnival cabin is occupied, with some cabins housing third and fourth passengers. Some sociologists worry that the hordes of passengers the line has unleashed across the Caribbean have forever altered island cultures, but these sociologists probably aren't making their living off the tourist trade. At least for the moment, Carnival's music is playing loudly, and ports around the tropics, plus passengers across the snowbelt, are dancing to its rhythm.

Something about this charismatic company attracts not only passengers but financial backers as well. In 1987, the Arison family disbursed a mere 20% of their holdings in Carnival's first public stock offering, quickly raising $400 million, yet managing to retain managerial control and an 80% ownership of the Carnival Group. The corporation's assets are enormous: In addition to its own fleet, Carnival holds substantial interests in several cruise lines, including a 50% ownership of the ultraluxurious Seabourn Line, a 43% stake in Epirotiki, and full ownership of both Windstar Cruise Line and Holland America. The company has been known to buy and sell holdings, including some of the largest hotels in the world, like other companies buy and sell company cars.

The origins of the Miami-based company were as shaky as they were accidental. Company patriarch Ted Arison, a reclusive billionaire now living in Israel, had sold an air-freight business in New York in 1966 and intended to retire to his native Israel to enjoy the fruits of his labor. After he negotiated terms for chartering a ship in the Mediterranean, he compiled a group of paying passengers, only to discover that the ship's owner could no longer guarantee the vessel's availability. According to latter-day legend, a deal was hastily struck whereby Arison's passengers would be carried aboard an underbooked ship then owned by Knut Kloster, a prominent Norwegian shipping magnate. The combination of Arison's marketing skill and Kloster's hardware created an all-new entity that, in 1966, became the corporate forerunner of Norwegian Cruise Line.

This coalition of convenience dissolved with much rancor in 1972. Arison reacted by buying an older vessel, *Empress of Canada,* known for its formal and somewhat stuffy administration, and reconfigured it into Carnival's first ship, the anything-but-stuffy *Mardi Gras.* Things did not go swimmingly on the ship's maiden voyage. Industry wags still tell the tale of how, loaded with rivers of liquor and 350 cynical travel journalists and hard-hitting travel agents, the brightly painted ship ran aground just off the coast of Miami. Infuriated, Arison managed to pick up the pieces after this initial debacle, forging ahead with a company that eventually evolved into the most influential trendsetter in the cruise-ship industry.

So how did he do it? Some of the most astute financiers in the western hemisphere (including executives of many competing lines) have spent years studying his technique. Micky Arison, chairman of the Carnival Group and son of the founding father, says that part of the company's success lay in the selection of a hard-hitting management team with nerves of steel, timing, and luck. Then there was advertising, with Kathie Lee Gifford and her undeniable charm powering one of the most successful advertising campaigns in the history of the leisure industry. Finally, the company established itself by linking middle Americans' exploding interest in cruising with a willingness to gamble big time on innovations in cruise-ship decor, vacation images, and perceived value in an all-inclusive holiday.

Carnival's success also derives in part from the ships' decor, and for that the credit goes to Joe Farcus, the eclectic and electric designer whose ideas permeate every Carnival vessel. Call it anything you like, but never call it subdued. Glitz, glitter, neon, and socko-on-socko colors that you'd be hard-pressed to find in the natural world are big aboard these megaships, whose overall effect is in deliberate, often provocative contrast to the everyday environment we all left behind when we board.

Anyone with an interest in art history will enjoy spotting the references in Carnival's often-whimsical decorative motifs. On the same ship, you might find a disco designed like an Andy Warhol collage, a "mingles bar" decorated with checkerboard patterns of yellow on black, and surprisingly comfortable chairs inspired by the network of pipes beneath New York City. Recent creations have used ancient mythological images in lieu

of the bold geometrics used on earlier vessels. One of our favorite rooms afloat would be wildly exotic anywhere else, but is completely appropriate aboard Carnival: It's a piano bar outfitted like King Tut's tomb, complete with thousands of hieroglyphs, effigies of long-ago Pharaohs, and settees fashioned like the wings of ancient Egyptian divinities Horus and Seth. Other Carnival rooms, whose themes vary with the ship, include a re-creation of a mogul emperor's palace, with domed shrines and replicas of elephants on either side of a bar, or a room featuring gilded representations of various winged or snake-draped deities of ancient Greece and Babylon. Atria are likely to soar overhead, glistening with mirrors, neon, and chrome. Both the *Fantasy* and *Ecstacy* have two of the most exciting atria ever built aboard a ship, seven-story extravaganzas that can change with the mood and the time of day or night thanks to special lighting. The *Imagination* and *Inspiration,* launched in 1995 and early 1996, respectively, boast decors that are a bit more subdued than their earlier counterparts, but are nonetheless very intriguing.

The effect of all this color and aesthetic foreplay might strike you as hilarious, and possibly leave you dumbstruck. Carnival vessels are theme parks on water, glitzy floating playlands where a San Francisco trolley car or an actual city bus might be used as decoration. Call it whatever you want—too vulgar, too plasticized, too cheap, too colorful, or simply too much— but whatever your conclusion, the effect is riveting and the ambience fun.

And don't think Carnival's adventure in decorating is over. The Fantasy-Class's *Inspiration,* launched in 1996, both subtly and shockingly blends art nouveau romanticism with elements from cubism and neoclassicism. And as newer ships equivalent to *Destiny* are brought online for the 21st century, subtle improvements, based on perceived glitches in earlier prototypes, will be put in place. Examples of Carnival's commitment to improving its product might include the shifting of traffic flows at poolside buffets, enlargements of pizza ovens to compensate for the popularity of pizzas at sea, and the addition of closed-circuit TV cameras that broadcast images of whatever's happening on the ship's dance floors to dozens of color monitors near the bars.

One frequently asked question is, "Aren't all Carnival ships alike?" Yes, for the most part. Except for their decor, a sail aboard the megaships *Ecstasy, Fantasy, Fascination, Imagination, Inspiration,* or *Sensation* is a pretty standardized experience. All were built from 1990 to 1996 at a cost of about $225 million each. The *Fantasy, Ecstasy,* and to some degree the *Sensation* probably contain more neon than the others, and provide an effect that's stimulating and calculatedly catalytic to letting the good times roll. The *Fantasy,* as befits its name, is the most bold and brassy, while the *Fascination* has a Hollywood motif complete with images of Gary Cooper, John Wayne, and Bette Davis perking up the Tinseltown decor.

Aboard a Carnival Cruise, the destination is the ship itself, with ports of call playing a secondary (and sometimes inconvenient) diversion. In other words, it's the complete opposite of American Canadian Caribbean Line. For Carnival's competition in this regard, you have to turn to Royal Caribbean Cruise Line or Princess Cruises, although ships owned by even these lines are much more subdued.

If you opt for Carnival, your only hope for happiness involves immersing yourself in the spirit of it all. A curmudgeon will stand out like a sore thumb, and there's no hope for escape, as "The Carnival" is all-encompassing, and seems even to spill off the gangplank with you during shore leaves. These fun ships *are* fun—a good antidote to snow belt winters and a 180° alternative to the aggressive tastefulness that permeates other, more upscale lines like Seabourn. For good times, Carnival simply has no equal on the high seas. You might as well join in the fun.

And in an industry that's increasingly geared to youthfulness, state-of-the-art

technology, and cutting-edge glamour, Carnival is well poised to compete for Caribbean business in the 21st century. It's fleet is uniformly new. Even the *Celebration,* one of the older Carnival vessels, was only launched in 1987, and it has as much Carnival neon flash and Las Vegas glitter as the 70,000-ton 1990s megaships. Even these pale in comparison to the 3,400-passenger *Destiny* that was launched in November 1996 as the first cruise ship to top the 100,000-ton mark. And the line isn't resting on its considerable laurels: It's already announced the scheduled launching of three new cruise ships, entering service in 1998 and 1999. The first two ships, *Elation* and *Paradise,* are 70,000-gross-register-ton vessels, and the final one, the 101,000-gross-register-ton *Triumph,* will rival *Destiny* in size and, we can only assume, *fun.*

PROS & CONS   There are ample arguments for and against sailing with what's possibly the most controversial cruise line afloat, but a strong point in the line's favor is its own success, and the sheer volume of passengers who have dipped their feet into the heady brew of seagoing life on a Carnival ship.

The company did not build the world's largest cruise line in less than four decades by being inept. This extremely well-run company delivers exactly what it says it will: almost unlimited "fun" opportunities for passengers to enjoy themselves in some of the most sprawling and excessive vessels afloat. And the fun atmosphere appeals to a wide demographic swath. The ships are clean and well maintained, crews are well trained, and the mass-produced food is about as good as it can get aboard a ship that seats 600 diners at one time.

The line doesn't call itself Carnival for nothing. Part of its success derives from its theme-park ambience, its tacit approval of bacchanalian behavior, and those deceptively potent sunset-colored drinks bartenders dispense from dozens of stations around each ship. Your dining partners may or may not be entirely sober before the first course is served, and might as likely order a tequila sunrise as an aged Bordeaux to accompany their beef Wellington. So if you're more than usually sensitive to adults rediscovering their second childhoods, you may want to skip these sailings. The ambience might grow tiresome after your initial good will has worn off, although if you find yourself losing your sense of indulgence, simply consider moving on to another area of the ship. Most Carnival vessels are big enough to be all things to all types of passengers, and, eventually, you're likely to find your own special niche.

The onboard entertainment is as good as it gets at sea, and recreational outlets are lavish. The fleet is newer, with many more innovations and an infinitely more interesting decor than vessels belonging to lines promoting themselves as cost-conscious alternatives to Carnival (including Norwegian Cruise Line).

If you tire of crowds easily, you might want to sail into the sunset on a Windstar ship instead. No matter how starry the night, the enormous capacity of most Carnival ships, coupled with an emphasis on action, almost guarantees there will be at least one person (and possibly several) invading your privacy or sense of solitude. The crowds are as dense as in any big-city nightclub on a Saturday night, and waiting in line gets to be routine after a while. The delay at any port of call is the most irritating. This is not the fault of the cruise line, but of bureaucratic port authorities who are understandably skeptical at the prospect of unleashing such a horde of rowdy and/or impatient passengers onto the shores of their tiny island nations.

One onboard annoyance, unfortunately, is common to many other companies whose fleet consists of large or megasized vessels: Too many announcements are broadcast at all times of the day about options for late-breaking fun. How you react to this depends on your attitude: It's either a banquet of fun, a bit much of a good thing, or maddening overkill.

If you're looking for love, you're more likely to find a suitable partner aboard Carnival than aboard smaller and more staid vessels where whatever candidates you see in your first two days afloat are likely to be all you'll ever see. Aboard the larger Carnival vessels, some romantic liaisons don't get ignited until late in the cruise, only because it took soul mates that long to discover each other. Our advice on the subject of late-blooming love at the Carnival? Enjoy it! Late aboard CCL is better than never aboard a smaller line.

Finally comes the question of cost. You'll pay more aboard Carnival than you would with an ultrabudget line like Dolphin, Commodore, or Cape Canaveral (with which Carnival is sometimes confused), but you won't pay nearly as much as you would aboard a chic and elegant line like Seabourn. For a nonstop round of parties held between some of the most fabled ports in the western hemisphere, you'll pay fees that are much more reasonable than such activities would cost if booked separately. So if you decide to come to Carnival, you'll get a lot of bang for your buck. The question is whether your stamina is up to it.

TYPES OF PASSENGERS   The line has a reputation for carrying lots of swinging singles (and a percentage of swinging married couples, too) from one sybaritic port to another. Although that's an image Carnival worked hard to spread, particularly during the company's infancy, it's only partially true.

Carnival is the only major cruise line where the majority of passengers are under 50, with the bulk of them booking in as first-time cruisers. Company officials estimate that around 20% of their clientele has taken a Carnival Cruise previously, and that they attract more singles than any other line. Industry insiders estimate the average age of passengers as 43.

Regardless of their age, passengers tend to be young at heart and deeply committed to a partying frame of mind where nonstop activities keep them involved in frolic around the clock. Many are already intimately familiar with the casinos of Atlantic City and/or Las Vegas, and can sometimes calculate the values of cards at a "21" table faster than a computer. They'll also tend to be familiar with the glitter of Florida's megaresorts and the pleasures of piña coladas before lunch, soaks in communal hot tubs, sunbathing, and late-night dancing. If you're an early-to-bed type, hate noise, and prefer tasteful jokes, subdued color schemes, and well-modulated voices, you'll probably wish you weren't sailing Carnival. But Carnival's ability to suspend disbelief is without equal; it evokes Fantasyland in an assortment of tropical colors that scream, "Do whatever you like because you're on vacation."

In addition to the number of unattached (or barely attached) people on board, you'll also find families. Children scamper around the edges of deck-side Jacuzzis overflowing with adults, suds, and sunset-colored cocktails in plastic cups.

In early 1997 the party line of all party lines finally decided to draw the line somewhere, and where they chose to draw it was right at the toes of the spring-break crowd, which in past years had turned some of the line's ships into veritable frat houses. According to Carnival's new rules, no one under 21 will be allowed to sail unless sharing a cabin with an adult over 25 (with exceptions made for married couples and young people whose parents are lodged in a different cabin.)

DINING Most Carnival ships have two dining rooms, each with two predefined seatings for each of three meals a day. However, several different restaurants allow guests a less structured alternative. Dining rooms are usually positioned on an upper deck and feature big windows, sunlight, and views over whatever port or seascape happens to be on the other side. There are usually very few tables for two; more prevalent are tables for eight and booths for six. A pianist or band plays during dinners and sometimes lunches,

too. Because of the hundreds of diners at each seating, Carnival dining rooms are invariably noisy; reserve *sotto voce* and romantic whispers for the privacy of your cabin. Megaships offer the option of dining cafeteria-style on the Lido Deck, and at least one and sometimes two late-night buffets are offered aboard every Carnival ship. In all, each ship offers about a dozen opportunities a day to throw away any semblance of dieting.

The largest array of dining facilities is found aboard Carnival's mammoth *Destiny,* which offers the two-level Galaxy and Universe dining rooms, with ocean views from both the main floor and the mezzanine level. Additionally, its Lido Sun and Sea Restaurant serves a variety of food in a more casual setting. Not only that, but *Destiny* has a number of specialty restaurants, including the Trattoria, with Italian fare, and Happy Valley, with a Chinese cuisine. There's also a 24-hour pizzeria plus a hamburger grill and a patisserie. All alternative dining options are available at no extra charge.

Carnival is big on changing its culinary themes throughout the duration of any cruise, with energy devoted to Italian food, French cuisine, Mexican specialties, seafood, and more. What Carnival ships lack in terms of culinary finesse is made up for in quantity. No one ever goes hungry aboard CCL.

Menus have improved noticeably since the early 1990s. Considering that thousands of meals need to be organized and prepared in cramped galleys, then hauled out on short notice to satisfy thousands of hungry passengers, each with a different and often unique gastronomic opinion, the line does a very professional job. Expect touches of culinary razzle-dazzle and a vague preference for middle-bracket Italian-American fare. Your surf and turf, huevos rancheros, smoked salmon omelets, blackened swordfish, and lobster ravioli with watercress coulis will be well prepared and copious. Buffets include sumptuous displays of salads, meats, and, from specially designed pasta stations, a "build your own rigatoni" option that combines good flavor with light-hearted snippets of humor. Soft ice cream and frozen yogurt are available 24 hours a day from self-serve machines, and some ships offer wine bars. Nautica spa menus, lower in calories, sodium, cholesterol, and fat content, are offered three times a day.

Despite this cornucopia, you won't get the gastronomic finesse you'd find on smaller, more upscale ships, such as Windstar or Seabourn. Carnival menus are varied and pleasing, however, with several selections at each meal designated as spa fare. There is also as much non-nutritious "comfort food" as even the most devoted junk food fan could ever want. All ships offer 24-hour room service from a standardized menu of ho-hum staples. All ships that made their debut in 1996 or 1997 feature 24-hour pizzerias.

There's never any genuine fuss made about wine, wine lore, or the precise temperature at which wine should be decanted. Selections from the wine list are likely to be presented by the same attendant who serves the food.

In the main dining rooms, kids can select from children's menus, which include easy-to-chew choices like ravioli. More appealing to children, however, is the fast-food available throughout each ship: soft ice cream and frozen yogurt from machines, late-night buffets laden with snack food, hot dogs or burgers from the Lido, and the constant flow of empty calories available from room service.

ACTIVITIES Carnival has based much of its success on keeping its passengers in almost perpetual motion. Anything you've ever heard of as a seagoing entertainment possibility will appear aboard a Carnival vessel. Plus, there's always the onboard staples of eating, sunbathing, and shopping.

Slot machines begin whirring and clanging at 8am (at least when the ships are at sea), and cocktails inevitably flow before lunch and continue throughout the rest of the day. Singles and newlywed parties are frequent. Learn to country line-dance,

ballroom dance, toss water balloons, or improve your skills at trivia contests. Practice your golf swing by smashing golf balls into a net. Join (or at least encourage) the participants in beer-drinking contests, or distract yourself with bingo or movies. For a supplemental fee, larger ships even offer skeet-shooting. It's all here aboard a Carnival ship, moving between public areas, between decks, and sometimes, between the cabins of your newfound friends.

One drawback is that there isn't much focus on quiet times, although there is a very handsome-looking library. If your idea of fun involves curling up in a deck chair with an original-language edition of Proust's *Remembrance of Things Past,* Carnival is not for you.

Incidentally, Carnival vessels have based part of their success on recognizing what adults desire. Each ship posts a small but obvious sign at the bottom of stairs leading to one of the sun-flooded upper aeries that reads, "Adults Only, Top Optional Sunbathing."

CHILDREN'S ACTIVITIES Carnival offers many onboard activities that can be enjoyed by the entire family. However, children can get away from their parents and play for all or part of a day in Camp Carnival facilities created especially for them. Carnival must be doing something right in the under-18 market—they carry some 100,000 children annually.

Youth counselors divide children into four different age groups: toddlers 2 to 4, intermediates 5 to 8, juniors 9 to 12, and teens 13 to 17. Programs are designed for each group, ranging from kiddie's pooltime to aerobics designed to reduce excess energy to karaoke parties. Activities begin at the breakfast hour, where teenagers might eat their eggs Benedict while listening to loud rap music. Ship entertainers offer special performances for children and lead backstage tours.

Children most enjoy the kiddie waterslides attached to the children's pools aboard all Carnival vessels, and every "Fun Ship" boasts a toy-stocked playroom. The ships also have ice cream parlors, teen discos, and 60 state-of-the-art video and arcade games.

If you want to bring your children along, consider taking them aboard one of CCL's larger vessels, where children's programs are more heavily emphasized and better developed than aboard Carnival's smaller and older ships. Families can take advantage of heavily discounted rates for third and fourth occupants of double cabins, and a fifth berth is sometimes available in the form of a cot that rolls away beneath another bed. The purser's office can even arrange for a crib to be set up in your cabin.

If part of your holiday fantasy involves heading off into the distant regions of a Carnival ship with your significant other (and without your children), baby-sitting can be arranged through the purser's office for a fee of $4 per hour for the first child, $2.50 per hour for each additional child. Don't expect a lot of one-on-one attention, or even any particular attempt to challenge your child's cerebral cortex: Baby-sitting aboard Carnival resembles a slumber party more than a carnival.

ENTERTAINMENT   Even aboard its smaller, older ships, Carnival consistently offers the most lavish entertainment extravaganzas afloat. Aboard the newer roster of megaships, the cruise line has spent enormous sums accumulating hardware and acoustical equipment that leave many other floating theaters in the dust. The most spectacular setting for entertainment is aboard the new *Destiny,* with its three-deck showroom, the largest afloat, plus a casino so large you'll think you were already in San Juan.

Carnival megaships each carry a dozen dancers. If you look carefully, you'll see that only one of them sings and the others, holding microphones, just lip-synch. The music of the 12-piece orchestra is sometimes augmented by prerecorded tapes, which make the setup sound like the London Philharmonic.

Shows, whose choreography and special effects typically cost millions of dollars to create and rehearse, are some of the best afloat, true testimonies to the glitz and show-biz allure of Atlantic City and Las Vegas. While they may not match the most sophisticated productions you might catch on Broadway, Carnival shows are pretty sensational.

The roster of onboard performers is incredibly diverse. You'll find comedians, jugglers, rock-and-roll bands, country-western bands, a cocktail pianist, and a Dorsey- or Glenn Miller–style big band, all performing, if not simultaneously, at least during the same cruise, and sometimes on the same night. There's also the glitter and electronic lights and music of floating discos, karaoke mikes in one of the cocktail lounges, and the cacophony of some of the largest casinos on the high seas. Outlets for your teenager include "Coke-tail" parties, karaoke contests, and teenage dance clubs.

All Carnival vessels sport an indoor promenade that stretches along one entire side of the ship. Each is lined with nightclubs, dance bars, lounges, and the inevitable casino. In carefully segregated compartments, theme bars appeal to your sense of romance, adventure, and fun. When a room is dark, it's deliberately very, very dark, but when it's not, its colors almost hit you in the face.

At one end of each promenade is a cabaret with risqué dance numbers and costumes worthy of a nightclub circa 1920s Paris. Smoke machines do their thing, stages pivot on their axes, and orchestra pits glide mysteriously from one end of the theater to the other.

During daylight hours you might hear a calypso or steel drum band performing on a deck somewhere, evoking a Caribbean ambience. You won't find the pseudo-academic lectures that preoccupy cruise directors aboard other lines. If there are any tenured college professors on board, they're probably covered with suds in a hot tub.

Even if the onboard entertainment should falter (an unlikely event, considering the razzmatazz this line is capable of), you'll always have the ingredients for creating your own party virtually everywhere you turn. On an average week at sea, the fleet of Carnival "fun ships" sells 261,000 glasses of beer and 43,750 bottles of wine, presumably enough to help lubricate the good times as they continue to roll.

SHOPPING Carnival shops are imbued with the Fun Ship esprit de corps and an inventory that includes many small, easy-to-pack items suitable for impulse purchases in a number of price ranges. Plus, a Galleria shopping mall on each Carnival vessel is filled with garments, notions, and souvenirs stenciled with the Carnival logo. If you decide to consummate last night's fling with an engagement party, you can buy a diamond ring or another gold trinket in the black-and-white marble boutique.

Regardless of the ship, there's a remarkable similarity of merchandise on each of the Carnival ships, a function of computerized inventory control by the line's concessionaire, Greyhound Leisure Services.

SERVICE Service tends to be attentive but brisk in the dining rooms, and slower and a lot less responsive in the cabins. Sometimes attempts to contact cruise directors or pursers by phone simply don't work, especially during high-volume periods or when embarkation and disembarkation are in progress.

When you board ship, you're welcomed by a polite and well-meaning staff at the gangway, given a diagram of the ship's layout, and then pointed in the right direction to find your cabin. Unfortunately, if you're laden with carry-on luggage, and disoriented by the vessel's vast size, you may get lost looking for your cabin or have a long wait for a crowded elevator.

It's a fact of life aboard megaliners like Carnival's that service is simply not as attentive as aboard smaller vessels. Some seasoned passengers quickly sum up the ship's layout, take matters into their own entrepreneurial hands, and pass out a tip or two. If you opt for this shortcut to quicker service, you won't be alone. Veteran Carnival

cruisers consider it as effective as such a technique would be in Atlantic City or Las Vegas.

There are takeaway laundry services on board, as well as self-service, coin-operated washing machines set on a deck conveniently near a cluster of fun-in-the-sun distractions. Be warned, however, that if you happen to pour spaghetti sauce all over your favorite garment, none of the ships have dry-cleaning facilities on board. Each ship also has an almost omnipresent photographer snapping away, recording moments you might not want to publicize after your return home.

ITINERARIES Carnival keeps costs low by skipping the beach outings favored by some competitors and allowing its parties to continue unabated during some days spent deliberately at sea. Plus, the additional revenues generated in onboard casinos and bars help the company meet its costs. This can be a lot of fun for passengers who care less about their destinations than they do about the "Fun Ship" format where the ship is often a destination unto itself. When you do make land, you can expect it to be at one of the larger and more obvious Caribbean destinations, where deep ports can accommodate Carnival ships' circus-sized girths and bulks.

Land/sea packages offered by the company usually combine a stay at Disney World with an experience aboard a Carnival ship. Ports throughout Florida have competed bitterly to become a Carnival vessel's port of origin, but the port of Miami seems to have won the jackpot, being home to more Carnival ships than any other. To attract the golden prize, Miami rebuilt many of its terminals at great expense, offering packages the giant company found hard to refuse.

Celebration—Year-round seven-day cruises originate in either Tampa or New Orleans and meander via Grand Cayman and Playa del Carmen/Cozumel to New Orleans or Tampa. Cruises on either of these routes incorporate three "fun" days at sea in either direction.

Destiny—Carnival's newest ship, launched late in 1996, departs from Miami and, partly because it's too big to navigate through the Panama Canal, remains in the Caribbean throughout the year. It alternates seven-day cruises through the Eastern Caribbean (with stops at San Juan and ports in the U.S. Virgin Islands) with excursions through such western Caribbean resorts as Playa del Carmen/Cozumel, Grand Cayman, and Ocho Rios.

Ecstasy—The ship makes three-day cruises from Miami to Nassau to Miami year-round, and four-day cruises from Miami to Key West, Playa del Carmen/Cozumel, and Miami. Both itineraries include at least one day at sea.

Fantasy—Three-day cruises from Port Canaveral to Nassau to Port Canaveral are booked year-round, as are four-day cruises from Port Canaveral to Nassau to Freeport to Port Canaveral. Both itineraries include at least one day at sea.

Fascination—Year-round, the ship makes seven-day cruises leaving from San Juan and calling at St. Thomas, Guadeloupe, Grenada, La Guaira/Caracas, Aruba, and San Juan, with one full day at sea.

Imagination—The ship makes seven-day cruises year-round from its home port of Miami, calling at Cozumel/Playa del Carmen, Grand Cayman, and Ocho Rios.

Inspiration—Year-round, the ship makes seven-day cruises departing from San Juan, calling at St. Thomas, St. Maarten, Dominica, Barbados, and Martinique.

Sensation—Year-round, the ship makes seven-day cruises through the Eastern Caribbean from its home base in Miami. Stops include San Juan, St. Croix, and St. Thomas.

SPECIAL DISCOUNTS The most successful cruise line in history offers special incentives for joining the Carnival. Examples are a Super Saver Program in which a seven-day cruise, booked early, includes a $1,000 discount that steadily diminishes in value as the percentage of occupied cabins increases. A third or fourth passenger in a cabin usually pays only $60 per diem (cruise only, without airfare, plus port taxes). During special promotions pertaining to specific ships during certain weeks of the year, a third or fourth passenger can be included for free.

AARP members receive a $200 discount per stateroom on cruises of 10 days or more, $100 on 7-day cruises, and $50 on 3- and 4-day Bahamas cruises.

If you arrange your own airfare, or drive to the port of embarkation, you receive a discount of $250.

There is no cost-conscious club per se for repeat cruise passengers, but second-, third-, and fourth-time cruisers are invited to special onboard cocktail parties for repeaters, and have easy access to the discount coupons that are a featured part of a magazine circulated to former passengers.

SINGLE SUPPLEMENTS Singles pay 150% to 200% of the per person double-occupancy rate. Carnival will house up to four adults of the same gender in a cabin for $650 each on some seven-day cruises.

PORT CHARGES Depending on the itinerary, port charges range from $84.50 to $119 per person.

Carnival's Vacation Guarantee

Introduced full-time in 1997, Carnival's Vacation Guarantee program has been extended through the 1998 cruise season. The program provides that guests who are dissatisfied with their cruise may disembark at their first non-U.S. port of call and receive a refund for the unused portion of their fare, plus reimbursement for coach air transport back to their ship's home port. To qualify, passengers must inform the ship's purser prior to their first port of call.

Does this mean Carnival is pretty confident of their product? You bet. And with a posted 42% year-over-year bookings increase for 1997, they have good reason to be.

Celebration

⇩ ⇩ ⇩

Specifications

Size (in tons)	47,262	Crew	670 (International)
Number of Cabins	743	Passenger/Crew Ratio	2.2 to 1
Number of Outside Cabins	453	Year Built	1987
Number of Passengers	1,486	Last Major Refurbishment	n/a
Officers	Italian		

Frommer's Ratings (Scale of 1–10)

Activities	7.8	Public Areas	7.5
Cabins	7.8	Public Comfort/Space	7.5
Cleanliness/Maintenance	7.6	Recreational Facilities/Pool	7.8
Entertainment	8.2	Service	7.0
Food & Beverage	6.8	Ship Crew/Officers	7.8
Interior Decor	6.5	Shore Excursions	6.0
Ports of Call	6.0	Worth the Money	8.0
		Overall Average	**7.3**

Based on standards that apply to many other ships and cruise lines, the *Celebration* is a very large vessel at 47,262 tons, but by the yardstick of other Carnival ships, it's downright average. Many passengers feel comfortable with its size, which makes the ship more intimate and easier to explore than the megaships. And even though it's smaller, it still hosts the shipboard activities for which Carnival is famous. You'll be moving and outside your cabin throughout the day and night. The entertainment is on par with (and just as glitzy as) what you'd find in Las Vegas, though, again, on a smaller scale than that aboard the line's megaships.

The *Celebration*'s decor encompasses every color in the rainbow and some the rainbow never heard of. When it was inaugurated in 1987, a Miami newspaper's architecture critic described the 1,486-passenger ship as "Mardi Gras meets *Animal House* in Las Vegas-by-the-Sea." Its original price tag (in 1987 dollars) was $130 million.

Cabins & Rates

Cabins	Average per diem	Bathtub	Fridge	Phone	Sitting Area	TV
Inside	$198	No	Yes	Yes	No	Yes
Outside	$216	No	Yes	Yes	No	Yes
Suite	$312	Yes	Yes	Yes	Yes	Yes

CABINS   Amid the often frenetic fun of a Carnival ship, you'll occasionally want to escape to the calm and quiet of your cabin. Cabins are fairly large, even spacious when compared to those of the standard Royal Caribbean Cruise Line vessel. Except for the suites, each stateroom is the same as all the others. Beds can be configured as twins or doubles, according to your romantic inclinations. Each cabin has piped-in stereo music, as well as a closed-circuit, wall-mounted TV that broadcasts films through most of the day and night. Unlike cabins aboard Carnival's larger vessels, only a few have both upper and lower berths. The medium-size bathrooms contain showers.

Especially prestigious are the 10 suites on the veranda deck that are as large and comfortable as those offered aboard vessels charging a lot more. Each has a whirlpool tub, a shower, an L-shaped sofa that converts into a foldaway bed, a safe, and sliding glass doors leading to a private balcony.

No cabins are designated specifically as singles. About a dozen cabins are wheelchair accessible.

RECREATION & FITNESS FACILITIES

You can swim in one of three pools or enjoy saunas and steam rooms (segregated by gender) and whirlpools.

The gym has a battery of high-tech workout machines, which rarely remain idle. There are free weights and Keiser progressive-resistance exercise machines. Classes combine instruction with low-key competitions for participants to outdo their earlier exercise records. Aerobics classes are among the most sophisticated aboard any line afloat, and include low-impact exercise for beginners, hour-long classes for participants already in shape, and sessions geared especially for seniors. Organized walks are held on the ships' upper decks.

"Spa Talks," infomercial-type lectures highlighting the ship's health and beauty enhancement facilities, are repeated regularly throughout each cruise, providing information on the Nautica Spa's facilities and activities. An array of skin, hair, body and scalp massages; aromatherapy treatments; and beauty regimes (choreographed by Steiner of London) are available.

Use of Carnival's exercise equipment, sauna, and steam rooms is included in the price of your cruise contract, but many supplemental treatments (such as massage, aromatherapy, skin or hair treatments) carry a sometimes hefty additional charge.

PUBLIC AREAS   Public areas are colorful and outrageous, like most everything that bears the name Carnival. Examples include a bar designed like the inside of a trolley car and a Red Hot Piano Bar outfitted in high-impact toreador colors of red and black. In all, there are seven bars, six entertainment lounges, a casino, a disco, a library, a card room, and, as if the ship's hyperkinetic stimulation weren't enough, a room devoted to electronic video games. There's also a barbershop/beauty shop, boutiques, and a small infirmary with a doctor and nurse on call. Elevators interconnect all eight decks.

Destiny

♨ ♨ ♨ ♨ ♨

Specifications

Size (in tons)	101, 000	Crew	1,000 (International)
Number of Cabins	1,321	Passenger/Crew Ratio	2.6 to 1
Number of Outside Cabins	806	Year Built	1996
Number of Passengers	2,642	Last Major Refurbishment	n/a
Officers	Italian		

Frommer's Ratings (Scale of 1–10)

Activities	8.5	Public Areas	9.2
Cabins	8.2	Public Comfort/Space	9.2
Cleanliness/Maintenance	9.0	Recreational Facilities/Pool	8.8
Entertainment	8.9	Service	7.2
Food & Beverage	7.0	Ship Crew/Officers	8.0
Interior Decor	8.5	Shore Excursions	6.5
Ports of Call	7.5	Worth the Money	8.2
		Overall Average	**8.2**

Late in 1996, Carnival inaugurated its largest ship to date, the 101,000-ton *Destiny*, which is taller than the Statue of Liberty, cost a staggering $400 million to construct, and carries 2,642 passengers based on double occupancy—and 3,400 with every berth filled. This was the first cruise ship ever built to exceed 100,000 tons, and its sheer size and spaciousness has so awed the cruise industry that ships of similar size are being constructed in the shipyards even as we type.

Destiny will ensure that Carnival, at least for the late 90s, will maintain its leadership in the mass-market cruise industry. At its launch, Carnival's president hailed the ship as "evolutionary rather than revolutionary," although it has many advanced features to complement its prodigious dimensions.

The ship will operate a year-round schedule of 7-day cruises from Miami, alternating weekly to the eastern and western Caribbean. Several days are spent at sea.

Cabins & Rates

Cabins	Average per diem	Bathtub	Fridge	Phone	Sitting Area	TV
Inside	$200	No	Yes	Yes	No	Yes
Outside	$215	No	Yes	Yes	No	Yes
Suite	$315	Yes	Yes	Yes	Yes	Yes

CABINS The configuration of decks aboard *Destiny* is a departure from the design of other "Fun Ships" in that the major entertainment and recreation decks are sandwiched between accommodation decks. This means that starting at the lowest passenger deck and moving up, there are two decks of staterooms followed by three public decks and then five more decks of staterooms and suites, these featuring balconies. This design centrally locates the indoor entertainment and recreation facilities for all guests, regardless of cabin location, and also allows for unobstructed views from dozens of balconied staterooms and suites.

More than 60% of the guest rooms on this ship offer ocean views, and some 60% of *these* have private balconies. Standard ocean-view staterooms measure a generous 220 square feet, and each includes a sitting area with a sofa and coffee table. There are two categories of suites: veranda suites measuring a mammoth 340 square feet and penthouse suites where you can live like the sultan of Brunei with 430 square feet, which is roomy indeed. Even the majority of standard outside doubles on this ship have private verandas. Specially designed family staterooms, at a modest 230 square feet (which is comfortable, but not roomy), offer connecting cabins located convenient to children's facilities. In lieu of a private veranda, these more economical family staterooms feature floor-to-ceiling windows providing ocean views. The cheapest cabins—the bottom bunks, so to speak—are inside and are equipped with upper and lower berths, a wall-mounted TV, a desk and a dresser, one chair, and a bath with shower.

A total of 23 cabins on the Lido, Upper, and Empress decks are wheelchair accessible.

RECREATION & FITNESS FACILITIES
They are the most generous of any Carnival vessel afloat, with four pools and seven whirlpools, and a slide pool featuring a 200-foot, three-deck-high slide.

The midship or Lido pool area features a swim-up bar, two whirlpools, and a multilevel terrace design that provides optimum viewing of deck activities and performances occurring on the adjacent stage. Located aft on the Lido Deck, the Sun and Sea pool features a Sky Dome, a retractable cover that can enclose the area and enable deck activities and entertainment to continue even in rainy weather. The pool area also includes a swim-up bar and two whirlpools.

In addition, *Destiny* has even more generous health and fitness facilities than the other "Fun Ships," including a two-deck-high, 15,000-square-foot Nautica Spa health and fitness center. There's even a bar dispensing fresh juice.

Children are especially catered to, with a two-deck-high, 1,300-square-foot indoor and outdoor play center, with its own pool. The inevitable game center has all the latest electronic gadgets.

PUBLIC AREAS Carnival interior designer Joe Farcus never had so much public space to play with, and he took full advantage. The ship is dominated by a staggering nine-deck atrium, and the three-deck-high showroom is the first of this magnitude on any cruise ship. It's the home of Carnival's trademark show-stopping Las Vegas–style productions, except now the chorus girls and boys have more room to strut their stuff. The ship also houses a casino whose size is unparalleled at sea, spanning some 9,000 square feet and featuring 324 slot machines and 23 table games. In addition, the Virtual World game center features high-tech virtual reality and other electronic games. A photography studio enables passengers to make appointments for portrait taking.

There's a large number of boutiques, along with a beauty salon/barber, and a drugstore.

Ecstasy • Fantasy • Fascination • Imagination • Inspiration • Sensation

⚓ ⚓ ⚓ ⚓

Specifications

Size (in tons)	70,367	Passenger/Crew Ratio	2.9 to 1
Number of Cabins	1,020–1,022	Year Built	1990 (*Fantasy*)
Number of Outside	620		1991 (*Ecstasy*)
Cabins			1993 (*Sensation*)
			1994 (*Fascination*)
Number of Passengers	2,040–2,044		1995 (*Imagination*)
Officers	Italian		1996 (*Inspiration*)
Crew	920 (International)	Last Major Refurbishment	n/a

Frommer's Ratings (Scale of 1–10)

Activities	8.0	Public Areas	8.5
Cabins	7.8	Public Comfort/Space	8.2
Cleanliness/Maintenance	9.0	Recreational Facilities/Pool	8.2
Entertainment	8.8	Service	7.2
Food & Beverage	6.8	Ship Crew/Officers	8.0
Interior Decor	8.5	Shore Excursions	6.5
Ports of Call	7.5	Worth the Money	8.2
		Overall Average	**7.9**

With names that vaguely reflect each ship's interior decor theme—and about which passengers are fond of making risqué remarks—these Fun Ships offer acres of teak decking plus all the diversions, distractions, and entertainment options for which Carnival is famous.

Billed as ships for the 21st century, each was built at a cost in excess of $225 million at the Kvaerner Masa shipyard in Helsinki, Finland, between 1990 and 1996. Each is identical in size (70,367 tons), profile, and onboard amenities, but it's the individualized application of Carnival-style colors, decors, wall hangings, artwork, and themes that sets them apart. The line's legendary designer, Joe Farcus, is responsible for each ship's unique personality.

The decor of the *Fantasy,* with a geometric, urban-metropolis kind of feel, is a tiny bit ragged and tired. Nevertheless, it has all the electric colors you expect from the line, and a full 15 miles of neon tubes to boot, so there's no mistaking that it's a Carnival cruise you're on, with all the lightheartedness and exuberance that entails.

Newest of the megaship sextet is the *Imagination,* where miles of fiber-optic cable make the mythical and classical artwork glow in ways the original Greek, Roman, and Assyrian designers never imagined. Medusas and winged Mercuries adorn the public areas, and the eclectic library contains copies of the columns Bernini added to St. Peter's Basilica in Rome. Although the ship has miles and miles of neon, it's more muted here, the feeling more elegant.

For its inspiration, *Inspiration* turns to styles exemplified by such artists and artisans as Toulouse-Lautrec, Fabergé, Frank Lloyd Wright, and Tiffany. The most striking part of this design is in the Brasserie Café, with its twisting tubes of lavender-colored aluminum illuminated by backlit stained glass and neon. Designer Joe Farcus saw these tubes as a fanciful interpretation of the flowers and vines adorning Métro stops in Paris. Another Carnival-like touch is the guitar-shaped rock 'n' roll dance club where closed-circuit TV cameras broadcast the dance floor antics to dozens of color monitors around the room.

The *Ecstasy* is a happy if somewhat subdued vessel—more subdued at least than the *Celebration,* where the colors and glitter are so loud they almost *hum.* The *Fascination* borrows heavily from Broadway and Hollywood movie-star legends, while the *Sensation* is the most subtle of the six ships, avoiding an obvious razzle-dazzle in favor of artwork enhanced with ultraviolet lighting, sound, and color to personify its theme: sensation. Even some of the surfaces in bars were selected to celebrate textures and the sense of touch. The ship contains rooms in which stately Ionic columns are disconcertingly arranged in very nontraditional patterns.

Since all these ships are so much alike, passengers are bewildered as to which one to select. Here are some guidelines:

- If it's your first cruise, or at least your first cruise on Carnival, let the itinerary of each megaship determine your choice. Also, find out the number of days spent at sea, as compared with days spent visiting ports of call.

- If you're already a dedicated Carnival fan, then rotate your choice of vessels. That way, you'll experience the latest design and any new pizzazz that might have popped out of Joe Farcus's imagination.

- A final suggestion, since all the ships are so similar, is to opt for the one offering the most appealing price at the time you plan to sail. Of course, this will have nothing to do with the decor and everything to do with how quickly cabins are selling on any particular cruise.

Cabins & Rates

Cabins	Average per diem	Bathtub	Fridge	Phone	Sitting Area	TV
Inside	$177–$198	No	No	Yes	No	Yes
Outside	$200–$220	No	Yes	Yes	Yes	Yes
Suite	$300–$310	Half	Yes	Yes	Yes	Yes

CABINS Each of the six vessels contains cabins whose configurations are neat, tidy, and almost utterly lacking in personality—pretty and comfortable, but definitely meant for sleeping and not as a daytime retreat. Who wants to hibernate anyway? There's too much happening on deck for that.

Each of the ships within the Fantasy-Class category contains 11 different cabin categories, as opposed to 12 available aboard the newer and larger Destiny-Class vessels. Accommodations range from an inside cabin far below the waterline with lower and upper berths, to large suites with verandas, king-size beds, and balconies. There are 26 demisuites and 28 suites with verandas on board, priced attractively considering the additional floor space and open-air views.

In contrast to the flamboyance prevalent in the public areas, cabins are decorated in a subdued fashion, with stained oak trim accents and conventional, usually monochromatic colors. They are efficiently designed, carpeted, and well upholstered with durable fabrics whose coordinated colors extend over both the floors and walls. They contain more space than you'd expect, a generous 185 square feet in the standard cabins. Even the least expensive have enough storage space to accommodate a reasonably diverse wardrobe, as well as safes for your valuables and TVs that broadcast an almost continuous

assortment of films. Bathrooms offer showers; suites also have tubs with whirlpool jets. The most expensive suites reward whoever can afford them with positions midway between stern and bow, on a middle deck subject to the least tossing and rocking during rough weather.

Some accommodations are wheelchair friendly, but there are no cabins outfitted with all the handrails and ramps required by a passenger with disabilities. Of course, as on all ships, a person with a disability should be accompanied by an able-bodied friend or companion.

RECREATION & FITNESS FACILITIES
Each ship contains saunas and steam rooms (segregated by gender), whirlpools, and three swimming pools.

Each Carnival vessel also contains a battery of high-tech workout equipment housed in enormous fitness centers. Most guests consider these the equivalent (or better) of the facilities they've been using (or avoiding) on shore. More than half of all passengers aboard any Carnival ship spend at least one session sweating and grunting, and many make a daily visit to the gym. The Sun Deck of each ship offers an unobstructed, $1/8$-mile jogging track covered with a rubberized surface.

On the *Ecstasy* and *Sensation,* electronic body composition analysis is available, a process in which electrodes are connected to various parts of the body to digitally measure fat, water, sodium, and muscle composition in proportion to height, weight, and age. Data are then fed into a computer and analyzed by resident experts to create a tailor-made exercise, nutrition, and fitness regimen for each participant. For the technologically squeamish, equivalent results can be derived by a staff member using such low-tech devices as a weight chart, scales, and calipers.

Nautica Spas are found aboard all Carnival ships, but none are better than the 12,000-square-foot spas on *Ecstasy, Fantasy, Fascination, Imagination,* and *Sensation.* Each spa features numerous exotic treatments, including one where you lie in an oval-shaped chamber while soothing aromas, sounds, and synchronized lighting surround you to induce a mood of total relaxation.

Use of Carnival's exercise equipment, sauna, and steam rooms is included in the price of your cruise contract, but many supplemental treatments (massage, aromatherapy, skin or hair treatments) carry a sometimes hefty additional charge.

PUBLIC AREAS   Each megaship in the Fantasy-Class category boasts the same configuration of decks, public lounges, hideaway cubbyholes, and entertainment venues. Each ship contains a four-story atrium flanked by glass-sided elevators, plus two big-windowed dining rooms and all the options you could want for drinking, dancing, flirting, and hot-tubbing. The line's casinos are the largest afloat, each with a different decorative theme and touches of green that suspiciously resembles U.S. currency. Each vessel contains at least 10 bars, many designed as "mood-specific," where you might allow your emotions to go with a flow that ranges from convivial and sometimes slightly manic to subdued, soothing, reflective, and contemplative. And there are enough Jacuzzi whirlpools scattered over the decks to allow virtually everyone on board to languish amid bubbling suds with a group of friends or acquaintances.

Celebrity Cruises

SHIPS   Century • Galaxy • Horizon • Zenith • Mercury (Preview)
5201 Blue Lagoon Dr., Miami, FL 33126. ☎ 800/437-3111 or 305/262-8322; fax 800/437-5111.

In 1915, cargo ships had to dodge German U-boats to get their goods to a safe port, and while this wouldn't seem the best time to launch a new cargo-shipping line, that's exactly what John D. Chandris did. He succeeded, too, although he never attained the legendary status of those titans of the sea, Stavros Niarchos and Aristotle Onassis.

In 1989, Celebrity Cruises spurted into life from its origins as this Mediterranean-based cargo venture, which also operates the down-market Fantasy Cruises. Bold and brash, and spending buckets of money, it rapidly inserted its cost-conscious cruises firmly into the middle-to-upscale bracket of the Caribbean cruise industry. Its allure was based on good value, great cuisine, and a Europeanized motif that was low-key and stylish instead of vulgar and ostentatious.

Since its debut, initial glitches and embarrassments have been ironed out, and the company's image has been defined and standardized among its growing armada of ships. It's developed into a wiser, more confident, and vastly more experienced cruise line that's weathered the storms and uncertainties of rapid growth in an emerging industry. Today, with five ships that are among the newest in the industry, and another, bigger-than-ever vessel (*Mercury*) being built, the line seems poised to thrive as we enter the 21st century.

When Chandris launched Celebrity Cruises, it retired its older ships, part of the mass-market Fantasy fleet, to the Mediterranean and replaced them with fresh new liners sporting a snappy new logo and corporate colors of red, white, and navy blue. All of the ships are spacious and comfortable, and retain the kind of old-fashioned, glamorous style that's associated with ocean cruising. It's the

kind you see on the late show in *Gentlemen Prefer Blondes* or *An Affair to Remember,* albeit with sleek new designs and a fresh, modern look.

The *Horizon* and *Zenith* (46,811 and 47,255 tons, respectively) are virtual twins. If you like variety in your cruising, don't sail on both of them, as you'll experience déjà vu.

The *Century,* launched with enormous fanfare late in 1995, and the *Galaxy,* inaugurated late in 1996, are the latest in the Celebrity fleet. Both are designed with the same crisp attention to detail and the same decorative panache as the *Horizon* and *Zenith,* only in a larger format. The company's newest and largest vessel, the *Mercury,* will take its maiden voyage from Port Everglades to the western Caribbean in early November 1997.

The 1963-vintage *Meridian* was always the odd-ship-out in the Celebrity fleet—which may explain why the line recently decided to sell it off. At press time, the ship was scheduled for an October 1997 delivery to its new owners, Metro Holdings of Singapore. If you're reading this in August or September there may be a slim chance of getting aboard, but we wouldn't bet on it—that's why we've decided not to profile the ship in this edition.

In a nutshell, Celebrity lives up to its promotion and advertising, especially in its cabins, service, and cuisine that's quite exceptional for a cruise line. In general, the line forgoes the hysterical pitch of organized activities offered by some of its competitors, notably Carnival. Activities tend to be low-key, and its summer children's programs are among the finest of any upscale cruise line.

PROS & CONS   Celebrity vessels attract people who prefer to pursue their R&R at a more relaxed pace, with a minimum of aggressively promoted group activities blared over the intercom. Entertainment, however, is strong, and some of the line's lavish shows are the best on the winter Caribbean seas, competing with those of Carnival.

Celebrity ships aren't for the serious partier, so singles and young couples might look elsewhere in planning their cruising adventure. A young couple on their winter honeymoon might find their fellow diners relate more to *I Love Lucy* and Rock Hudson than to *Seinfeld* and Antonio Sabato Jr.

One of Celebrity's biggest selling points is its cuisine. Unlike many cruise lines, where quantity is more important than quality, Celebrity actually gives some thought to the food served aboard its vessels. Of course, like the other lines, it puts on lavish, all-you-can-eat buffets, but it believes that potato salad needs more flavor than mayonnaise, and bottled seafood dressing doesn't do the job with a shrimp cocktail. Consequently, the line has poured time and money into researching and standardizing a culinary format that's meticulously repeated throughout its ships' galleys and service areas, and enables them to provide well-orchestrated, well-presented, and good-tasting meals to thousands of seagoing diners at the same sitting. For more on this, refer to "Dining," below.

Even with its long background in sailing, Celebrity Cruises can and did run into trouble. In 1994, there was an outbreak of Legionnaire's disease on the *Horizon*. In a lightning-strikes-twice mode, that same vessel was again afflicted with misfortune in 1995, when 299 cases of salmonella poisoning were reported during a July cruise to Bermuda. Both disasters made headlines, which led to some canceled bookings, a flurry of press speculation, and endless amounts of nervous hysteria for company insiders. However, bookings on Celebrity ships, even aboard the *Horizon,* remain high, the ship has received a clean bill of health, and no similar outbreaks have been reported aboard any other Celebrity vessel.

TYPES OF PASSENGERS   Celebrity vessels attract those who like to order wine with dinner instead of beer. The line focuses on middle- to upper-middle-income cruisers, although a handful of discreetly wealthy patrons might be on any given cruise or, conversely, a recent lottery winner. Most of the clientele give the impression of being prosperous but not obscenely rich, well behaved but not necessarily obsessed with the nuances of international protocol.

The clientele attracted to the line, especially on the winter Caribbean sailings, tends to be the graying, definitely past-45 set, three-quarters of whom live on the East Coast. A few honeymooners and many first-time cruisers show up to add a fresh note, but fully half the passengers have sailed before, enjoying their seasoned status as older, calmer, dignified cruisers. They're more likely to be seen reading a book authored by Newt Gingrich or Colin Powell than a biography of Curt Cobain, Michael Jackson, or Madonna.

Today's version of the swinging singles or swinging couples of the 1960s would not be at home here. Any shipboard romance might be far more discreet and less obvious, like Paul Henreid wooing Bette Davis in that favorite of the late, late show, *Now Voyager.*

DINING   Celebrity searched far and wide for a famous master chef/figurehead to define the culinary ambitions of its floating restaurants. The winner was Michel Roux, who gained culinary fame at Le Gavroche, one of London's best restaurants, and at the Waterside Inn, bordering the Thames at Bray, Berkshire, where the queen dines on occasion.

Critics doubted if Monsieur Roux's culinary endeavors could be imported into large-scale oceangoing galleys, where chefs must feed 800 or more diners a night at each of two seatings. Under such conditions, even a chef such as Roux can be stymied in the quest for gastronomic perfection. However, Roux has largely been able to satisfy Celebrity's desire for excellent cuisine by creating a series of first-class menus that can be prepared on board with ingredients slightly less fresh than those found on land. The food is plentiful, flavorful, and presented with style. If there's ever a murmur of discontent, it involves a deliberate down-scaling of peppery seasonings and strong flavors out of respect to the milder palates of older and more conservative cruisers. To compensate, waiters will sometimes ask diners the degree of spiciness preferred in a particular dish.

Culinary techniques have been perfected by kitchen staffs, who sometimes look askance at special requests such as, "Myrtle and I would like beef Wellington tonight." You can make a request like that in the deluxe dining room on the *QE2*, but on a Celebrity vessel, you might hit some resistance.

Meals are served five times a day, and dishes aren't concealed beneath gobs of decoration. A day's menu is likely to feature that 1950s favorite of Onassis: tournedos Rossini with foie gras and Madeira sauce. To balance such heartiness, an alternative, lighter dish such as veal scaloppini with lemon juice will be offered. In addition, all Celebrity dining rooms feature a rotating array of vegetarian dishes at both lunch and dinner, as well as one of the most extensive 24-hour in-cabin dining menus in the industry. Kosher and salt-free meals can be provided with some advance notice.

A recent innovation, in a line that manages to market its food more stylishly (and aggressively) than virtually any other afloat, is a late-night culinary soiree known as "Gourmet Bites," where a series of upscale hors d'oeuvres are served, buffet-style, between midnight and 1am on every oceangoing night.

Le Gavroche may have a wine list as exclusively French as the Eiffel Tower, but when chef Roux moved to Celebrity he branched out to vintages of a far wider scope and price range. Roux takes about three cruises a year on Celebrity ships, showing up undercover to check on the quality of the cuisine, which he revises and updates twice a year.

Dinner is served at two assigned seatings, one at 6:15pm and "dinner at eight," which attracts a younger crowd (if there's one aboard). Each seven-night cruise includes two formal evenings as well.

ACTIVITIES   A variety of different activities are presented aboard Celebrity vessels, although many clients prefer to remain firmly anchored in their deck chairs, enjoying a cup of bouillon and the seascape. In this regard you won't confuse a Celebrity cruise with Club Med, where overly enthusiastic *gentiles organisateurs* (social directors) urge you to participate in group activities, often with embarrassing results.

Activities during days at sea are fairly standardized on all ships. A typical morning might offer such amusement as bridge, darts, a culinary art demonstration, a trap-shooting competition, and a sports trivia game, followed by a basketball tournament. The afternoon might begin with a movie, a fitness fashion show, a fine art auction, "horse racing" shipboard style, a tour of one of the cabaret dancers' backstage dressing rooms, or a volleyball tournament.

CHILDREN'S ACTIVITIES   Celebrity is not a line that aggressively cultivates children as a vital part of its revenue base, but be warned that the line welcomes families at midsummer, especially between mid-June and early September. At that time, each Celebrity ship employs eight full-time counselors, mostly from the United Kingdom, Canada, and the United States, whose job it is to direct and supervise a camp-style children's program.

Activities are geared toward three different age groups. Kids ages three to six are dubbed "Ship Mates." They have their own clubhouse aboard Celebrity ships, where they can enjoy clown parties, summer stock theater presentations, movies, and ice-cream-sundae-making parties throughout the entire (eight-hour) day. "Cadets," ages 7 to 10, are awarded greater amounts of freedom, are less constantly supervised, and are kept amused by relay races, T-shirt painting, magic lessons, treasure hunts, a junior Olympics, and Nintendo. In any other circumstances, your 11-to-13-year-old might rebel against being labeled an "Ensign," but here they might find the appellation cool, and even the teenagers (age 14 to 17) think the program's infusion of nautical jargon is appropriate and fun. Activities include film festivals, reggae and Jacuzzi parties, dating games, dance parties, midnight film festivals, and lots and lots of karaoke.

Most of the youth programs on board are conducted within specially designated quarters that are, to many older passengers' relief, isolated from most of the ship's adult activities.

Baby-sitting on all vessels is available both day and night, and is sometimes offered at ports of call. In the playrooms, a group baby-sitting and pajama party is conducted from 9:45pm to 1am for children of all ages. Private sitters can be arranged by a cabin steward.

ENTERTAINMENT Although entertainment is not generally cited as a reason to sail on a Celebrity ship, the line does offer shows that have been praised for their innovation, sense of fun, and charisma. You won't find any big-name entertainers on the program, but at the same time you won't find any castoffs or obvious has-beens on their way down from the Atlantic City circuit either. What you will find is a lot of Broadway material, presented by hardworking professionals in a program that is, in a way so often encountered at sea, long on glitz and glitter and a bit short on plot and characterization. But then, who expects Ibsen on a cruise, anyway?

Shows are well conceived aboard all the line's ships, with some 4¹/₂ acres of interior or deck space devoted to the pursuit of pleasure, diversion, or entertainment. The theaters are big enough to accommodate Broadway-style productions, and include such features as telescoping walls, revolving stages, and a hydraulic orchestra pit. Showrooms aboard all Celebrity ships have excellent acoustics and sight lines

praised as some of the most panoramic and unobstructed at sea.

When you tire of Broadway-style entertainment, you'll find all the ships have cozy lounges and piano bars where you can retreat for a romantic nightcap. In these more intimate lounges, the music of choice is often laid-back jazz or music from the big band era. Each ship has a disco, usually open until 3am. Because Celebrity often attracts older passengers, many have either gone to bed or are only a couple of hours from getting up when the disco action ends. Karaoke and game rooms are aboard all ships.

Each ship has a casino, but they're rather low-key, except for the casinos aboard the *Century* and the *Galaxy*. If you're a serious gambler, you may prefer a Carnival ship.

One aspect of its cruises that Celebrity never tires of publicizing is its cooperative development, with the Sony Corporation of America, of a series of interactive video and audio systems that enhance the quality of the electronic entertainment and lighting on board. The prototypes for these systems were initially installed aboard the *Century*, with the intention of having the other ships retrofitted with the newfangled gadgetry. Frankly, this electronic wizardry is an aspect of its cruises that Celebrity tends to oversell. Most passengers seem merely to make a mental note of it all and then resume their preoccupation with other, less complicated aspects of their cruise experience. Of greater merit is the brace of Sony-sponsored personal computers available for test use by passengers, installed with the hope of exposing the cruise-going public to Sony's roster of electronic tools and toys.

SHOPPING Shopping is best aboard *Century* and *Galaxy,* which offer one of the largest areas devoted to retail shopping of any cruise ship afloat. *Horizon* and *Zenith* are not far behind.

To compete with shops at ports of call, Celebrity introduces occasional sales of unusual and constantly changing merchandise, announced in newsletters distributed on board. Its duty-free prices rival those ashore, and you shop in much more comfort, of course. Sale merchandise might include designer watches for $69.95 (admittedly not the finest), or French crystal at a 50% markdown. Art auctions are sometimes staged.

SERVICE   Celebrity allows passengers to indulge their sense of romance and desire for pampering by offering breakfast in bed, candlelight dinners, and formal white-gloved service in any of the line's main dining rooms.

Service spins about the way it should, although we've noted such bugaboos as relaxed (read slow) service at the onboard bars and a sometimes lethargic feeling at the casinos. In all fairness much of the blame for the latter will derive from the passengers themselves: If there aren't enough serious gamblers on board, the casino can be a dead zone.

These minor criticisms are more than offset by the polite, attentive, and cheerful service one receives in the dining rooms. In the cabins, service is efficient, but so discreet and unobtrusive you might never see your steward except at the beginning and end of your cruise. English is obviously a second language for many staff members, but their proficiency is such that this shouldn't cause a problem. Tips are accepted.

Five-star service can be had at the onboard beauty parlor or barber shop. The line is known for employing some of the most skilled beauticians afloat. Also, massages can be scheduled at any hour of the day, and laundry, dry cleaning, and valet services are fast and accurate. Shutterbugs desperate to see the results of their labor can get their film developed at the onboard lab.

Medical services are available to all passengers, and each ship has a doctor and nurse on board. A small pharmacy sells prescription drugs, but despite this service, you should take along any medication you might need.

If you occupy a suite on any of Celebrity's 7-, 10- or 11-night Caribbean cruises, you'll get a personal butler to handle your laundry, shine your shoes, make sewing repairs, deliver mail and messages, and serve complimentary hors d'oeuvres from 6 to 8pm. Your butler will even organize a small cocktail party for you and your newfound cruising friends.

ITINERARIES

Century—Celebrity aims to keep *Century*, one of its finest and newest ships, in the Caribbean throughout the year, departing and arriving from Fort Lauderdale and alternating visits to the western and eastern Caribbean at weekly intervals. Its eastern Caribbean route includes stopovers at San Juan, St. Thomas, Dutch St. Maarten, and Nassau, while its western Caribbean route takes in Ocho Rios, Grand Cayman, Cozumel, and Key West.

Galaxy—Unlike its older sibling, described above, *Galaxy* spends winters in the Caribbean and summers in Alaska, with interim cruises spent traversing the Panama Canal. Between October and April, San Juan is its home port, and tours depart every Saturday for Catalina Island (a beach island off the southeast coast of the Dominican Republic), Barbados, Martinique, Antigua, and St. Thomas. Repositioning tours that take the ship through the Panama Canal usually last from 15 to 17 days and stop at Caribbean and Pacific ports en route between Fort Lauderdale and Los Angeles.

Horizon—Between late October and mid-April, *Horizon* makes 10- or 11-day jaunts that depart from Fort Lauderdale and include visits to St. Maarten or Curaçao, St. Lucia or Grenada, Antigua or LaGuaira, and Martinique or Antigua, depending on the week of your journey. Regardless of the week you select, midwinter cruises usually stop at both Barbados and St. Thomas. For summer 1998, *Horizon* will be making weekly Sunday sailings to Bermuda from New York and other East Coast cities.

Zenith—Most of its 1998 cruises last between 10 and 17 nights and include such Caribbean ports as St. Thomas, Curaçao,

Cozumel, Grand Cayman, and Aruba. These are visited as part of a transit from such points as New York, San Juan, or Fort Lauderdale, en route through the Panama Canal to such Pacific ports as Acapulco, Cabo San Lucas, and Los Angeles.

SPECIAL DISCOUNTS The early bird gets the discount, so book as early as possible. A 14-day nonrepeating itinerary is offered at a discount, and a third or fourth passenger sharing a cabin with two others pays $125 per day. Children 2 to 12 traveling with and occupying the cabin of two full-fare adults are charged from $60 to $100 per day. Special single-parent discounts are offered, although not during

peak periods at Christmas and during January and February. Look for a deal, especially in the "shoulder" months of April and October. Except for port charges, which are mandated by law for all passengers, children under two sail free on most Celebrity cruises.

SINGLE SUPPLEMENTS A single passenger pays 150% to 200% of the going rate.

PORT CHARGES Subject to change, port taxes total $119.50 to $125 for most of the line's seven-night Caribbean cruises, $155 for an 11-day Caribbean cruise, and $225 for one of its 17-day Panama Canal transits.

Century • Galaxy

⇓ ⇓ ⇓ ⇓ ⇓

Specifications

Size (in tons)	70,000/77,713	Crew	853/909 (International)
Number of Cabins	875/935	Passenger/Crew Ratio	2 to 1
Number of Outside Cabins	569/639	Year Built	1995/1996
Number of Passengers	1,750/1,870	Last Major Refurbishment	n/a
Officers	Greek		

Frommer's Ratings (Scale of 1–10)

Activities	7.6	Public Areas	9.2
Cabins	8.8	Public Comfort/Space	9.2
Cleanliness/Maintenance	8.6	Recreational Facilities/Pool	8.8
Entertainment	8.0	Service	9.0
Food & Beverage	9.0	Ship Crew/Officers	8.2
Interior Decor	8.0	Shore Excursions	7.0
Ports of Call	8.0	Worth the Money	9.0
		Overall Average	**8.5**

When it was launched in December 1995, the $320 million *Century* received some of the most widespread publicity of any ship in the Celebrity fleet. This was partly a function of the way it symbolized Celebrity's entry into the megaship class of cruise operator and partly because it was, quite simply, a particularly well

conceived and beautiful ship. Until it was surpassed in December 1996 by a younger and larger sibling (*Galaxy*, weighing in at 77,713 tons), it was the largest ship ever built by its operators, with 48% more space than its next-largest sibling. Despite the fact that the newer *Galaxy* has slight variations in the number of staterooms, plus about 7,000 additional tons of displacement value, the two vessels are considered by the engineers at Celebrity as twin ships, with a deliberate similarity of decor, floor plan, amenities, and interior design.

The exteriors of both ships have a design that will probably remain in style for many years. The designer of the *Century*, from which the *Galaxy* was eventually modeled, was John Bannenberg, who earned initial acclaim with his plans for graceful, medium-scale yachts. Both *Century* and *Galaxy* are colossal by the standards of a decade ago, yet neither attains the megabulk of some of the new 100,000-ton behemoths run by and on the drawing boards of such competing lines as Carnival, Disney, and Royal Caribbean Cruises, Ltd. In the minds of its designers and operators, that's a good thing, untested as such supergiants are within the hurly-burly of the Caribbean cruise market.

Painted in dazzling contrast of bright white with patches of dark color, both vessels manage to be simultaneously bulky and streamlined-looking, with abrupt endings at their sterns and rakishly angled bows designed for speed and grace. A half-dozen firms based in London, Athens, Las Vegas, and New York collaborated on different aspects of these ships' interior decor. Because the *Century* was the prototype for Celebrity's planned trio of equivalent vessels (along with the *Galaxy* and *Mercury*), enormous amounts of time and effort went into its design. Each of the newer ships will repeat its carefully conceived decorative and entertainment-related themes.

The centerpieces of both *Century* and *Galaxy* are twin atria—soaring, three- and four-story nerve centers with serpentine staircases that seem to float without supports. Domed ceilings of painted glass illuminate the settings, with deliberate lighting changes throughout the day that simulate streaming sunlight, the glow of dawn, or moonlight.

Greater amounts of electronically sophisticated meeting space are available aboard the *Century* and *Galaxy* than on any of the other Celebrity vessels, a by-product of the line's collaboration with Sony of America. The ships could conceivably connect a multilingual onboard sales meeting with an audiovisual presentation at any corporate setting in the world, although few corporations have yet taken advantage of such services. The electronic finesse aboard *Century* is carried even further aboard *Galaxy*, where features include a special interactive voting system that enables audiences to be polled for their opinions, tastes, and preferences, with the results displayed on a projector screen after the poll is completed.

Both ships contain impressive artworks that sometimes greet you at unexpected moments and in otherwise not particularly noteworthy sections of each ship. They include works by such artists as Robert Rauschenberg, Jasper Johns, David Hockney, Pablo Picasso, Andy Warhol, and Helen Frankenthaler. For the *Galaxy* alone, Celebrity spent $3.5 million on works by emerging contemporary artists.

Cabins & Rates						
Cabins	Average per diem	Bathtub	Fridge	Phone	Sitting Area	TV
Inside	$278	No	Yes	Yes	No	Yes
Outside	$335	No	Yes	Yes	No	Yes
Suite	$475	Yes	Yes	Yes	Yes	Yes

CABINS   If the vast size of these ships unnerves you, you can find privacy, solace, and comfortable living space within the cabins, which are larger than those aboard either the *Horizon* or *Zenith*. Although inside cabins are about par for the industry standard, outside cabins are larger than usual, and suites (which come in five different categories) are particularly spacious. Some, such as the Penthouse Suites aboard the *Galaxy*, offer more living space (1,219 square feet, expandable to 1,433 square feet on special request) than you find in many private homes, and the *Galaxy*'s Sky Suites offer verandas that, with 179 square feet, are among the biggest aboard any ship.

Cabins aboard each of the decks are outfitted in a different color scheme, which permeates the entire deck. Regardless of their theme and which of the ships they're on, they're usually accented with rosewood trim and outfitted with built-in vanities, minibars, hair dryers, radios, and safes. Closets and drawer space are among the roomiest of any vessel within the Celebrity fleet, and all standard cabins have twin beds convertible to doubles. Bathrooms are roomy, stylish, and subtly distinctive because of their European inspiration and theme.

If you want to save money aboard either vessel, book an inside cabin, which won't be cramped or particularly inconvenient. Although the official brochure rate notes the price difference between equivalent inside and outside cabins as only about $25 per person per day, you can sometimes save as much as $100 per person per day by tapping into one of the line's special promotions, which come and go according to seasonal demand. The only drawback will be a lack of natural daylight within your cabin (which can be a boon to late sleepers), and the fact that you'll have to view seascapes from the public rooms instead of from the privacy of your cabin. Other than that, since there's practically no difference between the appointments and size of inside versus outside cabins, booking an inside cabin is often worth considering, especially if you don't plan to spend much time there. Unlike the situation on many cruise ships, such as Norwegian's dowager *Norway,* there are no really "bad" cabins aboard either the *Century* or the *Galaxy.*

As mentioned above, both *Century* and *Galaxy* have more electronic extras hardwired into their cabins than many competing ships afloat. Although computer neophytes might be confused by the array of cabin options, they're all there if you need, want, or understand them, including access to 14 TV channels, electronic versions of daily activities information, and videotaped previews of shore excursions. You can even order room service from on-screen menus, select the evening's wine in advance of dinner, or browse in "virtual" shops for a wide selection of merchandise for delivery directly to your home at the end of your cruise. From the privacy of your cabin, presumably in any state of undress or dishabille you prefer, you can even play casino-style games for "real money." Debits and credits for the games will be charged or credited directly to your shipboard account. Eight of the cabins aboard each ship (one inside and seven outside) were specifically designed for passengers with disabilities.

Suites aboard both vessels are particularly spacious and opulent, with walk-in closets big enough to house the fashion accessories of any traveling princess. Some suites are among the industry's largest, at 1,500 square feet. Decor is both conservative and contemporary, rife with the rich textures of varnished panels, plush fabrics, and touches of marble. Suite bathrooms have *lots* of marble and contain bathtubs fitted with whirlpools. Full-size windows open onto private verandas.

RECREATION & FITNESS FACILITIES
Decks aboard both vessels feature a pair of good-size swimming areas with cylindrical waterfalls flanked by a bridge and rimmed with teak benches for sunning and relaxation. Even when the ships are full, these areas don't seem particularly crowded.

Both vessels contain AquaSpa Health Clubs, whose motifs and layouts were inspired by a Japanese garden and bathhouse and whose services include hairdressing, pedicures, manicures, and massage. Also available are health and beauty treatments such as Thalassotherapy (where water jets massage different parts of the body), mud packs, and herbal steam baths. Generously sized gyms aboard both vessels are filled with computerized, high-tech workout equipment that, if programmed properly, tells you exactly how many of last night's tequila sunrises you've burned off. There are also aerobic classes, saunas, steam rooms, free weights, and "virtual bikes" where a natural woodland bike path is projected onto a screen ahead of you, and passes as you pedal. Both ships also contain a jogging track, a golf simulator, and one deck that's specifically designed for sports.

PUBLIC AREAS   In constructing the *Century* and *Galaxy,* Celebrity examined its competition's vessels and corrected some perceived flaws, such as the inadequate amount of open deck space aboard some Princess ships. Both *Century* and *Galaxy* boast lots of deck space, providing access to the wide skies plus quiet retreats when you want to be secluded but don't want to be confined in your cabin. The large size of both ships is matched by the number of food and beverage outlets aboard, more than on any other ship in the line.

Aboard both ships, breakfast is served from a vast buffet that manages to accommodate everyone's preferred waking hour. Lunch is presented on both ships in both formal and informal venues. Aboard the *Century,* sit-down luncheon service, with wait staff, is provided in the Grand Restaurant; aboard *Galaxy,* it's in the Orion Restaurant. The main dining rooms aboard each ship are decorated with subdued colors and vaguely art deco stylings based on the great age of transatlantic liners.

Persons not interested in the affable formality of a sit-down lunch aboard either ship can head for either of two other venues, one of which focuses on buffets and the other of which features grilled and/or barbecued meats and fish, as well as salads, sandwiches, and party-colored drinks. Tea, both hot and iced, is offered in even the most formal of venues, and getting a drink at any of the many watering holes scattered at strategic points around the ships is almost never a problem. At night, the formal dining rooms aboard both ships

are elevated to their full glory, filled with the noises of satisfied diners consuming good food served by competent wait staff.

Aboard the *Galaxy,* a retractable "magrodome" covers one of the swimming pools with a sliding glass cupola during inclement weather. Aboard both vessels, the more aft of the two atria opens onto a bar, one of the restaurants, a champagne bar, and the ship's casino. Each vessel boasts a mostly male enclave, Michael's Club, that's decorated like the parlor of a London men's club and devoted to the pleasures of fine cigars, fine cognacs, and stiff drinks. If you're a dedicated nonsmoker, don't even think of spending significant time there. Otherwise, puff away at some of the best cigars this side of Havana. For those who don't find that ambience appealing, Tastings Coffee Bar offers an alternative, with every kind of specialized, upscale caffeine you can imagine.

Both vessels contain two-deck theaters that have unobstructed views from every seat and scads of state-of-the-art equipment. Each boasts a cantilevered orchestra pit, and a wall devoted to video screens whose images enhance and complement the activities taking place on the stage below. Libraries aboard both ships are comfortable, but not as big or well stocked as they could be. The onboard casinos are the most comprehensive and largest aboard any Celebrity ships, offering blackjack, roulette, craps, and slots, and for those who care to try their hand at a hand, there always seem to be extra tables available in the card room.

You'll never have to search very hard for a place to get a drink on board either ship. In addition to many other venues, both vessels feature a high-tech video bar (Images) where great sporting events of the past are flashed on screen in sometimes bewildering juxtaposition. Various other bars, both indoor and outdoor, are tucked into nooks and crannies throughout the ship. Other onboard venues include a wind-sheltered Lido Deck where ocean breezes won't detract from your sunbathing.

Horizon

♇ ♇ ♇ ♇ ♇

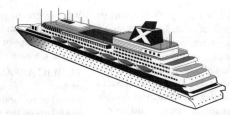

Specifications

Size (in tons)	46,811	Crew	645 (International)
Number of Cabins	677	Passenger/Crew Ratio	2.1 to 1
Number of Outside Cabins	542	Year Built	1991
Number of Passengers	1,354	Last Major Refurbishment	n/a
Officers	Greek		

Frommer's Ratings (Scale of 1–10)

Activities	7.5	Public Areas	9.0
Cabins	8.5	Public Comfort/Space	9.0
Cleanliness/Maintenance	8.5	Recreational Facilities/Pool	8.5
Entertainment	8.0	Service	9.0
Food & Beverage	9.0	Ship Crew/Officers	8.0
Interior Decor	8.0	Shore Excursions	7.0
Ports of Call	8.0	Worth the Money	9.0
		Overall Average	**8.4**

With its rakishly angled funnel and masts and its perpendicular (rather than angled) lines, *Horizon*'s profile ranks as one of the industry's most distinctive. Especially striking is the design of its rear decks, tiered in dramatically rising increments upward and forward, like the terraces in a formal garden. Many aspects of its design are identical to those of its slightly younger twin, the *Zenith*.

Even at peak capacity, *Horizon*'s well-designed passageways, hallways, seating arrangements, and traffic patterns create the feeling of more space than a ship of this size would ordinarily provide. Service in the dining room is excellent, and even the most jaded cruise-ship passengers are impressed with the variety and upscale presentation of the food, especially during buffets.

Cabins & Rates

Cabins	Average per diem	Bathtub	Fridge	Phone	Sitting Area	TV
Inside	$278	No	No	Yes	No	Yes
Outside	$335	No	No	Yes	No	Yes
Suite	$458	Yes	Yes	Yes	Yes	Yes

CABINS   Each of the accommodations bears a striking cookie-cutter similarity, but what you get isn't bad. A team of talented designers saw to that, combining efficiency and comfort in staterooms that are among the most spacious "average" accommodations in the cruise industry, putting such cramped cabins as those offered by American Canadian Caribbean Line to

shame. Aboard the *Horizon* you'll find large closets, roomy dressers for storing clothes and sundries, and a bathroom that's far larger than the bread boxes offered by many lines.

Surprisingly, units designed as regular suites are not appreciably bigger than regular cabins. They do, however, contain a scattering of amenities, including outdoor verandas and just enough extra room to squeeze in a pair of seats. Only the ship's presidential suites conform to most people's idea of a grand ocean-crossing suite. Regardless of status, all accommodations contain a radio, personal safe, glass-topped coffee table, twin or double bed, marble-topped vanity, and color-coordinated accoutrements. Some have both upper and lower berths, which are not available on many modern vessels. Some outside cabins on the Bermuda Deck have views blocked by lifeboats.

Four cabins are wheelchair accessible, with extra-large bathrooms.

RECREATION & FITNESS FACILITIES

The *Horizon* has an impressive amount of space devoted to recreation. Its two good-size swimming pools never seem to become overcrowded, even when the ship is sailing with a full passenger load, and its Olympic Health Club is bright, airy, and filled with sunlight. It's stocked with treadmills, step machines, weights, stationary bikes, and rowing machines.

Other recreation facilities and options include three outdoor whirlpools, a putting green, golf driving, snorkeling, trapshooting, and exercise classes. For joggers, eight laps of the unobstructed circuit on the Captain's Deck equals 1 mile.

PUBLIC AREAS   The uppermost decks of both the *Horizon* and *Zenith* were designed as panoramic aeries removed from the bustle of the rest of the ship. Rows of a generous number of deck chairs overlook the sea and the lower decks' swimming pools. The uppermost sundeck contains a bar, a jogging track, and the Olympic Health Club.

One level below is the Coral Seas Café, an informal eatery. Casual dining, both indoors and out, is also offered at The Grill. The Rendezvous Lounge and Bar is the preferred spot to sip a few drinks before hitting the Palladium showroom's glittery cabaret show. The 840-seat Starlight Restaurant features two different dinner seatings, at 6:15 and 8:30pm. To allow for more tableside ocean views, the restaurant was designed as a longish room, running along the side of the ship.

The ship's library is only adequate, but the card room is nearly always big enough.

Zenith

⚓ ⚓ ⚓ ⚓ ⚓

Specifications

Size (in tons)	47,255	Crew	657 (International)
Number of Cabins	686	Passenger/Crew Ratio	2.1 to 1
Number of Outside Cabins	540	Year Built	1991
Number of Passengers	1,374	Last Major Refurbishment	n/a
Officers	Greek		

Frommer's Ratings (Scale of 1–10)

Activities	7.5	Public Areas	9.2
Cabins	8.5	Public Comfort/Space	9.0
Cleanliness/Maintenance	8.5	Recreational Facilities/Pool	8.5
Entertainment	8.0	Service	9.0
Food & Beverage	9.0	Ship Crew/Officers	8.0
Interior Decor	8.0	Shore Excursions	7.0
Ports of Call	8.0	Worth the Money	9.0
		Overall Average	**8.4**

A big, sleek beauty in its own right, *Zenith* is a virtual twin of the *Horizon,* although the two do have design differences, such as the *Zenith*'s larger forward observation deck. Its clean, streamlined look makes the vessel appear much bigger than it is, yet it isn't a megaship and can still moor conveniently at the piers of such small ports as Key West.

Zenith was the flagship of the line until it was replaced by bigger and splashier ships such as the *Century* and *Galaxy*. It boasts an artfully elegant hull and rakishly angled smokestack. An exceptionally wide indoor promenade gives passengers the feeling of strolling along a boulevard within the ship's hull. Art and sculpture decorate the ship, but the works don't equal the premier collection aboard *Century*.

Cabins & Rates

Cabins	Average per diem	Bathtub	Fridge	Phone	Sitting Area	TV
Inside	$278	No	No	Yes	No	Yes
Outside	$340	No	No	Yes	No	Yes
Suite	$458	Yes	Yes	Yes	Yes	Yes

CABINS Special efforts were made during the ship's design to create roughly equivalent cabins, without the many permutations available on some older ships, such as the *Norway*. Accommodations have a generous amount of space, the same as on the *Horizon,* and pastel-colored appointments are tasteful, subdued, and well maintained.

Most cabins have twin or double beds, with generally roomy bathrooms, virtually the same as those aboard the *Horizon.* In cabins with twins, mattresses can be pushed together to create a king-size bed. All cabins contain the standard amenities, such as hair dryers and radio, plus televisions offering five channels (as opposed to the 14 aboard the *Century*). Six cabins are positioned all the way aft, with windows facing the wake. Some passengers who've sailed on the line before request these rooms, preferring to view the sea as they pass it by instead of confronting seascapes ahead. Since cabins are so similar, you can book on a lower deck to save money, unless you want to be nearer the sky.

Unlike some modern ships, the *Zenith* offers doubles with both upper and lower berths, which makes the ship a possible choice for families or friendly foursomes. Amenities include a glass-top coffee table, a desk, and a night stand with a solitary lamp that may be inadequate, especially if you're in a double. Suites are enormous, among the best in this price range. Regular suites, 20 in all, have a marble bathroom with whirlpool tub, a sitting area, safe, hair dryer, and even butler service. If you're Oprah or H. Ross Perot, you can ask for one of two royal suites with a separate living room, walk-in closet, marble bath, safe, and minibar.

Four spacious twin cabins are wheelchair accessible.

RECREATION & FITNESS FACILITIES Like the *Horizon,* the *Zenith* has two good-size swimming pools that are large enough even when the ship is fully booked.

The Olympic Health Club is a smaller version of the AquaSpa that appears on Celebrity's larger ships, and offers most of the same treatments. It's virtually the same though perhaps slightly better than the club aboard the *Horizon.* Its equipment includes six Aerobicycles, two computer rowing machines, five Tredex treadmills, a Universal stair machine, a Nordic Track cross-country ski machine, and an Aero-Step exercise machine. For a ship this size, this is a fairly impressive array of equipment, and is generally adequate to meet cruisers' demands.

PUBLIC AREAS They're as dramatic as anything afloat, but without the glitz and neon associated with some other lines (notably Carnival). *Zenith* has the same deck plan as the *Horizon,* including both a Fantasy and a Galaxy Deck. The major dining room is the Caravelle Restaurant, which seats 856 at two times: 6:15pm for the slightly older crowd, and 8:30pm for the younger set. The dining room architects added as many curves and circles as possible, and divided the room into smaller sections to place the greatest number of tables near picture windows. The decor is plush, metallic, and modern, rather than classical and conservative.

Amidships are the Rendezvous Lounge and Rendezvous Bar, where guests, especially on formal nights, can show off their finery. The Scorpio Disco can hold 135 dancers, but rarely does. The snuggest part of the ship, at the complete aft of the Fantasy Deck, is the romantic little Rainbow Room, to which you can retreat with that newly acquired special friend. Closer to amidships is Harry's Tavern, which is your last-chance watering hole before trying your luck in the nearby Mayfair Casino, where gaming machines ring and ding.

There's never a really bad seat in the 833-seat Celebrity Show Lounge, a two-level nightclub with state-of-the-art equipment for its splashy Las Vegas–style productions.

The uppermost Sun Deck, with a whirlpool at the aft end, is slightly better than the one aboard the *Horizon.* Like the *Horizon,* the *Zenith* also has a Marina Deck, with a lounge called the Fleet Bar. Casual dining and drinking take place at the Windsurf Bar and the Grill.

Of immense appeal is the sedate and contemplative library, with comfortable seating and a collection of in-house books, including many coffee-table creations about nautical themes or travel. There's also a good-size card room.

Mercury (Preview)

Celebrity's fifth ship, the *Mercury,* is slated to be launched in early November 1997, upping the line's number of itineraries to 40 worldwide and strengthening its foothold in the Caribbean, the base from which much of its initial success derived. The vessel will be similar in design and amenities to the *Century* and *Galaxy,* reviewed above, but with a somewhat larger physical capacity. Tonnage estimates vary between 73,000 and 77,713, with a passenger capacity of 1,870. In its inaugural season, the ship will sail seven-night cruises through the western Caribbean, using Fort Lauderdale as its home port and visiting Key West, Cozumel, Montego Bay, and Grand Cayman.

The *Mercury*'s contractor is Joseph Meyer GmbH of Papenburg, Germany, builders of four of the line's other ships. Special architectural features will include two atriums, a sliding glass roof that shelters one of the three onboard swimming pools, a special indoor/outdoor children's play area, and a specially designed lounge for teenagers. More than 30% of the cabins on board will have private verandas. In keeping with the line's focus on gambling and entertainment, the ship is conceived as a floating resort, providing virtually everything holiday makers might need to distract them during a week on the high seas. A word of warning for gamblers: Celebrity plans to equip the *Mercury* with ATM machines, which might encourage more betting than you'd otherwise planned.

As is the Celebrity way, the styles established in the line's other vessels (including those that affect the dining, drinking, entertainment, and health-club rituals) will remain entirely consistent here.

Clipper Cruise Line

SHIPS Nantucket Clipper • Yorktown Clipper
7711 Bonhomme Ave., St. Louis, MO 63105-1956. ☎ 800/325-0010 or 314/727-2929; fax 314/727-6576.

One of only a handful of cruise lines ever launched from the great American grain belt, Clipper's roots and marketing strategy are firmly rooted in St. Louis, Missouri, a city whose dependence on the navigation of rivers, rather than seas, profoundly influenced the design and vision of these ships.

Extolling the beauty of small-ship adventures, Clipper Cruise Line advertises that its ships are used for exploring the waterways of America. But Clipper explores the Caribbean as well, and the line's well-attended Caribbean sailings are taking up more of its time.

The company was founded in 1982 by Barney Ebsworth, creator of the Intrav group of wholesale travel and travel-related companies. Today, the ships are affiliated with the Windsor Group, a real estate and investment company managed by Paul Duynhouwer. The addition of a pair of cruise ships to the travel giant's roster of assets coincided neatly with its corporate emphasis on hosting thoughtful alternatives to conventional cruising.

You won't find glitter, glitz, or Las Vegas gambling aboard either ship within this line. Instead, the mood is perky, all-American, aggressively unpretentious, and not as cheap as you might think; you'll pay a hefty price for stripped-down amenities and an inexperienced staff.

The line it most resembles in spirit is American Canadian Caribbean Line (ACCL), to which its ships are frequently compared. Both are proud of their American crews, American food, and American interests, with pastel colors and additional Americana thrown in. Like ACCL, the Clipper ships leave something to be desired—there are no elevators, no stabilizers, the engines are noisy, and some landings at isolated ports of call can be downright wet.

Yet, don't be too quick to reject this line for its white-bread-with-mayonnaise approach, as you'll find some spicy onions in the middle of Clipper's sandwiches. Clipper fills a definite niche for the middle-of-the-road, mature, seasoned, non-demanding, relatively affluent older passenger seeking a casual (but not *too* casual) vacation experience, enjoying first-hand the natural beauties of the Americas and the Caribbean.

Clipper sends its ships to places in the Caribbean that larger vessels with deeper drafts won't or simply can't go. The *Nantucket Clipper* and *Yorktown Clipper* are small and maneuverable enough to access often unpopulated coral reefs of the southern Caribbean, isolated refuges in Panama and Costa Rica, isolated communities in the British Virgin Islands, and remote hideaways in the Grenadines and Anguilla. In addition, both Clipper vessels have U.S. registry, which is relatively rare in the Caribbean cruise industry. This status allows the ships to moor in and navigate between U.S. ports of call along the eastern seaboard.

Clipper should not, however, be confused with an adventure cruise line. Although their ports of call are more interesting than the well-trod landings favored by many larger lines, Clipper has only recently begun to venture into some of the wildly exotic ports that have long been favored by the more aggressively adventuresome American Canadian Caribbean Line (those of Central America, including excursions into the jungles of Panama). And whereas with ACCL you'll get to experience the Caribbean via the line's cutting-edge cruise technology, here you'll get the spectacular views but in a somewhat more cushy environment and with a somewhat lesser sense of novelty. As a company spokesperson notes, "We provide a soft adventure for travelers who may shy away from roughing it, and we think of ourselves not as a cruise line, but as a travel company that just happens to have ships."

The ambience is country clubbish, sometimes cliquish among repeat passengers, and ships are small enough (102 and 138 passengers, respectively) to make onboard conflicts embarrassingly obvious. Social life is at least partially catalyzed by an onboard cruise director, who's loaded with hints on what to do and how to do it safely during shore landings.

PROS & CONS   Early in its life, the company struggled with how to define ships larger than a yacht yet smaller than a cruise ship. For a brief time, Clipper called their craft "ultra-yachts," a term eventually dropped from their marketing. It's just as well, since the upscale connotations of "yacht" simply don't apply to these vessels. For example, when you step onto the stairs that interconnect various decks, the sound is apt to be a very navyish "clank" rather than the upper-crust tap of teakwood. The public areas are clean and cheerful, but certainly not plush, yet maintenance is generally high, and the ships are, pardon the expression, shipshape.

Be warned, however, that the ship design does not contribute to any great comfort during stormy or even choppy seas. Its lack of stabilizers is an amazing omission, since virtually every ship in the Caribbean seems to consider them part of their standard equipment. It means that if you're prone to seasickness, you'd best opt for a cruise on American inland waterways and not any of the repositioning cruises that tempt you with reduced prices and long stretches in the open seas.

The onboard atmosphere tends to be informal. There's almost no emphasis on dressing up, to the extent that any man who wore a button-down shirt would probably be considered overdressed. Staff members are mostly youthful and enthusiastic, mid-American college types working

their way to a series of exotic ports during summer holidays.

The ships are loosely structured in their activity schedules, but more strictly organized in mealtime regimens than some passengers would like. Also, the small size of each ship limits the number of passengers with whom you can bond, but maximizes your exposure to those passengers whom you might actively dislike. Luckily, there's not a hint of the false enthusiasm regarding party games or mindless activities that you'll find popping the rivets aboard some larger ships.

Regarding noise, the ship's engines are soundproof, yet they still emit an almost continuous drone that's louder than many people would really like. The sound is noticeable when engines are first engaged, and more so when they suddenly stop, leading to a blessed quiet and recognition of how loud the engines were when running. You'll also hear many onboard announcements, some almost interminable and many concerning subjects and activities that might not interest you in the least. While you can always shut off the amplifier in your cabin, they will still be faintly audible from speakers in the corridors.

Stopovers on islands bear some likeness to shore leave, with the difference being that here you're given rapid synopses of easy-to-digest information on the history and highlights of what you'll find ashore, rather than warnings on hygiene.

TYPES OF PASSENGERS   The majority of passengers are older than 50 and want to cruise in a manner that is culturally and physically comfortable. They don't want any emphasis on wardrobes or intricate social rituals. Many are "what you see is what you get" types: honest, unassuming, and not particularly indulgent of airs or pretensions in others. Passengers often hail from the Southeast or the Midwest, with annual household incomes in excess of $70,000. They are most interested in the cultural history and ecosystems of ports of call, not in extraneous hype, garble, marketing, or salesmanship. Many are quietly committed to their religious beliefs, and don't particularly care about gambling or shopping for big-ticket items.

Beachcombing is big, as are wash-and-wear clothes, Scrabble, John Grisham or Tom Clancy novels, and perhaps knitting or quilting a patchwork for a favorite bride-to-be. A high percentage might be repeaters who appreciate Clipper Line policies. Although some participants might bring a grandchild on board, the child might leave feeling he'd had a lesson in values rather than a whoop-it-up vacation.

There are no facilities for travelers with disabilities.

DINING   The fare is all-American, prepared by attendees of the Culinary Institute of America. A buffet-style breakfast is served at 8am. Lunch and dinners include a limited selection of main courses, usually two, plus a pasta and vegetarian dish. Soups are hearty and wholesome, rib-sticking fare. You can even order buttermilk with your meal. Whenever it's practical, local ingredients are incorporated into the daily menu. The cuisine, overall, is okay.

You'll see the world through the picture windows in each ship's one restaurant. Seating is open at tables set up for four to six diners. Tables for two are hard to come by and those who request them tend to be viewed as standoffish. So if your idea of fine dining is a romantic tête-à-tête with your significant other, get used to the idea of being overheard by other couples. Don't expect European restraint from the staff. Waitresses are perky young American women who sometimes forget (or never learned) proper attention to service rituals.

Meal hours are more strictly observed than many passengers would like, beginning promptly at 8am, 12:30pm, and 7:30pm. You won't feel particularly comfortable if you're a laggard, trailing in to meals when the crowd is digesting dessert.

There are no formal nights of any kind, although jeans are not appreciated at the dinner table.

If you prefer to skip the dining room and eat in, forget it. Room service doesn't exist, unless you're too ill to attend meals, in which event something nourishing might be brought to your cabin, but that's it. There are no midnight buffets, and almost no opportunities for snacking outside the regular meal hours. Among those following specific dietary regimes, only vegetarians can be accommodated.

ACTIVITIES   Unless your favorite pastime is hearing about your fellow passengers' grandchildren, you'd better bring along that novel you've wanted to finish. There's no disco, and none of the electronic, glittering diversions that contribute to the allure of the Caribbean's megaships. Lectures are big events, as is Scrabble. Much of your fun depends on how enthralled you are by the ports of call you'll visit, and on your ability to amuse yourself at such low-key activities as beach walking, beachcombing, and comparing the beach at one port of call to the beach at another.

CHILDREN'S ACTIVITIES   These ships have no facilities of any kind for children. If you want to bring a young niece, nephew, or grandchild, they'll be expected to behave like young adults. Although the dining and social rituals on board are not significantly different from home, most teenagers would be bored to death aboard a Clipper Cruise. Baby-sitting is not available.

ENTERTAINMENT   Even the strictest American puritan would not object too strenuously to the official activities sponsored aboard these ships. The "more substantive" travel experience, says Clipper, eschews casinos, professional singers and/or dance bands, comedy and/or magic acts. However, on rare occasions, a live band might play ashore at a port of call, ending the performance at a relatively early hour. Even if the line were to offer some of these distractions, you'd probably get the feeling that passengers might not particularly approve, or even be interested.

Many guests attend the onboard lectures, delivered in an anecdotal style by experts in such fields as botany, marine life, archaeology, and social history. Being able to meet, dine with, and challenge the opinions of the resident experts is an important part of the onboard entertainment. Overall, the tone is studious and unpretentious, with not a hint of frivolity.

The spot for a rendezvous with fellow passengers is the Observation Lounge, where you'll find a piano, a bar, a small library, and big windows for land- and seascape-watching. The room, by the end of any cruise, assumes a mess hall quality, since it's configured more for mass meetings than intimate conversational groupings. Each ship has two public TV sets with VCRs for watching nature films and the like.

SHOPPING   The best shopping opportunities are at off-the-beaten-track ports of call. Although even these have their fair share of T-shirts and suntan lotion, they also have crafts that aren't readily available at more popular stamping grounds. The fact that the person selling those carved coconut shells, woodcarvings, and woven goods either made them or is a friend or relative of the person who did allows you to avoid the supermarket mentality that seems to pervade the "native crafts" business on more commercialized islands.

On board, you can get such sundries as toothpaste, soap, and shampoo charged to your shipboard account. A display case is filled with craft items from whatever port of call the ship stopped at recently, although most passengers find it more appealing to negotiate directly with the merchants who appear wherever the ship docks. You'll get a wider choice of merchandise this way, too.

SERVICE   Staff, crew, and officers are selected as much for their abilities to relate to passengers as for their technical expertise. They are, almost without exception, American born and bred, and quite often young. Staff wear many hats simultaneously, usually with good cheer, and seem equally adept at cleaning up a galley or cabin, tossing a salad, or distributing lifejackets during a safety instruction drill. No one is particularly servile, but at the same time none gives the impression that they want to be captain someday. Passengers often "adopt" particular staff members as surrogate grandchildren for the duration of their cruise.

ITINERARIES   During the winter, the line features seven-day excursions into the central and southern Caribbean, focusing on such lesser-visited islands as Bequia, Dominica, Union Island, Nevis, and St. Kitts. Itineraries sometimes feature day excursions on the bounding main aboard locally chartered sailing yachts, which carry passengers for short-term jaunts to such islands as Mustique, Mayreau Island, or Petit St. Vincent. Recently, the line began dabbling in eight-night itineraries, about three a year, that combine two nights in a deluxe hotel in San Jose, Costa Rica, with six nights aboard the *Yorktown Clipper*. The trip includes a transit of the Panama Canal with excursions into the Darien Jungle and at least two of the region's wildlife sanctuaries.

SPECIAL DISCOUNTS   A third person in a shared cabin is charged from $600 to $2,100 for a cruise, depending on the itinerary, representing a major discount over what two persons are charged.

SINGLE SUPPLEMENTS   Add 50% to the cost of the per person rate for a double.

PORT CHARGES   Port charges are about $95 per person, depending on the itinerary.

Nantucket Clipper • Yorktown Clipper

⚓ ⚓

Specifications

Size (in tons)	95/97	Crew	32/40 (American)
Number of Cabins	51/69	Passenger/Crew Ratio	3.2 to 1/3.5 to 1
Number of Outside Cabins	51/69	Year Built	1984/1988
Number of Passengers	102/138	Last Major Refurbishment	n/a
Officers	American		

Frommer's Ratings (Scale of 1–10)

Activities	5.2	Public Areas	6.0
Cabins	6.0	Public Comfort/Space	6.2
Cleanliness/Maintenance	8.5	Recreational Facilities/Pool	2.0
Entertainment	4.0	Service	7.0
Food & Beverage	7.0	Ship Crew/Officers	8.0
Interior Decor	6.4	Shore Excursions	8.6
Ports of Call	8.0	Worth the Money	8.8
		Overall Average	**6.6**

These two ships hold few passengers, but population density aboard is high. There are only two public rooms, each of which is required to service a relatively large number of passengers due to the ship's small square footage. The four-deck ships have no elevators. Both were built in a riverfront shipyard in Jeffersonville, Indiana, a fact that helps reinforce the all-American image of this solid, Midwestern line. Both ships boast drafts of only eight feet, a fact that allows access to out-of-the-way ports where larger ships cannot go. Each, however, lacks some of the distinctive engineering innovations, such as bow ramps for disembarkation directly onto local beaches, that are standard features aboard the vessels of Clipper's most visible competitor, American Canadian Caribbean Line (ACCL). And although vessels are somewhat more plush, they lack the cutting-edge sense of engineering innovation that's ACCL's pride. Both the *Nantucket* and *Yorktown Clipper* emphasize such resorty activities as golf (whenever there's a suitable course nearby), art and history lectures with an emphasis on the geography of the region, and swimming and snorkeling, often directly off the sides of the ships.

Cabins & Rates

Cabins	Average per diem	Bathtub	Fridge	Phone	Sitting Area	TV
Outside	$350	No	No	No	No	No

CABINS   Cabins are neither particularly opulent nor particularly uncomfortable. Though small, they are adequate unless you bring lots of luggage, which is not the style of this cruise line and its passengers.

All cabins are outside, and except for those at the lowest level, most have picture windows. Rooms have showers but no tubs, and there are no phones or TVs. Prerecorded music (usually jazz) is projected into your room from a speaker. Decor is very far from glitzy, with a sort of affluent, no-nonsense, Midwestern WASP kind of quality to it.

Cabins come in five different categories, each based on location and their relative size. Each has two lower-level beds, permanently fixed in an L-shaped corner configuration or as two units set parallel to one another. Most passengers find this acceptable, but if moonlight and splashing waves make you romantic, you might not be pleased with this layout. Some cabins contain Murphy beds that unfold from the wall to accommodate a third person.

The half-dozen cabins in the stern of the Lounge Deck can be noisy, in part from socializing in the nearby public areas and in part from propeller and/or engine vibration. Note that the four cabins on *Yorktown*'s uppermost deck, which are listed among the line's top cabin category, are accessible only from the sometimes stormy, sometimes windy outside deck.

There are no special facilities aboard for travelers with disabilities and no cabins designed specifically for single occupancy.

RECREATION & FITNESS FACILITIES
Neither ship has a swimming pool and neither devotes a square inch to a health club. You can jog around the deck (18 laps equals 1 mile on the *Nantucket Clipper,* and 14 laps does the job on the *Yorktown Clipper*). Most joggers claim they lose track of their mileage on such small decks after a few laps anyway. Bring a hand-held "clicker" if you're concerned. The tracks are reserved for "power walkers" every day between 8 and 9am. And that's about it, fitness-wise, other than what you choreograph for yourself. You can get more exercise on beach junkets, usually on remotely isolated shores of natural or zoological interest.

PUBLIC AREAS   Each ship contains only two public areas: the dining room and the Observation Lounge. More passengers use the Observation Lounge, which has big windows, a bar, a small library, and enough space to seat everyone on board for lectures and meetings. You won't be threatened by the decor, although it's doubtful you'll find it thrilling either. The dining room aboard each ship is the most charming area.

Club Med Cruises

SHIPS   Club Med 1 • Club Med 2
40 West 57th St., New York, NY 10019. ☎ 800/4-LESHIP or 212/977-2100; fax 212/315-5392.

In the late 1980s, Club Med (CM) founder and CEO Gilbert Trigano heard the cruise industry's siren song. The man who shaped a version of *la vie en rose* into an exotic, all-inclusive holiday experience had another idea: a floating Club Med.

Realizing that there would be no reason for the venture if it simply siphoned off business from CM's land-based resorts, Club Med Cruises targeted as its potential passengers those people who haven't visited its other resorts, or would not. It's a strategy that's worked. Some 40% of the total passenger list has had no previous Club Med experience; they're attracted to the more luxurious accommodations offered at sea, as opposed to the stripped-down barracks of many Club Med villages.

There are many superlatives associated with this line. Its ships are the world's largest sail-equipped cruise ships, high-tech versions of 18th-century clipper ships that, while less dramatic, are far more stable. Each has five masts, seven computer-operated sails, and vague (but sometimes far-fetched) self-images as wind-driven private yachts.

Don't carry this image too far, however. Sails and masts à la Club Med are intended to be auxiliaries for the ships' motors, an aesthetic ornament aboard ships that are more than capable of dieseling their way into virtually any waters they want. The ships heel only slightly, and then only in the strongest of winds; sometimes CM captains induce a slight tilt to simulate the feeling of a ship under sail. The crew seems eerily absent from the minute-to-minute deck-side trimming of sails, and that's because the lines, ropes, riggings, and sails are set and fine-tuned via computer monitors from the bridge. Despite this mechanization, many passengers are awed by the vessel's sheer beauty, which adds to the romance of sailing

through Caribbean waters. Each ships' five masts and seven sails are merely a whimsical grace note, beautiful and evocative when viewed from the ships' decks, but oddly out of proportion to the bulk of the ships' hull when seen from afar. On some cruises, if the wind isn't cooperative, the sails are hoisted only occasionally, perhaps during exits and entrances from harbors, or at the debut and end of a cruise.

The line is often compared to Windstar, yet Windstar generally attracts a more affluent, sophisticated clientele and carries fewer passengers by half. Americans are most welcome; indeed, they make up between 20% and 30% of the passengers on board any Caribbean or Bahamian itinerary. But know before you go that *the* language on board is French, the currency is the franc, and the ethic of relaxed permissiveness is as Gallic as topless sunbathing or Bordeaux with pâté, both of which are part of the CM sailing experience. You also have to join Club Med; the one-time initiation fee of $30 per family includes travel insurance coverage. Club Med also imposes an annual fee of $50 per adult, which will add your name to the company's mailing list and provide easier access to the company's roster of products.

The aura that Club Med tries to project, both on sea and on land, is one of Gallic savoir faire. That aura is aggressively promoted by a cadre of attractive *gentiles organisateurs* (GOs), a veritable army of cheerleaders who encourage passengers to indulge in the many onboard activities. They are not "servants" per se, but function as quasi-passengers, participating in the activities along with paying guests. Many guests fall in love with these GOs (figuratively, of course—this isn't the Love Boat), whereas others find them irritating.

For some cruisers, though, the savoir faire doesn't hit the mark, and they comment snidely on a cliquish rowdiness that reminds them of a summer camp for adults. Potential passengers who feel this way would be better off sailing on a Windstar vessel.

If you opt to do business with Club Med before March 1998, you'll sail on *Club Med 1,* a 617-foot ocean liner painted an uncompromising brilliant white that's as much at home against the blue sky of the Aegean as it is against the turquoise reefs of the Caribbean. As of March, though, say good-bye to the *Club Med 1*—the company has sold it to Windstar, who will refit it, rename it the *Wind Surf,* and sail it on a new itinerary (see the news box in our Windstar review, page 333). After March, you'll sail aboard the *Club Med 2,* which is being transferred to the Caribbean from its current routes in the Mediterranean. The two ships are virtually identical, so you shouldn't experience any major feeling of loss if you had your heart set on the *CM1*. With its 3,000 square yards of sail, the *CM2* is just as impressive.

PROS & CONS   At its best, a Club Med trip offers an exposure to French culture, with many Americanisms thrown in to make the atmosphere more comfortable. At its worst, a Club Med experience is permeated with a French cultural nationalism that may make some Americans mightily uncomfortable. To mitigate too intense a Gallic dose, CM administrators have placed British, Canadian, German, Spanish, Australian, and sometimes American GOs on board. Yet cultural clashes are more likely to occur aboard a Club Med cruise than any other cruise line, including the Greek vessels of Celebrity, the Italian vessels of Costa, and the Norwegian vessels of Seabourn.

There are compensations for surrendering yourself to a company whose origins are distinctly non-American. Besides experiencing a taste of the Continent with its distinct style and taste, you'll find comfortable cabins, exotic itineraries (at least for the Caribbean), and water sports unlimited. The atmosphere is casual and laid back, without any of the stiff formality aboard such ships as *QE2.*

TYPES OF PASSENGERS   Many passengers are alumni from Club Med villages; others like the company's concept of relaxed informality, but want to avoid some of the bare-bone CM villages on land, and find the ship to be a luxurious introduction to the Club Med style. Some two-thirds of the passengers range from 35 to 55 years old. Among the French-born travelers on board there will almost certainly be some who become more outspokenly Gallic abroad than they ever were at home. If you're American, refrain from references to Disney and McDonald's and you should be OK. Among passengers who don't happen to be French, you'll find a number of Francophiles, who adapt to the cultural mix with ease. Many non-French passengers hope to improve their language skills or else wish to make friends with Europeans.

The Americans you'll tend to meet on a CM Caribbean itinerary often include youngish and relatively sophisticated urban professionals from New York, New Jersey, Connecticut, Massachusetts, Pennsylvania, and, to a lesser degree, California. This affluent group, ranging in age from 28 to about 55 years old, includes lawyers and medical professionals. They tend to be sports- and fitness-conscious, international in outlook, and appreciative of luxury without insisting on formality. They like to visit exotic ports of call, are not particularly upset by any shortcomings in cuisine or in availability of shopping options, and spend a lot of time playing at water sports.

Partying on board will probably not descend to the raunchiness that's the norm on some megaships. If it did, most passengers would be horrified by the blatant "Americanism" of that rowdiness.

Children under 10 are not admitted aboard a Club Med vessel.

DINING   Two dining areas both sport sea views. A single open seating at dinner lets passengers bond or break shipboard relationships at will. Officers and staff dine with the passengers, contributing to the clublike ambience. Tables for two are widely available, although if you drop the slightest hint that you're looking for company, one of the GOs will quickly bustle you to a communal table.

Cuisine is, you guessed it, French, with a few hints of Italian and other Continental traditions showing through occasionally. Charming touches include cheese carts featuring café au lait, espresso, and a selection of cheese that is very French indeed. Food is not gastronomically superlative, but is plentiful, eminently acceptable, and prepared and served with style and an occasional flourish. Meals are always accompanied by complimentary beer or red and white *vins de table* (usually one of Club Med's private-label wines). A surcharge is imposed for consumption of more esoteric vintages.

Somewhat formal and substantial fare is served during both the breakfast and the lunch hours in an indoor-outdoor bistro called the Odyssey. At lunchtime, both à la carte sit-down service and buffet spreads à la Med are featured. On some beach days, a crew sets up a buffet, usually with lobster, on whatever nearby beach happens to be most suitable.

Dinners are more formal, constituting a major social and gastronomic event in an otherwise relatively relaxed day. As on the French mainland, they can last for up to three hours, with not a ruffle of impatience from the diners and guests. Diners opt for meals served between 7:30 and 9:30pm in the Odyssey or the more formal Le Louisiane Restaurant. The dress code is usually casual or informal, with the exception of two gala dinners (dressy, but not necessarily black-tie) that are offered during the course of each seven-night cruise.

Room service is available 24 hours a day, although some items carry a supplemental charge and the menu is limited. Continental breakfast is always available in cabins. Upon request, special diets, such as low-calorie, nonfat, or vegetarian, are accommodated.

ACTIVITIES The teakwood decks support an ongoing, cross-cultural carnival that tries to be all things to all passengers. The outdoor areas invite sunbathing, although complaints are sometimes voiced (bilingually) when the ship's sails block the rays. Deck games with the GOs come with unbounded enthusiasm and the belief that fun and games can transcend linguistic differences. It can be a bit much, particularly if you don't feel as youthful as the GOs.

One benefit of each ships' relatively small size is the *Hall Nautique,* a private marina made accessible by opening a massive steel hatch at the ship's stern, allowing windsurfers, sailboaters, water-skiers, and snorkelers access to the open sea. Gear for all of these is provided free. A flotilla of tenders carry day trippers to the sands of isolated beaches.

Bridge has caught on recently, and a GO will organize lessons and tournaments for whomever is interested. There's also a complete 24-hour fitness center with saunas that are segregated (in a way that's not particularly French) according to gender.

CHILDREN'S ACTIVITIES Only children ages 10 and over are allowed on board, and even then they're not particularly welcome. Club Med does not advertise that it accepts children and does not encourage such patronage, as the ships, in theory at least, are "for sophisticated adults." If teenagers make it aboard, GOs will supervise daytime activities for them, but otherwise there are no special camps, workshops, or training sessions for children.

ENTERTAINMENT It's rather amateurish. GOs entertain on every cruise, lip-synching their way through Barbra Streisand or (on one dreadful night) Wayne Newton. Some passengers feel more professional entertainment should be provided, whereas others join in the fun and have a good time. Sometimes local bands come aboard for the evening at various ports of call. On the do-it-yourself front, the karaoke mike is a popular staple, and owing to the multinational nature of the Club Med experience you're likely to hear Dolly Parton segue disconcertingly into Edith Piaf. On Carnival night, passengers masquerade in stage makeup and stylized costumes provided by the staff.

The casino, offering blackjack and roulette along with the inevitable slot machines, is small but generally adequate for the number of players. The croupiers, for some reason, are usually women and usually British.

There's a piano bar on board, and a nightclub that's staffed by GOs who sing, dance, and tell jokes (often about the cruising experience) in several languages for the benefit of their international audience. Later, beginning around 10:30pm, Fantasia swings into action. That's a disco with lots of mirrors and chrome that rocks and rolls to a Francophilic beat till everyone decides to totter off to bed. It's hidden away behind an unmarked door on the vessel's bottom deck, a little too close to the engine room, far from any cabins where occupants might be sleeping.

SHOPPING   There's an angular, streamlined boutique aboard, where the inventory is about as upscale and glamorous as you'd expect: You can get cruise wear in varying degrees of naughtiness, accessories from the big names in European fashion, a predictable array of French perfumes, and souvenirs of your Club Med experience.

SERVICE   Remember that Club Med really is a *club* in many ways, and while efforts are made to attend to your needs and wants, the staff is much more laid back than the white-gloved, heel-clicking servants aboard Seabourn or Cunard's upscale vessels. In some ways, the army of GOs function on board as reliably energetic guests, rather than as hotel staffers in the traditional sense. You're as likely to see one sunbathing beside the pool as leading guests in songfests or lip-synching at karaoke.

Aboard Club Med, service relies on cooperation and cheerful coexistence. The illusion is maintained that whoever is serving you is a *copain* (French for jolly good fellow) and is doing so as a good-natured favor rather than as a duty. If you're too surly or demanding, the good will (and the subsequent service-related favors) might vanish. And in some cases, if staff find a request inconvenient, you may find that they conveniently forget it. More immature staff members can often be downright brusque, patronizing, or insulting, sometimes in two languages.

If you consider yourself talented in the fine and tactful art of persuasion, and enjoy talking, flirting, and fraternizing bilingually with a youthful and somewhat jaded staff that is known for its independent-mindedness, you'll fit in beautifully. Many guests actually develop seagoing (that is, short-term) friendships with the GOs, who are eventually viewed to some degree as facilitators, enablers, and catalysts for *laissez rouler les bon temps* ("let the good times roll").

Club Med maintains a "no tipping" policy at each of its resorts and on board each of its ships, a policy that's consistent with the company's all-inclusive price structures. Despite that, many staff members are pleased to discreetly accept a gratuity for exemplary service.

ITINERARIES   Between mid-November and mid-April, *Club Med* has its home port in Martinique, departing on five different seven-day itineraries that begin and end every Saturday. Two of the five focus on such northern Antillean destinations as St. Barts, St. Kitts, St. Martin, and Tintamarre, such offshore dependencies of Guadeloupe as the Iles des Saints, and scattered ports within the British and U.S. Virgin Islands. Itineraries through the southern Caribbean include stopovers at St. Lucia and Barbados, scattered destinations in the Grenadines, and such Venezuelan ports as La Blanquilla, Tortuga Island, and Los Roques. The ships' relatively shallow draft of 16 feet permits dockage off the shores of islands that are passed over by many other cruise lines.

SPECIAL DISCOUNTS Honeymooners who notify the line of their newlywed status receive bonus items like gift baskets, complimentary wine or champagne, custom-designed T-shirts, and strands of bar beads, which are legal tender on any Club Med ship or in any CM village worldwide. Special promotions and packages are aggressively marketed at Christmas/New Year's, when parties are especially gala and prices are, too.

A third passenger in any cabin pays 80% of the price he or she would have paid, per person, double occupancy, for a cabin on the ship's least expensive deck.

SINGLE SUPPLEMENTS Single occupants of double cabins pay a 30% surcharge. As in any Club Med village, the line will try to procure a same-gender roommate for you, allowing singles who share to benefit from the lower per diem rates available to couples who travel together.

PORT CHARGES Depending on the itinerary, port charges are $140 and up.

Club Med 1• Club Med 2

⚓ ⚓ ⚓

Specifications

Size (in tons)	14,745/14,983	Crew	188 (International)
Number of Cabins	188/191	Passenger/Crew Ratio	2.1 to 1
Number of Outside Cabins	188/191	Year Built	1990
Number of Passengers	386	Last Major Refurbishment	n/a
Officers	French		

Frommer's Ratings (Scale of 1–10)

Activities	6.5	Public Areas	8.5
Cabins	8.5	Public Comfort/Space	8.6
Cleanliness/Maintenance	8.4	Recreational Facilities/Pool	8.8
Entertainment	6.0	Service	7.8
Food & Beverage	8.0	Ship Crew/Officers	8.5
Interior Decor	8.5	Shore Excursions	8.4
Ports of Call	8.5	Worth the Money	8.8
		Overall Average	**8.1**

Every upper deck on these vessels is affected by the very masts, riggings, and sails that make them distinct—even the curiously understated smokestacks, with funnels that pivot so as to direct smoke away from them.

Sunbathing, for instance, can be challenging. You'll soon learn that settling down in one spot with your tropical oils and a copy of *Les Miserables* just won't cut it—five minutes later, the wind will shift, a synapse in the computer that controls the sails will click, and you'll be sitting in cool shade. It's a challenge, but you'll quickly develop your own way of dealing with it. Such is the way of the wind, and of ships with sails, and of the men and women who sail them.

Cabins & Rates

Cabins	Average per diem	Bathtub	Fridge	Phone	Sitting Area	TV
Outside	$270–$340	No	Yes	Yes	Yes	Yes
Suite	$405–$510	No	Yes	Yes	Yes	Yes

CABINS   Most cabins contain a generous 188 square feet each. The *CM1* has two suites, each measuring a generous 320 square feet, while the *CM2* has five suites at a somewhat smaller 258 square feet.

A prime incentive for a cruise aboard either of the *Club Med* ships is the care and attention devoted to cabin accoutrements. All cabins are outside, and have their own pair of brass-trimmed portholes, climate control, radio, minibar, safe, surprisingly generous closet, and telephone. Decor includes high-tech detailing, mahogany trim, and white walls offset by at least one other color, often navy blue. Bathrooms look like prefabricated modules, with amenities such as a hair dryer, pulsating shower head, terry-cloth robes, and scented soaps, shampoos, and body lotions. Cabins are outfitted with both 110- and 220-volt current, allowing appliances from both Europe and North America to be used without converters or adapters.

Turndown service and the accompanying cleanup rituals are performed every night during the dinner hour. Within the cabins, laundry service is available for a supplemental fee, but not dry cleaning.

Significantly, regardless of the deck on which it's located, each cabin on board each ship is almost exactly identical to every other one on board, with almost no variation for the height at which it sits above the waterline.

Some cabins contain upper bunks for a third passenger. There are no single cabins, and no cabins are especially suited for passengers with disabilities.

RECREATION & FITNESS FACILITIES

The onboard health clubs feature sauna, massage, weightlifting (both free weights and Nautilus), various aerobics machines, and stretching and aerobics classes, and there are two medium-size saltwater pools aboard each ship that have a somewhat voyeuristic/exhibitionistic fervor to them.

Don't underestimate the allure of spa treatment you might reject as too esoteric, too expensive, and too time-consuming back home. The mud packs, facials, hydro-jet therapies, and the like are aggressively marketed on board, and the French usually reserve treatments several days in advance.

PUBLIC AREAS   Various decorative details, including the use of Burmese teak as sheathing for all decks and a mixture of high-tech lines with lots of hardwoods, maintain the illusion that these are, indeed, small-scale yachts rather than 14,000-ton ships. The vessel contains four bars and lounges, a nightclub, a casino, and a medical center staffed by a doctor and nurse. Lounges are soothing if colorful, often done up with unusual murals and designs in a sort of postmodern interpretation of art deco. Large windows bring views of the sea indoors. Two elevators on board connect the eight decks.

There's a large lounge aboard each ship that serves as an all-purpose bar, lecture hall, and rendezvous point where the availability of a drink and the catalytic conviviality of at least one (and often two or more) GOs is only a few steps away.

In many cases, Club Med employs different public philosophies and phraseologies when comparing its ships and its land-based resorts, but in one respect, terminologies are the same: Decor and amenities within the *Club Med 1* and *Club Med 2* are on a par with the finest, most stylish, and most upscale resorts within the chain. Their designers qualify them as "Club Med's finest." Within the Club Med subculture, this is about as good as it gets.

Commodore Cruise Line

SHIPS   Enchanted Isle

4000 Hollywood Blvd., South Tower 385, Hollywood, FL 33021. ☎ 800/237-5361 or 954/967-2100; fax 954/967-2147.

Running second to its major competitor, Dolphin, Commodore Cruise Line's *Enchanted Isle* is one of the best bargains sailing the Caribbean, despite several drawbacks. The line's low rates make the dream of going on an ocean cruise a reality for many first-time cruisers on a budget. Fares are cheaper mainly because the vessel is old, slightly outmoded, and lacks many newfangled gadgets that appear as standard equipment on newer ships. But what the line lacks in technology, it makes up for with its personalized approach, its officers and crew working hard to imbue the setting with a humanity and communal warmth that many larger lines try (with varying degrees of success) to emulate.

When Commodore was launched in 1966, it was hailed as a trailblazer in seven-day cruises from the port of Miami to the West Indies. Dubbed the "Happy Ship," *Enchanted Isle* pioneered theme cruises; its Oktoberfest, with serious beer drinking and oom-pah-pah bands, was the most popular. Honoring the decade of its birth, the *Isle* still has sock hops and "Remember When" cruises, featuring music legends of the 1950s, and it's been successful adapting to new markets.

PROS & CONS   The biggest advantage to sailing with Commodore is the price. Some passengers' entire seven-day fare winds out to be less than one day's rate aboard one of the luxury lines, such as Seabourn. Not only is the price low, but most passengers say it's good value for the money.

The staff offers first-class service, or at least tries to. The cabins are large, having been originally designed for four or five passengers, as opposed to today's cozy duos. The cabin size makes Commodore ships a family favorite, as five can fit into one room without smothering each other.

Commodore also features a lively entertainment and activity calendar.

But, in spite of refurbishments, this Sputnik-era vessel sometimes shows its age. Time has taken its toll: Once-smooth wood finishings are often pitted or scarred, and surfaces can take only so many coats of paint. In spite of polishing, some brass remains corroded, and plumbing fixtures in cabin bathrooms are often tired and a bit worn.

There's no question about the vessel's seaworthiness: It's a veteran of seas much rougher than you're likely to encounter on your Caribbean jaunt, and the ship's basic solidity is actually quite reassuring. But if you're looking for a more modern or sleeker vessel with a decor that's spiffier, glossier, and more cutting edge, you might turn elsewhere—perhaps to one of the newer American Canadian Caribbean Line, Princess, Celebrity, or Carnival ships.

Food on board provokes widely different reactions, ranging from lackluster to raves, depending on the meal. Recently, a team of mostly German-trained head chefs has brought some life and zest to the cuisine, raising its standards to a level that's better, and sometimes much better, than you might expect from such a cost-conscious line. Lobster appears more frequently than before, as well as a roster of fish and steaks designed to appeal to most palates. Rich, luscious desserts go a long way toward either making you forget a so-so meal or perfectly capping a wonderful one. Unfortunately, the ship's restaurant is noisy, and while convivial in the right circumstances, isn't always conducive to a romantic, starry-eyed tête-à-tête between couples.

TYPES OF PASSENGERS   Commodore Cruises draws one of the widest spectrums of passengers in the business. Many passengers are first-time cruisers lured by the line's low per diem rates.

Nearly all the passengers are American, a few hailing from the Midwest and a handful from California. But since sailings depart from New Orleans, and because so many of the line's marketing efforts are aimed directly at the regions around the Mississippi Delta, the large majority of this line's passengers come from Louisiana, Mississippi, Alabama, Texas, and the Florida Panhandle. Unlike many other lines—including Carnival, whose business is heavily dependent on passengers from the Northeast—there are relatively few passengers from the New York/New Jersey/Connecticut tristate region.

Passengers' average family income is about $50,000 a year, with both husband and wife generally working either full or part time. Most cruisers are in middle-management positions, and half are university graduates. The line also draws many retirees, particularly on Caribbean winter voyages where about one in four passengers is retired. During school vacations, Commodore often becomes a floating family boat. Fewer singles sail here, but quite a few honeymooners who opt not to go broke immediately after their wedding book the line.

In recent months, more and more younger people are starting to travel Commodore, no doubt lured by the prices. Most are young professionals or work in blue-collar industries such as construction. Group travel makes up a huge percentage of Commodore's business, perhaps 35% or more.

Since the line specializes in theme cruises, the passenger mix might change drastically depending on what's offered. The 1950s theme cruises draw more people in their 50s and beyond, who remember that era nostalgically, while the Mardi Gras cruise attracts exactly the kind of revelers you'd expect.

DINING   As mentioned above, the cuisine is often inconsistent—some diners will rave about the food, whereas others will find it far off the mark. The soups, salads, and vegetables generally earn more

praise than the main courses. The recent addition of a new culinary team directed by a German-born, European-trained head chef has improved the quality and variety of the cuisine.

You're usually offered a choice of four main dishes, such as broiled lobster tail, coq au vin, and roast prime rib of beef, or perhaps veal Parmesan with pasta. Desserts include a Sacher torte (it's better in Vienna) or crêpes suzette, creating a little romance at night. Menus are coordinated to theme nights, such as Mardi Gras, the "Remember When" shindig, or a Mexican/Caribbean deck party.

There are two seatings, the first at 6pm, the second at 8:30pm. Tables are assigned, and there's a smoking section. Special menus are available, but you should indicate any dietary problems or requests when you book your cruise.

The Bistro Grill offers a buffet-style breakfast, while the dining room serves a full breakfast. Every Commodore cruise features a breakfast specialty from Brennan's Restaurant in New Orleans, such as eggs sardou, a flavorful version of poached eggs with hollandaise sauce atop creamed spinach and artichoke bottoms. A Continental breakfast is available from room service. In addition to a noon buffet at the Bistro Grill, there's full lunchtime dining room service, plus a poolside burger if you want it. The midnight buffet is sometimes less than tantalizing, and not especially worth staying up for unless you're absolutely ravenous.

ACTIVITIES   Routine activities include high-stakes bingo sessions (unless you're in port, where gambling is prohibited) and pool games such as finding out how many Ping-Pong balls your bathing suit will hold, or how fast you and your teammates can swim in the wet T-shirt relay. Game show addicts feel at home playing shipboard versions of the Liar's Club, Passenger Feud, Newlywed/Not So Newlywed, or Draw. Endlessly popular beyond anyone's ability to explain it is an onboard version of Quest, a treasure-hunt game.

Depending on the cruise, there are sometimes meetings of the "Friends of Bill W." (Alcoholics Anonymous).

CHILDREN'S ACTIVITIES   Activities for kids take place in public areas, including the outside decks. Commodore has two programs, one for "tweens" (4 to 12) and another for "teens" (13 to 17). During holidays and summer, counselors are brought aboard to supervise a playroom and run the youth programs, which include parties, movies, and games. Babysitting is available.

ENTERTAINMENT   Commodore Cruises is noted for its entertainment, which includes musical acts, Broadway-style revues, and various cabaret revues with singers, musicians, comedians, and members of the Ray Kennedy dance troupe, who lend a dash of choreography and glitter to the proceedings. Passengers particularly like the two shows *Broadway!* and *Jukebox USA.* Sock-hops and passenger lip-synch shows enliven the nighttime calendar. The main showroom is the Grand Lounge, where revues are backed up by small but able orchestras. Because some sight lines are much better than others you should arrive early to get a good seat. In the back you'll find a full-service bar.

The casinos are open until the last hand of Caribbean stud poker or blackjack is dealt, the last roulette wheel is spun, and the last coin is dropped into the slot machines. The vessel also features Spyglass Lounge, an observation room with a piano bar that's good for intimate meetings, and an indoor-outdoor bar that's ever popular. Neptune's Disco plays Top 40 dance music, and sometimes offers karaoke and the "everyone can be a star" self-entertainment. Two "gentleman dance hosts" are on hand to ensure that no lady who desperately wants to dance will be left wanting, at least in the short term. Passengers sometimes opt to escape from the maddening crowd and seek solace in the darkened confines of an onboard film-screening room.

In brief, the line goes a long way in compensating for its lack of an ultraglamorous, state-of-the-art vessel, putting its emphasis rather on interpersonal involvement and/or relationship-oriented activities. In the words of a company spokesperson whose enthusiasm seems to be mirrored by many among the onboard staff, "We deliberately emphasize a lot of 'people' stuff."

SHOPPING   Don't expect much in the way of shopping. The most patronized shop is the beauty/barber shop, found in the depths on the Aloha Deck. The ship also has the almost compulsory duty-free boutique, plus a small gift shop.

SERVICE   Service generally wins nothing but favorable comments. Dining room waitstaff manages beautifully in spite of noisy, overcrowded tables and the sometimes impossible demands made upon them. Yes, they'll even bring second helpings. And in the shipboard bars, you'll never have to explain how to make your favorite drink.

The cabin crew keeps the rooms immaculate, even if the cabins do look a bit faded. There is generally good camaraderie between the crew and officers and the passengers.

ITINERARIES   The ship departs on Saturday for seven-day cruises from New Orleans to the western Caribbean and along the west coast of Mexico. Stopovers include Plaza del Carmen/Cozumel and Grand Cayman, with Montego Bay (Jamaica) being the most distant point. In some cases, Key West or the Honduran ports of Roatan Island and/or Puerto Cortes might be substituted for Grand Cayman and/or Ocho Rios, a switch that repeat passengers already familiar with the line's somewhat repetitive itinerary tend to appreciate. Most cruises spend three days at sea.

SPECIAL DISCOUNTS   You'll receive a special discount for early bookings, in some cases up to $150 per cabin if a deposit is made 90 days before your departure. A third or fourth passenger pays only

$199 per cruise on selected trips. Repeaters or former passengers can usually book two cabins at a discount. Passengers booking a seven-day cruise, depending on the special promotion at the time, can receive a complimentary overnight stay in New Orleans. Couples celebrating their anniversary or honeymoon at sea can opt for special packages, priced at between $50 and $170, that include wine, champagne, party favors, photographs, and keepsakes. Families who opt to share a stateroom receive additional discounts that vary

depending on just how close-knit you want to be.

SINGLE SUPPLEMENTS Single travelers are charged from 135% to 200% of the double occupancy rate. To cut costs, the line will double up passengers of the same gender and charge the rate for double occupancy.

PORT CHARGES Port charges and a new charge designated as "handling" add another $107.50 per person to the overall cruise fare.

Enchanted Isle

⇩ ⇩

Specifications

Size (in tons)	23,395	Crew	350 (International)
Number of Cabins	367	Passenger/Crew Ratio	2.1 to 1
Number of Outside Cabins	290	Year Built	1958
Number of Passengers	729	Last Major Refurbishment	1994
Officers	European/ Scandinavian		

Frommer's Ratings (Scale of 1–10)

Activities	7.5	Public Areas	7.8
Cabins	7.8	Public Comfort/Space	7.5
Cleanliness/Maintenance	7.8	Recreational Facilities/Pool	7.6
Entertainment	8.2	Service	8.0
Food & Beverage	7.9	Ship Crew/Officers	7.8
Interior Decor	7.8	Shore Excursions	7.2
Ports of Call	7.0	Worth the Money	9.5
		Overall Average	**7.8**

This vessel, built in 1958 in the Ingalls Shipyard of Mississippi, has undergone more name changes than any other modern liner. It has been known as the *Argentina, Monarch Star, Bermuda Star,* and, in the 1970s, sailed as the *Veendam* for

the Holland America Line. Commodore acquired the ship in 1989 and named it the *Enchanted Isle.* For a time in 1994, it docked in St. Petersburg, Russia, and served as a floating hotel, the Hotel Commodore, before returning to the Caribbean.

Cabins & Rates

Cabins	Average per diem	Bathtub	Fridge	Phone	Sitting Area	TV
Inside	$136	No	No	Yes	Half	Yes
Outside	$162	Half	No	Yes	Half	Yes
Suite	$225	Yes	No	Yes	Yes	Yes

CABINS   There are 11 cabin categories, ranging from deluxe suites with sitting areas to cramped inside cabins with upper and lower berths. The smallest and most cramped cabins are only 120 square feet—only book these if you're on a tight budget—whereas the largest cabins are a generous 293 square feet.

Cabins show wear and tear, but the maintenance is top notch. Each attractively decorated cabin contains air-conditioning, radio, and carpeting. There's plenty of drawer and closet space, unless there's a fourth passenger, and then it's quite tight. Many cabins have single beds that can be converted to double beds. The spotless, tiled bathrooms are large if a bit worn, and contain no amenities, such as a hair dryer or bathrobe, though a few cabin bathrooms have bidets.

Commodore charges for such things as bottled water, which is free on most lines. You'll also note a scarcity of electrical outlets.

If ocean views are important to you, avoid outside cabins on the Navigation Deck, since the primary view there is of lifeboats. Rooms 222, 223, and 224 have unobstructed views. Cabins on the boat deck open onto the public promenade, which cuts down on your privacy a bit.

In the lower level cabins, passengers complain of noise, as the walls seem to be too thin; engine humming and the workings of the crew can be bothersome. There is also no elevator access to cabins on the lower deck, but all this inconvenience might be worth it if you're on a budget:

The per diem rate might only be $110, or even less.

Cabin bathrooms have a step that makes wheelchair accessibility impractical.

RECREATION & FITNESS FACILITIES
Deck space seems adequate for the number of passengers. The ship has an outside swimming pool on its promenade deck. On the sports deck, an active fitness program is offered, with aerobics, walking, jogging, and other exercise regimens. The minuscule Fitness Center, with Nautilus, free weights, cardiovascular equipment, and not much else, can get crowded fast.

PUBLIC AREAS   Although the rather plainly decorated public rooms are polished daily, they look as if they've hosted thousands before you—probably because they have. The public areas on the Promenade Deck stretch the full length aft to the site of the buffets and the main pool. Decks are spacious, but aren't arranged so you can walk the full distance around for your grand promenade.

The ship has a small video game room for children of all ages. There's also a small library, but serious readers should bring their own books. If you want to slip away, go to the lounge on the Observation Deck, which most passengers don't seem to discover until near the voyage's end.

Public rooms that have doorways with ledges are fitted with ramps, and elevators are accessible to wheelchair users. But there's no elevator service to the lowest passenger deck.

Costa Cruise Lines

SHIPS   CostaRomantica • CostaVictoria
World Trade Center, 80 Southwest 8th St., Miami, FL 33130-3097 (mailing address: P.O. Box 01964, Miami, FL 33101-9865). ☎ 800/462-6782 or 305/358-7325; fax 305/375-0676.

This company's origins are as Italian as Garibaldi. In 1860, Giacomo Costa established an olive oil refinery and packaging plant in Genoa. After his death in 1916, his sons (*il fratelli Costa*) bought a ship to transport raw materials and finished products from Sardinia through Genoa to the rest of Europe. Within 19 years, the family had acquired an additional half-dozen ships, whose fortunes rose and then collapsed with the fate of Italy during and after World War II. At war's end, only one tiny ship remained in the family's fleet, but within three years, as part of the postwar economic miracle, a dozen ships were flying the Costa flag, most of them carrying European passengers. Costa was the world's largest operator of passenger ships in the early 1960s, before the explosion of the U.S. cruise industry nudged it into fifth place.

In 1968, the Costa family made a major commitment to the U.S. market by establishing Costa Cruises, now a subsidiary of Genoa-based Costa Crociere. The size of both the ships and the fleet grew rapidly. In 1966, most of the line's ships weighed in at 30,000 tons; by 1993, the *CostaRomantica* was representative of the "new" Costa, at 54,000 tons. Today, the line boasts one of the most modern and beautiful fleets in the Caribbean, with the line's largest ship, the 76,000-ton *CostaVictoria*, rivaling the biggest megaships in the industry.

For whatever reason, Costa treats its Caribbean cruises somewhat differently than its Mediterranean cruises, marketing the latter to both North American and European markets, but with the former offering separate cruises, aboard separate ships, for its American and European clientele. Consequently, we have the odd situation in which Americans can easily sail aboard the *CostaClassica* and the

CostaAllegra on any of their summer trips to Europe, but they'd have to go through the labors of Hercules to book passage on the very same vessels' Caribbean sailings. We're not saying that it can't be done; you can book either of the above-mentioned ships through the office of a European travel agent or directly through the company's reservation office in Genoa. But the fervor with which Costa's Miami-based reservations center steers North American passengers away from those two ships in winter has induced us to not include reviews of them in this edition.

As a consequence of that policy—and even though Costa worldwide attracts greater numbers of European and South Americans than any other cruise line, with an estimated 25% and 38% share of those markets, respectively—you're not likely to see many Europeans on your Costa odyssey through the Caribbean. Even so, the line is infused with definite and highly visible continental flair—just no continentals, that's all.

Costa has had many innovative groundbreakers that now factor into the company's general lore. It pioneered the use of San Juan as a point of departure for cruises, which bolstered Puerto Rico's early attempts to restore San Juan's colonial core. Costa also recognized the allure of such southern Caribbean ports as Grenada long before that island and its much-photographed harbor of St. George's was recognized as a tourist gem. That year, Costa also became the first cruise line to inaugurate the air/sea package.

The company has never been afraid to sell off older, outmoded ships to other shipping concerns, or to rebuild newly acquired older ships. It's also not timid about building new ones, like the new *CostaVictoria*, or about adopting bold styles, such as the postmodern, vaguely austere designs of the *Romantica,* which spends part of every year in the Caribbean and has been carefully studied by the line's competitors.

Despite the glossy corporate veneer, the organization is still very much in the family. In 1996, at least 100 Costa relatives work full time for the related family companies. Key administrative positions affecting the North American market, however, are often filled from the ranks of Italian-born, U.S.-trained executives from outside the family. A good example is CEO Dino Schibuola, whose past experiences include stints at Celebrity Cruises and Athens-based Home Lines.

Each ship in the Costa line is easily identifiable by the blue and yellow smokestack emblazoned with a huge "C." Few other ships in the Caribbean, with the exception of Club Med, bear such an obvious national character as Costa, with its unswerving allegiance to all things Italian. And few other lines market their national origins in as likable a way: There's nothing but bonhomie in the *buongiorno* you're likely to hear from your cabin steward, and the Italian-ness of the line is never presented in any way other than charming and fun. Along with the red, white, and green colors of the Italian flag comes one noticeable gastronomic side benefit: The pasta, espresso, and gelati are better than aboard any other line afloat.

Recognizing that their identity (and success) is inextricably tied to a seagoing interpretation of la dolce vita, Costa is not above satirizing itself and its Italian origins. Some well-meaning staff member is always corralled into conducting a class in the Italian language and "Italian-ness," onboard pizza and toga parties are always well attended, and your waiter will likely urge you to *mangia, mangia!*

Despite lesser numbers of Italian-born stewards and crew members than in years past, and despite the fact that Costa vessels are registered in Liberia, and not Italy, the Italian aspects of a Costa cruise are still very strong, even if the steward who urges you to *mangia, mangia* does so with a Filipino accent, and the bartender who mixes your negroni is from South America.

PROS & CONS   The emphasis here is on style, humor, and escape from the workaday world, all offered with Italian finesse and charm. The combination can be effective, appealing, and sometimes romantic. Overall, Costa offers an excellent and very human experience, well worth an investment of your time and money.

Keep in mind that the ambience on board a Costa ship is distinctly foreign and very Mediterranean. Anyone who dislikes prosciutto with melon, thinks tira misu is a sexual technique (or just too sugary), and believes that drinking Chianti produces morning-after headaches will probably not like this line. You can always opt instead for the predictably unflappable Britishness at Cunard, or a Seabourn-style focus on seamless internationalism. Also, the line's familylike dynamic will probably grate against dyed-in-the-wool loners. Although on your Caribbean routing you're likely to get a less intense dose of rampant Italian-ism than you would aboard the line's Mediterranean sailings, you'll still get quite a lot, some of it directed to and abetted by the line's strength in the Italian-American market.

So, if you think the cool Nordic blue of your Norwegian steward's eyes is the most appealing thing afloat, you probably won't thrill to the more animated, more intimate, and considerably more jocular style of a steward who hails from Pisa, Palermo, or Padua—or the approximation offered by those from the Philippines or various regions of the Balkans. But if you ever loved Italy and its wonders, you'll probably love sailing with Costa.

TYPES OF PASSENGERS   This line attracts passengers who want to pay a reasonable price and who deliberately avoid all-American megaships like those of Carnival. Costa passengers are impressed with Italian style, appreciate a sense of cultural adventure and fun, and like the atmosphere of casual elegance at which the Italians excel.

Costa ships capture the fancy of any travelers who have ever gotten a lump in their throat during a Fellini movie, sipped espresso in a Rome cafe, or wished they had a warmhearted relative in Italy to welcome them with open arms when they came for a family reunion. So it should come as no surprise that Italian-Americans are heavily represented aboard every winter Caribbean cruise.

For its Caribbean cruises, the average age of Costa passengers is 45 to 50, with an annual household income of $50,000-plus. More than any other line, Costa appeals to retirees and young couples alike, partly because of its emphasis on Italy's cultural allure rather than more specific generational draws. Large numbers of good-looking and/or casually stylish passengers, regardless of their nationalities, mill about searching for the good life, the younger ones showing off expensive swimwear or sportswear during the day and a reasonable amount of décolletage at night. Banter on board is amusing and lighthearted, and usually of good will.

DINING   Food is well prepared, based on the bounty of Italian soil and traditions, and tailored for preparation within cramped, high-volume galleys aboard the high seas. Whereas the *CostaRomantica* has a single dining room, the newer and bigger *CostaVictoria* has two. In both cases, they maintain a two-seating policy where lunch is served at noon and 1:30pm and dinner at 6:15 and 8:30pm. You'll hear debate about which seating is better. Passengers tend to line up outside the restaurant doors in anticipation of feeding time, which can detract from the glamour of the occasion.

None of this, however, detracts from the basic bounty and allure of the cuisine. Food is flavorful and fragrant, spiced properly with Mediterranean seasonings. The fare is also appreciated as much for its entertainment as for its gastronomic value: Much emphasis, and a few theatrics, is placed on tossing a pasta, or energetically seasoning a salad while diners look on.

Display cases decorate the dining area, showing off the catch of the day or a medley of desserts.

No evening on board begins without a clearly defined theme, and in keeping with the line's Italian origins, three of the seven theme nights focus on Italian food and some aspect of Italian lore, legend, and ambience. They include *Festa Italiana, Notte Romantica* (where staff members dress up as Venetian gondoliers and present a red rose to each of the ladies during dessert), and versions of Roman bacchanals that are much, much tamer than the originals. The highlight of many cruises is Toga Night, when at least some of the guests seem reduced to helpless giggles and nearly every passenger dons a costume (usually a bedsheet fastened around the waist with a belt). Even the cruise director (who is usually American during Caribbean sailings aboard the *Romantica* and *Victoria*) is likely to threaten, "No sheet, no eat," so whether you look good in a toga or not, you'll be wearing one at dinner.

Service is efficient and alert, as quick-witted waiters intuitively grasp diners' needs. Naturally, the maître d' supervising the noisy room is as smooth and well rehearsed as they come, a well-trained impresario directing the many facets of the show.

There are, of course, plenty of places to eat between meals. Onboard pâtisseries serve espresso, chocolates, and pastries, while Romeo's Pizzeria offers many variations of its namesake throughout the day and night. Buffets, unfortunately, tend to be mediocre. Low-fat, low-salt, low-cholesterol menus are available in the dining room.

ACTIVITIES   Lecturers expound on Italian art, history, or wine-making, and coordinators organize small-stakes, small-scale betting pools on simulated horse racing. Good-natured representatives from each national group on board are selected to compete in mock-competitive social events referred to by Costa as their

"World Cup" series. These might include contests to decide which passenger looks best in a toga, which most closely resembles Al Pacino or Marlon Brando in the *Godfather* movies, or which non-Italian passenger can best imitate Luciano Pavarotti.

Whimsical diversions (such as a vegetable-carving demonstration) abound and are suited to sedentary, less physically active types. Each ship also contains a sedate and restrained-looking library and a card room.

An onboard priest conducts masses almost every day in a chapel (de rigueur aboard a line whose origins are strongly Catholic), and Costa captains offer to renew the vows of married couples in communal ceremonies. The line does a solid business performing weddings just before their ships pull out of Port Everglades before a Caribbean sailing. Any of these events might be followed by a poolside foccacia and pizza party.

CHILDREN'S ACTIVITIES Compared to other cruise lines, Costa places little emphasis on separating children from adult passengers, a practice that derives from (and enhances) the Italian atmosphere of *famiglia* promoted by the line.

However, even the most indulgent parent is sometimes happy to transfer the care of his or her children to someone else, and for this there's the "Costa Kids Club," a program designed to keep young sailors entertained while their parents enjoy la dolce vita, sans kids.

Two daily programs are offered on Caribbean cruises. In the program for ages 5 to 12, children enjoy jogging, aerobics, a puppet theater, mini-Olympics, and team treasure hunts, and in the program for ages 13 to 17, teenagers take part in sports and fitness programs, guitar lessons, movie-making sessions (using camcorders), and rock-and-roll hours. At least one full-time youth counselor is available aboard each Costa ship year-round, with additional staff pressed into service every time more than a dozen children are on the passenger list. While ships are at sea in Caribbean waters, supervised Kids Club hours are from 9:30 to 11:30am, 2 to 5pm, and 8 to 10pm. The program doesn't usually operate when ships are in port unless parents specifically request it.

Group baby-sitting for ages three and up is available on request every evening from 9:30pm to 1:30am, unless the vessel is in port, when hours are extended to include morning and afternoon sessions. Group baby-sitting costs $8 for one child and $10 for two children.

ENTERTAINMENT All aspects of a Costa cruise, regardless of the destination, focus on multilingual, multicultural events, linked by a shared appreciation of things Italian. Entertainment directors program amusements such as concerts, puppet or marionette shows, mime, acrobatics, or cabaret, none of which require audiences to know Italian.

Caribbean sailings for North American clients (see our note of explanation earlier) tend to be more monolingual than sailings in the Mediterranean, when onboard announcements and scripts of whatever cabaret act you're watching might ramble on in three or even five languages. But if the passenger roster justifies it aboard *Romantica*'s and *Victoria*'s Caribbean jaunts, the breadth of available translations expands as needed. When the crowd is particularly international, you might feel like you're trapped at the UN during a translators' strike.

If you're not looking for Las Vegas–style glitter, you'll likely find the entertainment programs amusing. But remember that the acts are conceived to be completely nonoffensive, remarkable in a time when expletives are rarely deleted.

Both ships contain state-of-the-art showrooms—two-tiered affairs that evoke the half moon–shaped amphitheaters of an 18th-century opera house—and casinos loaded with slot machines and tables for Caribbean stud poker and blackjack. Both the theater and the casino are bigger (and the casino consciously flashier) aboard the *CostaVictoria* than aboard the *CostaRomantica.*

SHOPPING   Costa shops are arranged in a circular, curving style inspired by an Italian piazza, albeit a glossy and slick one in Milan or Florence. Merchandise is heavy on Italian humor and style, and is sometimes fun if never particularly utilitarian. Shops rely heavily on impulse buying for their success, and aren't too grand to inventory key chains that read "Proud to be Italian" or T-shirts proclaiming their wearer an "Italian Stallion."

SERVICE   Quick to recognize how passengers relate, staff and crew handle the dynamics of extended families with grace and aplomb. Staff members are alert, hip, quick-witted, and at their worst, hysterically overworked.

Dining room staff is composed of career waiters of the type Italy excels at producing: charming, intuitive, and capable of handling most culinary requests. In recent years, greater numbers of the staff derive from South America, the Philippines, and many points in between, although at least two or three in any dining room crew are likely to be the genuine Italian article.

ITINERARIES

CostaRomantica—Every Sunday throughout the winter, the ship departs from Port Everglades (Fort Lauderdale) for two different itineraries that alternate weekly. The eastern Caribbean cruises call at San Juan, St. Thomas, Serena Cay (a private island off the coast of the Dominican Republic), and Nassau. The western Caribbean cruises dock at Key West, Playa del Carmen, Cozumel, Ocho Rios, and Grand Cayman.

CostaVictoria—Its winter itinerary is almost exactly the same as that of the *Romantica,* and alternates visits to the eastern Caribbean with visits to the western Caribbean. When *Romantica* does the eastern segment, *Victoria* does the western segment, and vice versa.

SPECIAL DISCOUNTS   Third and fourth passengers sharing a cabin during "value season" pay from $195 to $295 for a seven-night cruise. "Super Senior Discounts" allow passengers to deduct an additional 5% off fares booked 90 days before sailing, when at least one occupant of a cabin is 65 years or older.

Other discounts are offered if you book a suite or mini-suite at full tariff on selected sailings. Your traveling companion will pay only the price of the cheapest unit aboard ship for the same time period. The savings can reach almost $2,000 per couple. Children 12 years and younger sharing a cabin with two adults cruise for only $99 per child.

Clients booking two seven-day back-to-back cruises can sail both the eastern and western Caribbean for 14 days and take 50% off the price of the second seven-day stint.

SINGLE SUPPLEMENTS   Single travelers pay a 150% supplement over the double occupancy per person rate. If a solo passenger requests it, Costa can arrange to place a same-sex roommate in their cabin, in which event the single traveler will pay the double occupancy per person rate.

PORT CHARGES   For most Caribbean cruises, the port taxes are $121 per person.

CostaRomantica

Specifications

Size (in tons)	54,000	Crew	650 (International)
Number of Cabins	654	Passenger/Crew Ratio	2 to 1
Number of Outside Cabins	446	Year Built	1993
Number of Passengers	1,356	Last Major Refurbishment	n/a
Officers	Italian		

Frommer's Ratings (Scale of 1–10)

Activities	8.0	Public Areas	8.8
Cabins	8.5	Public Comfort/Space	8.4
Cleanliness/Maintenance	8.5	Recreational Facilities/Pool	8.2
Entertainment	7.5	Service	8.8
Food & Beverage	8.8	Ship Crew/Officers	8.8
Interior Decor	8.8	Shore Excursions	8.2
Ports of Call	7.5	Worth the Money	8.5
		Overall Average	**8.4**

CostaRomantica is the newer twin of the *CostaClassica,* which caters almost exclusively to Europe-based passengers. Built at a cost of $325 million, and weighing a respectable upper-middle-tier weight of 54,000 tons, the *CostaRomantica* was, along with its twin, the largest and most stylish ship in the Costa armada until 1996, when it was supplanted by the larger *CostaVictoria.* Many passengers are repeat customers, drawn to the ship for its emphasis on comfort and its restrained and almost sober dignity, based on contemporary Italian design accented with the best of Italy's traditions of arts and crafts.

Cabins & Rates

Cabins	Average per diem	Bathtub	Fridge	Phone	Sitting Area	TV
Inside	$137	No	No	Yes	No	Yes
Outside	$158	No	No	Yes	No	Yes
Suite	$382	Yes	Yes	Yes	Yes	Yes

CABINS   Except for the suites, all cabins aboard this ship are a standard size, although many are outfitted for berthing up to two additional passengers. This, plus the big discounts offered to children under 12, makes them a favorite of families. If you're traveling with just one significant other and anticipate quiet intimacy, it might be a problem if you're adjacent to a room with hyperactive children and their parents. But if you're from a big family yourself, or are traveling with one, just pretend you're living in a densely populated neighborhood in Genoa and try to remain amused.

Regardless of their configuration, all units have cherry-veneer cabinetry, bathrooms with showers and rather little square footage, private safe, radio, individual temperature controls, vanities, closets, and a table with chairs. Suites include all the above-mentioned amenities plus a Jacuzzi, double sink, minibar, separate sitting area, and, in some but not all cases, an outside veranda. Standard outside cabins average approximately 200 square feet, up to twice the size of equivalent cabins on some competing lines. Reflecting Italy's great musical legacy, suites are named after famous operas, including Parsifal, Manon, and Tosca.

Six cabins are wheelchair accessible.

RECREATION & FITNESS FACILITIES

The ship has two medium-size swimming pools surrounded by several levels of Burmese teakwood. These pools and the deck space are generally adequate for the number of passengers aboard.

You'll want to exercise at least once aboard ship, if only to assuage your guilt about consuming all that pasta. The ship has an exercise and jogging track, lifecycles, treadmills, saunas, plus the largest Turkish steam rooms afloat.

The decor of the Caracalla Spa is inspired by those hedonistic days of old Rome, though in high-tech versions that Nero and his pals wouldn't recognize. You can enjoy a seaweed, mud, or herbal body wrap, or a facial or exfoliation. You can flail your arms during Thalassotherapy, hydrotherapy, or an herb-based cure that the sometimes jaded attendants refer to as a "body blitz simpatico."

PUBLIC AREAS

The ship was designed by Gregotti Associati, creators of the Musee d'Orsay in Paris, who opted to infuse its public areas with what amounts to a public relations plug for Italy. Chandeliers from Murano, intricate mosaics, pear-wood inlays, and lots and lots of marble all testify to Italian taste and style, and the efficient and elegant lines are a tribute to modern Milanese design. Brilliant white Carrara marble is used more than on virtually any other ships afloat.

Public areas aboard *CostaRomantica* take their names from the heritage of Italy, and sometimes bear decors to match. Examples include the Excelsior Casino, the Via Condotti shopping arcade, the Caracalla Spa and Beauty Salon, the Piazza Italia Grand Bar, and the Botticelli Restaurant, in which murals and window blinds evoke themes from the Renaissance. (Unfortunately, its indented ceilings, though beautiful, seem to amplify the high noise level.) Some of the decor was influenced by one of the creative directors of La Scala in Milan. There's an outdoor Alfresco Café, with access to a frequently replenished buffet that sometimes gets a bit overcrowded.

Show time is presented in a half-moon–shaped theater, *L'Opéra Theater,* which presents a much less formal repertoire than its name implies. Rising two decks above the spectator seats, it contains 6 miles of fiber optics, mosaics inspired by 14th-century models, and a medley of eye-catching sets. Music in the ship's ballroom includes highly danceable down-memory-lane dance numbers performed by a six-piece band.

Deck names aboard *Romantica* reflect the national origins of Costa's cosmopolitan clientele (for example, Paris, Verona, Madrid), with the lowest, below-the-waterline deck named after the canals of Amsterdam. Staircases represent more than means of going up and down: Starkly architectural, they circle like birds from level to level, a celebration of both form and function. The nerve center of the ship is the central lobby, a five-story atrium flooded with overhead light. High overhead is a glass-walled circular observatory, the Diva Disco, where you can dance as close to the stars as any ship afloat will allow.

CostaVictoria

Specifications

Size (in tons)	76,000	Crew	800 (Italian/International)
Number of Cabins	964	Passenger/Crew Ratio	2.4 to 1
Number of Outside Cabins	573	Year Built	1996
Number of Passengers	1,950	Last Major Refurbishment	n/a
Officers	Italian/International		

Frommer's Ratings (Scale of 1–10)

Activities	8.0	Public Areas	9.0
Cabins	8.6	Public Comfort/Space	8.4
Cleanliness/Maintenance	8.6	Recreational Facilities/Pool	8.5
Entertainment	7.5	Service	8.8
Food & Beverage	8.8	Ship Crew/Officers	8.8
Interior Decor	8.8	Shore Excursions	8.2
Ports of Call	7.5	Worth the Money	8.8
		Overall Average	**8.5**

This ship launches Costa Cruises into the megaship era. Inaugurated in the summer of 1996 for a premier stint in Europe, this is the largest and most technologically sophisticated ship ever launched by the line—a flagship for the fleet and a vision of Costa's hopes for the millennium. It's sleek and stylish, its mammoth size allowing for more spacious and dramatic interior features and more options for dining and after-dark diversions than any other Costa ship.

Built in Bremerhaven, Germany, and with a cruising speed of between 21 and 23 knots, it has a streamlined, futuristic-looking design with four tiers of glass-fronted observation decks facing the prow.

As a nod to some of its mega-competitors, the interior is splashier and more colorful than that of any Costa vessel to date. A cadre of designers emphasized the decorative and artistic traditions of Italy, with ample use of pear wood, multicolored marbles, and Murano glass.

Cabins & Rates

Cabins	Average per diem	Bathtub	Fridge	Phone	Sitting Area	TV
Inside	$135	No	No	Yes	No	Yes
Outside	$165	No	No	Yes	No	Yes
Suite	$367	Yes	Yes	Yes	Yes	Yes

CABINS   These are among the best the Costa line offers, as some 60% of them feature large windows opening onto sea views. Especially desirable are 14 minisuites, which have generous living rooms, reading areas, and tubs with hydro-massage equipment, and are outfitted with one queen-size bed and two Pullman-style beds. What makes them a bargain is that they contain many of the same amenities and interior design features as the more expensive suites, and their space is very generous at 301 square feet. For those with imperial taste, six suites represent the epitome of seagoing luxury. These suites have one queen and two Pullman-style beds, and feel roomy even if bunking four passengers, as they're generously proportioned at 430 square feet. Furnishings in these suites are made of pear wood, with fabrics by Laura Ashley, who is not even remotely Italian. None of the suites or staterooms aboard this ship contains private balconies, but you get spacious portholes or big picture windows for wave-watching instead, and some of the suites have floor-to-ceiling windows for especially wide-angled views.

Instead of opulence, Costa has decorated its regular cabins in a severe, minimalist style that's short of ambience but perfectly adequate as a place to retreat between meals and bouts of cruise activities. It's the same comfortably restrained and conservatively modern Italian styling that appears aboard all Costa ships. Inside cabins, depending on their location, have between 120 and 150 square feet of floor space; outside cabins have 150 square feet, figures that are about the norm for the industry. (Surprisingly, they're smaller than those aboard the *CostaRomantica,* where inside cabins have 175 square feet and outsiders 200 square feet.) Some are rented as doubles, with two lower berths, whereas the larger staterooms can fit three passengers comfortably with two lower berths and one Pullman-style bed. Each cabin has standard amenities that include TV, radio, minibar, and safe.

Four of the ship's cabins are specifically outfitted for passengers with disabilities, and each has two bathrooms, one of which is accessorized for wheelchairs.

RECREATION & FITNESS FACILITIES

This is a good cruise for those addicted to seagoing health and beauty treatments. The Pompeii Spa stresses the use of skin and body-care products developed by Tuscany's Terme Saturnia. It's also the best-accessorized and largest spa in the Costa Line, and the only one that includes its own indoor pool. You can release your tensions in a steam bath, a sauna, or a Turkish bath, or sit and soak in the spa's Jacuzzi, perched artfully atop the spa's

pool. There's also a state-of-the-art fitness center with all the latest equipment.

Out on deck, there's a pair of swimming pools, as well as a "misting pool" that cools off overheated sunbathers with fine jets of water. Further decks wrap around the pools and their sunbathing area, providing plenty of space for passengers to stretch out and soak up the rays, even when the ship is fully booked. There are four Jacuzzis, a tennis court, and a 1,312-foot jogging track, four circuits of which equals 1 mile. There's also a beauty center aboard.

PUBLIC AREAS

In keeping with its role as Costa's largest and splashiest ship to date, public areas, especially the onboard casino, throb with color and energy. The ship's most notable feature is a grand observation lounge featuring a waterfall on one side and a floor-to-ceiling glass wall on the other. The area is conceived as an Italian piazza, a signature feature found on all Costa ships, with windows of the forward cabin corridors overlooking the lounge. The observation lounge serves first as a grand arena for socializing and special shipboard events, and second as a theater for evening entertainment.

In the Central Hall, an atrium begins in the lobby, rises seven decks, and is topped by a crystal dome that floods the interior with sunlight. Four glass elevators offer passengers a quick panorama of life on board at every level.

Two main dining rooms have two different seatings each night. The multifunction Tavernetta Lounge features the music of a three-piece dance band, stiff drinks, and wraparound paintings of other ships in the Costa Fleet, as painted by marine artist Stephen Card. Buffets, a grill, a pizzeria, and an ice-cream bar ensure that no one ever goes hungry between meals.

Gamblers gravitate to the big and brassy Monte Carlo Casino, the boldest, most dramatic, and biggest of any within the Costa Fleet. It's linked to the Grand Bar Orpheus, one floor below, by a curving stairway. This bar is the preferred spot aboard for sampling an espresso or a cappuccino.

Other public rooms include a play area for children, a club for teens, a chapel (not always a feature aboard today's megaships), three conference rooms, an array of boutiques, a card room, a library, and a disco (the Rock Star) that, unlike those aboard other Costa ships, lies amidships, not perched close to the stars on the uppermost deck.

Cunard

SHIPS   Sea Goddess I • Sea Goddess II

555 Fifth Ave., New York, NY 10017. ☎ 800/5-CUNARD or 212/880-7500; fax 212/949-0915.

Cunard is the grande dame of the cruise ship industry. No other cruise line in the world boasts such illustrious antecedents, or such a famous and frequently resurrected flagship, the *QE2,* which, though aging, is still the most famous passenger ship in the world.

Cunard's laurels, however, depend on more than just the prestige of one ship. Since its debut, the company's innovations, such as the first steam-driven turbine engines, in 1907, or oceangoing health spas, have had a major impact on the industry and been adapted by the line's competitors. Cunard has also entertained more British monarchs than any other afloat. They have, quite simply, the most impeccable pedigree in the cruiseship business.

In 1969, a smaller replacement for the original *Elizabeth* was inaugurated, the 70,327-ton flagship *QE2.* It's the only vessel that maintains the continuum between Cunard's grandiloquent past and a present where its fleet is much more diverse, less cohesive, and more difficult to define. In 1971, Cunard was acquired by a London-based multinational conglomerate, Trafalgar House Investments. In 1977, in a move that was widely criticized at the time as the sellout of a part of Britain's national heritage, Cunard's headquarters were moved from London to New York. In the years that followed, Cunard's sometimes stuffy, sometimes haughty management style caused it problems, and even some recent company spokespersons, including Peter Ward, who ruled briefly after the Kvaerner takeover before being abruptly replaced in 1996, have publicly condemned the secretive and indecisive fiefdoms that competed within its corporate labyrinth. Even travel agents, a group that cruise lines should, and do, tend to pamper and court, loudly criticized Cunard's clerical workers for their lack of helpfulness and clarity. Despite all this, the prestige and undeniable glamour of Cunard kept it going and helped it grow, and Cunard responded by buying a flotilla of ships from other carriers or, occasionally, commissioning vessels from scratch.

In 1983, Cunard bought the Norwegian American Line, in the process acquiring a pair of ships, the *Sagafjord* (which was subsequently sold in 1996) and the *Vistafjord.* In 1986, the company obtained its most consistently luxurious and upscale vessels: the sedate and yachtlike *Sea Goddess I* and *Sea Goddess II.* Small, socially correct, and difficult to operate at a consistent profit, they're doggedly maintained by Cunard in part for the prestige they afford the line. Beginning in 1996, Cunard began promoting the adventurous aspects of a cruise aboard these vessels, a new and not altogether convincing spin on ships that are otherwise noted for their exclusivity and formality. In 1992, Cunard added another luxury worldwide cruise ship: the *Royal Viking Sun,* acquired from a bankrupt competitor.

Recent streaks of bad luck involved a series of engineering, managerial, and logistical mishaps that wreaked havoc with the *QE2,* with two of the line's most upscale ships, and with Cunard's reputation. In 1995, the same year that Cunard declared a $25 million loss, Trafalgar House was bought by the Kvaerner Group, a Norwegian engineering and shipbuilding concern with a strong presence in London and a controlling interest in Finland's massive Kvaerner Masa Shipyards. Ironically, these yards, even at the time of the sale, were busy building megaships for both Royal Caribbean Cruises Ltd. and Carnival, two of Cunard's most potent rivals for Caribbean business.

Cunard listened in horror as Kvaerner announced that it had bought Trafalgar mainly for its engineering divisions, and that it didn't really want Cunard at all. Kvaerner offered Cunard for sale at a price substantially below book value, but when no other shipping line offered to buy it, Kvaerner somewhat reluctantly decided to keep it, albeit with a new, more savvy, and probably much more competent roster of managers. Cunard's director since 1996 has been Finnish-born Antti Pankakoski, a veteran shipbuilder and engineer and former executive vice president of the Kvaerner Masa Shipyards.

Since that takeover, there have been some decisive moves to cut costs and simultaneously re-emphasize Cunard as a cruise line for the affluent and demanding. In 1996, the company's least glamorous, most downscale ship, the *Cunard Countess,* was sold, and in May 1997 Cunard ended an arrangement with the Scandinavian shipping firm Effjohn in which it had managed that firm's downscale ship *Dynasty.* With these moves, a refreshing spirit of optimism began to gradually creep over the company's demoralized employees.

Today, venerable Cunard, despite humiliations and rejection by many suitors, still clings to its tattered vestiges of stiff-upper-lip Britishness. Ironically, one of the line's greatest challenges as it enters the 21st century will consist of finding and training competent shipboard staffs who are capable of consistently evoking spit-and-polish crispness of Cunard's finest hour: the Edwardian Age. This may provide the distinction the line needs as it faces such maritime giants as Carnival, Royal Caribbean, Celebrity, and Princess, whose ships are brilliantly designed, newer, and cheaper to operate, and whose skill at marketing their cruise products to the North American public is awesome.

Cunard remains the only company in the world to offer transatlantic service on a regular schedule, albeit aboard a flagship that has gobbled up millions of dollars in recent makeovers and in settlement of claims from past fiascoes. In addition to that, Cunard offers a cruise and a destination for almost everybody, many of them

extremely luxurious, and others much less so.

Cunard's current presence within the Caribbean is relatively limited, partly because of its 1996 and 1997 divestments of the *Cunard Countess* and the *Dynasty.* The line's two remaining vessels that spend significant time in the Caribbean are the *Sea Goddess I* and *II,* almost exact twins that provide some of the most luxurious experiences afloat, full of great style and pizzazz. The party you'll find aboard these small vessels (Cunard refers to them as "super-yachts") is sedate and cultivated, replete with white-gloved service and robust but ever-so-polite Britishness.

PROS & CONS Sailing Cunard is like taking a trip to a well-cultivated corner of Britain. The onboard ambience is quiet, sedate, and, in most cases, ever so polite. Public areas are tasteful to a fault, almost too much so.

The *Sea Goddess I* and *Sea Goddess II* are, however, in their own opulent category: Life aboard these tiny ships resembles something out of *Lifestyles of the Rich and Famous.* Service and cuisine are outstanding, but you will pay for it: Cruise prices are among the steepest in the industry. And the ships' small size might feel claustrophobic to some, and there's none of the architectural glitz that you'll find on most of the giant cruise ships on the seas today: These are not the ships to book if you're looking for a four-deck atrium with glass elevators zipping passengers from casino to cabaret.

TYPES OF PASSENGERS The line attracts a well-traveled, soft-spoken crowd of older passengers, many of them repeaters, whose median age is somewhere around and above 55. They're usually the type who would prefer a 4pm tea to a communal soak in a hot tub with a gaggle of strangers. All passengers, however, usually share a respect for all things British, and many British folks sail this line. Cunard cruisers are more likely to have read Trollope and Thackeray novels than the latest by Danielle Steel.

The *Sea Goddesses* appeal to the most upscale clientele: those who have tons of money or want their fellow passengers to think they do. Passengers demand, and get, many ego-reinforcing niceties.

Cunard probably carries more clients who sail just for the pleasures of sea- and star-gazing than any other line. If you crave solitude and the healing powers of a sojourn at sea, no Cunard staff member will ever disturb your self-imposed seclusion. The company and its crews will also understand and indulge whatever personal quirks and eccentricities you've brought with you on board.

Although many lines now openly solicit gay or lesbian travelers, Cunard is the most "gay friendly" cruise line. More and more, large groups of gay travelers are enjoying Cunard ships and their amenities. Pied Piper Travel, for example, often "escorts" gay groups on the *QE2* and other luxurious Cunard liners, all in grand style.

DINING   The fare on the *Sea Goddess I* and *II* is almost consistently excellent and the wine lists are outstanding. Service is flawless. Caviar, smoked salmon, foie gras, and truffles are available; lamb, steaks, and lobster are flown in at frequent intervals. Dining protocols are elegantly maintained by means of single-seating luncheon and dinner services, where passengers make and break the membership of their inner circles without regard for predesignated seating charts. You're likely to get a table for two if you ask for one.

In all Cunard dining rooms, maître d'hôtels encourage passengers to order dishes that don't appear on the menu. Some cruisers take advantage of this, telling the chef, for instance, how to prepare a perfect garlic chicken breast. This is unusual; you won't be so indulged on other lines.

A distinctive factor in Cunard dining rooms is a pleasantly low level of volume. Staff is eager to please, but remember that you're dealing with reserved Brits here, and they might seem unflappable and undemonstrative as compared to wait staffs aboard some other, more party-oriented

lines. Aboard all Cunard vessels, mid-morning bouillon and afternoon tea are standard bills of fare, and are especially pleasant when winds are chilly.

ACTIVITIES   On the *Sea Goddesses*, passengers set their own pace and schedules, yet sail knowing that if they want to play golf or tennis ashore at a difficult-to-get-into club, an obliging staff member will do his or her best to make it happen.

All Cunard cruises share a propensity for the spoken word. Guest lecturers might include the ex–press secretary for former Prime Minister Margaret Thatcher, or art auctioneers, noted chefs or wine connoisseurs, or economic advisors or professors known for their charm and affability.

On a much less edifying note, the line seems to enjoy booking authorities on the nuances and niceties of shopping. You might even sit in on a rather windy lecture on an upcoming port of call. Frankly, Cunard's lectures tend to be either highly erudite or highly frivolous—a medley of self-serving reminiscences from speakers whose references are, quite simply, worlds apart. Many are hit-or-miss.

You can also attend church services of the interdenominational variety (though we detected some Anglican overtones). Films are screened in a theater that doubles as a meeting room. All Cunard vessels contain libraries. Detective/mystery evenings are often held, where amateur Sherlock Holmeses and Miss Marples solve fictitious murders.

CHILDREN'S ACTIVITIES   Cunard is attentive to its passengers in a way one would expect from the best British butler, but the line falls short with its children's facilities. This is not an altogether unconscious omission. Cunard's image is not particularly suited to entertaining undisciplined children who might treat teakwood decks like a baseball or cricket field. Aboard the *Sea Goddesses*, children and teenagers would not be particularly welcome, and would probably be bored out of their minds anyway. In a pinch, babysitters can be arranged.

ENTERTAINMENT On the *Sea Goddesses,* passengers can socialize with one another after twilight, dine tête-à-tête in their cabins, and retire to bed early to hash out the problems of corporate and/or social life. Many passengers unwind at a piano bar, fussing over whatever minor star is tinkling the ivories. The *Goddesses* have no onboard showroom and no glittering cabaret shows. The mood is decorous and staid.

All Cunard vessels contain a casino, although they're nothing like the electronic, glittering altars to Las Vegas that you'll find aboard more high-charged vessels flying the Carnival or Royal Caribbean Cruise Line flags.

SHOPPING Even the least prestigious of the Cunard ships contains a small arcade of boutiques and gift emporiums, and those on the *Sea Goddesses* sell goods that are predictably more upscale and expensive. You'll find garments discreetly emblazoned with the Cunard logo and gifts (articles of pewter or Wedgwood, for example) that exemplify British homeyness.

SERVICE The *Sea Goddesses'* staffs are mostly young, affable Europeans with impeccable manners. Indeed, the excellent personal service, call it pampering, and cuisine are the two prime reasons passengers pay the high price to cruise on these vessels. Service is absolutely top notch, but with predictable British reserve. Aboard the *Sea Goddesses,* tipping is discouraged, but not absolutely forbidden.

ITINERARIES
Sea Goddess I—From March through October, the *Sea Goddess I* treks along the coast of Africa, Asia, and the Mediterranean and makes trips up the Amazon. It spends November through February in the Caribbean, transiting the Panama Canal and sailing on seven-day circular itineraries from a base in St. Thomas. Stopovers include St. John, St. Maarten, St. Barts, Antigua, Virgin Gorda, and Jost Van Dyke.

Sea Goddess II—During some months of the winter (usually January to April), this vessel maintains seven-day transits based in either St. Thomas or Barbados, and calling at points that include the Grenadines, St. Lucia, Martinique, St. Kitts, Grenada, St. Barts, and Tobago. The rest of the year *Sea Goddess II* tends to remain in the Mediterranean with excursions through the Suez Canal for cruises into the Indian and Pacific Oceans.

SPECIAL DISCOUNTS Cunard maintains one of the best-marketed and most lucrative rewards programs for frequent cruisers in the industry. "Cunard World Club Refined" is based on models set by the airlines years ago. If you enjoyed Cunard once before, it may be to your advantage to dip your feet into Anglophilic waters once again. Also, early booking discounts of 20% are available on any ship, as are specific promotions that vary with the ship, the season, and the destination. Examples include discounts on the second half of back-to-back cruises and discounts of up to 75% for a second passenger sailing with a companion who's booked a cabin within a predetermined price category.

SINGLE SUPPLEMENTS The *Sea Goddesses* charge from 150% to 175% of the per person rate for occupancy of a double.

PORT CHARGES Depending on the cruise and the ports of call, port charges can range from $80 to $186 per person.

Sea Goddess I • Sea Goddess II

⚓ ⚓ ⚓ ⚓ ⚓

Specifications

Size (in tons)	4,250	Crew	89 (European/American)
Number of Cabins	58	Passenger/Crew Ratio	1.3 to 1
Number of Outside Cabins	58	Year Built	1984
Number of Passengers	116	Last Major Refurbishment	1992
Officers	Norwegian		

Frommer's Ratings (Scale of 1–10)

Activities	6.5	Public Areas	9.5
Cabins	8.3	Public Comfort/Space	8.9
Cleanliness/Maintenance	9.2	Recreational Facilities/Pool	8.7
Entertainment	8.5	Service	9.8
Food & Beverage	9.6	Ship Crew/Officers	9.5
Interior Decor	9.2	Shore Excursions	9.2
Ports of Call	9.0	Worth the Money	9.0
		Overall Average	**8.9**

Cunard refers to a cruise aboard either of the *Sea Goddesses* as "an odyssey into the exquisite." We agree wholeheartedly. Overall, a *Sea Goddess* experience matches the top-notch echelons of service, cuisine, and amenities offered aboard some (but not all) compartments of Cunard's flagship, the *QE2*. Although some of Cunard's other vessels sometimes fall short, the *Sea Goddesses* provide service, grandeur, and yachtlike elegance that are nothing short of imperial.

This ultradeluxe pair of small ships is plush and meticulously maintained. Elegant and ever-so-polite service will make you feel pampered, and the cuisine equals meals served in a Michelin two-star restaurant—plus, all drinks and almost all wine is included in the price.

Drawbacks, if any, derive from the ships' small size. At 4,250 tons each, the *Goddesses* are truly petite. They are like a posh private club that just happens to move across the water. It is hoped you'll be comfortable with the other passengers aboard; if you aren't, the perfect manners of the staff will smooth over any embarrassing contretemps that might otherwise be conspicuous aboard a vessel this small.

Activities are almost completely unstructured. If you love Carnival vessels and its parties, you'll probably find either of the *Sea Goddesses* a real yawner. But if the idea of a Carnival rumpus makes you want to flee to your cabin, a *Goddess* might indeed be for you, assuming you can afford it.

Cabins & Rates*						
Cabins	**Average per diem**	**Bathtub**	**Fridge**	**Phone**	**Sitting Area**	**TV**
Suite	$650	Yes	Yes	Yes	Yes	Yes

Rates include airfare.

CABINS   Each cabin is an outside suite, but with only 205 square feet of floor space, they may feel claustrophobic. The plushly upholstered but "efficient" accommodations are cozy and romantically (or inconveniently, depending on your perspective) cramped, but since everything outside your cabin door is sheer grandeur, this may not matter. If you want larger and more comfortable lodgings, you'll find them aboard *Seabourn* vessels, whose prices are comparable.

Each *Goddess* accommodation contains a stereo, TV with VCR, a fully stocked complimentary bar with refrigerator, and many thoughtfully arranged grace notes. If you can afford it, two units can be interconnected, thereby creating a nest that's equivalent to a junior suite in a New York City hotel. Staff can arrange for dining within your suite and whip up elegant spreads, often with the requisite caviar and champagne as part of the panache.

This ship isn't good for passengers with disabilities, as doorways leading to staterooms and toilets are not big enough to accommodate a wheelchair. Persons in wheelchairs also can't go ashore, because the wheelchairs can't be taken on launches at ports where the vessel must anchor offshore.

RECREATION & FITNESS FACILITIES
There's a jogging track above the outdoor pool, but it's so small-scale you're likely to get dizzy if you run it at high speeds. There are also two whirlpools (yes, even Cunard allows its guests to stew among the bubbles) and a wading pool for children.

You can use the health club, with weight machines, free weights, stationary bikes, aerobics classes, and saunas, 24 hours a day. The facilities and amenities are smaller than the megarooms on other lines, but no one seems to mind. What the spas lack in space is compensated for by the pampering and ministrations of the staff, all representatives of the Golden Door health spa of California.

PUBLIC AREAS   Public areas are awash with marble, polished hardwoods, and Oriental carpets. So posh are they, and so yachtlike the feel of the vessels, that you expect an English lord to walk through the door at any moment to suggest a cocktail. There are flowers nearly everywhere, and a number of lounges, but no library.

Disney Cruise Line (Preview)

SHIPS   Disney Magic (early 1998) • Disney Wonder (late 1998)
210 Celebration Place, Suite 400, Celebration, FL 34747-1000. ☎ 407/566-7000; fax 407/566-7353.

Although it's taken almost to the millennium for the Disney company to introduce its first cruise ships, you might say that Walt Disney's roots were in the cruise business—after all, his first Mickey Mouse cartoon was named "Steamboat Willie."

The ships aren't slated to be launched until 1998, but Disney Cruise Line's reservations department was up and running in the summer of 1996. And passengers are booking. Call information for its toll-free number (at press time, the number had not been established).

Disney expects to accommodate half a million passengers a year on the ships, which could be a lethal blow to Premier Cruise Line, whose "Big Red Boat" has heretofore been the cruise ship of choice for the family market. Disney, being Disney, will be tough competition. Disney officials insist the ships will not be floating theme parks, but floating resorts—lavish, spectacular, and very, very Disney. Consistent with its orientation as a family-oriented cruise line, there won't be any casinos on board, although no one will take umbrage with an adult who orders a drink from an onboard bar.

The line's primary emphasis will be on "seamless" seven-day land/sea packages that immerse their participants in staggering doses of Disney-dom. Passengers wishing to book only the cruise portion may do so subject to space availability. Costs for a seven-day package for a family of four begin at $4,000 to $5,000, including air travel from virtually anywhere in continental North America. That's roughly equivalent to a week-long holiday at Walt Disney World in Orlando, and is very competitive with other Port Canaveral–based vessels, including those of Carnival, Royal Caribbean, Premier, and Cape Canaveral, each of which currently offers short sailings coordinated with vacations at or near Central Florida theme parks. Each of these established lines has, at least officially, slapped on a brave face and welcomed Disney's presence as an added draw in the burgeoning family cruise market.

Disney "tested the waters" of the cruise business long before it commissioned the construction of its own vessels: Its long-standing (and now defunct) arrangement with Premier Cruise Lines and their "Big Red Boat" designated the company as "The Official Walt Disney World Cruise Line." Now, jilted by its former partner, Premier has traded in its mouse ears for rabbit ears and struck up a deal with Looney Tunes, and the big question is how long it will take the public to forget a very visible association that both companies spent millions over the years to reinforce.

And speaking of millions, that's what's being poured into this new venture. In anticipation of their newest client's arrival, Port Canaveral is building a unique, $24 million Disney-designed cruise terminal that will be used solely by the new line. As for Disney itself, the company doesn't release information on how much it's investing, but with two ships costing around $350 million each, it's safe to guess they're putting as much as $1 billion into the project. If that's true, it would be the largest amount ever invested in a single Disney venture.

To shuttle passengers to and from the Orlando International Airport and any of Disney's eight theme parks, Disney has commissioned an armada of special entertainment buses unlike anything else on wheels. Their deployment will begin the immersion of passengers in Disney's orbit shortly after their airplanes touch down. At this writing, the entertainment program on board the buses hasn't been determined, but let's just say that the hour-long trips from the airport won't be dull. In keeping with the synergistic quality that Disney intends between its land and seaborne interests, the same computerized card that functions as a passenger's hotel room key will open their stateroom on board ship and also act as a credit card for the purchase of onboard extras.

Both *Disney Magic* and *Disney Wonder* will have the same size, layout, and, for the most part, decorative motifs, and there's a conscious emulation of the classic transatlantic liners in their outer design. Both will weigh in at 85,000 gross tons, measure 964 feet in length, and will carry 1,760 passengers at the rate of two per cabin, or up to 2,400 passengers depending on how fully occupied the upper berths are. An American staff and a crew of 945 will service 880 staterooms. (Disney prefers not to refer to them as "cabins.")

Do you think there will be a large, smiling mouse aboard? And perhaps a beautiful princess? And seven dwarves? We do. They're the fantasy, the make-believe, the stock-in-trade that's made Walt's little company into one of the largest financial empires in history, and you can bet that they'll be well represented. But you can expect more. Like what, you ask? Improvisational comedy, hideaway piano bars, ornate '30s-style movie palaces, jazz bands, sports bars, wine tastings, and the most decadent spa treatments. After all, Disney knows who's paying for that family vacation.

Disney Magic (Preview)

TYPES OF PASSENGERS Just walk around Walt Disney World and you'll see exactly the kind of people Disney expects to attract to its ships: families, honeymooners, adults without children, and seniors. Just about everybody, actually. Although Disney is certainly family oriented, it's estimated that 30% of the passengers will be married couples or singles, both without children. Also, Disney expects that 10% to 15% of passengers will be Europeans eager to experience that patented Disney magic.

DINING Disney will install three different theme restaurants aboard its ships, plus an alternative dinner restaurant reserved for adults only. Wait staff, guests, and tablemates will switch dining rooms every night, which means a new theme, a new experience, and a different menu. An indoor/outdoor cafe will serve breakfast, lunch, and snacks, as well as a buffet dinner for youngsters. A pool bar and grill will offer hot dogs, hamburgers, pizza, and sandwiches, along with ice cream and frozen yogurt. Those passengers on kosher, vegetarian, or low-salt/low-fat diets will be able to order special meals.

ACTIVITIES The cruise ships will not be a total kiddie romp. Disney officials are quick to point out that one-fourth of the visitors to Walt Disney World are "nonfamilies," a fact that they took into consideration when planning activities for these new vessels. Although childless couples might panic at the idea of sailing on a ship carrying some 500 to 800 children, there will be a number of adults-only areas to which they can escape, and even tables for two in the dining rooms.

Topside, the designated space for adults will be the forward swimming pool, a rather elegant area with a teakwood deck, adjacent to the bar and spa. Mickey Mouse will definitely not show up here to shake your hand.

Aboard each vessel there will be an adults-only alternative dining area called

Palo, which will feature Italian cuisine in a contemporary setting. Adults can even visit Beat Street, offering entertainment for those 18 and older. This section of each boat will have three themed nightclubs: Sessions, for romantic music, jazz, and blues; Off Beat, a comedy club; and the Rockin' Bar D, styled after an American roadhouse and featuring—what else?—rock 'n' roll.

CHILDREN'S ACTIVITIES As you might imagine, the line's children's program will be the most extensive in the industry. Each ship will allocate more space (15,000 square feet) to children than any other vessel afloat, and will offer supervised programs for age-specific groups. They will include a separate family/children's pool area, a special family lounge, and a designated teen club, plus an arcade devoted to video games. Naturally, you'll find the largest cadre of children's counselors aboard any ships at sea, plus a complete roster of the Disney characters. Supervised children's centers will be open for organized activities till 1am every evening for children over three, and in-cabin baby-sitting for children under three can be arranged for an additional, as yet undetermined, fee.

ENTERTAINMENT Guests will enjoy high-quality entertainment that's focused on good, clean family values and fun but nonetheless manages to incorporate Broadway-caliber entertainers and cabaret artists. The nightly entertainment program will be unique in the industry, featuring productions specially designed by and for Disney, with a different program for each night.

SHOPPING A 5,500-square-foot shopping area will be filled with Disney merchandise and memorabilia.

SERVICE Expect service in the dining rooms to be roughly equivalent to the top-level Disney World restaurants in Orlando. Services will include self-service laundry rooms (not always available, even on megaships), dry cleaning, one-hour photo processing, rentals of cameras and video recorders, and satellite phone service

that includes an in-cabin modem hookup for anyone interested in bringing a laptop computer on board. Strollers will be available at no extra cost. Modern medical facilities will be available.

ITINERARIES The huge majority of cruisers aboard either ship will precede their time at sea with a three- or four-day experience at Walt Disney World, where the number and variety of entertainment options is more staggering than many cruise passengers might realize: Scattered over 35,000 acres, an area the size of Manhattan, the components of Walt Disney World include the Magic Kingdom, Epcot, Disney-MGM Studios, Pleasure Island (devoted mostly to nightlife), a trio of water parks (Disney's Typhoon Lagoon, Disney's Blizzard Beach, and Disney's River Country), and, opening in 1998, Disney's Animal Kingdom. Passengers wishing to extend the land-based portion of their holiday will be able to do so, often at attractive package rates.

The waterborne portion of a Disney package will always follow the land-based portion, departing from Port Canaveral, 50 miles due east of Orlando International Airport. Cruises will always include a stop-over in Nassau and a day at Disney's private island, Castaway Cay, in the Abaco section of The Bahamas. Disney has invested staggering sums in the construction of a pier on this island long enough to accommodate mooring its megaships without resorting to the use of tenders.

CABINS Of the 880 staterooms, 73% will be outside units with four-foot-wide portholes, and 44% will have private verandas. Their standard stateroom size of 220 square feet is 25% larger than the industry average. Many are being specifically designed for persons with disabilities.

RECREATION & FITNESS FACILITIES Disney will offer three big swimming pools, one of which will be a place where adults can float aimlessly, soak up the rays, read, or nap in the sun. The second pool will be reserved for such sports activities as water volleyball, and the third will be a high-energy (and probably high-noise)

Stop the Presses! *Disney Magic* Is on Its Way

DATELINE: VENICE. On Tuesday, May 13, 1997, at approximately 2pm, the massive sea-gates of the Fincantieri Shipyard opened, the blue waters of the Adriatic poured into the drydock, and Disney Cruise Lines' first ship, the *Disney Magic,* embarked on its life at sea. This writer was there to see it and to have a special sneak-preview tour.

The *Magic* is, simply, a beautiful ship. Its long, lean construction, dignified prow, and smoothly contoured stern hark back to the classic transatlantic liners, while its color—a deep midnight blue in the hull, cut with bright golden filigree fore and aft—gives the ship a profile that's almost unreal. Seeing it float past, with horn sounding, confetti flying in the breeze, and doves—released from the anchor-windlass room—circling its stacks, it was hard to remember that the scene was real, so much did it seem like a fantasy, like a dream, like . . . Disney.

Which is to say that the company has done its job: They've created a ship that lives up to the Disney image and brings a taste of fantasy into the world at large. From this initial float-out the *Magic* goes to be outfitted, sheathing the bare steel walls and decks that I saw with all the features we've described in the review above. The massive Walt Disney Theater—constructed without any obstructing supports and so offering a good view from all seats—will be completed early so that rehearsals can begin for the first cruises' shows. Special effects for the innovative Animator's Palate restaurant will be installed so that during your meal the entire room will change slowly from a black-and-white sketch to full, vibrant color. And a thousand pagers will be tuned up so that parents and children can keep in touch even if junior is blazing through Buzz Lightyear's Cyberspace Command Post and Mom and Dad are relaxing in the spa's thermal bath.

All is on track for the ship's scheduled March debut, when Captain Tom Forberg, former master of Crystal's *Crystal Harmony* and Radisson's *Song of Flower,* pilots the boat from the new Disney Line terminal at Port Canaveral on a four-day voyage to The Bahamas. If what I saw is any indication, it will be quite a debut indeed.

—Matt Hannafin

area for children. A promenade deck will encourage strolling or jogging, and there will be a paddle tennis court, table tennis facilities, a basketball court, and shuffleboard.

The 8,500-square-foot Vista Spa will be devoted to spa, beauty salon, and fitness facilities, most areas of which will overlook the sea. Aerobics and Jazzercise instruction will be offered along with use of exercise equipment, saunas, and steam rooms. A full-service salon will feature massages, facials, and a variety of skin treatments, manicures, pedicures, haircuts, and styling.

PUBLIC AREAS   A three-story atrium will feature sweeping staircases and a preview of the Disney theatrics you'll encounter on board. The 1,040-seat Walt Disney Theater, a seagoing equivalent of a Broadway venue, will contain state-of-the-art equipment, and a 270-seat cinema will show first-run or classic Disney movies. Passengers can visit Sessions, a low-key bar and lounge for relaxed dialogues and quiet music; the Rockin' Bar D, a venue for live music; and Off Beat, the first area aboard any cruise ship devoted exclusively to comedy acts. There's also a disco and a sports bar, the ESPN Sky Box, located near the ship's forward funnel and featuring worldwide sports television coverage. An observatory that provides full 180° views over the bridge will, for the first time in the cruise industry, allow passengers to look down and get some idea of how a ship is operated.

Dolphin Cruise Line

SHIPS **IslandBreeze • OceanBreeze • SeaBreeze**

901 South America Way, Miami, FL 33132 (mailing address: P.O. Box 025420, Miami, FL 33102-5420). ☎ 800/222-1003 or 305/358-5122; fax 305/358-4807.

Dolphin Cruise Line claims to offer the best value in cruising, and while that may be a slight exaggeration, it's basically true. A Dolphin Cruise *is* good value for the money, but keep in mind that you may have to endure elbow-to-elbow people if your ship is full, and amenities that are acceptable but not cutting-edge. You won't find any frills or pretense aboard.

The company was born as a corporate answer to strife and controversy. In 1984, a shaky five-year coalition between two separate cruise lines—Ulysses Cruises and Paquet Cruises—came to a head, and the only vessel the coalition had ever shared, *Dolphin IV*, floated between the two antagonistic corporate forces. The settlement led to the creation of Dolphin Cruise Line—and to everyone's surprise, and despite formidable competition, the new entity thrived, with the trusty *Dolphin IV* running frequent, low-cost, three-day cruises between Florida and The Bahamas.

Few new cruise companies have come as far in so short a time as Dolphin. In 1991, the company established the somewhat more upscale Majesty Cruise Lines, with which Dolphin is closely affiliated, sharing a reservations network, corporate Miami-based headquarters, and many members of the same executive staff. Then, in 1995, it sold its company namesake, the *Dolphin IV*, to Cape Canaveral Cruises, which continues to operate the vessel under its original name, a fact that causes endless confusion. As replacements, Dolphin acquired a trio of sturdy veteran sea horses, refurbished them in a sensible modern style, and christened them *IslandBreeze*, *OceanBreeze*, and *SeaBreeze*. Together, these vessels have washed about a zillion miles of ocean beneath their bows, and weathered seas that would make lesser vessels cringe. They're

not opulent, but cruise liners don't come much tougher.(*Note:* See important, late-breaking corporate news on pages 5 and 6 in chapter 1.)

It's cost-effective to sail aboard any of Dolphin's trio of "Breezes," but you won't be sailing aboard state-of-the-art ships. All three are small to medium-size vessels (21,000 to about 32,000 tons each) that were long ago surpassed by the size and amenities of the new breed of megaships. They were effectively (but not opulently) reconfigured and renovated when acquired by Dolphin, but the idea was never to turn them into luxury yachts. These are sensible boats for sensible folks, but they're not PT boats. Aboard each, you will find a scattering of teakwood decks and occasional instances of interior paneling. You'll see the line's omnipresent dolphin logo everywhere, appearing on everything from T-shirts to cocktail napkins.

Facilities and daily activities are pretty standard aboard all three ships, and none attempts to overwhelm passengers with false promises or raise unrealistic expectations. What you see is what you get: good value, very few grace notes or frills, and an atmosphere that's conducive to camaraderie and fun. Bars usually dispense drinks at a rapid-fire rate, which certainly helps keep the good times rolling.

Dolphin has labored, with much success, to create an environment where staff members really seem motivated to satisfy the expectations of their passengers. This level of service is rare in the low-end cruise market. And while the ideal of a cashless society at sea is not always a reality aboard every low-cost vessel, Dolphin attempts to make it so by allowing passengers to sign for on-board notions, gift shop purchases, and bar tabs—another little touch of Cunard in the low-end market.

Decor à la Dolphin includes lots of curved chrome, patterned carpets, pastel colors, mirrors, and contemporary and durable furniture that's about as far from Chippendale or Queen Anne models as a designer could possibly get.

PROS & CONS Each "Breeze" specifically targets the low-budget end of the cruise-ship market, but wisely refrains from making unrealistic promises. Cabins are usually small, configured as little more than "bed-sits" (to use a British term). Onboard programs are the standard fare that appeals to first-timers but elicits a giant yawn from experienced cruisers. Any onboard shortcomings are generally overlooked because of the frequent distractions offered by numerous stops at ports of call.

Costs are low, but density is high. When the ships are full, there are long lines for shore excursions and even longer lines for buffets. If you're annoyed by diners who attack the buffet like cheetahs on a wildebeest, you won't be amused by Dolphin. You'll also be hard-pressed to find a comfortable, intimate nook or cranny that hasn't already been staked out by a half-dozen other passengers.

Despite the crowds, the ambience aboard a Dolphin ship is relaxed, positive, and upbeat, although far more casual than an equivalent experience aboard all but a handful of other lines. There's never a snooty maître d' or a deliberately arrogant or imperious staff member. The atmosphere is safe, relatively clean, and predictable, with very few surprises. Whether you consider that a drawback or not depends very much on your individual taste.

Thanks to the ships' small sizes, you'll feel you're on familiar ground about 30 minutes after you step aboard. And you may appreciate not needing formal wear, or even spiffy wear. It's hard to feel underdressed aboard a Dolphin ship, even though there are two nominally formal nights where evening wear is appropriate, but not required.

However, if you've already enjoyed upscale cruising experiences, skip Dolphin.

And don't opt for a Dolphin cruise if you demand instant room service (it's slow) or fancy entertainment (a sailor impersonating Fred Flintstone is not sophisticated by anyone's definition). Also, there are oft-repeated announcements, made in both English and Spanish, that may become tiresome and annoying after a while.

There's one final advantage to cruising Dolphin-style. The newest and largest of the line's trio of ships, the *IslandBreeze,* is the only cruise ship afloat that uses Montego Bay, Jamaica, as its home port, albeit only in winter. Although you'll pay more in airfare to Jamaica than you would to South Florida, you'll be rewarded with stops at some unusual ports of call, many of them often visited only by much more upscale vessels. Cruises depart every Sunday, with ports of call that include historic Cartagena (Colombia), the first stage of the Panama Canal (the Gatun locks), the Cuna Indian communities of the San Blas Islands off the Caribbean coast of Panama, and Puerto Limón, Costa Rica. With Dolphin, you'll do all this for a lot less money than aboard other lines, albeit in no-frills circumstances.

As the official cruise line of Hanna-Barbera cartoons, Dolphin includes frequent onboard references to the Flintstones, the Jetsons, and Yogi Bear, eccentricities and antics that are directed primarily at children and will either amuse or embarrass you.

TYPES OF PASSENGERS The line attracts those with limited budgets and a short block of time to fill. Many families have favorably compared the cost of a Dolphin Cruise with an equivalent land-based holiday (driving to New England, for example, with the kids and pets in a station wagon). Many passengers are first-timers; if they've sailed before, it's likely been aboard Dolphin or any of its most visible contenders—Commodore, Regal, or (to a lesser degree, because it's so new) Cape Canaveral Cruise Line.

The company scoops up a good percentage of the Florida-based family and honeymoon trade and also attracts college students. Many passengers are in their 20s and 30s. Retirees, particularly from the snowbelt, also find the line appealing, especially if they're on a budget and are concerned with avoiding the sometimes depersonalized experience of a jazzy megaship. Many passengers speak Spanish as their primary language.

Passengers have a good time aboard these boats, but it's not the all-night party circuit you'll find on Carnival. Dolphin passengers are usually more intrigued by the shore leaves.

DINING   Food aboard Dolphin ships is of the hotel-banquet-fare variety, somewhat limited in selection and presentation. If you don't expect much, you won't be disappointed with the cuisine, and you certainly won't go hungry.

All three vessels have two seatings each for breakfast, lunch, and dinner. Exact breakfast hours vary depending on the day; main seatings for lunch and dinner are at noon and 6pm, with late seatings at 1 and 8pm. Dining options, especially at lunch, are supplemented with offerings from an al fresco deck-side buffet. There's something of an ongoing battle on board, as more clients seem to prefer the late service to the inconveniently early main service, but inevitably, everyone gets fed. Late-night hunger pangs can be assuaged at the midnight buffets, a standard feature aboard all three ships.

Dining rooms aboard all three ships are relatively crowded, with tables for between 4 and 10 people, and not very many tables for two. All three ships feature background piano music during dinner, plus special culinary theme nights. Buffets of any ilk on board, although crowded, are lavish, although quantity usually wins out over quality.

Children can order from a special menu with a Hanna-Barbera theme. Though you might prefer that your child consume fruits and vegetables, he or she is likely to be distracted by such teasers as "Zoinks Sundaes," "Scooby Monster Burgers,"

and "Astro Dogs." No staff member is ever shy about offering sugared desserts, including endless amounts of ice cream.

Passengers who have special dietary requests must notify the line in writing seven days in advance of their arrival.

ACTIVITIES   The shorter the cruise, the more hectic the schedule of activities is likely to be. Dolphin crams activities into its calendar in much the same way it crams passengers into its cabins: tightly. Among the featured activities may be napkin-folding lessons, male nightgown competitions, name that tune, newlywed and not-so-newlywed games, and karaoke contests. Despite the corn, many find their days at sea richly overscheduled and a lot more fun than they had expected.

Most Dolphin Cruises, especially those lasting only three or four days, feature some kind of beach party, complete with buffets and easy availability of water sports. Some of these take place on the pinkish-white sands of Blue Lagoon Island, an isolated outpost in The Bahamas. There are also parties for the unattached, those who are single, widowed, or divorced—or who want to be. If you get bored with these activities, you'll always be able to entertain yourself with eating, eating more, and then eating again. The library stocks some rather banal titles, so you might want to bring your own if you plan to read.

CHILDREN'S ACTIVITIES   There's something about an actor stuffed into a giant, plush, cartoon-character outfit that makes children simply lose their minds, and you can be sure that's what will happen to yours aboard Dolphin, the official cruise ship for Hanna-Barbera cartoons. Kids participate in the on-board programs of Camp Jellystone, led by skilled and enthusiastic youth counselors. Activities include scavenger hunts, sand-castle building, kite-flying off the stern deck with Yogi, and making jewelry out of popcorn. The game room for children contains about a dozen whirring, clanging machines, and a playroom offers both indoor space and an outdoor area encircled with a net to keep children from falling overboard. Although *baby-sitting* is a word the line shies away from (it doesn't promote its facilities as day care), youth counselors are on hand to propose diversions for children, adolescents, and teenagers.

ENTERTAINMENT   Some passengers find the entertainment quite cheerful and upbeat, though few consider it top-tier. It never features any big-name talent, and, frankly, the line should probably spend more on entertainers' costumes. On the positive side, there's always some kind of pretty-girls-with-good-looking-legs-with-feathers-and-lots-of-glitter revue that's presented in a harmless, lighthearted, and utterly predictable variety-show format.

All three ships have casinos with an array of small-stakes slot machines. Largest and flashiest of the lot is the one aboard *IslandBreeze,* where memories of the ship's former life as a Carnival "Fun Ship" are especially pronounced. The casino aboard the *OceanBreeze* is built into a glittery two-story space interconnected via a spiral staircase. The one aboard *SeaBreeze* is small but serviceable, set amidships in the vessel's densest cluster of bars and lounges.

All three vessels contain glittery discos that rock and roll till late at night, far enough from passengers' cabins to allow most of them to sleep undisturbed by the pulsing rhythms. Areas within all three ships offer facilities for screening movies, in some cases on giant-screen TVs.

SHOPPING   In keeping with the line's cost-conscious, unpretentious atmosphere, the on-board shops focus on cost-conscious, unpretentious merchandise. You'll find many Hanna-Barbera souvenirs, including coffee cups, baseball hats, beer coolers with Flintstones logos, Yogi Bear crayon sets, comics, and videotapes.

SERVICE   Service on Dolphin lacks the polish, discretion, and finesse that higher-priced lines can more readily afford to provide. But for the money, the service is good, and staff morale seems to be high. Despite an occasional gaffe, usually the

result of inexperience, staff members really seem to enjoy the Halloween aspects of dressing up as Hanna-Barbera characters, particularly when young children are there to appreciate the effect.

ITINERARIES

IslandBreeze—It's one of the only cruise ships in the industry that uses Montego Bay, Jamaica, as its home port (at least during the months between October and April). From here, seven-day cruises depart every Sunday for Cartagena, the first stage of the Panama Canal (the Gatun lock), the San Blas Islands, and Puerto Limón, Costa Rica.

OceanBreeze—Throughout the year, depending on the season, it departs on an alternating series of three- and four-day cruises from either Miami or Fort Lauderdale. Three-day cruises visit Nassau and a small, sandy island in The Bahamas that the line refers to as Blue Lagoon. Four-day cruises make calls at Playa del Carmen/Cozumel and Key West.

SeaBreeze—Departing from Miami every Sunday, this vessel alternates seven-day itineraries that head for either the eastern or western Caribbean. Stops in the eastern Caribbean include Nassau, San Juan, St. John, and St. Thomas, with three days at sea. Stops along the western Caribbean include Playa del Carmen/Cozumel, Montego Bay, and Grand Cayman, also with three days at sea.

SPECIAL DISCOUNTS   With the company's SaleAway program, passengers who book early can save money, and sometimes lots of money. Airfares are booked as a separate expense and are not automatically included as part of the cruise package. If a passenger books at least 90 days in advance, the price of a cruise can be reduced by up to $200 per ticket per passenger. A third or fourth person sharing a stateroom pays $35 to $55 per diem. A "repeaters" program is being developed whereby discounts are offered to passengers who have taken at least one cruise on a Dolphin ship.

SINGLE SUPPLEMENTS   The single traveler pays 150% of the double occupancy rate.

PORT CHARGES   These range from $97.50 to $197.50 per passenger, depending on the destination.

IslandBreeze

⚓ ⚓

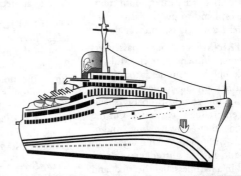

Specifications

Size (in tons)	38,125	Crew	612 (International)
Number of Cabins	508	Passenger/Crew Ratio	1.9 to 1
Number of Outside Cabins	272	Year Built	1961
Number of Passengers	1,146	Last Major Refurbishment	1995
Officers	Greek		

Frommer's Ratings (Scale of 1–10)

Activities	6.5	Public Areas	6.2
Cabins	7.2	Public Comfort/Space	7.2
Cleanliness/Maintenance	7.2	Recreational Facilities/Pool	5.0
Entertainment	6.6	Service	6.8
Food & Beverage	6.8	Ship Crew/Officers	7.8
Interior Decor	6.2	Shore Excursions	8.0
Ports of Call	6.5	Worth the Money	9.0
		Overall Average	**6.9**

Targeted to the first-time cruiser, the *IslandBreeze* is simultaneously the oldest, newest, and largest vessel in Dolphin's fleet. It was originally built in 1961, during a very different era of shipbuilding priorities, for a South Africa–based shipping line. Named the *Transvaal Castle* at the time, it became known for its frequent transatlantic runs between Southampton and Durban, near the southern tip of Africa. In 1977, it was dubbed the *Festivale* and became one of the early prototypes for the then-fledgling Carnival Cruise Lines. Until it was acquired by Dolphin in the mid-1990s and radically renovated to the tune of $1.8 million, it was viewed as one of the least technologically sophisticated and least well-accessorized of the Carnival fleet, a poor cousin when compared to that line's roster of new supercruisers.

As part of its renovations, this dowager of the early '60s has been given Dolphin's trademark blue and white paint job, and the distinctive Carnival "whale tail" fins atop its smokestack have been removed. What you'll see is a sleek-looking, not particularly classic ocean liner, with vestiges of Carnival mystique that include an art deco–inspired serpentine staircase. As was prevalent during the era it was built, this ship has a higher-than-usual percentage of inside cabins (more than half), and a public area and decks that can get crowded indeed whenever the ship is full.

There's one especially unusual aspect to this retrofitted, oft-upgraded veteran of endless corporate makeovers: It's one of the only cruise ships based part of the year in Jamaica (Montego Bay), and as such has earned the fervent cooperation of Jamaican authorities hoping that a demonstrable success will draw other lines to their shores.

Cabins & Rates

Cabins	Average per diem	Bathtub	Fridge	Phone	Sitting Area	TV
Inside	$127–$213	No	No	Yes	No	No
Outside	$199–$270	No	No	Yes	No	No
Suite	$277–$335	Yes	No	Yes	Yes	No

CABINS The range of cabins on board (10 different categories) reflects the vessel's debut during a radically different era of shipbuilding. More than half of them are inside cabins, necessarily without sea views, but some of these are larger than the outside doubles. Some (about 24 in all) are designated as suites, although the lower category of suites offers only a scant amount of additional sitting area. Regardless of their configuration or location, cabins are outfitted in a way that might remind you of a simple and cramped motel room in central Florida. Often the wash basin is in the cabin itself instead of in the bathroom. There are almost no concessions to frippery or frills, everything is angular and basic, and the overall effect will almost certainly not encourage you to spend your long days at sea in your room.

Suites are nominally better, more soothing, and fresher-looking. The Fantasy Suites come with private verandas, twin beds (they can be converted to queen-size if you're romantic), and a small sitting area with sofa. Unless you're *very* close to your traveling companions, think twice before deciding to share your nest with a third or fourth occupant: Packing more than two persons in a cabin might cause damage to your friendship.

RECREATION & FITNESS FACILITIES

There's a pool on the ship's sundeck, near the stern, that gets crowded—and sometimes very crowded—when the ship is full. There's also a wading pool closer to the bow that sunbathers tend to regard more as an ornamental reflecting pool, though it's sometimes splashed around in by children. The gym on board is a small affair no bigger than about five or six interconnected inside cabins, with a sauna and massage facility next door. A beauty salon and a children's playroom round out the facilities.

PUBLIC AREAS Most of the ship's promenade deck is devoted to the king of dining, drinking, gambling, and cabaret facilities that the ship's former owner, Carnival Cruises, developed into a multi-million-dollar floating industry. Subdivisions of that deck include the Gaslight Club Casino; a bar, the Tradewinds Club, that showcases a live dance band; two distinctly different show lounges, Le Cabaret and the Copacabana Lounge; a rendezvous point for large-scale gatherings called the Carnivale Lounge; and near the stern, the Fanta-Z disco. There's also a hideaway indoor/outdoor bar ("Little Bar and Grill") on the ship's Main Deck, where frosty, party-colored drinks seem to taste better in the sunshine and sea air. There's also a boutique for gifts and sundries, an on-board liquor store, a photo gallery and cinema (whose shows compensate for the lack of in-cabin TVs), and a children's playroom. No one leaves this ship without spending quality time in both the Lido Bar and Grill, adjacent to the stern-side swimming pool, and the Continental Restaurant, a glittering modern dining room that sprawls across the width of the ship on the vessel's Main Deck.

OceanBreeze

⇓ ⇓

Specifications

Size (in tons)	21,486	Crew	310 (International)
Number of Cabins	391	Passenger/Crew Ratio	2.5 to 1
Number of Outside Cabins	241	Year Built	1955
Number of Passengers	776	Last Major Refurbishment	1994
Officers	Greek/ International		

Frommer's Ratings (Scale of 1–10)

Activities	6.5	Public Areas	6.6
Cabins	5.8	Public Comfort/Space	6.0
Cleanliness/Maintenance	6.6	Recreational Facilities/Pool	4.8
Entertainment	6.6	Service	6.6
Food & Beverage	6.8	Ship Crew/Officers	7.8
Interior Decor	6.2	Shore Excursions	8.2
Ports of Call	7.0	Worth the Money	9.0
		Overall Average	**6.8**

The *OceanBreeze* is no slouch when it comes to impressive origins. A youthful Queen Elizabeth II christened this ocean-going "newborn" as *The Southern Cross* in 1954 in the port of Belfast, Ireland, marking the first time in British history that a monarch had christened a non-naval vessel.

Its design innovations included the placement of the funnel and engines near the stern, which makes its profile somewhat unusual and leads some myopic neophytes to believe that the stern is actually the bow, and vice versa. It was also one of the first cruise ships to abandon the concept of carrying both passengers and freight and concentrate solely on passengers.

Despite its many manifestations and makeovers, the ship still shows faint vestiges of its original styling, vaguely art deco lines, and classic ocean liner appeal. It's slightly more elegant (and more historically interesting) than the *SeaBreeze,* with which it otherwise has a lot in common.

Cabins & Rates

Cabins	Average per diem	Bathtub	Fridge	Phone	Sitting Area	TV
Inside	$84–$160	No	No	Yes	No	No
Outside	$136–$281	No	No	Yes	No	No
Suite	$189–$281	Yes	Yes	Yes	Yes	Yes

CABINS   In keeping with Dolphin's status as a budget cruise line, cabins are small, actually among the smallest in the industry, some comprising less than 100 cramped square feet. They are, however, attractively decorated, with sturdy accessories that even children will have trouble breaking. The color scheme is generally some combinations of earth tones and pastels (lots of blue), and most are outfitted with wall-to-wall carpeting, selectable music channels, and vanity desks with mirrors. Many portholes are rectangular instead of the usual round shape. Bathrooms are adequate, not plush, and might be considered cramped by some.

There are 12 suites, the largest (called "owner's suites") a generous 400 square feet facing forward over the bow.

OceanBreeze requires that passengers with mobility difficulties be accompanied by an able-bodied adult companion. Wheelchair users should note that cabin doors are 22 inches wide, bathroom doors are 20 inches wide, and there is a three-inch rise to the shower. Elevator service is not available to the Caravelle or Boat decks. Spokespersons for the line admit that passengers with disabilities would probably be more comfortable aboard the *Royal Majesty,* a vessel belonging to Dolphin's somewhat more upscale sister company, Majesty Cruise Line.

RECREATION & FITNESS FACILITIES

The *OceanBreeze* is one of the few ships afloat where joggers can make a complete circuit of one of its decks and remain mostly in the shade. In addition, there's a small gym area with up-to-date exercise equipment, but it's often crowded, particularly on days when the ship spends most of its time at sea, between ports. There's also a sauna, whirlpool bath, and table tennis, and aerobics classes are offered. Massage is available through the health and beauty facilities on all three ships. The barely adequate pool tends to be overcrowded whenever the ship is full.

PUBLIC AREAS   Much of what you'll see today, at least structurally, dates from the ship's 1971 rebuilding by Greek owners who retained everything of worth and removed lots of 1950s schlock, making it better than the original. After several subsequent refurbishments, the ship is an oceangoing classic, graced with old-fashioned, sheltered deck areas, often with wooden deck chairs and teakwood sheathing, and areas for sunning that, because of their wind protection, can be either warm, sunny refuges from blustery winds or uncomfortably hot areas devoid of any breeze. Unlike on many older ships, the teakwood decks are slickly varnished, so you'll probably want to stick with rubber-soled shoes for the duration of your cruise.

Low ceilings remain a standard fixture in many public areas of this high-density ship, although they're painted in light colors to appear higher than they are. Decor relies on a lot of reflective surfaces, mostly mirrors and glittery chrome, as well as bright colors that are relentlessly cheerful.

There are many onboard areas for reflective and/or quiet time, including a library, bistros with a corner-cafe ambience, and isolated areas so far removed from traffic patterns that many passengers never bother to hang out there. All but two of the most remote decks (the uppermost and the lowest) are interconnected by elevators.

SeaBreeze

⚓ ⚓

Specifications

Size (in tons)	21,010	Crew	400 (International)
Number of Cabins	421	Passenger/Crew Ratio	2.1 to 1
Number of Outside Cabins	263	Year Built	1958
Number of Passengers	84	Last Major Refurbishment	1993
Officers	Greek		

Frommer's Ratings (Scale of 1–10)

Activities	6.6	Public Areas	6.0
Cabins	6.0	Public Comfort/Space	5.8
Cleanliness/Maintenance	6.6	Recreational Facilities/Pool	4.8
Entertainment	6.6	Service	6.8
Food & Beverage	6.8	Ship Crew/Officers	7.8
Interior Decor	6.2	Shore Excursions	8.0
Ports of Call	6.5	Worth the Money	9.0
		Overall Average	**6.8**

When acquired by Dolphin in 1989, this older vessel (formerly the *Star/Ship Royale* of Premier Cruises, built in 1958 as the *Federico C.* by the Costa Lines) received a $5.5 million rebuilding and reconfiguration. Today, unlike its more eccentric-looking sibling, the *OceanBreeze,* it boasts a classic ocean liner design, an uncomplicated and forthright profile, and a decor that looks a lot fresher than you'd expect from such an aged ship. However, renovations over the years have produced a somewhat labyrinthine layout, so traffic flow can be awkward.

Cabins & Rates

Cabins	Average per diem	Bathtub	Fridge	Phone	Sitting Area	TV
Inside	$85–$142	No	No	Yes	No	No
Outside	$142–$178	Half	No	Yes	No	No
Suite	$192–$206	Yes	No	Yes	Yes	No

CABINS Due to the ship's vintage, the cabin roster is varied, both in configuration and size. There are 12 different price categories, which leads to endless passenger debate as to which represents the greatest comfort and/or greatest value.

Each cabin is small and cramped, but outfitted in pastel colors and mirrors that make them look nominally bigger. Furniture is minimal, with space-saving writing tables that pull out from the wall. Bathrooms are also noticeably cramped. Many cabins are advertised as suitable for up to five passengers, but tread cautiously here. Friendships, and a few marriages, have been damaged by cramming too many participants into too small a space.

Don't always expect unobstructed views from the porthole of your "outside" cabin. Cabins on the Daphne Deck look onto a busy walkway, and outside cabins on La Bohème Deck (Deck B) overlook a flotilla of hanging lifeboats.

Although most areas of the ship are accessible to persons with disabilities, that's not the case for those who are completely wheelchair-bound. Most cabin doors are only 22 inches wide, and bathroom doors are only 20 inches wide.

RECREATION & FITNESS FACILITIES Facilities include a sauna, whirlpool bath, a limited array of exercise equipment, and a pool that tends to be overcrowded whenever the ship is full. You can play table tennis or take an aerobics class, then pamper yourself with a massage.

PUBLIC AREAS Because this ship has been chopped up, renovated, refurbished, and rearranged over the decades, some public areas have assumed disjointed, labyrinthine patterns that require circuitous walks to get from one point to another. Despite this—and despite a close configuration of chairs and tables, especially in the dining room—public areas are cheerful and bright, and are often decorated with jazzy colors and hard-looking metallic ceilings. Sunning space on deck is limited.

Holland America Line—Westours

SHIPS   Maasdam • Nieuw Amsterdam • Noordam • Rotterdam VI (Preview) • Ryndam • Statendam • Veendam • Westerdam
300 Elliott Ave. West, Seattle, WA 98119. ☎ 800/426-0327 or 206/281-3535; fax 206/281-0351.

If you appreciate the thrift, industriousness, and cleverness of the culture that turned northern Europe's tidal flats into productive farmland, you'll love Holland America Line (HAL). Like the Netherlands itself, this company stresses steady profits over empire-building, and consistently delivers a worthy and solid product for a fair and honest price.

Its self-imposed conservatism hasn't been at all bad for profit margins. A. Kirk Lanterman, company president and CEO, claims his line to be the second most profitable cruise line in the world. Even if that statistic is occasionally contested by rivals at other cruise lines, it's still a testament to the fact that HAL is doing many things extremely well, including maintaining its balance sheet.

The line is as distinctive for what it isn't as for what it is. You won't find trendy or fashionable decor—HAL decors are never exhibitionistic or vulgar. Instead, the ships are Dutch squeaky-clean and thrifty. Plus, their excellent layouts ease passenger movement on their way to and from different activities. Each vessel looks good, too, with clean contemporary lines and impeccably maintained hulls and decks.

Holland America emphasizes tradition. In the public areas of its ships you'll see past trophies and memorabilia, and the very names of the vessels you'll sail on hark back to ships in Holland America's past. For example, the *Statendam* commemorates an older ship that was sunk by a German U-boat before it could board its first paying passenger, and the line's flagship, *Rotterdam*—a 38,000-ton vessel launched by the Netherlands' Queen Juliana in 1957—is the fourth Holland America ship to bear that name.

The company was founded in 1873 as the Nederlandsch Amerikaansch Stoomvart Maatschappij (Netherlands-America Steamship Company). In 1896, the company changed its name to Holland America Line. They worked hard to promote the port of Rotterdam (now Europe's largest) above that of Amsterdam, where some of the line's competitors were based.

During World War II, the company's headquarters moved from Nazi-occupied Holland to Dutch-owned Curaçao, then the site of a strategic oil refinery. Strong links were forged with North American interests beginning in 1947, when Westours, a Seattle-based company, began booking large blocks of Holland America cabins. In 1974, Westours and HAL were linked. In 1988, HAL acquired Windstar Cruises, expanding its midlevel services into the upper echelons of the cruise experience.

To everyone's surprise, both companies were acquired a year later by one of the most daring and innovative players in the cruise-line industry, Carnival Cruise Lines, whose brassy and sometimes confrontational style couldn't be more different from HAL's understatement and thrift. Many industry observers predicted the company's demise, yet the opposite occurred. Carnival improved entertainment quality and quantity (the line needed both) and poured money into upgrading HAL's cuisine. More importantly, Carnival used its new acquisition to clarify its own marketing niche. And to help promote its interests, Carnival also adapted the marketing infrastructure of Westours, always a potent force in the Alaska cruise ship market and in motorcoach tours.

Carnival has let Holland America Line discreetly update its fleet, its technology, and its marketing skill while retaining its understated, middle-of-the-road style. Plus, the cash and credit from Carnival allowed HAL to commission four additional vessels, with more to come. Each of HAL's newest ships—*Statendam* and *Maasdam* (both inaugurated in 1993), *Ryndam* (1994), and *Veendam* (1996)— are carbon copies of the same design, and were all built by Fincantieri shipyard in Monfalcone, Italy. Together, this quartet represents one of the most massive investments in hardware any shipping line has made during the 1990s. The *Maasdam, Ryndam, Statendam,* and *Veendam* each weigh in at 55,000 tons and provide a sedate, supremely well-crafted oceangoing experience in which all engineering kinks have been worked out. A fifth and sixth variation, both of them larger and more up-to-date, have been commissioned, but aren't expected to be operational until 1999.

Two additional, somewhat older ships in Holland America's Caribbean fleet, *Noordam* and *Nieuw Amsterdam,* each 34,000 tons, provide the amenities most passengers associate with a classic ocean liner. The ships have been refurbished to the standards of the fleet's four larger vessels, but the sheer scope and scale are pared down, as are rates and prices.

Finally, the fleet's most unusual vessel (in terms of engineering, anyway) is the *Westerdam*. Very experienced cruisers might remember this vessel as the *Homeric,* long-ago flagship of the Homeric Lines. In 1989, a German shipyard "stretched" this medium-size ship into a large ship by adding a 140-foot midsection, with all the electrical wiring, tubes, and plate steel such a feat requires. Although this is HAL's most densely populated ship, it's also one of the most conservatively decorated. Its fans often praise the thoughtful touches its staff provides.

Holland America vessels are the oceangoing personification of the thrifty, self-controlled, bemused, low-key, not-very-liberal-but-not-too-conservative, quietly prosperous bourgeoisie of Holland.

You'll find just a little bit of flash, a touch of glitter, and a dash of opulence, but nothing like what's aboard the sometimes psychedelic inspirations of Carnival. The passage you'll experience might not be as action-packed or cutting-edge as aboard many of the company's competitors, but that's not the point here. What you'll get instead is a voyage that's unthreatening, soothing, and restful.

PROS & CONS The line's even-handed consistency is both its greatest virtue and its greatest flaw. Holland America vessels are well designed, efficient, and comfortable, and what you'll get aboard them are well-choreographed but predictable amenities and activities, rather tame evening entertainment, and good value, but no surprises. On the other hand, HAL and its ships have won dozens of industry awards, including many different acknowledgments for "Ship of the Year," so your appreciation of the line is really a matter of temperament.

The name of the game is tame, with activities aboard being of the straightforward type: gambling, eating, and mingling with other passengers—but if you like that sort of thing you might find the atmosphere soothing. The line even addresses the ever-troublesome question of public announcements, keeping them to a quiet minimum instead of blaring them loudly and repetitiously throughout your trip.

However, if you regard variety as a spice to be savored, you might quickly grow bored on vessels whose entire pitch seems to be toward soothing the anxieties of older, middle-bracket clients. Night owls and single passengers fond of prowling might find the line quite dull, both for its calm quality and because the passenger list seems to be composed mostly of couples.

The one factor that tends to mitigate any of HAL's shortcomings is cost: It's among the least expensive of the giant, middle-bracket cruise operators, offering a maritime experience that's really very full, considering the price.

All of the above comments factor even more strongly if you have it in mind to sail Holland America more than once: So committed is HAL to consistency within its fleet that ships tend to be commissioned in identical clusters, decor of public areas retains many similar features, and even the names of many decks and public areas are identical from ship to ship. Upper and Lower Promenade Decks, Sky Decks, and Lido Decks will usually be the same regardless of which HAL ship you board. If you enjoy consistency and reliability, this is the line for you.

TYPES OF PASSENGERS HAL is simply too decorous and modest an outfit to ever define itself as a mass-market line in the sense of Carnival. Its allure and amenities fall into the "premium" category, a euphemism that implies a middle-market niche that's far from being the lowest but still has a long climb before ever making it to the top. Corporate priorities for shipboard ambience include an unstuffy lack of pretension, relaxed friendliness, good value for the money, and absolutely no illusions that its vessels fall into the loftiest tiers of the luxury market.

The clientele that HAL wants (and gets) tends to be set in its ways, not particularly flexible or adventurous, and not at all bohemian or nonconforming. Passengers are predictably middle-market, too, and not excessively active, experimental, or sports-oriented.

Before its acquisition by Carnival, HAL passengers tended to be older people, but Carnival's influence has moved the demographics toward a younger market. The transition is far from complete, though: HAL's passenger rosters tend to include some rapidly graying members of the baby-boomer generation, and overall many, many passengers tend to be 55 and over. They tend to be better educated than their equivalents aboard a Carnival ship, but a lot less affluent than those aboard a Seabourn vessel. Passengers are hospitable, and in most cases amiable

within certain limits, with reserved manners equivalent to what you might find at a golf and tennis club. It's a crowd that's sensible with its money, and likely to sport a lot of pastel-colored fabrics, double-knit trousers, and easy-to-care-for hairstyles. The line also attracts many groups traveling together, from incentive groups to social clubs on a lark or mission together.

In short, if you're aboard to swing, stay up late, carouse, or look for stimulating new adventures, HAL is not the line for you.

DINING The line knows how to appeal to passengers through their stomachs. On board, you'll begin to consider food as sustenance, food as entertainment, and food as diversion. Buffets with the inevitable queues are bountiful and frequent. These are supplemented by stands where you can make your own tacos, lavish displays showcasing anything you could possibly want to put into a salad, a different pasta every day, stir-fried dishes made to order, and tuckaway displays where you can make your own ice cream sundae as high and gooey as you want. Indonesian dishes are the theme of at least one buffet a week, and Indonesian *satay* (beef or chicken grilled on a wooden skewer and served with peanut sauce) appears at buffets almost as regularly as potato salad and coleslaw.

As its executive chef, HAL employs the renowned Reiner Greubel, formerly of Westin Hotels, New York's Plaza Hotel, and his own Reiner's Restaurant in Seattle. Instead of daring experimentation, he recognizes that some of the world's finest cuisine comes from classics prepared with fresh and high-quality ingredients, and that some of the more sophisticated palates still prefer traditional favorites: osso bucco, cassoulet, Alaskan king crab, Caribbean snapper. Greubel has also expanded the line's light and healthy cuisine with more fresh fish, such as pompano and grouper, and more pasta dishes with vegetable-based sauces. He also serves what he calls "fun foods," meaning spring rolls and sushi. We like his increased emphasis on offering the fare of the Caribbean, particularly at theme buffets. A major improvement in the cuisine is the desserts. Greubel has moved away from Grandmother's favorite cakes and heavy, cream-laden desserts in favor of newer creations with more flavorful sauces, including many desserts based on tropical fruit. His crème brûlée with fresh cherries is a delight, as is his tropical trifle with salmon berries, raspberries, pineapple, kiwi, and coconut cream.

Dinners are more formal than luncheon sittings. There are two dinner seatings with pre-assigned places; tables are available for between two and eight diners. At breakfast and lunch, you can sit where, when, and with whom you want.

Dinner items might be as straightforward as roast prime rib of beef with baked Idaho potatoes and horseradish cream, or as esoteric as warm hazelnut-crusted Brie with a compote of apples and onions. Menu descriptions are in plain American English (seared sea scallops, grilled halibut, rack of lamb), so you won't be put in the awkward position of having to ask for translations from the Dutch.

The line also pays attention to special dietary requests. If you're committed to kosher, low-salt, no-salt, low or no-fat, and make that clear at the time of booking, you'll receive food the way you like it. Then any bending or breaking of your doctor's dietary rules will be solely at your own discretion.

Children can enjoy four tried-and-true staples (pizza, hot dogs, burgers with fries, and chicken drumsticks) anytime they ask. These dishes are supplemented with chef's specials, such as small platters of pasta or tacos.

At least some tables aboard Holland America vessels will be dominated by corporate, family, or special-interest groups dining together. Two dining rooms aboard each vessel are usually reserved

exclusively for them, although their numbers are likely to spill out into the public dining rooms, too. Dining rooms are strictly segregated into smoking and non-smoking areas.

Breakfasts contain some vestiges of Dutch cuisine, such as Gouda cheese, and Dutch influences also prevail at least once during each cruise as a "Chocolate Extravaganza Late Show," a Holland-themed midnight buffet where the calories stack up so fast you might as well give up trying to count them. And the decoration aboard also contains a bow to the Dutch and their love of horticulture: HAL has a weekly budget for flowers that, according to company spokespersons, runs up to $20,000 a week, a figure some less well-funded cruise lines would probably consider lavish.

Room service is available 24 hours a day. Passengers have unlimited access to iced tea and coffee from self-serve dispensers. Midmorning bouillon and afternoon teas are well-attended events. Hot canapés are served in some of the bar/lounges during the cocktail hour.

During warm-weather cruises, lemonade is served on deck, one of many thoughtful touches provided at frequent intervals by the well-trained staff. Two evenings on each week-long cruise and three evenings on each 10-day cruise are designated as formal.

ACTIVITIES   Holland America activities are varied, relatively nontaxing, and fun. Seminars on upcoming ports of call are popular, as are deck games and tours of the galley. You can learn how to dance cheek-to-cheek, learn six ways to decorate a turnip, or play bingo. You can also just relax in a chaise lounge as the ship moves across tropical waters.

Activities pick up a bit at night, when dinner and predinner cocktails (and all their associated social imbroglios) are a major event of the day. You can then visit the show lounge and/or the casino for a sampling of Holland America's new and very unmistakably titled "Night Life" program. You might attend a "Fabulous 50s" party or a country-western night complete with hog-calling contest, take part in the "Champagne Slot Tournament" or "Night Owl Pajama Bingo," indulge yourself at the "Dutch Chocolate Extravaganza," or take in a midnight movie or the ever-popular "crew show," wherein Indonesian and/or Filipino crew members present songs and dances from their homelands.

Women of any age traveling alone or those whose escorts don't think of themselves as Fred Astaire need not fear: Cruises that last longer than 14 days come with a complement of unattached males who rescue wallflowers for a whirl across the dance floor.

Recently, HAL initiated onboard art auctions where you can bid on paintings and portable sculptures. The auctioneer is always entertaining, but you can be certain that there won't be any real bargains. Resident experts also present diverting lectures about each ship's art collection, which can sometimes be impressive.

With shore excursions, many passengers take organized bus tours to sites of historic or natural interest. Because of its association with Westours (which doesn't operate HAL's bus tours in the Caribbean), Holland America has developed and choreographed its motorcoach tours to a fine-tuned science. They're not particularly individualized, intellectually challenging, or taxing, but that's exactly what many participants want. Your view of St. Thomas or St. Maarten will be safe, hassle-free, undemanding, and will include lots of time for shopping.

Some cruises are designated as theme cruises, where the focus might be on photography, wine-tasting, Super Bowl trivia, country music, "grand bingo," or "grand shopping." In some cases, celebrity authors might be brought on board. Vintage films are shown, and great moments of opera sometimes played. In autumn, expect a seagoing emphasis on very Bavarian Oktoberfest activities.

CHILDREN'S ACTIVITIES Whenever demand warrants it, HAL offers supervised facilities for children, which go by the name "Club HAL" and tend to be about as tame as the offerings the line presents for adults. HAL emphasizes that its youth programs are neither a baby-sitting service nor a day-care center, and that parents who bring their children aboard will not be able to just drop them off and hit the decks, as it were. In theory, programs are designated for three different age brackets: 5- to 8-year-olds, 9- to 12-year-olds, and older teenagers. But, based on the greater or lesser number of young people aboard, these barriers are sometimes blurred.

Regardless of the age of the attendees, young people are diverted with pizza and soda parties, as well as tours of the bridge, the galley, and some areas below deck. There might also be group movie-watching sessions, ice-cream parties, arts and crafts lessons, storytelling sessions, games, karaoke, golf lessons, disco parties, charades, and kite-flying. Great ceremony is affixed to the first-night ritual where parents meet and mingle with whomever will be responsible for the care, "counseling," and feeding of their children. Activities are not scheduled while a ship is in port.

Baby-sitters are sometimes (but not always) available from volunteers among a ship's staff, who carve time out from their other duties or from their free time. If a staff member is available—and be warned: their availability is never guaranteed—the cost is usually around $5 per child per hour.

ENTERTAINMENT On-board entertainment has improved since HAL's acquisition by Carnival, which really understands how cabaret shows should be presented. Each ship features small-scale extravaganzas with live music and laser lights. There's enough glitter and exposed skin to attract everyone's attention, but never enough to offend. You can also trip the light fantastic before or after dinner thanks to musical trios or dance bands.

Nearly first-run movies are shown an average of three times a day in an onboard cinema, a diversion that perks up many an otherwise languid afternoon or early evening. Hot, freshly made popcorn is dispensed from a machine near the entrance.

The disco is often little more than a modern room with a bar, a dance floor, and loud prerecorded music. Passenger and/or crew talent shows are popular. On some holiday cruises, HAL might bring aboard some well-known personalities or well-known and rather sober authorities, none of them particular headliners but certainly of interest to some passengers. Past examples often cited by the line include economist Irving R. Levine and Col. James Reid.

SHOPPING   Holland America ships contain shopping arcades filled with merchandise that experienced cruisers consider predictable. You'll find collectibles like crystal whatnots and the inevitable blue-and-white Delft china—the kind of things you'll take home, set on a shelf, and leave to gather dust for several generations to come. You can also buy film and camera supplies, drugs, notions, and paperback books. At least two cocktail lounges are strategically positioned near the arcade, in case you get thirsty or tired between examining the merchandise. There are also racks of clothing (usually the kind where the logo of a name designer is prominent and obvious), plus perfume, cologne, and accessories to perk up whatever outfit you plan on wearing that night at dinner.

SERVICE   Onboard service is permeated with nostalgia for the Netherlands's past and its genteel traditions. During lunch, a uniformed employee might hold open the door of a buffet, and a steward ringing a chime will formally announce the two dinner seatings.

Holland America is one of the few cruise lines afloat that maintains a training school (a land-based facility in Indonesia known within HAL circles as the SS *Jakarta*) for the selection and training of its malleable, discreet, and appealingly shy staff. On the ships, a soft-spoken staff smiles more often than not as they labor to offer reasonably attentive service. You won't find a staff member rushing toward you every time you raise an eyebrow, but if you're only reasonably demanding, view your onboard experience with charity and a sense of humor, and phrase your needs in clearly enunciated English, someone will probably bring you almost anything you want.

Beginning in the mid-1990s, HAL hired more multilingual translators (usually Dutch, German, Spanish, and English) as part of its staff. Each functions as a social catalyst, or at least tries to, ensuring that the sedate unfurling of onboard activities aren't upset by language barriers.

There's an oft-mentioned no-tipping-required policy aboard all ships. Solicitation of tips is forbidden, but acceptance of tips is not. You can always press an unmarked white envelope into the palm of your favorite steward anytime during your cruise, and it will be gratefully acknowledged.

Each ship in HAL's line maintains a self-service Laundromat as an acknowledgment of the general thriftiness of many of the line's passengers, and onboard services aboard every ship in the fleet include take-away laundry and dry-cleaning.

ITINERARIES

Maasdam—Between November and April, the ship departs from Fort Lauderdale for 10-day cruises in the Caribbean, with an emphasis on transits through the Panama Canal and treks as far west as Acapulco.

Nieuw Amsterdam—Word is that this ship's presence in the Caribbean will be minimal in the coming years, as Holland America shifts it to primary service in Asia and the South Pacific. Look for the ship to run two 7-day holiday cruises (at Christmas and New Year), sailing from

New Orleans into the western Caribbean, with stops at Key West, Grand Cayman, and Playa del Carmen/Cozumel. Three days are spent at sea.

Noordam—From mid-October to April, *Noordam* leaves from Tampa for seven-day cruises through the western Caribbean, with stops that include Grand Cayman, Santo Tomás de Castilla, Guatemala (departure points for visits to the Mayan ruins of Tikal and Copán), and Cozumel.

Ryndam—From October to April, *Ryndam* sails from Fort Lauderdale for 10-day treks through central and southern Caribbean ports that include St. Lucia, Barbados, Guadeloupe, St. Maarten, and St. Thomas. It also makes a stop in Nassau before returning to its port of departure.

Statendam—From October to April, *Statendam* makes 10-day treks from Fort Lauderdale to St. John, St. Thomas, Dominica, Grenada, La Guaira/Caracas, and Curaçao, with three days at sea.

Veendam—Between October and April, *Veendam* spends 90% of its time making seven-day cruises from Fort Lauderdale with stopovers at Nassau, San Juan, St. John, and St. Thomas, with three days at sea. On rare intervals, these are interspersed with seven-day cruises from Fort Lauderdale that stop at Key West, Playa del Carmen/Cozumel, Ocho Rios, and Grand Cayman, with two days at sea.

Westerdam—From October to April, *Westerdam* makes seven-day cruises from Fort Lauderdale to Nassau and the eastern Caribbean ports of St. Maarten, St. John, and St. Thomas, with three days at sea. As of January 3, 1998, the *Westerdam* will assume a new seven-day itinerary that stops at Nassau, San Juan, St. John, St. Thomas, and Half Moon Cay, HAL's private island. Between May and August, the ship alternates this itinerary with weeks spent on a western Caribbean routing, whose stops include Key West, Playa del Carmen/Cozumel, Ocho Rios, and Grand Cayman.

SPECIAL DISCOUNTS Discounts of up to 40%, and in some cases even more, apply for early bookings. Depending on the cruise, "early" is sometimes defined as up to six months in advance, sometimes less, depending on how quickly the ship fills up. If a more favorable money-saving promotion is inaugurated after a client books and pays a deposit, he or she will receive the additional discount as a refund prior to departure.

HAL deliberately segregates the cost of its cruise fares from its airfares, and treats the packaging of its pre- and postcruise packages as obviously separate entities. Passengers are encouraged, therefore, to mix and match the components of their holiday to best suit their individual needs. Of course, this gives you even greater freedom to shop around for airline and hotel deals that are better, or cheaper, than those available through HAL.

AARP members receive a $100 discount when booking an outside stateroom for cruises of 7 days or longer, and $50 off shorter cruises.

Passengers can opt to buy a cancellation waiver, one of the most flexible in the industry, that will refund any monies paid if, for any reason, a client cancels a cruise up to 24 hours before the first component of the cruise package is activated. The cost of this waiver for most of HAL's Caribbean cruises ranges from $79 to $160 per person, depending on the duration and price of the cruise package. HAL emphasizes that this does not cover evacuations of a vessel for medical reasons of any kind.

A third or fourth passenger sharing a cabin with two other people pays between $60 and $100 per diem. Children ages two to seven are charged a flat rate for seven-day cruises of around $350 per child if they share their parents' room. Past passengers are granted automatic membership in the Mariner Club, and receive newsletters several times a year about special promotions and cabin upgrades on selected sailings. Once aboard, they're included in special receptions and parties, often with the ship's captain in attendance.

SINGLE SUPPLEMENTS Occupants of single cabins pay 150% to 200% of the cost of per person rates for double occupancy. Solitary occupants of a suite are charged 200% of the per person rate for a suite. The cruise line will place two same-sex occupants in a cabin (in selected categories only) at the double occupancy rate.

PORT CHARGES Depending on the cruise's duration and its ports of call, port charges for Caribbean/Bahamian itineraries range from $119 to $161 per person.

Maasdam • Ryndam • Statendam • Veendam

⚓ ⚓ ⚓ ⚓

Specifications

Size (in tons)	55,451	Crew	588 (Indonesian/ Filipino)
Number of Cabins	633	Passenger/Crew Ratio	2.1 to 1
Number of Outside Cabins	502	Year Built	1993/1994/ 1993/1996
Number of Passengers	1,266	Last Major Refurbishment	n/a
Officers	Dutch		

Frommer's Ratings (Scale of 1–10)

Activities	7.5	Public Areas	8.4
Cabins	8.0	Public Comfort/Space	8.5
Cleanliness/Maintenance	8.8	Recreational Facilities/Pool	7.6
Entertainment	7.2	Service	7.4
Food & Beverage	6.8	Ship Crew/Officers	8.2
Interior Decor	8.6	Shore Excursions	7.6
Ports of Call	7.0	Worth the Money	8.8
		Overall Average	**7.9**

These four nearly identical vessels represent the newest and most massive investment in hardware Holland America has ever made. Weighing in at 55,000 tons each, they're a bit shy of being megaships, but they're much, much bigger than HAL's long-standing flagship, the *Rotterdam V*, a comforting but somewhat tired 38,000-ton veteran scheduled for replacement in 1997. (See preview of *Rotterdam VI*, on page 208.) The four vessels were built within a three-year span at the Fincantieri shipyard in Monfalcone, Italy, and fifth and sixth siblings are scheduled for sometime during 1999.

The design kinks in this quartet were fine-tuned long before the first of the four was ever launched. The result is an extremely good use of space that pays attention to traffic flows. The ships have unusual squared-off sterns surrounded by windows, and interiors designed with practicality, cost-efficiency, and easy maintenance in mind. Each of the four has 10 decks interconnected via 8 elevators, and deck names are standard from ship to ship.

Interior components include leathers, glass, cabinets, textiles, and furniture from around the world. Touches of marble, teakwood, polished brass, and around $2 million worth of artwork for each vessel evoke the era of the classic ocean liners. Decorative themes usually emphasize the Netherlands' seafaring traditions, and the role of Holland America in opening commerce and trade between Holland and the rest of the world.

Although the ships are similar, the *Veendam* has the edge. An elegant vessel that avoids glitz, it contains some $2 million worth of antiques and art and presents a sleeker, more modern face than its siblings. Fresh flowers, white-gloved stewards, and bowls of fresh fruit in the cabins add a warm, hospitable touch.

Cabins & Rates

Cabins	Average per diem	Bathtub	Fridge	Phone	Sitting Area	TV
Inside	$292–$374	Yes	No	Yes	Yes	Yes
Outside	$342–$524	Yes	No	Yes	Yes	Yes
Suite	$664	Yes	Yes	Yes	Yes	Yes

CABINS   Cabins are roomy, unfussy, uncomplicated, and comfortable. Each contains about 25% more space than equivalently priced accommodations on competing lines. Suites begin at 243 square feet (larger than those aboard some of the most expensive ships afloat, such as Cunard's *Sea Goddess I*), move up to 600 square feet, and culminate at 1,200 square feet in a sprawling penthouse suite.

Cabins are outfitted with light-grained furniture, large mirrors, and, in some cases, floral-patterned curtains that separate the sleeping area from the sitting area. Accommodations also contain Indonesian batik and floral prints and artwork that reflects some aspects of Holland's history and aesthetic. Closets and storage space are larger than the norm. Bathrooms are well designed and well lit.

All cabins have twin beds that can be converted to a queen and, in some cases, to a king. About 200 cabins can accommodate a third and fourth passenger on a fold-away sofa bed. If you plan to do this, be sure you're very, very compatible with your traveling companions.

Outside cabins have picture windows that aren't blocked by dangling rows of lifeboats, although those on the Navigation Decks have pedestrian walkways (and consequently pedestrians) between you and your view of the sea. Special reflective glass prevents outsiders from spying in during daylight hours. To guarantee privacy at nighttime, you have to close the curtains.

On each ship, six cabins are wheelchair-accessible and specially outfitted for passengers with disabilities. That, plus spacious corridors, wide elevators, and wheelchair-accessible toilets, makes these ships popular with persons with disabilities.

RECREATION & FITNESS FACILITIES
The quartet of ships each has sprawling (112-foot) expanses of teak-covered decks surrounding a swimming pool that's always exposed to the sun and air. One deck above that, a second swimming pool can be sheltered from inclement weather with a sliding glass roof (Holland America calls it a magrodome).

These ships have an unobstructed track on an upper deck for power walking or jogging, and an Ocean Spa health club with rowing machines, weight machines, steam rooms, saunas, and stationary bicycles. You can also get facials or massages. In good weather, aerobics classes are held on deck. Points are awarded to passengers who show up for aerobics, and can be redeemed at cruise end for T-shirts, souvenirs, and so on.

PUBLIC AREAS   Joe Farcus, the brilliant designer who launched Carnival Cruise Lines' "Fun Ship" theme, played a role in the interior design of these ships, albeit with considerably more reserve and subtlety than he employed at Carnival.

Public areas are subdued, consciously tasteful, and soothing. Some of the most appealing areas are the Sky Decks, which offer a 360° panorama where the only drawback is the roaring wind. One floor below that, almost equivalent views are available from behind the shelter of glass. Each ship contains a three-story atrium—small compared to those aboard Carnival ships, but pleasingly designed and centered around an imaginative sculpture based on some aspect of marine mythology.

Showrooms aboard each are stylish, modern tributes to Holland's great artists: Aboard *Statendam* it's Van Gogh; *Maasdam* is Rembrandt; *Ryndam* is Vermeer (with references to Holland's national flower, the tulip); and *Veendam* is Rubens. Showroom seating is configured in a most unusual fashion, with groupings of overstuffed chairs and banquettes.

Likewise, each vessel's onboard library pays homage to some aspect of North European culture. The one aboard *Statendam* honors Erasmus, *Maasdam*'s honors Leyden, *Ryndam*'s honors Delft, and *Veendam*'s commemorates Hugo de Groot. Onboard libraries are tranquil and oft-visited retreats, each stocked with thought-provoking books.

Nieuw Amsterdam • Noordam

⚓ ⚓ ⚓

Specifications

Size (in tons)	33,930	Crew	542 (Indonesian)
Number of Cabins	607	Passenger/Crew Ratio	2.2 to 1
Number of Outside Cabins	411	Year Built	1983/1984
Number of Passengers	1,214	Last Major Refurbishment	1990
Officers	Dutch		

Frommer's Ratings (Scale of 1–10)

Activities	7.0	Public Areas	7.8
Cabins	7.8	Public Comfort/Space	8.0
Cleanliness/Maintenance	8.2	Recreational Facilities/Pool	6.8
Entertainment	6.8	Service	7.5
Food & Beverage	6.4	Ship Crew/Officers	8.0
Interior Decor	7.8	Shore Excursions	7.0
Ports of Call	7.0	Worth the Money	8.0
		Overall Average	**7.4**

These almost-identical vessels were built within a few months of one another at the Chantiers de l'Atlantique shipyard in St-Nazaire, France. Other than the *Rotterdam,* they're the oldest and most "classic" vessels in Holland America's fleet, smaller and more idiosyncratic than the quartet of newer ships described above, and almost nostalgically evocative of the pre-megaship age of cruising. Each was a trendsetter when it was inaugurated, although the technical innovations that set them apart then have since been eclipsed by today's vessels.

Passengers tend to be more sedate than those aboard the line's larger ships, and more conscious than usual of value for their dollars. Children are not particularly welcome on these two ships, so if you're planning on traveling with any, it might be wiser to opt for the larger HAL ships listed above.

Cabins & Rates

Cabins	Average per diem	Bathtub	Fridge	Phone	Sitting Area	TV
Inside	$185–$242	No	No	Yes	No	Yes
Outside	$215–$305	Half	No	Yes	No	Yes
Suite	$320	Yes	Yes	Yes	Yes	Yes

CABINS   Each cabin is a comfortable size and is representative of Holland America's low-key style. The furniture looks vaguely art deco, mirrors make the space seem larger than it is, and storage space is more than you'd expect. Cabins are kept sparkling by a steward who seems always on hand to polish metal and glass fixtures. Each cabin is insulated against noises emanating from neighboring cabins. Bathrooms are compact versions of the well-designed bathrooms you'd find in an upscale Florida motel.

A number of cabins are suitable for four passengers, allowing cost-saving options, but these cabins involve more crowding than you might be willing to endure. Cabins on the Boat Deck usually have obstructed views, and those on the Promenade Deck overlook an unending stream of joggers, walkers, and passersby. Cabins near the stern are subject to more than their share of engine noise and vibration. This applies to both ships, but especially to the *Nieuw Amsterdam.* Inside cabins usually include perpetually closed draperies that suggest the presence of a porthole where there is none. No cabins were designed specially for singles.

Four cabins in the B category—deluxe outside double rooms on the Navigation Deck—are suitable for persons with disabilities. Elevators are also wheelchair accessible.

RECREATION & FITNESS FACILITIES Each ship has two outside pools on the decks. You can power-walk or jog on an unobstructed track on an upper deck. The Ocean Spa health club has rowing machines, weight machines, stationary bicycles, steam rooms, saunas, and cubbyholes for facials and massages. Aerobics classes are held on the decks.

PUBLIC AREAS   The decor of the *Nieuw Amsterdam* pays homage to Dutch Colonial New York, whereas the *Noordam* decor is less specific and a lot less vivid. Each sports teakwood, polished rosewood, and discreet colors. Bouquets of fresh flowers are liberally scattered through public areas.

Many added features were inspired by the line's flagship, *Rotterdam.* The most visible is the 15-foot-wide teak-covered promenade that allows deck chairs, strollers, joggers, and voyeurs to mingle under the open sky. Some passengers consider it the ships' most endearing feature.

There are some unfortunate design flaws. For example, show lounges aren't large enough to seat all passengers, so there's standing room only in the cabaret theater, with some sight lines blocked.

Rotterdam VI (Preview)

Holland America has always enjoyed the tradition of naming its newest ships after the long-ago grandes dames of its cosmopolitan fleet, and the addition of the *Rotterdam VI* to its roster of ships is no exception. In September of 1997, the aging, relatively small *Rotterdam V,* the line's circa-1958 flagship, will be replaced with a newer and larger state-of-the-art version weighing in at 62,000 tons, with a "normal" passenger volume of 1,320 and a maximum speed of 25 knots—20% faster than most other cruise ships afloat. This *Rotterdam* will adopt the mantle of the line's flagship the day it's launched. Conceived as the first of a new generation of ships that will bring HAL into the first decade of the 21st century, it bears illustrious antecedents. Its predecessors *(Rotterdams I* through *V)* set dozens of speed records during their respective eras, and hauled millions of immigrants from their home port of Rotterdam to lives in the New World.

The vessel will mimic some aspect of such proven HAL successes as the *Staatendam, Maasdam, Ryndam,* and *Veendam.* Where it differs, however, will be within its configuration of cabins, many more of which will have verandas. The vessel will also contain some amenities that are available only to upper-tier cabins on the high end of the price range. These deluxe cabins will include 245 square feet of floor space (as opposed to a still-roomy 185 to 195 square feet of floor space within standard cabins) and will include access to the staff of a special concierge lounge. (Presumably, occupants can book tickets to shore excursions without enduring the long lines that are the norm within many large ships.)

The vessel also pays a lot of attention to children, and has designated a prime panoramic spot with wraparound windows and a semiprivate deck as the onboard playroom.

Dining options will be more versatile aboard *Rotterdam VI* than aboard any of its predecessors, partly because of the "alternative" onboard restaurant, where advance reservations are necessary. Cuisine will be upscale and Italian, and decor will be baroque and intimate, conceived as a foil to the expansive dining room.

The Lido Deck pool will be sheltered from the elements with a retractable, glass-topped "magrodome." Throughout the ship, HAL's emphasis on comfortable but understated decors will be the responsibility of design firms based in Utrecht, The Netherlands, who are committed to reinforcing the glamour of the line's most prestigious vessel with ample use of varnished hardwoods and dark colors. These will include lots of maroon and black (the latter a color favored by Holland's 17th-century burghers), usually offset with flashes of bronze, brass, and gilt.

The ship's centerpiece atrium will be oval-shaped rather than octagonal, as is the norm aboard many other HAL ships. One of its many distinctive features will be a double smokestack, an unusual, nostalgic touch that was added in homage to the *Rotterdam V,* and isn't seen on many other vessels presently afloat.

HAL's newest ship will spend only part of its year in the Caribbean, usually as part of 7- and 14-day jaunts along both sides of the Basin. It will also stop in the Caribbean at regular intervals during its roster of long-haul voyages to exotic ports around the world.

Other developments percolating at HAL? Two additional as-yet-unnamed vessels are being built right now for inauguration during February and September of 1999. Nearly identical, weighing in at 65,000 gross tons, and priced at around $300 million each, they'll have a passenger capacity of 1,440 each.

Westerdam

⚓ ⚓ ⚓

Specifications

Size (in tons)	53,872	Crew	642 (Indonesian)
Number of Cabins	747	Passenger/Crew Ratio	2.3 to 1
Number of Outside Cabins	495	Year Built	1986
Number of Passengers	1,494	Last Major Refurbishment	1990
Officers	Dutch		

Frommer's Ratings (Scale of 1–10)

Activities	7.2	Public Areas	7.8
Cabins	7.6	Public Comfort/Space	6.2
Cleanliness/Maintenance	8.2	Recreational Facilities/Pool	6.8
Entertainment	6.8	Service	6.8
Food & Beverage	6.8	Ship Crew/Officers	8.0
Interior Decor	7.6	Shore Excursions	7.0
Ports of Call	7.0	Worth the Money	7.5
		Overall Average	**7.2**

After HAL bought this ship in 1989, it sawed the boat apart and inserted a 140-foot midsection, an $84 million effort that added almost 14,000 tons and some 200 additional cabins to the ship. Experts say the enlargement is seamless, as do many passengers who search (unsuccessfully) for weld marks and disjointed traffic flows.

Despite its enlargement, *Westerdam* weighs a bit less than the four newer ships commissioned by the line since 1993, and

contains fewer decks. The result is an oceangoing hybrid with one of the densest passenger loads in HAL's fleet. And since most of the ship's rebuilding occurred before Carnival was around, the ship is completely and resolutely unglittery.

Fans of this seaworthy ship refer to it simply as "The West." You'll enjoy a sedate but well-run cruise, loaded with all the thoughtful touches for which Holland America is famous.

Cabins & Rates

Cabins	Average per diem	Bathtub	Fridge	Phone	Sitting Area	TV
Inside	$178–$242	No	No	Yes	No	Yes
Outside	$200–$305	Half	No	Yes	Half	Yes
Suite	$442–$465	Yes	No	Yes	Yes	Yes

CABINS The size of a standard outside cabin is a roomy 200 square feet, one of the largest in the industry. Cabins come in 15 different price and space configurations, many with one twin bed and one fold-away bed that functions during nonsleeping hours as a sofa. The cabins

are decorated in conservative colors (usually pastels) and batik prints that commemorate HAL's long-standing association with Indonesia. A fruit basket is refilled every day and everyone gets a canvas tote bag as a souvenir of their trip. Although compact, bathrooms are well designed and well lit, and come stocked with fine toiletries. Except for a few lower-priced cabins, all cabins have tubs as well as a shower.

Four cabins, plus all elevators, are wheelchair accessible.

RECREATION & FITNESS FACILITIES
The ship has two outside pools, one with a retractable dome for bad weather. There's an unobstructed track on an upper deck, and the Ocean Spa health club, with rowing machines, weight machines, stationary bicycles, steam rooms, and saunas. A tactful staff of attendants makes sure you're not overdoing your exercise. You can take an aerobics class or get a facial or massage.

PUBLIC AREAS   The public areas are more akin to the decor of the *Nieuw Amsterdam* and *Noordam,* with more deep jewel tones in the public areas. Unlike its siblings, however, *Westerdam*'s dining room is positioned below decks, with none of the ocean or port-side panoramas associated with the line's big-windowed newer versions. Otherwise, the vessel's layout is similar to the line's two older ships, although its larger format holds a greater number of passengers. Some distinctive features include seven bars (one with a piano), a cinema, a video arcade, and small meeting rooms for card playing, discussion groups, or whatever.

Majesty Cruise Line

SHIPS Royal Majesty

901 South America Way, Miami, FL 33132. ☎ 800/532-7788 or 305/530-8900; fax 305/358-4807.

Majesty Cruises is the upscale sibling of the less prestigious (and less expensive) Dolphin Cruise Lines. As such, it operates out of the same Miami-based executive offices, shares many members of the same executive staff, and saves money by ordering supplies for both lines together, taking advantage of bulk discounts.

The company's only vessel is the $220 million *Royal Majesty,* a small- to medium-size 32,000-ton ship that was originally conceived as a cruise ship and ferryboat in the Baltic Sea. Before its completion in 1992, and despite the rapid opening of the eastern Baltic to tourism, the vessel was reconfigured into a cruise ship for the Caribbean market and snapped up by the fiscal entity that today operates both Majesty and Dolphin.

Except for a handful of seven-night mid-summer cruises that navigate between Boston and Bermuda, the ship specializes in short-term Caribbean cruises of no more than four days, catering to a market that has traditionally included many not particularly affluent, cost-conscious travelers who might not have sailed on a cruise before. Consequently, Majesty has worked hard to present itself, with some justification, as the most upscale of the lines within the short-duration cruise market, offering grace notes that its more middle-brow competitors don't (or can't) provide. The demographic niche it aims for has sometimes been compared to that already occupied by Celebrity or Holland America, giant and savvy operators that are better-funded, better capitalized, and, in the case of HAL, much more experienced at what they do.

A relative newcomer to the cruise industry (the company was founded in 1991), Majesty finds itself in the difficult position of offering a middle-to-upscale product to a clientele that's usually perceived as relatively downscale/mass market. The innate conflicts this engenders sometimes lead to inflated expectations and consequent disappointments on the part of clients who don't get the posh experience they'd expected. As time goes by, and the ship ages and becomes less competitive when compared to the many newer ships being launched, it's anybody's guess as to whether it might slash its rates into something closer to those of its middle-market twin, Dolphin.

Therefore, before you book, take into account that Majesty is a small line that stands bravely alone in its middle-to-upscale appeal to a budget-conscious market. Also remember that its solitary vessel's small size can't provide the wealth of diversions available aboard any of the megaships, and that its cruising area is very limited and oft-traveled.

Something to watch for in the future? When the port of Havana eventually opens up (and industry pundits are fairly confident that it will), watch for the development of this vessel into a shuttle-ferry between and around South Florida and the newly opened Cuban waters.

PROS & CONS *Royal Majesty*'s strongest point is its good value and leadership in the three- to four-day cruise market from the Port of Miami. It is ideal for the first-time cruiser—that is, the slightly dubious passenger who wonders if he or she will like to be tossed around in a tub of steel for three or four days.

The pace is low key, and the deck plan is easy to follow, so even on short cruises, you quickly learn what's where. There is also an easy flow of passenger traffic, so you're not always bumping into someone. It's suitable for those who'd like to escape for a few days, with some style and without being spoon-fed high-energy activities.

The *Royal Majesty* is *not* for smokers, and is, in fact, the most smoker-unfriendly vessel afloat. Majesty was the first major cruise line to feature a non-smoking dining room. In addition, one-quarter of the cabins are nonsmoking. *Royal Majesty* even offers onboard "Kick-the-Habit" seminars.

Regrettably, the ship does not offer first-rate evening entertainment (some past passengers have referred to it as "adolescent") and you may decide to totter off to bed long before the show is over.

In spite of the ship's many strong points, one of which is a usually well-crafted design, it suffers from lackluster cuisine and service that's less than majestic. (Admittedly, some of these perceptions result from the line's self-proclaimed upscale nature causing passengers' inflated expectations. Aboard less costly or less pretentious lines, we doubt that passengers' perceptions of inefficient service would be so acutely noticed.)

Cruisers also tend to complain about "nickel and dime" charges, such as charging extra for sundries and some snacks (including ice cream between meals) on deck when other lines tend to offer equivalent goods for free. There seems to be an unspoken policy that tries to generate as much onboard revenue as possible, a policy that leads to onboard merchandising of booze, wine, gift items, bingo games, and such supplemental activities as skeet shooting that's sometimes a lot more strident than you might want.

TYPES OF PASSENGERS   The ship is appropriate for couples or honeymooners between 35 and 65 years old, with incomes of $50,000 or more. At least two-thirds of the passengers are in professions like dentistry or business-related activities like insurance. Most winter cruises are filled with passengers from Florida. You'll spot their suntans immediately. Single passengers tend to be few in number, so it's not a great ship on which to cruise for a date. Fortunately, the staff sometimes chitchats with lonely passengers, cajoling

and in some cases flirting away their blues.

There's a lot of emphasis on party-colored cocktails aboard, and some clients tend to overindulge. (Perhaps the relatively small size of the ship makes this behavior more obvious than aboard a ship with more places to escape to.) Readers have noted that alcohol-related rowdiness is especially apparent during afternoons around the pool and during tendering of passengers to and from shore leaves.

Although not aggressively promoted as a family fun cruise, families are welcomed and catered to. Most of the year-round children programs, however, take place on summer cruises to Bermuda. On Caribbean winter cruises, families are less prominent.

DINING   The main dining room, the Epicurean, unfortunately doesn't live up to its name. The room is intimate—too intimate, in fact, for some, who think the tables are too close together. However, it offers panoramic views on three sides, including a view over the stern. The restaurant is smoke free.

Apollo Catering out of Miami provides the food and service for the ship, and like many a catered affair the cuisine is only mediocre. Lobster is usually served at least once, even on the short cruises. The buffets draw more praise, probably because they offer such a wide array of food. The wine cellar contains a good selection of vintages.

Pizza ovens at the top of the ship attract many passengers. One confided to us the pizzas are so good he ordered one every day. The kitchen will accommodate your special dietary requests, but you should give notice when booking.

ACTIVITIES   From morning tai chi to late-night boogying at the Frame 52 disco, activities fill the cruise calendar. In keeping with the ship's low-key atmosphere, the decision to participate or not is entirely up to you; no one will hector you into an activity you want nothing to do with. The best activities are the scuba

Late-Breaking Majesty News

Things change with lightning speed in the cruise industry. As proof, we offer you Majesty Cruise Lines.

As this book goes to press, it was announced that Norwegian Cruise Line was in the final stages of purchasing Majesty and its *Royal Majesty*. (See "Late-Breaking NCL News" on page 232.) Some reports indicate that Majesty will be absorbed wholly into NCL rather than be maintained as a separate entity. On the other hand, Majesty president Paris G. Katsoufis is staying on in his position even as he resigns the presidency of Dolphin. Frankly, the situation could go either way. What we could confidently say is that the *Royal Majesty*'s itinerary will remain as we've reported it at least through the end of 1997 and probably through the first quarter of 1998.

If you've got your heart set on the *Royal Majesty* but think this corporate shuffling might put the kibosh on your plans, take heart: According to NCL executive vice president Bruce Nierrenberg, the line is "committed to making the operational transition between Majesty and NCL a seamless process to avoid any inconveniences to travel agents or the passengers. There will be no disruption of service whatsoever."

and snorkeling expeditions arranged by Club Nautica, especially in The Bahamas.

CHILDREN'S ACTIVITIES   Even though this is not the most ideal family cruise ship, a youth program is in effect year round. At the stern is the Little Prince Playroom, where little princesses can play, too. Facilities include a puppet theater, a slide, and a small outdoor splash pool. Yogi Bear, Fred Flintstone, Scooby-Doo, or George Jetson are likely to show up to entertain the kids. Activities of particular charm include face painting, kite-flying from the decks, and autograph hunts whereby children procure the signatures of adult passengers, partially as an exercise in overcoming shyness. Majesty tries to enliven dining hours for children by providing special menus with "Bam-Bam's Chilly-Willy Dog," and guest appearances by cartoon characters who urge kids to drink their milk.

Baby-sitting can be arranged between 10pm and 1am if you'd like to sample the ship's limited nighttime diversions.

ENTERTAINMENT   Regrettably, one of the line's best entertainment features, a policy of producing one-act plays that enlivened many a seagoing afternoon, was discontinued in 1996. Today, most diversions are along the lines of watered down song-and-dance Vegas clones that rely for much of their success on the audience being fairly deep into its collective cups.

We prefer the Polo Club, with its dim lights and live musicians; it's the warmest and most intimate place for a rendezvous. With 16 TV sets and flashing lights, Frame 52 draws what late-night disco crowd there is. Recently, some cruises have featured circus-style acrobats and jugglers who bravely and gamely jump through their hoops even during rough seas.

SHOPPING   A trio of gift shops with a limited array of merchandise occasionally attracts a bored passenger or two. Logo items, jewelry, boutique clothing—you've seen it all before. You may want to save your serious shopping money for The Bahamas, or elsewhere.

SERVICE   Service is a sore point with many passengers, and *Royal Majesty* will need to make far more progress in this area if it wants to retain an upmarket clientele. Although many crew members, especially the Greek officers, seem genuinely interested in pleasing passengers, other members of the international crew appear indifferent to requests.

Although the line touts its butler service for passengers in suites as much more substantial than its cabin steward service, it often falls far short of its promise. Passengers expect European panache and find instead nothing particularly extraordinary. Service is usually slow within the dining room, and passengers have complained of rude, sullen, or surly waiters. A few waiters, however, do offer well-rehearsed and thoughtful service—in fact, they're so good they often contrast glaringly with those who aren't.

Cruise directors don't take a lot of initiative about providing anything more than rudimentary insights into upcoming ports of call, and the activities on board often seem to lack any real vision and any purpose other than filling in the time between cocktail and meal times.

ITINERARIES   From mid-May until mid-October, *Royal Majesty* is the only ship that makes seven-day sailings to Bermuda from Boston. In winter, it sails from Miami to The Bahamas and Key West on three-day cruises and to Key West and Mexico (Playa del Carmen and Cozumel) on four-day cruises. Some itineraries are themed. For example, one three-day cruise is devoted to Elvis, with impersonators, Elvis costumes, Elvis dance contests, and Elvis trivia questions. Other themes include festivals of country-western music, Irish or Greek festivals (with their requisite food and music), and bobby-sock and bubble gum rock 'n' roll retrospectives.

SPECIAL DISCOUNTS   The earlier you book the more money you save, up to an astonishing 40% off brochure prices with the line's AdvanSaver Program. A third or fourth passenger sharing a cabin pays from $130 to $150 per diem. Discounts of up to $100 are granted if you arrange your own airfare.

SINGLE SUPPLEMENTS   Solo passengers pay 150% of double-occupancy rates.

PORT CHARGES   Port charges are $94.50 for three-night cruises, $103.50 for four-night cruises.

Royal Majesty

⚓ ⚓ ⚓ ⚓

Specifications

Size (in tons)	32,390	Crew	525 (International)
Number of Cabins	528	Passenger/Crew Ratio	2.1 to 1
Number of Outside Cabins	343	Year Built	1991
Number of Passengers	1,056	Last Major Refurbishment	n/a
Officers	Greek		

Frommer's Ratings (Scale of 1–10)

Activities	7.0	Public Areas	8.6
Cabins	8.0	Public Comfort/Space	8.8
Cleanliness/Maintenance	8.5	Recreational Facilities/Pool	8.5
Entertainment	6.0	Service	6.0
Food & Beverage	6.8	Ship Crew/Officers	7.0
Interior Decor	9.0	Shore Excursions	7.0
Ports of Call	9.0	Worth the Money	8.0
		Overall Average	**7.7**

If we were going to design and operate a medium-size ship for short cruises, we would build one just like *Royal Majesty*. The ship is well conceived and stylish throughout, based on the design of Michael and Ani Katzourakis of Athens. They avoid neon and glitz, preferring marble, large windows, polished woods and brass, and multitiered rooms. Blue, ranging from very light to intense, is obviously their favorite color, even though many of the upper-tier cabins, and many of the suites, tend to be outfitted in soft reds and burgundies.

Cabins & Rates

Cabins	Average per diem	Bathtub	Fridge	Phone	Sitting Area	TV
Inside	$196	No	No	Yes	No	Yes
Outside	$270	No	No	Yes	No	Yes
Suite	$356	No	Yes	Yes	Yes	Yes

CABINS It's unusual for such a small ship to have 12 different price categories, but that's just what this one has, and your cabin assignment will likely shape your opinion of *Royal Majesty*. You get what you pay for, beginning with a small, cramped cabin of only 118 square feet. Even the more expensive cabins, including the suites, are not overly spacious at 142 square feet. Regardless of their configuration and size, however, cabins are fine for short-term cruise vacations, especially any of the lines three- and four-day specials, and some passengers find them extraordinarily cozy and comfortable.

Various bed sizes are offered as well—convertible double, queen, sofa bed, and single. Less than a third of the beds convert to doubles; most are relatively narrow twins. You're usually separated from your traveling companion or spouse by a chest of drawers. All cabins are carpeted, containing ironing boards (unusual for ships on short cruises), and safes. Some cabins have berths that fold into the wall to sleep three or four passengers. No matter the size of your cabin, the bathroom will be cramped. All are equipped with showers.

A regular cabin has simple uncluttered lines and is decorated with natural wood surfaces and tasteful autumn color schemes. The most expensive cabins contain queen-size beds, a minibar, and good-size windows opening onto ocean views. Some guests request a cluster of cabins on the Duchess Deck, as they form a half moon opening onto the bow. In contrast, the vista from many cabins on the Queen's Deck is blocked by lifeboats. Cabins on the Princess Deck open onto a public promenade, which means a lack of privacy.

The 14 suites are medium size and nowhere near as impressive as aboard such industry leaders as *Seabourn*, but there is a 24-hour butler service, the value of which usually depends on how cooperative your butler is in responding to your whims. Although the line stresses the glamour-quotient of these butlers, passengers sometimes complain that they only provide a kind of window dressing, and perform far fewer, and more sporadic, duties than they'd been led to believe. Don't expect your butler to show up with white gloves, like Anthony Hopkins in *Remains of the Day*. Their role is much more limited.

Some suites are a bit too near the jogging track, and the sound of running shoes thumping by outside at early morning hours can be disruptive. Noises usually emanate from the ship's disco till around 3am.

Bathrooms within the suites are $2^1/_2$ times the size of those within the cabins.

Persons with disabilities gravitate to this ship, as it's fully accessible to persons in wheelchairs. Four staterooms are specially equipped for them, as are its four elevators and toilets on various decks.

RECREATION & FITNESS FACILITIES

The medium-size pool rarely seems over-crowded, but there's not enough space for sunning. Nearby shaded tents protect passengers from the sun's intensity. The flat, teak-covered expanse of deck near the bow is one of the few bits of deck space with full exposure to the sun and air. Designed without obstacles or barriers of any kind, it's a triangular frontal outpost that commands sweeping views over the vistas ahead, and as such, is quickly adopted as a favorite spot for outdoor strolls and contemplation. A jogging track covered with a material that minimizes leg strain runs completely around the deck.

The health center on the Princess Deck combines the Bodywaves aerobics gym with a sauna, massage rooms with licensed therapists, and a small sports boutique. The spa offers facial and body treatments. The fitness center has weights, a stair climber, rowing machines, tread-mills, a LifeCircuit, and stationary bikes. It's of adequate size, and usually not crowded with fitness fanatics, but it's not one of the vessel's strong points.

PUBLIC AREAS

Public areas aren't glitzy, decorated instead with a pleasant mixture of blues and grays, teak and brass. The Countess Deck has a variety of intimate bars, shops, and other small rooms where you can retreat with a companion or simply be alone. Many rooms are named descriptively: Queen of Arts (card room), Bookend (library), Boardroom (for conferences), Treasured Moments (photos), Crown Jewels (jewelry), and the Royal Fireworks lounge in the bow, which offers entertainment but rarely fireworks.

After a few hours aboard, you might wonder why all cruise ships don't have forward-facing rooms like the Royal Observatory on *Royal Majesty*. Theirs is located on Deck 9 (of 11), has a semicircular bar and grand piano, and is ideal for social gatherings, relaxing, or just watching the upcoming seascape or landscape. Some passengers spend their entire cruise in this delightful room—that is, if they can stand the karaoke.

Norwegian Cruise Line

SHIPS   Dreamward • Leeward • Norway • Norwegian Crown • Seaward • Windward

95 Merrick Way, Coral Gables, FL 33134. ☎ 800/327-7030 or 305/445-0866; fax 305/443-2464.

The earliest roots of Norwegian Cruise Line (NCL) were as the now-defunct Kloster Cruises, whose demise in 1996 represented one of the cruise industry's most wrenching shakeups. In 1966, Knut Knutson, the Norwegian owner of Kloster, had a cruise ship but no marketing system, and Ted Arison, an Israeli, had a deeply entrenched North American marketing system but no ships. They combined their assets and formed Norwegian Caribbean Line (corporate forerunner of NCL), and launched three- and four-day cruises from Miami to The Bahamas.

Alas, their union was short-lived and rancorous, and Arison and his entourage split from the company in 1972 to form Carnival Cruise Lines, which eventually became NCL's most vigorous competitor. Adding insult to injury, more than 20 years later Arison and his backers threatened a hostile merger of the two companies, on terms dictated by Carnival.

Part of the widely criticized financial weakness of NCL derived from Kloster's disastrous acquisition of Royal Cruise Line and Royal Viking Cruise Line, both of which eventually went bankrupt. Kloster was radically reorganized in 1996, throwing many employees of Kloster-controlled companies out of work but contributing to an enhanced financial stability for NCL. The reorganization also added an additional vessel (the *Norwegian Crown*) to NCL's roster of worthy but dissimilar ships.

One of the challenges the line faces involves the ongoing expense of maintaining the company's illustrious flagship, the *Norway,* a venerable but outmoded vessel that was originally built in 1961 as *Le France.* Today, Norwegian continues to struggle to adapt its fleet to the ever-changing cruise-industry marketplace, despite the fact that it's frequently outdistanced by more skilled and more cutting-edge competitors such as Carnival, Royal Caribbean, and Princess Cruises.

Despite its woes, NCL has some fine cruise ships, clustered into a hodgepodge armada whose differences the line does its best to downplay. Most of them are smallish (25,000 tons) to medium-size (42,000 tons), with the notable exception of the *Norway,* a floating city that, at 76,000 tons, was ranked as a megaship long before Carnival and Royal Caribbean Cruises, Ltd., were even heard of. Consequently, your experience and your opinion of NCL will depend on which of their widely disparate vessels you sail aboard.

To survive, the line hopes that its midsize ships will lure more upmarket travelers. If that doesn't happen, NCL is not too proud to offer some outrageous discounts during virtually any season as a means of filling empty berths. Recognizing that more cruise dollars are spent in the Caribbean than in virtually any other region of the world, NCL drops all pretensions of sending its vessels into exotic or faraway waters during the winter months, keeping its entire line, like snowbirds, almost entirely within the Caribbean, then sending them off to other scattered regions (usually Europe or Alaska) in summer.

You might enjoy the variety of options available at NCL. The *Leeward,* for example, feels more like an oversized yacht than a giant cruise ship. Passengers who reject megaliners such as the *QE2* or even the *Norway* may find NCL's more modern ships, such as *Dreamward* or *Windward,* to their liking. The newer vessels have all the equipment and facilities of their giant seagoing companions but are still small enough to offer a more intimate cruise experience and more personal service. The line has also been particularly savvy in its policy of promoting floating sports bars and alternative dining choices.

Following the bankruptcy of Royal Cruise Line in 1995, NCL launched its newest vessel in March 1996, the luxurious *Norwegian Crown,* formerly Royal's *Crown Odyssey.* This ship, which originally entered service in 1988, is a major and glamorous addition to the Norwegian fleet. To maintain the ship's former standards and maintain the goodwill former passengers feel toward it are still major challenges for NCL.

PROS & CONS   Here's where NCL excels. First, it excels in activities. If the line offered any more activities, passengers would be exhausted. Second, its entertainment, including Las Vegas–style shows, is first rate, even drawing headliners like Tanya Tucker. (Still, it doesn't equal the shows produced aboard Carnival's latest ships, which have better high-tech equipment.) Third, NCL excels in theme cruises and theme nights, including Viking Theme Night or SS *France* Theme Night. The latter takes place on the *Norway* each week.

The fleet further excels in recreational and fitness programs, with among the best and most comprehensive of any line. An incentive program rewards cruise passengers who join in the fun, whether they play volleyball or take an aerobics class. The line is also the leader in SuperSport theme cruises, devoted to tennis, golf, and other sports, in which sports celebrities take part.

The line also boasts what many competitors cannot: its own private island in The Bahamas. Sleepy little Great Stirrup Cay suddenly comes alive when an NCL vessel docks. Hardworking staffers leave the ship several hours before the passengers, transforming this uninhabited site into an instant party. Music plays, barbecues are fired up, and paddleboats and Sunfish are brought out from shoreside storage cabins or from the bowels of the ship.

Norwegian Cruise Line is a market leader in promoting a smoke-free environment for those who want it. At least half the cabins are nonsmoking. On any ship with more than one dining room, one restaurant will be nonsmoking. There are even blackjack tables in its casinos reserved for nonsmokers. Despite the presence of clearly defined smoking zones aboard each of NCL's ships, those who light up very frequently might be happier sailing elsewhere.

If cuisine is terribly important to your cruise experience, you'll find better food on some other more upmarket ships. Norwegian's vessels are not five-star ships, so those expecting service, cuisine, and cabins the equal of a deluxe hotel should also look elsewhere, to Seabourn, for example. And if you're a passive cruiser who's happier reading on deck than filling the hours with activities, you'll find more tranquil seas elsewhere, perhaps on the Windstar twins.

TYPES OF PASSENGERS   Passengers who book on NCL want to travel to a hot weather destination, especially in winter, but don't want to spend too much for the fare. The line offers a wide variety of cabins at a variety of prices to suit them.

The typical NCL passenger has an annual household income of around $40,000, and although the average age for European sailings might be a bit higher, those aboard most Caribbean cruises tend to range in age from 25 to 49. Most passengers hail from Florida, California, and New York. Many Europeans also travel this line, plus a few Canadians and the odd honeymooning couple from Argentina or count from Malta. The line has particular success with first-time cruisers who sometimes become repeaters. Families with children like NCL's activities calendar, which is full even during short cruises.

Norwegian Cruise Line has pioneered more theme cruises than any other line, so its passenger list is often composed of special-interest groups, including sports fans, *Wheel of Fortune* watchers, or older passengers who book Big Band Cruises to relive the days of Glenn Miller and Benny Goodman. Some NCL cruises are jazz, Dixieland, or blues festivals, sailings that tend to draw many young professionals.

Sports lovers particularly like the line, not only because of its fitness programs but because of its enhanced sports programs, pool and beach services, and even its aggressively promoted scuba programs, which the line tends to funnel off to independent concessionaires. All major weekend games, including NFL playoffs, are broadcast both into passenger's cabins and onto the video monitors of each vessel's sports bar. Carriers for these broadcasts include both ESPN and CNN.

Atmosphere through all NCL vessels is informal and well-suited to the serious party-maker taking a first or second cruise. An extremely chic passenger or a jaded, oft-afloat cruiser might prefer to sail elsewhere, if they can afford it, perhaps aboard one of the Windstar or Seabourn vessels.

DINING None of the Norwegian Cruise Line vessels is distinguished for its cuisine. Portions are exceedingly generous, but the food isn't that good. You can usually count on some marinated and smoked Norwegian salmon, but after that it's a typical veal piccata or broiled filet of flounder, or perhaps a pasta of the day or roast prime rib. The wine list appeals to standard mid-American tastes. Theme nights break the monotony of the cuisine, especially the Viking buffets filled with Scandinavian specialties. Sometimes strolling musicians add a grace note at dinner.

More attention has been directed to upgrading the cuisine aboard the *Norway,* whose modernized menus now offer lighter alternative dishes. The *Norway* has two main dining rooms, the domed-ceiling Windward and the balconied Leeward. Service varies because of personnel turnover. Both dining rooms are jammed with tables, and there are only a few tables for dining à deux. *Norway*'s midnight buffets are spread out amidst a Viking ship replica.

The *Dreamward* and *Windward* have smaller, more intimate dining rooms, with seating ranging from 76 to 282 passengers. Dining tables and rooms are assigned for dinner only, with two seatings nightly. The cuisine remains uneven aboard both vessels. The Sports Bar and Grill, with indoor/outdoor snacking and drinking, is a change of pace on either ship.

The *Seaward* has two main dining rooms, Four Seasons and Seven Seas, both located on the Main Deck with two dinner seatings and assigned tables. Its Lido restaurant, the Le Bistro Café, is best for its panoramic views and informal buffets.

The *Leeward*'s two main dining rooms are at the stern. Its Sports Bar and Grill is an informal spot for breakfast and lunch, with dining both inside and out.

All ships have "Le Bistro," which serves Italian specialties at no extra cost. The food here is better than in the main dining rooms. However, you might not get a table—seating is on a first-come, first-served basis.

Each vessel also offers a midnight buffet, and each, except the *Leeward,* also has an ice-cream parlor dishing out free treats. Aboard the *Norway, Dreamward, Windward,* and *Seaward,* you'll find the innovative Chocoholic Bar, offering everything from tortes to brownies. Also on the *Norway, Dreamward,* and *Windward,* white-gloved waiters serve English high tea.

Room service is available 24 hours a day from a very limited menu. The expansion of the *Norway* room service menu has met with success. Special diets, including vegetarian and kosher, are accommodated.

ACTIVITIES   Adult activities are one of the line's strongest points. You'll find the most action aboard the *Norway,* with some 75 or more different activities to try. You can take cha-cha lessons or compete in a shuffleboard tournament, play basketball or watch calypso performances, or take a beauty seminar. It's all here, more than on any other line.

CHILDREN'S ACTIVITIES   Norwegian Cruise Line offers a "Kids Crew" program year-round for children ages 6 to 17, and, during summer months and major holidays, for ages three to five. The program divides children into four age groups: junior sailors ages three to five; first mates ages six to eight; navigators ages 9 to 12; and teens ages 13 to 17. Activities vary within the fleet, and include sports competitions, dances, arts and crafts, and even a Circus-at-Sea. Children receive their own "Cruise News" detailing the day's events. The program is flexible, letting families spend time together as well as apart. You'll find the best year-round children's programs aboard the *Norway* and *Seaward.*

Dreamward and *Windward* have a playroom called Kids Korner, and *Norway'*s "Trolland" playroom offers activities for kids of all ages, and has more facilities than those aboard the other vessels.

Baby-sitting is available from noon to 2am aboard all ships within NCL's fleet for $8 per hour for the first child, and $1.50 per hour for each additional child. Baby-sitters are usually culled from among each ship's off-duty service personnel, who offer their time as a means of earning extra money.

ENTERTAINMENT   When the sun goes down, the allure of NCL truly shines. Productions are expensive, surprisingly lavish, and artistically ambitious. Each ship contains a fully equipped theater where creditable productions of such shows as *Crazy for You, Grease, 42nd Street, Will Rogers Follies,* and *Dreamgirls* have been presented. Norwegian Cruise Lines also produces its own Vegas-inspired extravaganza, *Sea Legs Review,* and brings aboard headliners such as George Jones, Tanya Tucker, and former Supreme Mary Wilson. While many are past their prime in box office allure, they are still major talents. Because passengers are diverse and have different interests, shows are tailored for everybody from the toddler to the octogenarian.

NCL pioneered the concept of theme-related cruising, and since then it's been among the most successful afloat at keeping the (themed) good times rolling. They've presented jazz cruises, blues cruises, Dixieland cruises, Big Band cruises, and country-western cruises. Comedy cruises, discontinued in 1996, may be re-inaugurated during the lifetime of this edition.

The *Norway,* being the giant of the fleet, presents the most lavish Las Vegas–style revues. It also boasts the fleet's biggest and splashiest casino, the Monte Carlo, a vision of art deco with mirrored walls. Actually, serious gamblers should sail the *Norway* only, as they may find the casinos inadequate aboard the other NCL vessels.

All the ships have bars where you can slip away for a quiet rendezvous, and small places for more intimate entertainment. Music for dancing is popular aboard all the ships, and takes place before or after shows. And you can dance into the wee hours of the morning in each ship's disco.

SHOPPING   The inventory aboard each of the NCL vessels bears a remarkable resemblance to that aboard many other cruise ships—due in part to the fact that the same concessionaire, Greyhound Leisure Services, is responsible for their shops' maintenance and style of marketing. Prices in each of the company stores are carefully calibrated to be competitive with equivalent goods you're likely to find at ports of call.

The widest selection of goods is aboard the *Norway,* mainly because it contains more space than the line's other, smaller ships. There are boutiques selling resort-wear, a gold and jewelry shop, the inevitable T-shirt outlet, a shop selling exclusive and very stylish dresses, and outlets for commemorative NCL souvenirs.

Shopping within the comparatively small *Leeward* is only somewhat more limited than that aboard the larger twins *Windward* and *Dreamward*, whose shopping options lie within the Galleria on the Star and Sun decks. If you look carefully, you can sometimes find something special, despite the fact that most of the merchandise is routine.

Don't get too carried away by the art auctions that draw a lot of attention aboard all NCL vessels. Passengers report they've never found any real bargains at these auctions, although some of the paintings and objets d'art are well chosen and interesting, and the pitter-patter of the auctioneer is always entertaining.

SERVICE *Uneven* is the word that keeps cropping up to describe service aboard NCL vessels. However, some passengers, especially first-timers, find the service excellent—but then, their expectations may not be as high as among more seasoned cruisers. We've found room service aboard these vessels to be generally speedy and efficient.

While service isn't bad aboard the other vessels, it's better on the *Norway,* whose staff seems more seasoned. If problems occur with service, it's usually in the main dining rooms. Cabin attendants generally win more passenger approval than the dining room wait staff.

ITINERARIES NCL's repeat clients sometimes place a high priority on special themes, sometimes to the extent that the theme overshadows their cruise's itinerary. If this describes you, be sure to talk theme-cruise schedules when you book. (*Note:* See page 232 for late-breaking news on the *Dreamward, Seaward,* and *Windward.*)

Dreamward—From January through April and from October through December, the ship departs every Sunday from Fort Lauderdale for seven-day cruises, stopping at Grand Cayman, Playa del Carmen/Cozumel, Cancún, and Great Stirrup Cay (NCL's private island in The Bahamas). During other months, trips leave from New York and include visits to Bermuda.

Leeward—Throughout the year, three-day cruises depart from the Port of Miami every Friday at 5pm, calling at Great Stirrup Cay and visiting either Key West or Nassau. Alternating four-day cruises leave Miami on Monday and stop in both Cozumel and Key West.

Norway—Seven-day cruises leave from the Port of Miami every Saturday. Most of the time they head for the eastern Caribbean, stopping at St. Maarten, St. John, St. Thomas, and Great Stirrup Cay, with three days at sea. On selected Saturdays, however, they depart for the western Caribbean, stopping at Ocho Rios, Grand Cayman, Cozumel, and Great Stirrup Cay, with two days at sea.

Norwegian Crown—From the first week of October through mid-April, the ship leaves Miami for seven-day cruises through the western Caribbean, stopping at Grand Cayman, Roatan (Honduras), Cancun, Cozumel, and Key West.

Seaward—From its home port in San Juan, Puerto Rico, the *Seaward* alternates weekly circuits that stop at Santo Domingo, St. Lucia, St. Kitts, St. Maarten, and St. Thomas. These alternate with week-long circuits that stop at Barbados, Santo Domingo, Dominica, Antigua, and St. Thomas. Both circuits include a full day at sea.

Windward—In autumn, winter, and early spring, the ship departs every Saturday from a base in San Juan for jaunts to islands that include Aruba, Curaçao, Tortola, and St. Thomas.

SPECIAL DISCOUNTS NCL maintains an aggressive policy of reducing its fares as needed to fill up cabins. Consequently, actual rates (NCL refers to them as "Leadership Rates") will in most cases be deeply discounted from the company's brochure rate. Distributed to travel agents across the country, they're revised frequently and unpredictably, based on market conditions and occupancy rates, and sometimes extend to selected cabins or to a predetermined number of cabins aboard every ship within its fleet. In addition to that, NCL sometimes offers two-for-one rates as well as reduced rates

for third and fourth occupants of cabins in selected categories.

SINGLE SUPPLEMENTS   Solo cruisers pay 150% to 200% of the double occupancy tariff.

PORT CHARGES   Depending on the itinerary, port charges range from $78.50 to $115.50.

Dreamward • Windward

⚓ ⚓ ⚓ ⚓

Specifications

Size (in tons)	41,000	Crew	483 (International)
Number of Cabins	623	Passenger/Crew Ratio	2.6 to 1
Number of Outside Cabins	531	Year Built	1992/1993
Number of Passengers	1,246	Last Major Refurbishment	n/a
Officers	Norwegian		

Frommer's Ratings (Scale of 1–10)

Activities	9.0	Public Areas	8.5
Cabins	8.5	Public Comfort/Space	8.5
Cleanliness/Maintenance	8.5	Recreational Facilities/Pool	8.6
Entertainment	9.0	Service	7.5
Food & Beverage	6.8	Ship Crew/Officers	9.0
Interior Decor	8.9	Shore Excursions	8.4
Ports of Call	8.2	Worth the Money	8.8
		Overall Average	**8.4**

Norwegian Cruise Line's identical twins, the *Dreamward* and *Windward,* are market leaders among quality, midsize, moderate-cost ships, and are known for their innovative designs by Bjorn Storbatten, the Scandinavian designer who set the tone for *Royal Viking Queen* and the Seabourn twins.

Even though the ships are midsize, they appear to be more spacious than they are. Both forward and aft, the ships' upper decks cascade down, resulting in panoramic views from the public areas, including the dining rooms. Walls of glass line the length of both vessels, each of which contains four intimate restaurants, two of which are arranged in terrace

fashion facing aft over the stern observation lounge. Eighty-five percent of the sleek contemporary cabins are outside cabins. However, in an attempt to save money, low-grade materials were used in the passageways and stairways, so you know you're not on a luxury yacht.

Both vessels draw greater numbers of upmarket clients than any others in the Norwegian Cruise Line fleet. First-time cruisers like these two vessels, although more seasoned cruisers may book elsewhere. An informal style permeates both vessels, and the Norwegian officers are very smooth and charming. Unfortunately, this grace isn't always apparent in other staff members.

Cabins & Rates

Cabins	Average per diem	Bathtub	Fridge	Phone	Sitting Area	TV
Inside	$245–$275	No	No	Yes	No	Yes
Outside	$295–$325	No	No	Yes	Yes	Yes
Suite	$345–$375	Partial	Yes	Yes	Yes	Yes

CABINS The big draw is that nearly all cabins are outside, and about 80% of the outside cabins have picture windows. Standard outside cabins measure 160 square feet, which is extremely generous in the industry. The inside cabins are almost as spacious, ranging in size from 130 to 150 square feet, so if you're not big on views (and aren't claustrophobic) it might not be worth the extra bucks for the more luxurious cabins.

The accommodations have a breezy decor with wood accents and pastels evocative of the West Indies. Unfortunately, storage space is minimal. Two people can just barely manage, but when a third or fourth person shares a cabin it can get truly cramped. Small closets with shelves are hardly adequate. Bathrooms are also tiny.

Fifteen cabin categories are available, most on the bottom 5 decks of the 10-deck vessels. Most cabins have a separate sitting and sleeping area, but to accomplish this the area around the beds was made smaller and is now rather cramped. Most cabins have twin beds that can be converted to queen size. Cabins on the port side are for nonsmokers. Note that lifeboats block the views of the Category 4 cabins at midships on the Norway Deck, and early morning joggers might disturb late sleepers who have cabins on the Promenade Deck.

Many families book the 76 accommodations that can be converted with berths to house a third or fourth passenger. There are no single cabins.

Suites are rather luxurious, with floor-to-ceiling windows, and many have private balconies. Guests are coddled with everything from buckets of champagne to concierge service. The half dozen "owner's suites" are the most dramatic, followed by 48 penthouse suites with balconies.

Six cabins are wheelchair accessible, and 16 cabins are equipped for those with hearing impairments, an innovation aboard cruise ships.

RECREATION & FITNESS FACILITIES
Each ship has two pools, but all are woefully small. The more theatrical (aboard each ship) is on the International Deck, where semicircular rows of chaise lounges and deck chairs surround a small and almost purely decorative keyhole-shaped pool. You really can't swim, but the view—whether of the ocean or of your fellow passengers—is panoramic. A larger pool lies two decks above on the Sun Deck. The focus here is less on sunbathing and more on swimming.

Both vessels have a fitness center and spa, with state-of-the-art exercise equipment including Lifecycles and Lifesteps. Aerobics and exercise classes are part of the activity-filled agenda, and the fitness center also offers massages and a sauna along with a whirlpool. Each ship has two Jacuzzis.

Sports fans gravitate to the Sports Deck, with its Ping-Pong tables, bar, and driving range for golfers. Snorkeling is available while sailing, with more active water sports programs pursued when the ships dock.

Both *Dreamward* and *Windward* become the most sports- and youth-oriented vessels afloat during major theme cruises devoted to golf, tennis, football, etc. During those cruises, the fitness center overflows its capacity.

Of all the ships within NCL's fleet, this pair of identical twins are the most likely to undergo radical alterations within the next four or so years, probably in the form of a "stretching" (cutting the ships into two parts and adding a midriff for additional passenger capacity).

PUBLIC AREAS   Both vessels have a terraced design, making for roomier lower-level public areas, generous amounts of deck space on upper levels, and good passenger flow.

Cruisers like the four onboard restaurants, which function with a variety of seating systems. Best are the rooms facing aft over the stern, whereas the rooms at the port side and amidships are less desirable. The largest dining room, the Terraces, on three levels, evokes a supper club in a 1930s movie.

The casinos are very small. Some lounges metamorphose into discos at night, but you can also find lounges where you can relax or engage in conversation. Try the Lookout Bar on the International Deck. The sports bars, with giant-screen TVs, are the most popular. Sometimes major sports figures come aboard to meet their fans or give talks.

Leeward

⇩ ⇩ ⇩

Specifications

Size (in tons)	25,000	Crew	400 (International)
Number of Cabins	475	Passenger/Crew Ratio	2.4 to 1
Number of Outside Cabins	217	Year Built	1992
Number of Passengers	950	Last Major Refurbishment	1995
Officers	Norwegian		

Frommer's Ratings (Scale of 1–10)

Activities	8.5	Public Areas	8.9
Cabins	8.0	Public Comfort/Space	8.0
Cleanliness/Maintenance	8.5	Recreational Facilities/Pool	7.8
Entertainment	8.5	Service	7.0
Food & Beverage	7.0	Ship Crew/Officers	9.0
Interior Decor	8.0	Shore Excursions	8.8
Ports of Call	7.5	Worth the Money	8.5
		Overall Average	**8.0**

Originally built as the *Viking Saga,* this ship was renamed the *Leeward* in 1995 when it was leased by NCL from Effjohn International for use in the lucrative three- to four-day cruise market from Miami.

Like a cat with nine lives, *Leeward* has had its ups and downs during a very short life. First launched as a car-passenger ferry in Scandinavia, it caught fire during a refit and was declared a total loss. Rebuilt, it became *Sally Albatross* and remained a car-passenger vessel operating in the Baltic Sea. However, it ran aground at a cruising speed of $19^{1}/_{2}$ knots and was again declared a total loss. (With a name like *Albatross,* what did its investors expect?) Insurance paid for the $60 million renewal to convert it to a Caribbean cruiser, and in spite of its past mishaps, it looks and feels like a new ship.

The *Leeward* is a small and somewhat chunky-looking ship, with a sharp, short bow; it's strong, sturdy, and in some ways the odd duck among NCL's ships. When full, it can seem very crowded, with only four elevators accommodating as many as 950 passengers. It's worse when one elevator is used to distribute luggage during embarkation. On the plus side, the ship is ideal for short cruises, appealing to a wide variety of passengers, some drawn to its short itineraries and others just wanting to try something new. The vessel's sports emphasis draws many men in the 25 to 45 age bracket. Plus, the meeting and convention facilities are good.

Activities are typical for a general-purpose short cruise, ranging from bingo and passenger talent shows to the popular and well-performed *Pirates of Penzance,* the *Sea Legs Review,* and cabaret solo acts. Movies are shown on cabin TV monitors.

Cabins & Rates

Cabins	Average per diem	Bathtub	Fridge	Phone	Sitting Area	TV
Inside	$190	No	No	Yes	No	Yes
Outside	$280	No	No	Yes	No	Yes
Suite	$330	No	Yes	Yes	Yes	Yes

CABINS   For the most part, cabins are very comfortable and quite spacious for the three- to four-day cruise market, except the very cheapest cabins that measure an ungenerous 60 square feet. There are 13 different types of cabins situated on the lower six decks.

All cabins are fully carpeted, have individually controlled air-conditioning and bathrooms with showers. Many have twin beds that can be converted to queen size. Port-side cabins are for nonsmokers. Most cabins in the lower price range can accommodate a third or fourth passenger, making them appealing for families or budget cruisers. There are no singles.

The two "owner's suites" have personal Jacuzzis on a private teak veranda, and eight Penthouse Suites offer a separate bedroom and living room, plus balconies. Five cabins are wheelchair accessible.

RECREATION & FITNESS FACILITIES
The one swimming pool, built for very limited use in chilly Baltic climes, hardly seems adequate for cruises from Miami to The Bahamas. If the ship is fully booked, there is serious overcrowding. The spacious expanse of teakwood sundecks is adequate, however. A children's pool is better than the inadequate children's playroom.

The onboard fitness center is adequate and reasonably well equipped with exercise equipment, saunas, a beauty salon, and a full-service spa. Also offered are exercise classes, aerobics, snorkeling lessons, skeet shooting, and table tennis. Joggers or walkers can enjoy a complete circumnavigation of the Promenade Deck.

Since space is limited and cruises are short, most athletes delay their water sports until arrival at NCL's private island, Great Stirrup Cay, where there's diving (if you're qualified) or snorkeling.

PUBLIC AREAS   The main drawback to this small ship's public areas is that what you see during the first few hours aboard is likely to be what you see again and again. The public areas are thoughtfully planned, comfortably decorated, and kept in good working and attractive decorative order, but during inclement weather these small spaces can get quite crowded. If you're at all claustrophobic, you may find this too much.

Full-scale Broadway or Las Vegas–type revues are presented in the two-story Stardust Lounge. The Monte Carlo Casino lures the gamblers, and the Tradewind Lounge has a dance floor with music. Boomer's Disco has a high-tech sound system for the late-night crowd. A piano bar and an observation lounge with a dance floor are in the aft section. Conference rooms have limited equipment for small groups.

The ship lacks certain facilities, such as a library or a forward observation lounge, which is a virtual requirement for some cruisers. Except for the elevator problem, there is generally a good flow of people.

Norway

⚓ ⚓ ⚓ ⚓

Specifications

Size (in tons)	76,049	Crew	875 (International)
Number of Cabins	1,016	Passenger/Crew Ratio	2.3 to 1
Number of Outside Cabins	656	Year Built	1961
Number of Passengers	2,044	Last Major Refurbishment	1996
Officers	Norwegian		

Frommer's Ratings (Scale of 1–10)

Activities	9.0	Public Areas	8.2
Cabins	8.2	Public Comfort/Space	8.7
Cleanliness/Maintenance	8.5	Recreational Facilities/Pool	9.0
Entertainment	9.2	Service	7.8
Food & Beverage	6.8	Ship Crew/Officers	8.8
Interior Decor	8.0	Shore Excursions	7.9
Ports of Call	7.2	Worth the Money	8.8
		Overall Average	**8.3**

The last of the 1,035-foot luxury liners, this ever-enduring legend is the only vessel of its kind sailing the seas today. Stretching the length of 3¹/₂ football fields, *Norway* was enormous by the standards of the year it was built. While many megaships rival it in size today, it still retains an aura of nostalgia they simply cannot match.

After a $65 million refurbishment begun in 1990, and with many facelifts over the decades, the ship still looks good, although not as fresh as it was when christened by Madame Yvonne de Gaulle. It is the only cruise ship flying the flag of the United Nations, in recognition of its international crew representing some 40 different countries.

In September of 1996, the *Norway* completed $15 million worth of refitting

at an English shipyard. Although new carpeting, fabrics, and signs were installed within the ship's public areas, most of the changes involved technical upgrades for compliance with the 1997 SOLAS (Safety of Life at Sea) standards. Expensive but inevitable, the rigorously enforced changes were a major hurdle that NCL seems to have successfully overcome. The year 1996 also witnessed a refreshing new assignment for the ship: treks between Miami, New York, Southampton, and Le Havre, France. Because those crossings were close to being sold out, look for NCL's flagship to play the transatlantic liner role during at least part of its summer schedule.

The *Norway* today is famous for its theme cruises, and the ship is credited with pioneering such jaunts to fill the cabins during off-peak periods. The first one was a week-long Mickey Mouse extravaganza, where the line teamed with Disney. In 1986, the *Today* show broadcast on board for a week. Whatever the subject—country music or jazz, basketball or fitness and beauty—these theme cruises, offered throughout the year, appeal to a wide variety of tastes. Owing to its many commodious public rooms and easy flow of traffic, the *Norway* is an ideal venue for these kinds of jaunts. The focal point of activities is the International Deck, with the Great Outdoor Restaurant at the stern.

The ship's size limits its access to certain smaller ports, which can't handle a vessel so huge. If your interest is in visiting smaller, more remote islands, this isn't the vessel for you. When you do stop at a port of call, the passenger count causes monstrous lines upon disembarkation, which can severely limit your time ashore. Lines can also be long at buffets.

Cabins & Rates

Cabins	Average per diem	Bathtub	Fridge	Phone	Sitting Area	TV
Inside	$225	No	No	Yes	No	Yes
Outside	$310	Partial	Partial	Yes	No	Yes
Suite	$365	No	Yes	Yes	Yes	Yes

CABINS   You can choose from 20 cabin categories, ranging from spacious "owner's suites" with private balconies to cramped and minuscule inside cells with upper and lower berths. Cabins are spread across ten decks, and the farther down you go, the cheaper the price.

Cabins are furnished traditionally, with some art deco touches. Since the cabin plans are so intricate, you might seek the advice of a good travel agent in selecting one. Bathroom size and amenities tend to be consistent regardless of your cabin's size. Plumbing seems a bit more solid than the cheaper plastic fixtures installed aboard many newer ships.

The first cabins to sell out are the 124 luxury cabins and suites on the two uppermost glass-enclosed decks. Half have verandas, but the veranda partitions aren't solid and don't ensure privacy. Views from cabins on the Olympic or Fjord decks are obstructed, completely or partially, by lifeboats.

Travelers with disabilities should book on the International Deck, near the major public rooms, where 10 cabins are wheelchair accessible.

RECREATION & FITNESS FACILITIES

The *Norway* has two large outdoor pools, the one near the Lido Bar being the larger, with ample room for sunning. There's also a cushioned circuit for jogging, and games include paddleball, table tennis, skeet shooting, shuffleboard, and basketball. Snorkeling classes are available aboard or offshore during excursions.

The fitness center and separate Roman Spa are excellent, roomy facilities. The former has floor-to-ceiling windows, an indoor pool, exercise equipment, Cybex and Bally fitness machines, two steam rooms, and two saunas, plus body-jet showers and a whirlpool.

It may be a bit of a hassle to reach the Roman Spa, located deep within the ship—only two elevators go there from the top decks, where many of its patrons reside. But once there, you'll find the most comprehensive spa at sea, with 16 treatment rooms. You'll find Jacuzzis for six (or a cozy eight), an aquacise pool, a sauna, Bally cardiovascular equipment, massage, and the first hydrotherapy baths ever on any cruise ship.

PUBLIC AREAS   There are 12 passenger decks, and their public areas are the most generously sized of almost any cruise line. The ship is filled with a vast treasure trove of art, including exquisite tapestries.

In lounges and bars, the *Norway* truly excels. You'll find three on the International Deck alone. If you're looking for a more cozy and intimate spot, try the Windjammer, a snug little box that holds no more than 48, has a piano, and serves lethal cocktails. If you want company, the North Cape Lounge on the pool deck accommodates 750 passengers.

The vast Monte Carlo Room is a gambler's heaven, with 206 slot machines and seven blackjack tables. The balconied,

two-story Saga Theater has some bad seats, but its sound, lighting, and audiovisual facilities are state of the art. This is not a conference ship, and the meeting rooms are severely limited. The library is very good for reading, escaping from the crowd, and wave-watching.

Myriad shops line both the port-side promenade (called "Fifth Avenue") and the "Champs Elysées," an equivalent thoroughfare on the starboard side.

Norwegian Crown

⚓ ⚓ ⚓ ⚓

Specifications

Size (in tons)	32,250	Crew	470 (International)
Number of Cabins	526	Passenger/Crew Ratio	2.2 to 1
Number of Outside Cabins	342	Year Built	1988
Number of Passengers	1,050	Last Major Refurbishment	n/a
Officers	Greek		

Frommer's Ratings (Scale of 1–10)

Activities	7.4	Public Areas	8.5
Cabins	8.5	Public Comfort/Space	8.2
Cleanliness/Maintenance	8.6	Recreational Facilities/Pool	8.0
Entertainment	7.5	Service	7.8
Food & Beverage	7.1	Ship Crew/Officers	8.0
Interior Decor	8.0	Shore Excursions	6.5
Ports of Call	7.5	Worth the Money	8.5
		Overall Average	**7.9**

The transfer of this fine vessel from the bankrupt Royal Cruise Line to Norwegian Cruise Line has significantly improved this line's competitiveness. Well designed and well built, the *Norwegian Crown* exudes style and grace. Marble and wood are used effectively, and gleaming brass and polished granite add to the luxurious ambience throughout. Classical motifs are blended with contemporary and art deco styling to create a sleek and handsome profile. The sometimes heavy-handed use

of mirrors and reflective surface is softened with touches of stained glass and lacquered walls. In many ways, it's the most "chic" member of NCL's fleet, rivaled only by certain upscale cabin categories within the fleet's dowager empress, the *Norway*.

Unlike some ships designed for short cruises—including most of those making the three- to four-day run from Florida to The Bahamas—this comfortable ship is suited for longer cruises and shorter

Caribbean jaunts. It rarely seems to be overflowing, even when all the berths are booked to their fullest capacity.

So far, NCL has maintained its high standards of food and service, and if there's any reason not to sail this ship, it isn't apparent yet.

Cabins & Rates

Cabins	Average per diem	Bathtub	Fridge	Phone	Sitting Area	TV
Inside	$245	Half	No	Yes	No	Yes
Outside	$295	Half	No	Yes	No	Yes
Suite	$345	Yes	Yes	Yes	Yes	Yes

CABINS The ship's staterooms are spread across seven decks and include "owner's suites" and penthouses, regular suites, and first-class inside and outside cabins. Some 80% of the staterooms are classified as deluxe outside cabins. All are generally spacious, although you may disagree if you book into one of the 155-square-foot cabins. Closet and drawer space is more ample than that aboard most ships this size. Soundproofing is effective (you don't know everything going on in the next room), and some staterooms are reserved for nonsmokers.

All cabins are equipped with a three-channel stereo music console, individually controlled air-conditioning, 110/220 volt electrical outlets, rich hardwood furniture and cabinetry, full vanities, two mirrored closets, twin or queen-size beds, and tie and shoe racks. Most outside cabins have exceptionally large windows. Bathrooms, in either tile or marble, have large mirrors, recessed toiletry shelves, and fine European fixtures. Many cabins on the Lido Deck, however, have obstructed views.

The ship contains a total of 90 suites, as opposed to 101 aboard both *Winward* and *Dreamward*, and 165 aboard *Norway*. The 16 penthouses, with furnished private decks, are especially luxurious. Four owner's suites have connecting doors to adjacent cabins, giving you the option of an extraordinary 1,000 square feet of living space. Each cabin on the penthouse deck has a remarkable 180° view. Some apartments are decorated with themes, as their names imply: Balmoral, Taj Mahal,

Sandringham, Tahiti, Hollywood. Suites on the Riviera Deck have unique, wood-paneled bay windows—a first on any cruise ship—that command panoramic views. Glass partitions separate the sitting rooms from the bedrooms in superior deluxe suites, where all the hand-crafted furnishings are of cherry wood.

Four cabins are designed specifically for persons with disabilities. They're wheelchair accessible, and are equipped with seated showers, handrails, tilting mirrors, and special lighting. These cabins are among the best of their kind in the industry.

RECREATION & FITNESS FACILITIES
The teakwood sunning area on the Penthouse Deck is generally adequate even when the ship is full. The penthouse pool is large and state of the art in design.

If you like to stay fit while floating, this is a good ship to sail. Its Romanesque health center is one of the best of its kind for a medium-size ship. You'll also enjoy a fully equipped gymnasium, juice bar, saunas, indoor pool, whirlpools, and a spa and beauty salon with a complete range of treatments. The ship's staff conducts exercise classes, many geared toward older passengers. One of the ship's best features is the unobstructed circuit for jogging. There's also a golf practice pit.

PUBLIC AREAS The public areas are exceedingly generous for a ship this size, and allow for good passenger flow. The wraparound outdoor promenade deck is one of the ship's finest features, much appreciated by strolling passengers.

The five lounges and six bars feel spacious, not overcrowded. The most dramatic lounge, the Top of the Crown, is a multipurpose room surrounded by glass and topped by two glass domes. It's a cocktail lounge in the afternoon and a disco at night, with a sunken and illuminated glass dance floor. Your coziest retreat, complete with granite tabletops and lots of stained glass, is the Rendezvous Bar, adjacent to the Stardust Lounge. For drama, the Monte Carlo Court, adjacent to the ship's outdoor pool, derives most of its lighting from topaz-colored pyramids affixed to the ceiling, a modernist/futuristic touch that many passengers find very appealing.

The two-level Seven Continents is the ship's main restaurant, with a central sunken section and large windows for panoramic ocean views. Some 590 diners are accommodated at two different seatings. Sounds tend to bounce off all this glass and stainless steel, however, making the room noisy.

During the day, the Penthouse Bar and Grill offers snacks and light lunches, and serves as a casual gathering place with an outdoor pool and whirlpools. The Yacht Club and Midnight Sun Café is a versatile poolside lounge, serving early morning coffee, buffet breakfasts and lunches, and then turning into a glass-floored dance area.

Nighttimes are lively, especially in the Stardust Lounge, where tiered seating and a raised orchestra platform evoke a small-scale theater. A movable dance floor transforms the lounge into an expansive stage for Broadway shows and musical revues. There's also an art deco theater, the Coronet, spanning two decks. A casino offers seven gaming tables and 82 slot machines—nothing special here.

Seaward

⇩ ⇩ ⇩

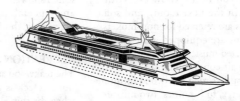

Specifications

Size (in tons)	42,000	Crew	630 (International)
Number of Cabins	767	Passenger/Crew Ratio	2.4 to 1
Number of Outside Cabins	486	Year Built	1988
Number of Passengers	1,504	Last Major Refurbishment	1991
Officers	Norwegian		

Frommer's Ratings (Scale of 1–10)

Activities	8.5	Public Areas	8.0
Cabins	8.0	Public Comfort/Space	8.2
Cleanliness/Maintenance	8.5	Recreational Facilities/Pool	8.1
Entertainment	8.5	Service	7.0
Food & Beverage	7.0	Ship Crew/Officers	8.8
Interior Decor	7.4	Shore Excursions	7.8
Ports of Call	7.5	Worth the Money	8.5
		Overall Average	**8.0**

This is not a glitzy ship, and some parts of it look the most spartan of anything in the NCL fleet. Nevertheless, the *Seaward* is seaworthy in every way and sleek in design, and it's been a hit for NCL, especially among Americans, who make up a good percentage of both its passenger list and its crew.

Seaward's Scandinavian designers, Petter Yran and Robert Tillberg, exercised restraint on this nine-deck ship, trying for a modern but not ostentatious look that would attract a more discriminating clientele than that sometimes sailing the *Norway*. A striking two-deck-high lobby has a water and crystal sculpture, along with a cascading fountain splashing into a marble-lined pool.

In effect, the *Seaward* is a larger version of the *Leeward*, offering the same cuisine, somewhat the same entertainment, and even some competitive itineraries. Most of the public rooms have the same names as aboard the *Leeward*, but everything's on a larger scale, as the *Seaward* accommodates more passengers.

If they are so similar, you ask, then which is better? It's a question of whether you prefer a smaller ship (the *Leeward*) or a larger ship (the *Seaward*). We personally give the *Seaward* an edge over the *Leeward*, because of its better and more ample facilities. Passengers with disabilities will also find the *Seaward* the better bet, as all public areas are wheelchair accessible.

Cabins & Rates						
Cabins	Average per diem	Bathtub	Fridge	Phone	Sitting Area	TV
Inside	$260	No	No	Yes	No	Yes
Outside	$300	No	No	Yes	No	Yes
Suite	$350	Yes	Yes	Yes	Yes	Yes

CABINS   Cabins come in 14 different price ranges, with the most expensive ones on the upper three decks. The bargains, which are almost equally as good, are on the lower three decks. Regrettably, many cabins are disappointingly small, and don't have balconies, which is an important consideration for some upmarket cruisers.

Standard cabins don't have sitting areas, and most contain twin beds, which can be converted to doubles by the steward. Storage space is tight but adequate for trips of up to a week. Bathrooms are compact but efficiently outfitted with good lighting, big mirrors, and easy-to-scrub all-white surfaces. Amenities include hair dryers. Port-side cabins are nonsmoking.

A quartet of deluxe suites was added during a 1990s renovation, and these are the best accommodations if you can afford them. Note that many cabins on both the Star and Norway decks have their views either obstructed or partially obstructed by lifeboats.

Four cabins are specially equipped for persons with disabilities.

RECREATION & FITNESS FACILITIES
There are two outside pools, plus twin outdoor Jacuzzis. One pool is a most generous 14 by 42 feet, one of the longest pools aboard any Caribbean cruise ship. The sunning and outdoor lounge areas are generally adequate.

The moderately sized health and fitness center has the necessary equipment. The Promenade Deck features a quarter-mile, 360° jogging and walking track, which has a nonslip metal surface instead of teak decking. The health club offers massages and a sauna, and standard aerobics and other exercise classes are a regular feature. A full-service spa is adjacent.

Sports on board include basketball, skeet shooting, and golf driving. Table tennis, shuffleboard, and snorkeling lessons can be arranged.

PUBLIC AREAS   Public areas are decorated in deep, jewel-toned colors, especially burgundy. One of the best public areas is the Observatory Lounge, where you can slip away from the activities below and commune with the seascape. Another hideaway is the intimate little piano bar called Oscars, and you can dance beneath the stars beside the top-deck swimming pools. The *Seaward* has a

Late-Breaking NCL News

As this book goes to press, Norwegian Cruise Line has announced a major program of expansion and reconstruction that will have a major impact on its fleet's positioning for the 1998 season.

First on the agenda, the *Dreamward* and the *Windward* will be sailed into the Lloyd Werft shipyard in Bremerhaven, Germany, where they'll each have a new 130-foot midsection grafted into their structure. The new sections will increase each ship's passenger capacity by 40%—the *Dreamward*'s from 1,242 to 1,754 and the *Windward*'s from 1,246 to 1,758. An additional casual restaurant will be added to each ship, as well as new gifts shops, lounges, a new spa and health club, a library, card room, cigar/cordial club, new meeting facilities, and improved children's facilities to cater to the fast-growing family cruise market. Additionally, in an effort to increase Norwegian Line's brand-name recognition, they'll both be renamed.

The *Windward* will depart San Juan for Bremerhaven on January 3, 1998, and return to service as the *Norwegian Wind* on March 29 with two 7-day Caribbean cruises, a 15-day Panama Canal cruise, and a 7-day Pacific Coastal voyage before resuming its regular schedule of 7-day summer Alaska cruises. Beginning October 4, 1998, the ship will sail a winter season of 7-day Western Caribbean cruises every Sunday from Miami.

The *Dreamward* will depart Miami for Bremerhaven on March 1, 1998, and resume cruise service as the *Norwegian Dream* on May 14. Rather than return to its regular Bermuda run from New York, the ship will offer a series of European cruises; then, beginning December 20, 1998, it will begin a winter season of 7-day Southern Caribbean cruises departing every Sunday.

Want more changes? The *Seaward,* which is being renamed *Norwegian Sea,* will switch its year-round alternating 7-day Southern Caribbean schedule from Sunday to Saturday departures beginning May 2, 1998.

OK, now for the new: NCL has an option to purchase a partially-completed 2,000-passenger cruise ship from Germany's Bremer Vulkan shipyard, but that's all we know at this point. We've also gotten word that NCL has signed a letter of intent to build a 2,000-passenger upscale ship at the Kvaerner Masa-Yard in Helsinki, Finland. If all goes according to plan, that ship would enter service in the second half of 1999. Stay tuned for next year's *Caribbean Cruises* for details.

More big news is Norwegian's purchase of Majesty Cruise Line and its ship the *Royal Majesty.* Whether they'll maintain the line as a separate entity or incorporate it into NCL has not yet been determined. The deal was still up in the air as we go to press, but all parties assure us that it's only a breath away from being signed and sealed. See "Late-Breaking Majesty News" on page 213 for more details.

number of places that cater to the romance-on-the-high-seas crowd.

Mealtime options include two dining rooms: the Four Seasons and the Seven Seas. The Big Apple Café is a less formal dining option.

High rollers head to the Monte Carlo Casino, with its roulette wheels, blackjack tables, and 178 slot machines. More contemplative types might retreat either to the Butterfly Card Room or to the not very well-stocked library. The Cabaret Lounge is big enough to mount a full scale production of *Grease* or even *A Chorus Line.* Unfortunately, the one-level seating in this room means that those in the back have a hard time seeing the show. The early bird gets the better seats up front.

Premier Cruise Lines

SHIPS   Star/Ship Oceanic

400 Challenger Rd., Cape Canaveral, FL 32920. ☎ 800/327-7113 or 407/783-5061; fax 407/784-0954.

In 1984, two ex-employees of Norwegian Cruise Line, Bruce Nierenberg and Bjornar Hermansen, founded Premier, and their success in tapping into the family holiday niche is now legendary. Their vision for a new cruise line coincided with the burgeoning appeal of central Florida's massive theme parks and with the emergence of then-tiny Port Canaveral as an acceptable port of embarkation. Within a few short years, the pair created one of the most recognizable logos and public images in the cruise-ship industry.

The partners developed their ideas while working at Norwegian Cruise Lines, but the NCL board of directors rejected their strategy, prompting the pair to take their show on the road. Backing for their new project eventually came from the Greyhound Corporation of Phoenix, Arizona, a company subsequently acquired by the Dial Corporation, later known as the Viad Corporation. In 1991, the industry's Goliath, Carnival Cruise Line, almost concluded negotiations to acquire Premier, but withdrew to pursue other ventures. In March 1997, Viad sold Premier to Cruise Holdings, Ltd., the entity that also owns Dolphin and Seawind Cruise Lines.

From the start, Premier hoped to link the draw of a holiday at sea to the already-proven success of central Florida theme parks and attractions, such as Walt Disney World and the Kennedy Space Center. To do this, Premier bought older, down-at-the-heels ships (the *Oceanic* and the now-divested *Atlantic*), sheathing them in catchy colors with a recognizable motif, and marketed them as waterborne, three-day excursions for the floods of visitors pouring into Florida.

Some of Premier's early publicity derived from its designation of Port Canaveral as its corporate headquarters and port of embarkation, since it was the first multiday cruise line to berth here. The line's official color, red, and its packaging as "The Big Red Boat" was one of Premier's all-time smartest moves, as the concept was picked up overnight by thousands of children reared on a diet of Saturday morning cartoons. The slogan also emphasized a cruise concept that parents could recognize, as well.

How was red designated as the official color? Apparently Nierenberg asked his marketing people to bring him various colored acetone sheets, which he laid over an outline of a ship to determine the hull color. He chose a bright Chinese scarlet and ordered that his ships would be called the "Big Red Boats." No other cruise ships in the world are *that* colorful.

Within a year of its inauguration, Premier was designated the official cruise line of Walt Disney World, a title that earned worldwide publicity and the right to feature Mickey and Minnie Mouse and other Disney characters as full-time personalities aboard ship. That designation lasted eight years, ending in March 1995 when the agreement with Disney was not renewed. Mickey and Minnie were unceremoniously ejected and replaced with a host of Looney Tune characters—Bugs Bunny, Yosemite Sam, Porky Pig, and Roadrunner—whose copyrights were owned by Warner Brothers.

If your family circle is looking for a week-long warm-weather holiday that's packed with things to do, some of the most comprehensive and cost-effective options anywhere are available at Premier. The company's holiday packages combine a three- or four-day cruise aboard their Big Red Boat with a three- or four-day land-based holiday that explores several or all of the Orlando area's half-dozen or so theme parks.

Premier is adept at configuring these diverse components into carefully predefined packages whose costs vary according to the number of children in tow, the quality and location of your hotel, the season, and the parks your entourage decides to visit. Just about every attraction and theme park in the Orlando area is included in the roster of possibilities, including the Magic Kingdom, Epcot, and Disney-MGM Studios. Packages usually come with an extra bonus visit to either the Kennedy Space Center or a local water park, Wet 'n' Wild.

The large majority of packages sold by Premier are seven-day affairs that include airfare and seven-day use of a rental car. Additional days can be added to the package if you wish. If you opt for any of these packages, we recommend the rental car, as it tends to be cheaper as part of the deal than if you had arranged it yourself.

If you only want to go cruising, and avoid Orlando's theme park razzmatazz, no one at Premier will object. Be warned that, package or no, you'll still be responsible for port charges, tips, and the inevitable odds and ends that crop up during trips, whether by land or sea, and with or without children.

Today, with the glow of its fire-engine debut pretty much worn off, Premier is facing serious problems. The most obvious is competition from larger and much wealthier cruise entities, whose bigger, glitzier, and more modern vessels threaten Premier's niche. First among these is Carnival, which has not only repositioned some of its ships to Port Canaveral, but has sent them off on the same itinerary as Premier. Plus, Carnival's pitch to the all-important children's market is a little more '90s, rejecting Premier's brand of cartoon and space-age fantasy, which some older or more cynical children and teenagers might reject as uncool.

Even more formidable a rival is Disney, an as-yet-untested line whose inaugural vessel—the 85,000-ton *Disney Magic*, scheduled to launch in 1998—will be the largest afloat. The *Magic* will carry all the Disney characters that had previously cruised Premier, and will boast more modern and sophisticated amenities than those aboard the somewhat antiquated *Oceanic*.

What is Premier's official response to the looming threat posed by Disney? Spokespersons say, perhaps a bit too sweetly, that vast populations of potential cruisers will have their cruising appetites whetted by Disney's ad campaigns, and that Premier—which will inevitably offer a less expensive alternative to Disney—will reap the rewards. Whether there will really be room at the banquet for both companies remains to be seen.

PROS & CONS The line's short itineraries and unpretentious and undemanding style make it a good choice for first-time passengers who aren't sure that life at sea is really their thing.

But Premier's *Oceanic* is by no means a modern, state-of-the-art megaship with all the newfangled gadgets. No matter how many coats of red paint get slapped on, it's a middle-aged ship whose wrinkles will inevitably show. However, most passengers, both children and adults, seem more concerned with the magic of their first ocean voyage than with architectural niceties.

This ship isn't for travelers who believe children should be seen only at rare intervals. Cabin walls are not so thick as to muffle the sound of unruly or noisy youngsters, and any conversations you might strike up with fellow passengers will almost surely bear constant interruption from a child demanding his or her parent's attention.

This is not the line of choice for singles, either. Even if you were to become emotionally involved with another passenger on a Premier cruise, the chances are very, very good that your newfound soul mate's life will already revolve around his or her own children.

But if you do take the plunge into Looney Tune Land, you'll find much to do that's amusing, whimsical, and escapist, with more of an "us" mentality than the "me" or "I" you might encounter aboard a line like Carnival.

The major question you'll need to ask yourself is how much of this you can take before *you* go loony. Fortunately, there's a more grown-up world adults can escape to whenever children's activities simply get too cloying: There's gambling in the casino, drinking sunset-colored cocktails in one of the onboard bars, catching the show in the onboard theater, or people-watching. For the budding sociologist interested in observing other families' bonding and pecking rituals, a Premier experience simply has no equal.

Possibly the worst part about a Premier cruise is the noise level in the dining room. This is not necessarily caused by the children (most of whom opt for the first seating), but rather by the fact that the U.S. Coast Guard wouldn't let the line enlarge its dining rooms. Thus, with the hordes of people and children aboard, dining is crowded and noisy to the point of inducing headaches.

Finally, Premier's itineraries are among the most standardized and tourist-trodden in the industry—three- or four-day roundabouts between Port Canaveral and the tried-and-true Bahamian ports of Nassau and Freeport. There's no hint of exotica, but these itineraries are entirely appropriate for parents who want to expose their children to the "international" allure of another country. They're also ideal as fun-in-the-sun shopping cruises.

TYPES OF PASSENGERS Premier's *Oceanic* contains children, many children, endless numbers of children. Parents usually fall into the 30- to 45-year-old-range, with household incomes in excess of $35,000 a year, and are most concerned with amusing their progeny during a limited time at sea, for a reasonable price. Many consider their cruises the highlight of their long-awaited annual vacations, and arrive with an understandable sense of anticipation.

Passengers are a cross-section of middle-class America, with the majority of families hailing from the suburbs of Northeast cities (especially the Philadelphia-to-Boston corridor), the Southeast, California, and Chicago. The line also attracts a fair number of international guests, so your children are likely to develop a friendship, or at least a dialogue, with a child from another culture.

Midweek cruises are likely to be less crowded than weekend cruises, and with noticeably fewer children. Cruises during school holidays—Christmas, Easter, summer vacations—have the highest percentages of children and are the most crowded.

DINING The line believes in food as sustenance, diversion, and entertainment, and creates a lot of hoopla around its presentation. Expect dishes like fried calamari, catch of the day, piccata of veal Milanese, or fettuccine with seafood. It's family fare with pizzazz: flavorful, competently prepared, and served in generous portions.

There are themed dinners, midnight buffets, 24-hour room service, a poolside grill, and pizza and ice-cream parlors where you can specify the ingredients of your favorite "space pie" or build your own sundae as high and gooey as you want. Afternoon tea is a regular feature, and you can get something to eat, no matter how late the hour, from onboard bistros.

The main concern when dining is that the dining rooms are too small for the number of passengers on board, and are therefore quite noisy. Premier is devoted, however, to making the most of their constricted spaces. Dining room artwork is changed to reflect the culinary themes of French, American, or Italian nights, and there's a good chance an actor swathed in a cartoon costume will emerge at midmeal to entertain you.

Within the dining rooms, both lunch and dinner are served in two assigned seatings. The early seating is extremely popular due to the number of children aboard.

Children's menus get almost as much play as the regular adult menus. Even if it's a theme night, you can almost always order some version of easy-to-eat food such as chicken nuggets, burgers, catfish fingers, spaghetti circles, and in some cases, tacos.

If requested in advance, special diets and kosher meals can be prepared. The line also serves "fitness" cuisine that's low in salt, fat, and calories.

ACTIVITIES Premier is the only cruise line whose adult facilities seem secondary to those crafted for children. Recognizing this—and perhaps recognizing also the fragile state of some vacation-frazzled passengers' nerves—the line does make a bit of a fuss over its adults. You can bet on handicapped horse races, attend a party hosted by the captain, or play golf during shore leaves in The Bahamas. You can also snorkel in shallow waters off Bahamian shores with a guide who knows the most interesting underwater sites. There are also bridge playoffs, wine tastings, auctions, a "guess that tune" game, and a mock-serious oceangoing version of *The Newlywed Game*.

If you're looking to immortalize your kids (or yourself) in one of those Kodak Moments, such characters as Porky Pig or the Tasmanian Devil are always willing to provide a photo-op.

CHILDREN'S ACTIVITIES By some yardsticks, Premier's children and teen programs are the most complete and comprehensive in the cruise-ship industry. Each ship employs at least 15 full-time youth counselors whose skill at involving children who are strangers to one another has been praised by many parents. Each counselor has past training in child care, education, nursing, or some related field.

Children are divided into five different age categories—2 to 4, 5 to 7, 8 to 10, 11 to 13, and 14 to 17—for supervised activities that continue from early

morning until 10pm. Many diversions are mindless fare that at best help develop social and cooperative skills. Others are sports related, and some are of the "edutainment" category, incorporating lessons on the natural environment and science. Children even have the option of heading off on their own (chaperoned) shore excursions, allowing parents to pursue their own land or sea activities.

There's an accessory-packed area aboard called Pluto's Playhouse, which is the largest children's recreation center in the short-cruise market. Kids also have their own swimming pools, ice-cream parlors, video arcades, and even a "Teen Nite Club" for the older children. A teen center is awash with images that somebody really believes are cool.

Group baby-sitting, available around the clock, is midway between a day-care center and a slumber party. Children ages 2 to 12 can spend a few hours or stay overnight (for a nominal fee) in Pluto's Playhouse from 10pm to 9am. Private baby-sitting fees are about half those charged by more upscale and adult-oriented cruise lines: $4 per hour for the first child and $2 per hour for each additional child. For an additional fee, you can arrange to have a costumed Looney Tune character tuck your child into bed.

ENTERTAINMENT Premier's entertainment has a distinct and not-always-subtle theme: Families that sail together stay together. Although that theme permeates every aspect of a Premier cruise, the strongest dose is spooned out during show time. So don't expect the sophistication, raunchy humor, and top entertainers you'd find aboard lines such as Carnival. Premier has worked hard to establish itself as a family values cruise line.

Onboard shows include Broadway-style revues with all the requisite glitter, dancing, and lights, interspersed with jugglers, PG-rated comedians, and magicians pulling (what else?) Daffy Duck dolls out of a hat. Lenny Bruce it's not; what it is is thoroughly competent and entertaining for all ages, and that's the way Premier wants it.

Karaoke is an ongoing staple, with adults and teenagers trying out their lungs on an Elvis, Buddy Holly, Reba McEntire, or Madonna tune. Theme nights like "The Big Chill 1960s Oldies Hour" are also popular.

Passengers under 18 are not allowed to play games of chance, though if you *look* like you're 18 you might get away with plunking a few coins into the slot machines. Underaged players who can't quite pull off the Cary Grant act are tactfully directed to a whirring and clanging video game arcade nearby.

Premier shows absolutely no reserve or ambivalence about such tried and true adult activities as drinking, smoking, and gambling, and configures its bar areas as adult havens where you can share memories and horror stories about child-rearing or put all that aside for an hour or two. Bartenders are well-trained in switching between adult and children's venues.

Singles parties take on an unusual aspect aboard Premier, as there's a higher percentage of single parents than aboard any other line afloat. For those determined to kick up their heels—children or no—there's dancing in the disco, dance bands in some lounges, the odd calypso show, and, if you still want to rock and roll after the midnight buffet, an occasional after-midnight Bahamian dance party on deck. Too tired for all that? Then relax in your cabin with a recent movie, and order in.

SHOPPING There's a walkway of shops called the Milky Way. The inventory, selected by Greyhound Leisure Services, includes gift and souvenir items, children's memorabilia, resort-casual clothing, and such luxury items as perfume, makeup, and middle-bracket jewelry. There's also duty-free liquor for sale. You may find some charming and whimsical items that are reasonably priced. Of course, there's tons of cartoon character

memorabilia—everything from stylish clothing to just plain junk.

SERVICE The multinational staff from Asia, the Caribbean, and Europe is hardworking, patient, and seems to smile more than you would've thought possible. The staff is patient and indulgent with children, even in difficult moments. Potty problems between the first and second course at dinner? No problem. Seasick tummies after too much ice cream on deck? No problem. Actually, the staff seems superhuman.

ITINERARIES Sojourns last either three or four nights. The four-night cruise spends an extra day chugging slowly along in the waters between Nassau and the Florida mainland. Ports of call on all cruises include only Nassau and Port Lucaya.

SPECIAL DISCOUNTS Premier offers discounts for passengers booking their cruise and Orlando theme park reservations more than three months in advance in selected cabin categories. These discounts can total $350 for a family of four or $400 for a family of five.

Premier also offers discounts for groups. A family reunion package allows reductions of up to 10% for the first six occupants in accommodations suitable for 10. Single-parent plans grant discounts for a parent and any child or children (up to a total of five) sharing a cabin with them. Amounts differ according to bookings and departure dates, and apply only to certain accommodations.

Honeymoon plans offer supplemental bonus packages for a relatively modest cost of $150 per couple. Senior citizens (defined by Premier as anyone over 55) and their spouse or guest (of whatever age group) receive discounts of between 10% and 20% off their cruise package, depending on the time of year they sail. Family reunion packages make the cost of a communal sail very competitive with equivalent holidays on land, and passengers who have sailed with Premier before receive special favors and amenities.

The line features packages that incorporate airfare from the snow belt, visits to various Florida theme parks, and a cruise. If you arrange your own airfare or drive to Port Canaveral on your own steam, you can save $200 to $250 off the cost of a cruise package, depending on your point of origin and the season.

SINGLE SUPPLEMENTS   Since this line does not cater to single travelers without children, Premier charges solitary occupants of cabins a whopping 200%

of the per person rate for a double accommodation.

That policy changes radically if a child is involved. If a single parent shares a cabin with a child or children under 17, the single parent's rate will fall to 125% of the per person rate for a double, and their progeny will pay discounted rates to fill up that cabin's extra berths.

PORT CHARGES   All passengers pay an additional $85 in port charges on both the three- and four-day cruises.

Star/Ship Oceanic

⇩ ⇩

Specifications

Size (in tons)	39,241	Crew	518 (International)
Number of Cabins	590	Passenger/Crew Ratio	2.3 to 1
Number of Outside Cabins	255	Year Built	1965
Number of Passengers	1,180	Last Major Refurbishment	1993
Officers	Greek		

Frommer's Ratings (Scale of 1–10)

Activities	6.8	Public Areas	7.0
Cabins	6.5	Public Comfort/Space	7.8
Cleanliness/Maintenance	7.8	Recreational Facilities/Pool	7.0
Entertainment	6.8	Service	8.0
Food & Beverage	7.5	Ship Crew/Officers	8.0
Interior Decor	7.5	Shore Excursions	6.5
Ports of Call	5.0	Worth the Money	7.5
		Overall Average	**7.1**

Built in the style of a classic ocean liner, the *Oceanic* boasts a layout of decks and public areas that was originally conceived for long-haul cruise odysseys. There's more weight and metal in this ship's design than in more modern vessels, where lighter materials are used and where modern structural innovations sometimes reveal a cookie-cutter similarity from ship to ship. Here you'll find teakwood decks and heavy doors with the traditional raised sill; children often have to experiment to learn to open the doors. Portholes, when they

appear, are usually round, as traditionalists think they should be.

The *Oceanic* is a dignified and stately vessel, a worthy example of the way ocean liners used to be built. Premier payed $20 million for the ship in 1985 and spent another $17 million on refurbishments and renovations—which included, naturally, a trademark red paint job. The purchase and renovations cost considerably less than building an all-new vessel, but there's no hiding the fact that this is an older ship.

Cabins & Rates

Cabins	Average per diem	Bathtub	Fridge	Phone	Sitting Area	TV
Inside	$165	Half	No	Yes	No	Yes
Outside	$225	Yes	No	Yes	Yes	Yes
Suite	$250	Yes	No	Yes	Yes	Yes

CABINS Some of the outside *Oceanic* cabins are gratifyingly large, with suites up to 500 square feet. Some of the suites have private verandas. The cheapest cabins are truly minuscule—only 137 to 139 square feet. These inexpensive lodgings are positioned near the bow, so there's lots of pitching and rolling.

Cabins sleep between two and five occupants, depending on their configuration and the family arrangements of their occupants. Upper berths (and, in some cases, convertible sofas) have enlarged many cabins originally configured for two occupants. This makes shipboard density high. It also creates the impression that you're lodged in a glamorized dormitory.

Each cabin contains a radio, a welcome-aboard basket, and an endless supply of chocolate chip cookies (Premier calls them "Chocolate Ship" cookies). Furniture is durable and solid, and as indestructible as cabin accessories come. To make it easier for kids to find their way home, cabin doors are color-coded. Bathrooms are durable and as family friendly as possible, with rounded angles and no potentially dangerous glass objects.

Don't expect undisturbed slumber. Doors tend to bang open and shut at all hours, and you'll hear an ongoing undertone of kid noises regardless of your cabin's location. Compared to most other cruise lines, there's lots more activity in hallways, especially during embarkation and disembarkation.

If an outside cabin with a view is important to you, make this very clear before you commit yourself. There's a higher-than-expected percentage of inside cabins aboard the *Oceanic,* and many of the outside cabins on the Premier Deck have views that are partially blocked by lifeboats.

Only one cabin is designated as a single, and only one is designed for passengers with disabilities. Others are designated "wheelchair friendly," meaning they're okay for passengers with partial mobility but not a good idea for anyone who really needs wall railings.

All landings at Port Lucaya and the (optional) excursions to the beaches at Salt Cay, near Nassau, require passengers to ride aboard a tender. This is complicated if you require a wheelchair, and probably unwise.

RECREATION & FITNESS FACILITIES
There are two swimming pools and two whirlpools on board. The pools are often full to overflowing, and are covered by retractable greenhouse-style roofs that Premier refers to as magrodomes.

There's a spa with weight equipment, Lifecycles, sit-up boards, and mini-trampolines that are more frequently jumped on by children than by adults. There are also massage facilities, setups for volleyball, aerobics classes, basketball, table tennis, real tennis, shuffleboard, skeet shooting, and an unobstructed, small-scale jogging track. There are communal morning walks on the deck, and services by Steiner of London that include the usual assortment of facials, hairdressings, and toning/slimming regimes.

For an additional fee, passengers can sign up for introductory scuba lessons, which include video presentations and practice sessions with scuba equipment in one of the ship's pools.

PUBLIC AREAS The interior design of public areas features cheerful decors by the husband-wife team of A. and M. Katzourakis. There are lights twinkling along shiny metallic surfaces, bright but not jarring color schemes, and features

Late-Breaking Premier News

As this book goes to press, word has come down that Cruise Holdings, the company that owns Premier, Dolphin, and Seawind Cruise Lines, will be merging the three lines into one during the fall of 1997. The name of the new line had not yet been finalized, though the buzz is that it will seek a market niche as the "classic cruise ship" alternative to today's mega-colossal megaships. This strikes us as a positive idea. The new line's ships are all fine old vessels that, without a concerted effort to promote them, might have gotten lost in the megaships' advertising wake.

Unfortunately, details of the merger's effects are still unavailable at this writing, though we predict few or no major changes in the short term regarding the Big Red Boat's itineraries, its family focus, or its general shipboard ambience. So, for those of you who are leaning toward a cruise aboard the *Oceanic* (or one of the new line's other ships), the reviews in this edition of *Caribbean Cruises* will still provide the information you'll need, and your travel agent or cruise agent can fill you in on any new info. You can also call the line at ☎ **800/327-7113.** Tell 'em Frommer's sent you.

that add an instant showtime aspect to otherwise not-very-noticeable corners. The only somber-looking place aboard either ship is the deliberately darkened, artsy-looking Heroes and Legends jazz pub, where adults can hide from the constant barrage of kiddie-dom.

The *Oceanic* is a sleek, bullet-shaped vessel, built before wider, sports-oriented decks came into vogue, and apparently before passengers took to migrating around the ship—some traffic flows make getting from point A to point B rather awkward. For instance, to get from one end of the Lounge Deck to the other, you have to pass through the already-crowded casino, which is difficult for the pedestrian and distracting for the committed gambler.

The names of the public areas derive from a combination of Looney Tune characters and the looming nearby presence of the Cape Canaveral Space Center. You'll find the Satellite Café, the Mars Bar, the Milky Way Shops, and the Space Station Teen Center and Disco.

Adults aren't ignored in all the kiddie play. There are five bars on board, plus a casino and between three and four lounges where some kind of entertainment is presented. There's no library aboard.

Princess Cruises

SHIPS   Crown Princess • Dawn Princess • Grand Princess (Preview) • Regal Princess • Sea Princess (Preview) • Sun Princess

10100 Santa Monica Blvd., Los Angeles, CA 90067-4189. ☎ 800/421-0522 or 310/553-1770; fax 310/284-2845.

Princess is dynamic. Princess is diverse. Princess cooks up marketing plans that assume most people, regardless of lifestyle, age, or values, can benefit from a Princess cruise. Princess fancies itself the best of all possible cruise lines.

Their vessels carry 10% of all passengers taking Caribbean cruises. More than virtually any line afloat, and without apologies, they offer a niche for everyone, and configure ships to virtually every taste. As such, Princess is a good and worthy choice for the first-time cruiser, but whether Princess is the right choice for children depends on the individual vessel you choose.

Few other cruise lines, except Carnival, have managed to start so small and grow so rapidly in such a short time. In 1974, Princess was an obscure West Coast cruise outfit with a small-scale, somewhat outmoded fleet of mostly leased vessels. Today, it's a hyper-modern upper-middle-class giant with a billion-dollar budget for acquiring new megaships.

The company's success resulted in part from decisions made when the cruise industry was gearing up for some major changes and some bitter competitive battles. In 1989, Princess was far-sighted and daring enough to launch one of the world's first megaships built specifically for holiday cruises, the 63,500-ton *Star Princess,* which no longer sails Caribbean waters. The line continued its commitment to megaship investments and within a year added the 70,000-ton twins *Crown Princess* (1990) and *Regal Princess* (1991).

Princess was also smart enough to associate itself with the multimillion dollar TV series *The Love Boat.* The show's forgettable plots and sometimes far-fetched romantic triangles created a flood of paying customers anxious to experience amour on the high seas, all skippered and shepherded by tactful Gavin McLeod and his witty crew, or some reasonable facsimile.

Company spokespersons give the series enormous credit for promoting cruises in general and Princess in particular. Nevertheless, *The Love Boat* theme is growing just a bit tired, and is being increasingly downplayed. The campaign could perk up again, however, as vague rumors about a rebirth of *The Love Boat* are bandied about in Hollywood—perhaps as a full-length feature film.

After mergers, acquisitions, and explosive growth in the 1980s, Princess today is an amalgam of corporate entities welded together into a not always smoothly functioning whole. Princess controls one of the most diverse fleets in the industry, but downplays the differences among its various ships to the cruising public. Most passengers opt for "the Princess experience," but don't realize how varied the experience can actually be.

The company's products are geared one notch above mass-market and its most aggressive competitors, Carnival and Royal Caribbean. Yet Princess never attempts to emulate the ultraglamour of lines such as Seabourn or vessels such as Cunard's *Sea Goddesses.* Likewise, it rarely attempts to provide adventure experiences in wildly exotic Caribbean locales. What Princess delivers is a semiformal product on a mass scale, and in this it succeeds quite well. Aboard Princess, you'll get a lot of bang for your buck, attractively packaged, well executed, and with the odd grace note or two.

More than any other cruise line, Princess succeeds in satisfying the widest range of passengers with the broadest levels of taste. The onboard atmosphere is neither high-brow nor low; it's middle- to upper-middle-class, but not bourgeois, and infused with some glitter and an undeniable panache. It's definitely the most mainstream cruise line plowing Caribbean waters. But, of course, any line so mainstream can turn off prospective cruisers with more adventurous, more esoteric, or more refined tastes.

Our overview of Princess' role in The Bahamas and Caribbean doesn't begin to describe the company worldwide. Its vessels and those of its parent, P&O, call at 200 ports around the world, with many in Alaska, Europe, and Asia. P&O and Princess share a combined annual total of cruise-ship passengers that exceeds 450,000, and it's carried more passengers through the Panama Canal than any other line in the world.

Princess Cruises as we know it today originated in 1962, when the company's founder, Stanley McDonald, chartered the long-gone *Princess Patricia* as a floating hotel for the Seattle World's Fair. He then continued to charter ships for cruises between Los Angeles, Alaska, and the Pacific coast of Mexico. Soon after, two additional ships, one of them brand-new, were leased from Costa Cruises to meet demand. In 1974, the company was snapped up by P&O Group, which has intensified its efforts to market Princess vessels and Caribbean itineraries within markets on both sides of the Atlantic.

In 1988, Princess received a massive influx of staff, equipment, and hardware when P&O bought Italian-owned, Los Angeles–based Sitmar cruises. As part of this deal, Princess acquired three huge, cutting-edge ships: the *Star Princess*, whose construction was almost completed at the time of the sale (and which has since then been commandeered by P&O and removed from Princess' inventory), and the futuristic-looking *Crown Princess* and *Regal Princess*, identical 70,000-ton twins whose avant-garde design at this point appear somewhat dated in comparison with the line's newer roster of ships. These two ships are to an increasing

degree being assigned routes in and around the Panama Canal.

Princess' image has begun to change and come into sharper focus through its launch of a new "Grand Class" of megaships. The new lineup represents billions of dollars worth of investment, endless design-related debates, and a real focus on long-term planning. The new ships, cutting edge and costing no less than $300 million each, are good-looking vessels, more youthful and up-to-date than those of most other lines afloat. The design of each has catered to what cruise passengers really want: private verandas and a balance of small-scale intimacy and megaresort amenities.

First in the new line were the long-awaited *Sun Princess* and *Dawn Princess,* launched in 1995 and 1997, respectively. The third ship in the trio, the *Sea Princess,* is scheduled to be launched in 1999. The line will unveil its biggest ship to date, the 105,000-ton *Grand Princess,* in 1998, at about the same time Carnival, Disney, and Royal Caribbean launch roughly equivalent vessels. You can be sure that these most youthful and spectacular of Princess ships will be deployed for at least part of their year in the Caribbean, and will be heavily marketed to the North American cruise market.

What are the factors that have propelled Princess into its role as one of the most profitable and financially stable lines afloat? Much of it has to do with the quality of its products, which remain remarkably consistent regardless of the vessel on which they happen to be featured.

When a Princess product is good, it's wonderful. Princess cruises tend to be mainstream, conservative, quietly stylish, and moderately upscale, but with prices that are discounted to levels that make them appealing to the mass market. They also have a bit more upper-crust appeal and razzle-dazzle than products offered by such competitors as Holland America.

PROS & CONS   Princess appeals to greater numbers of cruisers from all walks of life than any other line afloat. Its fleet is competently managed, with enough gloss and glitter to titillate, but not so much that it fatigues. There's very little wrong here, unless you're looking for a more adventurous cruise or a theme cruise, two things that Princess doesn't offer.

There are enough single passengers to appeal to soloists, enough been-married-since-forever couples to appeal to the hearth-and-home type, and enough honeymooners to add poignancy and zest to gatherings of folks married since the age of Sputnik. There's also enough racial diversity to keep the place from looking too much like a suburban country club. Middle-aged, middle-class passengers always find lots of people to bond with.

Princess value derives in part from spacious cabins, a trait that is especially visible aboard ships inaugurated since 1990. With the line's new breed of Grand Class vessels, enormous emphasis is placed on the addition of private verandas. By 1999, the line will boast more than 2,500 of them, more than any other line afloat.

Officers tend to be British or Italian, and are very conscious of their role as solid but charming spokespersons for the line. Dining and cabin stewards are culturally diverse and well trained in handling hordes of shipboard passengers. Don't be disappointed that Gavin McLeod and his merry band of soap-opera cronies won't be aboard with you.

In spite of the number of cruisers aboard, the line still markets efficient shore excursions, often better than many competing lines, such as Carnival.

One definite pro for Princess is its adaptability to changes in perceived industry demands. This might range from installing frozen yogurt dispensers at the ice-cream buffets to offering discounted prices to keep Princess vessels constantly competitive with Holland America, Carnival, and Royal Caribbean.

Princess works hard to keep onboard amenities consistent within all its ships. Nonetheless, the ships in its fleet are uneven, so your evaluation of Princess will depend on the vessel you select. Getting a grip on what each vessel is like is a bit of a challenge, as the worldwide fleet contains mostly individual ships, with only two pairs of twins. The older of the line's vessels are tried-but-true workhorses whose activities and diversions are pure Princess style and pizzazz. Despite their age and relative lack of cutting-edge style, they're often heavily booked. Architecture in the newer vessels is among the most pleasing afloat, but while these newer ships are more stylish, they do have some layout flaws.

At Princess, when you're presented with surprises, they'll tend to be pleasant much more often than not. One of the more pleasant is the impressive art collection aboard each ship. To stumble across a painting by David Hockney, Helen Frankenthaler, Frank Stella, Andy Warhol, or Robert Motherwell in one of the public areas is not at all uncommon.

There's an additional advantage for beach buffs aboard any of Princess' Caribbean vessels: the line's private island, Princess Cays, off the southwestern coast of Eleuthera in The Bahamas. Aside from the presence of service and storage buildings, hammocks, picnic facilities, barbecue pits, and play areas for children, the site looks artfully rustic and "natural" looking. Don't be fooled: Princess spends millions of dollars annually on maintaining the beaches, barging sand in as needed and ferrying in ingredients for beach parties before passengers disembark. The only drawback? To maintain their position offshore as tenders carry beach-goers in, the ships are forced to use a bow anchor in conjunction with very noisy stern thrusters. That, however, is a small price to pay for a barbecue on some of the most perfect beaches.

One high-tech virtue that comes with sailing Princess? Shore-to-ship phone calls are made directly through equipment belonging to the cruise line, and as such are a lot less complicated than the labyrinthine INMARSAT system used by other lines. Consequently, one call through a

"900" number connects a land-based caller directly to whatever Princess ship is requested, at the relatively low rate of $8.95 per minute.

TYPES OF PASSENGERS Passenger demographics are wider than aboard virtually any other line afloat, but tend to concentrate on middle-aged middle America.

The youngest among Princess passengers tends to be around 35, with the average around 50. The average annual household income for passengers ranges upward from $40,000, and can be much higher. Most travelers come from the Northeast (especially the Philadelphia-to-Boston corridor), California, Chicago, and Texas. Some might be British.

The passenger roster is educated and genuinely curious about new people and new experiences. They're not as rowdy and boisterous as clients aboard Carnival, not as rich as those aboard Seabourn, and not as staid as those aboard Holland America. They tend to be the quiet and respectable neighbors who live on your block, from whom scandals, temper tantrums, and disagreeable behavior patterns are rarely seen or heard. And at least some will have been motivated by the images they digested on *The Love Boat* series. Some might have been influenced by some aspect of the line's image as an upper-crust carrier, and might even be quietly impressed with the line's Anglo-American pedigree. Many appreciate the traditional cruise experience offered by Princess, enjoy the rituals of dressing up for dinner (the evening atmosphere is formal), and like dancing to the onboard bands.

DINING Princess' dining draws the most varied reactions from passengers. Some say that it satisfies all of their needs, with requisite panache and flair. Others claim that the dining rooms are noisy (hardly surprising, considering the size of some of the line's ships), service is sometimes uncooperative and slow, and food presentation is uninspired.

We think the food is on a par with that of other mass-market lines such as Royal Caribbean, Norwegian Cruise Line, or Carnival. However, the line doesn't seem to focus on food and beverage presentations as assiduously as Celebrity, for example, whose food is better and more stylish, or Seabourn, which serves the most cultivated cuisine. The rule about Princess Line's dining is the same as the one that applies to the line as a whole: If your expectations are reasonable, and you've opted to have a good time instead of finding fault, you'll have no complaints about the food or service.

It's true that no passenger goes hungry aboard a Princess cruise. On this line, dining is part of the onboard entertainment. Mealtime niceties include theatrical preparation of some dishes at tableside, changing silverware between courses, and maître d'hôtels who are, within reason, willing to prepare special dishes according to a passenger's instructions. A wine "cellar" with at least 10,000 bottles is standard issue aboard each ship.

Princess dining rooms have two seatings at dinner and usually two at breakfast and lunch as well. If the ship is in port for a day, however, one of the lunches is usually dropped, as many passengers choose to dine ashore. Smoking is prohibited in all dining rooms. Smokers have to head out on deck to indulge, or else look for specially designated indoor areas.

The same passengers who find Princess dining rooms competent and predictable sometimes seem quite pleased with the food, service, and themes in the line's satellite restaurants. Frequently praised is the pizza served in an ersatz trattoria after the main meals and late into the night. We think it's really very, very good.

The newer the ship, the greater the emphasis on the supplemental dining areas. These are best developed aboard Princess' newer vessels, beginning with the *Sun Princess'* Horizon Court and continuing with slight variations on each of the line's subsequent ships. What they are is all-you-can-eat 24-hour buffets boasting

180° panoramas over the waves—a far cry from the linoleum-floored Lido restaurants aboard less glamorous ships. Some passengers prefer this informal dining and its flexibility of seating to the ships' more formal dining areas.

Aboard Caribbean jaunts, live musicians—perhaps a harpist wearing something diaphanous, or a jazz duet or trio—add grace notes to the rituals of afternoon tea-drinking.

Formal dinners, such as the captain's party, feature fare more elegant than on other nights, and might include dollops of caviar or slices of foie gras, rich sauces, and dishes that, while not particularly experimental, do tend to please the bulk of passengers' tastes. Alternative choices of low-calorie, low-sodium dishes are available as spa-style substitutes.

There's 24-hour room service in the cabins, and coffee is available around the clock somewhere aboard every Princess ship.

ACTIVITIES The line that wants to be all things to all people is expert at programming activities to please a wide range of tastes. Each activity tends to start promptly as scheduled and never contains any of the potential embarrassments you might find on rowdier lines like Carnival. No one aboard Princess will ever pressure you to test how many Ping-Pong balls you can stuff into your bathing suit.

Activities are equivalent to those of such lines as Holland America and Celebrity, and range from the relatively stressful (water volleyball, paddle tennis, putting and virtual-reality golf) to the more sedate (bingo, handicap horse racing, dance classes, bridge tournaments, and trivia contests).

Regardless of what vessel you sail, Princess believes in the value of audience participation as a means of breaking the ice. Game shows such as "The Liars' Club" and "The Newlywed Game" are big, as is karaoke, and passengers with or without talent can participate in "Love Boat Legends," a latter-day takeoff of the TV series, with the requisite emotional

complications. Try-outs are held on the first day at sea, rehearsals follow, and before the end of the cruise, an entire sitcom has been rehearsed, refined, and staged for your fellow passengers. Princess also emphasizes get-togethers, both for singles (of whatever ilk) and for members of service clubs.

Before a port of call is reached, Princess presents lectures about that port and its shopping possibilities. There are even refresher courses in French, Spanish, Portuguese, and Italian, to make sure that you know such rock-bottom basics as "How much?" and "Which way to the big ship?"

Although you'll almost always have beach-time at whatever Caribbean port you visit, Princess also maintains a private island—Princess Cays, off the coast of Eleuthera, in The Bahamas—that functions exclusively as a "fun in the sun" stop. You can swim and snorkel, and make use of Princess' fleet of Hobie Cats, sun fish, Banana Boats, kayaks, and paddle wheelers. There's live music, a beach barbecue, and tree-shaded hammocks for anyone who wants to sleep off too many rum punches. However, be particularly alert to water safety during these deceptively carefree beach holidays. If you're not in good physical shape and opt for too strenuous a regime, you could hurt yourself. The high-speed banana boat rides are especially accident-prone.

Aboard Caribbean sailings on the *Dawn Princess* and *Sun Princess* (and *Grand Princess*, when it comes into service), passengers can earn PADI certification for scuba diving, a rare and worthwhile expenditure of time and effort that's not available aboard many other ships. (Regrettably, this opportunity is not available on the *Regal Princess* or *Crown Princess* Panama Canal cruises.) Full certification costs $299—less than you'd spend at some land-based resorts—and requires that you successfully complete a written exam. Included in the cost are a PADI open-water dive manual, a workbook and dive log book, classroom and video instruction, four supervised dives in one of the ship's pools, and four supervised open-water dives at one of the ports of call. Sign up in advance or the moment you get aboard, as the course requires that you attend at least 15 hours of classroom and practice sessions. If you opt to pursue this, approach it with the seriousness it deserves, and plan to spend some time alone in your cabin, studying.

Princess devotes a lot of attention to its onboard libraries, and spent a goodly sum of money to upgrade each of them in 1996. They're viewed as havens of quiet and reflective calm, and each includes the services of a resident librarian to assist with the procurement of VCR tapes and headphones that allow you to listen to recorded versions of popular novels, memoirs, and other titles. Also, every vessel since the *Sun Princess* contains a business center with phones, fax machines, and computers.

CHILDREN'S ACTIVITIES Princess ships are not and never will be kiddie playland free-for-alls. Any person under 21 on board a Princess Cruise should be accompanied by an adult, and babies under 18 months of age are not allowed on board at all. These guidelines aside, the line has made greater efforts since 1996 at trying to synchronize niche marketing for children, without upsetting its traditional emphasis on escapist cruises for mature adults.

If you really want the Princess experience and think your children are well behaved enough to travel with you, the Caribbean itineraries are probably a good bet. Princess recognizes that the region attracts a higher percentage of families than do more exotic ports in Europe or Asia, and consequently these cruises are somewhat more child-friendly.

Architecture aboard the line's post-1995 ships, such as the *Dawn* and the *Sun Princess* (and the upcoming *Grand Princess*), contains more space and more sophisticated amenities devoted to the care, maintenance, and diversion of shipboard youth. Specially designated "fun zones" include entertainment centers and promote activities guaranteed to have parents whipping out their cameras. Participants are segregated by age into "Princess Pelicans" (ages 2 to 12), and PTCs (Princess Teen Club, ages 13 to 16). There's lots of emphasis on karaoke fests, movie fests, weight-training classes, swimming and snorkeling lessons, tours of the galley, scavenger hunts, arts and crafts, coloring contests, ice-cream sundae–making contests, birthday parties, dance marathons in a teen-only disco, hula parties complete with grass skirts, and teenage versions of the *Dating Game,* which you may or may not view with abject horror. On a more educational note, there are lessons in marine ecology ("Save our Seas") that were conceived by the California Coastal Commission and the Center for Marine Conservation. Youth counselors make it a point to visit any young person suffering from his or her first bout of seasickness.

ENTERTAINMENT The Princess vision about how to keep passengers amused remains remarkably consistent from ship to ship, despite any differences in the vessels' size, age, and architecture. More than virtually any other line afloat, Princess makes it a point to tap into the circus, mime, and performance subcultures of former eastern bloc nations. Shows have more costume changes and troupe members than you might be able to count, much razzmatazz, and some awe-inspiring acrobatics. On the opposite end of the spectrum, retrospectives of the major 20th-century musical movements, often performed with verve, authenticity, and skill, are sometimes presented. One of the most unusual performances on the high seas is "Odyssea," a whimsical fantasy based on the underwater society of Atlantis, with plenty of acrobats from Eastern Europe and Asia and inflatable scenery that seems to magically swell and grow in front of you.

Karaoke is big, as are audience-style game shows focusing on trivia, sometimes plucked directly from the plot lines of such shows as *The Love Boat.* Each ship contains a theater that screens recently released movies that are clearly delineated to appeal either to children (early seatings) or to adults (later seatings). These supplement the two all-movie channels that are broadcast directly into passengers' cabins throughout the day and night.

Every ship has a casino, and discos witness lots of energetic dancing on at least some nights of any given cruise. Aboard more modern ships, a glass floor covers a grid of TV monitors where you can watch Whitney Houston sing while watching your own feet swing.

There are well-upholstered and nicely hidden-away bars where you can get away from it all for a while, but a musical duo sometimes drowns out conversation. At least one bar aboard any Princess vessel is a venue for "outrageous" drinks that come in every size and shape imaginable. Plus, all Princess ships covered in this review offer a wine bar selling caviar by the ounce and vintage wine, champagne, and iced vodka by the glass.

SHOPPING   Princess is a middle-bracket cruise line catering to upper-middle-bracket tastes. Consequently, within each ship's Galleria Shopping Arcade you'll find a good selection of collector or gift items such as Lladró porcelain or Wedgwood figurines, clothing accessories for any of the two or three formal dinners you'll be facing on board, and all the film supplies, resort wear, paperback books, and sundries you'll need to make it through the night. Shopping boutiques are interspersed with cocktail lounges, presumably allowing buyers to reflect on their purchases over a drink.

SERVICE   As far as officers are concerned, you'll get the feeling that their public presentation really was influenced by *The Love Boat* series. Mostly British and Italian, and noteworthy for their nautical as well as social skills, the officers often function as semiofficial company spokespersons. Their uniforms, based on

tropical British colonial models, include knee socks and Bermuda shorts.

Cabin stewards do their jobs well, and everyone likes the jovial and good-natured Italian dining room stewards. The service personnel are hardworking, well trained, and as efficient as is humanly possible considering the vast size of some of the line's vessels, and the hordes of passengers demanding time, attention, and another glass of beer. Although the staff won't grovel, you'll get whatever you want, within reason and within a reasonable amount of time. Remembering a staff member's name and being as polite as possible is effective aboard this line.

All of the Princess vessels in the Caribbean have their own self-service Laundromats.

ITINERARIES
Crown Princess—Beginning in 1997–98, this vessel, along with its identical twin, the *Regal Princess,* will specialize in midwinter transits through the Panama Canal, launching or ending its route in either Los Angeles or Fort Lauderdale and following itineraries that last between 10 and 15 days each. A limited number of the itineraries will not make a complete transit of the canal, but rather pass through the canal's Atlantic-side Gatun Locks and sail across Lake Gatun before continuing with a 10-day tour that incorporates visits to Cartagena, Puerto Limón, the San Blas Islands, and Cozumel.

Dawn Princess—From its home port of San Juan, this twin of the *Sun Princess* sails on a series of seven-day cruises, departing every Saturday. About half of its routes visit Aruba, Caracas, Grenada, St. Thomas, and Dominica. That schedule alternates, on a weekly basis, with a route that stops at St. Thomas, St. Maarten, Barbados, Martinique, and St. Lucia.

Grand Princess—This megaship, scheduled for launch in 1998, will be too large to fit through the Panama Canal, so Princess plans to keep it in the Caribbean year-round. Itineraries should be released some months before the launch date; check with your travel agent for up-to-the-minute information.

Regal Princess—It benefits from a size that permits it to (barely) squeeze through the Panama Canal, and so spends most of its winter making transits of the canal, moving between Acapulco and San Juan. Most of these cruises last for between 10 and 11 days, with the exception of a late spring "repositioning cruise" that requires 15 days and ends in San Diego.

Sun Princess—From its home port in Fort Lauderdale, this vessel makes seven-day circuits throughout the winter, stopping at ports that include Princess Cays (Eleuthera), Ocho Rios, Grand Cayman, and Cozumel. In summer, it sails off the coast of Alaska.

SPECIAL DISCOUNTS   As one of the savviest and most market-conscious entities afloat, Princess is sure to float some special deals, so keep an eye out. Some cabins may be reduced to half-price on selected cruises; others may go for as little as $700 per person, double occupancy, even during the peak of midwinter. Because of the large numbers of cabins the line moves every week, it really pays with Princess to keep phoning cruise discounters to see what's available.

Children (except for those under 18 months of age, who are not allowed on board) pay 50% of the minimum rate (regardless of the cabin) if they fill a third or fourth berth in their parent or guardians'

cabin. Otherwise, they pay the standard double occupancy tariff. A third or fourth passenger in any cabin can sometimes pay as little as $90 to $140 per day.

Discounts of up to 25% or 50% are offered for early bookings, depending on the sailing date and itinerary. Prices are also reduced if you arrange your own transportation to the port of embarkation, usually by around $250 per person.

Repeat passengers are feted with inclusion in special cocktail parties. If you cruise with Princess 10 times, you might get a piece of expensive silver or cut crystal. Newsletters go out at frequent intervals with information about special discounts and coupons good for credit in onboard boutiques during specific sailings.

Passengers who combine two cruises back-to-back receive hefty discounts on the second cruise. If you intend to extend your holiday with land-based sightseeing before or after a cruise, ask about hotel and sightseeing packages, which are an extremely good value, even if you only stay one night pre- or postcruise.

SINGLE SUPPLEMENTS   Singles pay from 150% to 200% of the per person rate in a double.

PORT CHARGES   Most Caribbean seven-day cruises carry supplemental charges of between $114 and $149 per person. Cruises that include a transit through the Panama Canal carry port charges of between $211 and $269 per person.

Crown Princess
Regal Princess

⬦ ⬦ ⬦ ⬦

Specifications

Size (in tons)	70,000	Crew	696 (International)
Number of Cabins	795	Passenger/Crew Ratio	2.3 to 1
Number of Outside Cabins	624	Year Built	1990/1991
Number of Passengers	1,590	Last Major Refurbishment	n/a
Officers	Italian		

Frommer's Ratings (Scale of 1–10)

Activities	7.6	Public Areas	7.6
Cabins	8.4	Public Comfort/Space	7.0
Cleanliness/Maintenance	8.2	Recreational Facilities/Pool	8.0
Entertainment	8.0	Service	7.7
Food & Beverage	7.4	Ship Crew/Officers	8.5
Interior Decor	7.8	Shore Excursions	8.5
Ports of Call	7.0	Worth the Money	8.8
		Overall Average	**7.9**

From 1991 to 1995, these identical twins were the company's most modern and dramatic vessels. Their designer, Renzo Piano, has been responsible for such high-profile designs as the Centre Beaubourg in Paris and reconstruction plans for the reunited Berlin, projects that were among the most talked about in Europe since the building of the Eiffel Tower in the 1880s.

When these ships were launched in 1990 and 1991, their futuristic design was shocking. Industry insiders either adore or despise the look of these ships. The designer compares their curiously hooded hulls to a porpoise moving through the water. Others compare them to the helmeted Darth Vader of *Star Wars,* about to free themselves from the forces of gravity and fly off for an intergalactic mission. Even the smokestacks' design—jutting directly upward, almost in rebellion against the raked stacks of most other modern vessels—has attracted criticism.

We find the design appealing and dramatic, but with two noteworthy flaws. One is a lack of deck space, which leads to congestion at deck-side buffets and around swimming pools whenever the

ship is full (which is often). There's no place to take a brisk circular constitutional on deck; if you want to stroll, you'll have to walk back and forth along the ship's sides or get on a treadmill in the health spa. All in all, you'll find that there's more of an emphasis on indoor space rather than on exposure to the wide blue sea.

The other problem is one of the ship's nerve centers, a massive observation deck glassed in by 270° of panoramic windows. It's an ill-conceived multipurpose area combining a casino, a bar/lounge, and an observation area—a combination of functions that doesn't really please anybody. Public areas have many pillars and columns, a somewhat disjointed internal layout, incidental noise from engines, and only a nominal connection with events happening outside on deck.

These avant-garde, futuristic-looking ships contain all the amenities offered by competing megaships. Their interiors are stunning and, for such large vessels, surprisingly intimate and cozy. Despite their flaws, these vessels were absolutely the best in the Princess repertoire until the company's newest ship, *Sun Princess,* surpassed them.

Cabins & Rates

Cabins	Average per diem	Bathtub	Fridge	Phone	Sitting Area	TV
Inside	$220–$265	No	Yes	Yes	Yes	Yes
Outside	$275–$330	No	Yes	Yes	Yes	Yes
Suite	$375–$570	Yes	Yes	Yes	Yes	Yes

CABINS We're willing to forgive almost any flaws in these ships' design because of the large size of their cabins. Of 795 total, 624 are outside cabins, and

many have a first-class feature: private verandas. Standard cabins range from 190 square feet to 210 square feet—a generous allowance.

Grand Princess (Preview)

Scheduled for an inauguration in early 1998, the *Grand Princess* will be the largest, most dramatic, and most cost-effective ship Princess has ever built. At 105,000 tons, and with a passenger capacity of 2,600, the vessel will be a giant, sprawling resort that just happens to float. Built in northern Italy for $400 million, the ship will have 16 decks, contain 1,300 cabins, and have a girth that will prevent it from navigating through the Panama Canal, meaning it will be deployed full-time in the Caribbean, from a home base in Fort Lauderdale.

The ship will be so large you couldn't possibly take advantage of all its amenities without the aid of track shoes and a week's supply of No-Doz. It would be like trying to experience a happening medium-size city in a few days. With three show lounges, each with different after-dinner entertainment, this vessel is the closest approximation of Las Vegas on the high seas.

Three different dining rooms will alleviate the crush of diners (and subsequent loss of intimacy), and a gaggle of supplemental dining areas will include outdoor buffets, bistros, pizzerias, a Mexican restaurant, a wine and caviar bar, ice-cream parlors, and a late-night restaurant for casual, after-casino fare.

One deck will be devoted entirely to suites, 750 cabins with verandas (whose appeal to cruisers far surpassed anyone's expectations), and no fewer than five swimming pools. The uppermost swimming pool will be sheltered with a retractable roof. Access to a nightclub on the 15th deck will be via a moving, glass-enclosed walkway. Other facilities will include a health club and spa, a business center with a battery of computers for passenger use, every imaginable kind of bar, and social centers for teenagers and younger children. The mammoth onboard casino will be 14,000 square feet, an area three times the floor space of many rambling, generously proportioned five-bedroom houses.

For passengers with disabilities, there will be 28 specially designed cabins, more than aboard any other ship afloat.

Each cabin has a safe and beds that can be adapted into either twins or a queen, and terry-cloth robes are provided for passengers' use. (But only while aboard. No making off with those, now.) Decor includes light-grained wood, color schemes of warm beiges and peaches, comfortably upholstered chairs and sofas, and framed artwork. Portholes are rectangular, which makes wave-gazing easier. Bathrooms are compact but comfortable, well-lit, modern, and standardized down to every detail of their layout and amenities.

If you're booking a standard cabin, opt for one of the four classified as category GG on the Plaza Deck, if available. These outside doubles with queen-size beds are the ship's most convenient cabins and the best of the standard lot. Note that views from some cabins on the Dolphin Deck have partially obstructed views.

The lowest priced outside cabins are category G on the Fiesta Deck, with both lower and upper berths and round portholes. These cabins are good buys, specially for budget-minded friends or families traveling together. If you're on a budget but fear the cheapest cabins will have cramped closets, you'll be safe aboard Princess. Inside double staterooms at the lower end of the price scale have almost the same facilities and furnishings as the standard cabins.

Twenty-two cabins aboard each of these ships are designated as singles, and ten cabins are wheelchair accessible.

RECREATION & FITNESS FACILITIES
Two pools on the Lido Deck of both ships can become crowded when either ship is completely booked.

The health clubs/spas aboard the *Crown*

Princess and *Regal Princess* lie below decks, so you won't have any inspiring views of the waves while you're working out on the Nautilus machines or getting yourself pampered. There are saunas, massage, and health and beauty regimes, and health club staff can create a personalized workout schedule.

PUBLIC AREAS An army of designers worked hard to create as many divergent styles on board as possible. The plush and sleek interiors, studded with some of the most intriguing artwork afloat, feel more like a hotel than a ship, making one wonder at the logic behind a cruise ship that gives the impression that you aren't at sea.

At each ship's core is a three-story Plaza atrium with a grand staircase. The lower level houses the lobby and reception area, as well as a bar devoted exclusively to pastries. A duty-free shopping arcade is on the upper levels. Lying forward at the top of each ship is "The Dome," a massive, all-purpose room that includes an observation area, a bar, a casino, and a dance floor. Curved glass outer windows are framed by polished, rounded, bone-white "ribs" arching from ceiling to floor. In the casino, craps, roulette, blackjack, and slot machines lie close to a stage whereon a piano player or a band keeps you entertained between hands.

The dining room—named Crown Court on the *Crown Princess* and Palm Court on the *Regal*—boasts two-level terracing. There's also a two-level lounge for nightly entertainment. At midship on the *Crown* is a bar with a British India theme; on the *Regal* it's the Bengal Bar. Each bar has floor-to-ceiling mirrors, a raised stage featuring a piano, a dance floor, ceiling fans, and potted palms. But if you'd like to escape the hordes, seek out Intermezzo on the *Crown* or Adagio on the *Regal*.

The children's facilities are not as good as those aboard the *Sun Princess,* profiled below.

Dawn Princess • Sea Princess (Preview) • Sun Princess

⚓ ⚓ ⚓ ⚓ ⚓

Specifications

Size (in tons)	77,000	Crew	900 (American/European)
Number of Cabins	1,011	Passenger/Crew Ratio	2.2 to 1
Number of Outside Cabins	603	Year Built	1995/1997/1999
Number of Passengers	1,950	Last Major Refurbishment	n/a
Officers	Italian		

Frommer's Ratings (Scale of 1–10)

Activities	8.8	Public Areas	8.8
Cabins	8.8	Public Comfort/Space	9.0
Cleanliness/Maintenance	9.4	Recreational Facilities/Pool	8.8
Entertainment	9.0	Service	7.8
Food & Beverage	8.6	Ship Crew/Officers	8.2
Interior Decor	8.8	Shore Excursions	8.0
Ports of Call	7.0	Worth the Money	8.8
		Overall Average	**8.6**

The December 1995 inauguration of the *Sun Princess* represented the emergence of a new type of cruise vessel, Princess' Grand Class series. It also demonstrated Princess' commitment to radically upgrading its fleet before the millennium. The *Sun Princess* wasn't alone for long. Its debut was followed in April 1997 by an identical twin, the *Dawn Princess*.

Knowing a good thing when it saw one, Princess ordered another ship, the *Sea Princess*, which is scheduled to enter service in early 1999. It will be identical to the *Sun* and *Dawn*, weighing 77,000 tons and carrying 1,950 passengers, and is being built at a cost of $295 million. Once the *Sea Princess* is launched, the number of Grand Class berths will be 8,500 out of a total of nearly 17,000 in the Princess fleet. The *Sea Princess* will also bring to nearly 2,500 the number of staterooms with private balconies offered fleetwide.

Currently, *Sun* and *Dawn* are the line's most exciting ships, largely because of their size and drama, rising 14 floors above the waterline. Their decor is a return to classic yet modern styling, using expensive materials such as varnished hardwoods, marble, etched glass, granite, and richly textured fabrics. The decor doesn't sock you between the eyes with its daring; instead, it's comforting.

These innovative and awe-inspiring ships have many superior virtues, including double atria. Plus, the large amount of interior space means that there's less crowding aboard than on virtually any other ships of comparable size and price range. A feeling of intimacy is engendered with two separate dining rooms, equal in every way and each with its own galley, a feature that contributes to greater culinary finesse than aboard other Princess vessels.

Cabins & Rates

Cabins	Average per diem	Bathtub	Fridge	Phone	Sitting Area	TV
Inside	$225	No	No	Yes	No	Yes
Outside	$285	No	Yes	Yes	Yes	Yes
Suite	$425	No	Yes	Yes	Yes	Yes

CABINS   Even the smallest cabin on board these vessels, measuring 235 square feet, is larger than the suites aboard such ultra-expensive vessels as Cunard's *Sea Goddess I*. Suites can be as large as a sprawling 754 square feet. More than 400 cabins on each vessel boast private verandas, more than any other vessel currently afloat, and a marvelous feature that other cruise vessels will almost certainly emulate.

Furnishings are tasteful and amenities are state of the art, including excellent and spacious bathrooms. There are no really bad cabins, as there are on some older ships like Norwegian Cruise Line's *Norway*. No cabins are configured as singles.

Some 19 cabins on each vessel are wheelchair accessible.

RECREATION & FITNESS FACILITIES
On board are a half-dozen swimming

pools—one a 40-foot-long lap pool—and five whirlpools scattered around the decks, usually near some dispensary of frothy, sunset-colored drinks. Some pools are designated specifically for children.

These ships, functioning as they do as a prototype for all Princess vessels to follow, also contain the best-designed, most appealing health clubs of any of the line's vessels presently afloat. Called "The Riviera Spa Gymnasium," it offers all the requisite massage and spa treatments and is flanked with an open-air pool and a pair of whirlpools. A teakwood deck encircles the ship for joggers and walkers, and a computerized golf center called Princess Links simulates the trickiest aspects of some of the world's best and most legendary golf courses.

PUBLIC AREAS   As the showcase vessels of a cruise line that increasingly wants

Cruise Now, Pay Later

As if cruise lines weren't running enough special deals to entice you onto their boats, here's a new one: Princess Cruises has worked out a credit program called Love Boat Loans, whereby U.S. residents can finance every aspect of their cruise, from deposit through final payment (though not including a $50 nonrefundable down payment), through MBNA America Bank.

Prospective financees can call ☎ 800/PRINCESS for details or to register for the program. If you're arranging your cruise through a travel agent, the agent can contact the bank through Princess' reservations department while you wait. Interest rates start at 14.99 percent APR and may vary up to 26.99; repayment can be scheduled over 24, 36, or 48 months. What's all that translate to? A seven-day Caribbean cruise for $35 a month, with payment stretched over 36 months.

to show off its style, the *Sun* and *Dawn* have many fine public rooms. Many (some observers say too many) are sheathed with marble and outfitted with light-grained wood, and in the case of the bottom atrium deck, $70,000 rugs. The overall effect is restrained contemporary elegance.

Both ships feature a decidedly un-glitzy decor that relies on lavish amounts of wood, glass, and marble, and features a $2.5 million collection of original paintings and lithographs, grouped into schools and art periods. You'll also notice more than $400,000 worth of tropical plants, cared for by a full-time gardener. Exotic cacti and 18-foot-tall palm trees enhance the forest effect.

One of the most outstanding features of both ships is a Broadway-style theater with velvet, theater-style chairs and excellent sight lines. There's no bar in the theaters, and passengers are not allowed to bring in drinks. Entertainment is so heavily featured on board that you're likely to find a half-dozen musical shows in several areas every night, making the *Sun* a showboat in every sense of the word.

Many bars and lounges are truly expansive, extending to two or more decks. The ships' stern contains the Vista Lounge, a well-designed watering hole and rendezvous point where part of the fun involves drinking "sundowners" and watching the ship's wake fade into the distant horizon.

Radisson Seven Seas Cruises

SHIPS   Radisson Diamond
600 Corporate Dr., Suite 410, Fort Lauderdale, FL 33334. ☎ 800/477-7500 or 305/776-6123; fax 305/772-3763.

In 1992, Minneapolis-based Radisson Hotels Worldwide began a venture that has evolved into Radisson Seven Seas Cruises, which manages (but does not own) some of the most talked-about luxury vessels anywhere.

Part of the incentive for Radisson's expansion into cruising stemmed from its wide experience in resort and hotel management, its bulk purchasing power, and its already established network of telephone booking agents. The company gambled that cruise ship owners might relish putting sales, marketing, and managerial tasks into the hands of such experienced hoteliers—and they were right.

Since the line's inauguration, it has assumed management responsibility for five different ships: the Japanese-owned *Song of Flower,* the small-scale luxury adventure ships *Bremen* and *Hanseatic,* the as-yet-unlaunched *Paul Gauguin,* and the ultra-top-notch *Radisson Diamond.* All of them are either mainstream luxury vessels or niche-market vessels catering to affluent travelers headed to the Amazon or Antarctica. Of them, only the *Diamond* spends significant time in the Caribbean, but it's created such a stir since its much-publicized 1992 launch that it's enabled Radisson to become a force in the Caribbean luxury cruise market.

Carrying only 350 passengers, the ship has such an unusual design that it tends to stop traffic on coastal highways and maritime seaways whenever it sails. Owned by a group of Finnish investors and built at a price of $125 million, it is basically a gigantic catamaran, its vast, wide shell supported by a pair of submarine-like hulls that are 28 feet in diameter and 123 feet longer than a football field. The six-deck superstructure they support rides 28 feet above the water and is 103 feet wide by 420 feet long.

Compare that to Cunard's *QE2,* which is 963 feet long, but only two feet wider than the *Diamond.*

From its snub nose to its hydraulically lowered marina in the stem, the boxy-looking ship is a show-stopper. Once on board, passengers find some of the most carefully crafted interiors, most upscale amenities, and most superb cuisine afloat. As such, the ship has become a favorite of North America–based big-ticket spenders, many of them repeaters. It has also become a favorite choice for full charters (which must be arranged at least 18 months in advance) and oceangoing conventions. So many top business executives from Fortune 500 companies have conducted meetings aboard the *Diamond* that industry pundits have occasionally referred to it as "The Write-Off Boat." The vessel is intimate enough, and its staff is savvy enough, to pull off such combinations of business and pleasure with high style.

The vessel's catamaran-style SWATH (Small Waterplane Area Twin Hull) design provides extraordinary stability, embodying features that will still be novel well into the next century. Yet, amazingly, the original concept was created in the mid-1800s by an English marine architect. It was picked up almost 150 years later by a group of Helsinki shipbuilders who, in crafting the design, studied structural features of wide-beamed, very stable car ferries operating in the Baltic and submersible drilling platforms used in the North Sea. Special features they added to the *Diamond* included two sets of stabilizers welded to pontoons that remain at a more or less constant depth of five feet below the water line. Technicians and marine insurance experts refer to the vessel as SSC (semisubmersible craft) *Radisson Diamond.*

The ship's unusual design has been appreciated by virtually everyone in the shipbuilding and design industries. Even the relentlessly middle-brow *Popular Mechanics* awarded it their highest honors in 1994. Nor is the vessel's appeal lost on the Europeans, as judges in Paris and Brussels have awarded it with everything from Grand Seals of Excellence to "World's Best Cruise Ship for 1995." Despite all of this, the vessel's design isn't likely to be duplicated anytime soon. *Diamond* was extraordinarily expensive to build and uses lots of fuel to propel its twin hulls from port to port, and though the cruise-ship market has been appreciative of *Diamond*'s design eccentricities, it's not rushed to scrap traditional single-hull vessels in their favor. Consequently, 30 years from now, you might remember your time aboard the *Diamond* the way some people remember the time they drove a Tucker or a DeLorean.

PROS & CONS Because of its wide stance and unusual design, the ship wins hands down as one of the most unflappably stable in the cruise industry, providing a platform where glasses of champagne can be perched on tabletops with barely a spill, even during choppy seas. It has encountered winds that broke the anemometer at more than 75 miles per hour without any damage to the vessel, whereas other vessels in equivalent storms have suffered. Consequently, we highly recommend the *Radisson Diamond* for landlubbers who'd like to go on a cruise but suffer from severe motion sickness (or have queasy companions who do). You might still experience *mal de mer,* but it won't be as bad as aboard more conventional, single-hulled ships.

However, you pay for this stability in speed. *Diamond* is an absolute slowpoke, with a cruising speed that rarely exceeds a maximum of around 12.5 knots—about 40% slower than many other cruise ships. As it ages, it will increasingly be left in the wake of such ships as Holland America Line's soon-to-be launched *Rotterdam VI,*

which will boast an everyday speed in excess of 22 knots. Consequently, cruises tend to last longer for the number of sea miles (and ports of call) covered, when compared to faster vessels. Overall, though, considering the elegance and high quality of the service, amenities, and cuisine on board, no one seems to object.

Speed considerations aside, the extraordinarily low density of passengers and the high ratio of crew members to passengers makes an experience aboard this vessel eminently worthwhile.

TYPES OF PASSENGERS The ship attracts independent and self-reliant types, many of whom have already sailed the seven seas. They're no-nonsense folks who prize the intimacy and camaraderie that's available aboard a small-scale ship and have no interest in the resorty "all this plus the kitchen sink" experience available aboard some of the industry's megaships. They shun mass-market travel and demand instead deluxe food, service, and accommodations—and are willing to pay the price.

Passenger rosters typically include CEOs and professionals such as lawyers and doctors. They tend to be around age 50 and up, with an average annual income of $100,000 or more, and are the type that might fly the Concorde to Paris or take the *Orient Express* to Istanbul. Many belong to country clubs and favor such shipboard policies as allowing passengers to sit and dine with whomever they wish, instead of arranging them according to a seating chart. About three-fourths of the passengers are from the United States, with the rest coming from pockets of posh around the world.

Some passengers traveling independently complain that the ship is too heavily oriented to conventioneers, as it was almost exclusively after its debut. Even so, most conventioneers are top executives, or top producers, for their respective organizations, who fit very well into the ship's passenger demographics. Nevertheless, when a sizable group is on board, the group might take over the lounge, and other passengers might feel excluded. To avoid this, Radisson tries not to book more than three corporate groups at a time onto any individual sailing, and does its best to handle the inevitable awkward moments caused by cohabitation of groups with individual passengers.

DINING If the *Diamond's* kitchen were in New York or San Francisco, it would be one of the best in the city. Among ships sailing the Caribbean, we'd rank its cuisine second only behind Seaborne, and it's a close second.

The cuisine aboard the *Diamond* is prepared with first-class ingredients by award-winning chefs who fashion the dishes to please the eye as much as the palate. A typical meal can be overwhelming. You might start with Sevruga Malosso caviar, follow this with a soup like essence of duckling with a garnish of dumplings, and then maybe have a Caesar salad. Main courses might be Norwegian salmon with a chive sauce or roast pheasant breast with a creamy tarragon sauce. There's also a special selection for those watching their diets, and each dinner offers a wok selection as well as the pasta of the day.

Many of the chefs, dining room captains, and waiters came to Radisson after serving aboard the *Sea Goddess I* or one of the Seabourn vessels, so they're accustomed to serving deluxe cuisine. Professional waitresses from Austria and elsewhere make every meal a delight, and they serve each food item as if it were individually prepared just for you, which it might very well have been.

The *Diamond* has an open seating policy in its two dining areas, the Grand Dining Room and the Grill, so you'll never have your dining companions forced on you. The Grand Dining Room is spacious, with ample space between tables. Large picture windows open onto three sides and overlook the stern. Either or both of the dining room wings can be cordoned off for separate groups.

The Grill, which seats 55, features a glass enclosure that allows for open-air dining. It features Italian cuisine and often hosts "Evenings in Italy," at which such regional specialties as herb-flavored lamb chops are served. The menu changes every evening. Be warned, the Grill is so popular you might not be able to get a table unless you reserve.

In lieu of midnight buffets, passengers can obtain just about anything they want 24 hours a day from room service. During dining hours, the dining room menu selection is available in the cabins.

ACTIVITIES The best program is the lecture series, which brings aboard well-known authors, producers, oceanographers, and others. Otherwise, this is more of an amuse-yourself ship, where you're provided with a tall ship and a star to steer by, but after that you're on your own. Arm yourself with a good book or interesting companion and you should be okay. If the afternoon starts to drag, there are card games, shuffleboard, dance lessons, and backgammon for your amusement. Videotapes are available 24 hours from the library, with no schoolmarm to check out your selection.

In port, *Diamond* often tries to come up with something better than a hot bus ride around a dry island. On Dutch St. Maarten, for instance, it might offer you a race on an America's Cup 12-meter sailboat.

CHILDREN'S ACTIVITIES The ship is geared to adults, and mature ones at that. There's no child care and no special activities for children.

ENTERTAINMENT The entertainment is all casual and laid-back, and might include a small bevy of dancers (*very* small—say, four) backed up by a five-piece band. One headliner is also brought aboard, either a soloist or a comedian. Plus, a resident quartet offers a variety of programs. Otherwise, you amuse yourself.

There's a late-night disco for anyone still up at midnight. The small Chips

Casino, which a serious gambler would not pay much attention to, offers black-jack, roulette, and slots.

SHOPPING The gift shop is limited, but the changing array of merchandise tries to appeal to very discriminating customers.

SERVICE The service is a delight, the equal of Seabourn, which is the best in the business. Those Austrian waitresses in the dining room are quite professional, and some are so charming they make you think you like a particular dish even when you don't. The service in the cabins is first class as well, although some staff members seem inexperienced.

Many nationalities are represented among the crew, including English, German, Finnish, Swedish, and Danish. It's truly astonishing to see how quickly they learn passengers' names, even though there's a no-tipping policy. (Actually, some passengers tip anyway.)

ITINERARIES In winter, the *Diamond* departs on a series of 7-day, 12-day, and 15-day cruises that make a transit of the Panama Canal and finish up with stops at Puerto Caldera, San José, and some of the rain forests and volcanoes of Costa Rica. Stops on the Atlantic side often include the San Blas Islands of

Panama, Cartagena, Curaçao, Aruba, Cozumel, Puerto Limón, and Grand Cayman and its satellite island, Cayman Brac. Depending on the itinerary, passengers board in either Aruba, Fort Lauderdale, San Juan, or Charleston, South Carolina.

SPECIAL DISCOUNTS Conscious of its status as a high-end, high-priced cruise operator, Radisson tends not to actually reduce its price, but configures its promotions as value-added perks that are thrown into the pot as a commercial "teaser." Examples include a half-price reduction for any companion of a full-fare passenger, two free nights at a deluxe hotel, or the inclusion of a free city tour of San José that includes a visit to a nearby volcano. Unless you specifically request cruise-only rates, price quotes almost always include airfares from virtually any major airport east of the Mississippi. Discounts of 50% are usually granted off the second cruise when itineraries are combined for a sailing of two weeks or more.

SINGLE SUPPLEMENTS The solo cruiser pays an average of 125% of the double occupancy rate, per person.

PORT CHARGES Port charges range from $240 to $360 aboard the vessel's Caribbean itineraries.

Radisson Diamond

⇃ ⇃ ⇃ ⇃ ⇃

Specifications

Size (in tons)	20,295	Crew	192 (International)
Number of Cabins	177	Passenger/Crew Ratio	1.8 to 1
Number of Outside Cabins	177	Year Built	1992
Number of Passengers	354	Last Major Refurbishment	n/a
Officers	Finnish/ American/ International		

Frommer's Ratings (Scale of 1–10)

Activities	7.0	Public Areas	8.5
Cabins	9.0	Public Comfort/Space	9.0
Cleanliness/Maintenance	9.5	Recreational Facilities/Pool	8.5
Entertainment	7.0	Service	9.0
Food & Beverage	9.0	Ship Crew/Officers	9.5
Interior Decor	9.5	Shore Excursions	8.2
Ports of Call	8.5	Worth the Money	9.0
		Overall Average	**8.7**

Space is what the *Diamond* is all about. From the dramatic three-deck-high forward lounge to the underwater viewing room in the starboard hull, the ship gives you plenty of space to stretch out.

Cabins & Rates

Cabins	Average per diem	Bathtub	Fridge	Phone	Sitting Area	TV
Suites	$450–$550	Yes	Yes	Yes	Yes	Yes

CABINS   The cabins are among the largest and most luxurious in Caribbean waters. All cabins are actually suites, all the same size (245 square feet) and configuration except for 53 cabins that have bay windows and 121 cabins that open onto balconies. Best of all are the two master VIP suites. Views are wide open and unobstructed from every cabin aboard.

For its floating hotel, Radisson hired noted interior expert Vincent Kwok, who spent an estimated $664,000 per cabin (compared to an average price of around $160,000 per cabin aboard most recent Caribbean cruisers). Done in a mix of modern and art deco styling, the cabin decor is subdued, with a lavish use of blond woods, pastel tones, and comfortable settees, and generally meets with approval. All cabins have a VCR, minibar, individual cabin temperature control, direct ship-to-shore phone, and a safe. Bathrooms have marble-topped vanities, bathtubs with showers, hair dryers, and thick terry-cloth robes, but are not as opulent as you might expect given how glamorous and spacious the cabins are. A very limited number of cabins accommodate a third or fourth occupant on a foldaway couch. According to your wishes and/or lifestyle, twin-size beds can be fitted together to create a queen-size bed.

Two cabins are specially outfitted for persons with disabilities.

RECREATION & FITNESS FACILITIES
While some passengers think the pool is too small and others consider it large, the truth lies somewhere in between. Its size is adequate unless the cruise is fully booked.

The perimeter of Deck 11 has been turned into a jogging track that encloses the ship's health club/spa, which is stocked with Nautilus machines, treadmills, and stationary bicycles. The spa offers all the upscale pampering that you'd expect from such a state-of-the-art vessel, including steam and massage rooms, beauty treatments, herbal wraps, and daily aerobics and yoga lessons.

From the stern, a floating marina is lowered at various ports of call to provide a platform for sailing, windsurfing, and waterskiing. In some ports of call, the line arranges scuba diving through outside concessionaires, providing you have dive certification.

PUBLIC AREAS   The ship has a mostly North American feel. It's roomy, but since most public rooms are inside the ship, they get little daylight. There's strict adherence to the rules regarding smoking and nonsmoking areas of the public rooms.

One complete deck, called the Constellation Center, is almost solely devoted to a convention and meeting center (à la Radisson Hotels), with in-house publishing facilities, a computer workshop, conference facilities, an auditorium that seats 240, and devices to record the minutes of your meeting in either audio or video.

A five-deck atrium with two unusually shaped glass-enclosed elevators and a winding staircase facilitate easy access to all public rooms. However, there is no outdoor wraparound promenade deck,

which many passengers consider a serious omission.

The Lounge, a three-tier room with a dramatic forward view of the sea, serves as an observation post, cocktail lounge, teatime rendezvous, after-dinner dance floor, and late-night disco. On the deck below is "The Club," a quiet, comfortable, and commodious yet windowless lounge. Usually when passengers want privacy and quiet, they retreat to their suites, but you might also find a secluded spot on an out-of-the way deck chair, in a quiet corner of the cocktail bar, or within an unused conference room. The library contains a roster of popular videotapes, films, and books.

Regal Cruises

SHIPS   Regal Empress

4199 34th St. South, St. Petersburg, FL 33711. ☎ 800/270-7245 or 813/867-1300; fax 813/867-1046.

Despite the name, there's very little that's regal about this outfit. Founded in 1993, Regal Cruises has only one aged and rather tired ship that offers three- to seven-day itineraries at rock-bottom prices. Some, but not all, of its cruises encourage a party hearty atmosphere, so if you're on a tight budget and are looking for a Carnivalesque cruise experience, this might be a line to consider.

The *Regal Empress'* name creates quite a lot of consumer confusion, similar as it is to Princess Cruises' *Regal Princess*. The similarity stops at the name, though. While the *Regal Princess* is a stylish, futuristic-looking megaship, the *Regal Empress* is older, smaller, and much less luxurious.

Built in Scotland in 1953 as a two-class ocean liner, the ship made its debut sailing from Glasgow and Liverpool to New York. Between 1974 and 1983, the ship was mothballed at a pier in Piraeus, Greece, the victim of an economic recession brought on by the increasing power of the airline industry. In 1984, after a major refitting, it sailed as the *Caribe I* ("The Happy Ship") for Commodore Cruise Lines.

In 1993, the owner of two enormous travel agencies, GoGo Tours and Liberty Travel, paired up with another investor and bought the vessel for a reasonable price, changing its name and marketing it through Liberty and GoGo's formidable army of sales representatives. Cruises aboard the vessel, whose prices are almost unbeatable, are presented to clients who presumably might have sailed on another line.

Despite the many triumphs of this joint marketing effort, the *Regal Empress* suffered several embarrassing faux pas from the very start. The ship flunked its first two sanitation inspections and required expensive reconfigurations. During its first summer of operation, inexperienced crew members battled glitches in an operation schedule that demanded grueling four-hour turnarounds between cruises. The beginning was rocky, but some of the most obvious errors have been corrected. And those that remain? Well, let's just say that the siren song of reduced costs does a lot to alleviate complaints.

Frankly, this is the perfect line for anyone who's unwilling to spend a lot of money and who doesn't particularly care about glamour. Fares are sometimes so cheap that if you happen to live near the ports of Florida, and can drive to Port Manatee, you might conceivably spend less on a cruise than you would entertaining yourself back home, especially if you can get in on one of the line's seasonal promotions.

During the summer, the *Empress* docks in New York and turns up the proverbial volume, using that city as a base for rowdy and raucous "cruises to nowhere" and somewhat more sedate excursions up and down the coast of Canada and New England, and, less frequently, to Bermuda. During the winter, its home is Port Manatee, Florida.

We know what you're saying: Port Manatee? Where the heck is Port Manatee? It's set in the southern boondocks of Tampa Bay, has difficulty attracting any other cruise lines to its bare-bone facilities, and usually devotes its energy to the loading of phosphates. So why does Regal dock its ship there? Well, remember that old saw about "In the land of the blind, the one-eyed man is king"? At Port Manatee, the *Empress* is queen of all that it surveys—and port charges are less than at the nearby Port of Tampa. Another reason involves legal restrictions as to when onboard parties can begin. It's quicker to get into the Gulf of Mexico from Port Manatee than it is from Tampa, and this means that onboard casinos can open about an hour sooner. Incidentally, Port Manatee is a 45-minute drive south of the Port of Tampa. Take exit 45 off I-75 and follow the signs.

PROS & CONS The vessel, now in its mid-40s, shows its age despite dedicated efforts to keep it in shape. If you can overlook the ravages of time and tide, you can take one of the least expensive cruises sailing out of any Florida port.

The vessel is not totally without charm and a certain antiquated appeal. Some nautical connoisseurs enjoy wandering through public areas admiring vestigial old-time details such as lovely wood paneling in the dining room, inlaid wood clocks, beautiful marquetry, wood sheathing around some interior structural columns, and glass-fronted bookcases and fixtures in the library.

On the down side, if the ship is full, it not only feels crowded, it *is* crowded, and regardless of how isolated your retreat is, it's likely to be invaded. Your only option for solitude during a crowded cruise is to take refuge in your cabin. All in all, you'll be happiest aboard this ship if you lower your expectations to reflect the lower price you paid.

Onboard dress is pretty much whatever you want to wear. So-called "formal" nights are rather informal, but still tend to please those who enjoy dressing up.

TYPES OF PASSENGERS Passengers run the gamut from very young to very old, though there are many older passengers because zillions of retirees live in the Clearwater/Tampa/St. Petersburg area. You'll find hard-drinking, hard-playing passengers determined to get their money's worth aboard this vessel, though the cruises out of Port Manatee tend to be slightly more sedate than the rowdy mid-summer party cruises out of New York.

If you're fussy, sensitive to the nuances of service rituals, or a cruise industry veteran looking for a cost-conscious escape, don't even consider choosing this line unless you can switch off your value judgments while aboard.

DINING This low-budget cruise company maintains its dining standards with cost control as an ever-present factor. The galley staff, however, does a relatively good job. The cuisine is heavily Italian/Hispanic/Caribbean, and comes in generous portions.

Food in the main dining room is generally good, and surprisingly good if you factor in the price you paid for the cruise. Staples tend to include grilled steaks and lobster thermidor; pastas such as fettuccine with smoked chicken, Parmesan, basil, and diced tomatoes; roasted breast of duckling with peppercorn sauce; and at least one calorie-conscious and one vegetarian dish per meal.

The dining room offers two seatings each for breakfast, lunch, and dinner, with tables configured in groups of between four and eight. There are a few tables for two. There's also a Lido-style indoor-outdoor buffet, but it's not as good as the dining room, with dishes sometimes overcooked, depleted, or in disarray, and too many passengers attacking too small a display.

Regal emphasizes eating and more eating, just like the more expensive cruise lines, but with fewer of the grace notes and frills. You can enjoy early morning coffee, juices, and pastries; three square meals a day in the dining room; afternoon tea; a midnight buffet; and 24-hour room service from a limited menu.

ACTIVITIES There are many of the usual cruise-ship activities, like bingo, card parties, and audience participation in shows. Shuffleboard tournaments, limbo contests, skeet shooting, and shipboard-style handicap horse racing are big events. You can improve your golf putting skills on an AstroTurf green or participate in R-rated, adults-only scavenger hunts. During days at sea, everyone will sunbathe on deck, but the chaise lounges are rather close to one another. If you get really bored, you'll always find food being served, or about to be served, in some venue.

Shore excursions are frequent, and part of almost any day at sea is devoted to lectures on the upcoming port of call. Cruise directors request that at least one member of every family on board attend.

CHILDREN'S ACTIVITIES Youth counselors arrange activities appropriate for several age groups, and there's a children's activity room with video arcades and Nintendo, but Regal lacks the awesome array of children's activities offered by Premier, Celebrity, or Carnival. Aboard Regal, the number and variety of children's activities varies according to how many children are on board a particular cruise. Activities might include arts and crafts lessons, Nintendo contests, and guided tours of the ship.

The ship doesn't provide baby-sitters for children under five. A counselor will watch children over five during morning and afternoon sessions, but not during mealtimes.

ENTERTAINMENT Entertainment varies according to what and who is hired to perform in the Grand Lounge or the Mirage. There is dance music before and after dinner, although sometimes the combos sound like they're playing a wedding reception. There's always karaoke, and the ship thoughtfully provides props (a wig, a cane, or whatever) that might make your rendition more believable. Disco music begins around 1am.

Set near the stern, on the same deck as the restaurant, the ship's casino is hardly the most spectacular afloat, but it might be one of the busiest, especially when the ship is packed. If you're not familiar with the rules of roulette, blackjack, or craps, a croupier will usually be glad to teach you. Failing that, play the slot machines.

Crowds congregate at the ship's half-dozen bars, where much fuss is made over whatever exotic-looking cocktail is being promoted at the moment.

SHOPPING Two gift shops are located across from one another on the port and starboard sides, midway between the main dining room and the casino. Inside, you'll find jewelry (gold chains, gold charms, earrings), cosmetics and sundries, postcards, and souvenirs such as coffee or beer mugs or warm-weather clothing with the cruise line's logo. Nothing is particularly riveting.

SERVICE Service is one of the weakest links in Regal's budget-conscious chain, a problem that derives from lack of experience among staff members. But to everyone's credit, the staff seems able and willing to get into the good-spirited flow of things. We found that a bit of tact and lowered expectations go a long way in resolving any frustrations you might feel about overworked and/or inexperienced waiters, bartenders, and cabin stewards.

There's a high turnover rate of onboard employees, so it's almost guaranteed that at least some percentage of the staff will be in training.

ITINERARIES Regal's itineraries are more varied, both in their duration and in their destinations, than many of its cost-conscious competitors. Caribbean itineraries, offered every year between late October and late May, include options for 4-day, 6-day, 7-day, and 10-day jaunts to warm-weather ports. The least comprehensive itinerary departs from Port Manatee for a two-day stopover in Playa del Carmen/Cozumel and includes two days at sea. Seven-night itineraries vary from week to week, but include stopovers at at least four ports of call that might include Grand Cayman, Ocho Rios, Montego Bay, Key West, and Playa del Carmen/Cozumel. The outfit's 10-night cruise stops at some relatively exotic Central American ports—including the Colombian island of San Andrés, the Panamanian archipelago of San Blas, and Puerto Limón, Costa Rica—and include a traversal of the first lock of the Panama Canal, as far as Gatun Lake.

In summer, the ship migrates north to a base in New York City for two-day "cruises to nowhere"; sailings along the coast of Canada and New England; and five-night round-trips to Bermuda, with a stop in Newport, Rhode Island.

SPECIAL DISCOUNTS The usual per diems for Regal are so consistently low that the company's offers of special discounts almost make it more expensive to stay at home. Third, fourth, and fifth passengers sharing a cabin with two full-fare adults pay between $199 and $349, depending on the length of their cruise. But in some slack seasons, a third or fourth passenger might pay only $99 for the full duration of a seven-day cruise when sharing a cabin occupied by two adults paying full fare. There are no special rates for children, just the normal discounts offered to third and fourth passengers in a double cabin.

During periods of low demand (say, November and April), the company might initiate a "one pays, one sails for free" promotion for sailings with excess capacity. Taking advantage of this will almost certainly make a sojourn at sea cheaper than an equivalent holiday on land.

SINGLE SUPPLEMENTS Single rates are levied at 150% the per person rate for a double.

PORT CHARGES Depending on the cruise, port charges range from $84 per person for the outfit's 4-night cruise to $195 for its 10-night cruise.

Regal Empress

⚓ ⚓

Specifications

Size (in tons)	22,979	Crew	386 (American/International)
Number of Cabins	453	Passenger/Crew Ratio	3 to 1
Number of Outside Cabins	226	Year Built	1953
Number of Passengers	1,180	Last Major Refurbishment	1993
Officers	European		

Frommer's Ratings (Scale of 1–10)

Activities	5.6	Public Areas	6.2
Cabins	6.4	Public Comfort/Space	5.8
Cleanliness/Maintenance	5.8	Recreational Facilities/Pool	5.0
Entertainment	5.0	Service	6.0
Food & Beverage	6.0	Ship Crew/Officers	7.5
Interior Decor	6.2	Shore Excursions	5.0
Ports of Call	5.0	Worth the Money	8.5
		Overall Average	**6.0**

Despite years of hard use and ownership by at least four fiscal entities (one of which abandoned it for several years on an out-of-the-way wharf near Athens), vestiges of this ship's original elegance and good taste still remain. It boasts ample amounts of deck space, although when it's full, much of it might be taken up by sunbathers. Another appealing feature is the glass-enclosed promenade on, where else, the Promenade Deck, whose virtues might be best appreciated during windy weather in the North Atlantic. During hot days in the Caribbean, you'll wish it was open.

Cabins & Rates						
Cabins	Average per diem	Bathtub	Fridge	Phone	Sitting Area	TV
Inside	$100–$150	No	No	No	No	No
Outside	$112–$188	No	Yes	Yes	Yes	Yes
Suite	$195–$213	Some	Yes	Yes	Yes	Yes

CABINS   The 453 cabins vary widely in size, location, and configuration, with the smallest measuring a cramped 80 square feet and the largest an only slightly bigger 125 square feet. Suites are a more spacious 216 to 408 square feet. The price is right, but the cabins have seen better days, and a high percentage are inside units without views.

Decor is universally uninspired, angular, and rather bleak except for touches of wood trim and, more rarely, paneling. In-cabin music is available via a radiolike gizmo, and each unit contains wall-to-wall carpeting and, in most cases, round portholes rather than rectangular picture windows. Bathrooms are small and somewhat old-fashioned; only the largest of the ship's 19 suites contains a bathtub.

Most cabins can be configured for up to four occupants through bunk-bed arrangements. Some can be configured to accommodate five. Each cabin, thankfully, has enough storage space and a reasonable amount of elbow room, at least for a cruise of short duration. Even in the lowest category, an inside cabin might have two lower beds, two closets, and two dressers that will store most of a couple's possessions. If you cram four into a cabin, however, you'll be pressing your luck. Twelve cabins are singles.

Only one cabin—no. P20A, on the Promenade Deck—is wheelchair accessible. This rather undesirable inside cabin has no sills on the entrance to the bathroom, and cabin and bathroom doors are wide enough to accommodate a wheelchair.

RECREATION & FITNESS FACILITIES
There is one small and rather ornamental "dipping" pool aboard, more a spot for sunbathers than a place to swim.

You won't find a full-fledged health and beauty spa aboard the *Regal Empress*. There's a few exercise machines in a rather bland room on the top deck, but no sauna or showers. There are two whirlpools on deck. Stretch-and-tone classes are led by one of the showroom's dancers.

PUBLIC AREAS   Except for the library, whose wood paneling offers a scholarly feel, public areas contain glittering chrome and strong, sometimes strident colors. Pedestrian traffic is heavy as passengers migrate from one area of the ship to another.

A two-level disco (The Mirage), a busy casino, a dining room with mirrors and vestiges of the room's original wood detailing and murals (scenes are of New York and Rio), and a half-dozen bars are the most active public areas. Somewhat more sedate are a hideaway lounge called The Club and a cozy piano bar called the Tradewinds Lounge.

Royal Caribbean Cruises, Ltd.

**SHIPS   Enchantment of the Seas (Preview) • Grandeur of the Seas •
Legend of the Seas • Majesty of the Seas • Monarch of the Seas • Nordic
Empress • Rhapsody of the Seas (Preview) • Sovereign of the Seas •
Splendour of the Seas • Vision of the Seas (Preview)**
1050 Caribbean Way, Miami, FL 33132. ☎ 800/327-6700 or 305/539-6000; fax 305/
371-8399.

Royal Caribbean Cruises, Ltd. (RCCL), is one of the steadiest cruise companies in the industry, having perfected a well-rehearsed arsenal of better-than-average crowd pleasers. Rather than sell prospective passengers on any one specific vessel in their fleet, RCCL sells a style of cruise. The Royal Caribbean allure goes beyond ship design into something subtler. There's very little that's wrong with an RCCL experience, and many things that are right. Prices are reasonable—good value for the dollar and geared to compete with the fares charged by every other megaliner afloat. Activities are varied enough to appeal to virtually everyone, modern enough to impress even the most jaded of hipsters and conservative enough not to offend reactionaries.

Royal Caribbean was the first company to launch a fleet specializing exclusively in Caribbean ports of call—thus the company name. In the late 1980s, it expanded its base of operations beyond the Caribbean basin. Will its name change? It hasn't so far, and the company's savvy marketing department explains that the word *Caribbean* represents a *style* of cruising, rather than a reference to specific destinations or ports of call. (RCCL is big on this "style" thing.)

What began in 1969 as a consortium of Norwegian ship owners has blossomed into a company with a staggering volume and a flotilla of megaships valued in the billions. Today, RCCL is comprised of an evenhanded mixture of Norwegian and North American business partners, a blend of ship owners and hotel owners that has proven immensely profitable. In 1990, the Pritzker family (creative force behind the Hyatt empire) bought a major

stake in the company, and funds from the sale, coupled with all the creditworthiness of Hyatt, helped finance the line's massive expansion during the 1990s. In 1993, corporate coffers were enriched even further thanks to a stock offering, the company's first. Since then, shares have been traded on the New York Stock Exchange using the symbol RCL.

Before the present crop of megaships had been launched, the fledgling company solved its capacity problems in a then-unusual way. Two vessels within RCCL's fleet were stretched—that is, cut in half and enlarged by inserting carefully constructed midsections. Although the technique had been successful with car ferries, cargo vessels, limousines, airplanes, and buses, RCCL was the first cruise line to attempt it. Others, including Holland America, later adopted the technique.

This makeshift solution of stretching vessels didn't remain a company priority for long. Royal Caribbean ushered in a new generation of megaships in 1988 with the 73,192-ton *Sovereign of the Seas*. This vessel was the largest passenger ship built in the previous 50 years and was between two and four times as large as any other vessel in the RCCL fleet as it then stood. Its debut at the Port of Miami was the oceangoing equivalent of the first 747's unveiling. Highways and byways all along the seafront of Miami Beach came to a standstill as motorists craned their necks, trying to get a look at this new generation of supercruiser.

The *Sovereign of the Seas* contained features that were lavishly innovative at the time, but which have since been included almost as standard issue in megaships throughout the industry. Those features included a five-story atrium with glass-sided elevators, enough potted plants to form a small jungle, sweeping staircases, and fountains splashing into marble pools. It also contained the prototype of a design feature that has been incorporated into every RCCL vessel since: an observation lounge 10 or 11 stories above sea level, wrapped around the rear smokestack in a style reminiscent of big-windowed airport control towers. Its designer admitted that his inspiration derived from Seattle's Space Needle, built for the 1962 World's Fair.

The *Sovereign of the Seas* and the ships that followed, such as the twin vessels *Majesty of the Seas* and *Monarch of the Seas,* tripled the cabin capacity of Royal Caribbean between 1988 and 1992. Today, the company is dominated by megaliners. The line's ship construction program is so large that if the six vessels launched or proposed for launching between 1995 and 1998 were segregated as an independent cruise line, it would be the third largest in the world.

The ships are remarkably equivalent in amenities, allure, and decor. Some observers have called them cookie-cutter vessels, while others call RCCL the NASA of the cruise-ship industry, rehearsing and fine-tuning its product as if prepping for a moon launch. That prototype has led to product recognition that is the envy of many other cruise lines. Contrast RCCL's megaship predictability to such fleets as Norwegian Cruise Line, whose flotilla contains vessels that differ radically in size and levels of luxury. Some travel agents have declared that even the doughnuts taste the same aboard RCCL vessels, the result of systematized and ritualized line-wide galley procedures.

This corporate homogenization doesn't come without a price: Black sheep employees refer to the line as the "IBM of the cruise line industry," citing a corporate culture that's probably more deeply entrenched, oppressive, and rigidly enforced than that of virtually any other cruise line.

The company often sponsors a series of theme-related gimmicks to sell cabin spaces. Regardless of the ship, there's a consistent use of Broadway themes used as monikers for show lounges and music bars. When a sales and marketing theme or architectural configuration aboard any one ship proves successful, RCCL duplicates it throughout its fleet.

PROS & CONS   Royal Caribbean's most obvious asset is its consistency. Except for a handful of small ships that remain outside of the Caribbean, RCCL's Caribbean vessels are usually around the same size, age, and configuration. Activities, daily programs, cuisine, bar service, and cabin service have long ago been hammered into a format that both travel agents and members of the public swear by.

The line was one of the first to promote year-round, seven-day cruises that depart like clockwork every Saturday from Miami. In fact, the Port of Miami credits RCCL, Norwegian Cruise Line, and Carnival with transforming their once-sleepy industrial port into the cruise capital of the world. Today, the ships' itineraries remain rigorously predictable, rarely changing either ports of call or the length of their voyages.

One drawback for sophisticated, oft-traveled cruisers is the fact that the ports of call RCCL visits are not particularly exotic; RCCL tends to concentrate on such glittery but oft-visited ports as St. Thomas and St. Maarten, and on isolated beaches owned by the company. RCCL trips are thus safe and standardized, and so not a good bet if you're looking for a little adventure in your cruise diet.

Shipboard ambience remains constant as well—witty, classy, refined but not stuffy and, well, *sane.* It's not particularly giddy, with the fantasyland make-believe of Premier or the soon-to-be-launched Disney line, but RCCL shipboard ambience is easy to live with and can be a lot of fun. There's not a hint of slapstick, no cornpone, and no gratuitous tastelessness—as opposed to a line like Carnival, with its ongoing round of parties and indulgent or even encouraging attitude toward raucous merrymakers. Karaoke is about as out-of-control as activities aboard RCCL gets. One bylaw that applies to RCCL and is pretty handy to keep in mind generally is that the shorter the cruise, the more raucous and party-oriented it's likely to be. When there's less time available, passengers tend to make the most of it. So if you're looking for a relaxing holiday to catch up on your sleep, consider one of the 7- to 10-day sojourns, rather than one of the three-day quickies.

Daytime dress codes are unwritten, but tend to be dictated by peer pressure from other passengers. Dress is casual but neat during the day and informal most evenings. Every seven-day cruise will include two semiformal or formal nights, where men will be encouraged to wear tuxedos or suits with ties, and women can wear something dressier or more glittery than usual.

In one arena, Royal Caribbean competes specifically with Norwegian Cruise Line, Carnival, and Princess, all of which either own or make stops at privately owned islands astride most of the sea routes. RCCL far outstrips the others in this domain, thanks to its outright ownership of two tropical beaches and its discreetly conducted efforts to buy at least one more. At CocoCay (Little Stirrup Cay), an otherwise uninhabited 140-acre landfall in the Berry Islands of The Bahamas, you'll find enough hammocks, barbecue pits, and small sporting craft to keep you and all your fellow passengers amused and entertained. As if the natural attractions weren't enough, RCCL even built and sank a replica of one of the pirate Bluebeard's schooners, to enhance the underwater vistas for anyone interested in snorkeling.

The line also maintains an idyllic beachfront, Labadee, along the northern coast of Haiti, far from teeming Port-au-Prince. Developed by RCCL on an isolated, 270-acre peninsula in 1987 and closed for several years during the worst of Haiti's civil unrest, it reopened again in 1995. The site is unusual in that it boasts five separate beaches, each with different characteristics, evoking everything from the gravel and rocks of New England to the sandy atolls and palm trees of the southern Caribbean. If it weren't for souvenir stands hawking Haitian paintings, you'd never know you were in poverty-stricken Haiti, so removed does the site seem from the rest of the country.

What are the drawbacks with Royal Caribbean Cruises? There are two: anonymity and cabin size. It's an undeniable fact that big ships are more anonymous than small-scale cruisers. Royal Caribbean is a mass-market line with middle- to upper-middle-class tastes and a flotilla of behemoth vessels. If you feel confused on a large ship, or if you can never, absolutely never, remember what deck your cabin lies on, you won't like the line's mall-sized ships. But if you're not a shrinking violet or wallflower, don't spend more than a usual amount of time within your cabin, and enjoy ships that offer plenty to do, RCCL might very well be for you. When it comes to activities and diversions, bigger is much, much better than smaller. But you'll experience the inevitable lines for buffets, disembarkation, and boarding of buses during shore excursions, and will sometimes have to wait a while for your drink when a bar or lounge is particularly crowded.

A more important bone of contention involves the size of cabins aboard RCCL's pre-1995 vessels, where standard inside cabins measure as little as a cramped 119 square feet, and outside cabins aren't much better at 122 square feet—almost guaranteeing that you'll bump knees and elbows with whomever you happen to be sharing the space with. With the first of RCCL's "Project Vision" vessels, 1995's *Legend of the Seas,* cabin dimensions were upsized to a more comfortable 138 square feet for inside cabins and 153 square feet for outsides. This change was no doubt made in reaction to the larger cabins offered by Carnival, an outfit that jolted RCCL into a new awareness of how important cabin dimensions are to the cruise-going public. Each of the half-dozen ships for which *Legend* was the prototype will feature these expanded cabin dimensions.

Although cabins aboard the older ships are moderately inconvenient, we wouldn't cite them as a reason to avoid sailing the line. After all, the reason Royal Caribbean originally decided on smaller cabins was its assumption that active, involved cruisers who are up and busy with shipboard activities retreat to cabins only in the event of seasickness, for romantic trysts, or to sleep.

TYPES OF PASSENGERS   Defining the typical passenger aboard a line that is noted for its broad-based, mass-market appeal is about as treacherous as sailing a megaship over a shallow Bahamian reef. Forced to generalize, though, we'd define Royal Caribbean's typical passengers as couples (and, to a lesser extent, singles) aged 30 to 60. There are a good number of families thrown in the mix as well.

Caribbean passengers have an average age in their early 40s. Average age, income, and education level for passengers taking three- and four-night cruises are slightly lower than among passengers booking cruises longer than 10 nights. Passengers in general tend to be active. They participate to some extent in shipboard activities and, to varying degrees, in evening revelries. They also look carefully at how much money they're spending and what they're getting for it. About half of RCCL passengers have taken a cruise before, and about a quarter have previously sailed with RCCL.

Income levels for the typical RCCL passenger have dropped in recent years, especially since more of the line's revenues derive from short-term cruises of between three and four days in length and since, in the present market climate, cruises are being deeply discounted from their brochure rates. Past averages for household annual income hovered around $50,000

a year, whereas present averages are just above $30,000 a year. The majority of passengers are professional, white-collar types.

Ninety percent of the passengers come from somewhere in North America, and there's about an equal division between men and women. You won't find the Bacchanalian playland aspect that dominates aboard Carnival. Passengers on RCCL are more sedate—or perhaps we'll call them *dignified*—preferring to let their hair down in a slightly different way. This is not to suggest that RCCL passengers are prudish, as many surely get involved in some sybaritic and/or abandoned activity during their time on board, perhaps losing themselves in the whirl of the casino or in the flash and glitter of the showrooms. No one objects to a bit of serious tippling in any of the bars, either. Basically what we're saying is that you won't see too many people wandering around wearing lampshades on their heads.

If you have a fire-and-brimstone approach to morality, the party atmosphere aboard an RCCL vessel might upset you. And if you require punctilious service at any moment's notice, you'll probably throw at least one temper tantrum during your time aboard this line. But if you're normally indulgent and permissive, you might have a perfectly marvelous time aboard RCCL.

In recent years, many large, extended families have held family reunions aboard RCCL, and to an increasing degree, large numbers of Latin Americans, Europeans (15% to 20%), and Australians book with the line. This growth in foreign markets isn't accidental. Since 1994, RCCL has placed sales representatives in 40 countries. To prevent language barriers from standing in the way of the good times' continued rolling, it offers multilingual interpreters (usually German, Spanish, French, and, as needed, Portuguese and Dutch) aboard each of its ships.

DINING   The line (and by definition each of its vessels) is a member of France's Chaîne des Rôtisseurs. Food aboard is good and sometimes even very good. It's not gourmet, but dishes are flavorful and well conceived, using as many fresh ingredients as are possible aboard a ship. However, the sheer size of RCCL's dining operation makes the occasional culinary faux pas, such as frozen lettuce, inevitable. Cuisine is often presented in an array of different themes, with table settings, menus, and waiters' costumes reflecting the theme. Evening buffets have a lot of self-indulgent pizzazz.

Dining rooms feature two seatings with assigned tables at breakfast, lunch, and dinner (which is served at 6:15pm and 8:30pm). Tables are, for the most part, ovals or rectangles, seating between four and eight diners. Tête-à-têtes are difficult to arrange aboard RCCL ships, so it's better to save your romantic trysting till you get back to your cabin.

The dining room decor varies from ship to ship, but is always patterned on a theme inspired by a successful Broadway play or Hollywood film. Perhaps because of the line's usually well-mannered clientele, the noise level in the dining rooms is much lower than in equivalent rooms aboard Costa or Carnival vessels. You can eat breakfast and lunch in the main dining room or in a self-service cafeteria on deck, near one of the pools. Lines, unfortunately, can grow long.

Inventories in RCCL wine cellars fall far short of what's available on more upscale lines, but are peppered with choices whose economy and bouquet will please both connoisseur and neophyte.

Every menu contains selections designed for low-fat, low-cholesterol, low-salt dining, as well as vegetarian and children's dishes. Other than that, special diets are obtained only with difficulty. At lunch, afternoon tea, and dinner, you can make your own sundae from an ice cream bar with all the fixings. In addition to the midnight buffet, sandwiches are served throughout the night in the public lounges.

Room service is available 24 hours a day. The selection is fairly routine, with an array of cold sandwiches and cheese and fruit plates. During normal dinner hours, however, a cabin steward can bring you anything being served that night.

RCCL's children's menus, even more so than virtually any line except Premier, seem devoid of nutrients and heavy on everything a growing child should probably avoid: Desserts are even identified as the best part of the meal. However, it's well known that children (like adults) can survive on a diet of pizza, burgers, ravioli, and macaroni and cheese, so your youngsters won't starve.

ACTIVITIES Royal Caribbean activities are not staid. There are plenty of opportunities for partying on board, although in a less raucous and uninhibited manner than aboard Carnival. If you want to remain seated in a deck chair and watch the world go by, no one will bother you and embarrass you into joining.

The line maintains two private beach resorts, and many of its cruises feature a day at one or the other of them. CocoCay in The Bahamas, and Labadee, an isolated and sun-flooded peninsula along Haiti's north coast, are tropical retreats RCCL has transformed into fun-in-the-sun playlands. Shore excursions, usually aboard buses or minivans, are carefully structured (or, depending on your point of view, regimented), and are fairly effective at shuttling large numbers of visitors around to what RCCL considers the most important sights and attractions. Informal volleyball tournaments are held either aboard ship or at either of the line's beach resorts.

Daytime activities are typical cruise line fare. You can join in white elephant sales to get rid of souvenirs you decided you really didn't want, bet on wooden horses that race (with the help of staff members) across imaginary finish lines, or play bingo, shuffleboard, or other deck-side games. Many passengers like the line-dancing lessons, where you can wear jeans and a cowboy hat, but don't need a partner to pace your way through the country-western steps. RCCL has even adopted an entertainment motif that's been popular aboard competing lines, staging auctions where worthy but not particularly famous paintings are sold to the highest bidder.

Royal Caribbean features one of the most elaborate golf-training sessions afloat. The program, known as "Golf, Ahoy!," lets golfers play the best local course in any of 16 ports of call and in four pre- and postcruise ports—courses that are difficult to get onto without membership privileges. Tee-off times are reserved, guaranteed, and timed to coincide with your ship's arrival and departure.

The line has also developed one of the cruise industry's most comprehensive onboard fitness regimes, the ShipShape Fitness Program. Available aboard every ship in the fleet, it extends its boundaries far beyond the premises of the usual health club/exercise room. Passengers can participate in as many or as few activities as they want, selecting from low-impact aerobics, up-tempo aerobics, "gut-buster" exercises, dance classes, basketball free-throws, Ping-Pong tournaments, and early-morning walk-a-thons that challenge cruisers to walk at whatever speed they want for 30 hard minutes. Other classes are specifically designed for senior citizens or anyone prone to injuries of the tendons and ligaments. These feature a series of fitness routines conducted entirely from the relative comfort of your chair.

CHILDREN'S ACTIVITIES   Programs for children ages 3 to 17 are maintained year-round throughout the Royal Caribbean fleet. RCCL refers to them as "Adventure Ocean." Partly because of each vessel's massive size, they're some of the most extensive afloat, and include a teen disco that might, depending on the individual trip, be outfitted with replicas of the rings of Saturn. Children's play areas boast environments conceived for their creative stimuli and, depending on the vessel, may evoke the interior of a

space station, complete with accessories that children presumably find cool.

Activities include pin the tail on the donkey, costume parades, poster-painting classes, hat-making, face-painting, wacky races, freeze dances, midnight dancing, or late-night basketball. Teenagers tend to most enjoy the "abnormal formal" party, where everyone seems to emulate one of the Munsters. Counselors are on hand to do what they do best: counsel, advise, stimulate, supervise, and amuse their charges. Kids' agendas are slipped under cabin doors every night.

Baby-sitting is usually available in the evenings and sometimes during the day and in port. There's no charge for group baby-sitting, although it's a good idea to tip anyone who has supervised your cherubs during your night out. Private sitters, culled from the ranks of well-meaning chambermaids and stewards during their off-hours, are available from 8am to 2am and charge $8 per hour for up to two children in the same family, $10 per hour for three. Payment for their services is expected in cash and cannot be charged to a shipboard account.

ENTERTAINMENT   The line is one of the savviest of any afloat when it comes to producing razzle-dazzle at sea, and even though each shipboard production follows a cliché-ridden, tried-and-true format, it still manages to convey its own kind of excitement and enthusiasm. The line accentuates some aspects of Las Vegas, with the requisite skin and glitter that never crosses the border into sleaze, and brings aboard such headliners as Lou Rawls, Phyllis Diller, David Brenner, Diahann Carroll and Vic Damone, Connie Stevens, and Jerry Lewis.

The line doesn't stint on its entertainment budgets, incorporating sprawling, high-tech cabaret stages into each of its ships, usually with as many as 50 video monitors to complement live performances. Like a Las Vegas showroom, entertainment begins before dinner and continues late, late into the night.

Megaships carry additional music acts, as well as comedy acts that are piquant enough to be absorbing and mainstream enough not to offend. Passengers can always amuse themselves (and others) using an assortment of karaoke machines.

Aboard the occasional country-western, big band, or rock 'n' roll theme cruises, passengers come armed with the appropriate costumes.

SHOPPING Royal Caribbean has a lusty appreciation for the pleasures of shopping. On each ship, boutiques and gift shops supplement their inventories with local booty from ports of call such as San Juan and St. Thomas. The megaships have about a dozen shops. Unlike many of its competitors, who hire outside concessionaires to inventory and maintain their onboard boutiques, RCCL does everything in-house.

You can find some bargains on board, particularly on liquor, certain jewelry, and such luxury items as porcelain. The line's awesome buying power almost guarantees that prices might be as low, and sometimes lower, than equivalent products on shore. Plus, inventories are kept up-to-date by a computer and a central buying committee. We recommend you visit the onboard boutiques the first day of your cruise, rather than the last; this way you'll learn the prices of whatever strikes your fancy and can comparison shop during stopovers at your ports of call. The line occasionally holds special sales, during which prices can be really attractive.

In San Juan and Charlotte Amalie, RCCL makes shopping more pleasant by maintaining "Crown and Anchor Clubs," hospitality centers outfitted with sofas, chairs, rest rooms, a bar, and a snack bar. Passengers can leave packages here before returning to the ship, or use the center as a rendezvous point. Staff will offer information about local tourist options, as well as provide first aid if necessary. Look for the addition of several others of these Crown and Anchor Clubs in the future, at locations to be announced.

SERVICE Vast armies of personnel are required to maintain a line as large as RCCL, and so it's a miracle that staff members appear as motivated and enthusiastic as they do. Part of this derives from fair compensation, part from the pride inherent in doing a job well.

You're likely to be greeted with a smile by someone polishing the brass in a stairwell, a greeting that supervisors encourage on the part of even the lowest-ranking employees. Service might be a bit slower whenever many passengers congregate in one place at the same time, but this is to be expected aboard any megaship. At their worst, some RCCL staff members might appear robotic, performing their duties as if on automatic pilot.

Tipping rituals are surprisingly brash, with guidelines clearly delineated by the cruise line. But because most passengers are content with the onboard service, few mind passing out the requisite gratuities. Be warned that many staff members will change from solicitous to unsubtle whenever it comes time to pass out tips.

As a guideline, RCCL recommends that each passenger give about $8 total per day on board, distributed between cabin attendants ($3), dining room stewards ($3), and assistant waiters ($1.50).

Also note that both staff members and the cruise line place great emphasis on favorable reports from passengers about satisfactory service. Staff questionnaires and complaints are reviewed within a few hours of receipt. Some former staff members, especially those working RCCL dining rooms, have complained of close supervisor scrutiny producing a virtual reign of terror. Everywhere aboard RCCL's armada, the possibility of a passenger jotting a negative comment in his staff evaluation is much-dreaded, and it's probable that at least one staff member will ask you—quietly, when no one else is listening—to fill out a favorable passenger survey card. Considering the perks that such reports entail, such behavior is both understandable and predictable.

ITINERARIES

Enchantment of the Seas—Between October and April, it departs every Sunday from Miami on alternating tours of the western and eastern Caribbean. Eastern Caribbean stops include St. Maarten, St. John, St. Thomas, and CocoCay; western Caribbean circuits stop at Key West, Cozumel, Ocho Rios, and Grand Cayman.

Grandeur of the Seas—Based in Miami, and departing every Saturday throughout the year, it makes seven-day circuits of the eastern Caribbean, with stops at Labadee, San Juan, St. Thomas, and CocoCay.

Legend of the Seas—Throughout the winter, from a base in San Juan, it departs on 10- or 11-day transits through the Panama Canal, as far as Acapulco. Cruises heading west make stops in St. Thomas, Catalina Island (off the coast of the Dominican Republic), Curaçao, and Caldera (Costa Rica). Eastbound transits call at the port of Aruba.

Majesty of the Seas—Every Sunday, year-round, it departs from Miami for tours of the western Caribbean, making stops at Playa del Carmen/Cozumel, Grand Cayman, Ocho Rios, and Labadee.

Monarch of the Seas—Using San Juan as its home port, it departs every Sunday throughout the year on seven-day cruises that stop at St. Thomas, Martinique, Barbados, Antigua, and St. Maarten.

Nordic Empress—Between June and August it uses Port Canaveral as its base, departing for three- and four-night treks to Nassau and CocoCay. From September to May, it moves to San Juan, from which it makes an alternating series of three- and four-night cruises. Three-night cruises stop at St. Thomas and St. Maarten; four-night cruises add an additional stop at St. Croix.

Rhapsody of the Seas—Between October and April, it departs every Saturday from San Juan for southern Caribbean ports that include Aruba, Curaçao, St. Maarten, and St. Thomas. Twice a year, in spring and autumn, it migrates through the Panama Canal on its way to warm-weather sailing in Alaska.

Sovereign of the Seas—Throughout the year, it embarks on three- and four-night circuits that begin and end in Miami. Three-night cruises stop at Nassau and CocoCay; four-night cruises add an additional stop in Key West.

Splendour of the Seas—Between November and March, from a base in Miami, it embarks on 10- and 11-night circuits through the Caribbean. Ten-night itineraries stop at Cozumel, Grand Cayman, Ocho Rios, St. Thomas, San Juan, and Labadee. Eleven-night itineraries stop at Key West, Curaçao, Aruba, Ocho Rios, Grand Cayman, and Cozumel.

Vision of the Seas (launching in 1998)— No itineraries have yet been announced. Check with RCCL or a travel agent.

SPECIAL DISCOUNTS   Savvy at marketing (among the most skilled in a competitive industry), RCCL manages to keep its fares on a par with those offered by competitors Carnival, Holland America, and Princess. So, if one of those lines has drastically reduced its fares during a particular season or sailing, chances are good that RCCL has done the same thing. Cruise industry insiders have noted that cruises at RCCL are usually priced, regardless of the market conditions, at around $10 per person per day more than its biggest rival, Carnival. Part of this stems from RCCL's self-image (and self-promotion) as just a bit classier than Carnival. But when bookings are really slow, expect to see the price differences between the two lines get pretty close.

Early bookings sometimes benefit from what RCCL refers to as "breakthrough discounts," which might be up to 40% off the brochure rates. Their availability is capacity controlled, and RCCL ensures that no subsequent booker will get an equivalent cabinet cheaper than the early booker. Cruises over such holidays as Christmas, Thanksgiving, or Easter sometimes require

Enchantment of the Seas • Rhapsody of the Seas • Vision of the Seas (Previews)

Scheduled for launchings in 1997 and 1998, too late to be reviewed in this guide, these look-alike vessels are slated to be the last in the "Project Vision" series, which includes three other ships: *Legend of the Seas* (1995), *Splendour of the Seas* (1996), and *Grandeur of the Seas* (also 1996). The collective presence of these half-dozen floating cities represents a multibillion-dollar program of expansion rivaling that of many national navies across the globe. It's one of the most aggressive enlargement policies of any single cruise line in history.

Though they're being built at different shipyards—*Enchantment* at Finland's Kvaerner Masa-Yards and *Rhapsody* and *Vision* at France's Chantiers de l'Atlantique—each will be almost identical to the other ships in the Vision Line, with the same configuration of outdoor swimming pools, casino, indoor/outdoor buffet restaurant, library, fully equipped conference room, and card rooms, and featuring a shopping mall, RCCL's trademark Viking Crown Lounge perched 10 stories above sea level, and a seven-deck atrium with glass elevators and glass walls. Although exact layout and decorative themes will evolve as each ship is built, company insiders say that each will probably contain enough razzmatazz and visual excitement to compete, albeit more discreetly, with Carnival's fancifully decorated vessels.

After the *Vision* is complete, what next? Eagles, that's what. Royal Caribbean has finalized a deal with the Kvaerner Masa-Yards to build two—and possibly three—130,000-ton, 3,100-passenger "Eagle Class" vessels on a design developed in conjunction with the long-range planners at Japan's Mitsubishi Heavy Industries. The ships will likely debut in 1999 and 2000. If RCCL exercises its option to order the third ship, the Eagles would increase RCCL's total fleet capacity to over 33,000 berths—a 40% increase from the number it floats today. Ambitious? Yes. Audacious? Sure. And what will these vessels be like? Stay tuned for next year's *Caribbean Cruises* to find out.

payment of a $75 supplement per person, and a $150 to $250 per person travel allowance may be deducted from most cruises for passengers who don't book combined air/sea packages.

A third or fourth passenger in a cabin usually pays between $65 and $100 per day, regardless of the itinerary. Senior citizen discounts are offered whenever too many cabins remain unbooked for any particular vessels.

Discount packages are offered at many hotels (especially Hyatt, which is owned by some of the same people that run RCCL) throughout Florida, either before or after a cruise.

Past passengers are offered special discounts on selected cruises and receive a magazine four times a year and news of other discount plans more regularly than

that. Repeaters are invited to special parties during their cruise. Sometimes the line's discounts will be reduced air/sea packages for specifically designated ships or markets—discounts that sometimes come in below the already discounted "Breakthrough Rate."

SINGLE SUPPLEMENTS Solo passengers usually pay around 150% of the per person rate for occupancy of a double. However, if you're flexible and willing to wait till boarding to be assigned a cabin category, that percentage might be less, depending on circumstances or cabin availability.

PORT CHARGES Beginning in spring 1997, RCCL began including port charges in its advertised rates, so you can expect no additional fees.

Grandeur of the Seas • Legend of the Seas • Splendour of the Seas

↓ ↓ ↓ ↓ ↓

Specifications

Size (in tons)		Officers	Norwegian/International
Grandeur	74,000	Crew	
Legend	69,130	*Grandeur*	760 (International)
Splendour	69,130	*Legend*	720 (International)
Number of Cabins		*Splendour*	720 (International)
Grandeur	975	Passenger/Crew Ratio	
Legend	902	*Grandeur*	2.5 to 1
Splendour	902	*Legend*	2.5 to 1
Number of Outside Cabins		*Splendour*	2.5 to 1
Grandeur	576	Year Built	
Legend	575	*Grandeur*	1996
Splendour	575	*Legend*	1995
Number of Passengers		*Splendour*	1996
Grandeur	1,950	Last Major Refurbishment	n/a
Legend	1,804		
Splendour	1,804		

Frommer's Ratings (Scale of 1–10)

Activities	7.8	Public Areas	8.8
Cabins	7.8	Public Comfort/Space	8.5
Cleanliness/Maintenance	8.4	Recreational Facilities/Pool	8.0
Entertainment	8.5	Service	7.8
Food & Beverage	7.8	Ship Crew/Officers	8.0
Interior Decor	8.0	Shore Excursions	7.6
Ports of Call	7.6	Worth the Money	7.8
		Overall Average	**8.0**

This trio of identical megaships, whose launchings began in 1995, are the newest hardware in Royal Caribbean Cruises' fleet. The first of the six-ship "Project Vision" series, each weighs in at between 69,130 and 74,000 tons and was constructed at a price of around $325 million.

Built according to basically identical plans at French or Finnish shipyards, they borrow heavily from the tried-and-true forerunner of the line, *Sovereign of the Seas*, albeit with subtle design and layout differences to improve layout and performance.

Each takes the use of glass at sea to new heights, containing about two acres of glass canopies, glass windbreaks, skylights, and suspended glass window walls with sweeping views. That's more than aboard any other cruise ship afloat. The focal point of each vessel is a dramatic seven-story atrium that features a series of 18-foot sculptures, hundreds of potted plants, and all the bustle of a hotel lobby. Don't expect too many straight lines on board: An army of interior designers added as many graceful and sinuous curves as they could to the interior of these ships, trying to emulate the flow of the sea and the curve of the horizons, as viewed through the wide expanses of glass.

Some of the fastest cruise ships built in the past quarter century, these three were designed mostly for warm-weather deployment, but since they're relatively speedy, with a cruising speed of between 22 and 24 knots, they are certainly capable of visiting the far-flung ports of the world. As market priorities for the cruise industry change, at least one of them might conceivably be deployed outside the Caribbean.

Cabins & Rates*						
Cabins	Average per diem	Bathtub	Fridge	Phone	Sitting Area	TV
Inside	$245	No	No	Yes	No	Yes
Outside	$285	No	No	Yes	No	Yes
Suite	$400	Yes	Yes	Yes	Yes	Yes

Rates include port charges.

CABINS Although cabins are somewhat compact, they're noticeably larger (by about 17%) than the cramped cubicles that were standard issue on RCCL megavessels in the past. Inside cabins begin at a cozy 138 square feet and move up to the Royal Suite's mammoth 1,150 square feet. Nearly one-fourth of the cabins aboard each ship have private verandas, a reflection of the most modern trends in cruise-ship construction and a response to the number of private verandas available aboard such lines as Princess. A total of 388 cabins per ship can hold third and fourth passengers, but most RCCL passengers don't opt to take advantage of this. Each vessel contains 17 staterooms, within a variety of price ranges, specifically designed for persons with disabilities.

RECREATION & FITNESS FACILITIES
Each contains an 18-hole, 6,000-square-foot miniature golf course and a two-story, big-windowed health club/exercise room/spa. This segues gracefully into an outdoor deck area whose pool and entertainment facilities can be covered during inclement weather by a futuristic-looking glass canopy. The onboard fitness program is named "Ship-Shape."

PUBLIC AREAS Wood (usually teak and cherry wood) and brass, luxuriant fountains and foliage, and carefully chosen artwork and textures highlight the public areas. Some public areas evoke a private Roman villa; others are deliberately glitzier and flashier, with more glitz than any of RCCL's previous ships. Different areas of the ship were designed to evoke different places in America—for example, a wine bar in New York or a gambling hall in Las Vegas. Aboard both ships, multimillion-dollar art collections give you something to look at as you explore.

Focal points of both ships are the soaring seven-story atriums known as "Centrum." Each is crowned by a sloped two-deck-high skylight. Glass elevators, à la Hyatt, take passengers up through Centrum into the Viking Crown Lounge, a glass-sided aerie high above the waves. Accessorized with a superb sound and light system, it's high on the roster of everybody's favorite space for wave-watching and sightseeing, especially during transits of the Panama Canal. In deliberate contrast to such massive, showcase spaces, each ship contains many hideaway refuges, including an array of cocktail bars (usually with themes), a library, card rooms, and a conference room that can hold up to 200 people. Eleven very busy elevators interconnect the ships' many decks. Humanity and warmth are maintained with more than 1,800 potted plants and more than 3,000 original artworks aboard each ship.

Dining rooms aboard both vessels span two decks that are interconnected with a very grand staircase and flanked with walls of glass nearly 20 feet high. Each seats 1,050 passengers within a milieu that's contemporary and tasteful, replete with lots of stainless steel, mirrors, dramatic chandeliers, and a massive grand piano that provides highly digestible music throughout the dinner service.

Full musical revues are staged in glittery auditoriums, each of which seats 800 and spans two decks. Each has an orchestra pit that can be raised and lowered hydraulically to provide dramatic effect during cabaret shows.

The ship's casinos are deliberately glittery, and consciously overaccessorized with hundreds of gambling stations so densely packed that it's sometimes diffi-

cult to move and always difficult to hear. Expect all the sound and fury of Atlantic City within the casino precincts.

Each ship has a higher-than-expected amount of open deck areas. One of the most dramatic is the Sun Deck, which manages to incorporate a swimming pool, whirlpools, and a food service area whose comfortable seating and potted plants can be covered with a huge glass roof. Because of its engineering, this roof allows more light to filter through than any equivalent transparent dome afloat.

On a decidedly downscale note, some passengers regret the lack of self-service Laundromats, although few passengers really seem to want to interrupt the fun to do their wash.

Majesty of the Seas • Monarch of the Seas

⚓ ⚓ ⚓ ⚓

Specifications

Size (in tons)	73,941	Crew	822/825 (International)
Number of Cabins	1,177	Passenger/Crew Ratio	2.9 to 1
Number of Outside Cabins	732	Year Built	1992/1991
Number of Passengers	2,354	Last Major Refurbishment	n/a
Officers	Norwegian		

Frommer's Ratings (Scale of 1–10)

Activities	7.8	Public Areas	8.0
Cabins	7.2	Public Comfort/Space	7.9
Cleanliness/Maintenance	8.2	Recreational Facilities/Pool	7.8
Entertainment	8.3	Service	7.6
Food & Beverage	7.8	Ship Crew/Officers	8.0
Interior Decor	7.8	Shore Excursions	7.6
Ports of Call	7.6	Worth the Money	7.8
		Overall Average	**7.8**

Built at the same Breton shipyard in western France (in 1992 and 1991, respectively) for a cost of $300 million each, these mirror-image twins are about 4,000 tons heavier than most of the megaships

they're in competition with and boast dimensions that rival the great transatlantic liners of the 1930s. Their oceangoing profiles are clean, distinguished, and accented with architectural features unique to RCCL. Foremost among these is the glass-sided circular observation platform that completely encircles the smokestack. Their proportions are monstrous, with 14 passenger decks and 11 passenger elevators (plus several others for baggage and crew), a dazzling lineup of public spaces, and a roster of activities and entertainments that rivals those offered in many small cities.

Cabins & Rates*

Cabins	Average per diem	Bathtub	Fridge	Phone	Sitting Area	TV
Inside	$230–$245	No	No	Yes	No	Yes
Outside	$275–$285	Half	No	Yes	Half	Yes
Suite	$380–$400	Yes	Half	Yes	Yes	Yes

Rates include port charges.

CABINS   Small cabins are these vessels' only flaw, but bear in mind that Royal Caribbean's belief when this ship was constructed was that cabins are for activities that most passengers perform with their eyes closed, and therefore could be designed without undue amounts of space.

There are 16 different size and amenity categories, and cabins within each are rigidly standardized in their floor layout and size. Standard cabins, scattered over nine decks, average a not-very-generous 120 square feet. In 64 of the outside cabins, some of the cramped feeling is relieved by verandas. About 116 of the cabins contain both upper and lower berths in order to house four, albeit quite tightly. Suites are larger, of course, and moderately more comfortable than the standard cabins. The Royal Suites and the owner's suites are significantly larger. In each cabin, beds can be moved to form either doubles or twins. Bathrooms are adequate but not frilly or plush.

None of the cabins is designated explicitly as a single. About a dozen staterooms aboard either vessels are configured for complete wheelchair access.

RECREATION & FITNESS FACILITIES

Two good-sized swimming pools are located on the Sports Deck, and each is ringed with chaise lounges. Looking at this space when it's empty, you'd think there's all the room in the world, but when the ship is full, the rows of sunbathers resemble sardines in a tin.

As part of RCCL's ShipShape fitness program, you can work out in some very large exercise areas, and some activities spill out onto the decks. On both ships, a state-of-the-art gymnasium has weight-training facilities, ballet bars, Stair-Masters, treadmills, rowing machines, and stationary bicycles. Flashing lights and digital displays show how much energy you've expended on the machines. There are seven massage cubicles, plus separate saunas for men and women.

A jogging track encircles one deck. At $1/3$ mile, it's much, much longer than those aboard most other vessels. There's a basketball court near each vessel's stern.

PUBLIC AREAS   The public areas glitter with as much pizzazz as those aboard all RCCL megaships, featuring the glass-ringed observation lounges set midway up the ship's smokestack, 150 feet above sea level. If prompted, any of the perky bartenders there can mix you a drink color-coordinated to whatever you happen to be wearing.

Public areas are wisely clustered aft of the atrium to minimize noise in the forward section of the ship, where cabins are. Broadway musicals and Hollywood films inspired the names and decor of most public areas: the Brigadoon dining room, the Ain't Misbehavin' Nightclub, the April in Paris Lounge. The five-story atrium, with a color scheme that glows in a metallic shade of either bronze or champagne, is the ship's interior focal point.

Public rooms include a paneled library any passenger would be proud to have at home, a massive showroom suitable for up to 350 guests, and a host of other bars and cubbyholes scattered throughout the ship, some with modern art nouveau decors. One of the largest casinos afloat whirs and clangs with a bustle worthy of Vegas or Atlantic City.

Traffic flow within these ships is surprisingly graceful. Passengers don't seem to get lost very often, thanks to intelligent layouts, clear markings, and the interconnections provided by the ship's huge atrium. Although this is a monstrous cruise ship, it's so well designed that only when you find yourself standing in long lines does it become irritating and uncomfortable.

Nordic Empress

⬇ ⬇ ⬇ ⬇

Specifications

Size (in tons)	48,563	Crew	671 (International)
Number of Cabins	800	Passenger/Crew Ratio	2.4 to 1
Number of Outside Cabins	471	Year Built	1990
Number of Passengers	1,600	Last Major Refurbishment	n/a
Officers	Scandinavian		

Frommer's Ratings (Scale of 1–10)

Activities	7.8	Public Areas	7.5
Cabins	7.2	Public Comfort/Space	7.4
Cleanliness/Maintenance	8.2	Recreational Facilities/Pool	7.2
Entertainment	8.0	Service	7.5
Food & Beverage	7.6	Ship Crew/Officers	8.0
Interior Decor	7.5	Shore Excursions	6.5
Ports of Call	7.0	Worth the Money	8.5
		Overall Average	**7.6**

This hefty 48,000-ton vessel looks small when compared to the megaships comprising the rest of Royal Caribbean's modern fleet. Originally part of Admiral Cruises, a now-defunct subsidiary of RCCL during its early days, the vessel was retained by RCCL in an bid to capture a segment of the short-term cruise market—that is, jaunts of three and four days. In many ways, *Nordic Empress* is one of the best among vessels contending in the whoopee-oriented Florida-to-Bahamas short-haul sweepstakes. It was specifically created for this type of cruise, where passengers tend to hurl themselves into onboard activities, knowing they don't have a languorous week to explore

their surroundings, and its designers built in the most bang for the buck. *Nordic Empress* is consistently flooded with sunlight from big windows, which dominate most of the ship's stern end, and is almost always illuminated after dark. This contrasts with RCCL's longer-haul vessels, which are often decorated in soothing colors that passengers won't tire of.

The short duration and relatively inexpensive price of cruises aboard the *Nordic Empress* tend to attract passengers who are younger and less prosperous than those taking the line's seven-day outings. A higher percentage of families are also likely to be on board, so there's more energy and high jinks. In addition, many corporate incentive groups have discovered the cost-effectiveness of short three- or four-day seminars aboard this vessel, so a higher percentage of incentive groups may be traveling en masse than you're likely to find aboard RCCL's longer (and more expensive) excursions.

Cabins & Rates*

Cabins	Average per diem	Bathtub	Fridge	Phone	Sitting Area	TV
Inside	$235	No	No	Yes	No	Yes
Outside	$310	Yes	Yes	Yes	Yes	Yes
Suite	$485	Yes	Yes	Yes	Yes	Yes

Rates include port charges.

CABINS   Aboard this ship, which was specifically designed for short cruises, RCCL stuck firmly to its belief (subsequently changed) that cabins are for activities that most passengers perform with their eyes closed, and therefore can be designed without undue amounts of space. Consequently, cabins are small, not more than 130 square feet, equivalent in size and amenities to those aboard the *Sovereign,* the *Majesty,* and the *Monarch.* There are a dozen different cabin categories.

Although small, the cabins are carefully designed, which makes them seem more livable. But a large number of cabins are inside and downright claustrophobic, practically guaranteeing passengers will spend as much time as possible on deck or in public areas. Cabins in the upper echelon and suites have their own verandas. Outside cabins have rectangular picture windows, not the less panoramic round portholes. Even if you upgrade for one of the smaller suites, you won't gain that much additional elbow room, although amenities and location within the vessel are more convenient.

Each cabin has a multichannel music system, closets with barely adequate storage space, and twin beds that can be reconfigured as doubles. Soundproofing is fairly good. Most cabins are decorated with blonde wood trim and pale colors. There are no singles.

Four cabins are wheelchair accessible, and wheelchair users will find the ship friendly, with level floors and oversize bathrooms with rails. Most elevators also accommodate the standard wheelchair. However, the line still requires that an able-bodied person accompany a person with a disability.

RECREATION & FITNESS FACILITIES On the Sun Deck, where virtually everything seems to happen, there are three whirlpools, a generous swimming pool fed by a fountain, a wading pool for children, and enough shady spots to protect your skin from the sun.

Although the exercise area isn't the largest afloat, it contains representative samplings of all the facilities you'd find aboard RCCL's megaships. There's a sauna, plus massage, and the ship has an unobstructed jogging track where five laps equals a mile.

During days ashore at RCCL's private Bahamian island, CocoCay, the ShipShape program swings into high gear. You can participate in virtually any kind of water sport or fitness activity, under trained supervision.

PUBLIC AREAS   Considering the relatively small size of this vessel, the inclusion of a nine-deck atrium, which penetrates the ship's center, was an astonishing design choice. (Atriums aboard RCCL's megaships extend through only five or seven decks.) Aboard the *Empress,* light floods into the atrium from above and from big windows flanking five decks on either side. So intent were the designers on creating a razzle-dazzle venue for exciting parties that they sacrificed space that might otherwise have gone toward cabins. Adding to the decor are a splashing fountain ringed with tropical plants and unusual and original artwork based on Nordic themes.

It's easy to navigate through the *Nordic Empress,* even after a round of sunset-colored drinks. Pedestrian thoroughfares run along one side of the ship, not down the center as you might expect.

More than aboard any other ship in RCCL's fleet, the Sun Deck is an important venue for both daytime and nighttime diversions. Loaded with sunbathers during the day, the deck is transformed into a starlit dance floor at night. Fountains, a gazebo, and canopies inspired by the sails of an old-fashioned ship add to the outdoor decor.

Whimsical themes abound, including a bar designed like a children's merry-go-round, and the Windjammer, a cafe

perched high above the officer's bridge, where passengers can scan the seas ahead. *Nordic Empress,* like every other RCCL ship in the Caribbean, boasts its own version of the Viking Crown Lounge. Positioned at the ship's stern like all the others and sitting 11 stories above the waterline, it's a bit less dramatically cantilevered from the ship's smokestack than its equivalents aboard RCCL's megaships.

Public lounges adopt the same Broadway/hip-hip-hooray themes as other vessels within the RCCL fleet, with perhaps more emphasis on giddiness and high energy. The Strike Up the Band Showroom, for instance, is very Atlantic City and very, very pink. In all, there are six bars, three entertainment lounges, a vibrant disco, a video game room, a conference center, and a three-level casino spread over two decks.

Sovereign of the Seas

⇩ ⇩ ⇩ ⇩

Specifications

Size (in tons)	73,192	Crew	808 (International)
Number of Cabins	1,138	Passenger/Crew Ratio	2.8 to 1
Number of Outside Cabins	722	Year Built	1988
Number of Passengers	2,276	Last Major Refurbishment	1996
Officers	Norwegian		

Frommer's Ratings (Scale of 1–10)

Activities	7.8	Public Areas	7.8
Cabins	7.2	Public Comfort/Space	7.2
Cleanliness/Maintenance	8.2	Recreational Facilities/Pool	7.8
Entertainment	8.3	Service	7.6
Food & Beverage	7.8	Ship Crew/Officers	8.0
Interior Decor	7.6	Shore Excursions	7.6
Ports of Call	7.6	Worth the Money	7.8
		Overall Average	**7.7**

When it was launched in 1988, after costing $185 million to build, the *Sovereign of the Seas* stopped traffic along freeways all up and down the Miami harbor front. Most travel agents, as well as RCCL itself,

tend to classify this ship in the same category as two later models, *Monarch of the Seas* and *Majesty of the Seas;* however, the *Sovereign* has a slightly different deck layout and weighs a bit less. When launched, it was the largest passenger vessel built during the previous 48 years and the largest cruise ship in history. Enough steel went into its construction to rebuild Paris's Eiffel Tower twice.

The ship's design was fussed over, fretted over, and debated long and intensely within the corridors of RCCL. The result included features that were exotic and radical at the time, but have since been copied (with subtle improvements) in the *Monarch* and the *Majesty,* as well as closely observed by competing line's designers.

As happens with all neophytes that are celebrated during their debuts and later relegated to less prominent status, the *Sovereign,* prototype for at least eight other vessels either afloat today or soon to be launched, is now a piece of nautical history, a sea horse with a sense of nostalgia that doesn't apply to any other vessel in the RCCL fleet. In 1996, it was relieved of its duties in the seven-day cruise market (a niche that's traditionally favored by older, more affluent cruisers) and commissioned for a series of three- and four-day itineraries that are usually the domain of older, more battered vessels whose hard-partying and relatively inexperienced passengers inflict lots of wear and tear. To their credit, RCCL poured about $6 million that same year into a complete restoration of the craft, an act that brought the ship to a level that's close to the standards of newer members of its fleet. But basically, the vessel is congenially outmoded.

Passenger's complaints about the vague sense of anonymity that prevailed on board during the vessel's heyday was to a large part overcome during the 1996 refurbishment. Overall, despite its many virtues, cabin size is the ship's major drawback, corresponding as it does to RCCL's now-scrapped policy of building compact, small staterooms.

Cabins & Rates*

Cabins	Average per diem	Bathtub	Fridge	Phone	Sitting Area	TV
Inside	$200	No	No	Yes	No	Yes
Outside	$270	Half	No	Yes	Half	Yes
Suite	$450	Yes	Half	Yes	Yes	Yes

Rates include port charges.

CABINS   Arched ceilings and light-toned colors try to make the cabins appear larger than they are, but can't really disguise the fact they average a mere 120 square feet. There are also a surprisingly large number of inside cabins (419 in all), proof of RCCL's commitment to devote as much room as possible to spacious and appealing public areas.

All cabins, regardless of their size, location, or configuration, have music channels, double beds that can convert into twins, and limited closet space. Unless you opt to upgrade to a suite, you won't find much difference in the sizes of cabins. Price differences depend on the cabin's position within the various decks. Bathrooms have a standard comfort level and are adequate but not frilly or plush.

Sovereign isn't as well equipped for wheelchair users as *Monarch* or *Majesty.* However, 10 staterooms have extrawide doors. Corridors tend to be wide, and elevators for the most part are wheelchair accessible.

RECREATION & FITNESS FACILITIES Deck layout and the two good-sized swimming pools are stylish and impressive when they're empty, but the staggering number of passengers aboard this ship almost guarantees that they'll fill up. Other than that, virtually all aspects of the fitness programs aboard *Sovereign of the Seas* are equivalent to those aboard the *Majesty* and the *Monarch.*

PUBLIC AREAS   A five-story atrium interconnects most of the ship's many splashy and airy public areas, which are outfitted in appropriately theatrical styles.

As in RCCL's later ships, public areas are clustered stern side. Cabins are mainly near the bow, creating the illusion that this mighty vessel is more intimate than it is. The ship features the RCCL architectural trademark, the Viking Crown Lounge that encircles the smokestack and offers views from an altitude almost as high as the crown of New York's Statue of Liberty. There is the same medley of restaurants (here named Gigi and Kismet), show lounges, bars, and lounges already described under reviews of the *Monarch* and *Majesty*.

The layout, however, is somewhat more awkward than that aboard the abovementioned vessels. Lines tend to be longer at elevators, and there are fewer intimate hideaways and cubbyholes. Any design glitches, however, are balanced out by the art collection, worth an estimated $2.7 million.

Royal Olympic Cruises (Sun Line / Epirotiki)

SHIPS Stella Solaris

1 Rockefeller Plaza, Suite 315, New York, NY 10020. ☎ 800/872-6400 or 212/397-6400; fax 212/765-9685.

Royal Olympic was created from the merger of the well-respected Sun Line Cruises with the more middle-brow Epirotiki Cruises in 1995. Although it operates an aging fleet, it is known for its onboard lectures, well-conceived entertainment, and unique itineraries that combine treks through the Caribbean with some other attraction, usually tours up the Amazon or through the Panama Canal. Its main appeal, though, lies in warm personal service. The average staff member has been with the line 14 years, and some crew members and officers, most of whom are Greek, have been around since the early 1970s. They make a point of remembering names and faces and are unusually cheerful about welcoming passengers aboard "their home." This has led to an enormous repeat business among mature, affluent, frequent travelers.

The *Stella Solaris* is the only Greek-registered ship making regular runs through the Caribbean, and this fact contributes to the heights of seagoing affability the staff typically achieves. By Greek law, ships registered in Greece must hire a predesignated number of Greek nationals to staff its ships, and as most Greek sailors and stewards are members of the powerful Greek maritime union, their pay is higher, and often much higher, than aboard many other cruise ships. As such, many of the staff have made service aboard the *Stella Solaris* into a career, and so imbue their jobs with a commitment that doesn't always appear aboard lines with a more transient staff.

PROS & CONS With the *Stella Solaris*, what you see is what you get. In spite of its age, it has been well maintained over the decades. Its last major refurbishment occurred in 1995, with additional changes of a less all-encompassing nature completed late in 1996.

The ship's crew is the most homogeneous and friendly of any major cruise line. There are no bells and whistles, just good service and convivial warm attention, enjoyed by the mainly repeat passengers. There's no better authentic Greek hospitality in the Caribbean.

Its second biggest draw is its size: only 620 passengers. In this age of megaliners, it's refreshing to be on a medium-size ship that year in and year out maintains a steadfast level of quality service and cleanliness. The ship has the intimacy of a smaller vessel without sacrificing some of the first-class amenities and services of the largest ships afloat.

If you're seeking a new ship with glitz and glamour, you're on the wrong boat, but if you like trustworthy comfort, absolutely no neon, and a sense of cruising on a scale less gargantuan than that proposed by many newer lines, consider the *Stella Solaris*.

TYPES OF PASSENGERS The repeat passengers, especially on the Caribbean winter cruises, tend to be in the 40 to 70 age bracket, and are often married. In winter, some three-quarters of the passengers are 55-plus, many with incomes ranging upward from $75,000. The greatest number of travelers are from Florida, the New York metropolitan area, Texas, and California.

These well-traveled folks are on this older ship because they know what they can expect, and like it. Many passengers are adventure-oriented and come aboard hoping that *Solaris'* unique cruises, especially trips to the Amazon following stopovers in the Caribbean, will give them something new and different. The *Solaris* also attracts those people, largely drawn from the professions, who are interested in the food, culture, and life of Greece.

The *Stella* is not for the sequin crowd who want to strut their finery, enjoying casinos and late-night disco action. Most passengers are in bed by midnight. There are also no provisions for children, except for a handful of organized activities that might appear aboard the Christmas cruise.

DINING   The food is what you'd expect at a good Greek restaurant, with an emphasis on popular international dishes. The line doesn't even try to compete with the haute cuisine and the high-priced chefs aboard Seabourn or Celebrity ships, but it's justifiably proud of its dinner cuisine and the variety of offerings presented at each course.

The kitchen is best when it serves Greek food. Mezes (appetizers) and psarosoupa (fish soup) are served along with souvlaki (meat kebabs) and moussaka (meat pie). The feta cheese alone is eaten at the rate of a ton a year. There's regular and standard cruise fare for those who don't want to go Greek.

The dining room is spacious, the noise level under control, and there are two assigned seatings. Breakfast and lunch are open seatings. The wine list has the popular names and bottles. Don't ask for Greek retsina, either regular or fortified, as it's not available. But ouzo certainly is.

Fairly routine breakfast and luncheon buffets are served on the Lido Deck. Each mealtime features a spa cuisine, conforming to what the chef calls low-sodium, low-cholesterol, and low-fat recipes.

ACTIVITIES   This is not an action-oriented ship, and there are no unusual surprises in the activities department. Dance lessons are given, fitness classes conducted, and bridge tournaments staged, along with arts and crafts demonstrations, backgammon, and films shown daily in the theater. Best are the lectures given en route and in the Amazon after leaving the major Caribbean ports of call.

Activities sometimes center around whatever theme happens to be promoted during any particular cruise. Greek nights are likely to include joining in the Greek dancing. If lessons are offered before that event, it's wise to attend. During cruises that coincide with solar eclipses or the vernal equinox, there will be lots of attention paid to lectures on Mayan art and architecture, examining and explaining the mystical patterns the shadows make as they fall across Mayan ruins.

CHILDREN'S ACTIVITIES   There are few children aboard a *Solaris* cruise except at Christmas, and consequently there are extremely limited facilities for them. However, if 15 children are on board, the line offers a special program, led by trained counselors. Activities include games, scavenger hunts, ice-cream parties, and other diversions. With several hours advance notification, baby-sitting can be arranged. The cost is around $5 per hour, paid directly to whatever staff member has volunteered his or her service during off-hours.

ENTERTAINMENT   Each evening there's a wholesome floor show—a magician, solo singer, dance team, or other specialty act. The best night is "Greek Night," when the crew puts on a Greek show that always wins a standing ovation. While entertainment is obviously presented on a limited budget, most passengers seem pleased. The Main Lounge (aka the Solaris Lounge) is quite a large room, holding up to 550 passengers. There is a slight tiering around the edges, but this doesn't do much for the sight lines, which are not very good due to the deck-level dance floor and entertainment area, not to mention the columns rimming it.

In the Bar Grill Room you'll find bartender Simos Tzagos, who has dispensed his special Bloody Marys since 1967 and seems to remember everyone's name and drink choice. Whatever he puts into that Bloody Mary should be available commercially—but it's not. Likewise, the potato chips are made fresh every day and are served with a sauce as secret as the Bloody Mary. Pianist Billy Dare has been a fixture here since 1990.

Sternward is the Piano Bar, which stretches across the breadth of the ship. The bar stools offer an excellent sea view over the stern. Other than the vista, the number-one attraction is the affable Stelios (Steve) Likuris, who has officiated here since the ship was christened.

There are two small but separate gambling areas; one contains games involving croupiers, whereas the other, less glamorous room is devoted exclusively to slot machines. There is also a disco and a large video screen and bar.

Two specially designated "dance hosts" are aboard the ship to dance, socialize, play cards, accompany passengers on shore excursions, and generally keep the good times rolling.

SHOPPING   One small shop, located just outside the main dining room, carries some souvenir Greek items, sweaters, women's clothing, the usual T-shirts, coffee mugs, and jewelry (some very expensive).

SERVICE   The staff and crew are among the best in the industry, rivaled only by the more upmarket Seabourn vessels. The tradition of Greek hospitality is maintained by all of them, and it's obvious they take pride in their ship and in pleasing passengers.

Published criticisms that the waiters hustle you in and out of the dining room aren't substantiated by our experience, nor the experience of any of the *Solaris* passengers we interviewed. In our view, the dining room presentation is unhurried and gracious.

Housekeeper Irene Kragt deserves a special star for her industry and her ability to keep the vessel spick-and-span. Tips are pooled. Only the barber, beautician, and masseuse get individual tips.

ITINERARIES   Unlike cruise lines that repeat the same seven-day Caribbean itinerary with little or no variation, *Stella Solaris* offers cruises that tend to be very different one from another, and usually feature Caribbean ports as diversions en route to either the Amazon or the Panama Canal. Depending on the itinerary, cruises of between 12 and 16 days offer stopovers at such ports as Key West, Cozumel, Trinidad, St. Vincent, Antigua, San Juan, Curaçao, St. Lucia, St. Thomas, Bequia, and Barbados. Other stops on these junkets, which sometimes chug on toward the Mediterranean, include such Amazonian ports as Manaus, Santarem, and Boca de Valeria. Fort Lauderdale and Galveston, Texas, are the points of origin for many of these cruises, a fact that offers easy access to clients based in Texas.

SPECIAL DISCOUNTS   An early booking could mean a discount of anywhere from 10% to 50%. If the company quotes a fare with airfare included, and you arrange your own airfare, you'll receive a discount, but know in advance that arranging economically priced airfare into such ports of departure as Manaus, Brazil, will be difficult at rates less than those the line quotes. Repeaters, of which there are many, get special discounts on predesignated sailings. On some promotional round-trip Amazon cruises, or during spring or fall repositionings between the eastern and western hemispheres, twofers are usually offered.

Children ages 2 to 14 who share their cabin with two full-fare adults pay half the minimum tariff, and babies under age two travel free. If three or four persons agree to share a communal cabin, each will receive a discount of around 15% off the brochure rate, plus whatever other discounts apply at the time of their booking.

SINGLE SUPPLEMENTS   A solo passenger is charged 150% to 200% of the regular double-occupancy rate. If requested, the cruise line can arrange for singles to share a cabin with another same-sex traveler, paying the regular double occupancy rate.

PORT CHARGES   Port charges for Caribbean sailings vary from $160 to $190 for cruises of between 12 and 16 days.

Stella Solaris

⇓ ⇓ ⇓

Specifications

Size (in tons)	17,832	Crew	310 (Greek/Filipino)
Number of Cabins	541	Passenger/Crew Ratio	2 to 1
Number of Outside Cabins	329	Year Built	1953
Number of Passengers	620	Last Major Refurbishment	1995
Officers	Greek		

Frommer's Ratings (Scale of 1–10)

Activities	5.8	Public Areas	7.4
Cabins	7.2	Public Comfort/Space	7.1
Cleanliness/Maintenance	8.2	Recreational Facilities/Pool	5.0
Entertainment	6.2	Service	9.0
Food & Beverage	7.3	Ship Crew/Officers	9.5
Interior Decor	7.4	Shore Excursions	9.0
Ports of Call	8.5	Worth the Money	9.5
		Overall Average	**7.6**

Stella Solaris was built in France in 1953 and features a relatively deep keel of 29 feet, a fact that keeps it fairly stable during stormy weather. It was originally conceived as a cargo ship, *Camboge,* for long-haul transits across rough seas to what was then known as French Indochina. In 1973, it was bought by Greek-owned Sun Line, stripped to its hull at a shipyard in Piraeus, and radically reconfigured into the comfortable but unpretentious cruise ship you'll see today. Of the original vessel, only the hull and the engines remained in place. Today, with an exterior painted in the dark blue that was the trademark of Sun Line, it's the most obviously Greek ship sailing the Caribbean.

Cabins & Rates

Cabins	Average per diem	Bathtub	Fridge	Phone	Sitting Area	TV
Inside	$265	No	No	Yes	No	Yes
Outside	$315	Half	No	Yes	No	Yes
Suite	$420	Yes	Yes	Yes	Yes	Yes

CABINS   There are 11 different price categories, and these staterooms come in all shapes and sizes. Most cabins are generously proportioned, especially the outside cabins on the Golden, Ruby, and Emerald Decks. No cabins have balconies, however, and unlike the walls on a Seabourn vessel, for instance, the walls in the *Solaris* have inadequate soundproofing.

Furnishings are comfortable and include a dresser with drawers that can be locked. Closet and drawer space is reasonably generous, but don't bring everything you own aboard. The better rooms often contain a small sofa and coffee table. All cabins have four-channel music programs. If you're with a third or fourth passenger, you can ask for a standard outside cabin or else a superior inside. You may be able to connect some cabins if you're traveling with a family. There are no single cabins.

If you're looking for a bargain, book the most cost-conscious cabins in category 11 on the Sapphire Deck. They are not serviced by an elevator, so you'll have to walk down one deck to reach them. These cabins are a bit cramped, but adequate, and they have both a lower and an upper berth.

The smoothest sailing we have found is in one of the smaller but first-class suites amidships on the Ruby Deck. Those prone to motion sickness might want to book here. You get portholes instead of windows, however.

The best bet, if you can afford it, are the Fantasy Suites on the Boat Deck. They come in a variety of styles, but all have sitting areas with queen-size or twin beds. Closets here are the most generous on the ship, and baths have tubs, unlike most other cabins, which have a shower only.

On the Boat Deck, the 34 deluxe outside cabins live up to their high rank, but a drawback is that when the curtains are open fellow passengers can peer into your suite. Those wanting greater privacy can book one of 16 deluxe cabins on the Ruby Deck, which are about the same size and have windows that open onto the sea.

There are no cabins for persons with disabilities.

RECREATION & FITNESS FACILITIES

Since not every passenger wants to use the twin swimming pools at the same time, these public bathing facilities are generally adequate. The lounging area around these pools is narrow, but allows for deck chairs. The *Solaris* has a much-photographed figure-eight swimming pool. Usually a "mermaid" reclines on the small platform separating the two pools. Waiters from the Lido Bar serve tropical drinks to sunbathing passengers.

After the most recent renovations, the heretofore modest gym was vastly improved. New equipment includes a step machine, free weights, slant boards for sit-ups, and exercise bicycles. Massage and

sauna rooms are also available, as are the services of a modest spa, with beauty and health treatments available.

Joggers or strollers use the outside promenade; if you go around it about seven times, you'll have gone a mile. Regular aerobics classes are also given.

PUBLIC AREAS The 1995 renovations have improved the public rooms considerably. The main show lounge and the casino, for example, have been enlarged, and new carpets and fresh flowers make the public rooms more inviting than they've been in years.

The public areas have a European-style elegance. Even when the ship is fully booked, the passenger flow through them moves smoothly.

From the spacious 450-seat dining room forward to the 550-seat Main Lounge and Piano Bar aft, the Solaris Deck is *the* passenger activity deck. The commodious lobby and purser's office amidships is the crossroads of the *Solaris*. If you're looking for someone, stand here and they'll eventually pass by.

One of the most unusual rooms on the *Solaris* is the disco. Its walls are a replica of the hull of an old wooden ship, and red carpeting contrasts vividly with ivory chairs, hassocks, and a black tile dance floor.

Only eight of the nine decks, named after gems such as sapphire, ruby, or emerald, are in use. The unused top deck offers a great deal of space, but it's in front of the amidships smokestack. Gusty winds often sweep this top deck, and exhaust noise from the turbines make the back of the deck unusable.

From the Lido Bar, lifeboats obscure the view of the seascape, but there's a clear view from the Lido Deck's sunning area. You have to walk to the Lido Bar, as there is no elevator. That can be quite a feat when the decks are swept by rains and winds.

To imbue you with the Greek mystique, the ship's owners purchased a mammoth bronze screen to separate the

Piano Bar from the Solaris Main Lounge. Luzzati, the Italian artist who is known mainly for his set designs for La Scala in Milan, depicted scenes from the *Iliad* and the *Odyssey*, including the Trojan Horse legend. Whatever becomes of the aging *Solaris* in years to come, we hope this creative art is saved for posterity—there is nothing quite like it in the world.

You'll find a cozy nest one flight up on the Boat Deck, a reading room and card room that provides a tranquil retreat.

Seabourn Cruise Line

SHIPS   Seabourn Pride

55 Francisco St., Suite 710, San Francisco, CA 94133. ☎ 800/929-9595 or 415/391-7444; fax 415/391-8518.

All things considered—size, design, decor, cuisine, service, itineraries—Seabourn offers the best cruise product at sea. It has unprecedented amounts of onboard space for each passenger, service worthy of the grand hotels of Europe, and the hushed, ever-so-polite ambience that appeals to prosperous, usually older clients who shun publicity and like having logistical details taken care of for them. This line is a genuine aristocrat, with perfect manners. If you're the type of client who responds to discretion and a subdued good taste, it might be perfect for you. A travel agent faced with a "which ship is for us" query from Henry and Nancy Kissinger would definitely book them on Seabourn.

If you opt for a ride aboard Seabourn, you'll be entering an absolutely stratospheric microniche of the cruise-ship industry: The fees it charges are about three times the industry average, and its passengers account for only one-half of 1% of the industry's berths. In fact, the 8,000 passengers the line carried in 1995 equals only about a third of the passengers that Carnival, Seabourn's mass-market co-owner, carries in an average week. This is luxury sailing at its most exclusive, as small-scale and big-ticket as you'll find without buying your own yacht.

Seabourn was established in 1987 by Warren Titus, the creative force behind Royal Viking Line and a patriarch of the luxury cruise industry. (Titus is still senior vice president of the line, and president of the mostly ceremonial Seabourn Club.) Titus was financed in his venture by Norwegian shipping mogul Atle Brynestad, then in his 30s, who had single-handedly established a knitting factory at age 16 and subsequently amassed a billion-dollar fortune.

The line got off to a jerky start when its owners announced its debut as Signet Cruises, spending loads of money on ad campaigns showing the distinguished-looking, tuxedo-clad Mr. Titus standing on a pier. Industry gossips and visionaries predicted a level of luxury not seen since the days of Cleopatra's barge. But, to everyone's dismay, an obscure outfit in Texas immediately sued, claiming to have already trademarked "Signet Cruises" for a venture that was never developed. So Titus switched the name to Seabourn and established joint headquarters in San Francisco and Oslo. Seabourn remains the only cruise line functioning from a San Francisco base.

Soon thereafter, Titus and Brynestad commissioned a trio of ultra-upscale vessels from a North German shipyard, each weighing 10,000 tons, more than twice as much as Cunard's ultra-upscale *Sea Goddess* vessels (4,250 tons each) with which they were designed to compete. Business boomed during the early years, and remarkably prescient management has kept the line riding high. To meet its vision of the perceived needs of the cruise industry, the line has taken risks other companies dared not. For example, as early as 1995, it scheduled, with appropriate publicity, many stopovers in Havana, Cuba—a bold step that many other lines were reluctant to rush into.

The following traits make the ships unusual: their roominess, their excellent service, and their stylishness. Much money was spent on streamlined, yacht-inspired designs that will probably remain in vogue for the next half-century. They manage to look both aggressive and elegant, and are small enough to venture safely into exotic harbors where mega-ships cannot go. Seeing one of the Seabourn vessels moored at St. George's Harbour in Grenada, one of the world's most colorful ports, is an especially beautiful sight. Neither grotesquely over-sized nor puny, the ship just seems to fit, subtly dominating every other vessel in the harbor. The whiteness of its hull is whiter than white, a white that the U.S. Navy would envy, a white almost blinding in bright sunlight.

Seabourn maintains strong links with its Norwegian roots, registering each of its ships in the country and preferring to re-stock many of its marine supplies there. This fact reinforces the understated sense of Norwegian nationalism on board. Plus, Norway is among the most prestigious places in the maritime world to register a ship—though it's also one of the most expensive.

In 1992, one of the oddest marriages in the shipping industry occurred. Carnival, an extremely wealthy and large mass-market outfit, bought 25% of Seabourn. Three years later, in December 1995, Carnival exercised its option to buy an additional 25%, bringing its ownership of the company to half, a co-ownership it shares today with company founder Atle Brynestad. With this acquisition, Carnival's influence extended up and down the cruise industry ladder, from the very prosperous (Seabourn) and rather prosperous (Windstar) to the upper-middle to middle-of-the-road (Holland America) and mass-market (Carnival).

Seabourn's roster of vessels is small—only three, the *Legend, Pride,* and *Spirit*—but each is choice. Of the three, only the *Pride,* built in 1988 for a cost of about $65 million, sails the Caribbean.

PROS & CONS The line's vessels of-fer unusual and creative itineraries that focus on ports that larger ships, with less well traveled clients, usually don't visit. Shore excursions are also suitably esoteric and upscale, more expensive and more unusual than a typical bus ride through hot, sweaty tropical landscapes.

Seabourn knows that many (if not most) of its clients are accustomed to spacious homes and would be unwilling to seques-ter themselves in oceangoing cubbyholes.

Consequently, each of the line's standard accommodations has an extremely gener-ous 277 square feet of space (compared to the 205-square-foot suites on the Cunard *Sea Goddesses*). Although many ships afloat have some suites that size, virtually none devote that amount of space to their standard units. Add in the fact that each Seabourn vessel carries only 200 passen-gers (as opposed to the 400 that most 10,000-ton vessels cruising today accom-modate), and you have an astonishing amount of space for each person aboard.

Therein lies the expense of a Seabourn cruise. Fees must be proportionally high to justify such space, but most passengers consider the cost completely justified. This is borne out by the fact that al-though housing third or fourth passengers in any accommodation would technically be possible, very few passengers opt to in-vite friends or children to share their space.

Then there's the service, which is flaw-less, and the strongly stated policy that passengers are not expected to tip—a fact that anyone, no matter how affluent, seems to appreciate.

What are the disadvantages of an expe-rience on Seabourn? There really aren't any, as long as you don't come aboard ex-pecting something the line has no inten-tion of providing. If you come aboard expecting to find romance, and upon scan-ning the dining room on your first night you see slim pickings for finding a soul mate, you're basically relegated to reading a good book and enjoying a pleasant, if passionless, cruise. You'll find none of the party atmosphere of a Carnival ship, and you will never, *ever* see an overstuffed car-toon character listing down the deck to-ward you. Lastly, entertainment on board is rather bland, and activities are limited because of the ships' relatively small size—but again, this is by design. This is the way the line's clientele wants it.

In the end, the only really glaringly un-attractive aspect to Seabourn is the ex-pense, which is higher than that charged for most luxury vessels, and much, much higher than the cost for more egalitarian lines. But if you can overcome that hurdle, the Seabourn experience can be delightful.

TYPES OF PASSENGERS Even Seabourn is reluctant to define a typical passenger. Obviously, most have comfortable household incomes, usually in excess of $200,000. Many are retired (or never worked to begin with), and many have net worths above $4 million—and sometimes much higher. Few seem to come aboard with children or grandchildren in tow. Seabourn simply isn't that kind of line. While children are allowed on board, there aren't any special facilities for their amusement.

In many ways, the passenger roster looks like the membership of a posh and somewhat reactionary country club, where old money judges new money, and new money had better do its best to look as well established as possible. Most passengers are North American, and dress in expensive clothes that aren't the least bit flashy. Passengers are not particularly chatty, giddy, or outgoing, and may exhibit their share of icy aloofness and judgmental toughness, both toward their fellow passengers and toward Seabourn. Many are likely to have sailed aboard other luxury cruise lines and stayed in five-star hotels. Passengers who expect to receive good service in an atmosphere of discreet gentility are the norm here.

If you're looking for the razzle-dazzle of a megaship and the company of only moderately self-disciplined people, don't sail with Seabourn. And if you're rich and bohemian, and consider yourself something of a wayfaring black sheep, stay well away. Onboard ambience can be rather stiff and self-consciously haute bourgeois. We also get the feeling that some clients might be rich enough to afford a one-time Seabourn experience, yet not so rich they don't slightly resent the line's high price tag. So if you consider yourself a maverick, hate to dress up, and are uncomfortable amid retired corporate moguls and status-conscious wannabes, you might not thrill to a Seabourn setting.

Those who appreciate the line, however, tend to come back for more: The line's history of repeaters is among the highest in the industry, sometimes as many as 50% aboard any given cruise.

DINING Cuisine is one of Seabourn's strongest points, matching what you'd find in a world-class European resort hotel. The line assumes that most of its passengers are used to getting what they want, usually whenever they want it, so meals are served in a manner that satisfies both appetite and the expectation of high-class service.

Tables seat up to 10, and you'll almost never have a problem getting a table for two, if that's your wish. Also, tables are spaced far enough apart so you'll never feel crowded. There are no set seating arrangements, so passengers can dine with whomever they want, just like at a private dinner party.

Service is high-style and intensely formal, but with humor, humanity, and an almost military precision. Staff members almost run at a trot through the elaborate, seven-course European service. It's all enormously appealing and extremely civilized.

Gentlemen are expected to wear jackets and, on most evenings, neckties as well. Two formal evenings are held during the course of any one-week cruise. Virtually every male present appears in a tuxedo, and the events are, indeed, very, very formal.

According to one company chef, Seabourn cuisine is an eclectic mix that allows each vessel's head chef to exercise his imagination, whimsy, and creative vision. There are old favorites such as beef Wellington, Dover sole, and broiled lobster; ethnic dishes reflecting the itinerary of wherever the ship happens to be at the time; and a mixture of light Pacific Rim and California cuisine. Dishes are prepared to order, spa menus are available at every meal, and passengers can make virtually any special request they want. Cuisine is more contemporary than the nouvelle cuisine of the '80s, and is permeated with contemporary French touches.

Yet don't expect troughs of caviar and buckets of foie gras whenever you want it. The food is less exhibitionistic than that, and less conspicuously self-indulgent. Caviar does appear once or maybe twice on the dinner menu, smeared atop a cunning assortment of canapés served during the cocktail hour, but Seabourn is not a line that feels the need to drench its passengers in culinary finery to ensure their goodwill.

If your mood doesn't call for the dining room, you can choose another venue. The Veranda Cafe serves bountiful breakfasts every morning, with omelets made fresh to your specifications, rows of herring and smoked salmon reflecting the ship's Norwegian origins, and every imaginable kind of food laid out as a decorative art form. The same Veranda is open at lunchtime, with salads, sandwich makings, pastas made at a moment's notice, and ice-cream buffets. Beach barbecues are held in grand style, with impeccable food and service.

Room service is available 24 hours a day. During normal lunch or dinner hours, your private meal can mirror the dining room service, right down to the silver, crystal, and porcelain. After hours, the menu is more limited, with burgers, salads, sandwiches, and pastas.

ACTIVITIES Warren Titus, the much-respected Seabourn patriarch, bristles at the notion that Seabourn vessels are small. He prefers to stress that they are ships with an unusually high amount of space per passenger, and the room to include many amenities that usually appear only on much larger vessels. However, that's not entirely accurate. Seabourn is weak on organized activities, but many passengers, as they say, just don't give a damn.

A daily schedule of activities is slipped under your cabin door every evening, but you'll never find any of the occasionally inane games—bingo, karaoke, men-in-lingerie contests—that are so beloved by more mass-market cruisers. The atmosphere is ever-tasteful, with never a hair out of place except during sporting activities, which are well organized and well supervised. There's also absolutely no pressure to participate in anything, which many passengers appreciate.

Activities include card games and tournaments, tours of the ship's galley, and visits to a cozy library with coffee-table books as well as tomes on philosophy and ethics. You'll soon realize that many passengers are aboard to read, quietly converse with their peers, and be ushered from one stylish, ever-so-polite spot to the next. For water sports, a platform is lowered into the sea from each vessel's stern, resulting in an instant marina, complete with Sunfish, kayaks, snorkeling gear, and high-speed banana boats for waterskiing or just letting it rip.

There are also few, if any, public announcements to disturb your solitude, which is a relief when compared to the barrage of noise broadcast aboard many other lines.

CHILDREN'S ACTIVITIES Children can come aboard Seabourn and are greeted with genuine warmth by the staff. After that, however, they're on their own: The line provides no special programs, no special menus, and no special concessions for children. This is exactly what most of the very adult passengers on board prefer. If there's a teenager on board, he or she will almost certainly appreciate the roster of land-based activities in the ports of call, but may be bored while at sea.

ENTERTAINMENT Entertainment is not Seabourn's strong suit. Generally speaking, it's so tasteful as to be dull and so polite as to be repressed, and simply isn't up to par with the programs offered by most mass-market cruise lines.

Star billings aboard Seabourn might fall to likable no-name singers taking a break from some touring Broadway show, piano meisters or affable personalities from southern cabarets, or starlets who have either faded or were never all that bright to begin with. Part of the problem derives from the fact that each Seabourn entertainer is expected to do double duty as social host or hostess, presiding over dinner tables and exhibiting perfect manners and a well-groomed appearance whenever they're not performing. The concept adds warmth to the general ambience, but only rarely heats up the stage. While the intention of the line's entertainment might be to emulate the style, wit, or charm of an urban supper club, it just doesn't hit the mark. At its best, it's tepid. At its worst, it's lackluster, pretentious, and dull. A resident dance band performs a likable but tame roster of old favorites.

The line offers lectures on whatever port of call is about to be visited from well-meaning resident travel experts. But since their talks are video-recorded and broadcast later on the ship's television network, only a handful of passengers actually attend. From time to time, the line manages to bring on glitterati like Patricia Neal, Art Buchwald, ambassador and Middle East negotiator Sol Linowitz, Mercury astronaut Wally Schirra, and Ian Campbell, general director of the San Diego Opera. Regrettably, the onboard participation of any of these stars can be very iffy, and when they do appear, they tend not to be featured on Seabourn's Caribbean sailings.

Gamblers take note: Each ship has a small-scale, staid, and rather sterile-looking casino sequestered behind glass near a piano bar. They rarely manage to be exciting, titillating, or fun, and most passengers tend to wander into them only once or twice during their cruise.

One bright spot in all of this involves the extraordinarily reasonable price Seabourn charges for drinks at its bars and for wines in its dining room. Even though a cruise is quite expensive, liquor is not. In this regard, the line is among the fairest in the cruise-ship industry.

SHOPPING Each Seabourn vessel contains a stylish boutique with the kind of merchandise upscale passengers seem to like and buy. Garments emblazoned with the Seabourn logo are well made and certainly not something you'd be embarrassed to wear after your return to the snow belt. There's also a worthy collection of perfumes, accessories for formal wear (cummerbunds, cuff links), and some awesomely beautiful gemstones of the kind a traveling millionaire might impulsively buy for his traveling companion. You won't find junk or petty souvenirs in any Seabourn boutique, as the line's purchasers fully understand that there's plenty of that available at any port of call.

SERVICE Seabourn maintains the finest roster of service staff of any line afloat. Most staff are young northern Europeans, many Norwegian, who are aggressively recruited after they've gained experience at one of the grand hotels of Europe, then put through a training program on the rigors of seagoing life. Most are in their 20s and 30s, and many develop discreet romantic links with other employees on board (marriages between employees are not infrequent). They are, overall, universally charming, competent, sensitive, and discreet—a joy, in short, and among Seabourn's most valuable assets.

Service is alert, sensitive, tactful, and ever-present. Seabourn recognizes the vital role its staff plays in the creation of a successful cruise line, and usually agrees, within reason, to pay for any additional training any of its employees want at Cornell University's School of Hotel Management.

Once you've paid the price of your initial cruise contract, this elevated degree of service comes for free. No tipping is allowed aboard a Seabourn vessel, a policy that makes many passengers wonder why other lines with less exemplary service make tipping such a heavy-handed aspect of each end-of-cruise experience.

ITINERARIES   Because of Seabourn's fleet expansion in early 1996, itineraries were less clearly defined and also dependent on the potential opening of Cuba as a possible port of call for passengers with American passports. Check with your travel agent or with Seabourn for an up-to-the-minute roster of ports of call and schedules, and remember that a second Seabourn vessel might put in a Caribbean appearance for at least part of the year, sometimes as one leg of a longer cruise.

Seabourn Pride—In winter, the *Pride* will depart from Fort Lauderdale on 16-day cruises that stop at Cozumel, Grand Cayman, Port Antonio (Jamaica), St. Barts, French St. Martin, Virgin Gorda, San Juan, Key West, and, pending U.S. government approval, Havana. Also available are seven-day cruises from Curaçao to Barbados, with an excursion into the mouth of the Orinoco River (Venezuela). In addition, 14-day trips from Fort Lauderdale to Curaçao will make intermediary stops at Havana (pending approval), ports along the Caribbean coast of Mexico, Honduras, sections of the Panama Canal, and Colombia. Other 14-day cruises from Fort Lauderdale go to San Juan, the British Virgin Islands, French St. Martin, St. Kitts, Antigua, St. Barts, Virgin Gorda, St. Thomas, and Havana (if approved). Passengers can opt to book segments of any of the longer cruises.

SPECIAL DISCOUNTS   As the cream of the world's passenger cruise lines, Seabourn does not encourage the belief that it actually discounts its products whenever ships aren't full enough. So while you can't telephone Seabourn and bargain a cruise contract down to what you think you can afford, there are ways to save some money.

An early payment program means that if you book and pay for your cruise a year ahead of your departure, you'll save 10%. If you book six months ahead of time, you'll save 5%. Yes, these advance savings programs don't sound as generous as those offered by some other lines, but remember that 10% of a lot is a lot: These savings can add up to $1,000. Two or more cruises can be combined for a savings of up to 50% on the price of the second or third cruise. Any repeat passenger who brings friends aboard a Seabourn vessel is rewarded with some kind of credit toward future cruises, a fact that has contributed to the sense that Seabourn is to an increasing degree an oceangoing private club. A third passenger in a suite pays between 25% and 50% of the per person rate for a double.

Seabourn believes that the most effective way to retain its standards is to encourage loyalty among previous passengers. Consequently, second-time Seabourn passengers are given membership in the Seabourn Club and receive invitations to private onboard receptions (some of them very gala), and deep discounts on trip cancellation/interruption insurance. These policies are surprisingly comprehensive, providing medical and evacuation coverage, baggage protection, and even reimbursement of an airline's cancellation penalties if you have to cancel your trip for medical reasons. Anyone who completes 28 days of Seabourn cruising receives a 25% savings on subsequent cruises, and anyone who completes 140 cumulative days aboard any combination of Seabourn vessels gets the next cruise of up to 14 days free.

In 1996, Seabourn initiated a policy whereby cruise contracts are sold separately from conventional airfare (or other modes of transport, such as chartered jet) to the port of embarkation. The policy supposedly allows clients greater flexibility in arranging pre- and postcruise commitments and distractions.

SINGLE SUPPLEMENTS   Seabourn derives more than the usual percentage of its business from older passengers traveling alone, and consequently is lenient in charging supplements for their accommodations. Depending on the cruise, they cost from 110% to 150% of the per person rate for double occupancy of the same standard suite. Any single traveler who wants to book any of a Seabourn vessel's larger-than-standard "specialty suites" will pay 200% of the per person rate.

PORT CHARGES   Port charges for Caribbean cruises range from $95 to $285 per person, depending on the length of the itinerary.

Seabourn Pride

⚓ ⚓ ⚓ ⚓ ⚓

Specifications

Size (in tons)	10,000	Crew	145 (European)
Number of Cabins	100	Passenger/Crew Ratio	1.4 to 1
Number of Outside Cabins	100	Year Built	1988
Number of Passengers	200	Last Major Refurbishment	n/a
Officers	Norwegian		

Frommer's Ratings (Scale of 1–10)

Activities	7.0	Public Areas	8.5
Cabins	9.8	Public Comfort/Space	9.5
Cleanliness/Maintenance	9.5	Recreational Facilities/Pool	8.0
Entertainment	6.8	Service	9.8
Food & Beverage	9.8	Ship Crew/Officers	10.0
Interior Decor	9.5	Shore Excursions	8.0
Ports of Call	9.5	Worth the Money	8.5
		Overall Average	**8.9**

The *Pride* is the first of the three ships acquired by Seabourn, and like its siblings is an elegant, gleaming tribute to Seabourn's vision of cruising luxury.

Cabins & Rates

Cabins	Average per diem	Bathtub	Fridge	Phone	Sitting Area	TV
Suite	$774	Yes	Yes	Yes	Yes	Yes

CABINS   True to its upscale nature, Seabourn refers to its standard units not as cabins or staterooms but as suites, and indeed, at 277 square feet each is very large by seagoing standards. Technically, however, they *are* staterooms, although many expensive accoutrements (curtains, partial partitions) clearly delineate sleeping areas from the comfortably spacious sitting areas. Beds can be configured either as twins or queen-size beds.

Everything about a Seabourn cabin has the impeccably maintained feel of an up-scale Scandinavian hotel—no surprise, considering the origins of both line and staff. Each cabin has a five-foot-wide rectangular picture window overlooking the blue beyond, with an electric blind to shut out the glare of the noonday sun. Each unit contains a fully stocked bar, a walk-in closet with a safe operated by a combination you define the first time you use it, and a TV/VCR concealed behind efficient, curved cabinets of bleached oak. Videotaped movies are available from the ship's library, and the purser's office broadcasts films from their own collection of European esoterica. Units also contain some of the most luxurious bathrooms afloat, sheathed with white marble and featuring large mirrors, double sinks, and the kind of bathtub even lanky or large-framed passengers can stretch out in. Soundproofing is extremely effective between cabins, so you won't usually be in on the minutiae of your neighbors' lives.

The line also maintains a handful of even larger units that are really bona-fide suites, many with jazzy architectural features such as private verandas and acutely angled walls with rows of rectangular, brass-trimmed windows. Ask to see a floor plan before you book one, as layouts vary widely from unit to unit. Suites range in size from a very generous 400 square feet to a truly spacious 575 square feet. Unfortunately, some suites located near the bow can be very uncomfortable during rough seas.

Everything about the cabins is soothing, conservative, and relentlessly upscale. With regard to decor, there's an almost universal use of light-grained wooden trim, mirrors, and spotlights that allow for varied lighting treatments. A staff member is available at any hour for room service or tidying up. Just pick up the phone.

RECREATION & FITNESS FACILITIES

On the uppermost deck, a swimming pool is crammed into too small an area of deck space, and a whirlpool tub, perched oddly above a platform, isn't particularly inviting.

Each vessel sports a health spa with exercise machines and treadmills, and an area with padded floor mats for aerobics classes. There's also a steam room and sauna, two or three beauty technicians for hairstyling and manicures, cubbyholes for massage and herbal wraps, three outdoor whirlpools, and a small outdoor swimming pool. You can sunbathe on a teakwood deck.

Seabourn excels in water sports. When it lowers its stern platform into the sea, an instant marina is created, complete with a submersible steel mesh tank that when lowered into the sea becomes a saltwater swimming pool. A miniflotilla of small watercraft includes sailboats, kayaks, and paddle-boats; plus, you can water-ski.

PUBLIC AREAS

Public areas are not Seabourn's forte—surprising, considering the line's high prices. For anyone who thrills to a razzle-dazzle atrium of the kind the megalines have almost perfected, walking onto a Seabourn ship is a bit of a disappointment. Similarly, public areas aboard Seabourn are so low-key as to be ordinary-looking, relieved only by a sweeping glass and metal staircase that interconnects five of the decks. Even in key nerve centers of heavy pedestrian traffic, the only ornamentation might be a lackluster series of award plaques. Art is conspicuous by its absence. It's almost as if in its zeal to create conservative decors, management couldn't decide on the appropriate artwork and so omitted it completely.

The least successful layout is that of the uppermost deck, with a cramped swimming pool and deck space and an oddly perched whirlpool tub. The crescent-shaped Veranda Cafe located here is simply too small and awkwardly configured for the function it serves. The cafe's outdoor veranda is accessible only through heavy and awkwardly positioned doors. Luckily, the hardworking staff usually lends a hand to passengers navigating their way around the many obstacles.

Even the show lounge, outfitted aboard many vessels as a tour de force of the set decorator's art, is blander than anything else afloat, a decorative disappointment in an otherwise superbly crafted floating jewel.

The most spectacular exception to this trend of boring public areas is the ship's dining room, which despite its lack of any panorama (it's positioned on the lowest passenger deck) is very upscale indeed. Contemporary but subdued, it sprawls across an amount of space that designers of more crowded ships would probably consider obscene. There's actually room between tables.

Each vessel contains a cozy library of interesting and/or edifying books, accented with memorabilia from Seabourn's past triumphs. There's a selection of VCR tapes you can borrow for viewing within your suite.

Near the bow, on an upper deck, is the Constellation Lounge. With its wraparound windows and panoramic view, it's ideal for watching the waves while you sip your extremely genteel afternoon tea. What's surprising is that the area is not used more than it is. On the same deck, but outside and exposed to the sea air and sunshine, is the Sky Bar, an all-teakwood staple.

Seawind Cruise Line

SHIPS   Seawind Crown
4770 Biscayne Blvd., Suite 700, Miami, FL 33137. ☎ 800/258-8006 or 305/573-3222; fax 305/576-1060.

In its own way, this small and relatively new company is among the most savvy marketers in the cruise-ship industry. Thanks to a handful of clever tricks, and an unwavering consciousness of its own niche, its product is one of the best values on the market.

Seawind offers a cruise experience whose focus is more on the "there" than on the getting there, a concept that's distinctly opposed to lines that market their vessels as vacation destinations in their own right. The line exhibits a genuine respect for the cultures and ecology of the Caribbean, and plans enough time in each port that its passengers can actually get a good look at the place. Plus, you can book a land stay in Aruba, Martinique, or St. Lucia for three to seven nights. The combination allows you more flexibility and better value, albeit in decidedly middle-bracket circumstances, than what's available with many other cruise lines.

The company's single ship, the *Seawind Crown,* is a seaworthy but not at all glamorous 1961 vessel whose fans refer to it as "a very comfortable lady." Middle-bracket but not bare-boned, *Seawind Crown* is completely devoid of aesthetic tricks, computer-controlled lights, and anything that might be defined as "trendy." It weighs in at 24,000 tons, more than twice the size of the 10,000-ton Seabourn vessels, but much smaller than the 70,000-ton megaships.

The ship has had a long career and taken its share of hard knocks. Previously configured as a classic, long-range ocean liner, its 1994 renovation added at least 50 cabins in space previously devoted to cargo storage, transforming it into a cruise ship able to replenish its stocks at frequent intervals. The vessel is comfortable in a way that many passengers find vaguely dowdy and to some degree endearing. Corridors are wider than those aboard many newer ships, and intricate examples of wooden marquetry are visible on some walls. Don't expect glamour, as much remains drab and threadbare. In fact, the line's administrators caution travel agents not to oversell or overly promote the vessel to prospective passengers, for fear of raising unrealistic impressions of glamour.

Boat aside, the line itself has its threadbare side. Seawind is a relatively underfinanced outfit that's experienced a brief and occasionally turbulent history. Established in 1991, it has already experienced at least two abrupt changes in management. Its first incarnation combined business interests from Portugal, Greece, and Sweden into a not-very-smoothly functioning whole. Shortly after its start, the Sweden-based shipping and hotel company Nordisk bought control of the line, then seemed to lose interest in it. In July 1995, Nordisk sold the vessel and its charter to a New York–based outfit, Holding Capital, who, with a handful of limited partners, seems committed to capitalizing on the niche they've carved. On Seawind, you can enjoy reasonably priced holidays in the deep Caribbean within a milieu more polyglot and international than that of any Florida-based vessel.

Seawind maintains the only cruise ship based in Aruba, a thriving tourist destination in its own right, but a remote outpost with much less cruise-related congestion than that experienced at points closer to the Florida mainland. A competitor, Dolphin, moved its limited roster of operations away from Aruba in the mid-1990s.

Why Aruba? For one thing, it's closer to the Latin American markets (especially

Argentina and Brazil) that Seawind has successfully tapped. Plus, Aruba sounds more exotic to European ecotourists than does the Florida mainland. Lastly, since there are limited air routes in and out of Aruba, it's not likely that any megaship will adopt the island as a home port any time in the near future, so the older, smaller *Seawind Crown*—which would be lost among the behemoths at, say, the Port of Miami—has no local competition and can remain the king of Aruba's hill.

PROS & CONS The company's embarkation point in Aruba means some passengers face a sometimes grueling all-day transit from their point of origin. Getting there almost invariably involves taking a very early morning flight. The inconvenience, however, is offset by closer access to the southern Caribbean and ports of call that are rarely visited as part of seven-day cruises originating from Florida.

The ship is among the oldest of any plying the Caribbean's waters, with very few of the eye-popping decorative features distinguishing the new crop of megavessels. Despite that, enough interesting original features remain to counteract the effects of its advancing age.

Nothing about the standard aspects of this cruise experience are top-notch, but, with some indulgence, flexibility, and good will, you can have an absorbing good time afloat. The company's land-based programs seem to have a genuine respect for the Caribbean cultures you visit. Plus, if you book a suite or an outside cabin in middle and upper-bracket categories, you'll receive a free land-based holiday—up to a week's vacation in Aruba, Martinique, or St. Lucia at no additional charge.

You won't find intimacy at La Cabana, the Aruba hotel Seawind uses to house its clientele. One of the Caribbean's biggest hotels, it's a sprawling, modern complex that rises from a dusty, sun-drenched landscape that's sure to get shadier as its gardens mature. Each unit is furnished like a comfortable condominium and has

its own kitchen. There are swimming pools (naturally), and the nearby beach is superb. Overall, the place is very mass market, but considering you can stay here for free, it's hard to beat.

(Please note that booking inexpensive cabins, including any inside unit without a sea view, does not qualify you for any of the extra bonuses that are the trademark of this cruise line.)

TYPES OF PASSENGERS Seawind cruises have a definite international clientele, with a roster of passengers that's as multicultural as anything you'll find afloat. About half are from the United States and Canada, one-quarter from Europe (including many Dutch, Italians, Scandinavians, French, British, and Germans), and one-quarter from Latin America (mainly Argentina and Brazil), so anyone with a thirst and curiosity for foreign cultures will find the mix more appealing than the culturally homogenized clientele aboard many megaships.

Passengers share one common denominator: They're all on a budget.

English is the ship's official language, but just to be sure everyone gets the message, broadcasts are announced in at least six languages, which can be a bit trying. Even guest lecturers are generally proficient in two or more languages.

DINING The names of the ship's main dining room, the Vasco da Gama, and the less formal buffet restaurant, the Madeira, celebrate the vessel's Portuguese origins. The inspiration for the cuisine and service is pan-European, with soups and salads offered as a matter of course at dinner, and with European waiters remaining cheerful and cooperative despite sometimes daunting odds. During days spent exclusively at sea, an additional luncheon buffet is usually set up in the Taverna, which sunbathers appreciate because of its convenience to the swimming pools and sun decks.

Cuisine is filling and sometimes savory, but isn't spectacular. Dishes are pan-continental, and are described in ways that appeal to American tastes. Examples might include baked Alaskan salmon with a dill mousseline sauce, roast prime rib of beef with horseradish sauce, duckling à l'orange, and flaming cherries jubilee. As a change of pace, some meals might feature Greek cuisine, such as lamb kebabs, souvlaki, or moussaka.

Dinner and lunch are served at two pre-assigned seatings. Romantic tables for two can be finagled, although it might require a bit of juggling between you and whoever is administering the dining room. Much more common are tables for between four and eight.

The emphasis is on buffets, which are displayed with a certain artfulness and usually have Latin American or Caribbean themes. If you're finicky about maintaining the division between smoking and nonsmoking areas, you won't be pleased, as a lot of passengers light up wherever and whenever they feel like it.

Room service is very limited, although continental breakfast will be brought to your cabin if you request it. Within reason, special diets, including vegetarian, can be arranged.

ACTIVITIES   There are two distinct kinds of days aboard the *Seawind Crown:* days in port, when activities on board ship come to a sleepy standstill, and days at sea, when many activities are conducted in several different languages. There's no danger of forgetting the starting time of your favorite pastime, as announcements are loud, too frequent, and annoying, blaring out in many languages when volleyball, shopping, or whatever is about to begin.

Activities and daily programs mimic those aboard most mainstream cruise lines cruising tropical waters. There's a card room for bridge or poker, afternoon dance classes (learn to waltz, polka, or samba, depending on who happens to show up), lessons in how to play the steel drums, and even an occasional cooking lesson. Photography is emphasized; you can buy film and have your pictures developed, enlarged, and duplicated in the photo gallery.

The real focus of this line, however, is its stops at various ports of call. The line exhibits a real awareness of the Caribbean's cultures and ecology, and the ship spends a full day (at least eight hours) in each port of call, so passengers have time to do more than just shop. Fortunately, the ship is small enough to be able to dock beside the piers at each of its ports of call, eliminating the need for slow ferrying back and forth by tender and allowing you to devote every possible minute to your port experience.

CHILDREN'S ACTIVITIES   Recognizing that most children appear on board during their summer vacation, Seawind devotes more time and energy to its children's program during the summer than during winter months. What the specially designated children's playroom lacks in terms of megaship glitz and electronic glitter it makes up for with its international mix of children and staff. In fact, the greatest asset of the children's program is its kind and attentive international staff, additional members of whom are added to the children's programs even in winter if advance bookings justify it.

Baby-sitting can be arranged with several hour's advance notification.

ENTERTAINMENT   Onboard entertainment is ordinary but can sometimes be good. If you go with the swing of things, you're likely to find it endearing, if only because of the enthusiasm of the troupers.

Most evenings, there's a cabaret act with an ambitious agenda, presented in a show lounge that's packed almost to the ceiling when the ship is full. Music, glitter, and magic acts don't rely on passengers understanding a specific language. Before and after this gala act, a singer, sometimes accompanied by computer-generated music, performs in one of the bars.

The ship contains a 208-seat movie theater nestled on the next-to-lowest deck, below the water line. It screens European and American films several times a day. A casino is styled on low-key European models, and is rather surprisingly devoid of any Vegas-style glitz. You'll also find five bars, one which is charmingly but incongruously outfitted like a woodsy European beer hall. After hours, it's transformed into a disco that continues pulsing until sunrise.

Two nights of any seven-day cruise are designated as formal nights, where passengers tend more often than not to dress formally.

SHOPPING Two small shops lie on the Pacific Deck, stocked with essential sundries plus resort wear, Caribbean souvenirs, a smattering of whimsical jewelry, and gold items such as chains and earrings.

SERVICE The staff is likable and hardworking. Hailing from a wide variety of countries, including some that the ship visits, many staff members are in seagoing service as a long-term career, and usually have families they support in their country of origin.

Some staff members have been aboard during the ship's earlier incarnations, going back to when the boat was more stylish. Owing to this experience, the staff manages to maintain a level of style and degree of protocol you might not have expected from such a reasonably priced line.

Waiters circulate around the sundecks, offering to bring drinks to a passenger's chaise lounge or sun chair. "Suggested" tipping is $7.50 per day per passenger, divided among the cabin and dining room staffs.

ITINERARIES Year-round, the *Seawind Crown* departs every Sunday from Aruba on seven-night sailings in the "South Seas" of the Caribbean, stopping at Curaçao, Caracas, Barbados, and St. Lucia, with two full days at sea.

SPECIAL DISCOUNTS Seawind's most spectacular discount deal is a free land package of between three and seven nights at a hotel in Aruba or St. Lucia.

The duration of the land package and its locale vary according to the category of cabin you book.

Regardless of the island and hotel you select, Seawind's programs offer an excellent way to prolong your pre- or post-cruise time in the Caribbean sunshine at tremendous savings. Before booking, note what kind of vacation you enjoy, and what kind of hotel you're attracted to. Where you'll stay in Aruba (described above in "Pros & Cons") is much larger and more anonymous than where you'll stay in St. Lucia. We recommend Aruba stays for beach lovers and sun worshippers; stays in St. Lucia are more suited to nature lovers and ecotourists.

Seawind also offers more conventional discounts. Anyone booking back-to-back seven-night cruises receives heavy discounts on the second week of cruising. Advance purchase discounts of $320 to $520 per person are offered to anyone who pays a deposit and makes firm reservations at least 60 days before sailing. A third or fourth passenger sharing a cabin with two full-fare passengers receives heavy discounts, and children under two sharing a cabin with their parents pay only $100 each per week of cruising. Honeymooners and couples celebrating their anniversary within a week of their cruise receive gifts, a $20 onboard credit per couple, complimentary champagne and fruit baskets, a commemorative gift. Anniversary couples are invited to renew their vows in the *Seawind Crown*'s chapel.

Seawind favors repeat passengers with after-market programs in which they receive a special savings certificate, valid for one year. These certificates result in the lowest price available to individual passengers.

SINGLE SUPPLEMENTS Passengers traveling alone pay between 150% and 200% of the per person rate for a double, but some of the smallest and least desirable inside cabins are exempt from this charge. As cramped as they are, it's likely they were originally designed as single cabins anyway.

PORT CHARGES Cruise fares include all costs in the various ports of call visited, including port charges. Should the passengers purchase air add-ons, they will be required to pay the U.S. airport/customs fees of $25.95.

Seawind Crown

⇩ ⇩ ⇩

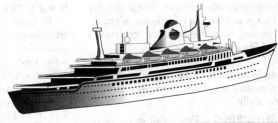

Specifications

Size (in tons)	24,000	Crew	311 (International)
Number of Cabins	367	Passenger/Crew Ratio	2.3 to 1
Number of Outside Cabins	246	Year Built	1961
Number of Passengers	728	Last Major Refurbishment	1995
Officers	Greek		

Frommer's Ratings (Scale of 1–10)

Activities	6.2	Public Areas	7.8
Cabins	6.6	Public Comfort/Space	7.6
Cleanliness/Maintenance	7.0	Recreational Facilities/Pool	6.5
Entertainment	6.5	Service	8.0
Food & Beverage	7.5	Ship Crew/Officers	8.4
Interior Decor	7.6	Shore Excursions	8.8
Ports of Call	8.0	Worth the Money	9.0
		Overall Average	**7.5**

This ship, built in 1961, was once one of the most visible passenger ships in Portugal. Originally dubbed the *Infante Dom Enrique,* and later rechristened the *Vasco da Gama* in honor of Portugal's legendary navigator, it was one of the few ships afloat to bear two names simultaneously.

For several years, records in Panama listed both *Vasco da Gama* and *Seawind Crown* as this vessel's name. In the early 1990s, the Portuguese name was dropped when its other moniker was judged more likely to attract North Americans.

Cabins & Rates

Cabins	Average per diem	Bathtub	Fridge	Phone	Sitting Area	TV
Inside*	$139–$248	No	Yes	Yes	No	Yes
Outside**	$231–$368	Half	Yes	Yes	No	Yes
Suite**	$282–$448	Yes	Yes	Yes	Yes	Yes

*Rates include airfare. **Rates include airfare and a land package of between three and seven days.*

CABINS The ship has more than a dozen cabin categories, most of them located on middle decks. The average cabin size is a fair 160 square feet, although the smallest inside cabin, outfitted with bunk beds, is only 120 cramped square feet. Some suites have a generous 500 square feet.

Late-Breaking Seawind News

As this book goes to press, word has come down that Cruise Holdings, the company that owns Premier, Dolphin, and Seawind Cruise Lines, will be merging the three lines into one during the fall of 1997. Unfortunately, the name of the new line has not been determined yet, though the buzz is that it will seek a market niche as the "classic cruise ship" alternative to today's mega-colossal megaships.

Unfortunately, details are still unavailable at this writing regarding any possible changes—though we don't expect there will be any major ones in the short term, so the information provided here will still serve you well in deciding whether this is the ship for you; your travel agent or cruise agent can fill you in on any new info. You can also call the line at ☎ **800/258-8006.** Tell 'em Frommer's sent you.

Outside cabins have enough room to be comfortable, with big closets and touches of wood trim. The new cabins added during the 1995 renovation are mostly outside cabins. Regardless of size, each contains a small refrigerator, a multichannel music system, a telephone geared only for calls within the ship, and a hair dryer. Many are oddly configured, with odd angles and, in many cases, views that overlook pedestrian walkways. Most annoying to North American travelers are the European-style hand-held shower nozzles.

Note that electrical current in the cabins corresponds to European models: 220 volts. There's also a 110-volt outlet in the bathrooms for electric razors and other appliances.

Two cabins are wheelchair accessible. Passengers confined to wheelchairs must make this clear at the time of their initial bookings, and must travel with a fully mobile adult.

RECREATION & FITNESS FACILITIES
The ship has two adequate outdoor swimming pools near the stern of two contiguous decks, and lots of chaise lounges for sunbathing. Latin music is broadcast around the swimming pools throughout the day.

Deep below the water line, on the ship's lowest deck, is a fitness center with volleyball, facilities for practicing your golf swing, cubicles for massage, and a sauna. Sauna use is carefully designated to suit all degrees of modesty, with some men-only sessions, some women-only sessions, and some mixed sessions. Exercise machines include treadmills, rowing machines, and weight machines. In 1996, the ship's gym was enlarged by taking over an area hitherto reserved for (but rarely used for) tennis practice. A beauty salon is staffed by Steiner of London.

Anyone interested in jogging or power-walking usually heads for the Promenade Deck, where an uninterrupted circuit attracts walkers at sundown and joggers before breakfast. Someone from the staff usually leads exercise programs twice a day. Programs are also available for scuba divers and snorkelers whenever the ship pulls into a port of call.

PUBLIC AREAS   Public areas are decorated with pastel colors, and are not at all flashy but rather comfortable, functional, well used, and easy to live with. One of the most charming touches is a chapel, a windowless vestige of the days when the ship was Portuguese and observed religious rituals more stringently than it does today.

Some public areas lie near the ship's bow, others near the stern, and the distance you have to walk between them makes the vessel seem moderately larger than it is. The ship doesn't feel cramped; the number of passengers (700) is relatively low compared to other lines that would try to pack 300 more aboard.

Star Clippers

SHIPS   Star Clipper

4101 Salzedo Ave., Coral Gables, FL 33146. ☎ 800/442-0553 or 305/442-0550; fax 305/442-1611.

Vessels modeled on the clipper ships of the 1860s appear least frequently in the world of Caribbean cruising. Full-sailed, built for speed, and undeniably romantic, these magnificent vessels reigned for only a brief time on the high seas before being driven out by steam-driven engines, iron and then steel hulls, and the philosophy that bigger is better.

During their heyday, however, clipper ships engendered more romantic myths than any vessels before or since. These ships helped open the Pacific Coast of California during the Gold Rush of 1849, carrying much-needed supplies around the tip of South America from Boston and New York. Even after the opening of the Suez Canal in 1869, names like *Cutty Sark, Ariel,* and *Flying Cloud* remained prestigious, and no sailing ship has ever surpassed the record of *Sea Witch,* a vessel that once sailed from Canton, China, to New York in 74 days.

Until Star Clippers became a player in the cruise-ship industry in 1991, large-scale sailing vessels ("tall ships") were the almost exclusive domain of national governments, who maintained a handful of the antique ships as training vessels for naval cadets. But despite the nostalgia and sense of reverence that surrounded every aspect of their maritime history, nothing that could be technically classified as a clipper ship had been built since the *Cutty Sark* in 1869. In fact, their return to the high seas as viable commercial ventures could only have been realized by a nautical visionary with a passion for ship design and almost unlimited funds. The right combination of these factors emerged in Mikael Krafft, a Swedish-born industrialist and real-estate developer who invested vast amounts of personal energy and more than $80 million in the construction of two modern-day clippers at a

Belgian shipyard in 1990 and 1991. The ships were the *Star Clipper*, which spends its winters in the Caribbean, and the *Star Flyer*, which operates in the Far East and the Aegean.

Before this venture, Krafft had sailed a series of high-tech yachts, including a particularly spectacular version 128 feet long. Krafft supervised the construction of a fleet of cargo ships, whose hydrodynamics are vastly different from those that apply to a clipper. To construct his clippers, he procured the original drawings and specifications of Scottish-born Donald McKay (a leading naval architect of 19th-century clipper-ship technology) and employed his own team of naval architects to solve such engineering problems as adapting the square-rigged, four-masted clipper design to modern materials and construction.

Krafft established his wind-driven line as Clipper Cruises, and was promptly sued by a Missouri-based line that already had rights to the name, though its cost-conscious vessels didn't have sails. After several messy and expensive legal battles, Krafft adopted Star Clippers as the name of his line, and successfully wedged his way into a small but distinctive niche in the cruise-ship market.

Technically, the *Star Clipper* and *Star Flyer* should not be designated as ships at all; *360-foot barkentines* is the term most nautical experts prefer, but who are we to quibble? Today, the twin vessels are at once traditional and radical. They're the tallest and among the fastest clipper ships ever built. With dimensions about 100 feet longer than the average 19th-century clipper ship, and 25 feet longer than the largest ever built, they're so beautiful that even at full stop they seem to soar.

Part of the new ships' success derives from a skillful blend of traditional aesthetics and newfangled materials and technology. The configuration of the vessels' sails is not quite traditional, having been adapted by Krafft to include a higher percentage of triangular sails and fewer of the square-rigged sails that are usually associated with clippers. Also, sails are made of lightweight Dacron rather than canvas, which rotted easily and was so heavy that the amount of sail each of Krafft's ships flies (36,000 square feet) would probably have capsized an original clipper. Further innovations include masts crafted from steel and aluminum alloys instead of tree trunks and a network of electric winches that eliminates the backbreaking labor historically involved in the sails' raising and lowering. Fewer than 10 deckhands can manipulate the ships' sails, as contrasted to the 40 to 55 that were needed to control and maintain sails aboard the 19th-century ships. Concessions to modern design include a bow thruster and a single propeller that's used to navigate in and out of tricky harbors or during dead calms. When used together, they can spin each craft around on a very tight axis. Star Clippers almost never use their bow thrusters for such basic tasks as coming about into the wind—both crew and ships are simply too proud for that.

One of the great challenges Krafft and his designers faced was taking a type of ship originally intended to haul tea, wool, and opium and adapting it to carry vacationing passengers. The new clippers needed the amenities of a private yacht: a paneled library with its own fireplace, a piano bar, two swimming pools, four tenders to carry passengers from ship to shore, a dining room big enough to accommodate all passengers and officers at the same time, and all the sports-related paraphernalia—including scuba and snorkeling gear—that contributes to a modern Caribbean holiday. An added factor almost made the project completely impractical: The line's intention to undertake transatlantic cruises meant its vessels needed considerable space to store provisions and large enough cabins so

that passengers wouldn't go stir-crazy at midvoyage. Whatever alchemic formula they came up with apparently worked, and the line was off and running.

As opposed to the *Club Med 1,* a rather bulky cruise ship that just happens to be outfitted with sails, Star Clipper's ships sail under wind power much more often than they do by motor. During meals, however, the use of sails is limited, as they tend to raise the ships' prows to an incline, which terns to disturb place settings.

Each ship performs superlatively, and can reach a speed of 17 knots. During the *Star Clipper*'s maiden sail in 1992 off the coast of Corsica, it sustained speeds of 19.4 knots, thrilling its owner and designers (who had predicted maximum speeds of only 17 knots). During most conventional sessions afloat, however, the crew tries to keep passengers comfortable and decks relatively horizontal, and so the vessels are kept to speeds of 9 to 14 knots. In fact, if you're an avid sailor, you might be frustrated that these greyhounds of the sea aren't allowed to run to their potential.

In its short history, Star Clipper has assembled quite a list of firsts: the first commercial sail-driven vessel to cross the Atlantic in 90 years; the first ship ever to pass full U.S. Coast Guard certification and safety exams on the first try; and one of the only ships to ever enter the Port of Miami under full sail—a daunting feat, considering the motorized traffic barreling through on all sides. Also impressive is the fact that both ships received the highest rating available by Lloyd's Register—the "+100 A-1-a" rating, which hadn't been awarded to a sailing vessel since 1911. On Star Clippers, you'll be sailing aboard vessels where safety and nautical logistics are more visible and more all-encompassing than aboard most other lines, where operations are kept safely hidden away.

How do their prices and amenities compare to the products of Windjammer Barefoot Cruises and Windstar Cruises, two other companies that have replicated the sailing ships of yore? Star Clippers represents a midpoint between the two—more luxurious and usually a bit more expensive than the bare-boned, no-frills Windjammer excursions and less opulent, less formal, and less expensive than Windstar. Onboard ambience is freewheeling and uncluttered, permeated with a sense of rugged individualism and salty enough to make you feel like a fisherman keeling off the coast of Maine, without the physical hardship of actually being one.

PROS & CONS   On Star Clipper, the happiest passengers are those who know what they're getting into. These vessels are not mainstream cruise ships trying to overwhelm your senses with bright lights, high-tech gizmos, endless banquets, and glitzy entertainment, and therein lies their potent allure and appeal. If your idea of happiness is playing virtual-reality golf while sipping a toucan-colored drink, Star Clippers is not for you. If, however, you long for a tall ship and a star to steer by, a quiet ocean and the moon above, this might be your line.

Star Clippers are *hearty* ships, and they're sailed by hearty people. Something about the line seems to attract, celebrate, and even enhance glowing good health. Even if you feel lackluster when you step on board, chances are that by the time you leave there'll be a spring in your step and a glow in your cheeks.

The ships themselves are under-accessorized when compared to larger, motorized vessels, but they're endlessly rich in atmosphere, which is probably what attracts potential clients to this line anyway. Passengers typically have a hankering for the sea life, but the question always arises about the degree to which passengers should (or can) get involved in day-to-day operations. Crew members are indulgent and, usually, good-natured about clients who want to tie knots, raise and lower sails, and keep the deck shipshape. Some crew members, though, to whom English is not their mother language, might simply give up at the

challenge of explaining the difference between an upper topgallant and a flying jib to a novice who doesn't speak Swedish or German.

Overall, you'll quickly learn where the boundaries are and when you should probably stay out of the way. This is another challenge to consider: When told that you can't spend the afternoon in the crow's nest, scanning the horizon, will you (a) grab a book and do some sunbathing instead, or (b) grow frustrated and bolt yourself in your cabin? Consider well.

Destination-wise, Star Clippers' have the advantage of relatively small size, which allows them to visit smaller, more exotic ports of call than those usually visited by larger ships. Plus, there's the dramatic aspect to consider: Even if you're visiting a large port packed to the gills with megaships, the entry of a clipper under full sail is going to cause a stir.

But what about those sails? They're beautiful, yes, and generally very efficient, but there are a couple of potential drawbacks. If sunbathing is a big goal on your cruise, you might find that as the sails change their position relative to the deck and the position of the sun, your once-sunny spot of deck is thrust into deep shade. Also, as is inevitable aboard any ship with high masts, there's more side-to-side rolling. Even though elaborate configurations of stabilizers and ballast tanks were built into the ships to reduce this rolling, you might find the movement more troublesome and seasick-inducing than aboard commercial cruisers—especially such ultrastable ships as the catamaran-shaped *Radisson Diamond.*

You may also be disappointed on a cruise where there is very little wind. Wind and its velocity are of no concern at all aboard diesel-driven vessels, but take the wind out of Star Clippers sails and you have one no-going boat. (Here we exaggerate: Thankfully, engines will chug the vessels along to the prearranged ports of call, though you might feel quite let down if you'd envisioned yourself as a latter-day Errol Flynn beneath the roiling and blustering sails.)

If you're looking for love on the high seas, keep in mind that Star Clippers' passenger rosters are not particularly rich in single travelers. If you're eager to travel aboard a ship with sails and find love at the same time, you'd do better to stick to Club Med, despite the fact that *Club Med 1*'s sails are more cosmetic than functional.

TYPES OF PASSENGERS With only 170 passengers aboard, each cruise seems like a triumph of individuality and intimacy. The line's unusual niche appeals to passengers who might recoil at the lethargy and sometimes enforced enthusiasm of cruises aboard larger, more typical vessels. Forty percent of any passenger roster is comprised of people who have never cruised before, perhaps for this very reason.

As the line has matured and increased both its stature and its prestige, many passengers tend to be repeaters. About half are European, the remainder North American (including many stressed-out urbanites) and a steadily growing number of Latin Americans. Each tends to be active, sports-conscious, and curious, and, as you might expect, many come from boating or yachting backgrounds of their own. Passengers tend to fall between the ages of 30 and 60, with an average age of around 45, and most travel as couples. Many are devoted conservationists who appreciate a vessel that relies for the most part upon wind power rather than diesel fuel. Many have also taken a safari in Africa, and are well versed in the pros and cons of unusual and exotic holidays. Incomes run the gamut from average to way above average. You'll find goodly numbers of stockbrokers and doctors. When extreme wealth does appear, it tends to be understated and without ostentation. Mikael Krafft himself may even be on board, in many cases with his wife and children, traveling as a low-key, highly accessible, and semianonymous guest.

Onboard atmosphere is quite casual. During the day, Bermuda shorts with Lacoste shirts and topsiders are standard issue, and for dinner many passengers simply change into cleaner and better-pressed versions of the same, with perhaps a change from shorts to slacks for most men.

DINING Star Clippers has evolved into a more upscale, more glamorous outfit since its somewhat raw-boned debut in the early 1990s, and in the process, it's upgraded its dining rituals considerably. Meals are served in a dining room that's cozy and classy instead of glitzy and bright. When it's full, the room tends to be noisier than those aboard many equivalent ships, as its designers considered the room's shape and size less important than the design of the hull that contains it.

Theoretically, the room was designed for a maximum of 200 diners at a time, but in actual practice, it's a lot more comfortable, and less cramped, when the ship sails at its average passenger load of between 130 and 150 passengers. Plus, the dining room layout has several odd features. Rather than creating a warren of small dining areas, the designers opted instead for an area large enough to seat all passengers and all officers simultaneously. The result is a crowded room with mahogany trim and a series of thin steel columns that pierce the center of many of the dining tables. While, from an engineering status, the columns were the best way to solve the structural problem inherent within such a large open space, they sometimes slightly block sight lines across the tables. In the convivial rush of things, however, few diners seem to mind or even notice.

Don't expect secluded spots for tête-à-têtes with your beloved: There are no tables for two. Places adjacent to the portholes are booths configured for six, and when they're fully occupied (as they often are), you'll have to stand up and sit down a lot to accommodate the people seated farthest from the aisle, and might sometimes have to pass platters of food to them as well. The remaining seating is at tables that are bolted into place and almost always configured for eight. The room's port side, aft, is reserved for smokers. In other areas, smoking is usually discouraged.

Food is plentiful and well seasoned, designed for appetites whetted by exposure to bracing winds and sea air, with enough flourishes to appeal to a somewhat epicurean audience. Meals are well prepared but not intensely esoteric, nourishing and flavorful but not at all gastronomically fussy. Selection is limited every night to two main courses (usually a meat and a fish), plus a vegetarian platter. Gala nights might focus on steak, lobster, or prime rib. There's a worthwhile selection of wines on board, with a heavy emphasis on medium-priced selections from California. Coffee, served in Styrofoam cups, is available from a "coffee station" 24 hours a day, and there's an informal tea every afternoon where snack items might include a well-conceived, health-conscious platter of crudités. In 1996, breakfasts were enhanced with the addition of an omelet station, where a uniformed employee will make your eggs the way you like them.

Room service is available on a minimalist basis, with nothing approaching the full complement of dishes available in the main dining room.

ACTIVITIES   Many activities involve simply exploring these extraordinary ships. A daily highlight is practical instruction in "know thy sailing ship" subjects by either the captain or a "guest captain." Knot-tying might be the topic of the day, or you might get to participate in a man overboard drill. Many instructors are members of the Society of Cape Horners, all of whom have skippered a ship, by sail, around the tip of South America. Many passengers spend time reading pertinent texts and doing their homework in preparation for these lectures. Within reason, passengers can lend a hand with deck-side duties, observe the mechanics of navigation, and have a token try at handling the wheel when circumstances and calm weather permit. Each ship maintains an "open bridge" policy, allowing passengers to wander up to the navigation center at any hour of the day or night. Crew members will either welcome or tolerate such visits, depending on their mood and the moment.

Other activities are not of the megaship variety. Instead of bingo games or toga parties, you can lie on a woven net suspended between the ship's hull and the bowsprit, just a few feet above the sea foam, feeling the spray from waves ricocheting against the bow. Known as a "widow's net," it's everyone's preferred spot for dolphin sightings.

Many passengers view the crew's deck-side work as their entertainment, so there's an inherent conflict in scheduling daily activities: Many passengers prefer to spend daylight hours on deck than on shore. Consequently, Star Clippers tend to arrive relatively late (between 9am and noon) at their ports of call.

Very unusual in the cruise-line industry, Star Clippers' tenders accommodate 52 passengers each, and each is powered by high-powered underwater jets instead of conventional propellers. This allows tenders to run right up onto a beach. Each is then winched off the sands and back into the water with a stern-mounted anchor.

Ships tend to depart from their island ports of call early enough so they can be under full sail during sunset. Many passengers order sunset-colored cocktails and effuse over the superiority of their experience as compared to other sunset cruises marketed all around the Caribbean.

CHILDREN'S ACTIVITIES   We don't recommend taking very young children aboard this line, but if you do, the staff will make it very clear that supervision is your responsibility. That said, an experience aboard a sailing ship can be a wonderful educational experience, especially for children between 7 and 18, to whom the ships' adventurous aspects are extremely appealing.

No baby-sitting is available, unless a well-intentioned crew member agrees to volunteer his or her off-duty hours, a gesture that's entirely voluntary.

ENTERTAINMENT Entertainment is quite simple: a resident piano player/keyboard player who provides digestible music before and after the dinner hour. That's really about it, except for the occasional stray steel band that comes aboard during late-night departures from ports of call. There are no cabaret-style dancers, no dance bands, and no casino. There's just you, the sea, and the conversation of your fellow passengers.

Oh yes, there's a disco too, set beneath the stars on the Main Deck, midway between the library and the Tropical Bar. Plus, four movies a day are piped into passenger cabins, along with news broadcasts from Britain, France, Germany, and the United States, which alternate with one another every quarter hour or so.

SHOPPING Armani tuxes you won't find. The shop mostly carries the kind of clothing you'd wear on deck, which is pretty much the Land's End look you'd expect. There's also an inventory of toilet articles and sundries, and gift items reflecting Star Clippers' nautical sensibilities.

SERVICE There are few, if any, attempts to provide haute service aboard these ships, particularly since everyone on board seems hip to the roughing-it nature of clipper ship life. Service is congenial, low key, unpretentious, cheerful, and reasonably attentive. This is not a "snap your fingers and whatever you want will magically appear" kind of line. After you watch the crew steer your ship through the wind, waves, and splashing surf for a while, you'll certainly understand when they don't slip on the white gloves for dinner service. Expect efficient but sometimes slightly distracted service in the cramped dining room, and realize that you'll have to fetch your own ice, bar drinks, and whatever else you might need during your time on deck.

ITINERARIES Since the *Star Clipper* and its faraway mate, the *Star Flyer*, rely on wind power for their locomotion, they are more directly influenced by storms, wind, and weather patterns than any diesel-powered vessel. During periods of prolonged calm, the ship's engine can chug it toward its ports of call, but occasional last-minute changes in any itinerary are sometimes necessary. This is not at all the norm, however: In the mid-1990s, one of the vessels' captains was dismissed for a series of infractions, one of the most glaring of which involved his habit of motoring, rather than sailing, between destinations.

A pair of week-long sojourns can be combined into 14-day expeditions where very few of the same islands are visited twice. Pre- and postcruise hotel packages can be arranged in Barbados and several other islands.

Between November and April, the *Star Clipper* operates from bases in Antigua and Barbados, site of some of the strongest and most constant trade winds in the Antilles. Seven-day routings leave on Saturdays and include stops at St. Vincent, Grenada, Carriacou, Bequia, and Martinique. On alternate Saturdays, the itinerary includes stops at St. Lucia, Martinique, Dominica, and the Tobago Cays. Both routes defer to prevailing wind patterns, so that as much time as possible is spent running before a stern-side breeze. In summer, the ship moves into the Mediterranean.

SPECIAL DISCOUNTS Discounts of around $300 per person are granted to anyone making a booking more than four months in advance, and discounts of around $500 per person are available for booking a cabin more than a year in advance. Booking of two back-to-back cruises saves around $300 per person on the price of the second cruise, plus whatever other discounts are offered for early bookings of both cruises. Special discounts are routinely offered to veterans of previous Star Clipper cruises. A third passenger in a cabin already occupied by two people pays $395 for a one-week cruise.

SINGLE SUPPLEMENTS   Singles are charged 100% to 150% of the per person rate for a double, depending on how flexible they are regarding cabin selection.

PORT CHARGES   For seven-day Caribbean cruises, port charges are about $118 per person.

Star Clipper

⇩ ⇩ ⇩ ⇩

Specifications

Size (in tons)	2,298	Crew	70 (International)
Number of Cabins	84	Passenger/Crew Ratio	2.5 to 1
Number of Outside Cabins	78	Year Built	1991
Number of Passengers	172	Last Major Refurbishment	n/a
Officers	European/ American		

Frommer's Ratings (Scale of 1–10)

Activities	7.0	Public Areas	7.0
Cabins	6.5	Public Comfort/Space	6.8
Cleanliness/Maintenance	7.5	Recreational Facilities/Pool	5.0
Entertainment	6.0	Service	6.5
Food & Beverage	6.8	Ship Crew/Officers	8.0
Interior Decor	6.5	Shore Excursions	7.5
Ports of Call	9.5	Worth the Money	9.0
		Overall Average	**7.1**

Life aboard the *Star Clipper* means life on deck: Since there are no other hideaways, that's where most passengers spend their days. Made from teakwood (as they would have to be) and with a cozy, cluttered feeling, these decks were planned with more space per passenger than virtually any other vessel afloat. More sail-trimming activity occurs amidships and near the bow, so if you're looking to avoid all bustle, take yourself off to the stern.

Cabins & Rates

Cabins	Average per diem	Bathtub	Fridge	Phone	Sitting Area	TV
Inside	$199–$250	No	No	Yes	Yes	Half
Outside	$240–$370	No	No	Yes	Yes	Yes

CABINS   There are six cabin categories, but all cabins include some type of wood and brass trim and subdued decor. Least comfortable are four inside cabins with upper and lower berths and only 95 square feet of floor space. A limited number of slightly larger inside cabins contain 120 square feet of floor space, which is still relatively cramped. The remaining cabins are outside cabins, most measuring a compact 120 to 130 square feet, with round portholes and a double bed that can be reconfigured as two twins. About eight outside cabins are slightly larger (150 square feet each), with full, rectangular picture windows, Jacuzzi tubs, and small refrigerators. Regrettably, these larger units are so close to deck-side action that you might not feel as private and isolated as you might have wished.

Each cabin contains carpeting, a hair dryer, a safe for valuables, and TV with an ongoing roster of videotaped movies. Smoking is forbidden in the cabins but is allowed on deck and in the rear of the dining room. Cabins are cleaned daily. Very compact cabin bathrooms have touches of marble and are rather annoyingly outfitted with push valves, which release water only when they're compressed.

Room service is minimal, viewed only as a means of sustaining life if you fall gravely ill. None of the units are suites, except for one carefully guarded owner's suite that's not normally part of the roster of cabins marketed to the public, unless it's offered as a prize or award during any of the company's frequent charity drives.

Be warned that the ship's generator tends to drone on through the night, annoying passengers who had hoped to sleep only with the sound of waves slapping against the *Clipper*'s side. Cabins on lower decks, near the stern, are the most susceptible to this.

No cabins were designed for wheelchair accessibility, and as such, these ships are not recommended for passengers with mobility problems.

RECREATION & FITNESS FACILITIES
Each ship contains two swimming pools, one with glass portholes peering from its depths into the piano bar. Both are suitable only for dips, not for swims, and, when the ships are under sail, they might be closed completely. The pool near the stern tends to be more languid, the favorite of sunbathers, whereas the one at amidships is more active, with more noise and splashing. At both, the ship's sails might occasionally block the sun's rays, although this happens amidships much more frequently than it does at the stern.

Neither vessel contains a health club, as the designers chose to eliminate it in favor of sports-related activities that passengers might pursue during shore leaves. There is, however, a Jacuzzi, and someone will probably conduct an aerobics class on deck every day. Partly because Mikael Krafft is an avid scuba diver, and partly because itineraries focus on waters that teem with marine life, each ship offers (for an extra charge) the option of PADI-approved scuba diving and snorkeling. Certified divers will find all the equipment they'll need on board. Even uncertified/inexperienced divers can pay a token fee (usually around $125) for comprehensive training that, while short of certification, will allow them to make a roster of relatively simple dives. Waterskiing is also available.

PUBLIC AREAS   There are a few overused public rooms on each vessel: a dining room, piano bar, and a cozy library with a decorative, nonfunctioning fireplace and a good stock of coffee-table books and tracts on naval history and naval architecture. An extension of the piano bar stretches from the ship's interior, adjacent to the dining room, to a deckside space that's sheltered from the sun by a fluttering canopy.

The inside piano bar has a space that's almost as large as the ship's dining room, but is configured for fewer people. That area and the outdoor "tropical bar" are the most important spots for socializing and rendezvousing aboard either ship.

The interior decor is rather conservative, mostly white with touches of brass and mahogany or teakwood trim. The decor is well crafted and unpretentious, but simply does not compare to the more upscale interiors cultivated by *Star Clipper*'s competitor, *Wind Star*.

Tall Ship Adventures

SHIPS   Sir Francis Drake

1389 South Havana St., Aurora, CO 80012. ☎ 800/662-0090 or 303/755-7983; fax 303/755-9007.

If you've always wanted to sail on a true old clipper ship, here's your chance. For as long as it remains seaworthy, you can cruise aboard *Sir Francis Drake,* one of the fewer than 100 remaining "tall ships" originally built to navigate under sail only.

Tall Ship Adventures was formed to administer this remarkable ship, a sturdy sailing craft that was built as the *Landkirchen* during the most violent days of World War I. Launched in 1917 from a berth beside Germany's Weser River, it boasted a riveted steel hull and a shape and dimensions that have changed little since then. Before a diesel motor was added in the 1930s, it operated exclusively under sail. The ship visited most of the Baltic ports, and made five sail-driven trips between Germany and the Pacific coast of Chile, hauling supplies outbound and copper on the return trip.

World War II did more to cramp this ship's style than the corrosive effects of sea and salt. All of the records associated with its past journeys went up in flames during the Allied bombings of northern Germany early in 1945. In December of that year, the ship was sold at auction as an Allied war prize to new (German) owners. It carried cargo through the Baltic until 1979, when it was given a much-needed refitting. Rechristened as the *Godewind,* the vessel hauled day-trippers off the coast of Martinique for a few years.

Then a New Zealander, Capt. Bryan Petley, persuaded his partner, Eckart Straub, to purchase the ship. In 1988, it was refurbished and renamed *Sir Francis Drake,* since the partners planned to sail the waters of the British Virgin Islands that had so fascinated this English admiral. (The deep-water channel that bisects the British Virgin Islands is also named for Drake.) Today, Straub, a sometimes-resident of Stuttgart, is the sole owner of the line, the only cruise line in the world headquartered in Colorado. In 1996, after brief stints of registry in both Honduras and Panama, the *Drake* was re-registered in Equatorial Guineau—a highly unusual legal home in the world of Caribbean cruising.

PROS & CONS   As you can imagine, there are many obvious differences between this ship and a modern, more conventional cruise ship. The *Drake* doesn't cater to passengers who desire the anonymity of a large crowd or the amenities and activities available aboard a megaship. Instead, aboard the *Drake* you'll experience what passengers aboard sailing ships of the 18th and 19th centuries experienced: the wind, sun, rain, and waves. And very little will divert your attention from semitropical panoramas over an archipelago that many sailors consider one of the most spectacular sailing venues in the western hemisphere.

The onboard atmosphere is like that of a very small town (or a very small planet). Depending on your point of view, this could be an asset or a drawback. Gossip and opinions, shared beliefs, divergent beliefs, feuds, cliques, and pecking orders, if any, quickly make themselves known, so if you shy away from close scrutiny, you might be uncomfortable aboard this ship. And if you're looking for love, you'll know after the first night afloat whether or not Mr. or Ms. Right is sitting at your dining table.

For many travelers, a Tall Ship Adventure is just their cup of rum. The experience here is straightforward and loosely scheduled, and can be very appealing.

TYPE OF PASSENGERS   Passengers aboard this line tend to be less demanding and more self-reliant than those aboard more typical cruise lines. They're more interested in nautical terms and sailing techniques, too, though few will actually insist on hoisting a yardarm, or be stalwart enough to pull on rain gear during foul weather and help the crew lash down the deck chairs. These passengers entertain themselves by watching waves and listening to the wind, and understand that ships with sails don't always follow a rigid itinerary.

The passenger list used to be mainly North American, but the line has recently pursued a more aggressive marketing campaign in Britain, Germany, and Switzerland, which might increase the number of Europeans booking berths aboard this vessel in the next few years.

The line whose passengers are the most roughly equivalent is Windjammer Barefoot Cruises. Both lines attract hardy, young-at-heart, salty types who have a certain degree of earthy humor. Aboard *Sir Francis Drake* there's less focus on heavy-duty consumption of liquor as an incentive to letting the good times roll.

DINING Because of the vessel's small size and small passenger roster, *Sir Francis Drake*'s stewards have enormous flexibility in defining and altering their menus based on what they find fresh in port markets. Where larger lines must sock away carloads of provisions at the beginning of every trip, this small-scale contender is always on the lookout for lobster, fresh fish, and fresh vegetables, which local merchants present whenever the ship arrives in port. These supplement a roster of frozen goods that are either carried on board or picked up from local suppliers.

This is a line with absolutely no pretensions toward fancy food or elaborate presentations. As the galley prepares the same meal for everyone aboard, there's really no choice at most dinners as to what you'll eat; instead, the wait staff will recite the evening's menu to the assembled crowd. Don't be surprised to hear baked chicken actually called "baked chicken," grilled sirloin steaks called "grilled sirloin steaks," and lobster called "lobster"—this is a straightforward line. Relatively simple lunches might feature burgers, fried shrimp, salads, pizzas, and sandwiches. Dinners are usually more elaborate than lunches, but there's nary a hint of gourmet pretension, with the emphasis being more on simple, solid North American staples, plus a hint of Caribbean overtones. If you're absolutely opposed to eating red meat, you should inform the reservations agent when you book, and chicken or fish can usually be prepared for you on the side, but if you're a strict vegetarian, you might pretty quickly grow tired of the boiled vegetables you're given. At some lunches, and during at least one dinner, burgers and meat might be barbecued atop a gas-fired grill on deck. Room service is extremely limited in both menu and hours, and is mainly viewed as a means of keeping you alive during bouts of seasickness.

There's a single seating for both lunch and dinner, at 12:30pm and 7pm, respectively. When weather permits, deck-top barbecues or beach picnics are prepared.

ACTIVITIES The activities program is more noteworthy for what it isn't than for what it is: There are no scheduled activities of any kind. Instead, passengers read, chitchat with staff or fellow passengers, watch the waves, watch the crew manipulate the sails, or just relax.

But you won't lack for things to do. Mornings are usually spent sailing for periods of between one and four hours, covering distances that vary in mileage based on the wind's intensity and direction. Lunch is usually consumed on board or on a beach somewhere, with afternoons (about four hours) devoted to exploring any of the sparsely inhabited islands that Tall Ship Adventures designates as its ports of call. After an afternoon ashore, around dusk, the ship repositions itself to a new site. Dinner is served in the main lounge; recorded music is played and cocktails are served on deck. Because of the many submerged rocks and reefs in this part of the British Virgin Islands (BVI), the ship does not sail in the dark, allowing passengers to slumber as their craft rolls gently at anchor.

Snorkeling is big aboard every Tall Ship cruise, with one favorite spot for exploration being the mouths of sea caves peppering the rocky coast of Norman Island (a deserted BVI island that inspired Robert Louis Stevenson's *Treasure Island*). During afternoon stopovers at, say, The Baths at Virgin Gorda, virtually everyone afloat dons face masks and fins for views of underwater reef life.

CHILDREN'S ACTIVITIES   There are no special activities of any kind for children. As a matter of fact, very few children or teenagers are even allowed on board. If you do manage to sneak one on (not literally, of course), you'll find that the lack of organized activities encourages either monumental boredom or a gleeful sense of adventure in your tot, depending on his or her demeanor.

ENTERTAINMENT   It's about as low key and do-it-yourself as anything afloat. Recorded calypso music playing on the deck might induce some passengers to dance (briefly) during the cocktail hour, but overall, entertainment comes down to whatever party you create on your own. Vaguely structured afternoon get-togethers, "promptly scheduled at fiveish," feature "snacks and swizzles" whose social lubricant comes out of a complimentary bowl of rum-based pirate's punch. Sometimes it clicks, and sometimes it doesn't, depending on who happens to show up.

Sometimes the good times have a theme, as when palm fronds might be shaped into a headdress or a bedsheet pressed into duty as a toga. There might even be a good-natured contest or two, to determine, say, who is the best dancer aboard, or who was the most cheerful during an attack of seasickness. More frequently, landfalls are scheduled to coincide with the evening festivities at isolated bars and marinas on the British Virgin Islands. Known mostly to the yachting crowd, they include the Bitter End Yacht Club on Virgin Gorda, Cane Garden Bay

on Tortola, Foxy's on Jost van Dyke, and Pusser's Bar and Grill on Marina Cay, near the east end of Tortola. Here, even if you don't happen to own a yacht, you can mingle with lots of people who do.

SHOPPING   Forget it. A staff member might be able to dig up an extra, unused toothbrush out of the back storeroom if you really need it, and the deck-top bar usually stocks an inventory of baseball caps, beach towels, and shirts with the Tall Ship logo. But other than that, any shopping you do will have to be on shore.

SERVICE   This is not by any means a "snap your finger and the gin-and-tonic will magically appear" kind of vessel. Because the ship is so small, it's not a good idea to complain too loudly if you don't like the way someone has sliced the lime that garnishes your drink—you might find yourself tossed overboard. (Just kidding.) Service in fact is reasonably attentive. Cabin service is perfunctory but efficient, involving brief cleanups in the morning. Towels are changed only every other day, and sheets will be changed once during the duration of a seven-day cruise, if you're lucky.

Unless you're deathly ill, don't expect room service (there's no phone to call for it anyway) or any of the social graces (mints on your pillow, fresh flowers in a vase) that are de rigueur aboard larger, more expensive cruise lines. If you're ever tempted to demand English-butler precision, take a good look at the crew in their uniform of shorts and knit shirts, reconsider your idea of service, and relax.

ITINERARIES   Between November and June, the ship is based in the British Virgin Islands, using the capital of Roadtown in Tortola as a base. Landfalls include Peter Island, Cooper Island, Marina Cay, Long Bay, and sites on or off the coast of Virgin Gorda, including the Bitter End Yacht Club, The Baths, and the uninhabited cay of Norman Island. Itineraries from week to week follow basically the same route, although there are moderate variations depending on wind and weather. So, although such archipelago highlights as The Baths at Virgin Gorda or the caves at Norman Island are always featured, passengers can book for a second week and expect some variation in what they'll see en route.

Between June and November, the ship heads to the Grenadines, making weekly circuits (Saturday to Saturday) between Kingstown, St. Vincent, and Grenada, with stops at many of the small, isolated islands along the way. These might include Bequia, Canouan, Tobago Cays, Petit Martinique, Petit St. Vincent, Isle de Ronde, Carriacou, and Mayreau.

SPECIAL DISCOUNTS   Special discounts are offered frequently and cover a wide range of possibilities, including a 20% discount for early bookings more than eight weeks in advance. If you want

to create your own party, there's a 5% discount for members of groups of 10 participants, and a 10% discount for members of groups with 20 participants. There are no discounts offered for senior citizens, but repeat passengers get "a good deal" as well as some souvenir-style awards and bar credits once they're aboard.

PORT CHARGES   Week-long BVI treks will cost you $35 in port charges; Grenadines treks cost $50.

SINGLE SUPPLEMENTS   Solo travelers who don't want to share a cabin will pay 175% of the per person rate for double occupancy. However, Tall Ship guarantees a roommate for any solo passenger; you'll just pay the per person rate for a double. If no roommate can be found, you won't pay the supplement even though you'll be alone in a cabin.

Sir Francis Drake

⇓ ⇓

Specifications

Size (in tons)	450	Crew	10 (International)
Number of Cabins	14	Passenger/Crew Ratio	3 to 1
Number of Outside Cabins	14	Year Built	1917
Number of Passengers	30	Last Major Refurbishment	1992
Officers	English/ International		

Frommer's Ratings (Scale of 1–10)

Activities	4.0	Public Areas	3.0
Cabins	4.2	Public Comfort/Space	5.0
Cleanliness/Maintenance	6.5	Recreational Facilities/Pool	3.0
Entertainment	4.0	Service	5.0
Food & Beverage	5.0	Ship Crew/Officers	8.0
Interior Decor	4.0	Shore Excursions	8.5
Ports of Call	8.8	Worth the Money	8.5
		Overall Average	**5.5**

The vessel is tiny and as hopelessly anti-quated next to modern megaships as the *Spirit of St. Louis* would be next to the space shuttle. But loyal clients, who sail almost every year, find those traits just add to its charm. *Sir Francis Drake* is an authentic three-masted top-sail schooner, measuring only 28 feet wide and (with the spearlike bowsprit included) 128 feet long. Its shallow draft of 9.2 feet allows it to go into bays and coves that most cruise ships can't enter.

Other than its navigational aids, which are housed in a deckhouse near the stern, very few aspects of its operation are computerized. The ship's nine sails (6,456 square feet of them) are furled and unfurled the way they've always been: manually (albeit with modern winches). You can always help.

Cabins & Rates

Cabins	Average per diem	Bathtub	Fridge	Phone	Sitting Area	TV
Outside	$142–$170	No	No	No	No	No
Suite	$199	No	No	No	Yes	No

CABINS   Each cabin is a spartan, durable, no-nonsense cubbyhole that's a lot less roomy than you might hope. Standard cabins measure only a cramped 8 by 10 feet, and some smaller ones with bunk beds measure only 8 by 8 feet. Even the ship's only suite, at 11 by 18 feet, is smaller than the size of standard cabins aboard some upscale conventional cruise lines. No cabins have anything approaching adequate storage space.

Even though the line designates its accommodations as "outside cabins," none of them have portholes. Instead, light filters down from overhead skylights, eliminating the need for artificial lighting during daylight hours. Severe claustrophobics might find the arrangement confining, but then, severe claustrophobics probably won't be booking the *Drake* in the first place.

Each cabin is air-conditioned, and set more or less at the water line, which adds the soothing sound of water splashing against the hull to your seagoing experience. Interior decor is not worth mentioning except to say that the "simulated mahogany" plastic panels are easy to clean after a bout of seasickness. Beds are bolted into position, thereby preventing configurations of twins, doubles, and bunks from ever being changed. For this reason, it's very important to state your sleeping preferences in advance, at the time of your initial reservation.

The spartan nature of the cabins extends to the bathrooms. Even the line's reservations staff refers to them as "wet heads," meaning that they're tiny tile-sheathed cubicles containing a toilet, a sink, a closable door, a drain in the floor, and a shower head. First-time users of this inconvenient arrangement invariably forget to remove the toilet paper and the bath towels before turning on the spray, thereby soaking both.

RECREATION & FITNESS FACILITIES
Not surprisingly, there's no state-of-the-art health club, or any health club at all for that matter. Passengers get their exercise participating in a well-choreographed water sports program. The ship carries a motorboat for tendering passengers from anchorage to pier, water skis, a sea kayak and a Sunfish or two, snorkeling gear, and a Sea Biscuit, which is an inflatable, hard-bottomed boat pulled behind the motorboat for high-speed joy rides. Because some parts of the British Virgin Islands restrict the use of these motorized recreational craft, they're used only sparingly.

Many passengers make it a point to swim to shore from the ship's nearby anchorage, swim laps around the ship as it bobs at anchor, and dive (water depth permitting) into the water from the ship's jutting bowsprit. For insurance reasons, the ship does not have scuba gear among its playthings, preferring to point scuba enthusiasts in the direction of land-based outfitters.

One activity aboard this antique vessel seems among the least widely available in the cruise-ship industry: Each of the ship's three masts has its own crow's nest, and if you're fit enough—and are granted the captain's permission—you can climb to one of them and enjoy sweeping panoramas over land and sea.

PUBLIC AREAS   No one would define the *Sir Francis Drake* as a luxurious vessel, although it likely looks more glamorous today than it did as a cargo vessel. Despite decorative upgrades installed during the vessel's refittings in the 1980s and 1990s,

however, there's absolutely nothing fancy or elaborate aboard this ship. The vessel's small size limits public areas to a few that are used, and used, and used again.

Other than the deck areas, the Main Salon is the ship's catch-all public area. It serves as an all-purpose drinking area, dining area, lecture hall, card room, and general hangout. Tastefully and durably outfitted with dark paneling and blue-and-white upholstery, it's a room you'll see plenty of, because there's really no other place to go, other than the upper decks, which you'll see plenty of as well. There are bars both on deck and within the Main Salon.

Windjammer Barefoot Cruises, Ltd.

SHIPS **Amazing Grace • Fantôme I • Flying Cloud • Legacy (Preview) • Mandalay • Polynesia • Yankee Clipper**

1759 Bay Rd., Miami Beach, FL 33139 (mailing address: P.O. Box 190120, Miami Beach, FL 33119-0120). ☎ 800/327-2601 or 305/672-6453; fax 305/674-1219.

When British poet Thomas Beddos wrote, "The anchor heaves, the ship runs free, the sails swell full, to sea, to sea," he might as well have been describing the Windjammer operation. There's no pretense here—this is sailing in its purest form. On these authentic vessels, which have withstood the test of time and tide, you can taste the salt air as it blows among the riggings, and feel the sails stretch to the wind, propelling you toward adventure.

Windjammer has the largest fleet of sailing ships at sea today (the runner-up is reportedly the Norwegian government). From an inspired if unintentional beginning, it has grown into one of the major lines for cruisers who wish to forgo the orchestrated regimentation on the giant cruise ships.

The patriarch who founded the company in 1947 is Mike Burke—Cap'n Mike, as he's been known for the past half century. Company legend has it that Burke, released from navy submarine duty in 1947, headed for Miami with $600 in back pay, intending to paint the town red. He succeeded. The next morning, he awoke with a blinding hangover and no money, on the deck of a 19-foot sloop moored somewhere in The Bahamas. Mike Burke had apparently bought himself a boat. Using a mostly empty bottle of Scotch, he christened the boat *Hangover,* and the rest is history. The *Hangover* was followed by the *Tondeleyo,* a 70-foot ketch for which Burke traded the house he'd wound up with after a divorce. He lived aboard to save money, then started ferrying friends out for weekends of sailing and fishing. Demand escalated, and Burke quit his full-time job to become a one-man cruise line.

After another year, Burke acquired a 150-foot schooner named *Janeen,* which had run aground and was in need of serious repairs, and thus began his life's work as a restorer of tall ships. After refurbishing *Janeen* himself, Burke rechristened her *Polynesia,* hired a crew of four, and began carrying passengers on week-long cruises. *Polynesia* was followed by the *Brigantine Yankee* and the *Polynesia II,* and then by the ships that comprise the current Windjammer fleet. Some people collect antique cars; Mike Burke collects tall ships.

Burke works on a principle that anyone who's ever bought an old house will understand: Buy them cheap and decrepit, fix them up, and then stand back and admire your handiwork. His six children (including company president Susan) have assisted him in his ventures, renovating most of the vessels at a shipyard the line owns and maintains near Miami. Burke says that the saddest thing he's ever seen is a tall ship permanently tethered to a pier, serving as a museum.

The fleet's flagship is the *Fantôme,* a 282-foot barkentine that was built as a destroyer by the Italian navy, reconfigured into a glamorous yacht by the duke of Westminster, and later bought by Aristotle Onassis as a showy present for the 1956 wedding of his nemesis and rival, Prince Rainier of Monaco, to Grace Kelly. When Onassis didn't receive a wedding invitation, he decided to retain the yacht's title. When Burke heard about the ship, it had been languishing at a harbor in Kiel, Germany, for 14 years. After negotiating a trade with Onassis, Burke flew to Keil and found the ship lying on its side. Extensive restoration brought the *Fantôme* back to its former glory, and a second, $6 million renovation in 1992 enlarged the dining area and added an upper teakwood deck and some additional cabins.

The *Mandalay* was once one of the most famous and luxurious ships in the world, the dream boat (*Husar IV*) of financier E. F. Hutton and his wife, Marjorie Merriweather Post. Later, it was commissioned as a research vessel by Columbia University, which sailed it for 1.25 million miles trying to develop theories (since proven correct) about continental drift. It's estimated that at the time (the early 1980s), half of the knowledge of the world's ocean floor was gathered by instruments aboard this ship.

The *Yankee Clipper,* the only armor-plated sailing yacht in the world, was built by arms baron Alfred Krupp, whose armaments influenced the outcome of the Franco-Prussian War of 1870. Hitler once stepped aboard to award the Iron Cross to one of his U-boat commanders. Seized by the United States as war booty after World War II, the ship eventually became George Vanderbilt's private yacht. While the Vanderbilts owned it, the *Yankee Clipper* was the fastest two-masted sailing vessel off the California coast, once managing an almost frightening 22 knots under full sail. Burke bought the ship just before it was due to be broken down for scrap, then gutted, redesigned, and rebuilt it. Renovations in 1984 added a third mast, additional deck space, and cabin modifications. Although not as light and streamlined as it was originally, it's still a fast and very exciting ship.

The *Flying Cloud,* built in Nantes, France, in 1935, functioned long ago as a training vessel for French cadets. During World War II, the ship served as a decoy and spy ship for the Allied Navy. Its moment of glory came when Charles de Gaulle decorated it for sinking two Japanese submarines while it was carrying nitrates from Tahiti. More than any other vessel in the Windjammer fleet, this one resembles a pirate ship of old.

The *Polynesia,* built in Holland in 1938, was originally known as the *Argus,* and served as a fishing schooner in the Portuguese Grand Banks fleet. Windjammer bought it in 1975. Its original fishiness has disappeared, thanks to a complete reconfiguration of the cabins and interior spaces and the addition of varnished wood. Less stylish-looking than many of its thoroughbred siblings, it nonetheless remains as one of the fleet's most consistently popular ships.

Amazing Grace is the largest, most diligent, and most dogged workhorse in the bunch, functioning as the freight-carrying diesel-driven ship that keeps the other members of the fleet supplied and provisioned. Because of its large hold, it's the most stable ship in the fleet, with no apologies for its role as a relatively slow but reliable umbilical cord to its younger and more high-strung siblings. Its itineraries are more comprehensive than those of any other ship in the fleet, stopping at each port the others use, as well as supply depots en route.

Which is the line's best ship? Each of them is nearly human, according to crew members who helped restore the vessels, with distinctive personalities to match their distinctive lines. All are roughly equivalent in amenities, activities, and priorities, and since each has been extensively refurbished—usually by the same company-owned shipyard and by the same management team—they have more or less equivalent interior decors.

Are these cruises fun? No cruise can be all bad when it includes complimentary Bloody Marys in the morning, Rum Sizzles at sunset, and wine or beer with dinner. Since service for each meal involves two separate seatings, passengers have plenty of time to enjoy another drink or two while waiting for (or recovering from) dinner.

Swimming pools? There's no need, as the crystal-clear Caribbean is the swimming hole. Shuffleboard? Are you kidding? That's for those *other* cruise ships. Work the sails? Well, no. The crew handles that. This is a barefoot adventure, not a Shanghai special: Your duty is to sit back and live it up, not winch up a topsail whenever the captain barks an order.

This is a T-shirt and shorts adventure, with itineraries that are only partially finalized before a ship's departure and are based on such elusive factors as wind and tides. Vessels tend to sail during the late afternoon or night, arriving each morning at landfalls, allowing passengers to enjoy the local terrain and diversions. Favored waters include the Grenadines and the Virgin Islands, miniarchipelagos that offer some of the most challenging and beautiful sailing in the hemisphere, as well as esoteric landfalls such as cone-shaped Saba, historic Statia, or mysterious Carriacou, sites that are almost never visited by larger, diesel-driven ships. *Amazing Grace,* because of its restocking duties (and, of course, its engines) maintains a more rigid schedule.

Despite the fact that the company's fleet is worth millions and its clear public image is the envy of many larger operators, Windjammer continues to think of itself as a mom-and-pop cruise line—and therein lies at least part of its allure for the many iconoclasts who flock to the line's vision of wind-in-the-face adventure.

The line's role as a nonstandard entity with intimate, nonstandard ships and an amused and nonchalantly permissive nature becomes even more obvious whenever it runs theme cruises. Don't expect the kind of tame country music or big band themes that such lines as Holland America and Norwegian Cruise Line have run through like phases of the moon for years. Aside from cruises scheduled to catch the last eclipse of the millennium (February 23, 1998), Windjammer's themes are a lot more raffish and a lot wilder. Examples? Nude cruises, gay cruises (five were scheduled for 1997 alone), and "swingers cruises" where, theoretically, you should bring a spouse with you, even if he or she is abandoned en route. The line also offers "Parrothead Cruises," where fans of Jimmy Buffet wear hats, drink margaritas, and proclaim their love for Caribbean living. Theme cruises tend to be marketed by agents, rather than by the line itself.

PROS & CONS Amateur historians and anyone else who admires the beauty of wind-powered vessels will enjoy these ships. Crews are amicable and easy to talk to, and many other like-minded passengers who appreciate completely unstructured holidays will be traveling with you. As aboard any small ship, however, you're going to be affected by the dynamic of a situation that becomes a kind of cramped miniuniverse unto itself. If you fit in, you'll have a marvelous holiday. If personalities clash, the tensions will be much more visible than aboard larger ships where strains can be more easily concealed.

Don't sign up for one of these cruises unless you enjoy partying. Other than reading and watching the sea, there's not much else to do. Also, if you have certain standards about formality of dress codes, know in advance that there is none here. On the other sartorial hand, some passengers consider it a vacation in itself that they can step aboard with nothing more than a second pair of shorts, clean underwear, and a couple of T-shirts.

Some aboard will already be accustomed to the rocking and rolling of sailing craft on the high seas, but those who aren't sometimes find themselves with a nasty case of *mal de mer.* Newcomers sometimes complain of dreadful seasickness aboard these small vessels, which have no stabilizers and ballast tanks to control the rock and roll. You may grow used to it quickly; if not, the staff can usually provide medication or an ear patch to alleviate motion sickness.

Exactitude of itineraries (or the lack thereof) is another factor you'll need to understand in advance. Sailings will usually follow the routes described in the brochures, although one destination might be substituted for another if a particularly adverse wind is blowing, or if there's a storm between you and your scheduled destination. If your heart is absolutely, positively set on stopping off in Carriacou or the Isles des Saintes, you might be disappointed if Canouan or Dominica is substituted instead. How can you ensure your exposure to as many islands as possible? Register for a two-week odyssey aboard the *Amazing Grace,* the doggedly reliable diesel-driven commissary ship that keeps its sail-driven siblings stocked with provisions, regardless of most wind and weather patterns.

Together, the benefits of Windjammer tally up to a nice package: You'll see natural beauty, be exposed to some offbeat landfalls, and not have to endure the sometimes inane activities that dominate shipboard life on other lines. Windjammer cruises are also relatively inexpensive. Although you'll need to be hardy and something of a rugged individualist to enjoy these excursions, their per diem rates tend to be lower than those of Star Clipper and significantly lower than Windstar Cruises.

Speaking of the competition, Windstar's computer-guided ships don't approach the windblown authenticity of these rebuilt antiques. On the other hand, Windstar and Star Clippers' level of luxury is much, much higher.

TYPES OF PASSENGERS Unlike some "all things to all people" lines, Windjammer is for a particular kind of passenger. Informality is the operative word, and those who appreciate this kind of experience tend to return again and again. (The record is held by "Pappy" Gomez, of Cleveland, Ohio, who has sailed with Windjammer more than 160 times.)

A detailed survey conducted by the line tells us some things about its passengers' lifestyles: Percentages of men and women aboard were 46.5% and 53.5%, respectively; 17% of the passengers identified themselves as single; 3% identified themselves as members of male couples, and 6% as members of female couples. Almost 63% of all passengers were relatively young, between 26 and 45 years old. Passengers aboard the *Amazing Grace* commissary ship, however, tended to be older than those aboard the wind-driven sailing ships.

Some compare the Windjammer experience to a continuous fraternity party, with a crowd that's usually younger than those aboard more conventional lines. You may feel that you spend more time and energy partying (and recovering from partying) than you do experiencing sailing. Whether you consider this fulfilling or exhausting depends on you and the chemistry you develop with fellow passengers.

The sailing vessels tend to attract young, single or divorced, high-energy folks who don't necessarily cotton to highly regimented scheduling, at least not when they're on vacation. Young children should probably not go, nor should anyone prone to seasickness (there's quite a bit of that the first days afloat) or anyone wishing to be pampered (there's none of that during any day afloat). These ships are not for persons with disabilities, either.

DINING   Elaborate dining rituals and fussed-over food are not the reason to sail aboard this line. Food is wholesome, communal, and simple—definitely not Cordon Bleu. Lunches include as many beach barbecues as can be crammed into the week's schedule. There are two open seatings for dinner.

A representative sampling from a peak evening—the Captain's Dinner, say—might include seafood chowder, Caesar salad, prime rib with baked potatoes and vegetables, and bananas flambé. Anyone not interested in prime rib could opt for grilled tuna, but otherwise, what you see is what you get. Lunches are even simpler, with pizzas, deli-style sandwiches, and tried-and-true recipes straight from the Antillean matriarch cookbook, such as Creole-style flying fish. Many dishes overall are rooted in Caribbean tradition. The chef will accommodate special diets, including vegetarian and low-salt.

ACTIVITIES Windjammer deliberately de-emphasizes the activities that dominate shipboard life aboard larger vessels, although it might occasionally host a deck-side crab race after all observers have had just enough cocktails. Your entertainment depends on you, and whatever diversion, dialogue, or reading list you happen to have brought on board. If the weather's fine and you want to lend a hand with shipboard maintenance, trim the sails, or whatever, you might be allowed to help. If the weather gets dicey, however, don't even think about it.

Theme cruises don't begin to match those aboard larger vessels, although two of Windjammer's ships, the *Polynesia* and the *Flying Cloud*, host singles cruises several times a year. Windjammer refers to these as "an alternative to smoky discos," which we couldn't have said better ourselves.

CHILDREN'S ACTIVITIES No children under seven are allowed on board, and children under age 16 must be accompanied by an adult. The line prefers that children be at least 10 years old. Teenagers divert themselves the same way adults do, with conversation, shore excursions, reading, and watching the wide blue sea. Otherwise, few concessions are made for their amusement. Baby-sitting is not available.

ENTERTAINMENT Social interaction around the bars is emphasized. Otherwise, there's almost no organized night life unless you and your fellow passengers work up your own.

SHOPPING A very limited number of toilet articles and some souvenir items are offered, including logo-adorned towels, hats, coffee mugs, T-shirts, shorts, and "Barefoot Bears."

SERVICE Service is adequate, but not elaborate. Depending on the weather, crew members might be more preoccupied with the anchor cables and rigging than with color-coordinating the place mats for that night's dinner, as they should be.

You won't find elegance or anyone willing to provide Grand Hotel service on board. Unlike dozens of more upscale cruise lines, Windjammer never defines a master/servant relationship between passengers and staff. Windjammer staffers fit comfortably into their role as fellow travelers who just happen to serve dinner or drinks whenever their schedules call for it.

Windjammer tends to attract a staff that shares founder Mike Burke's appreciation for the wide open sea and barely concealed scorn for corporate agendas and staid, suburban priorities. Also, many staff members are from the same Caribbean islands Windjammer ships might visit, making for increased conviviality and excitement whenever a vessel pulls into an employee's home port.

ITINERARIES More than virtually any other line afloat, Windjammer adjusts its itineraries in midcruise to reflect changing wind and weather patterns, as well as any island event of particular interest. The itinerary of each cruise is up to the ship captain, as long as the ship leaves the port of embarkation and returns at the scheduled time. The haphazard nature of any voyage is part of the excitement.

Amazing Grace—As a motorized, diesel-driven supply ship whose duty involves replenishing the stocks of each of its siblings, *Amazing Grace* navigates its way through the Caribbean with a more rigid timetable than any of the other ships in the fleet. Cruises are 13 days each and call at most of the ports between Freeport, The Bahamas, and Port-of-Spain, Trinidad. This radically divergent route encompasses greater distances and more ports of call (almost 20) than those promoted by most mainstream cruise ships.

Fantôme—Throughout the year, *Fantôme* embarks from its home port in Belize City on alternating round-trip six-day cruises that stop at various points along the Belize Reef, the Gulf of Honduras, and the Bay Islands. The "Bay Island Cruise" stops at Goffs' Cay, Lighthouse Reef/Half Moon Cay, Roatan, Cayos Cochinos, and Glovers Reef/Northern Cay. The "Spanish Main Cruise" visits Placencia, Puerto Cortes, Roatan, and Utila/Half Moon Cay.

Flying Cloud—Six-day cruises depart every Monday from Tortola, British Virgin Islands, calling at a selected roster of some of the archipelago's least-visited, least-touristy sites, such as Jost van Dyke, Virgin Gorda, Peter Island, and Norman Island.

Mandalay—Thirteen-day cruises depart on Mondays from either Grenada or Antigua and feature stops in St. Vincent and isolated harbors in the Grenadines that usually include Bequia, Palm Island, St. Lucia, Guadaloupe, Martinique, St. Kitts, and Carriacou. About one in five of the cruises follows an abbreviated six-day circuit of the same route.

Polynesia—Six-day cruises depart every Monday from St. Maarten, with stops at a selection of islands including St. Barts, St. Kitts, Saba, Statia, Prickly Pear, Anguilla, Nevis, and Montserrat.

Yankee Clipper—Six-day cruises depart every Monday from Grenada with stops at islands throughout the Grenadines.

SPECIAL DISCOUNTS   Do you want to at least imagine that you're a stowaway on board Errol Flynn's ship in *Captain Blood*? Stay aboard the night before any cruise and the charge will be a relatively modest $45 per person, double occupancy.

If you opt for more than one consecutive cruise, the nights prior to each sailing (usually as the ships are anchored in port) are free. Children under 12 sharing a cabin with two adults are charged 50% of the adult fare.

Payment of a $25 membership fee entitles clients to receipt of special mailings and $25 discounts on an unlimited number of future Windjammer cruises.

SINGLE SUPPLEMENTS   Solo passengers pay from 175% to 200% of the per person cost for double occupancy. If a solo traveler wants the line to assign him or her a same-sex roommate, there won't be any imposition of the surcharge. Even during the well-attended singles cruises—such as those aboard the *Polynesia*, departing from St. Maarten—many single people check in expecting Windjammer to assign them a roommate who will, it is hoped, be compatible.

PORT CHARGES   Six-day outings for all ships except the *Fantôme* require payment of only $25 worth of port charges, less than that charged by larger cruise lines and ships. Port charges for 13-day outings cost $50 per person. Aboard *Fantôme*, charges for four-day trips are $20; five-day trips, $25; and eight-day trips, $45.

Amazing Grace

⇕ ⇕

Specifications

Size (in tons)	1,526	Crew	40 (International)
Number of Cabins	47	Passenger/Crew Ratio	2.4 to 1
Number of Outside Cabins	47	Year Built	1955
Number of Passengers	94	Last Major Refurbishment	1995
Officers	American		

Frommer's Ratings (Scale of 1–10)

Activities	5.0	Public Areas	4.8
Cabins	5.5	Public Comfort/Space	4.5
Cleanliness/Maintenance	8.2	Recreational Facilities/Pool	2.0
Entertainment	5.0	Service	6.0
Food & Beverage	5.5	Ship Crew/Officers	8.5
Interior Decor	5.8	Shore Excursions	9.2
Ports of Call	9.5	Worth the Money	9.5
		Overall Average	**6.4**

This dowdy but reliable sea horse, moving its way doggedly and regularly through most of the Caribbean archipelago, is the only vessel in the Windjammer fleet that does without sails. The *Amazing Grace* is the closest thing to a banana boat in the cruise industry, with all the leisure that life aboard a slow-moving freighter entails.

Built as the *Pharos* in Dundee, Scotland, in 1955, it mostly carried supplies to isolated lighthouses and North Sea oil rigs, though once or twice it was pressed into service as a weekend cruiser for the queen of England. The vessel was acquired by Windjammer in 1988 and, despite many modernizations, still retains some vestiges of its British past. Today, it's still a freighter servicing remote outposts, albeit in the warm Caribbean rather than the chilly North Sea. If you come aboard expecting to be treated like the queen, however, you'll be sorely disappointed.

Some of the line's least dramatic (but cheapest) cruises are its languid odysseys aboard the *Amazing Grace*. Few other seagoing options emulate the "slow boat to China" motif that is this vessel's dominant characteristic. The lack of organized activities is a drawback, however, so you'll be forced to create your own. Clients are noticeably more sedentary, older, and less party-oriented than those aboard the line's more raffish sail-powered vessels.

While the overall rating for this ship appears unnaturally low when compared to other ships, it does not indicate a lack of enthusiasm. *Amazing Grace* simply doesn't have the facilities of most other cruise ships. However, for adventure and ports of call, it's top-notch.

Cabins & Rates

Cabins	Average per diem	Bathtub	Fridge	Phone	Sitting Area	TV
Inside	$75–$100	No	No	Yes	No	Yes
Outside	$95–$225	No	Yes	Yes	Yes	Yes

CABINS   As you might have guessed, cabins are utterly without frills and very small, though they're a tad roomier than others in Windjammer's fleet. About half contain the varnished paneling from the ship's original construction; the others are more modern, with almost no nostalgic value. Although there's a sink in each cabin, you'll have to share shower and toilet facilities with passengers from two other cabins. The honeymoon suite, near the stern, is often rented by nonhoneymooners because of its somewhat larger size. There are no wheelchair-accessible cabins.

RECREATION & FITNESS FACILITIES
This is the only Windjammer ship with a whirlpool, which is on the (relatively) spacious deck. There's no swimming pool, health club, or fitness facilities. Instead, you'll get your exercise during snorkeling and scuba sessions at the ports of call. Snorkeling gear (mask, fins, snorkel, and carrying bag) rents for $20 per week, and one-tank dives offered at some ports of call cost around $50 each. Novice divers pay $80 for a "resort course." Shore outings sometimes include strenuous hiking expeditions. All excursions and scuba

expeditions are conducted by outside agencies, not by Windjammer, and passengers are required to sign a liability release before participating.

PUBLIC AREAS   You can have a lot of fun aboard this ship, though there's no avoiding reminders that it is indeed a glorified freighter. A bar/lounge faces forward across the bow, and there's a library. Some of the greatest authenticity preserved from the ship's early days is a piano room and a smoking room. Because large sections of this vessel (the storage areas) are off-limits to passengers, many people tend to gravitate to the deck areas for reading, napping, or whatever.

The dining room has booth-type tables that seat up to eight passengers. There are two open seatings, generally at 6:30pm and 8pm.

Fantôme • Flying Cloud • Mandalay • Polynesia • Yankee Clipper

⚓ ⚓

Specifications

Size (in tons)		Officers	British/Australian
Fantôme	676	Crew	
Flying Cloud	400	*Fantôme*	45
Mandalay	420	*Flying Cloud*	25
Polynesia	430	*Mandalay*	28
Yankee Clipper	327	*Polynesia*	45
Number of Cabins		*Yankee Clipper*	29
Fantôme	64	Passenger/Crew Ratio	2.2–3.1 to 1
Flying Cloud	33	Year Built	
Mandalay	36	*Fantôme*	1927
Polynesia	46	*Flying Cloud*	1927
Yankee Clipper	64	*Mandalay*	1923
Number of Outside Cabins		*Polynesia*	1938
Fantôme	54	*Yankee Clipper*	1927
Flying Cloud	33	Last Major Refurbishments	
Mandalay	36	*Fantôme*	1992
Polynesia	46	*Flying Cloud*	1991
Yankee Clipper	64	*Mandalay*	1982
Number of Passengers		*Polynesia*	1990
Fantôme	128	*Yankee Clipper*	1984
Flying Cloud	74		
Mandalay	72		
Polynesia	126		
Yankee Clipper	64		

Frommer's Ratings (Scale of 1–10)

Activities	5.0	Public Areas	5.0
Cabins	5.2	Public Comfort/Space	4.5
Cleanliness/Maintenance	8.2	Recreational Facilities/Pools	1.0
Entertainment	5.0	Service	6.0
Food & Beverage	5.5	Ship Crew/Officers	8.5
Interior Decor	6.5	Shore Excursions	9.2
Ports of Call	9.5	Worth the Money	9.5
		Overall Average	**6.3**

Despite different origins, different histories, and subtle differences in the way they react to the wind and weather, each of these sailing ships shares many things in common with the others. We've opted to cluster them into one all-encompassing review because of the extent to which each has been rebuilt and reconfigured to the Windjammer ideal. For the ships' individual histories, refer to the pages above.

How to select one or another if you're a first-time Windjammer client? We advise you to select your ship based on its itinerary rather than its aesthetics, taking into account the frequent cruises for singles that are held aboard the *Polynesia* and the *Flying Cloud*. Other than that, which boat you float will depend on such vagaries as your schedule and any special promotions the line might be offering.

The overall rating for these ships appears unnaturally low when compared to other ships, but that doesn't indicate a lack of enthusiasm. These Windjammer ships simply don't have the facilities of most other cruise ships. However, for adventure and ports of call they're absolutely top-notch.

Cabins & Rates

Cabins	Average per diem	Bathtub	Fridge	Phone	Sitting Area	TV
Cabins	$125–$155	No	No	Yes	No	Yes
Suites	$155–$185	No	Yes	Yes	Yes	Yes

CABINS Cabins are cramped; there's no getting around that. Few retain any glamorous vestiges of their original owners, and most are about as functional as they come. On sojourns of longer than two weeks they become claustrophobic.

Each cabin has a minuscule bathroom with a shower that sprays water everywhere, regardless of how careful you are. Remember to hide your toilet paper and towels before you turn it on. The flood of water tends to leave bathrooms perpetually wet. On many vessels, hot water is available only during certain hours of the day; that is, whenever the ships' galleys and laundries aren't using it. Be prepared for toilets that don't always function properly, and retain your sense of humor as they're repaired.

Storage space is very limited, but this isn't a serious problem because few passengers bring very much with them. Many cabins have upper and lower berths, and those aboard the *Flying Cloud* and the *Polynesia* even have dormitory-style cabins with six bunks arranged merchant-marine style. If you crave even a modest degree of privacy and look forward to retreating to your cabin when shipmates grow wearying, these dormitory-style beds are probably a very bad idea. However, they're sought out by families traveling with young children, and during any of the line's singles cruises (when some are designated for "bachelors" the others for "bachelorettes") they're invariably sold out.

Some vessels contain several suites which, although not spacious by the standards of larger, diesel-driven ships, seem to be of generous proportions when contrasted to standard cabins. There are no wheelchair-accessible cabins on any of these ships.

RECREATION & FITNESS FACILITIES
Ships are too small to provide health clubs or any of the sauna and fitness regimes so heavily promoted aboard larger ships. None of the vessels has a swimming pool. You'll get an adequate amount of exercise, however, during snorkeling and scuba sessions conducted at the ports of call. Snorkeling and diving fees/specifications are the same as aboard *Amazing Grace* (see page 324.)

PUBLIC AREAS   What glamour may have been associated with these ships in the past is long gone, lost to the years or in the gutting and refitting they required before entering Windjammer service. You may note a few touches of rosewood or mahogany, but otherwise the decors are durable, washable, and practical, and appropriate backdrops for a passenger roster so laid-back that few bother to ever change out of their bathing suits, T-shirts, and shorts. Dining rooms are durable and designed with efficiency in mind. In contrast, teakwood decks look positively opulent; many passengers adopt some preferred corner of the decks as a place to hang out, because views of the wide blue sea and sky make the vessel appear less crowded and cramped than it really is.

In fairness to Windjammer, many of the factors outlined above (and the criteria used throughout this guide) are simply not pertinent to this kind of niche-specific line. It's like comparing the proverbial apples and oranges. If passengers have any complaints at all, they're often offset by the rare and heady thrill of sailing aboard such evocative craft.

Legacy (Preview)

Windjammer's newest and largest ship was originally designed as a motorized research vessel for the French government. Designed in 1963 with a deep keel that gave it additional balance during North Atlantic and North Sea storms, it was one of several government-owned ships sending weather reports to a central agency in Paris, which used them to predict storm patterns on the French mainland. The advent of global satellites made the vessel obsolete. It was bought by Windjammer in 1986, and, over the course of a decade, cleaned of the residue of its earlier incarnation.

The massive refitting of the vessel, which cost in excess of $10 million and was conducted at Windjammer's family managed shipyard in Trinidad, completely reconfigured the ship's interior. Four steel masts and 11 sails were added, plus accoutrements the vessel needed for seven-day barefoot (and bare-boned) jaunts through the eastern Caribbean. Its configuration of sails will most closely resemble that of the *Polynesia,* but, at 1,121 tons, it's larger than any other vessel in the Windjammer fleet, although still tiny compared to a megaship.

Because it corresponds to the strict engineering standards of the American Bureau of Shipping (ABS), the U.S. Coast Guard has approved it for dockage at ports on the U.S. mainland. As such, expect the ship to be based in Miami for several months before being sent off to a home port of St. Thomas and a usual cruising ground in the Virgin Islands. Unclear at press time was the specific launch date (though a good rumor of April 1997 was heard) and the exact itinerary the ship will follow. Consult your travel agent for late-breaking news.

Nautical engineers hail the ship's revised design as a "staysail schooner." Windjammer, faced with a lack of antique sailing vessels suitable for restoration, anticipates that its newest ship will set a trend for the adaptation of deep-keeled but relatively modern vessels into replicas of sailing ships of yore.

Windstar Cruises

SHIPS Wind Spirit • Wind Star

300 Elliott Ave. West, Seattle, WA 98119. ☎ 800/258-7245 or 206/281-3535; fax 206/281-0627.

Launched in 1986, Windstar Cruises combines the best of 19th-century clipper design with the best of modern yacht engineering. As you see *Wind Star* or *Wind Spirit* approach a Caribbean port, with their four masts the height of 20-story buildings, you'll think the seafaring days of Joseph Conrad or Herman Melville have returned.

But Captain Ahab wouldn't know what to do with a Windstar ship. Million-dollar Hewlett-Packard computers control the six triangular sails with their 21,489 square feet of Dacron, flying from masts that tower 204 feet above deck. They automatically trim the sails and control fin stabilizers, rudder tab, anti-heeling devices, and much, much more. Sails can be retracted in two minutes to a diameter of less than a foot. Nothing like this has ever been attempted before in ship design.

The original designs were developed by Warsila Marine Industries in Helsinki. The French government assisted with subsidies, and the ships were built at Le Havre in France. The catalyst behind the program was flamboyant Jean Claude Potier, a native Parisian, who, in a 25-year-span, has led the French Line, the Sun Line, and Paquet (this last based in North America).

In the late 1980s, Windstar was acquired by Holland America Line, which is itself wholly owned by Carnival Cruise Lines. As such, Windstar is the most adventure-oriented of Carnival's many cruise-line divisions, and although not as luxurious as Carnival's most upscale branch, Seabourn, it nonetheless prides itself on a cruise experience that's much, much more upscale than the ones offered aboard any of Carnival's megaships. Today, Windstar operates a trio of ships, one of which, the *Wind Song*, remains in the Pacific throughout most of the year.

Windstar offers an unabashedly sybaritic type of cruise aboard superior resorts that just happen to float. Under full sail, the calm tranquility of the cruises is utterly blissful. Windstar cruising is a top-class, ultracomfortable experience, with superb food and deluxe service. It's not a barefoot, rigging-pulling, chowder-down, paper plates in lap, sleep-on-the-deck, or let-it-all-hang-out adventure.

Passengers can visit the bridge at any time to watch the computers at work. If sail control is switched off, you can actually steer the ship under the careful supervision of the officers at an old-time wheel located aft on the flying bridge. Because of the antiheeling devices, Windstars rarely lean more than $2^1/_2°$ (maximum 6°). The ships are so stable in fact that at times the bridge induces a tilt so passengers feel they're actually on a sailing ship.

PROS & CONS For a commercial cruise line, Windstar is about as close as you can get to experiencing the lifestyles of the rich and famous at sea, with nearly all the pampering inherent on a private yacht.

Windstar's exclusivity, not to mention its high price, makes it the wrong choice for certain people. First-timers to cruising should look elsewhere for their inaugural trip. Likewise, single passengers, unless they are firmly independent and used to being alone, may feel left out, since everybody seems to be a couple. (Another factor that tilts the passenger roster toward couples is the line's price structure, which is not particularly attractive for single passengers.) Families with children should also book elsewhere, as these are ships for adults, and sophisticated adults at that.

Windstar cruises are basically for those who wish to provide their own entertainment, and don't expect glittering floor shows or glitzy gambling casinos in the evening. (There's a small casino aboard each Windstar vessel that's staffed with employees selected by Carnival—the admitted experts at that sort of thing—although each casino is downright drab compared to those aboard Carnival vessels.) Passengers don't pack formal clothes. Dress is casually elegant in the evening, but hardly formal.

Complaints are generally few, and most are minor, such as that spirits are expensive or that it's difficult to communicate with some crew members. There are no elevators, so persons with disabilities would have great difficulty getting around the vessel.

TYPES OF PASSENGERS   These cruises are recommended for people who say that they wouldn't be caught dead on a Carnival cruise, or even a Royal Caribbean cruise. The passengers are those normally on the A list for parties instead of the B list or below, and tend to be interested in tennis, corporate hierarchies, blue-chip stocks, and well-maintained real estate. Many hail from Florida and California, and somewhat fewer others are from New Jersey, Connecticut, and Delaware. They tend to range in age from 30 to 70, with an average age of 48, and enjoy an average annual household income in excess of $80,000. Many are retirees, although some relatively youthful passengers enjoying either their first or second honeymoons might be on board too. About a third of all passengers are repeaters, a figure that represents one of the best recommendations for Windstar.

Many passengers want something different from the regular cruise-line experience. These cruises are for those seeking a romantic escape, who like to visit islands not often touched by regular cruise ships, including the Grenadines, the Tobago Cays, and relatively isolated dependencies of Guadeloupe such as the Ile de Saints.

DINING   The food is among the best of any vessel sailing the Caribbean, ranking up there with Seabourn and Cunard.

The signature cuisine is known as "180 Degrees from Ordinary," the creation of the renowned chef/restaurateur Joachim Splichal, winner of many culinary awards (including some from the James Beard Society) and owner of Los Angeles's Patina Restaurant and Pinot Bistro. Splichal's recipes include goodly numbers of "Heart Smart" items that are low in virtually everything that might be bad for you.

Splichal's food is most inventive and imaginative, as reflected by such appetizers as a corn risotto with wild mushrooms and basil followed by a "seafood strudel" of lobster, scallops, mussels, king crab, and shrimp with lobster sauce. Windstar recently added a new healthy choice menu available for breakfast, lunch, and dinner and designed by expert Jeanne Jones. The aim is for moderation in calories and fat grams, not deprivation.

With regard to wine, Windstar vessels stock some more interesting California labels, including Robert Mondavi, Cuvaison, Merryvale, Dry Creek, and Iron Horse. In 1996, the line revamped its onboard inventories to include greater numbers of unpretentious but well-recommended vintages priced from $15 to $30 a bottle.

Each ship contains two dining rooms, one used during breakfast and lunch (The Veranda) and another, more formal room (The Restaurant) that's the stage for dinner. Whereas The Veranda is a sunny, window-lined room whose tables extend from inside out onto a covered deck, The Restaurant is enclosed and accented with nautical touches that include teakwood trim and pillars wrapped decoratively in hempen rope. At breakfast and lunch, meals can either be ordered from a menu or selected from a buffet. Made-to-taste omelets are available at breakfast, and luncheons feature a special pasta dish of the day. There is open seating for meals, at tables that are designed for between two and eight diners. The captain presides over one large table for 14.

Windstar chefs do their very best to fulfill special requests, but special diets should be ordered in advance. On some cruises there is a barbecue ashore.

The Restaurant is "casually elegant," which covers a multitude of dressing sins. Normally the passengers conform to contemporary and acceptable social garb. No tuxedos are really necessary, but one would be perfectly in vogue at a captain's party. Room service is available 24 hours.

ACTIVITIES   Activities are generally livelier when the ships dock than when they sail. Passengers can enjoy a watersports platform lowered at the stern where almost every conceivable aquatic activity can be enjoyed. But when the vessel leaves port, there are no scheduled bingo or wooden-horse-racing type of activities.

The island tours are more creative than usual. Staff are willing and able to point passengers toward good spots for such activities as bird-watching, butterfly collecting, geology tours, or snorkeling, all depending on weather conditions.

CHILDREN'S ACTIVITIES   As children are not encouraged to sail with Windstar, there are no activities planned for them.

ENTERTAINMENT   Passengers entertain themselves, generally. There's a low-key pianist aboard, and perhaps a vocalist or a combination of both during cocktail hour in the lounge. Local entertainment, such as steel bands, calypso bands, or limbo dancers, is sometimes brought aboard at a port of call. A small, very modest casino offers slots, blackjack, and Caribbean stud poker. In lieu of a Broadway or Las Vegas–inspired floor show, there's an intimate piano bar.

SHOPPING   Each ship has a cluster of small shops, one with upscale merchandise and one for sports. Other than the usual cruise-ship junk items, the merchandise is tailored to discriminating passengers, most of whom have just about everything they want anyway. There's also an onboard jewelry shop whose inventory contains baubles suitable for impulse buying, even if your impulse is to shell out $5,000.

SERVICE   The service is exemplary. Room service is prompt, almost on the run. Windstar is a class operation, as reflected by its service personnel. The staff smiles hello and makes every effort to learn a passenger's name. The lower-level staff are far too shy for that and may not communicate at all until spoken to first. The line operates under a "tipping not required" policy, though no member of the staff will refuse if you're inclined to give them a little something extra for exemplary service.

ITINERARIES

Wind Spirit—The ship uses Charlotte Amalie, St. Thomas, as a base for its seven-day cruises in fall, winter, and spring. Stops are made at Saba, French St. Martin, Ile des Saints, St. Barts, Virgin Gorda, Jost van Dyke, and St. Thomas. This circuit is interrupted only by a 14-day holiday cruise, conducted over Christmas and New Years, that includes visits to Aruba, Bonaire, and/or Curaçao. In summer, the ship sails the Mediterranean.

Wind Star—In fall, winter, and spring, the ship uses Bridgetown, Barbados, as a home port for seven-day cruises. A route that includes stopovers at Bridgetown, Nevis, St. Maarten, St. Barts, Ile des Saints, and Bequia alternates on a weekly basis with one that includes stops at Bequia, Martinique, Ile des Saints, Tobago, the Tobago Cays, and Pigeon Island off the coast of St. Lucia. The ship sails the Mediterranean in summer.

SPECIAL DISCOUNTS   Windstar offers an early booking discount program whose savings can reach 50% off the regular brochure fare. Discounts typically range from 10% to 50%, depending on the departure date and the season. Discounts almost never increase as a sailing date nears, although special promotions sometimes make last-minute deals especially desirable. If a special promotion is activated after an early booker has already paid, the savings are credited back to his or her account. Windstar publishes a price sheet, distributed to former passengers and travel agents at frequent intervals, that reflects last-minute price adjustments and special promotions. A third person occupying a double cabin pays 50% of the per person rate for a double.

SINGLE SUPPLEMENTS   Solo passengers pay 150% of the published per person rate.

PORT CHARGES   On Caribbean sailings, port charges range from $145 to $225, depending on the sailing.

Wind Spirit • Wind Star

⚓ ⚓ ⚓ ⚓ ⚓

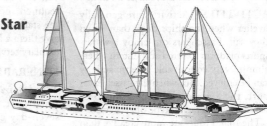

Specifications

Size (in tons)	5,350	Crew	91 (Indonesian/ Filipino)
Number of Cabins	74	Passenger/Crew Ratio	1.6 to 1
Number of Outside Cabins	100%	Year Built	1986/1988
Number of Passengers	148	Last Major Refurbishment	1995/1996
Officers	British		

Frommer's Ratings (Scale of 1–10)

Activities	8.0	Public Areas	9.0
Cabins	8.9	Public Comfort/Space	9.2
Cleanliness/Maintenance	9.5	Recreational Facilities/Pool	7.0
Entertainment	6.0	Service	9.0
Food & Beverage	9.0	Ship Crew/Officers	8.0
Interior Decor	8.5	Shore Excursions	9.0
Ports of Call	9.5	Worth the Money	9.0
		Overall Average	**8.6**

The most noticeable thing about these ships is their beauty. Despite their high-tech nature and their size, which is significantly larger than virtually any private yacht afloat, they nonetheless have the grace and line of a clipper ship, with virtually none of the associated discomforts.

There's even a needle-shaped bowsprit jutting into the waves. Getting around is usually easy, except for the fact that there is no inside access to the breakfast and luncheon restaurant, so during high winds or rain, access via an external set of stairs can be both inconvenient and uncomfortable.

Cabins & Rates

Cabins	Average per diem	Bathtub	Fridge	Phone	Sitting Area	TV
Outside	$485–$513	No	Yes	Yes	Yes	Yes

CABINS   All cabins are outside with large portholes. They are all very similar and there are no class distinctions among them. Although cabins are perfectly adequate for two occupants, they'd be uncomfortably crowded for the rare third

Late-Breaking Windstar News

In early May 1997, it was announced that Windstar Cruises had purchased Club Med's *Club Med 1,* and would take delivery of the ship in March 1998. Reports are that the ship will be refit, remodelled, and renamed the *Wind Surf.* When finished, the ship will actually have *fewer* cabins than before—accommodating 312 passengers instead of 386 but reconfiguring the ship to include 30 more suites than it currently carries.

In its inaugural season, the new Windstar ship will sail a Mediterranean itinerary May through October before repositioning to the Caribbean to spend November through March sailing from Barbados.

According to Richard Meadows, vice president of marketing and sales for Windstar Cruises, "This ship is perfect for Windstar. It was built by the same shipyard as Windstar's other three vessels, and with planned modifications, we believe this ship will fit quite well within the Windstar fleet." Windstar plans to debut a comprehensive new spa program aboard the new ship, and in keeping with the line's tradition will distribute artwork throughout to evoke a casual yet refined atmosphere.

person booking. Mattresses can be adapted into either one queen-size or two twin-sized beds. Each cabin contains a TV with VCR, a CD player, a minibar, and a closet that's more compact than most passengers feel really comfortable with. Teakwood-decked bathrooms are better than those aboard many luxury cruise liners, and contain a hair dryer and plenty of fluffy towels,

We recommend getting a cabin either amidships, or maybe forward, on deck two. Note that the engines, when run at full speed, tend to be noisy. No cabins are designated as singles.

This line is not recommended for passengers with serious disabilities or those who are wheelchair bound. There are no elevators on board, access to piers is often by tenders, and ramps over door sills are not adequate.

RECREATION & FITNESS FACILITIES
The swimming pool is tiny, as you might expect aboard such a relatively small-scale ship. There's also a hot tub and a barely adequate fitness room. You can continue your exercise routines on Nautilus equipment, stationary bikes, treadmills, and free weights.

PUBLIC AREAS Public areas are adequate in size, given that the maximum 148 passengers are rarely carried aboard. The interiors are classy and tasteful; furnishings are rich-looking, conservatively contemporary, and tasteful. Fabrics are offset with ample use of wood, especially burls. Large glass windows allow in plenty of light.

The open decks seem to invite a camaraderie among passengers and crew, but there are places to go and hide out and be by yourself (or with a companion) if that's your desire. One of the most appealing of these is the library, where dark colors and lots of exposed wood create a feeling that manages to be both nautical and collegiate at the same time. Each contains books, magazines, CDs, and videotapes.

10 Ports of Call

You've picked your Caribbean cruise, and you're ready to sail. How you spend your time aboard ship is entirely dependent on your personal preferences, but when you anchor at a port of call, you need to know how to make the most of your time. Should you take a shore excursion or arrange a tour yourself? Where are the best beaches? Are there outfitters that can arrange scuba diving or snorkeling? Where can you find the best duty-free bargains or island handcrafts? What's the best place on the island to have lunch? We'll answer all those questions, and more, as we take you to 21 ports of call, mainly in the Caribbean, but also including The Bahamas, Mexico, and Key West.

This chapter features complete A-to-Z coverage, telling you how best to see each port of call. On some islands, it's best to take an arranged shore excursion, because roads may be poor and driving difficult. We'll tell you where that's the case, and we'll also tell you how to get around on your own in other places, whether on foot, by taxi, or by renting a car. In some cases it may be cheaper to book an excursion yourself, and we'll share our insider advice on how to do that. We'll give you all the options so you can choose whether to go it alone or go on a tour.

As a general rule, most cruise ships arrive in port around 7am and passengers start disembarking around 9am. (This can vary considerably depending on the individual cruise.) You rarely have to clear customs or immigration, because your ship's purser has your passport or documents and will have done all the paperwork for you. When local officials give the word, you go ashore. Sometimes you can walk down the gangplank right onto the pier, but if the port isn't big enough to accommodate large cruise ships your ship will anchor offshore and ferry passengers to land via a tender. You may have to wait in line to get ashore.

Most passengers start heading back to the ship around 4pm or not much later than 5pm. By 6pm you're often sailing off to your next destination. In the appendix to this book we've included a few sample "port day" activity calendars, which should give you an idea of how some lines structure and schedule their days at anchor.

All shore excursions are carefully organized to coincide with your time in port. Taxi drivers meet all cruise ships and will quickly take you to the beach you've selected, and it's a good idea to arrange with the driver to pick you up at a certain time to bring you back to the port. If you opt to explore an island on your own, you should always make car-rental arrangements in advance, especially during the popular winter

What the Anchors Mean

⚓ ⚓ ⚓ ⚓	The best in the Caribbean
⚓ ⚓ ⚓	A close runner-up of wide appeal
⚓ ⚓ ⚓	Lots to see and do, plus good shopping
⚓ ⚓	Minor attractions and limited shopping
⚓	Let's stay on board

months. To cut costs, form a car pool with another couple or two.

With regard to duty-free shopping, the savings on duty-free merchandise can range from as little as 5% to as much as 50%. Unless there's a special sale being offered, many products will carry comparable price tags from island to island. If you have particular goods you're thinking of buying this way, it pays to check prices at your local discount retailer before you leave home, so you'll know whether you're really getting a bargain or not.

It's also a good idea to talk with your cruise-ship director before you reach a port if you want to do something special, like take a submarine ride in St. Thomas, or pursue a sport, be it scuba, golf, tennis, horseback riding, or fishing. You'll need to reserve spots for many of these activities before you land, because facilities might be filled by land-based vacationers or by passengers from other cruise ships. It goes without saying that if you arrive at a port of call and find the harbor filled with ships, expect the shops, restaurants, and beaches—everything, as a matter of fact—to be crowded. Call from the docks for a reservation.

1 Antigua ⚓ ⚓ ⚓

Rolling, rustic Antigua (*an-TEE-gah*) claims to have a different beach for every day of the year. Though this may be an exaggeration, its numerous sugar-white, reef-protected beaches are reason enough to visit, even if just for a day. Antigua is also known for the yachting facilities centered at English Harbour, home of Nelson Dockyard National Park, one of the Caribbean's major historical attractions.

Sleepy St. John's, the capital, has seen better days and is a bit tattered. It's a large, neatly laid out town, 6 miles from the airport and less than a mile from Deep Water Harbour Terminal. Protected in the throat of a narrow bay, the town is full of cobblestone sidewalks, weather-beaten wooden houses, corrugated iron roofs, and louvered Caribbean verandas. The port is the focal point of commerce and industry, as well as the seat of government and visitor shopping.

COMING ASHORE

Only smaller ships anchor directly at English Harbour; everyone else reaches it via taxi or shore excursion from Deep Water Harbour Terminal in St. John's. Passengers landing here can head directly to the nearby duty-free shopping centers, Heritage Quay (pronounced *key*) and Redcliffe Quay. You don't need a guide to walk around this sleepy town. Credit-card phones are located on the dock.

FAST FACTS

Currency   The **Eastern Caribbean dollar (EC$)** is used on these islands; however, nearly all prices are quoted in U.S. dollars. For a long time, the EC dollar has been worth about 37¢ in U.S. currency ($1 U.S. = EC$2.70).

Information   Head to the **Antigua and Barbuda Department of Tourism** at Long and Thames streets in St. John's (☎ 268/462-0480). Don't expect the staff here to tell you very much; they offer only cursory data. Open Monday to Thursday from 8am to 4:30pm and Friday from 8am to 3pm.

Language The official language is English.

SHORE EXCURSIONS

Since we don't recommend renting a car here, it's best to take the ship's shore excursions, which are less expensive than hiring a private taxi. The major excursion is to Nelson's Dockyard and Clarence House at English Harbour. On the way you'll get to view some of the island's lush countryside. Most shore excursions offered by the cruise lines cost anywhere from $30 to $40, depending on the line, and last three hours. That will still leave you plenty of time for shopping or beaching. If you're in an Indiana Jones mood, you can call **Tropikelly** (☎ 268/461-0383), which takes you by four-wheel drive through an Antigua rarely seen by foreigners. In five hours and for a cost of $60 per person, you're shown the ruins of old forts or sugar mills, taken along rainforest trails and through land that was once thriving plantations, and finally arrive at Boggy Peak, which is Antigua's loftiest citadel. The tour even includes a picnic lunch with drinks.

GETTING AROUND

Taxis meet every cruise ship. The one-way fare from the airport to English Harbour is an expensive $25 or more. The taxis don't have meters; although the government fixes the rates, it's always wise to negotiate the fare before getting in. While costly, the best way to see Antigua is by private taxi, since the drivers are also guides. Most taxi tours cost $16 and up per hour.

We don't recommend renting a car here, since the roads are seriously potholed and local taxi drivers remove the signs. While buses exist and are cheap, we don't recommend them for visitors

because of the low comfort level and inconvenience of their schedules.

SEEING THE SIGHTS

If you don't want to go to English Harbour, you can stay in St. John's to shop and explore its minor attractions. All this can be done on foot from the cruise-ship dock.

ST. JOHN'S

The **market** in the southern part of St. John's is colorful and interesting, especially on Saturday morning when vendors are busy selling their fruits and vegetables. The partially open-air market lies at the lower end of Market Street.

You'll see the Anglican **St. John's Cathedral** between Long Street and Newgate Street at Church Lane (☎ 268/461-0082). The **Museum of Antigua and Barbuda,** at Long and Market streets (☎ 268/462-1469), traces the history of the two-island nation from its geological birth to present day.

Established in 1893, the $3^1/2$-acre **Antigua and Barbuda Botanical Gardens,** at the corner of Nevis and Temple streets (☎ 268/462-1007), is filled with tropical blossoms, herbal plants, ferns, dripping philodendrons, rare bromeliads, and a colorful carpet of flowers.

✪ NELSON'S DOCKYARD NATIONAL PARK

One of the major attractions of the eastern Caribbean, **Nelson's Dockyard** (☎ 268/460-1379) sits on one of the world's safest landlocked harbors, 11 miles southeast of St. John's. This centerpiece of the national park is the only existing example of a Georgian naval base. English ships used the harbor as a refuge from hurricanes as early as 1671, and Adm. Horatio Nelson made it his headquarters from 1784 to 1787. The dockyard played a leading role in the era of privateers, pirates, and great 18th-century sea battles.

Restored by the Friends of English Harbour, the dockyard is sometimes

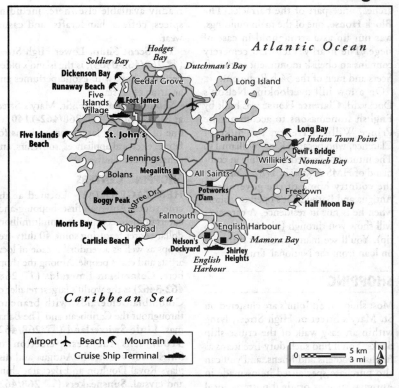

Atlantic Ocean

Hodges Bay
Soldier Bay
Dutchman's Bay
Dickenson Bay
Runaway Beach
Cedar Grove
Long Island
Five Islands Village
Fort James
Long Bay
Indian Town Point
St. John's
Parham
Devil's Bridge
Five Islands Beach
Willikie's
Nonsuch Bay
Jennings
Megaliths
All Saints
Bolans
Potworks Dam
Freetown
Boggy Peak
Figtree Dr.
Half Moon Bay
Falmouth
Morris Bay
Old Road
English Harbour
Carlisle Beach
Nelson's Dockyard
Shirley Heights
Mamora Bay

Caribbean Sea

English Harbour

Airport ✈   Beach 🏖   Mountain ▲▲▲
Cruise Ship Terminal ⚓

0   5 km
    3 mi
N

---

known as a Caribbean Williamsburg. Its colonial naval buildings stand now as they did when Nelson was here. He never lived at Admiral House, however, which was built in 1855. The house has been turned into a museum for nautical memorabilia.

The park itself is worth exploring, filled with sandy beaches, cacti, and other tropical vegetation, including mangroves that provide shelter for a migrating colony of African cattle egrets. Archaeological sites date well before the Christian era. You can take in the vegetation and coastal scenery along the nature trails. Dockyard tours last 15 to 20 minutes, whereas tours along nature trails can last anywhere from 30 minutes to five hours. The cost is $2.50 per person to tour the dockyard; children under 13 are admitted free. The dockyard and its museum are open daily from 8am to 6pm.

Dow's Hill Interpretation Center (☎ 268/460-1053), 2¹/₂ miles east of English Harbour, uses multimedia to present a journey through six periods of the island's history. A belvedere provides a panoramic view of the park. Admission, including the multimedia show, is $5 for adults, $3 for children under 16. The center is open daily from 9am to 5pm. It's best reached by taxi from English Harbour.

A footpath at the entrance to English Harbour leads to **Fort Barclay,** a fine specimen of old-time military engineering. The path starts just outside the dockyard gate; the fort is about a half mile away.

For an eagle-eye view of English Harbour, take a taxi up to the top of **Shirley Heights,** directly to the east of the dockyard. Still standing are Palladian arches, once part of the barracks. **The Block House,** one of the main buildings, was put up as a stronghold in case of siege. The nearby Victorian cemetery contains an obelisk monument to the officers and men of the 54th Regiment.

On a low hill overlooking Nelson's Dockyard, **Clarence House** was built by English stonemasons to accommodate Prince William Henry, the duke of Clarence, who became King William IV. The future king stayed here while in command of HMS *Pegasus* in 1787. Currently the country home of the governor of Antigua and Barbuda, it's open to visitors when he is not in residence. A caretaker will show you through (it's customary to tip). You'll see many pieces of furniture on loan from the National Trust.

SHOPPING

Most shops in St. John's are clustered on St. Mary's Street or High Street, lying within an easy walk of the cruise-ship docks. You'll find such duty-free items as English woolens and linens, and you can also purchase specialized items made in Antigua, such as original pottery, local straw work, Antiguan rum, fabrics with hand-printed local designs, mammy bags, floppy foldable hats, and shell curios. If you want an island-made bead necklace, don't bother shopping; just lie on any beach and a "bead lady" will find you.

Antigua no longer offers some of the lowest liquor prices in the Caribbean, but if you're in the market for alcohol, **Quin Farara's Liquor Store,** Long Street and Corn Alley in St. John's (☎ 268/462-0463), has the island's largest collection of wines and liquors.

Caribelle Batik, St. Mary's Street (☎ 268/462-2972), is an outlet for the Romney Manor workshop on St. Kitts. The Caribelle label consists of batik and tie-dyed items such as beach wraps, scarves, and casual wear for both women and men. **Island Hopper,** Jardine Court, St. Mary's Street (☎ 268/462-2972), features Caribbean-made products not readily available elsewhere, including spices, coffees, handcrafts, and casual wear.

The Scent Shop, Lower High Street (☎ 268/462-0303), is the island's oldest perfume shop, with exotic perfumes and an array of crystal.

Shoul's Chief Store, St. Mary's Street at Market Street (☎ 268/462-1140), is one of Antigua's largest emporiums for fabric, electrical appliances, souvenirs, and general merchandise.

SHOPPING CENTERS

HERITAGE QUAY   Located at the cruise dock, Antigua's first shopping-and-entertainment complex is a multimillion-dollar center featuring some 40 duty-free shops as well as a vendors' arcade of local artists and crafts people. Among the shops here, **Colombian Emeralds** (☎ 268/462-3462) is the world's largest retailer of Colombian emeralds, with branches throughout the Caribbean and The Bahamas. **Little Switzerland** (☎ 268/462-3108) sells the best selection of Swiss-made watches in Antigua and displays Royal Doulton and Baccarat china and crystal. **Sunsneakers** (☎ 268/462-4523) has one of the largest selections of swimwear available in the Caribbean.

Island Arts (☎ 268/461-6324) was founded by Nick Maley, a makeup artist who worked on *Star Wars* and *The Empire Strikes Back.* You can purchase one of his own fine-art reproductions, including the provocative *Windkissed & Sunswept.*

REDCLIFFE QUAY   Near Heritage Quay, this historic complex is the second best center for shopping and dining in St. John's. **A Thousand Flowers** (☎ 268/462-4264) sells Indonesian batiks, crafted on the island into sundresses, shirts, sarongs, rompers, and accessories such as necklaces and earrings. **Jacaranda** (☎ 268/462-1888) tempts you with the art of John Woodland or place mats and prints by Jill Walker. The shop also stocks local clothing, herbs and spices, and artwork by local artists, as well as gels, soaps, and bath salts.

Base (☎ 268/462-0920), the brain-child of English designer Steven Giles, carries an intriguing line of casual comfort clothing in stripes, colors, and prints, all made here at the company's world head-quarters. Prices are extremely reasonable. **The Goldsmitty** (☎ 268/462-4601) presents the designs of the well-known Hans Smit in precious stones and gold.

BEACHES

"Beaches, beaches, and more beaches" best describes Antigua. Some are excel-lent, and all are public. There's a lovely beach at **Pigeon Point,** in Falmouth Harbour, about a four-minute taxi ride from Admiral's Inn. The superior beach at **Dickenson Bay,** near the Rex Halcyon Cove Hotel, is a center for water sports; for a break, you can enjoy meals and drinks on the hotel's Warri Pier.

Other beaches are found at the Curtain Bluff resort, where long, sandy white **Carlisle Beach** is set against a backdrop of coconut palms. **Morris Bay** attracts snorkelers. **Long Bay** is on the somewhat remote eastern coast, but most visitors consider it worth the effort to reach its beautiful beach. **Half Moon Bay** is fa-mous in the Caribbean and attracts aris-tocratic types to a stretch of sand that goes on for almost a mile. Site of such hotels as the Barrymore Beach, **Runaway Beach** is one of Antigua's most popular; its white sands make it worth fighting the crowds. **Five Islands** is actually a quartet of remote beaches with brown sands and coral reefs located near the Hawksbill Hotel.

Warnings: (1) It's unwise to have your fun in the sun at what appears to be a de-serted beach. You could be the victim of a mugging in such a lonely setting. (2) Readers increasingly complain of beach vendors hustling everything from jewelry to T-shirts. Since the beaches are open to all, hotels can't restrain these bothersome peddlers, so don't bother to complain.

Taxis will take you from the cruise-ship dock in St. John's to your choice of beaches. You can make arrangements to be picked up at an agreed-upon time. A typical fare to Pigeon Point or Long Bay, both about 15 miles or a 25-minute ride from St. John's, is $20 per car. To Run-away, a distance of only 3 miles or a five-minute ride, the charge is $8 per car. For Five Islands, 6 miles or 10 minutes from the capital, the fare is $12. Confirm all fares with your driver before setting out.

GOLF, SAILING, DIVING, TENNIS & WINDSURFING

GOLF   The 18-hole, par-69 **Cedar Val-ley Golf Club,** Friar's Hill Road (☎ 268/462-0161), is 3 miles east of St. John's, a five-minute, $11 taxi ride from the cruise dock. It's the island's largest golf course, with panoramic views of Antigua's northern coast. It was designed by the late Richard Aldridge to fit the contours of the area. Greens fees are $35 for 18 holes, plus another $35 for cart rentals.

SAILING   Antigua's famous "pirate ship," the *Jolly Roger,* at Redcliffe Quay in St. John's (☎ 268/462-2064), is one of the island's most popular attractions, lying within walking distance of the cruise-ship docks. You can arrange to be picked up if your ship is anchored farther out in the deep-water harbor. This perk is included in the admission price. For cruise-ship passengers, there is one sail daily at 9:30am to 3pm. The $50 per per-son fee includes cocktails, swimming, snorkeling, dancing, and other activities.

SCUBA DIVING   Scuba diving is best arranged through **Dive Antigua,** at the Rex Halcyon Cove, Dickenson Bay (☎ 268/462-3483). They are Antigua's oldest and most experienced dive opera-tion. Instruction and a boat dive with all equipment costs $85 (compared to $120 on a big cruise line's boats). Dive Antigua is about a 10-minute or $6 taxi ride from the cruise-ship dock.

TENNIS   The major resorts have tennis courts. The most convenient is **Rex**

Halcyon Cove, at Dickenson Bay (☎ 268/462-0256), which is a 15-minute or $11 taxi ride from the cruise-ship dock. Call from the dock to reserve court time, which costs $10.

WINDSURFING Located at the Lord Nelson Beach Hotel, on Dutchman's Bay, **High Wind Centre** (☎ 268/462-3094) beckons absolute beginners, intermediate sailors, and hard-core windsurfers. A two-hour introductory lesson costs $45 and includes use of equipment. The center is a $6 or 5-mile ride from the cruise-ship dock.

DINING

Most cruise passengers dine either in St. John's, English Harbour, or nearby Shirley Heights. Reservations usually aren't needed for lunch unless it's a heavy cruise-ship arrival day. If it is, call from the dock before going to a particular restaurant.

IN ST. JOHN'S

In Redcliffe Quay, **Big Banana Holding Company** (☎ 268/462-2621), serves the best pizza on the island as well as frothy coconut or banana crushes that are practically desserts in themselves. It's known as the "Hard Rock Café of Antigua."

✪ **Hemingway's,** Jardine Court, St. Mary's Street (☎ 268/462-2763), is close to the cruise docks on the second floor of a building in the heart of St. John's. View this charming and bustling cafe as more of a "refueling stop" than as a place that serves topnotch food. There's good people-watching from its upper verandas. Menu items include the usual array of salads, sandwiches, burgers, and an array of brightly colored tropical drinks.

Also close to the cruise docks, ✪ **Julians,** Church Lane and Corn Alley (☎ 268/462-4766), is the island's finest dining choice, offering the inspired cuisine of an Englishman, Julian Waterer. The menu is eclectic, wandering the world for inspiration. No place in St. John's equals the temptation found here

at lunch, everything from breast of home-smoked duck with spicy Italian-style sausage layered on a bed of fresh endive and radicchio to a tenderloin of beef stuffed with a mousse of chicken livers and mushrooms.

AT ENGLISH HARBOUR

Set right in the heart of Nelson's Dockyard, ✪ **Admiral's Inn** (☎ 268/460-1027) is charming and atmospheric, with a menu that changes daily. The cuisine is good home-style cooking. The favorite appetizer is pumpkin soup, which is followed by a choice of four or five main courses, such as local red snapper, grilled steak, or lobster.

AT SHIRLEY HEIGHTS

A short taxi ride away from English Harbour, **Shirley Heights Lookout** (☎ 268/460-1785) is a panoramic spot, one of the most romantic on Antigua. In the 1790s, this was the lookout station for unfriendly ships. You can sit on the stone battlements below the restaurant, but we prefer the upstairs restaurant itself, with large, old-fashioned windows all around. This is the next best alternative to the Admiral's Inn and is popular with cruise ship passengers, who come here more for the grand view than the food and seafood, which can be overcooked. Less expensive hamburgers and sandwiches are available in the pub downstairs.

ELSEWHERE AROUND THE ISLAND

Coconut Grove, in the Siboney Beach Club at Dickenson Bay (☎ 268/462-1538), is the best place outside St. John's for lunch on the beach. It's about a 10-minute or $11 taxi ride north from the docks. Each day, a tangy soup is prepared fresh from local ingredients.

Harmony Hall (☎ 268/460-4120), overlooking Nonsuch Bay in Brown's Bay Mill near Freetown, makes an ideal luncheon stopover or a shopping expedition. This partially restored 1843 plantation house and sugar mill displays Antigua's best selection of Caribbean arts and crafts. Lunch features Green Island lobster, flying fish, and other specialties; Sunday is barbecue day. It's a 40-minute taxi ride from St. John's; you'll have to negotiate the fare, which can range from $20 to $30.

2 Aruba ⚓ ⚓ ⚓

Today, Aruba is one of the most popular destinations in the Caribbean, so much so that the government has had to call a moratorium on hotel construction. The capital, Oranjestad, isn't a picture-postcard port, but it has one of the Caribbean's finest white-sand beaches and some glittering casinos. With only 17 inches of rainfall annually, Aruba is dry and sunny almost year-round.

COMING ASHORE

Cruise ships arrive at the **Aruba Port Authority,** a modern terminal with a tourist information booth and duty-free shops. From the pier, it's just a five-minute walk to the major shopping districts of downtown Oranjestad. You can make your way around on your own, allowing some time for Aruba's famous beaches between lunch and shopping.

FAST FACTS

Currency The currency is the **Aruba florin (AFl),** which is divided into 100 cents. Silver coins are in denominations of 5, 10, 25, and 50 cents and 1 and 2¹/₂ florins. The 50¢ piece, the square "yotin," is Aruba's best-known coin. Currently, the exchange rate is 1.77 AFl to $1 U.S. (1 AFl is worth about 56¢).

Information For information, go to the **Aruba Tourism Authority,** 172 L. G. Smith Blvd., Oranjestad (☎ 297/8/23777), open Monday to Friday from 7:30am to 4:30pm.

Language The official language is Dutch, but nearly everybody speaks English. The language of the street is often Papiamento, a patois that combines Dutch, Spanish, and English

with Amerindian and African dialects. Spanish is also widely spoken.

SHORE EXCURSIONS

Instead of opting for a dull guided excursion around the island, many passengers prefer to take an *Atlantis* submarine tour, go shopping, or head to the beach. The typical countryside tour offered by cruise ships usually lasts three hours and costs about $25 per person. Cruise ships can also book you on the *Atlantis* submarine tour. As an alternative, you might join a glass-bottom boat tour offered by the cruise lines. You're taken in a 60-passenger vessel to view the extensive marine life around the coast of Aruba. The tour costs $25 per person and lasts 1¹/₂ hours.

GETTING AROUND

It's easy to rent a car and explore Aruba. The roads connecting the major tourist attractions are excellent. Try **Budget Rent-a-Car,** 1 Kolibristraat (☎ 800/527-0707 in the U.S., or 297/8/28600); **Hertz,** 142 L. G. Smith Blvd. (☎ 800/654-3001 in the U.S., or 297/8/24545); or **Avis,** 14 Kolibristraat (☎ 800/331-1084 in the U.S., or 297/8/28787).

Since roads are good and the terrain flat, you might prefer to explore on moped or motorcycle, which costs an average of $37 and $40 per day, respectively. They're available at **George's Scooter Rental,** L. G. Smith Blvd. 136, Oranjestad (☎ 297/8/25975), or **Nelson Motorcycle Rental,** 10A Gasparito, Noord (☎ 297/8/66801).

Taxis don't have meters, but fares are fixed. Tell the driver your destination and ask the fare before getting in. The main office is on Sands Street between the bowling center and Taco Bell. A **dispatch office** is located at Bosabao 41 (☎ 297/8/22116). A ride from the cruise terminal to most of the beach resorts, including those at Palm Beach, costs about $5 to $8 per car, plus a small tip. A maximum of five passengers is allowed.

It's next to impossible to locate a taxi on some parts of the island, so when traveling to a remote area or restaurant, ask the taxi driver to pick you up at a certain time. Some English-speaking drivers are available as guides. A one-hour tour (and you don't need much more than that) is offered at $25 per hour for a maximum of five passengers.

Aruba has excellent bus service, with regular daily service from 6am to midnight. The round-trip fare between the beach hotels and Oranjestad is $1. Try to have exact change. Buses stop across the street from the cruise terminal on L. G. Smith Boulevard and will take you to any of the hotel resorts or the beaches along the West End.

SEEING THE SIGHTS

Bustling **Oranjestad** attracts shoppers rather than sightseers. The capital has a very Caribbean flavor, with both Spanish and Dutch architecture. The main thoroughfare, L. G. Smith Boulevard, runs from the airport along the waterfront and on to Palm Beach, changing its name along the way to J. E. Irausquin Boulevard. Most visitors cross the road heading for Caya G. F. Betico Croes, where they find the best free-port shopping.

After shopping, you might return to **Schooner Harbor,** where colorful boats dock along the quay and boat people display their wares in open stalls. A little farther along, fresh seafood is sold directly from the boats at the fish market. **Wilhelmina Park** is on the sea side.

Aside from shopping, Aruba's major attraction is **Palm Beach,** among the finest in the Caribbean. Most of Aruba's high-rise hotels sit in a strip along pure white-sand stretches on the leeward coast.

DRIVING AROUND ARUBA

AYO & CASIBARI Rocks stud the *cunucu,* which means "the countryside" in Papiamento. The most impressive are stacks of building-size diorite boulders at

Ayo and **Casibari,** northeast of Hooiberg. Ancient Amerindian drawings are painted on the rocks at Ayo. At Casibari, you can climb the boulder-strewn terrain to the top for a panoramic view of the island. Casibari is open daily from 9am to 5pm. No admission is charged. There's a lodge at Casibari where you can buy souvenirs, snacks, soft drinks, and beer. In the center of the island, **Hooiberg** is affectionately known as "The Haystack." It's Aruba's most outstanding landmark. On a clear day you can see Venezuela from atop this 541-foot hill.

SAVANETA On the east side of Aruba, the area called Savaneta has caves with Arawak artwork, the oldest traces of human habitation on the island. This has been an industrial center since the days of phosphate mining in the late 19th century, and here you'll see the storage tanks of the Lago Oil and Transport Company Ltd., the Exxon subsidiary around which the town of **San Nicolas** developed. A "company town" until the refinery closed in 1985, San Nicolas, 12 miles and a 25-minute taxi ride from Oranjestad, is called the Aruba Sunrise Side. A PGA-approved golf course has sand "greens" and cactus traps.

The one good reason to visit tacky San Nicolas is Aruba's most famous local dive—and we don't mean the kind you do with tanks and flippers. **Charlie's Bar and Restaurant,** at Blvd. Veen Zeppenfeldstraat 56 (Main Street; ☎ 297/8/45086), dates from 1941 and qualifies as one of the most authentically raffish bars in the West Indies. Where roustabouts and roughnecks once brawled, you'll find tables filled with contented cruise-ship passengers admiring thousands of pennants, banners, and trophies dangling from the high ceiling. Two-fisted drinks are still served, just like they were when San Nicolas was one of the toughest towns in the Caribbean. The chow—soup, fish, and steak—isn't bad, but most patrons come here for the good times and the brew. Open Monday to Saturday from noon to 10pm.

Aruba

0   12.4 mi
0   20 km

California
Lighthouse

Caribbean Sea

Malmok Beach

California
Sand Dunes

Fisherman's Hut Beach

Palm Beach

Eagle Beach

Noord

Altovista Chapel

Manchebo
Beach

Divi Beach

Bushiribana

Druif Bay

Natural Bridge

Oranjestad

Casibari

Ayó

Queen Beatrix Airport

Santa Cruz

Hooiberg

*Spanish
Lagoon*

Fontein Cave

Boca Prins

Guadarikiri Cave

Huliba Cave

Savaneta

Boca Grandi

Sint Nicolas
(San Nicolas)

Grapefield
Beach

Rodgers Beach

Seroe
Colorado

Caribbean Sea

Baby Beach

Cruise Ship Terminal   Airport   Beach   Lighthouse

AN UNDERWATER JOURNEY ON THE SUBMARINE *ATLANTIS*

An underwater journey on the submarine *Atlantis* (☎ **800/253-0493** or 297/8/36090) is one of the Caribbean's best opportunities for nondivers to see the underwater life of a coral reef. The ride carries 46 passengers to a depth of up to 150 feet, and departs from the Oranjestad harbor front every hour on the hour, daily from 10am to 2pm. Each tour includes a 25-minute transit by catamaran to Barcadera Reef (2 miles southeast of Aruba), a site chosen for the huge variety of its underwater flora and fauna. At the reef, participants transfer to the submarine for a one-hour underwater lecture and tour.

Allow two hours for the complete experience. It costs $69 for adults and $29 for children ages 4 to 16 (no children under four are admitted). You must reserve in advance. The company's offices are at Seaport Village Marina (opposite the Sonesta) in Oranjestad.

GAMBLING THE DAY AWAY

Aruba's gaming establishments are second only to San Juan. Most casinos are open both day and night, and most are at the big hotels on Palm Beach, a $7 taxi ride from the cruise terminal. Those mentioned below are open throughout the day.

The casino at the **Holiday Inn Aruba Beach Resort,** J. E. Irausquin Blvd. 230 (☎ **297/8/67777**), wins the prize for all-around gambling action. Closer to Oranjestad is the **Crystal Casino** at the Aruba Sonesta Resort and Casino at Seaport Village (☎ **297/8/36000**).

Casino Masquerade, at the Radisson Aruba Caribbean Resort and Casino, J. E. Irausquin Blvd. 81 (☎ **297/8/66555**), is Aruba's newest casino. The **Casablanca Casino** occupies a large room adjacent to the lobby of the Wyndham Hotel and Resort, J. E. Irausquin Blvd. 77 (☎ **297/**

8/64466). **Casino Copacabana,** in the island's most spectacular hotel, the Hyatt Regency Aruba, L. G. Smith Blvd. 85 (☎ **297/8/61234**), evokes France's Côte d'Azur. More than just a casino, the **Alhambra,** L. G. Smith Blvd. 47 (☎ **297/8/35000**), offers a collection of boutiques.

Outdrawing them all, however, is the **Royal Cabaña Casino,** at the La Cabaña All-Suite Beach Resort and Casino, J. E. Irausquin Blvd. 250 (☎ **297/8/79000**). Aruba's largest casino, it has 33 tables and games, plus 320 slot machines.

SHOPPING

An easy walk from the cruise terminal, Oranjestad's half-mile-long **Caya G. F. Betico Croes** compresses six continents into one main shopping street. While this is not technically a free port, the duty is low at 3.3% and there is no sales tax. Delft blue pottery is an especially good buy, as are Edam and Gouda cheeses from Holland. Philatelists can purchase colorful and artistic stamp issues at the post office in Oranjestad.

The Aruban hand-embroidered linens at **Artistic Boutique,** Caya G. F. Betico Croes 25 (☎ **297/8/23142**), are the most exquisitely crafted on the island. The shop also has the best collection of Indonesian imports, plus jewelry, oriental antiques, handmade dhurries and rugs, and fine linens.

Wulfsen and Wulksen, Caya G. F. Betico Croes 52 (☎ **297/8/23823**), offers some of the finest and most varied clothing in the Dutch islands, and has done so for more than a quarter of a century. Continental fashions for both men and women range from the straitlaced to the far-out.

For a wide selection of perfumes, stop by **Aruba Trading Company,** Caya G. F. Betico Croes 14 (☎ **297/8/22602**); **D'Orsy's,** in the Oranjestad Strada Complex II (☎ **297/8/31233**); or **Penha,** Caya G. F. Betico Croes 11–13 (☎ **297/8/24161**).

At **Gandelman Jewelers,** in the Royal Plaza, L. G. Smith Boulevard (☎ **297/8/32121**), you'll find fine gold jewelry and such famous-name timepieces as Gucci and Swatch at reasonable prices, plus gold bracelets, Gucci accessories, and exceptional handbags.

Aruba's leading department store, the **New Amsterdam Store,** Caya G. F. Betico Croes 50 (☎ **297/8/21152**), is best for linens, with its selection of napkins, place mats, and embroidered tablecloths.

SHOPPING CENTERS

Much of the best shopping in Aruba is found in clusters, including the **Port of Call Marketplace,** L. G. Smith Blvd. 17 (☎ **297/8/36706**), where shops feature perfumes, duty-free liquors, batiks, fine leather goods, jewelry, French perfumes, and stylish clothing.

The Holland Aruba Mall at Havenstraat 6, also right in the center of Oranjestad, has an array of stylish shops and some not-so-stylish food joints.

ALHAMBRA MOONLIGHT SHOPPING CENTER This shopping bazaar is adjacent to the Alhambra Casino on L. G. Smith Boulevard. Merchandise at this blend of international shops and outdoor marketplaces ranges from fine jewelry, chocolates, and perfume to imported craft items, leather goods, clothing, and lingerie.

SEAPORT VILLAGE Housing Seaport Village Mall, the Crystal Casino, and the Aruba Sonesta Resort and Casino, this complex, with more than 130 stores and boutiques, is located across from the harbor at the "entrance" of the center of downtown, only five minutes from the cruise terminal. If you need books or sundries stop at **Boulevard Book and Drugstore** (☎ **297/8/27358**). **Les Accessories** (☎ **297/8/37965**) is where award-winning American designer Agatha Brown sells her exclusive designs of quality leather purses handmade in Florence, Italy.

BEACHES

Called the **Turquoise Coast,** Aruba's western and southern shore attracts sunseekers. A $7 taxi ride from the cruise terminal will take you to **Palm Beach** and **Eagle Beach,** the best two stretches on the island. The latter is closer to Oranjestad. The island's beaches are open to the public, so you can spread your towel anywhere along 7 miles of uninterrupted sugar-white sand, including **Manchebo Beach** or **Druid Bay Beach.** On the other hand, you'll be charged for using the facilities at any of the hotels on this strip.

In total contrast to this leeward side of Aruba, the north or windward shore is rugged and wild.

GOLF, TENNIS & WATER SPORTS

GOLF Visitors can play at the **Aruba Golf Club,** Golfweg 82 (☎ **297/8/42006**), near San Nicolas, on the southeastern end of the island. Although it has only 10 greens, they are played from different tees to simulate 18 holes. Twenty-five sand traps add an extra challenge. Greens fees are $10 for 18 holes and $7.50 for nine holes. The course is open daily from 7:30am to 6:30pm; anyone wishing to play 18 holes must begin before 1:30pm. The pro shop has golf carts and clubs for rent.

Aruba's long-awaited **Tierra del Sol Golf Course** (☎ **297/8/67800**) opened in 1995. Designed by the Robert Trent Jones II Group, the 18-hole, par-71 course is on the northwest coast, near the California Lighthouse. Greens fees are $120 in winter, including golf cart, or $72 after 3pm. Off-season, the fees drop to $85, or $65 after 12pm. The course is open daily from 7am to 5pm.

TENNIS Most of the island's beachfront hotels have tennis courts, often swept by trade winds. It's best to hit the courts soon after you disembark to avoid playing in the noonday sun. The best tennis is at the **Aruba Racket Club** (☎ 297/8/27000), part of the Tierra del Sol complex on Aruba's northwest coast, near the California Lighthouse. It's about an $8 ride from the cruise terminal.

WATER SPORTS   Snorkelers will find the waters to be rather shallow here, but scuba divers can explore stunning marine life. At some points, visibility is up to 90 feet. Most divers want to see the German freighter *Antilla*, which was scuttled in the early years of World War II off the northwestern tip of Aruba, near Palm Beach.

De Palm Tours, L. G. Smith Blvd. 142, in Oranjestad (☎ 297/8/24400), combines boat rides with snorkeling. For $38 per person, they'll take you on a 1¹/₂-hour "fun cruise" aboard a catamaran, after which passengers stop for three hours at the company's private De Palm island for snorkeling. Lunch and an open bar aboard are included in the price. If there are enough takers, the tour departs Tuesdays and Saturdays at 10am and returns at 4pm, just in time to return to the ship. De Palm Tours also offers a one-hour glass-bottom boat cruise that visits two coral reefs and the German shipwreck *Antilla*. The cruise costs $17.50 per person and operates Monday, Tuesday, Wednesday, Friday, and Saturday.

Red Sails Sports, Palm Beach (☎ 297/8/61603), is the island's best water sports center. The scuba-diving course is tailored for cruise-ship passengers. Certified divers with their own gear pay $35 and up for one-tank excursions.

Divi Winds Center, J. E. Irausquin Blvd. 41 (☎ 297/8/23300, ext. 623), near the Tamarind Aruba Beach Resort, is the windsurfing headquarters of the island. Equipment rents for $15 to $18 per hour, $30 per half day, or $50 all day. The resort is on the tranquil Caribbean side of the island. Sunfish lessons can be arranged, and snorkeling gear can be rented.

DINING

If there are many cruise ships in port, call from a pay phone in the cruise-ship terminal to make a reservation. If it's a light day for cruise traffic, though, chances are you won't need them. If you're going to the beach, you can eat lunch at one of the big resort hotels that line the sands.

IN ORANJESTAD

Named after the legendary beach parties of Jamaica, **Boonoonoonos,** Wiihelminastraat 18 (☎ 297/8/31888), offers a culinary tour of the Caribbean, including Aruban keshi yena (chicken casserole), Jamaican jerk ribs, and curried chicken Trinidad style.

Although expensive, most satisfied customers agree that **Chez Mathilde,** Havenstraat 23, near the Sonesta hotel complex (☎ 297/8/34968), is worth the price. The lunch menu features homemade soups and fresh salads. Main courses are limited, but a definite delight is the filet of red snapper that's topped with onions, tomatoes, green peppers, fresh herbs, and a dash of rum and baked in parchment paper.

Overlooking a manicured mall at the most desirable end of a shopping complex in downtown Oranjestad, the **Waterfront Crabhouse,** Seaport Market, L. G. Smith Boulevard (☎ 297/8/35858), offers crabs and seafood galore. All fish served here are caught with hook and line.

A shopper's favorite in Oranjestad is **Le Petit Café,** Emmastraat 1 (☎ 297/8/26577), a local hangout where the chef's special is "Romance on the Stone"—meals cooked on hot stones, including steak, chicken, and jumbo shrimp. Although you can get full hot meals here at lunch, many patrons opt for one of the freshly made salads such as chicken, tuna, fruit, or chef, or else a well-stuffed sandwich.

3 Barbados ⚓ ⚓ ⚓ ⚓

No port of call in the southern Caribbean can compete with Barbados when it comes to diversions, attractions, and fine dining. What really puts this former British colony on world tourist maps, however, is its seemingly endless stretches of pink and white sandy beaches, among the best in the entire Caribbean Basin.

COMING ASHORE

The cruise-ship pier is one of the best docking facilities in the southern Caribbean. You can walk right into the modern cruise-ship terminal, which has a tourist office, car rentals, taxis, sightseeing tours, and other services, plus shops and scads of vendors. You can also purchase postage stamps from the bureau. There are credit card telephones, and the port authority sells phone cards.

FAST FACTS

Currency The **Barbados dollar (BD$)** is the official currency, available in $100, $20, $10, and $5 notes and $1, 25¢, and 10¢ silver coins, plus 5¢ and 1¢ copper coins. The Bajan dollar is worth 50¢ in U.S. currency. Most stores take traveler's checks or U.S. dollars.

Information The **Barbados Tourism Authority** is on Harbour Road (P.O. Box 242), Bridgetown, Barbados, W.I. (☎ 246/427-2623), and has an office in the cruise terminal.

Language English is spoken here.

SHORE EXCURSIONS

It's not easy to get around Barbados quickly and conveniently, so a shore excursion is the best way to see the major places of interest. Most cruise lines offer a three-hour tour to Harrison's Cave, usually costing about $33 for adults. The second most popular tour is aboard the *Atlantis* submarine.

Since most cruise lines don't really offer a comprehensive island tour, many passengers deal with a local tour company. **Bajan Tours,** Glenayre, Locust Hall, St. George (☎ 246/437-9389), offers an island tour covering all the highlights, which leaves between 8:30 and 9am and returns to your ship before departure. On Friday, a heritage tour visits primarily major plantations and museums. And on Tuesday and Wednesday, an ecotour explores the island's natural beauty. Each tour costs $50 per person.

Touring by taxi is far more relaxing than touring by bus. Nearly all Bajan taxi drivers are familiar with their island and like to show it off to visitors. The standard rate is $16 per hour, so an average day tour by taxi will cost about $50. Be sure to agree on a price in advance.

GETTING AROUND

Blue-and-yellow **public buses** fan out from Bridgetown every 20 minutes or so onto the major routes; their destinations are marked on the front. Buses going south and east leave from Fairchild Street, and those going north and west depart from Lower Green and the Princess Alice Highway. Fares are BD$1.50 (75¢) and exact change is required.

Privately owned **minibuses** run shorter distances and travel more frequently. These bright yellow buses display destinations on the bottom left corner of the windshield. In Bridgetown, board at River Road, Temple Yard, and Probyn Street. Fare is BD$1.50 (75¢).

Taxis aren't metered, but their rates are fixed by the government. They're identified by the letter "Z" on their license plates.

We don't advise renting a car. Roads are bad, driving is on the left side of the road, and the signs are totally inadequate.

Barbados

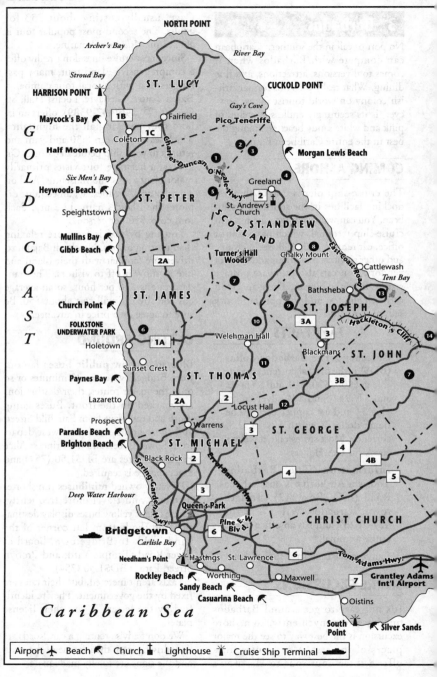

NORTH POINT

Archer's Bay

River Bay

Stroud Bay

HARRISON POINT

ST. LUCY

CUCKOLD POINT

1B

Fairfield

Gay's Cove

Maycock's Bay

1C

Coleton

Pico Teneriffe

Half Moon Fort

❷ ❸

Morgan Lewis Beach

G O L D

❶

O'Neale Hwy.

❹

Six Men's Bay

Greeland

Heywoods Beach

❺

2

St. Andrew's Church

ST. PETER

Charles Duncan

Speightstown

SCOTLAND

ST. ANDREW

Mullins Bay

Gibbs Beach

2A

Turner's Hall Woods

❽

Chalky Mount

East Coast Road

Cattlewash

C O A S T

1

❼

Tent Bay

Bathsheba

Church Point

ST. JAMES

❾

ST. JOSEPH

❶❸

FOLKSTONE UNDERWATER PARK

6

❿

3A

Hackleton's Cliff

❶❹

Holetown

1A

Welchman Hall

3

Sunset Crest

Blackmans

ST. JOHN

Paynes Bay

ST. THOMAS

❶❶

3B

❼

Lazaretto

2A

2

Locust Hall

❶❷

Prospect

Paradise Beach

Warrens

3

ST. GEORGE

Brighton Beach

ST. MICHAEL

4

4B

Black Rock

2

4

5

Deep Water Harbour

3

Queen's Park

CHRIST CHURCH

Bridgetown

Pine E-W Blvd.

Carlisle Bay

6

6

Tom Adams Hwy.

Needham's Point

Hastings

St. Lawrence

✈

Rockley Beach

Worthing

Maxwell

7

Grantley Adams Int'l Airport

Sandy Beach

Casuarina Beach

Oistins

Caribbean Sea

South Point

Silver Sands

Airport ✈ Beach 🏖 Church ✝ Lighthouse 🗼 Cruise Ship Terminal ⚓

Caribbean Islands

Barbados

Andromeda
  Botanical Gardens **13**
Barbados Wildlife Reserve **1**
Chalky Mount Potteries **8**
Cherry Tree Hill **3**
Codrington College **15**
Farley Hill National Park **5**
Flower Forest
  of Barbados **9**
Gun Hill Signal Station **12**
Harrison's Cave **11**
Morgan Lewis Sugar
  Windmill & Museum **4**
Sam Lord's Castle **16**
St. James Church **6**
St. John's Church **14**
St. Nicholas Abbey **2**
Sunbury Plantation House **17**
Villa Nova **7**
Welchman Hall Gully **10**

Atlantic Ocean

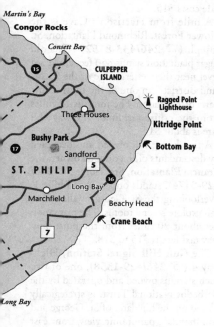

Martin's Bay
Congor Rocks

Consett Bay

**CULPEPPER
ISLAND**

15

☀ **Ragged Point
Lighthouse**

Three Houses

Kitridge Point

Bushy Park

⚓ **Bottom Bay**

17 Sandford

ST. PHILIP

5

16

Marchfield

Long Bay

Beachy Head

7

⚓ **Crane Beach**

Long Bay

0 ▭▭▭▭ 3 km
        1.9 mi

N

SUBMERGED SIGHTSEEING

You can see the wonders beneath the seas as well as a shipwreck lying upright and intact aboard *Atlantis II* and *Atlantis III,* air-conditioned sightseeing submarines that seat 28 to 48 passengers. The vessels make several dives daily from 9am to 6pm. Passengers are taken to the submersible via ferry from the Careenage in downtown Bridgetown, a ride that passes the island's west coast, home of luxury resort hotels and expensive real estate. *Atlantis II* and *III* sail on two different trips. The first, called the Odyssey, is a dive onto a reef where professional divers leave the vessel and perform a 15-minute show, costing $84.50 for adults or $42.25 for children. The Expedition, the second trip, costs $73.50 for adults and $36.25 for children. For reservations, contact **Atlantis Submarines (Barbados),** Shallow Draught, McGregor Street, Bridgetown (☎ **246/436-8929**).

The company also offers rides in the *Atlantis Seatrec,* a semisubmersible boat that gives a snorkeler's view of the reef. This tour costs $29.50 for adults; children ages 4 to 12 are charged half fare. (The tour is not suitable for those three and under.) For reservations, call the number above.

Most cruise ships offer the *Atlantis II* excursion, or you can save money by reserving three to four days before you arrive in Barbados. The submarine company will pick up do-it-yourselfers at the cruise terminal.

SEEING THE SIGHTS

Barbados is too diverse and spread out, and its attractions too difficult to reach, to see everything here in a day. The capital, Bridgetown, is a short taxi ride (the one-way fare is $3 to $4) or a hot, dusty walk of at least 30 minutes.

Bridgetown is not one of the Caribbean's picturesque ports. It's hot, dry, and dirty, and unless you want to go shopping, you should spend your time at calmer oases. One thing the capital has going for it, however, is an old **synagogue** (☎ 246/432-0840). Dating from 1833, the present building sits on the site of an even older synagogue that was erected by Jews from Brazil in 1654.

Welchman Hall Gully, St. Thomas (Highway 2 from Bridgetown; ☎ 246/438-6671), is a lush tropical garden owned by the Barbados National Trust. The gully is eight miles from the port and features some plants that were here when the English settlers landed in 1627. It can be reached by bus from the terminal.

All cruise-ship excursions visit ✪ **Harrison's Cave,** Welchman Hall, St. Thomas (☎ 246/438-6640), Barbados's top tourist attraction. Here you can see a beautiful underground world from aboard an electric tram and trailer. If you'd like to go on your own, the 30-minute taxi ride costs $15.

A mile from Harrison's Cave is the **Flower Forest,** Richmond Plantation, St. Joseph (☎ 246/433-8152). This old sugar plantation stands 850 feet above sea level near the western edge of the "Scotland district," in one of the most scenic parts of Barbados. The forest is 12 miles from the cruise terminal; one-way taxi fare is about $15.

A fine home still owned and occupied by descendants of the original owner, the **Francia Plantation,** St. George (☎ 246/429-0474), stands on a wooded hillside overlooking the St. George Valley. You can explore several rooms. The plantation lies about 20 miles from the port; one-way taxi fare is $15 to $18.

The **Gun Hill Signal Station,** Highway 4 (☎ 246/429-1358), one of two such stations owned and operated by the Barbados National Trust, is strategically placed on the highland of St. George and commands a panoramic view from east to west. Built in 1818, the station is 12 miles from the port; the one-way taxi ride costs $15.

Sam Lord's Castle Resorts, Long Bay, St. Philip (☎ 246/423-7350), was built in 1820 by one of Barbados's most notorious scoundrels, Samuel Hall Lord. Legend says he made his money by luring ships onto the jagged, hard-to-detect rocks of Cobbler's Reef. You can explore the architecturally acclaimed centerpiece of this luxury resort, which has a private sandy beach. It's an $11 taxi ride from the cruise terminal.

SHOPPING

The cruise terminal contains 20 duty-free shops, 13 local retail stores, and a plethora of vendors selling arts and crafts, jewelry, liquor, china, crystal, electronics, perfume, and leather goods. But you'll find a wider selection and better prices in Bridgetown.

Good duty-free buys include cameras, watches, crystal, gold jewelry, bone china, cosmetics and perfumes, and liquor (including locally produced Barbados rum and liqueurs), along with tobacco products and British-made cashmere sweaters, tweeds, and sportswear.

Among Barbados handcrafts, black-coral jewelry is outstanding. Local clay potters turn out different products, some based on designs centuries old. Crafts include wall hangings made from grasses and dried flowers, straw mats, baskets, and bags with raffia embroidery. Bajan leather work includes handbags, belts, and sandals.

The best place for tax-free merchandise is **Cave Shepherd** (☎ 246/431-2121), which has an outlet at the cruise terminal. The Broad Street branch is the island's largest department store. The store offers perfumes, cosmetics, fine crystal and English bone china, cameras, gold and silver jewelry, swimwear, leather goods, men's designer clothing, handcrafts, T-shirts, and souvenirs. They sell more than 70 brands of liqueurs.

In Bridgetown, **Articrafts,** on Broad Street (☎ 246/427-5767), offers an impressive display of Bajan arts and crafts.

Part of an island-wide chain of 12 stores, the **Best of Barbados,** in the Southern Palms, St. Lawrence Gap,

Christ Church (☎ 246/420-8040), is best for local products, including coasters, mats, T-shirts, pottery, dolls, games, and cookbooks.

Next to the Waterfront Café, on the Careenage, **Colours of De Caribbean** (☎ 246/436-8522), sells unique tropical clothing that's all made in the West Indies, as well as jewelry and decorative objects.

Fashion magazines have praised **Cotton Days,** Bay Street, St. Michael (☎ 246/427-7191), as the most stylish of Barbados's many boutiques. It has a wide array of casually elegant, one-of-a-kind garments, inspired by the island's flora and fauna and underwater world.

At **Little Switzerland,** in the Da Costas Mall, Broad Street (☎ 246/431-0029), you'll find a wide selection of fragrances and cosmetics, plus fine china and crystal and other goodies. The shop also specializes in 14- and 18-karat gold jewelry, watches, and Mont Blanc pens.

The main **Harrison's,** 1 Broad St. (☎ 246/431-5500), and 14 other branches sell duty-free merchandise, including china, crystal, jewelry, leather goods, sweaters, and perfumes, all at fair prices. They also sell some good leather products handcrafted in Colombia.

Featuring specimens from all over the world, **The Shell Gallery,** Carlton House, St. James (☎ 246/422-2593), is a shell collector's delight. They also offer hand-painted chinaware, shell jewelry, local pottery and ceramics, and imported batik and papier-mâché art depicting shells and aquatic life.

Near the Southern Palms Hotel, **Walker's Caribbean World,** St. Lawrence Gap (☎ 246/428-1183), offers many locally made items, as well as handcrafts from other Caribbean countries.

SHOPPING COMPLEXES

MALL 34 On Broad Street, Bridgetown's most modern shopping complex offers duty-free watches, clocks, china, jewelry, crystal, linens, sweaters, liquor, souvenir items, and tropical fashions.

PELICAN VILLAGE   Near the cruise terminal on Princess Alice Highway (which leads down to the city's deepwater harbor), this tiny colony of thatch-roofed shops features a collection of island-made crafts and souvenirs.

BEACHES

Barbadians will tell you that their island has a beach for every day of the year. With clear waters, those on the island's western side—the luxury resort area called the Gold Coast—are far preferable to those on the surf-pounded Atlantic side. All Barbados beaches are open to the public, even those in front of the big resort hotels and private homes. At most, you can buy food and drink.

ON THE WEST COAST   Take your pick of the west coast beaches, which are a 15-minute, $8 taxi ride from the cruise terminal. **Payne's Bay,** with access from the Coach House, is a good beach for water sports, especially snorkeling. It can get rather crowded, but the beautiful bay makes it worth the effort. Directly south of Payne's Bay, at Fresh Water Bay, are three fine beaches: **Brighton Beach, Brandon's Beach,** and **Paradise Beach.**

Church Point lies north of St. James Church, opening onto Heron Bay, site of the Colony Club Hotel. Although the beach can get crowded, it's one of the most scenic bays in Barbados, and the swimming is idyllic.

Mullins Beach's blue waters have been called "glassy," and snorkelers in particular seek it out. There's parking on the main road.

SOUTH COAST   Depending on traffic, South Coast beaches usually are easily reached from the cruise terminal. Figure on an $8 taxi fare. Windsurfers like the trade winds that sweep across **Casuarina Beach.** Access is from Maxwell Coast Road, across the property of Casuarina Beach Hotel. This is one of the wider beaches of Barbados.

Silver Sands Beach is to the east of Oistins near the very south point of Barbados, directly east of South Point Lighthouse and near the Silver Rock Hotel. This white sandy beach is a favorite with many Bajans. Windsurfing is good.

Sandy Beach, reached from the parking lot on the Worthing main road, has tranquil waters opening onto a lagoon. This is a family favorite.

SOUTHEAST COAST   The southeast coast is known for its big waves, especially at **Crane Beach,** a white sandy stretch set against a backdrop of cliffs and palms. Britain's Prince Andrew owns a house here. It offers excellent body surfing, but this is ocean swimming, so be careful. The one-way taxi fare is $17 from the cruise pier.

GOLF, RIDING, DIVING, TENNIS & WINDSURFING

GOLF   The 18-hole championship golf course of the west coast **Sandy Lane Hotel,** St. James (☎ **246/432-1311**), is open to all. Greens fees are $100 in winter and $75 in summer for 18 holes, or $65 in winter and $45 in summer for nine holes. Carts and caddies are available. Make reservations the day before you arrive in Barbados. It's a 25-minute, $12.50 taxi ride from the cruise terminal.

HORSEBACK RIDING   **Caribbean International Riding Centre,** Cleland Plantation, Farley Hill, St. Andrew (☎ **246/422-7433**), offers trail rides for equestrians of all experience levels. The shortest ride is a 75-minute escorted trek through tropical forests. The most scenic tour goes through the Gully Ride and continues to a cliff with a view of almost the entire east coast. Prices of various rides range from a 1-hour trek for $30 to a $2^{1}/_{2}$-hour jaunt for $65, including a drink and transportation to and from the cruise terminal. Advance reservations are required.

SNORKELING & SCUBA DIVING
The clear waters off Barbados have a visibility of more than 100 feet most of the year, providing great views of several

wrecks and of lobsters, moray eels, sea fans, gorgonias, night anemones, octopuses, and innumerable fish swimming over coral reefs.

The **Dive Shop,** Pebbles Beach, Aquatic Gap, St. Michael (☎ **246/ 426-9947**), offers the best scuba diving on Barbados. It charges $48 per one-tank dive or $70 for a two-tank dive, and also offers snorkeling trips and equipment rentals. Visitors with reasonable swimming skills who have never dived before can sign up for a resort course at $60. You can sign up for scuba at a booth next to the dock. The Dive Shop provides transportation to and from the cruise terminal.

TENNIS The deluxe **Sandy Lane** resort at St. James (☎ **246/432-1311**) focuses on tennis, with two pros on hand, five courts, and an open-door policy to nonresidents. Court rentals are $20 per hour, or $10 per half hour. It's a 20- to 25-minute taxi ride from the cruise terminal, with a one-way fare of $12.50.

WINDSURFING **Silver Sands** is rated the best spot in the Caribbean for advanced windsurfing (skill rating five to six). **Barbados Windsurfing Club,** at the Silver Sands Hotel in Christ Church (☎ **246/428-6001**), rents boards and gives lessons. Boards cost $20 per hour, or $40 for a half day. To reach the center, take a taxi from the cruise terminal, a $10 one-way fare.

DINING

John Moore Bar, on the waterfront, Weston, St. James Parish (☎ **294/ 422-2258**), is the most atmospheric and least pretentious bar on Barbados. Most visitors opt for a rum punch ($3.50) or beer (75¢), but if you're hungry, you can order a fish platter. It's about an $8 taxi ride from the cruise terminal.

SOUTH OF BRIDGETOWN

The chefs at **Brown Sugar,** Aquatic Gap, St. Michael (☎ **294/426-7684**), prepare some of the tastiest Bajan specialties on the island. Good-value lunches are served

buffet style. Try hot gungo-pea soup, broiled pepper chicken, stuffed crab backs, or garlic pork, and the walnut-rum pie with rum sauce for dessert. The restaurant is about a $4 taxi ride from the cruise terminal.

ON THE SOUTH COAST

The following restaurants are about an $8 one-way taxi ride from the cruise terminal:

Josef's, St. Lawrence Gap (☎ **246/ 435-6541**), is one of the most durable upscale restaurants in Barbados, serving Caribbean and Continental cuisine. Tropical dishes include garlic shrimp, jerk shrimp, blackened kingfish, seafood crepes, and curried chicken. The menu is roughly the same for both lunch and dinner.

Also at St. Lawrence Gap is **The Ship Inn** (☎ **246/435-6961**), a traditional English-style pub with a tropical garden. The inn itself serves substantial bar food, and the more formal **Captain's Carvery** restaurant offers a buffet of prime roasts and traditional Bajan dishes such as fillets of flying fish. Its all-you-can-eat lunchtime carvery is one of the best dining values on the island. Come here for the libations and hearty portions, not for refined cuisine.

Four miles south of Bridgetown, near Rockley Beach along Highway 7, ✪ **T.G.I. Boomers,** St. Lawrence Gap (☎ **246/428-8439**), offers some of the island's best bargain meals. You can always count on seafood, steaks, and hamburgers. For lunch, try a daily Bajan special or a jumbo sandwich. A special 16-ounce daiquiri will put a glow into your afternoon.

ON THE WEST COAST

These restaurants lie an $8 to $12 taxi ride (depending on traffic) from the cruise terminal:

✪ **Bagatelle Restaurant,** Highway 2A, St. Thomas (☎ **246/421-6767**), one of Barbados's finest and most elegant dining choices, occupies the circa-1645 residence of the colony's first governor. This five-acre sylvan retreat lies in the cool uplands, just south of the island's center. Your best bet is the local catch of the day grilled, barbecued, or seasoned and sautéed. Cruise ship passengers can take advantage of light lunches served from 11am.

On the island's western coastline, south of Holetown, ✪ **The Fathoms,** Paynes Bay, St. James (☎ **246/432-2568**), serves meals both inside and on a terrace shaded by a mahogany tree. A fairly ambitious lunch menu offers shrimp and crab étouffée, herbed conch cakes, and caramelized barracuda or local rabbit stewed with onions, rum, rosemary, and raisins.

The wine bars of London inspired the informal **Nico's Champagne and Wine Bar,** Derrick's, St. James (☎ **246/ 432-6386**). Wines from around the world are dispensed by the glass or bottle. Meals are flavorful and designed to accompany the wine. Nico's serves some of the best lobster in Barbados.

ON THE ATLANTIC COAST

If you opt for a taxi tour of the island, the best luncheon stopover on the eastern side of Barbados is the **Atlantis Hotel,** Bathsheba, St. Joseph (☎ **246/433-9445**), which has a generous and filling two-course fixed-price lunch that's served daily beginning at 11:30am. The place is shabby and run-down, and beloved by the locals. The food is authentically Bajan, with such dishes as pumpkin fritters and Bajan pepperpot stew on the menu. No one leaves here hungry.

4 British Virgin Islands: Tortola & Virgin Gorda ⚓ ⚓ ⚓

With its small bays and hidden coves that were once havens for pirates, the British Virgin Islands (B.V.I.) are among the world's loveliest cruising grounds. Strung over the northeastern corner of the Caribbean, this British colony has some 40 islands, of which only Tortola, Virgin Gorda, and Jost Van Dyke are of signifi-

cant size, with the rest being tiny rocks and cays. Norman Island is said to have been the inspiration for Robert Louis Stevenson's *Treasure Island.* And remember "Fifteen men on a dead-man's chest / yo, ho, ho and a bottle of rum"? Blackbeard inspired that famous ditty by marooning 15 pirates and a bottle of rum on the rocky cay known as Deadman Bay.

TORTOLA

Road Town, the colony's capital, sits about midway along the southern shore of 24-square-mile Tortola. Wickhams Cay, a 70-acre landfill development and marina, brought a massive yacht-chartering business to Road Town and transformed this sleepy village into a bustling center.

The island's entire southern coast is characterized by rugged mountain peaks. On the northern coast are beautiful bays with white-sand beaches, banana trees, mangoes, and clusters of palms.

COMING ASHORE

Visiting cruise ships dock in Road Town at Wickhams Cay 1. The pier is a five-minute walk to Main Street, where you'll find restaurants, bars, and shopping. The place is small and everybody speaks English, so you should have no trouble finding your way around town.

FAST FACTS

Currency The **U.S. dollar** is the legal currency.

Information The **B.V.I. Tourist Board Office** is at the center of Road Town, near the ferry dock south of Wickhams Cay 1 (☎ **809/ 494-3134**). Pick up a copy of the *Welcome Tourist Guide.* Open Monday to Friday from 9am to 5pm.

Language English is spoken here.

SHORE EXCURSIONS

The shore excursions and even the organized activities here are very modest. The cruise ships don't offer excursions, but

The British Virgin Islands

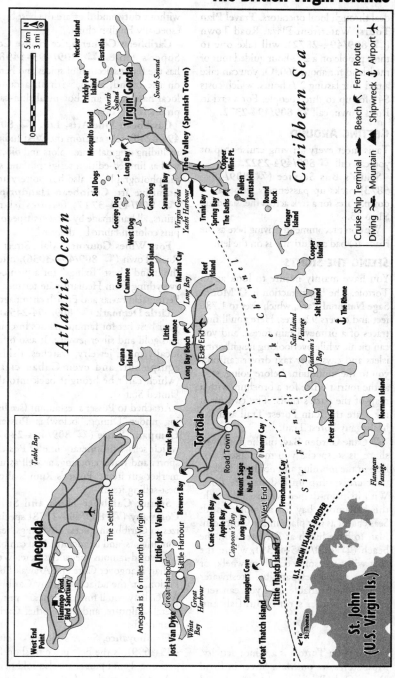

Legend:
- Cruise Ship Terminal
- Diving
- Beach
- Ferry Route
- Mountain
- Shipwreck
- Airport

Caribbean Sea

Virgin Gorda
- Necker Island
- Prickly Pear Island
- Eustatia
- Mosquito Island
- North Sound
- South Sound
- Seal Dogs
- George Dog
- West Dog
- Great Dog
- Long Bay
- The Valley (Spanish Town)
- Savannah Bay
- Copper Mine Pt.
- Virgin Gorda Yacht Harbour
- Trunk Bay
- Spring Bay
- The Baths
- Fallen Jerusalem
- Round Rock
- Ginger Island
- Cooper Island
- Salt Island
- The Rhone
- Salt Island Passage
- Deadman's Bay
- Cooper Island

Atlantic Ocean

- Great Camanoe
- Scrub Island
- Marina Cay
- Long Bay
- Beef Island
- Little Camanoe
- Guana Island
- Long Bay Beach
- East End
- Trunk Bay
- Brewers Bay
- Cane Garden Bay
- Apple Bay
- Cappoon's Bay
- Long Bay
- Smugglers Cove
- West End
- Road Town
- Mount Sage Nat. Park
- **Tortola**
- Nanny Cay
- Frenchman's Cay

Sir Francis Drake Channel

- Peter Island
- Norman Island
- Dead Chest
- Flanagan Passage

St. John (U.S. Virgin Is.)
- U.S. VIRGIN ISLANDS BORDER
- To St. Thomas

Anegada
- West End Point
- Table Bay
- The Settlement
- Flamingo Pond Bird Sanctuary
- *Anegada is 16 miles north of Virgin Gorda*

Jost Van Dyke
- Little Jost Van Dyke
- Great Harbour
- Little Harbour
- White Bay
- Great Harbour
- Great Thatch Island
- Little Thatch Island

Scale: 5 km / 3 mi — N

355

deal through local operators. **Travel Plan Tours,** Waterfront Plaza, Road Town (☎ 809/494-2872), will take one to three people on a 2½-hour guided tour of the island for about $60. Or you can take a taxi tour lasting 2½ hours, which costs $45 for up to three people. For a taxi in Road Town, call ☎ 809/494-2322.

GETTING AROUND

Taxis meet every arriving cruise ship or you can call ☎ 809/494-2322.

Scato's Bus Service (☎ 809/494-5873) picks up passengers who hail it down. Fares for a trek across the island are $1 to $3.

We don't recommend driving here as the roads are bad and driving is on the left.

SEEING THE SIGHTS

You have mainly nature to look at on Tortola. The big attraction is ✪ **Mount Sage National Park,** which rises to 1,780 feet and covers 92 acres. Here you'll find traces of a primeval rain forest, and you can picnic while overlooking neighboring islets and cays. Any taxi driver can take you to the mountain. Before going, stop at the tourist office for a brochure with a map of the park's trails. The two main hikes are the Rain Forest Trail and the Mahogany Forest Trail.

✪ **Cane Garden Bay,** on the northwest shore, is so special you may take a taxi here in the morning and not head back to your cruise ship until departure time. With its palm-draped white-sand beach, this half-moon bay has as much South Seas charm as any place in the Caribbean. Plan to have lunch at **Rhymer's** on the beach (☎ 809/495-4639), where the chef will cook some conch or whelk, or perhaps barbecue spareribs. Freshwater showers are available, and you can rent towels. Rhymer's rents Sunfish and Windsurfers.

SHOPPING

Shopping on Tortola is a minor activity. Most stores are on Main Street in Road Town. Only British goods are imported

without duty, and they are the best buys, especially English china.

Caribbean Corner Spice House Co., Soper's Hole (☎ 809/495-4498), has the finest selection of spices and herbs on the island, along with an array of local handcrafts and botanical skin-care products.

Caribbean Fine Arts, Ltd. (☎ 809/494-4240), sells art from the West Indies, including original watercolors and oils, as well as limited-edition serigraphs and sepia photographs. It also has pottery and primitive art. **Caribbean Handprints** (☎ 809/494-3717) features island prints, all handmade by local craftspeople, plus colorful fabric by the yard.

Fort Wines Gourmet, Main Street in Road Town (☎ 809/494-3036), offers the island's best "fixings" for a picnic—everything from Hediard pâté terrines to Petronssian caviar and French champagne.

Little Denmark (☎ 809/494-2455) is your best bet for famous names in china and gold and silver jewelry. It also offers locally made jewelry, watches, fishing equipment, and even Cuban cigars (which can't be brought back into the United States).

Attached to Pusser's restaurant (see listing under "Dining," below) is **Pusser's Company Store** (☎ 809/494-2467), which sells a proprietary line of Pusser's sports and travel clothing, as well as up-market gift items. Pusser's Rum is also a best-selling item.

Sunny Caribbee Herb and Spice Company (☎ 809/494-2178) specializes in Caribbean spices, seasonings, teas, condiments, and handcrafts. You can buy two world-famous specialties here: West Indian Hangover Cure and Arawak Love Potion. In the adjacent Sunny Caribbee Art Gallery you'll find original art, prints, metal sculpture, and many other Caribbean crafts.

Flamboyance, Soper's Hole (☎ 809/495-4699), is the best place to shop for perfume. Fendi purses are also sold here.

Across from the Methodist church,

J. R. O'Neal, on Upper Main Street (☎ 809/494-2292), is a decorative and home-accessories store that sells terra-cotta pottery, wicker and rattan home furnishings, Mexican glassware, Dhurrie rugs, baskets, and ceramics, plus fine crystal and china.

BEACHES

Most of the beaches lie a 20-minute taxi ride from the cruise dock. Figure on about $15 one way, but agree with the driver before setting out. You can also ask the taxi driver to pick you up at a certain time.

The finest beach is at **Cane Garden Bay,** which compares favorably to the famous Magens Bay Beach on the north shore of St. Thomas. It's on the northwest side of the island, across the mountains from Road Town.

Surfers like **Apple Bay,** on the northwest side. A hotel here, Sebastian's, caters to the surfing crowd who visit in January and February, but the beach is ideal year round.

On the northwest shore near Cane Garden Bay, **Brewers Bay,** which has a campground, attracts both snorkelers and surfers.

Smuggler's Cove is at the extreme western end of Tortola, opposite the offshore island of Great Thatch and very close to St. John in the U.S. Virgin Islands. Snorkelers also like this beach, which is sometimes known as Lower Belmont Bay.

Long Bay Beach is on Beef Island, east of Tortola and the site of the major airport. This mile-long stretch of white-sand beach is reached by crossing the Queen Elizabeth Bridge, then taking a left on a dirt road before the airport.

Marina Cay, off Tortola's East End, is known for its good snorkeling beach, and we also recommend the one at **Cooper Island,** across Drake's Channel. Underwater Safaris (☎ 800/537-7032 in the U.S., or 809/494-3235) leads snorkel expeditions to both sites, weather permitting.

RIDING & DIVING

HORSEBACK RIDING Shadow's Ranch, Todman's Estate (☎ 809/494-2262), offers horseback rides through Mount Sage National Park or down to the shores of Cane Garden Bay. The cost is $25 per hour. It's about 15 miles from the cruise dock; taxi fare is $12.

SCUBA DIVING *Skin Diver* magazine has called the wreckage of the **HMS Rhone,** which sank in 1867 near the western point of Salt Island, the world's most fantastic shipwreck dive.

Baskin in the Sun, a PADI five-star facility (☎ 800/233-7938 in the U.S., or 809/494-5854), caters to divers of all experience levels, offering a half-day resort course for beginners. Regular dive trips go to such sites as the HMS *Rhone,* Painted Walls (an underwater canyon with walls formed of brightly colored coral and sponges), and the Indians (four pinnacle rocks that jut up out of the water; divers trace them down to coral reefs along the ocean floor, some 40 feet below the surface). You can hook up with Baskin in the Sun at the Prospect Reef Resort, a three-minute, $3 taxi ride from the dock. It has other locations at Sopher's Hole and at Tortola's West End.

Underwater Safaris (☎ 800/537-7032 in the U.S., or 809/494-3235) takes you to all the best sites, including the HMS *Rhone.* Associated with the Moorings yacht charter company, it offers a complete PADI and NAUI training facility. The company's Road Town office is a five-minute or $4 taxi ride from the docks.

DINING

✪ **Bomba's Surfside Shack,** Cappoon's Bay (☎ 809/495-4148), is the oldest, most memorable, and most uninhibited bar on the island. It sits on a 20-foot-wide strip of unpromising coastline near the West End. Despite its makeshift appearance, the shack has the means, the will, and the technology to create a really great party at any time of the day. The Sunday barbecue is $7 per person.

Standing on the waterfront across from the ferry dock, **Pusser's** (☎ 809/494-3897) serves Caribbean fare, English pub grub, and good pizzas. The complete lunch and dinner menu includes English shepherd's pie and New York deli–style sandwiches. The drink to have here is the famous Pusser's Rum, the same blend of five West Indian rums that the Royal Navy has served to its men for more than 300 years.

It's certainly worth venturing to ✪ **Sky-world,** Ridge Road (☎ 809/494-3567), which sits on one of the island's loftiest peaks. From here you can see both the U.S. Virgin Islands and the British Virgin Islands. The pumpkin soup is the best on the island, and you might also opt for mushrooms stuffed with conch. Other dishes are French-inspired, but we like the fresh fish grilled to order. You can finish with homemade tropical ice cream or terrific Key lime pie.

VIRGIN GORDA

Instead of visiting Tortola, some small cruise ships put in at lovely Virgin Gorda, famous for a boulder-strewn beach that's known as The Baths. The second-largest island in the colony, it got its name ("Fat Virgin") from Columbus, who thought the mountain framing it looked like a protruding stomach.

The island was a fairly desolate agricultural community until Laurance S. Rockefeller established Little Dix Bay Hotel here in the early 1960s. Other major hotels followed, but the privacy and solitude he envisioned still reign supreme on Virgin Gorda.

COMING ASHORE

Virgin Gorda doesn't have a pier or landing facilities that suit any of the large ships. Most vessels tender at anchor outside the island, sending small craft ashore. Many others dock at the pier in Road Town, then send tenders across the channel to Virgin Gorda.

SHORE EXCURSIONS

Many taxi drivers await visitors who debark from tenders and small boats at Spanish Town. They can take you to the Baths and the beach.

GETTING AROUND

The best way to see the island is to call Andy Flax at the Fischers Cove Beach Hotel (☎ 809/495-5252). He runs the **Virgin Gorda Tours Association,** which gives island tours for about $20 per person. The tour leaves twice daily. You can be picked up at the dock.

BEACHES

The major reason cruise ships visit Virgin Gorda is **The Baths,** where house-size boulders long ago toppled over one another to form saltwater grottoes suitable for exploring. The pools around The Baths are excellent for swimming, and the snorkeling nearby is wonderful (equipment can be rented on the beach).

Neighboring the Baths is **Spring Bay,** one of the best of the island's beaches, with white sand, clear water, and good snorkeling. **Trunk Bay** is a wide sand beach reachable by boat or along a rough path from Spring Bay. **Savannah Bay** is a sandy beach north of the yacht harbor, and **Mahoe Bay,** at the Mango Bay Resort, has a gently curving beach with vivid blue water.

Devil's Bay National Park can be reached by a trail from the Baths roundabout. The walk to this secluded coral-sand beach takes about 15 minutes through a natural setting of boulders and dry coastal vegetation.

SCUBA DIVING

Kilbride's Underwater Tours, at the Bitter End Resort at North Sound (☎ 800/932-4286 in the U.S., or 809/495-9638), offers the best diving in the B.V.I. at 15 to 20 dive sites, including the *Rhone.* Prices range from $80 to $90 for a two-tank dive on one of the coral reefs. Equipment is supplied at no extra charge.

DINING

At the end of the waterfront shopping plaza in Spanish Town, **Bath and Turtle Pub,** Virgin Gorda Yacht Harbour (☎ 809/495-5239), is the island's most popular bar and pub. You can join the regulars over midmorning guava coladas or peach daiquiris. From its handful of indoor and courtyard tables, you can order fried fish fingers, nachos, very spicy chili, pizzas, Reubens or tuna melts, steak, lobster, and daily seafood specials such as conch fritters.

Chez Bamboo (☎ 809/495-5963) lies beside the main road, a short walk north of the Yacht Harbour at Spanish Town. Menu items include Carib-Creole specialties, many with a New Orleans flavor. Try the fresh catch of the day or else the barbecue shrimp.

Mrs. Ilma O'Neal, a teacher in the island's public school for 43 years, began ✪ **Teacher Ilma's** (☎ 809/495-5355) by cooking privately for visitors and island construction workers. She serves dishes that are local in origin and flavor. Her hearty lunches might feature chicken, local goat, lobster, conch, pork, or your choice of grouper, snapper, tuna, dolphin, swordfish, or triggerfish. Desserts include homemade coconut, pineapple, or guava pies.

5 Cozumel & Playa del Carmen ⬇⬇⬇

Cozumel has white-sand beaches and fabulous scuba diving, but its greatest draw is its proximity to the ancient Mayan ruins at Tulum and Chichén Itzá. Some ships also stop at nearby Playa del Carmen on the Yucatan Peninsula, as it's easier to visit the ruins from there than from Cozumel.

COZUMEL

The ancient Mayans who lived here for 12 centuries would be shocked by the million cruise passengers who now visit Cozumel each year. Their presence has greatly changed San Miguel, the only town, which now has fast-food eateries and a Hard Rock Cafe. However, development hasn't touched much of the island's natural beauty. Ashore you will see abundant wildlife, including armadillos, brightly colored tropical birds, and lizards. Offshore, the government has set aside 20 miles of coral reefs as an underwater national park, including the stunning Palancar Reef, the world's second largest natural coral formation.

COMING ASHORE

Ships arriving at Muelle Fiscal on Cozumel tender passengers directly to the heart of San Miguel. From the downtown pier you can walk to shops, restaurants, and cafes. Other ships anchor off the international pier, 4 miles from San Miguel. The beaches are close to the international pier.

You can make telephone calls from **The Calling Station,** Avenida Rafael Melgar 27 (☎ 987/2-1417), at the corner of Calle 3 in San Miguel, three blocks from Muelle Fiscal. They issue prepaid phone cards, operate an international money exchange, and have a fax machine.

FAST FACTS

Currency The Mexican currency is the nuevo peso, or new peso. Mexican coins come in denominations of 1, 2, 5, and 10 pesos and 20 and 50 centavos (100 centavos equals one new peso). Paper currency comes in denominations of 2, 5, 10, 20, 50, and 100 new pesos. Since the peso has fluctuated wildly in recent years, prices in this section are in U.S. dollars.

You can change currency at the following banks, all a block or less from the Meulle Fiscal pier and open weekday mornings: **Banpais,** Rafael Melgar 27A (☎ 987/2-0318); **Bancomer,** Avenida 5A at the Plaza (☎ 987/2-0550); **Banco del Atlantico,** Avenida 5A Sur at Calle 1 (☎ 987/2-0142); or **Banco**

Serfin, Calle 1 Sur between Avenidas 5A and 10A (☎ 987/2-0930). You could also stop by **American Express,** Calle 11 Sur 598 between Avenida 25 and Avenida 30 in San Miguel (☎ 987/2-0831), in the Fiesta Cozumel, 15 blocks from the pier of Muelle Fiscal.

Information The **Tourism Office,** Plaza del Sol (☎ 987/2-0972), distributes *Vacation Guide to Cozumel* and *Cozumel Island's Restaurant Guide;* both have island maps. Open Monday to Friday from 9am to 2:30pm and 5:30 to 8pm.

Language Spanish is the tongue of the land, although English is spoken in most places frequented by tourists.

SHORE EXCURSIONS

If your ship is going to Playa del Carmen, it will be easier to see the ruins at Chichén Itzá, Tulum, and Cobá from here. From Cozumel, a shore excursion is the only way to visit the ruins in a day.

Tour agencies offer various one-day tours to the ruins. One of the best, **Intermar Caribe,** Calle 2 N 101B, between Avenidas 5A and 10A, two blocks from Muelle Fiscal pier (☎ 987/2-1535), offers airplane trips to Chichén Itzá, followed by tours of the ruins, that are conducted Tuesday to Friday for $90 per person. The flight takes 40 minutes each way, and transfers and entrance to the ruins are included. The company also offers a full-day guided tour by bus and ferryboat to the ruins at Tulum and Cobá for $79 per person. Entrance to the monuments is included in the price.

Intermar Caribe also offers an island tour of Cozumel, which includes visits to the locale's Mayan ruins and trips to the island's major sights, including the museum, with a brief stop for snorkeling from a beach within the national park. This tour costs $35 per person. The same company offers an even more comprehensive snorkeling tour, whereby you'll be transported by boat to a point above one of the world's greatest reefs. The tours depart Monday to Saturday from 9am to 2pm, including lunch and use of snorkeling equipment. The outfit can also arrange scuba diving daily, with dives starting at $50 for qualified divers.

If you prefer to visit ruins in the style of the Spanish conquistadors, you can sign up for a three-hour guided tour on horseback that begins at **Rancho Buenavista,** Avenida Rafael Melgar at Calle 11 in San Miguel (☎ 987/2-1537). Limited to eight participants at a time, tours depart four times a day, or whenever business justifies it, and takes its participants to ruins on Cozumel Island that include San Gervasio. The cost is $60 per person. No tours are conducted on Thursday or Saturday.

GETTING AROUND

The town of San Miguel is so small you can walk anywhere you want to go. Essentially there is only one road in Cozumel, which runs from the northern tip of the island, hugs the western shoreline, then loops around the southern tip and returns to the capital.

Taxi service (☎ 987/2-0236) is available 24 hours a day. Taxis are relatively inexpensive, but it's tradition to overcharge cruise-ship passengers, so settle on a fare before getting in. The average fare from San Miguel to most major resorts and beaches is $4.50. More distant island rides cost $12.

Mopeds are a popular means of getting about despite heavy traffic, hidden stop signs, potholed roads, and a high accident rate. Try **Auto Rent** (☎ 987/2-0844) in the Hotel Ceiba, a block from the pier at Muelle Fiscal. They charge about $25 per day. Mexican law requires helmets.

A number of passenger ferries link Cozumel with Playa del Carmen. The most comfortable are two big speed boats and a water jet catamaran run by **Aviomar** (☎ 987/2-0477) that operate Monday to Saturday from 8am to 8pm, Sunday from 9am to 1pm. The trip takes 45 minutes. Other vessels include the

The Yucatán's Upper Caribbean Coast

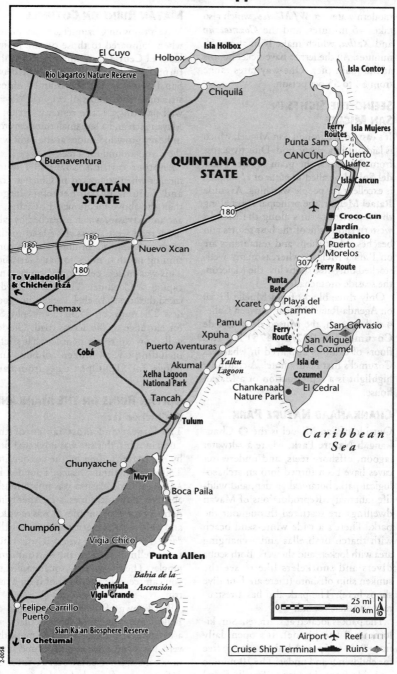

El Cuyo

Río Lagartos Nature Reserve

Holbox

Isla Holbox

Chiquilá

Isla Contoy

Ferry Routes

Isla Mujeres

Punta Sam

CANCÚN

Puerto Juárez

Isla Cancun

Buenaventura

QUINTANA ROO STATE

YUCATÁN STATE

Croco-Cun

Jardín Botanico

180

Puerto Morelos

Nuevo Xcan

307

Ferry Route

180 D

180 D

180

To Valladolid & Chichén Itzá

Chemax

Punta Bete

Xcaret

Playa del Carmen

Pamul

Xpuha

Ferry Route

San Gervasio

San Miguel de Cozumel

Cobá

Puerto Aventuras

Akumal

Yalku Lagoon

Isla de Cozumel

Xelha Lagoon National Park

Chankanaab Nature Park

El Cedral

Tancah

Tulum

Caribbean Sea

Chunyaxche

Muyil

Boca Paila

Chumpón

Vigía Chico

Punta Allen

Bahía de la Ascensión

Peninsula Vigía Grande

Felipe Carrillo Puerto

0   25 mi
        40 km

N

Sian Ka'an Biosphere Reserve

To Chetumal

Airport ✈   Reef

Cruise Ship Terminal 🚢   Ruins ◆

2-0058

modern water-jet *WJ México,* which also takes 45 minutes, and the *Cozmeleño* and *Xelha,* which make it in about 55 minutes. All the ferries have ticket booths at the main pier. One-way fares range from $4 to $5 per person.

SEEING THE SIGHTS IN SAN MIGUEL

It's easy to get around San Miguel, which is laid out in a classic grid. Directly across from the docks, the main square, **Plaza del Sol** (also called *la plaza* or *el parque*), is excellent for people-watching. **Avenida Rafael Melgar,** the principal street along the waterfront, runs along the island's western shore, site of the best resorts and beaches. Most shops and restaurants are on Rafael Melgar, whereas many well-stocked duty-free shops line the Malecón, the seaside promenade.

Only three blocks from Muelle Fiscal on Agenda Rafael Melgar between Calles 4 and 6 north, the **Museo de la Isla de Cozumel** (☎ 987/2-1475) has two floors of exhibits displayed in what was Cozumel's first luxury hotel. A charming highlight is a reproduction of a Mayan house.

CHANKANAAB NATURE PARK

Outside of San Miguel is the ✪ **Chankanaab Nature Park,** where a saltwater lagoon, offshore reefs, and underwater caves have been turned into an archaeological park, botanical garden, and wildlife sanctuary. Reproductions of Mayan dwellings are scattered throughout the park. There's a wide white-sand beach with thatch umbrellas and a changing area with lockers and showers. Both scuba divers and snorkelers like to see the sunken ship offshore (there are four dive shops here). The park also has a restaurant and snack stand.

The park is located at Carretera Sur, kilometer 9 (no phone). It's open daily from 9am to 5pm. Admission is $5, free for children 9 and under. The 10-minute taxi ride from the pier at Muelle Fiscal costs about $5.

MAYAN RUINS ON COZUMEL

Mayan ruins on Cozumel are very minor when compared to those on the mainland. **El Cedral** lies 2 miles inland at the turnoff at kilometer 17.5, east of Playa San Francisco. It's the island's oldest structure, with traces of original Mayan wall paintings. Little remains except a Mayan arch and a few small ruins covered in heavy growth. Guides at the sight will show you around for a fee.

Another ruin on Cozumel Island, meager when compared to Chichén Itzá and Tulum, but nonetheless larger than the above-mentioned El Cedral, is at **San Gervasio,** which is reached by taking a road west across the island to the army air base, then turning right and continuing north 4 miles to San Gervasio. This was once a ceremonial center and capital of Cozumel. The Mayans dedicated the area to Ix-chel, the fertility goddess. The ruins cost $5.50 to visit, plus $1 for entrance to the access road. Guides will show up to six people what's left, including several broken columns and lintels, for $12. Open daily from 8am to 5pm.

MAYAN RUINS ON THE MAINLAND
✪ Chichén Itzá

The largest and most fabled of the Yucatán ruins, this site was inhabited first by the Mayans, then by the conquering Toltecs of Central Mexico. Founded in A.D. 445, Chichén Itzá was mysteriously abandoned two centuries later. After lying dormant for two centuries, it was resettled and enjoyed prosperity again until the early 13th century, when it was once more relinquished to the surrounding jungles. The site covers 7 square miles, so you can see only a fraction of it on a day trip.

Best known of the ruins is **Castillo of Kukulcán,** a pyramid that's actually an astronomical clock designed to mark the vernal and autumnal equinoxes and summer and winter solstices. A total of 365 steps, one for each day of the year, ascend to the top platform. During each equinox, light striking the pyramid gives the illusion of a giant snake slithering down the steps to join its gigantic stone head mounted at the base.

The government began restoration on the site in the 1920s. Today it houses a museum, restaurant, and shop. Admission is included in shore excursions; otherwise, the site and museum cost $6.50 Monday to Saturday, free on Sunday. You may shoot video footage of the site, using your own camcorder, for a fee of $8. The site is open daily from 8am to 5pm.

✪ Tulum

Eighty miles south of Cancún, the walled city of Tulum is the single most visited Mayan ruin. It was the only Mayan city built on the coast and the only one inhabited when the Spanish conquistadors arrived in the 1500s. With panoramic views of the Caribbean, the walled city consists of 60 individual structures. As with Chichén Itzá, its most prominent feature is a pyramid topped with a temple to Kukulcán, the primary Mayan/Olmec god. Other highlights include the Temple of the Frescoes, with well-preserved friezes, plus the Temple of the Descending God, the House of Columns, and the House of the Cenote (a well). Entrance is included in shore excursions; otherwise, it's $5.50 Monday to Saturday, free on Sunday. Use of a video camera costs $8. The site is open daily from 8am to 5pm.

Cobá

Cobá is the site of one of the most important city-states in the Mayan empire. Excavation work began in 1972, and archeologists estimate that only 5% of this dead city has been uncovered. Cobá flourished from A.D. 400 to A.D. 1100, its population numbering perhaps as many as 40,000 inhabitants. The site lies on four lakes. Because of its still-primitive nature, its 81 acres provide exploration opportunities for the truly adventurous hiker. Cobá's pyramid, Nohoch Mul, is the tallest in the Yucatán. The price of admission is included in shore excursions; otherwise, it's $6.50 Monday to Saturday,

free on Sunday. The site is open daily from 8am to 5pm; it's located 105 miles south of Cancún.

SHOPPING

You can walk from the pier at Muelle Fiscal to the best shops, which are centered in San Miguel. Prices are relatively high here.

To stock up on your reading, head a block from the pier to **Agencia Publicaciones Gracia,** Avenida 5A (☎ 987/2-0031), Cozumel's best source for English-language books, guidebooks, newspapers, and magazines.

You'll find handcrafts made of wood and tin at **El Sombrero,** Avenida Rafael Melgar 29 (☎ 987/2-0374), plus pottery, ceramics, and onyx. Although it's likely to be packed with cruise-ship passengers, **La Fiesta Warehouse,** Avenida Rafael Melgar 101 (☎ 987/2-2032), sells a good selection of handmade Mexican crafts in wood, paper, silver, and pottery. Shipping is available.

In front of the international port, **Casablanca,** Avenida Rafael Melgar 33 (☎ 987/2-1177), has a fine selection of Mexican jewelry and loose stones, plus a good collection of Mexican crafts.

Two blocks from Muelle Fiscal, **Talavera,** Avenida 5A Sur 349 (☎ 987/2-0171), is your best bet for Yucután ceramics. You can also purchase interesting crafts here, including wooden animals from Oaxaca or masks from Guerrero.

Local artist **Gordon Gilchrist,** Studio 1, Avenida 25 S 981 at Calle 15 S (☎ 987/2-2659), produces Cozumel's finest etchings of local Mayan sites. He also displays and sells pencil drawings and limited edition lithographs of the ruins.

Joyería Palancar, Avenida Rafael Melgar N15, between Calles 2 and 4 (☎ 987/2-1468), has an amazing collection of loose stones such as topaz and amethyst, as well as pearls in 14- or 18-karat gold settings. Silver Mexican coins are also available. **Rachat and Romero,** Avenida Rafael Melgar 101 (☎ 987/2-0571), also sells loose stones that they will mount while you wait.

Ultra Femme, Avenida Rafael Melgar 341 (☎ **987/2-1251**), is an important jeweler in Cozumel and the exclusive distributor of Rolex watches on the Mexican Riviera. It also sells such famous names as Ebel, Rado, and Gucci, as well as perfumes, body oils, and skin-care products.

A block from the pier, the department store **Prococo,** Avenida Rafael Melgar N99 (☎ **987/2-1875**), has great Mexican crafts as well as religious artifacts. You'll also find Mexican pottery and leather goods, plus everything from French perfumes to Swiss knives. Another department store with a bit of everything at reasonable prices is **Los Cinco Soles,** Avenida Rafael Melgar N 27 (☎ **987/2-0132**). Its selection of handcrafted items is the largest in Cozumel.

BEACHES

Cozumel's best beach of powdery white sand, **Playa San Francisco,** stretches for some 3 miles along the southwestern shoreline. You can rent water sports equipment here and eat lunch at one of the many *palapa* restaurants and bars. The beach is a $4 taxi ride south from San Miguel's downtown pier. If you dock at the international pier, you're practically at the beach already.

Since many of your fellow cruisers have heard of the fine **Playa del Sol,** about a mile south of Playa del San Francisco, it'll probably be crowded. **Playa Bonita** is one of the least crowded beaches, but it lies on the east (windward) side of the island and is difficult to reach unless you drive or take a taxi. It sits in a moon-shaped cove sheltered from the Caribbean Sea by an offshore reef.

SCUBA DIVING & SNORKELING

In Cozumel, Jacques Cousteau discovered black coral in profusion, plus hundreds of species of rainbow-hued tropical fish. Underwater visibility here can reach 250 feet. All this gives Cozumel the best diving in the Caribbean.

Cruisers may want to confine their adventures to the finest spot, **Palancar Reef.**

Lying about a mile offshore, this fabulous system is a water world of wonder, including gigantic elephant-ear sponges and black and red coral, plus deep caves, canyons, and tunnels.

The best scuba outfitter is **Aqua Safari,** in the Hotel Plaza las Glorias between Calles 5 and 7 (☎ **987/2-0101**), about eight blocks from Muelle Fiscal. A one-tank dive costs $5; a day of diving starts at $50.

One of this outfit's worthwhile competitors is **Diving Adventures,** Calle 5 Sur no. 2, near the corner of Avenida Rafael Melgar (☎ **987/2-3009**), whose prices, itineraries, and diving skills are equivalent.

DINING

Right in front of the in-town cruise dock, ✪ **Café del Puerto,** Avenida Rafael Melgar 3 (☎ **987/2-0316**), is a local favorite. The kitchen bridges the gap between Mexico and Europe with dishes like a superbly prepared mustard steak flambé, succulent lobster, and Yucatán chicken wrapped in banana leaves.

Just north of the ferry pier, **Carlos 'n' Charlie's,** Avenida Rafael Melgar 11 (☎ **987/2-0191**), is Mexico's equivalent of the Hard Rock Cafe. People come here for good times and the spicy, tasty ribs. You can dine surprisingly well on Yucatán specialties, and the best chicken and beef fajitas in Cozumel.

There's always the real thing: the **Hard Rock Cozumel,** Avenida Rafael Melgar 2A (☎ **987/2-0885**). Its juicy burgers aren't as good as at the stateside outlets, but they're still the best in Cozumel. This branch also serves grilled beef or chicken fajitas.

El Capi Navegante, Avenida 10A Sur 312 at Calles 3 and 4, five blocks from Muelle Fiscal (☎ **987/2-1730**), offers the freshest fish in San Miguel. We thought the kitchen was at its best with red snapper flambé, until we sampled the lobster soufflé. There's also a shrimp soufflé and excellent conch ceviche. You can dine inside or out.

Two blocks from the Muelle Fiscal pier, **La Choza,** Calle Rosada Salas 198 at Avenida 10A Sur (☎ **987/2-0958**), offers real local cooking that's a favorite of the town's savvy foodies. The Mexican specialties are the most authentic in town, including a savory *puerco entomatado* (pork in tomato sauce) or their famous chicken mole. Red snapper is delectable in a rather sweet-tasting mustard sauce, and they will also grill or fry fresh fish as you like it.

A half block from the pier, **Las Palmeras,** Avenida Rafael Melgar (☎ **987/2-0532**), is ideal for casual eating. If you arrive in time, it serves one of the best breakfasts in town. You can also drop in during the day for the best margaritas and piña coladas. For lunch, they offer tempting seafood dishes or Mexican specialties.

When you can't face another taco, head to **Pizza Prima,** Avenida Adolfo Rosada 109 (☎ **987/2-4242**) for the best pizza on the island, but the restaurant only opens at 3pm daily.

If your ship is leaving late enough for an early dinner ashore, two grills near the port are so good you'll wish they had branches in your hometown. **Pepe's Grill,** Avenida Rafael Melgar at Salas (☎ **987/2-0213**) serves succulent flame-broiled prime rib, filet mignons, and steaks. The grilled red snapper at **Santigo's Grill,** Calle Rosada Salas 299 at Avenida 15A Sur (☎ **987/2-2137**), is a delectable choice and never allowed to stay on the fire until it's dried out. Fresh lobster appears frequently on the menu, and it's seldom overcooked either.

PLAYA DEL CARMEN

Some cruise ships spend one day at Cozumel, then another at Playa del Carmen, on the Yucatán mainland.

The famed white-sand beach here was relatively deserted not many years ago, but today tourists have replaced the Indian families who used to gather coconuts to extract the oil. If you can tolerate the crowds, snorkeling is excellent over the offshore reefs. Turtle-watching is another local pastime.

Avenida Juárez in Playa del Carmen is the principal business zone for the Tulum-Cancún corridor. Part of Avenida 5 running parallel to the beach has been closed to traffic, forming a good promenade. Most visitors at some point head for Rincón del Sol, a tree-filled courtyard built in the colonial Mexican style. This has the best collection of handicraft shops.

COMING ASHORE

Cruise ships dock at anchor or at the pier of Cozumel, and then send passengers to Playa del Carmen by tender. Plans are under way to construct a massive pier here.

SHORE EXCURSIONS: SEEING THE RUINS

Other than the beach, which is spectacular and almost blindingly white, there are no significant attractions in Playa del Carmen except Xcaret, an ecologically sensitive theme park described below. Consequently, most visitors head for the region's Mayan ruins the moment their cruise ship ferries (or tenders) them ashore, making a stop in the town of Playa del Carmen almost as an afterthought. Virtually every cruise ship that stops here will offer shore excursions to the Mayan ruins in venues that make efficient use of your limited time ashore, but if you opt to handle your tour independently, one of the region's largest agencies is **Aviomar,** Calle 5 at Calle 24 Norte 8A (☎ **987/2-0588**). Depending on which cluster of ruins you decide to visit, their tours cost between $69 and $79 per person, depart at 9am daily, and return between 6 and 6:30pm.

GETTING AROUND

Taxis are readily available to take you anywhere, but you can walk to the center of town, to the beach, and to most major shops.

If you decide to rent a car for the day, try **National,** Hotel Molca, 1A Avenida Sur 5A (☎ 987/3-0360), or **Econo Mobile,** Hotel Diamond at Playacar (☎ 987/3-0340). Cars at either agency—usually Volkswagen beetles, Chevettes, and Jeeps—usually come with unlimited mileage and most forms of insurance included, renting for between $55 and $70 a day.

AN ECOLOGICAL THEME PARK

You can spend your day at **Xcaret,** a 250-acre ecological theme park four miles south of Playa del Carmen on the coast. Mayan ruins are scattered about the lushly landscaped acres. On an underwater river ride, you float on currents that run through a series of caves. There's also a botanical garden, plus a dive shop. Admission costs $30. Frequent buses run from Playa del Carmen to Xcaret. A taxi costs $4.

DINING

Both local residents and visitors flock to ✪ **Máscaras,** Avenida Juárez (☎ 987/3-1053), for the best pizzas, pastas, and other Italian dishes. They also grill some of the freshest fish in town.

If you get hungry for some stateside home cooking, you can head to **Mom's,** Avenida 30 at Calle 4 (☎ 987/3-0315), for homemade soups, salads, and maybe a good meat loaf. Even the vanilla ice cream is made here, and it's yummy with apple cobbler. Mom's also serves rib-sticking breakfasts.

Across from La Plaza is **El Tacolote,** Calle 5 at its junction with Avenida Juárez (☎ 987/3-0066), a branch of a popular Cozumel restaurant that specializes in fresh seafood and the most succulent grilled meats in town. All the Mexican staples accompany these platters.

6　Curaçao　⚓ ⚓ ⚓

As you sail into the harbor of Willemstad, a quaint "floating bridge" swings aside to welcome you into the narrow channel set against a backdrop of pastel rows of gabled Dutch houses. Welcome to Curaçao, the largest and most populous of the Netherlands Antilles, just 35 miles north of the coast of Venezuela.

A tropical Holland in miniature, this island has the most interesting architecture in the West Indies. Its Dutch-colonial structures give Willemstad a storybook look, while the rest of this desertlike island seems like the American Southwest, with three-pronged cacti, spiny-leafed aloes, and divi-divi trees bent by trade winds.

COMING ASHORE

Cruise ships dock at the terminal just beyond the Queen Emma pontoon bridge, which leads to the duty-free shopping sector and the famous floating market. You can call home from the terminal's phone office. It's a 6- to 10-minute walk to the center of Willemstad, or you can take a taxi from the stand.

FAST FACTS

Currency　The official currency is the **Netherlands Antillean florin (NAf)**, also called a guilder, which is divided into 100 cents. Currently the exchange rate is $1 U.S. to 1.77 NAf (or 1 NAf = 56¢ U.S.). Canadian and U.S. dollars are accepted for purchases.

Information　Go to the **Curaçao Tourist Board,** Pietermaai 19 (☎ 599/9-616000). Open Monday to Friday from 7:30am to 5pm.

Language　Dutch, Spanish, and English are spoken, along with Papiamento, a patois that combines the three major tongues with Amerindian and African dialects.

SHORE EXCURSIONS

Excursions are minor here. You can easily see the town on your own in 2 or 3 hours, leaving plenty of time for the beaches or water sports. If you don't want to rent a car, most cruise lines will arrange

Curaçao

0 — 5 km
0 — 3 mi

Caribbean Sea

Noordpunt

Westpunt
Playa Abao
Knip Bay

Westpunt
■ **Boca Tabla**

Christoffel National Park
▲ **St. Christoffelberg**

Barber

Santa Marta Bay
Soto

San Juan Bay

St. Willibrordus

Daaibooi

Boca St. Marie

St. Michiel

Blauwbaai

Piscadera Bay

Curaçao International Airport
Boca Hato
■ **Hato Caves**

Julianadorp

Brienvegat

Emmastad
■ Santa Catarina

St. Anna Bay
Santa Rosa
St. Joris Bay

Willemstad
Seaquarium ■
Montagne

Jan Thiel Bay

Santa Barbara Beach
Spanish Water

Curaçao Underwater Marine Park

Oostpunt

Caribbean Sea

Airport ✈ Beach 🏖 Diving 🤿 Mountain ▲ Cruise Ship Terminal ⛴

367

a 3¹/₂-hour countryside tour for $25 per passenger. You get to see the Westpunt, Mt. Christoffel, the towering cacti, and rolling hills topped by landhuizen (plantation houses) built more than three centuries ago. You'll also be taken to a beach, but stops at the Museum of Natural History and the grotto known as Boca Tabla may leave you wondering if the tour was worth the price. Excursions also include a submarine trip at Curaçao Seaquarium, but you can do that yourself.

You'll save money by booking your own shore excursions. Up to four passengers can share a taxi tour, which costs about $25 per hour. **Taber Tours,** Dokweg (☎ 599/9-376637), also offers several day and night excursions. Its tour through Willemstad, to the Curaçao Liqueur distillery, through the residential area and the Bloempot shopping center, and to the Curaçao Museum costs $12.50 for adults, $6.25 for children under 12, including museum admission.

GETTING AROUND

Taxis don't have meters, so settle on a fare before getting in. Drivers are supposed to carry an official tariff sheet. Generally there is no need to tip. The best place to get a taxi is on the Otrabands side of the floating bridge or call ☎ 599/9-690747 or 599/9-690752. A fleet of DAF yellow buses operates from Wilhelmina Plein, near the shopping center, and runs to most parts of Curaçao. You can hail a bus at any designated bus stop.

Driving is on the right on paved roads. If you want to rent a car, try **Avis** (☎ 800/331-1084 or 599/9-681163), **Budget** (☎ 800/527-0700 or 599/9-683420), or **Hertz** (☎ 800/654-3001 or 599/9-681182).

SEEING THE SIGHTS

Willemstad is the major attraction. The town grew up on both sides of a canal, and today it's divided into the **Punda,** with an Old World Dutch feel and great shopping, and the more contemporary **Otrabanda,** meaning "the other side." Both sections are connected by the **Queen Emma Pontoon Bridge,** a pedestrian walkway that swings open to let ships pass in and out of the harbor. Vehicles take the **Queen Juliana Bridge,** which rises 195 feet over the harbor.

A statue of Pedro Luis Brion dominates the square known as Brionplein at the Otrabanda end of the Queen Emma Pontoon Bridge. Born in Curaçao in 1782, he became the island's favorite son and best-known war hero.

The **Waterfront** originally guarded the mouth of the canal on the eastern or Punda side, but now it has been incorporated into the Plaza Hotel. The task of standing guard has been taken over by **Fort Amsterdam,** site of the Governor's Palace and the 1769 Dutch Reformed church. The church still has a British cannonball embedded in it. The arches leading to the fort were tunneled under the official governor's residence.

A corner of the fort stands at the intersection of Breedestraat and Handelskade, the starting point of the island's major shopping district.

A few minutes' walk from the pontoon bridge, at the north end of Handelskade, is the **Floating Market,** where scores of schooners tie up alongside the canal. Boats from Venezuela, Colombia, and elsewhere sell tropical fruits and vegetables—a little bit of everything. The modern market nearby has not diminished the fun of watching the activity here.

Between the I.H. (Sha) Capriles Kade and Fort Amsterdam, at the corner of Columbusstraat and Hanchi Snog, is the **Mikve Israel–Emanuel Synagogue** (☎ 599/9-611633). Dating from 1651, the Jewish congregation here is the oldest in the New World.

Next door, the **Jewish Cultural Historical Museum,** Kuiperstraat 26–28 (☎ 599/9-611633), is housed in two buildings dating from 1728. They were the rabbi's residence and the mikvah, or bath, for religious purification purposes.

WEST OF WILLEMSTAD

You can walk from the Queen Emma Bridge to the tiny **Curaçao Museum,** Van Leeuwenhoekstraat (☎ 599/ 9-626051). The building, built in 1853 by the Royal Dutch Army as a military hospital, has been carefully restored and furnished with paintings, objets d'art, and antique furniture, and houses a large collection from the Caiquetio tribes. On the museum grounds is an art gallery for temporary exhibitions of both local and international art.

The **Curaçao Seaquarium,** off Dr. Martin Luther King Boulevard (☎ 599/9-616666), displays more than 400 species of fish, crabs, anemones, and other invertebrates, sponges, and coral. A rustic boardwalk connects the hexagonal buildings, which sit on a point near the site where the *Oranje Nassau* broke up on the rocks and sank in 1906. The Seaquarium also has Curaçao's only full-facility, white-sand, palm-shaded beach. In the "shark and animal encounter," divers, snorkelers, and experienced swimmers are able to feed, film, and photograph sharks, stingrays, lobsters, tarpons, parrot fish, and other marine life in a controlled environment. Nonswimmers can see, but not touch, the underwater life from a 46-foot semisubmersible observatory.

If you're here in the late afternoon, the semisubmersible *Seaworld Explorer* departs daily at 4:30pm on hour-long journeys. You'll see submerged offshore wrecks and rainbow-hued tropical fish swimming over coral reefs. Reserve a day in advance by calling (☎ 599/ 9-604892). Fares are $30.75 for adults, $19 for children 11 and under.

A NATIONAL PARK & CAVES

Cacti, bromeliads, rare orchids, iguanas, donkeys, wild goats, and many birds thrive in 4,500-acre **Christoffel National Park,** about a 45-minute taxi ride from the capital near Curaçao's western tip (☎ 599/9-640363). The park rises from flat, arid countryside to 1,230-foot-high St. Christoffelberg, the tallest point in the Dutch Leewards. Along the way are ancient Arawak paintings and the Piedra di Monton, a rock heap accumulated by African slaves who cleared this former plantation.

The park has 20 miles of one-way, trail-like roads. The shortest is about 5 miles long, but it takes about 40 minutes to drive it because of the rough terrain. Several hiking trails go to the top of St. Christoffelberg. It takes about 1 1/2 hours to walk to the summit (come early in the morning before it gets hot).

There's a museum in an old storehouse left over from plantation days. Guided tours of the park are available; admission is $9 per person. Next door, the park has opened the **National Park Shete Boka (Seven Bays),** a turtle sanctuary.

The stalagmites and stalactites mirrored in an underground lake in **Hato Caves,** F. D. Rosseveltweg (☎ 599/9-68037), have been called "mystical." This limestone terrace was actually a coral reef that was uplifted by geological forces. After crossing the lake, you enter two caverns known as the Cathedral and La Ventana, or "The Window." Displayed here are samples of ancient Indian petroglyphs. Professional local guides take visitors through the caves every hour. Admission is $4.25 for adults, $3 for children.

SHOPPING

Curaçao is a shopper's paradise, with some 200 stores lining streets in the Punda, a five-block district. Many stores open for a few hours on Sunday and holidays if cruise ships are in port.

Look for good buys on French perfumes, Dutch Delft blue souvenirs, finely woven Italian silks, Japanese and German cameras, jewelry, silver, Swiss watches, linens, leather goods, liquor, and island-made rum and liqueurs (especially Curaçao liqueur), some with a distinctive blue color. The island is famous for its five-pound "wheelers" of Gouda or Edam cheese. Some stores also offer good buys on intricate imported lacework. Street vendors at any main plaza hawk carvings and flamboyant paintings from Haiti and the Dominican Republic.

Although collection of black coral has been made illegal by the Curaçao government, an exception was made for Bert Knubben, a diver who has been harvesting corals from the sea and fashioning them into fine jewelry and objets d'art for more than 35 years. The **Bert Knubben Black Koral Art Studio** is located in the Princess Beach Resort and Casino, Dr. Martin Luther King Boulevard (☎ 599/9-367888).

Boolchand's, Heerenstraat 4B (☎ 599/9-612262), has Seiko and Citizen watches, French perfume, Italian silk ties, Dutch dolls, British cashmere sweaters, and cameras and photo equipment. Your best bet here is audio and video equipment. If you can't find what you want, try **Palais Hindu,** Heerenstraat 17 (☎ 599/9-616897).

Gandelman Jewelers, Breedestraat 35 (☎ 599/9-611854), is the island's best and most reliable jeweler, stocking a large, often exquisitely designed selection. If you want something local, ask to see their Curaçaoan gold pieces. Exclusive here is the line of Prima Classe leather goods with the world map.

At **Obra Di Man,** Bargestraat 57 (☎ 599/9-612413), you'll find the best selection of authentic local handicraft items, especially dolls that represent island folkloric characters. The store also sells hand-screened fabrics and carved driftwood.

Penha and Sons, Heerenstraat 1 (☎ 599/9-612266), in the town's oldest building, is known for its perfumes and brand-name clothes. You'll also find Hummel figurines and Delft blue souvenirs.

The Yellow House (La Casa Amarilla), Breedestraat 46 (☎ 599/9-613222), has the best perfume selection, plus an impressive array of cosmetics and accessories. But don't expect cut-rate prices.

BEACHES

Curaçao's beaches are not as good as Aruba's 7-mile strip, but the island does have some 38 beaches, ranging from hotel sands to secluded coves. The seawater remains an almost-constant 76°F year-round, with good underwater visibility.

You have to pay to use the island's only full-facility, white-sand, palm-shaded beach at the Curaçao Seaquarium.

A good private beach on the island's eastern side is **Santa Barbara Beach,** near the primary water sports and recreational area known as Spanish Water. There is also Table Mountain, a remarkable landmark, as well as an old phosphate mine. The natural beach has pure white sand and calm water. Restrooms, changing rooms, a snack bar, and a terrace are available. You can rent water bicycles and small motorboats. The beach has access to the Curaçao Underwater Park.

Daaibooi is a good beach about 30 minutes from town, in the Willibrordus area on the island's west side. It's free, but there are no changing facilities.

Blauwbaai (Blue Bay) is the largest and most frequented beach on Curaçao. Along with showers and changing facilities, there are shady places to retreat from the noonday sun.

Located on the island's northwestern tip, **Westpunt** is known for its gigantic cliffs and the Sunday divers who jump from their heights into the ocean. **Knip Bay,** just south of Westpunt, has beautiful turquoise waters, and on weekends, live music and dancing make the beach a lively place. Changing facilities and refreshments are available. **Playa Abao,** with crystal turquoise water, is at the island's northern tip.

Taxi drivers at the cruise dock will take you to any of the beaches at fares to be negotiated. You can also make arrangements to be picked up at a certain time.

Warning: Beware of stepping on the sea urchins that sometimes abound in these waters. While not fatal, their hard spines can cause several days of real discomfort. If you do step on one, the locals suggest applying vinegar or lime juice.

GOLF, DIVING, SAILING, TENNIS & WATER SPORTS

GOLF   The **Curaçao Golf and Squash Club,** Wilhelminalaan, in Emmastad (☎ 599/9-373590), has the island's only course. This nine-holer is open to nonmembers Friday to Wednesday from 8am to 12:30pm, Thursday from 10:30am until sundown. Call the day before you wish to play. Greens fees are $20; you can rent clubs and carts.

SAILING   Tabor Tours, Dokweg (☎ 599/9-376637), offers a handful of seagoing tours, such as a snorkel/barbecue trip to Port Marie, which includes round-trip transportation to excellent reef sites and use of snorkeling equipment. The cost is $70 per person.

Day trips are offered on the *Insulinde,* Handelskade (☎ 599/9-601340), a 120-foot, traditionally rigged sail clipper that sails to Port Marie on the island's northwestern shore. Trips are offered on Wednesday and Thursday or for cruise passengers by special arrangement. Included in the $55 per person charge is a barbecue lunch and use of snorkeling equipment. Advance reservations are necessary.

SCUBA DIVING & SNORKELING Scuba divers and snorkelers will see steep walls, at least two shallow wrecks, gardens of soft corals, and more than 30 species of hard corals at **Curaçao Underwater Park,** which stretches 12½ miles along Curaçao's southern coastline. The park has placed 16 mooring buoys at the best dive and snorkel sites, and a snorkel trail with underwater interpretive markers is laid out just east of the Princess Beach Resort and Casino. There's also shore access at Santa Barbara Beach in Jan Thiel Bay.

Underwater Curaçao, in Bapor Kibrá (☎ 599/9-618131), has a complete PADI-accredited underwater sports program and a fully stocked modern dive shop with retail and rental equipment. Dives cost $33 if you're certified. An introductory dive for novices is priced at $65. A snorkel trip costs $20, including equipment.

TENNIS   The best tennis courts are at the hotels. Call to make sure courts are available. You'll have to take a taxi to the **Curaçao Caribbean Hotel and Casino,** Piscadera Bay (☎ 599/9-625000); **Princess Beach Resort and Casino,** Dr. Martin Luther King Boulevard (☎ 599/9-367888); and **Holiday Beach Hotel and Casino,** Pater Euwensweg 31 (☎ 599/9-6254000).

WATER SPORTS   The most complete water sports facilities are at **Seascape Dive and Watersports,** at the Curaçao Caribbean Hotel, Piscadera Bay (☎ 599/9-625905). Among the offerings are snorkeling excursions in an offshore underwater park for $18 per person, submarine rides for $29, waterskiing for $50 per half hour, and jet-ski rentals for $38 per half hour. A Sunfish rents for $20, and an introductory PADI scuba lesson is $45. A package of four dives costs $124. Deep-sea fishing (all equipment included) costs $336 for a half day.

DINING

Opposite the cathedral in the center of town is **Wine Cellar,** Ooststraat/Concordiastraat, (☎ 599/9-612178), which, as you might've guessed, has an extensive wine list. The kitchen turns out an excellent lobster salad and a sole meunière, and game is imported throughout the year from Holland. Meals are flavorful and hearty.

De Taveerne, Landhuis Groot Davelaar, Silena (☎ 599/9-370669), on the east side of St. Anna Bay, is the island's most elegant choice. We were won over by the smoked Dutch eel, and the lobster

bisque is velvety smooth and perfectly flavored. We also like the shrimp thermidor
and the salmon gratiné.

Near Point Juliana, **Fort Nassau**
(☎ 599/9-613086), sits on a hilltop
overlooking Willemstad in the ruins of a
fort dating from 1796. From its Battery
Terrace, you have a 360° view of the sea,
the harbor, Willemstad, and the island's
vast oil refinery. We like some dishes, like
the goat cheese in puff pastry and a cold
terrine layered with salmon and sole.
Also, the fried tuna served with stir-
fried vegetables and rice is simple and
satisfying.

Legends, Orionweig 12, Salinja
(☎ 599/9-618222), features a medley of
Italian and French cuisine. The menu is
the same for lunch and dinner. Try the
Legends salad that combines steamed
shrimp and fresh avocado in curry sauce.
All offerings in each course are the same
price, so checks are easily divided among
shipboard friends dining together.

**Rijstaffel Restaurant Indonesia and
Holland Club Bar,** Mercuriusstraat 13,
Salinja (☎ 599/9-612999), is the best
place to sample Indonesian rijstaffel, the
traditional rice table with all the zesty side
dishes. You'll have to take a taxi to this
villa in the suburbs near Salinja southeast
of Willemstad. At lunch, the selection of
dishes is more modest. There's even an
all-vegetarian rijstaffel. You may want to
go with a party from your ship so all of
you can share in the feast.

7 Freeport / Lucaya ⚓ ⚓

Bold and brassy Freeport/Lucaya on
Grand Bahama Island is the second most
popular tourist destination in The Bahamas. Its cosmopolitan glitz may be too
much for some visitors, but there are alternatives to the glamour—sun, surf, and
excellent golf, tennis, and water sports.
And because the island is so big and relatively unsettled, there are plenty of places
to get close to nature. Or else you can
gamble the day away or shop till you
drop.

COMING ASHORE

On Grand Bahama Island you're depos-
ited in the middle of nowhere: the west
end of the island where there's little of
interest. You'll want to take a taxi ride ($9
to $12 for two passengers) over to
Freeport and its International Bazaar.

FAST FACTS

Currency   The legal tender is the
Bahamian dollar (B$1), which is on
a par with the U.S. dollar. Both U.S.
and Bahamian dollars are accepted
on an equal basis.

Information   Go to the **Grand
Bahama Tourism Board,** International Bazaar, Freeport (☎ 242/
352-6909). Another information
booth is at Port Lucaya (☎ 242/
373-8988). Open 9am to 5:30pm
Monday to Saturday.

Language   The language of The
Bahamas is English, though there are
some words left from the Arawak
tongue (like *cassava* and *guava*).

GETTING AROUND

You can explore the center of Freeport or
Lucaya on foot, but to get to the East End
or the West End you'll either need a car
or will have to use highly erratic public
transportation.

Roads are generally good on Grand
Bahama Island, and it's easy to
drive around. For car rentals, try **Avis**
(☎ 800/331-1084 in the U.S., or 242/
352-7666); **Hertz** (☎ 800/654-3001 in
the U.S., or 242/352-2950); or the local
Star Rent-a-Car, Old Airport Rd.
(☎ 242/352-5953).

The government sets the taxi rates. The
meter starts at $2 and 30¢ is charged for
each additional quarter mile for two passengers. Most taxis wait at the cruise-ship
dock to pick up passengers, or you can
call **Freeport Taxi Company** (☎ 242/
352-6666) or **Grand Bahama Taxi
Union** (☎ 242/352-7101).

Bicycles and motor scooters are also a good way to get around. You can rent them at any of the major hotels such as **Princess Country Club,** West Sunrise Highway (☎ **242/352-6682**). A two-seater scooter requires a $100 deposit and rents from $40 per day; bicycles require a $50 deposit and cost $12 for a half day, $20 for a full day.

Public bus service runs from the International Bazaar to downtown Freeport and from the Pub on the Mall to the Lucaya area. The typical fare is 75¢.

SHORE EXCURSIONS

The offerings here are weak. You can often manage better on your own. Most cruise ships, however, offer a 25-mile round-trip sightseeing trip. You spend about 30 minutes at the Garden of the Groves and then get led around the International Bazaar, which is better explored on your own. The three-hour trip costs $12 per passenger.

PARKS & GARDENS

The prime attraction is the 11-acre **Garden of the Groves,** at the intersection of Midshipman Road and Magellan Drive (☎ **242/373-5668**). Seven miles east of the International Bazaar, this scenic preserve of waterfalls and flowering shrubs has some 10,000 trees. The **Palmetto Café** (☎ **242/373-5668**) serves snacks and drinks, and a Bahamian straw market sits at the entrance gate.

Hydroflora Garden, on East Beach at Sunrise Highway (☎ **242/352-6052**), is an artificially created botanical wonder, featuring 154 specimens of indigenous Bahamian plants. A special section is devoted to bush medicine.

Filled with mangrove, pine, and palm trees, the 40-acre ✪ **Lucaya National Park,** Sunrise Highway (for information, contact Rand Nature Centre at ☎ **242/ 352-5438**), is about 12 miles from Lucaya. The park contains one of the loveliest, most secluded beaches on Grand

Bahama. A wooden path winding through the trees leads to this long, wide, dune-covered stretch. You'll cross Gold Rock Creek, fed by a spring from what is said to be the world's largest underground freshwater cavern system. You can enter two caves, exposed when a portion of ground collapsed. The pools there are composed of six feet of freshwater atop a heavier layer of saltwater.

Located 2 miles east of Freeport's center, the **Rand Nature Centre,** E. Settlers Way (☎ 242/352-5438), is the regional headquarters of The Bahamas National Trust, a nonprofit conservation organization. Forest nature trails highlight native flora and bush medicine in this 100-acre pineland sanctuary. Wild birds abound. Other features include native animal displays, a replica of a Lucayan Indian village, an education center, and a gift shop.

GAMBLING THE DAY AWAY

You can try your luck at two of the largest casinos in The Bahamas and the Caribbean. The **Lucayan Beach Casino,** in the Lucayan Beach Resort, Royal Palm Way (☎ 242/373-7777), offers 550 super slots. Novices can take free gaming lessons daily at 11am or 7pm. But most of the action occurs at the **Princess Casino,** at the Mall at W. Sunrise Highway (☎ 242/352-7811), a giant, glittering, Moroccan-style palace.

SHOPPING

INTERNATIONAL BAZAAR

There's no place in The Bahamas quite like the **International Bazaar,** at East Mall Drive and East Sunrise Highway. It's one of the world's most unusual shopping marts, a veritable 10-acre shopper's theme park. There are nearly 100 shops, where you can choose from African handcrafts, Chinese jade, British china, Swiss watches, Irish linens, and Colombian emeralds—and that's just for starters.

Freeport/Lucaya

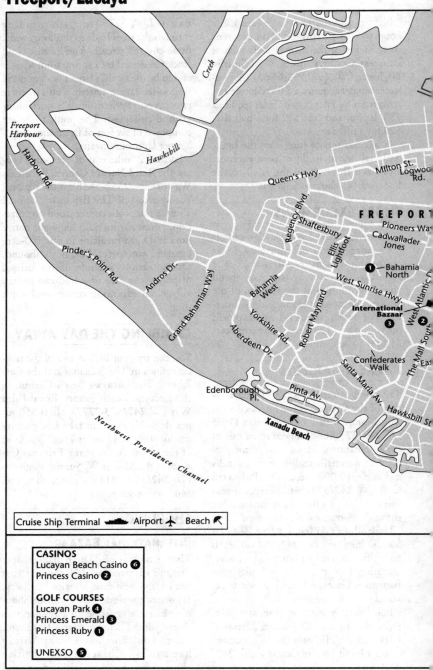

Freeport Harbour

Creek

Hawksbill

Harbour Rd.

Queen's Hwy.

Milton St.

Logwood Rd.

FREEPORT

Pioneers Way

Cadwallader Jones

Regency Blvd.

Shaftesbury

Ellis
Lightfoot

Pinder's Point Rd.

Andros Dr.

Grand Bahamian Way

Bahamia West

Yorkshire Rd.

Robert Maynard

West Sunrise Hwy.

①—Bahamia North

West Atlantic

International Bazaar ③

②

The Mall South

Aberdeen Dr.

Confederates Walk

Santa Maria Av.

Hawksbill St

The Mall East

Edenborough Pl.

Pinta Av.

Xanadu Beach

Northwest Providence Channel

Cruise Ship Terminal	Airport ✈	Beach 🏹

CASINOS
Lucayan Beach Casino ❻
Princess Casino ❷

GOLF COURSES
Lucayan Park ❹
Princess Emerald ❸
Princess Ruby ❶

UNEXSO ❺

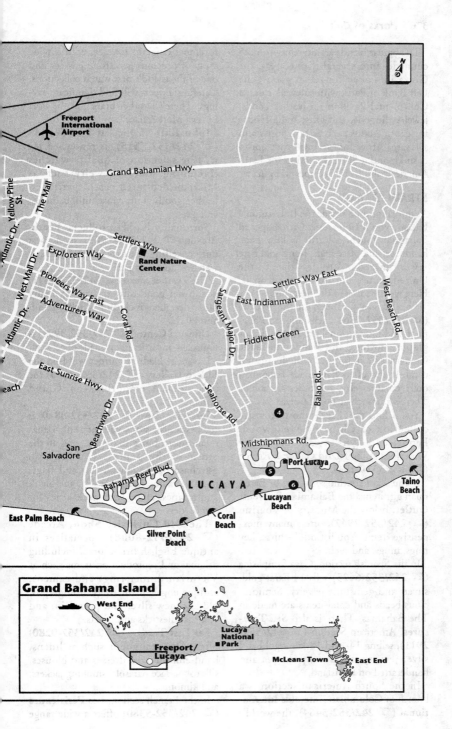

Freeport
International
Airport

Grand Bahamian Hwy.

Atlantic Dr. Yellow Pine St.

The Mall

Settlers Way

Explorers Way

Rand Nature Center

West Mall Dr.

Pioneers Way East

Adventurers Way

Atlantic Dr.

Coral Rd.

Sargeant Major Dr.

Settlers Way East

East Indianman

Fiddlers Green

West Beach Rd.

East Sunrise Hwy.

Beach

Beachway Dr.

Seahorse Rd.

Balao Rd.

4

San Salvadore

Midshipmans Rd.

5

Port Lucaya

6

L U C A Y A

Taino Beach

Bahama Reef Blvd.

East Palm Beach

Lucayan Beach

Coral Beach

Silver Point Beach

Grand Bahama Island

West End

Lucaya National Park

Freeport/ Lucaya

McLeans Town

East End

The bazaar blends architecture from 25 countries into several theme areas: the Ginza in Tokyo for Asian goods; the Left Bank of Paris, with sidewalk cafes; a Continental Pavilion for leather goods, jewelry, lingerie, and gifts; India House for exotic goods such as taxi horns and silk saris; Africa for carvings or a colorful dashiki; and a Spanish section for Latin American and Iberian serapes and piñatas.

STRAW MARKET

At this emporium beside the International Bazaar, you'll find items with a special Bahamian touch: colorful baskets, hats, handbags, and place mats. Items sold here *might* run about 40% less than in the United States, but don't count on it. Here we list some of the best shops.

The **Flovin Gallery,** in the Arcade (☎ 242/352-7564), sells original Bahamian and international art, frames, lithographs, posters, and Bahamian-made Christmas ornaments and decorated coral. It also offers handmade Bahamian dolls, coral jewelry, and other gift items. There's a branch at Port Lucaya.

You'll find the island's most extensive collection of China by Wedgwood, Lenox, and Aynsley, and crystal by Waterford at the **Island Galleria,** Arcade (☎ 242/352-8194).

If you want routine souvenirs or Bahamian gift items, the **Bahamian Souvenir Outlet,** below the Ministry of Tourism (☎ 242/352-2947), offers many inexpensive items. You'll find T-shirts, key rings, mugs, and such.

In the Spanish section, **Casa Simpatica** (☎ 242/352-6425) sells 14-karat gold, silver, and gemstone jewelry. Semiprecious beads and coral items are made in The Bahamas. There is also **Sea Treasures,** American Section (☎ 242/352-2911), selling 14- and 18-karat gold and silver jewelry inspired by the sea and handcrafted on the island.

In the South American section is a branch of **Colombian Emeralds International** (☎ 242/352-5464), the world's foremost emerald jeweler, with a wide array of precious gemstone jewelry and one of the island's best watch collections. Careful shoppers will find significant savings. There's another branch at the Port Lucaya Marketplace.

John Bull, in the Far East Section (☎ 242/352-7515), is renowned for its fine selection of quality watches (including Rolex), jewelry such as Mikimoto cultured pearls, perfumes, leather goods from Moschino, cameras, and gifts.

For quality leather products, **Fendi,** Arcade (☎ 242/352-7908), is the best outlet, selling suitcases, purses, coats, watches, and even perfume.

The Leather Shop (☎ 242/352-5491) is another good outlet, carrying many other designers including Vitello, Land, and HCL.

Unusual Centre (☎ 242/352-3994) is unusual—it carries items made of eel skin.

Lovers of Lladró figurines will find the **Lladró Gallery** (☎ 242/352-2660) the best-stocked emporium on Grand Bahama Island.

Intercity Music (☎ 242/352-8820) is the best music store, with not only Bahamian music, but soca, reggae, and all the music of the islands. You can also purchase Bahamian posters and flags, portable radios, Walkmans™, and blank audio tapes, along with accessories for camcorders.

The Old Curiosity Shop, Arcade (☎ 242/352-8008), specializes in antique English bric-a-brac, including original and reproduction items such as Victorian dinner rings and cameos, antique engagement rings, lithographs, old and new silver and porcelain, and brass candlesticks and trivets.

Far East Traders (☎ 242/352-9280) offers Oriental goods such as linens, hand-embroidered dresses and blouses, silk robes, lace parasols, smoking jackets, and kimonos.

In the French section, **Les Parisiennes** (☎ 242/352-5380) offers a wide range of perfumes, including the latest from Paris, and Lancôme cosmetics and skin-care products. Nearby is **Parfum de Paris** (☎ 242/352-8164), which sells French perfumes at a discount. You'll find another branch at Port Lucaya Marketplace.

The **Perfume Factory/Fragrance of The Bahamas** (☎ 242/352-9391) is the top fragrance producer in The Bahamas, housed in a reproduction of an 1800 mansion. In the "mixology" department you can create your own fragrance. The shop's well-known products include Island Promises, Goombay, Paradise, and Pink Pearl.

Bahamas Coin and Stamp Ltd., Arcade (☎ 242/352-8989), specializes in Bahamian coin jewelry, ancient Roman coins, and relics from sunken Spanish galleons. It also carries antique U.S. and English coins and paper money.

PORT LUCAYA MARKETPLACE

This six-acre shopping and dining complex is near the Lucayan Beach Resort and Casino, Flamingo Beach Resort, and Clarion Atlantik Beach and Golf Resort. Many restaurants and shops overlook a 50-slip marina. Free entertainment, such as steel-drum bands and strolling musicians, adds to the festival atmosphere. Merchandise ranges from leather to lingerie to wind chimes. Here are some of our favorite stores.

Photo Video Center (☎ 242/373-1244), is the best place to buy video and photo equipment. The outlet also makes camera repairs.

UNEXSO Dive Shop (☎ 242/373-1244) is the premier dive shop of The Bahamas, selling swimsuits, wetsuits, underwater cameras, shades, hats, souvenirs, state-of-the-art diver's equipment, and computers.

Jeweler's Warehouse (☎ 242/373-8400) is for bargain hunters looking for up to 50% discounts on close-out 14-karat gold and gemstone jewelry.

Coconits by Androsia (☎ 242/373-8387) is the Port Lucaya outlet of the famous batik house of the Andros Islands. Fabrics are handmade on the island of Andros, and the store sells quality, 100% cotton resort wear.

BEACHES

Grand Bahama has some 60 miles of white-sand beaches rimming the blue-green waters of the Atlantic. The mile-long **Xanadu Beach,** at the Xanadu Beach Resort, is the premier beach in the Freeport area. Most beaches are in Lucaya, site of the major resort hotels. The resort beaches tend to be the most crowded in winter.

Other island beaches include **Taíno Beach,** lying to the east of Freeport, **Smith's Point,** and **Fortune Beach,** one of the finest beaches on Grand Bahama. Another good beach about a 20-minute ride east of Lucaya, is **Gold Rock Beach,** a favorite picnic spot with the locals.

CRUISES, DOLPHIN ENCOUNTERS, RIDING, DIVING & MORE

CRUISES   Any tour agent can arrange an excursion on the *Mermaid Kitty* (☎ 242/373-5880), supposedly the world's largest twin-diesel-engine glass-bottom boat. You'll see the panoramic underwater life that lives off the coast. Departures from behind Port Lucaya's Straw Market, on the bay side, are at 9:30am, 11:15am, 1:15pm, and 3:15pm. The 1 1/2-hour tour costs $15 for adults, $8 for children.

Superior Watersports in Freeport (☎ 242/373-7863) offers fun cruises on its *Bahama Mama,* a 72-foot double-decker catamaran with a semisubmarine that goes down five feet. Best is its Robinson Crusoe Beach Party daily from 11am to 4:30pm, costing $49 per person. If your ship stays late, there's a sunset booze cruise costing $25 and running from 6 to 8pm EST, or 6:30 to 8:30pm daylight saving time.

You'll get to see dolphins up close with ✪ **The Dolphin Experience,** operated by the Underwater Explorers Society (UNEXSO), in Port Lucaya opposite Lucayan Beach Casino (☎ **242/373-1250**). The animals are released daily to swim with scuba divers in the open ocean, and all ages can step onto a shallow wading platform and interact with them. The shore encounter costs $25, and diving with the dolphins in the ocean goes for $105. Advance reservations are essential (call ☎ **800/992-DIVE** in the U.S., or 305/351-9889).

GOLF All courses are open to the public year-round, and clubs can be rented from all pro shops on the island.

Fortune Hills Golf and Country Club, 5 miles east of Freeport in Richmond Park, Lucaya (☎ **242/373-4500**), was designed as an eighteen-hole course, but the back nine were never completed. You can replay the front nine for a total of 6,916 yards from the blue tees. Par is 72. Greens fees are $18 for nine holes, $28 for eighteen.

Lucayan Park Golf and Country Club, at Lucaya Beach (☎ **242/373-1066**), is the best-kept and most manicured course on Grand Bahama. Greens are fast, and par is 72. Greens fees are $50 for nine holes or $70 for 18 holes, including mandatory shared golf cart.

Princess Emerald Course, The Mall South (☎ **242/352-6721**), is one of two courses owned and operated by The Bahamas Princess Resort and Casino. The course has plenty of trees along the fairways, as well as water hazards and bunkers. Greens fees are $51 for nine holes or $72 for 18 holes, including use of an electric cart.

The championship **Princess Ruby Course,** on West Sunrise Highway (☎ **242/352-6721**), was designed by Joe Lee in 1968. Greens fees are $51 for nine holes and $72 for 18, including electric carts.

HORSEBACK RIDING **Pinetree Stables,** N. Beachway Drive, Freeport

(☎ **242/373-3600**), offers trail rides to the beach Tuesday to Sunday from 9am to 12pm and at 2pm. A 1 1/2-hour ride costs $35 per person.

SEA KAYAKING To explore the waters off the island's north shore by kayak, call Erika Moultrie, at **Kayak Nature Tours** (☎ **242/373-2485**), who arranges trips through the mangroves. The trip costs $75 per person, including a picnic lunch and transportation from any major hotel; the tour begins at 8:30am and ends at approximately 5pm.

SCUBA DIVING & SNORKELING The ✪ **Underwater Explorers Society (UNEXSO),** at Port Lucaya, opposite the Lucaya Resort Hotel and Casino (☎ **242/373-1244**), has daily reef trips, shark dives, wreck dives, and night dives. A popular three-hour learn-to-dive course is offered every day for $89. For experienced divers, a guided reef dive is $35. A snorkeling trip to the reef costs $18, all equipment included, and a half-hour snorkeling lesson is $10.

TENNIS You can play at The Bahamas Princess Resort and Casino, The Mall at West Sunrise Highway, for $10 per hour at the **Princess Country Club's** three courts (☎ **242/352-6721**) or for $7 per hour at the three lighted courts at the **Princess Tower** (☎ **242/352-9661**).

WATER SPORTS **Paradise Watersports,** at the Xanadu Beach Resort and Marina (☎ **242/352-2887**), offers a variety of activities. With snorkeling trips, you cruise to a coral reef on a 48-foot catamaran for $18 per person. Paddleboats rent for $7 for a half hour, $10 per hour. Waterskiing is priced at $15 for a 1 1/2-mile ride. Parasailing costs $30 for a four-minute ride. A glass-bottom boat ride runs $15 for adults and $8 for children under 12.

Clarion Atlantik Beach and Golf Resort, on Seahorse Road (☎ **242/373-1444**), is the best place for parasailing and windsurfing. Parasailing costs $25 for from 5 to 7 minutes.

DINING

The most amusing place for cruisers seeking lunch is **Kaptain Kenny's** at Tino Beach (☎ 242/373-8689), which, in spite of its Disneyesque overtones and corny name, actually serves good food. A great beachy restaurant, it's an ideal choice for an inexpensive lunch. Try the grilled conch sandwich, a Bahamian version of the New Orleans "Po Boy." Diced conch, tomatoes, and onions are mixed with a tangy lime juice, then piled high on a seasoned bun and cooked on an open grill.

If you'd like to see what's left of The Bahamas "the way it was," head for the West End to the **Star Club,** Bayshore Road (☎ 242/346-6207), built in the 1940s as the first hotel on Grand Bahama. It's been a long time since any guests have checked in, but the place is still going strong as the island's only 24-hour snack bar and drinking bar. Come here for the good times, not the food. You can also drop in next door at **Austin's Calypso Bar,** a real Grand Bahama dive if there ever was one.

In the International Bazaar, **Becky's Restaurant** (☎ 242/352-8717) offers authentic Bahamian cuisine. Breakfasts, either all-American or Bahamian, are available all day. Stick to the Bahama Mama specialties, as the American dishes are lackluster. **Café Michel** (☎ 242/352-2191) is a coffee shop serving platters, salads, and sandwiches throughout the day.

Opposite the International Bazaar is **The Pub on the Mall,** Ranfurley Circus, Sunrise Highway (☎ 242/352-5110), with three distinct eating areas. The only one open for lunch is the Prince of Wales Lounge, evoking medieval Britain and serving a lunch menu of shepherd's pie, fish and chips, platters of roast beef or fish, and real English ale.

✪ **Geneva's,** Kipling Lane, The Mall at W. Sunrise Highway (☎ 242/352-5085), is more the type of place the locals are likely to patronize. This restaurant sticks to the local mainstays such as conch, and is one of the best places for it. You can have conch stewed, cracked, or fried, or in a savory chowder. There's also no escaping grouper, prepared in every imaginable way. The bartender's rum-laced Bahama Mama special will get you into the mood.

Next to The Bahamas Princess Tower, the **Ruby Swiss Restaurant,** W. Sunrise Highway at W. Atlantic Avenue (☎ 242/352-8507), serves a continental menu. For lunch, enjoy a Reuben or club sandwich, seafood or Caesar salad, or the inevitable burger. A Creole-style shrimp is also worth trying. Finish off with a Viennese strudel.

Before moving to Port Lucaya Market Place, ✪ **Fatman's Nephew** (☎ 242/373-8520) catered mostly to locals. Now it's touristy, but the local fare remains a delight. Dishes include game fish, such as wahoo and Cajun blackened snapper. If you don't want fish, try the zesty curried chicken, and start your meal with a freshly made conch salad or conch chowder.

8 Grand Cayman ⭗⭗⭗

Grand Cayman is the largest of the Cayman Islands, a British colony 480 miles due south of Miami (Cayman Brac and Little Cayman are the others). Despite its name, Grand Cayman is only 22 miles long and 8 miles across at its widest point. George Town is the colony's capital and its commercial hub. Grand Cayman has some of the Caribbean's best diving and snorkeling, plus the famous Seven Mile Beach.

COMING ASHORE

Cruise ships anchor off George Town and ferry their passengers to a pier on Harbour Drive, which is set conveniently right in the heart of the shopping district. Taxis line up to meet cruise-ship passengers.

FAST FACTS

Currency   The legal tender is the **Cayman Islands dollar (C.I.),** which is valued at $1.25 U.S. ($1 U.S. = 80¢ C.I.). The Cayman Islands dollar breaks down into 100 cents. Coins come in 1¢, 5¢, 10¢, and 25¢. Bills come in denominations of $1, $5, $10, $25, $50, and $100. Canadian, U.S., and British currencies are accepted, but you'll save money if you exchange your U.S. dollars for Cayman Islands dollars. Many restaurants quote prices in Cayman Islands dollars. Unless otherwise noted, prices in this section are given in U.S. dollars.

Information   The **Department of Tourism** is in the Pavilion Building, Cricket Square (P.O. Box 67), George Town, Grand Cayman, B.W.I. (☎ **345/949-0623**). There's also a tourist information booth at the pier. Open Monday to Friday from 9am to 5pm.

Language   English is the official language of the islands.

SHORE EXCURSIONS

Nearly all the shore excursions here are underwater adventures, which you can book on your own or through your cruise ship. The favorite is a two-hour snorkeling trip to Stingray City that costs $30. You can also ride in the submarine *Atlantis XI,* which costs $8 per person. A Seaworld Explorer Cruise on a glass-bottom boat sails over tropical fish, stunning coral reefs, and sunken ships. The hour-long tour costs $29.

You can also take a taxi tour for $37.50 per hour. Taxis can hold up to five people. You'll need about three hours to cover all the sights in a leisurely fashion.

GETTING AROUND

Taxi fares are fixed; typical one-way fares range from $10 to $12. **Cayman Cab Team** (☎ **345/947-1173**) and **Holiday Inn Taxi Stand** (☎ **345/947-4491**) offer 24-hour service.

The roads are good by Caribbean standards, so driving around is relatively easy, as long as you remember to drive on the left side of the road. Reserve a car in advance with **Cico Avis** (☎ **800/331-1084** in the U.S., or 345/949-2468); **Budget** (☎ **800/527-0700** in the U.S., or 345/949-8223); or **Ace Hertz** (☎ **800/654-3131** in the U.S., or 345/949-7861).

The terrain is relatively flat, so motorcycles or bicycles are another way to get around. **Soto Scooters Ltd.**, Seven Mile Beach (☎ **345/947-4363**), located at Coconut Place, offers Honda Elite scooters for $25 daily, bicycles for $15 daily.

SEEING THE SIGHTS ON LAND

The only green sea turtle farm of its kind in the world, **Cayman Turtle Farm,** Northwest Point (☎ **345/949-3894**), is the island's most popular land-based tourist attraction. Once a multitude of turtles lived in the waters surrounding the Cayman Islands, but today these creatures are an endangered species. The turtle farm's purpose is two-fold: to provide the local market with edible turtle meat and to replenish the waters with hatchlings and yearling turtles. You can look into 100 circular concrete tanks containing turtles ranging in size from six ounces to 600 pounds, or sample turtle dishes at a snack bar and restaurant.

In George Town, **Cayman Islands National Museum**, Harbour Drive (☎ **345/949-8368**), is housed in a veranda-fronted building that once served as the island's courthouse. Exhibits include Caymanian artifacts collected by Ira Thompson (beginning in the 1930s), and other items portraying the natural, social, and cultural history of the Caymans. There's a gift shop, theater, and cafe.

On 60 acres of rugged wooded land, **Queen Elizabeth II Botanical Park,** off Frank Sound Road, North Side (☎ **345/947-9462**), offers visitors a one-hour

The Cayman Islands

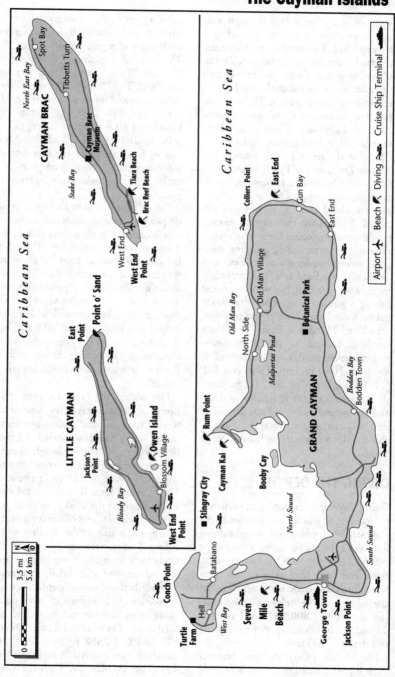

walk along an 8-mile trail through wetlands, swamps, dry thicket, and mahogany trees. You might spot hickatees, the freshwater turtles found only on the Caymans and in Cuba, the rare Grand Cayman parrot, or the anole lizard with a cobalt-blue throat pouch. There are six rest stations along the trail, plus a visitor center and a canteen. There's also a heritage garden, a floral garden, and a lake.

One of the newest attractions is the **Mastic Trail,** west of Frank Sound Road (☎ 345/949-1996), a restored 200-year-old footpath through a two-million-year-old woodland area in the heart of the island. Named for the majestic mastic tree, the trail showcases the reserve's natural attractions, including a native mangrove swamp, traditional agriculture, and an ancient woodland area. You can follow the trail on your own, but we recommend taking a guided tour. The three-hour guided tours, limited to eight participants, are offered Monday to Friday at 8:30am and 3pm, on Saturday at 8:30am. Reservations are required; call Monday to Friday from 10am to 3pm. Tours cost $25 C.I. ($31.25) per person. Participants should wear comfortable, sturdy shoes and carry water and insect repellent. The trail, adjacent to the Botanical Park, is about a 45-minute drive from George Town.

DIVING THE DEPTHS

Grand Cayman is the top of an underwater mountain, whose side, known as the Cayman Wall, plummets straight down for 500 feet before becoming a steep slope that falls away for 6,000 feet to the ocean floor. You don't have to be a scuba diver to explore these underwater wonders, for the submersible ✪ *Atlantis XI,* on Goring Avenue (☎ 800/887-8571 or 345/949-8296), has three types of dives going to a depth of 100 feet.

The "Atlantis Odyssey" dive features such high-tech extras as divers moving about on underwater scooters or communicating with submarine passengers by wireless underwater phones. Operated both day and night, the dive costs $82. The "Atlantis Expedition" dive visits the Cayman Wall; it lasts 55 minutes and costs $72. The "Atlantis Discovery" lasts 40 minutes and introduces viewers to the marine life of the Caymans. It costs $55. Children ages 4 to 12 are charged half price on all dives. *Atlantis XI* dives Monday to Saturday, and reservations are recommended 24 hours in advance. Your cruise staff can make arrangements for you.

The Atlantis company also operates two deep-diving research submersibles, each of which carries two passengers and a pilot. They go as deep as 800 feet. These trips last just more than an hour and allow passengers to see the variety of sea life at different depths. Weather permitting, each dive goes down to the wreck of the *Kirk Pride,* a cargo ship that sank in 1976 and lodged on a rock ledge at 780 feet. These deep dives cost $295 per person, and are available to anyone over the age of eight. Reservations should be made as early as possible.

The waters off Grand Cayman are home to ✪ **Stingray City,** one of the world's most unusual underwater attractions. Set in the sun-flooded, 12-foot-deep waters of North Sound, about 2 miles east of the island's northwestern tip, the site gained notoriety in the mid-1980s, when local fishers cleaned their catch, dumped the offal overboard, and quickly noticed scores of stingrays (which usually eat marine crabs) feeding on the debris. Today, between 30 and 50 relatively tame stingrays hover in the waters around the site for their daily handouts.

About half a dozen entrepreneurs lead expeditions to Stingray City from points along Seven Mile Beach. One well-known outfit is **Treasure Island Divers** (☎ 800/872-7552 or 345/949-4456), which charges divers $45 and snorkelers $25. They go Monday, Wednesday, Friday, and Sunday at 1:30pm. Most of the stingrays here are females, the males preferring to remain in deeper waters offshore. Stingrays possess viciously barbed stingers, so never try to grab one by the tail. Despite the dangers, divers and snorkelers feed and pet these velvet-skinned creatures without incident.

SHOPPING

You'll find duty-free shopping in George Town for silver, china, crystal, Irish linen, British woolen goods, and such local crafts as black-coral jewelry. But the prices on many items are similar to those in the United States. Don't purchase turtle products, since they cannot be brought into the United States or most other Western nations.

Generally recognized as the premier outlet on the island for back issues of rare Caymanian stamps, **Artifacts Ltd.**, across from the cruise tender landing dock on Harbour Drive (☎ 345/949-2442), is managed by Charles Adams, one of the country's philatelic authorities. Stamps range in price from 17¢ to $900, and inventory includes the rare War Tax Stamp issued during World War II. Other items include antique Dutch and Spanish coins retrieved from shipwrecks, enameled boxes, and antique prints and maps.

Connoisseurs of unusual fine jewelry and unique objets d'art are drawn to **Black Coral and . . . ,** on Fort Street (☎ 345/949-0123), for the stunning black-coral creations of acclaimed sculptor Bernard K. Passman. Signed, limited-edition pieces are excellent investments.

In front of the cruise-ship landing, the **English Shoppe,** on Harbour Drive (☎ 345/949-2457), sells watches, black-and pink-coral jewelry, gold jewelry, T-shirts, and souvenirs.

On Seven Mile Beach, **Kennedy Gallery,** West Shore Centre (☎ 345/949-8077), specializes in watercolors by local artists and by its founder, Robert Kennedy. The artwork ranges in price from $15 to as much as $7,000.

The largest store of its kind in the Caymans, **Kirk Freeport Plaza,** Cardinal Avenue and Panton Street (☎ 345/949-7477), contains a treasure trove of gold jewelry, watches, china, crystal, porcelain, perfumes, and cosmetics sold at discount prices. With the island's Cartier franchise, it sells handbags, valises, and perfumes priced 15% to 35% below suggested stateside retail prices.

The Jewelry Centre, Fort Street (☎ 345/949-0070), is a real jewelry department store. Its six departments specialize in loose or set diamonds, gold, black coral, colored gemstones, and caymanite, the pinkish-brown striated rock found only on the Caymans.

The **Sunflower Boutique,** S. Church Street (☎ 345/949-4090), sells hand-painted skirts and blouses, T-shirts and shorts, coral jewelry, gift items, and Caribbean paintings.

BEACHES

Grand Cayman's ✪ **Seven Mile Beach,** which begins north of George Town, has sparkling white sands against a backdrop of Australian pines. An easy taxi ride from the cruise dock, the beach is really only about $5^{1}/_{2}$ miles long, despite its name. You'll find great water sports here.

GOLF, DIVING, SNORKELING & WATER SPORTS

GOLF The major golf course is at the **Britannia Golf Club,** next to the Hyatt Regency on West Bay Road (☎ 345/949-8020). Designed by Jack Nicklaus, it incorporates three different courses in one: a nine-hole championship layout, an 18-hole executive set-up, and an 18-hole Cayman course. The last was intended for play with the Nicklaus-designed Cayman ball, which goes about half the distance of a regulation ball. The Britannia charges $50 to $80 for greens fees in the winter season, $40 to $65 in the off-season. Cart rentals are $15 to $25; club rentals, $25.

Nonguests can reserve no more than 24 hours in advance.

SCUBA DIVING & SNORKELING

Coral reefs and formations encircle the island and are filled with marine life. It's easy to dive close to shore, so boats aren't necessary, though plenty of boats and scuba facilities are available. Many dive shops rent scuba gear or supply air to certified divers.

The best dive operation is **Bob Soto's Diving Ltd.,** P.O. Box 1801, Grand Cayman, B.W.I. (☎ **800/262-7686** for reservations, or 345/949-2022), with full-service dive shops at the Treasure Island on Seven Mile Beach, the SCUBA Centre on North Church Street, the Cayman Islander Hotel, and Soto's Coconut in the Coconut Place Shopping Centre. A full-day resort course for beginners costs $90. Certified divers can choose from a wide range of one-tank ($40 to $45) and two-tank ($60 to $65) boat dives daily on the west, north, and south walls, plus shore diving from the Scuba Centre. Nondivers can take daily snorkel trips ($20) to such sights as Stingray City.

WATER SPORTS Red Sail Sports (☎ **800/255-6425** or 345/945-5965) is beside the beach at the Hyatt Regency Grand Cayman on West Bay Road. Their half-day deep-sea fishing excursions for four to six people depart daily at 7:30am and 12:30pm and cost $500 ($700 for a full day).

Red Sail also rents 16-foot Hobie Prindle for $40 an hour. A daily 10am to 2pm sail to Stingray City, including snorkeling equipment and lunch, costs $60.50 per person. Waterskiing can be arranged for $75 per half hour; parasailing costs $45 per ride.

Red Sail also offers scuba diving for all levels. A two-tank morning dive costs $66. A resort course for beginners is offered daily at $99 per person.

DINING

❂ **Chef Tell's Grand Old House,** S. Church Street, 1 mile south of George Town past Jackson Point (☎ **345/949-9333**), is situated in a turn-of-the-century plantation house. We think the chef is the island's best, and many dishes reflect his German background. Try such appetizers as home-smoked marlin and salmon or else coconut beer-battered shrimp. Then perhaps order the catch of the day prepared Cayman style with tomatoes, peppers, and onions.

The best seafood can be found 2 miles north of George Town at **Hemingway's,** in the Hyatt Regency Grand Cayman, West Bay Road (☎ **345/949-1234**). The imaginative menu includes pepper pot soup, grouper stuffed with crabmeat, mahimahi with a sweet potato crust, or macadamia-crusted pork with mango juice.

On a stony plot of seafront land near the start of West Bay Road, the ❂ **Hog Sty Bay Café and Pub,** N. Church Street (☎ **345/949-6163**), combines an amusingly decorated pub and a Caribbean-inspired dining room open to a view of the harbor. You can eat either British pub staples or a Caesar salad topped with marinated conch, fresh catch of the day, shrimp, or pasta.

At the George Town harbor front, **Island Taste** (☎ **345/949-4945**) sits across from the *Atlantis* submarine base. There's an indoor and outdoor bar area and a few indoor tables, but most guests head for the wraparound veranda. The restaurant has a large appetizer selection and most of the menu is devoted to seafood. Perennial favorites include the turtle steak and spiny lobster.

Lobster Pot, N. Church Street (☎ **345/949-2736**), overlooks the water from its second-floor perch at the western perimeter of George Town near what used to be Fort George. True to its name, it offers lobster prepared in many different ways: Cayman style, bisque, and salad. At lunch you might be offered English fish and chips, perhaps a seafood jambalaya, or a freshly made pasta. Sometimes the seafood is a bit overcooked, but most dishes are right on the mark. The

Lobster Pot's pub is a pleasant place for a drink.

Most tables at **Whitehall Bay**, N. Church Street (☎ **345/949-8670**), overlook the coral reef and piers that jut out into the sea. The kitchen is known for turning out typical West Indian fare, and it does so with some charm.

9 Grenada ⇩⇩⇩⇩

St. George's, the capital of Grenada, is one of the most colorful ports in the West Indies. Nearly landlocked in the deep crater of a long-dead volcano, and flanked by old forts, it reminds many visitors of Portofino, Italy. Here you'll see some of the most charming Georgian colonial buildings in the Caribbean. Frangipani and flamboyant trees add even more color. Criss-crossed by nature trails, Grenada's interior is a jungle of palms, oleander, bougainvillea, purple and red hibiscus, crimson anthurium, bananas, breadfruit, birdsong, ferns, and palms.

Grenada's lush tropical scenery and natural bounty attract visitors who want to snorkel, sail, fish, or loll the day away on 2-mile-long Grand Anse Beach, one of the best in the Caribbean.

COMING ASHORE

Ships either dock at a pier right in St. George's or anchor in the harbor and tender their passengers to shore. At the pier you'll find a tourist information center and telephones. The Carenage, St. George's main street, is only a short walk from the pier, or you can take a taxi into the center of town for about $3. You can either take a regular taxi or a water taxi to Grand Anse Beach.

FAST FACTS

Currency The official currency is the **Eastern Caribbean dollar (EC$)**, currently worth about U.S. 37¢. Always determine which dollars, EC or U.S., you're talking about when someone quotes a price.

Information Go to the **Grenada Board of Tourism,** the Carenage, in St. George's (☎ **809/440-2001**), for maps and general information. Open Monday to Friday from 8am to 4pm.

Language English is commonly spoken on this island, but you'll also hear people speaking in a French-African patois.

SHORE EXCURSIONS

Because of Grenada's lushness, we recommend spending at least three hours touring its scenic interior. The best deal is the four-hour Grenada Tour, which costs $40. The tour takes you through the interior and along the coast, including Grand Anse Beach. You'll see the most luxuriant part of Grenada's rain forest, a nutmeg-processing station, and many small hamlets along the way.

The offerings of various cruise lines can vary, but most of them feature a Grand Etang Tour that takes you through the touristic highlights of St. George's, after which you head north through the lush central mountain range to the rain forest, visiting Grand Etang Forest Centre and Crater Lake—all in three hours at a cost of $30. For only $16, and lasting just two hours, you can take another nature tour, usually called "Bay Gardens Tour," exploring the historic sights of the capital, including forts, before being driven to Bay Gardens, a private horticultural enclave where nearly 500 species of island flora are cultivated.

GETTING AROUND

St. George's can easily be explored on foot, although parts of the town are steep as it rises up from the harbor.

Minivans charge EC$1 to EC$6 (40¢ to $2.20), and the most popular run is between St. George's and Grand Anse Beach. Most minivans depart from Market Square or from the Esplanade area of St. George's.

Taxi fares are set by the government. Most cruisers take a cab from the pier to somewhere near St. George's. You can also tap most taxi drivers as a guide for a day's sightseeing. The charge is about $15 per hour, but be sure to negotiate a price before setting out.

An ideal way to get around the harbor and to Grand Anse Beach is by water taxi. The round-trip waterborne fare to the beach is $4. A water taxi will take you from one end of the Carenage to the other for another $2.

We don't recommend driving here.

SEEING THE SIGHTS

In St. George's, you can visit the small but interesting **Grenada National Museum,** at the corner of Young and Monckton streets (☎ **809/440-3725**), set in the foundations of an old French army barracks and prison built in 1704. It houses finds from archaeological digs, plus native fauna, the island's first telegraph, a rum still, and an exhibit tracing the native culture of Grenada. There are also two bathtubs worth seeing—the wooden barrel used by the fort's prisoners and the carved marble tub used by Joséphine Bonaparte during her adolescence on Martinique.

The Outer Harbour is also called the **Esplanade.** It's connected to the Carenage by the Sendall Tunnel, which is cut through the promontory known as St. George's Point.

You can take a taxi up Richmond Hill to **Fort Frederick.** From its battlements you'll have a panoramic view of the harbor and of the yacht marina.

In the afternoon, we suggest exploring the mountains northeast of the capital. After a 15-minute drive, you reach ✪ **Annandale Falls,** a tropical wonderland. You can picnic surrounded by liana vines, elephant ears, and other tropical flora and spices. The **Annandale Falls Centre** (☎ **809/440-2452**) offers gift items, handcrafts, and samples of

Grenada's indigenous spices. A nearby trail leads to the falls, where you can swim.

Opened in 1994, the 450-acre **Levera National Park** has several white-sand beaches for swimming and snorkeling. Be aware that the Atlantic meets the Caribbean here, creating rough surf. Offshore you'll find coral reefs and seagrass beds. It's also a hiker's paradise. The park contains a mangrove swamp, lake, bird sanctuary, and an interpretation center (☎ **809/442-1018**). About 15 miles from the harbor, it can be reached by taxi, bus, or water taxi.

SHOPPING

As you stroll along the waterfront Carenage, spice vendors besiege you. This "Spice Island" boasts more spices per square mile than anywhere else in the world.

Local stores sell luxury-item imports, mainly from England, at prices that are not quite duty free. This is no grand Caribbean merchandise mart, so if you're cruising on to such islands as Aruba, St. Maarten, or St. Thomas, you should wait to shop there. In Grenada, you may find worthwhile local handcrafts, gifts, or art.

Bon Voyage (☎ **809/440-4217**) is the island's leading purveyor of diamonds, precious stones, gold and silver jewelry, china and crystal. It also sells sunglasses, scarves, and accessories. **Creation Arts and Crafts** (☎ **809/440-0570**) sells handcrafts from off-island, including Venezuela, St. Maarten, and Cuba. Look hard enough and you'll find Cuban cigars, cinnamon-scented soaps, sundresses and other casual wear, and painted masks and bird sculptures crafted by Grenadian artisans from coconut shells, calabash, and local gourds.

It's easy to bypass **Frangipani** (no phone) as you walk from the cruise-ship docks along the Carenage. But it's worth seeking out—its imaginative inventory includes hand-painted tiles, batiks, woodcarvings, baskets, and soap scented with

Caribbean
Sea

Levera Beach and
National Park

Sauteurs

Victoria

Mt. St. Catherine

Gouyave
(Charlottetown)

Grand Etang
National Park

Grand Roy

Grenville

Mt. Qua Qua

Grand Etang

Annandale
Falls

Marquis

Mt. Sinai

Constantine

Beaulieu

St. George's

St. David's

Grand Anse Beach

Morne Rouge

Woburn

Atlantic
Ocean

Point
Salines

L'Anse aux Epines

Cruise Ship Terminal
Airport ✈ Beach 🏖 Mountain ▲▲

0   5 km
3 mi
N

coconut, frangipani, cloves, and pimiento.

In the cramped and crowded **Sea Change Bookstore** (☎ 809/440-3402), you'll find British and American newspapers plus paperback books, island souvenirs, postcards, and film.

If you're a collector of exotic scents, **Spice Island Perfumes, Ltd.** (☎ 809/440-2006) is a virtual treasure trove of perfumes, potpourri, and teas made from locally grown flowers and spices. After a few sprays from the testers, you'll come back to the ship smelling of island flower, spice, frangipani, jasmine, patchouli, and wild orchid. The shop is near the harbor entrance, close to the Ministry of Tourism, post office, and public library.

Tikal, on Young Street (☎ 809/440-2310), is off the Carenage, next to the museum. It sells handcrafts from around the world, as well as the finest selection of crafts made on Grenada, including batiks, ceramics, wood carvings, paintings, straw work, and clothing.

A two-minute walk from Market Square, **Yellow Poui Art Gallery,** on Cross Street (☎ 809/440-3001), is the most interesting shop for souvenirs and artistic items. Here you can see oil paintings and watercolors, sculpture, prints, photography, rare antique maps, engravings, and woodcuts, with prices starting at $10. Also on Cross Street, **Gift Remembered** (☎ 809/440-2482) sells handcrafts, straw articles, jewelry, stamps, film, postcards, good-quality T-shirts, books, and magazines.

Imagine, in the Grand Anse Shopping Centre (☎ 809/444-4028) is your best bet near the Grand Anse Beach for handcrafts, including dolls, ceramics, and straw items.

BEACHES

One of the best beaches in the Caribbean is ✪ **Grand Anse Beach,** with 2 miles of sugar-white sands. Most of Grenada's best resorts are within walking distance of Grand Anse. You can also take off and discover dozens more beaches on your own, as they're all public. From the port, Grand Anse Beach is about a 10-minute, $10 taxi ride, although you can take a water taxi from the pier for $4 round trip.

GOLF, SAILING, DIVING, SNORKELING & TENNIS

GOLF   The **Grenada Golf Course and Country Club,** Woodlands (☎ 809/444-4128), has a nine-hole course with views of the Caribbean and the Atlantic. Greens fees are $12.

SAILING   The *Rhum Runner* and *Rhum Runner II,* c/o Best of Grenada, P.O. Box 188, St. George's (☎ 809/440-4FUN), are two large "party boats," designed for 120 and 250 passengers respectively, that operate out of St. George's harbor, making shuttle-style trips three times a day, with lots of emphasis on strong liquor, steel-band music, and good times. Four-hour daytime tours, conducted every morning and afternoon, coincide with the arrival of cruise ships, but will carry independent travelers if space is available. Rides cost $20 per person and include snorkeling stops at reefs and beaches along the way.

SCUBA DIVING & SNORKELING   Grenada offers the diver an underwater world rich in submarine gardens, exotic fish, and coral formations, sometimes with visibility up to 120 feet. Off the coast is the wreck of the ocean liner *Bianca C.* Novice divers might want to stick to the west coast, whereas more experienced divers can search out the sights along the rougher Atlantic side.

Daddy Vic's Watersports, directly on the beach in the Grenada Renaissance, Grand Anse Beach (☎ 809/444-4371,

ext. 638), is the premier dive outfit, with a two-tank dive for $45. It also offers snorkeling trips for $18 (1¹/₂ to 2 hours), Windsurfer and Sunfish rentals at $16 per half hour, parasailing for $30 per 10 minutes, and waterskiing for $15 per run. If you call, they'll pick you up at the pier in a courtesy bus and bring you back to the ship afterward.

Giving Daddy Vic's serious competition is **Grand Anse Aquatics,** at Coyaba Beach Resort on Grand Anse Beach (☎ 809/444-4129). They offer both scuba diving and snorkeling jaunts to panoramic reefs and shipwrecks. A single dive costs $40; snorkeling trips are $18. Diving instruction, including a resort course, is available.

Warning: Grenada doesn't have a decompression chamber. In the event of an emergency, divers are taken to Barbados to use the facilities there.

TENNIS   The best tennis courts are at the major resorts, which allow cruise-ship passengers to use courts that haven't been previously booked. In L'Anse aux Epines, the best courts are at **Secret Harbour** (☎ 809/444-4439) and **Calabash** (☎ 809/444-4334); and on Grande Anse Beach, at the **Grenada Renaissance** (☎ 809/444-4371) and **Coyaba Beach Resort** (☎ 809/444-4129).

DINING

Right on the harbor above the Sea Change bookstore, the **Nutmeg** (☎ 809/440-2539) has been a rendezvous site since the mid-1960s for the yachting set and expatriates. This low-key spot is suitable for a snack or a full-fledged meal, or you can drop in just for a drink and the view. Try one of the Grenadian rum punches made with Angostura bitters, grated nutmeg, rum, lime juice, and syrup. We think the lobster thermidor is the best in town. Lambi (the ubiquitous conch) is also done very well. You may be asked to share a table.

On the north center of the Carenage, long-established **Rudolf's** (☎ 809/440-

2241) overlooks the deep, U-shaped harbor. It's busy at lunch and a good spot for drinks in the late afternoon. The food from the extensive menu is well prepared. The steaks, Wiener schnitzel, and octopus stew are Grenada's finest, and several flying fish dishes also deserve praise. On occasion, wild game such as rabbit and duck are offered.

OUTSIDE ST. GEORGE'S

Your last chance to enjoy food from old-time island recipes is at ✪ **Betty Mascoll's Morne Fendue,** at St. Patrick's (☎ **809/442-9330**), 25 miles north of St. George's. Lunch might include a yam and sweet-potato casserole or curried chicken with island-grown spices. You get all of grandmother's favorites, including fritters made of tannia (a starchy tuber) and corn coo coo (resembling spoonbread). The most famous dish is Betty's legendary pepperpot stew. A fixed-price lunch for EC$45 ($16.45) is served Monday to Saturday from 12:30 to 3pm; call ahead to reserve a place.

Set on a hilltop with a view of Grand Anse Beach, ✪ **Canbouley,** Morne Rouge (☎ **809/444-4401**), serves some of the most unusual Antillean food on Grenada. Specialties include coconut crepes stuffed with crabmeat, cornmeal baked or fried in coconut milk, blackened flying fish, and fried conch served with a local citrus sauce.

On Grand Anse Beach, the raffish and informal ✪ **Coconut's Beach Restaurant** (☎ **809/444-4644**) specializes in lobster dishes, including an imaginative stir-fry with ginger chili. Fish predominates, however, and curried conch West Indian style is a favorite. Chicken and meats are also savory, especially breast of chicken cooked in local herbs and lime juice.

On the road leading to Grenada Yacht Services, **Mamma's,** on Lagoon Road (☎ **809/440-1459**), is a trip unto itself. You'll get large meals that capture the taste of Grenada. Dishes include callaloo soup with coconut cream, shredded cold crab with lime juice, freshwater crayfish,

and a casserole of cooked banana, yams, and rotis made of curry and yellow chickpeas, followed by sugar-apple ice cream. Mamma is also known for her "wild meats," including armadillo, opossum, monkey (yes, monkey), game birds, and even iguana.

10 Guadeloupe ⚓⚓⚓

Guadeloupe actually consists of two islands separated by a narrow channel known as the Rivière Salée. **Grande-Terre,** the eastern island, is typical of the charming Antilles, with rolling hills and sugar plantations. The western island, **Basse-Terre,** is rugged and mountainous, dominated by the active 4,800-foot volcano La Soufrière. Basse-Terre's mountains are covered with tropical forests, and the island is ringed by beautiful beaches. The surf pounds hard against its east-facing Atlantic coast, but calmer seas rule on the leeward bathing beaches.

Guadeloupe's charm is not readily apparent when your ship arrives at Pointe-à-Pitre, the capital. This rather tacky port doesn't have the old-world charm of Fort-de-France on Martinique. The rather narrow streets are jammed during the day with a colorful crowd creating a permanent traffic jam. At sunset, however, the town becomes quiet again and almost deserted.

COMING ASHORE

Cruise ships dock right in the commercial center of Pointe-à-Pitre at Centre St-Jean-Perse. This modern center, located near the open-air markets and small shops, has its own duty-free shops selling Guadeloupean rum and French perfume.There's also a renowned restaurant, La Canne à Sucre.

The cruise center also has a bank, where you can get some French francs. There are phones that accept ATM cards or Telecartes, prepaid discount phone cards that can be used in booths marked Telecom. Purchase these from outlets labeled *Telecart en Vente Ici.*

FAST FACTS

Currency   The official currency is the French franc (Fr). We have used an exchange rate of Fr 4.98 to U.S.$1 (1 Fr = 20¢) to calculate prices. Most restaurants quote prices in francs; however, shops in and around the cruise dock generally have prices in both francs and U.S. dollars, with rates lower than the official exchange rate.

Information   The major tourist office is the **Office Départmental du Tourisme,** Square de la Banque, 5, in Pointe-à-Pitre (☎ 0590-82-09-30). Open Monday to Friday 9am to 5pm.

Language   The official language is French, and creole is the unofficial second language. English is spoken only in the major tourist centers.

SHORE EXCURSIONS

Most cruise ships offer a three-hour tour for $40 per person that takes in many scenic highlights of Grande-Terre, which is closer to the cruise terminal. Although Grande-Terre is not without its charms, Basse-Terre has far more scenic wonders. Ask at the tourist office if a local company is offering an excursion to Basse-Terre. If one is, and you can get back to the ship on time, you'll find Basse-Terre more interesting. If no tours are running, you'll have to rent a car or take a taxi tour. We've described a driving tour later in this section.

GETTING AROUND

You'll find taxis, but no limousines or buses at the cruise dock. The taxi drivers charge whatever they can, although technically the government regulates fares. Always agree on the price before getting in. Call ☎ 0590-82-99-88 for a radio-dispatched cab. If you're traveling with people or can put together a party, it's possible to sightsee by taxi. Fares are negotiable.

You can rent a car and drive around Basse-Terre; the road all the way around it is one of the loveliest drives in the Caribbean. Driving is on the right side of the road and is relatively easy. Reserve a car in advance from **Hertz** (☎ **800/654-3001** or 0590-82-00-14), **Avis** (☎ **800/331-2112** or 0590-82-33-47), or **Budget** (☎ **800/527-0700** or 0590-82-95-58).

Buses link almost every hamlet to Pointe-à-Pitre, and these jitney vans going to Basse-Terre leave from the Gare Routière de Bergevin. Those heading to other parts of Grande-Terre depart the Gare Routière de Mortenol.

SEEING THE SIGHTS

As you might expect of a port town, **Pointe-à-Pitre** is tops for shopping on Guadaloupe, particularly in the morning when the **covered market** at the corner of rue Frébault and rue Thiers is quite lively. The town center is **place de la Victoire,** a park shaded by palm trees and poincianas. If you want to explore outside the town, here's some sights to see.

A DRIVING TOUR OF GRANDE-TERRE

LE BAS DU FORT   From town, head to the "South Riviera," which runs along the coast from Pointe-à-Pitre to Pointe des Châteaux at the eastern end of Grande-Terre. At the tourist complex of Bas du Fort, 2 miles east of Pointe-à-Pitre near Gosier, you'll come to the **Aquarium de la Guadeloupe** (☎ 0590-90-92-38), just off the main highway near Bas-du-Fort Marina.

GOSIER   Some of Guadeloupe's biggest and most important resorts are found at Gosier, with its nearly 5 miles of beach stretching east from Pointe-à-Pitre. Most shore excursions stop at **Fort Fleur-d'Epée,** dating from the 18th century. The well-preserved ruins command the crown of a hill. From here you'll have

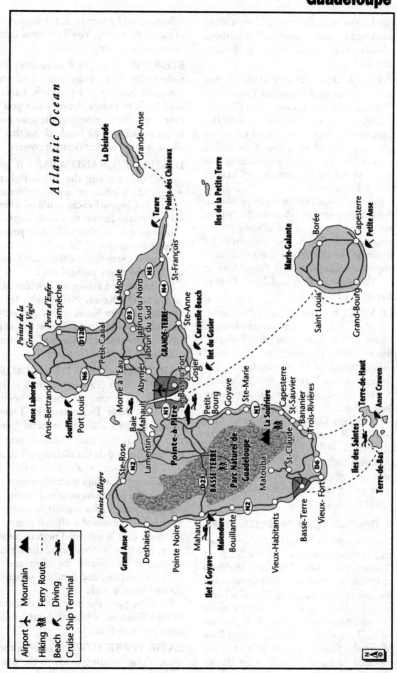

Atlantic Ocean

La Désirade

Grande-Anse

Pointe des Châteaux

Tarare

St-François

Îles de la Petite Terre

Pointe de la Grande Vigie

Porte d'Enfer

Campêche

Le Moule

N5

N4

Jabrun du Nord

Jabrun du Sud

GRANDE-TERRE

Ste-Anne

Caravelle Beach

Îlet du Gosier

Marie-Galante

Borée

Capesterre

Petite Anse

D3

Anse Laborde

Souffleur

Port Louis

N6

Anse-Bertrand

Petit-Canal

D120

Abymes

Morne à l'Eau

Le Bas du Fort

Gosier

Saint Louis

Grand-Bourg

Ste-Rose

N2

Baie Mahault

Lamentin

Pointe-à-Pitre

N1

Petit-Bourg

Goyave

Ste-Marie

Capesterre

St-Sauvier

Bananier

Trois-Rivières

N1

Terre-de-Haut

Anse Crawen

Pointe Allegre

BASSE-TERRE

Parc Naturel de Guadeloupe

La Soufrière

St-Claude

Matouba

D23

Îles des Saintes

Terre-de-Bas

Deshaies

Pointe Noire

Malendure

Bouillante

Vieux-Habitants

N2

Basse-Terre

Vieux-Fort

D6

Grand Anse

Îlet à Goyave

Airport	✈	Mountain	▲
Hiking	🚶🚶	Ferry Route	---
Beach	↖	Diving	🚶
Cruise Ship Terminal	🚶🚶		

N↻

good views over the bay, and on a clear day you can see the neighboring offshore islands of Marie-Galante and Iles des Saintes.

POINTE DES CHÂTEAUX Seven miles east of St-François is Pointe des Châteaux, the easternmost tip of Grande-Terre, where the Atlantic meets the Caribbean. With the sound of waves crashing around you, you'll see a cliff sculpted by the sea into castlelike formations. At the top is a cross placed here in the 19th century.

You might walk to Pointe des Colibris, the extreme end of Guadeloupe, where you'll have a view of the island's northeastern sector. To the east is a view of La Désirade, another island that looks like a huge vessel anchored far away. Among the coved beaches found here, **Pointe Tarare** is au naturel.

LE MOULE You can use N5 as an alternative route from St-François back to Pointe-à-Pitre from Pointe des Châteaux. After 9 miles, you reach the tiny coastal fishing village of Le Moule, founded at the end of the 17th century. A holiday center is developing along its more than 10-mile crescent-shaped beach.

The **Edgar Clerc Archeological Museum La Rosette,** Parc de la Rosette, Le Moule (☎ **0590-23-57-43**), shows an extensive collection of Amerindian artifacts, including both Carib and Arawak relics gathered from various islands of the Lesser Antilles.

A DRIVING TOUR OF BASSE-TERRE

You can explore Basse-Terre's northeastern, or windward, coast via the N1 from Pointe-à-Pitre. After $1^1/2$ miles, the Pont de la Gabarre crosses the Rivière Salèe, the narrow strait separating Grande-Terre from Basse-Terre. For the next 4 miles the road runs straight through sugar cane fields. Turn right on the N2 toward **Baie Mahault.** Don't confuse this with the town of Mahault, which is on Basse-Terre's western coast. Leaving Baie Mahault, head northwest to Lamentin, a

village settled by corsairs at the beginning of the 18th century. You'll see some colonial mansions scattered about.

STE-ROSE From Lamentin, drive $6^1/2$ miles to Ste-Rose, where you'll find several good beaches. On your left, a small road leads to **Sofaia,** from which you'll have a panoramic view over the coast and forest preserve. The locals claim that a sulfur spring here has curative powers.

DESHAIES / GRAND ANSE A few miles farther along the N2 is Pointe Allègre, the northernmost point of Basse-Terre. At **Clugny Beach,** you'll be where the first settler landed on Guadeloupe. A couple of miles farther will bring you to **Grand Anse,** one of Guadeloupe's best beaches. It's very large, still secluded, and sheltered by many tropical trees.

Snorkeling and fishing are popular pastimes at **Deshaies.** Nine miles from Deshaies, **Pointe Noire** comes into view. Its name derives from black volcanic rocks. Look for the odd multicolored cenotaph monument in town.

PARC NATUREL DE GUADE-LOUPE You reach Mahaut 4 miles from Pointe Noire. On your left begins the **route de la Traversée,** the Transcoastal Highway. We recommend going this way, as you pass through scenic **✪ Parc Naturel de Guadeloupe.** Taking up 74,100 acres, or about one-fifth of Guadeloupe, this huge tract of mountains and tropical forests is home to a variety of tame animals, including titi (a raccoon adopted as the island's official mascot), and birds such as the wood pigeon, turtledove, and thrush. Small exhibition huts, devoted to the volcano, the forest, and to coffee, sugarcane, and rum, are scattered throughout the park.

From the park, the main road descends toward Versailles, a hamlet about 5 miles from Pointe-à-Pitre.

BASSE-TERRE TOWN You can continue along winding roads to the town of Basse-Terre, Guadeloupe's seat of government. Founded in 1634, it's the oldest town on the island. Although there's not much to see here other than a 17th-century cathedral and Fort St-Charles, it still has its charms. The market squares are shaded by tamarind and palm trees.

LA SOUFRIÈRE The big attraction of Basse-Terre is the famous sulfur-puffing ✪ **La Soufrière** volcano. The appearance of ashes, mud, billowing smoke, and earthquakelike tremors in 1975 proved that this old beast is still active. Rising some 4,800 feet high, it's flanked by banana plantations and lush foliage. You can drive from Basse-Terre to **St-Claude,** a suburb 4 miles up the mountainside at an elevation of 1,900 feet. St-Claude has a perfect climate and tropical gardens. From here, you can drive up the narrow, winding road the Guadeloupeans say leads to hell—that is, the summit of La Soufrière. The road ends at a parking area at La Savane à Mulets, at an altitude of 3,300 feet. Hikers can climb right to the volcano's mouth. You can touch the ground in the parking lot and feel its heat. Steam emerges from fumaroles and sulfurous fumes from the volcano's "burps."

STE-MARIE In the town square of **Ste-Marie,** 4¹/₂ miles past Capesterre, you can stop and see the statue of Guadeloupe's first tourist: Christopher Columbus. He anchored a quarter of a mile from Ste-Marie on November 4, 1493, on his second voyage.

ROCHES GRAVÉES The country along the northeast, or windward, coast of Basse-Terre is richer and greener than elsewhere on the island. Here, near the pier in Trois Rivières, are the **Roches Gravées** ("Carved Rocks") onto which the island's original inhabitants, the Arawaks, carved petroglyphs of humans and animals. They most likely date from A.D. 300 or 400. You'll also see specimens of plants, including cocoa, pimento, and banana, which the Arawaks cultivated long before the Europeans set foot on Guadeloupe.

SHOPPING

We suggest that you skip a shopping tour of Pointe-à-Pitre if you're going onto Martinique, as you'll find far more merchandise there.

Your best buys here will be anything French—perfumes from Chanel, silk scarves from Hermès, cosmetics from Dior, crystal from Lalique and Baccarat. Sometimes we've found some items discounted as much as 30% below U.S. or Canadian prices, provided you pay by traveler's checks. Many eager shopkeepers stay open longer than usual and even on weekends when cruise ships are in port.

You may want to seek out some native goods in little shops along the backstreets of Pointe-à-Pitre. The straw hats or salacos made in Les Saintes islands are considered collector's items. Native doudou dolls are also popular gift items.

Open-air stalls surround the **covered market** (Marché Couvert) at the corner of rue Frébault and rue Thiers. In madras turbans, local Creole women sell oranges, papayas, bananas, mangoes, and more.

On Rue Frébault, **Rosébleu**, at no. 5 (☎ **0590-82-93-44**), has Pointe-à-Pitre's biggest stock of fine crystal, fine porcelain, and tableware. The best crystal made in France is sold here. At no. 8, **Phoenicia** (☎ **0590-83-50-36**) is the best place to purchase French perfumes, at prices lower than those charged in Paris. It also has the best selection of imported cosmetics. Next door at 8–10, **Vendôme** (☎ **0590-83-42-84**) sells imported fashions for both men and women, as well as gifts and perfumes.

A little antique shop called **Tim-Tim** (the local creole patois for "once upon a time"), at 15 Rue Henri IV 15 (☎ **0590-83-48-71**), offers a sometimes whimsical collection of Creole furnishings, baskets, madras table linens, and even dolls and maps.

The "essence of the island" on Guadeloupe is rhum agricole, a pure rum fermented from sugarcane juice.

Currently, only two distilleries still process it. At **Distillerie Bellevue,** Rue Bellevue Damoiseau, La Moule (☎ **0590-23-55-55**), you can taste before purchasing.

BEACHES

Beaches dot the island, from the surf-brushed dark strands of western Basse-Terre to the long stretches of white sand encircling Grande-Terre.

Outstanding beaches include **Caravele Beach,** a long, reef-protected stretch of sand outside Ste-Anne, about 9 miles from Gosier, site of many leading resorts. Hotels welcome non-guests, but charge for changing facilities, beach chairs, and towels. On Basse-Terre, one of the best beaches is **Grande Anse,** a palm-sheltered beach north of Deshaies on the northwest coast.

Sunday is family day at the beach here. Public beaches are generally free, but some charge for parking and have few facilities. Topless sunbathing is common at hotels, less so on village beaches. Nudist beaches include Ilet du Gosier, off Gosier. Another nudist beach, Plage de Tarare, lies near the eastern tip of Grande-Terre at Pointe des Châteaux.

GOLF, DIVING & TENNIS

GOLF   Guadeloupe's only golf course is the well-known **Golf de St-François** (☎ **0590-88-41-81**) at St-François, opposite the Hôtel Méridien. The 6,755-yard, par-71 course is challenging, with water traps on six holes, massive bunkers, and prevailing trade winds. Greens fees are Fr 250 ($50) per day per person. Rental golf clubs cost Fr 100 ($20), an electric golf cart is Fr 200 ($40).

SCUBA DIVING   Scuba divers are drawn to the waters off Guadeloupe, which lack underwater currents and are relatively calm. The **Cousteau Underwater Reserve** has many attractive dive sites. During a typical dive, sergeant majors become visible at a depth of 30 feet, spiny sea urchins and green parrot fish at 60 feet, and magnificent stands of finger, black, brain, and star coral come into view at 80 feet.

Centre International de la Plongée (C.I.P.), B.P. 4, Lieu-Dit Poirier, Malendure Plage (☎ **0590-98-81-72**), is the island's most professional dive operation, located at the edge of the Cousteau Underwater Reserve. Dive boats depart three times a day, usually at 10am, 12:30pm, and 3pm. Certified divers pay Fr 200 ($40) for a one-tank dive. A one-on-one course for first-time divers costs Fr 230 ($46).

TENNIS   All the large resort hotels have tennis courts. Your best bet is to call **Le Relais du Moulin,** Chateaubrun, near Ste-Anne (☎ **0590-88-23-96**), and arrange for a playing time. A taxi will take you there from the cruise dock.

DINING

Guadeloupe is fabled for Creole women operating simple little bistros, sometimes in their own homes.

ON GRANDE-TERRE

Although Guadeloupe has some of the finest dining choices in the Caribbean, you won't know that if you stay only in dreary Pointe-à-Pitre. There's an exception, however, open only for lunch. **Le Big Steak House,** 2 rue Delgrès at Quai Lardenoy (☎ **0590-82-12-44**), near the cruise docks, serves the best midday meal in town. Decorated with a Wild West motif, it imports its meats twice a week from mainland France, and will prepare your steak any way you like it, and serve it with your choice of five different sauces. Fish such as red snapper culled from local waters is also a hot item.

La Chaubette, Route de Ste-Anne (☎ **0590-84-14-29**), is a "front porch" Creole restaurant with lots of local color. About a 12-minute taxi ride east of Pointe-à-Pitre, it's the Guadeloupe version of a roadside inn. When available, the langouste is peerless, as is the hog's-head cheese with a minced-onion vinaigrette. Begin your meal with a lethal and filling rum punch served with a lime wedge and sugar, and finish with coconut ice cream or a banana aflame with rum.

At the far eastern end of Gosier village, en route to Ste-Anne, **Chez Violetta,** Perinette Gosier (☎ **0590-84-10-34**), is the most formally decorated of all the island's Creole restaurants. Try stuffed crabs, cod fritters, or classic *boudin* (blood sausage). The chef also makes a fine conch ragout that's best when served with home-grown hot chiles.

If you have transportation, you can visit St-François, 25 miles east of the cruise docks at Pointe-à-Pitre. The area has always been known for its authentic Creole and French dining. Sample the delights of **La Louisiane,** Quartier Ste-Marthe, 1¹/₂ miles east of St-François (☎ **0590-88-44-34**), which works as hard on its luncheon menu as it does on its dinner. The French owners feature some of the best regional cuisine from their native Provence and Vosges. Dishes such as scallops in a lime and ginger sauce pay homage to the Caribbean.

ON BASSE-TERRE

You'll find good food in the family run **Chez Paul de Matouba** (☎ **0590-80-29-20**), beside the banks of the small Rivière Rouge (Red River). It's the best choice if you've decided to visit La Soufrière. The cooking is Creole, and crayfish dishes are the specialty. In winter, the restaurant may be filled with the tour-bus crowd.

On the waterfront near the center of Ste-Rose, **Restaurant Clara** (☎ **0590-28-72-99**) combines fine French dining with authentic, spicy Creole cooking. Specialties at lunch may include ouassous (freshwater crayfish), brochette of swordfish, or sea-urchin omelets. The sauce chien is a blend of hot peppers, garlic, lime juice, and "secret things" that go well with the house drink, which is made with six local fruits and ample quantities of rum. Your dessert sherbet might be guava, soursop, or passion fruit.

11 Jamaica ⇩⇩⇩⇩

Jamaica lies 90 miles south of Cuba and is the third largest of the Caribbean islands, with some 4,400 square miles of predominantly green terrain, a mountain ridge peaking at 7,400 feet above sea level, and, on the north coast, many beautiful white-sand beaches rimming the clear blue sea.

Most cruise ships dock at Ocho Rios on the lush northern coast, although others are increasingly going to the city of Montego Bay ("Mo Bay"), 67 miles to the west. Both ports offer comparable attractions and some of the same shopping possibilities. Don't try to do both ports in one day, however, since the four-hour round-trip ride will leave time for only superficial visits to each.

FAST FACTS

Currency The unit of currency is the **Jamaican dollar,** designated by $, so we use the symbol **J$** to denote prices in Jamaican dollars. Currently, the rate of exchange is J$35 to U.S.$1 (J$1 = 2.8¢ U.S.). You can use U.S. dollars, but always determine whether a price is being quoted in Jamaican or U.S. dollars.

Information In Ocho Rios, the tourist board office is located at the Ocean Village Shopping Centre (☎ **809/974-2570**) and is open Monday to Friday from 9am to 5pm. In Montego Bay, the tourist board office is located at Cornwall Beach, St. James (☎ **809/952-4425**), and is open Monday to Friday from 9am to 5pm.

Language The official language is English, but most Jamaicans speak a richly nuanced patois.

OCHO RIOS

Once a small banana and fishing port, Ocho Rios is now Jamaica's cruise-ship

Jamaica

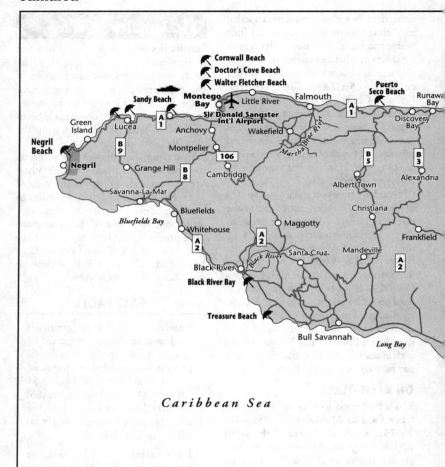

capital. The bay is dominated on one side by a bauxite-loading terminal and on the other by resort hotels with palm tree–fringed beaches.

Although the Ocho Rios area has some of the Caribbean's most fabled resorts, the town itself is tacky and not a romantic place to walk around. Its quaint charm has disappeared under the weight of mass tourism.

COMING ASHORE

Most cruise ships dock at the port of Ocho Rios, which is near Dunn's River

Falls. Only a mile away is one of the most important shopping centers, Ocean Village.

Vendors are particularly aggressive in Ocho Rios. Don't expect to shop in the markets without a lot of hassle and a lot of very pushy salesmen hawking their merchandise.

SHORE EXCURSIONS

We recommend shore excursions to see Ocho Rios, because of the town's inadequate public transportation. Also, renting and driving a car is a hassle.

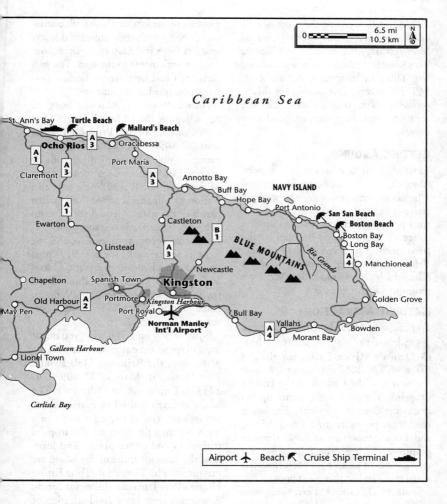

The most popular tour, which lasts 3½ hours and costs $35 per passenger, visits Dunn's River Falls, which gets quite crowded when many cruise ships are in port. This tour also visits Shaw Park Botanical Gardens, Fern Gully, and other local attractions, with time allocated for shopping. Be prepared: Wear a bathing suit underneath your clothes if you take this tour.

Other tours include one of still-operational Prospect Plantation, which lasts 3½ hours and costs $39. Another tour, which lasts three hours and costs

$49, takes you trough the Jamaican countryside to visit Brimmer Hall Plantation, a working property with a Great House and tropical crops. On the way back, you pass the estates once occupied by Noël Coward and Ian Fleming.

Other tours include a two-hour snorkeling jaunt for $25. A coral reef near the cruise pier is one of the best places on the northern coast for snorkeling, with panoramic underwater visibility. Another tour, which lasts one hour and costs $16 per person, takes you on a glass-bottom boat for a look at underwater Jamaica.

Traditionally, one of the most heavily booked tours, from Ocho Rios or Montego Bay, is rafting on the Martha Brae River in a 30-foot, two-seat bamboo raft. This tour lasts four hours and costs $45. However, most people are disappointed with this tour, and we think there are more interesting ways to spend your time.

GETTING AROUND

Taxis are your best means of transport. Always agree on a fare before you get into a Jamaican taxi. Rates are charged per taxi, not per person. You can also negotiate a price for a taxi to take you around to see the sights. Taxis licensed by the government display red Public Passenger Vehicle (PPV) plates. All others are gypsy cabs, which you should avoid. We don't recommend renting a car.

NATURAL ATTRACTIONS

You can relax on the beach or climb with a guide to the top of the 600-foot ✪ **Dunn's River Falls,** on the A3 (☎ **809/974-2857**). You can splash in the waters at the bottom of the falls or drop into the cool pools higher up between the cascades of water. The beach restaurant provides snacks and drinks, and dressing rooms are available. If you're planning to climb the falls, wear old tennis shoes to protect your feet from the sharp rocks and to prevent slipping.

South of Ocho Rios, **Fern Gully** was originally a riverbed. Today, the main A3 road winds up some 700 feet among a rain forest filled with a profusion of wild ferns, hardwood trees, and lianas. Roadside stands sell fruit and vegetables, carved-wood souvenirs, and basketwork. The road runs for about 4 miles. At the top of the hill you come to a right-hand turn onto a narrow road leading to Golden Grove.

SEEING THE SIGHTS

A mile from the center of Ocho Rios, at an elevation of 420 feet, **Coyaba River Garden and Museum,** Shaw Park Road (☎ **809/974-6235**), was built on the grounds of the former Shaw Park plantation. The Spanish-style museum displays artifacts from the Arawak, Spanish, and English settlements in the area. The gardens are filled with native flora, a cut-stone courtyard, and fountains.

Three miles east of Ocho Rios along the A3, adjoining the 18-hole Prospect Mini Golf Course, working **Prospect Plantation** (☎ **809/994-1058**) is often a shore excursion stop. On your leisurely ride by covered jitney through the scenic beauty of Prospect, you'll readily see why this section of Jamaica is called "the garden parish of the island." You'll see pimento (allspice), banana, cassava, sugarcane, coffee, cocoa, coconut, pineapple, and the famous leucaena "Tree of Life," plus Jamaica's first hydroelectric plant. Horseback riding is available on three scenic trails. The rides vary from 1 to $2^1/_4$ hours; you'll need to book a horse 1 hour in advance.

If you're here on a Thursday, you might want to spend the day at another working plantation, the **Brimmer Hall Estate,** Port Maria, St. Mary's (☎ **809/974-2244**), 21 miles east of Ocho Rios. The estate is often visited as part of shore excursions. You're driven around in a tractor-drawn jitney to see the tropical fruit trees and coffee plants, and learn how the luscious fruits of the island are produced. The Plantation Tour Eating House offers Jamaican dishes for lunch. A souvenir shop has a good selection of ceramics, art, straw goods, wood carvings, rums, liqueurs, and cigars.

There are old-timey exhibits at ✪ **Columbus Park Museum,** located in a large, open area between the main coast road and the sea at Discovery Bay (☎ **809/973-2135**). Here you'll see a canoe fashioned from a single piece of cottonwood in the same way the Arawaks did it more than five centuries ago. There's also a tally, used to count bananas carried on men's heads from plantation to ship, and a planter's strongbox with a weighted lead base to prevent its theft. You can learn how Khus Khus, a

Jamaican perfume, is made from the roots of a plant, and how black dye is extracted from logwood. A taxi will take you here from the cruise dock.

Firefly, Grants Pen, 20 miles east of Ocho Rios above Oracabessa (☎ **809/ 997-7201**), was the home of Sir Noël Coward and his longtime companion, Graham Payn, who, as executor of Coward's estate, donated it to the Jamaica National Heritage Trust. The recently restored house is as it was on the day Sir Noël died in 1973.

SHOPPING

In general, the shopping is better at Montego Bay if you're going there. If not, wander the Ocho Rios crafts markets, although much of the merchandise seems the same from shop to shop and stall to stall.

Hundreds of Jamaicans pour into Ocho Rios hoping to sell something to cruise-ship passengers. Be prepared for aggressive selling and some fierce haggling. Every vendor asks too much for an item at first. Is shopping fun in Ocho Rios? No. Do cruise-ship passengers indulge in it anyway? Yes.

Warning: Some so-called "duty-free" prices are indeed lower than stateside prices, but then the government hits you with a 10% "General Consumption Tax" on all items purchased.

There are seven main shopping plazas. **Island Plaza** is right in the heart of Ocho Rios. You'll find some great Jamaican art. You can also purchase local handmade crafts (though you should be prepared to haggle over price and quality). **Beautiful Memories** (☎ **809/974-2374**) stocks Jamaican art and exhibits local crafts, pottery, woodwork, and hand-embroidered items.

The **Ocean Village Shopping Centre** has numerous boutiques, food stores, a bank, sundries purveyors, travel agencies, service facilities, and **Ocho Rios Pharmacy** (☎ **809/974-2398**). **Swiss Stores** (☎ **809/974-2519**), sells all the big-name Swiss watches, as well as duty-free hand-crafted jewelry.

Just east of Ocho Rios, **Pineapple Place Shopping Centre** is a collection of shops in cottages roofed with cedar shingles and set amid tropical flowers. **Casa de Oro** (☎ **809/974-2577**) sells duty-free watches, fine jewelry, and classic perfumes.

Ocho Rios Craft Park has some 150 stalls. An eager seller will weave a hat or a basket while you wait, or you can buy ready-made hats, hampers, handbags, place mats, and lampshades. Other stands stock hand-embroidered goods. Wood carvers work on bowls, ashtrays, wooden-head carvings, and statues chipped from lignum vitae, and make cups from local bamboo.

Shops at the **Coconut Grove Shopping Plaza** sell mainly local craft items. Many of your fellow shoppers may be cruise-ship passengers.

If you'd like to flee from the hustle and bustle of the Ocho Rios bazaars, you can take a taxi to **Harmony Hall / The Garden Café,** Tower Isle, on the A3 (☎ **809/975-4785**), 4 miles east of Ocho Rios. One of Jamaica's Great Houses, the now-restored Harmony Hall was built near the end of the 19th century as the centerpiece of a sugar plantation. Today, it's the focal point of an art gallery and restaurant that showcases the painting and sculpture of Jamaican artists as well as a tasteful array of arts and crafts. Among the featured gift items are Sharon McConnell's Starfish Oils, with natural additives harvested in Jamaica. Sportswear that's sold includes Reggae to Wear, designed and made in Jamaica.

The Garden Café, which is also known as Alexander's after the name of its co-owner, serves Jamaican cuisine as part of full meals. You can also stop in just for a cup of tea and a slice of homemade cake.

BEACHES

Most visitors head for the beach. The most crowded is **Mallards Beach,** shared by hotel guests and cruise-ship passengers. Locals may also steer you to **Turtle Beach.** It's less crowded, with white sand and clear waters.

GOLF, RIDING & TENNIS

GOLF Super Club's Runaway Golf Course, at Runaway Beach near Ocho Rios on the north coast (☎ 809/973-2561), is one of the area's better courses. Cruise-ship passengers should call ahead to book playing times. The charge is $58 for 18 holes, with carts and clubs rentals.

You can play nine holes for $50 or 18 holes for $70 at the **Sandals Golf and Country Club** (☎ 809/975-0119), a 15-minute drive from Ocho Rios.

HORSEBACK RIDING Jamaica's most complete equestrian center is the **Chukka Cove Farm and Resort,** at Richmond Llandovery, St. Ann (☎ 809/972-2506), located less than 4 miles east of Runaway Bay. A one-hour trail ride costs $30, and a two-hour mountain ride goes for $40. The most popular ride is a three-hour beach jaunt where, after riding over trails to the sea, you can unpack your horse and swim in the surf. Refreshments are served as part of the $55 charge. A six-hour beach ride, complete with picnic lunch, costs $130.

TENNIS Ciboney Ocho Rios, Main Street, Ocho Rios (☎ 809/974-1027) has three clay surface and three hard-surface courts. Call to make arrangements with the manager.

DINING

The **Almond Tree,** in the Hibiscus Lodge Hotel, 87 Main St. (☎ 809/974-2813), is a two-tiered patio restaurant overlooking the Caribbean at this resort three blocks from the Ocho Rios Mall. Lobster thermidor is the most delectable item on the menu and lobster Almond Tree is also a specialty. Also excellent are the roast suckling pig, medaillons of beef Anne Palmer, and a fondue Bourguignonne. Have an aperitif in the unique "swinging bar" (the chairs swing; you may also, but that's a matter of personal preference).

A five-minute taxi ride south of Ocho Rios, ✪ **Evita's Italian Restaurant,** Eden Bower Road (☎ 809/974-2333), is the most fun restaurant along the north coast. Half the menu is pasta, and the fish dishes are excellent, especially snapper stuffed with crabmeat or the lobster and scampi in a buttery white cream sauce.

You'll think you're at Tara in *Gone with the Wind* when you arrive at the ✪ **Plantation Inn Restaurant,** in the Plantation Inn, Main Street (☎ 809/974-5601). You can sit indoors or on the outdoor Bougainvillea Terrace, with the Peacock Pavilion annex a few steps away, where afternoon tea is served daily. The continental cuisine is spiced up a bit by Jamaican specialties. Our favorite appetizer is "Fire and Spice," a chicken and beef kebab with a ginger pimiento sauce. For the main course, we always ask the chef to prepare a whole roast fish, based upon the catch of the day, served boneless and seasoned with island herbs and spices.

At **Ruins Restaurant, Gift Shop, and Boutique,** Turtle River, DaCosta Drive (☎ 809/974-2442), you lunch at the foot of a series of waterfalls in the center of town. You may want to climb the stairs to the top, where bobbing lanterns and the illuminated waters below afford one of the most delightful experiences on the island. The setting is more dramatic than the cuisine, which is basically Chinese-American. Dishes include several kinds of chow mein or chop suey and sweet-and-sour pork.

MONTEGO BAY

Montego Bay is sometimes less of a hassle than the port at Ocho Rios. Its beaches, shopping, and restaurants are also better, and you can play some of the Caribbean's best golf. Aside from shopping, the good stuff to do here lies in the environs, which you'll have to reach by taxi or shore excursion.

COMING ASHORE

Montego Bay has a modern cruise dock, with duty-free stores, telephones, tourist information, and plenty of taxis to meet all ships. This rather dull cruise port isn't at the center of town, however, so you'll have to take a $5 taxi ride to get to the main tourist board in the heart of "Mo Bay."

SHORE EXCURSIONS

Most cruise ships offer weak shore excursions that are not worth your time or money. One of the most highly touted is the rafting on the Martha Brae River, described above. You can book independent tours yourself.

The **Croydon Plantation,** Catadupa, St. James (☎ 809/979-8267), a 25-mile ride from Montego Bay, can be visited on a half-day tour on Tuesday, Wednesday, and Friday. Included in the $45 price are round-trip transportation from the dock, a plantation tour, a tasting of pineapple and tropical fruits in season, and a barbecued chicken lunch.

Another plantation tour is offered Tuesday, Wednesday, Friday, and Sunday by the **Hilton High Day Tour,** with an office on Beach View Plaza (☎ 809/952-3343). The tour includes a plantation tour, breakfast, lunch, and transportation for $50 per person, with an additional $10 fee for 30 minutes of horseback riding.

GETTING AROUND

If you don't book a shore excursion, a taxi is the way to get around. See "Getting Around," under Ocho Rios, above, for taxi information, as the same conditions apply to Mo Bay.

Montego Honda/Bike Rentals, 21 Gloucester Ave. (☎ 809/952-4984), rents Hondas for $35 a day, plus a $300 deposit.

SEEING THE SIGHTS

These attractions can be reached by taxi from the cruise dock.

Charging a very steep admission, the most famous Great House in Jamaica is the legendary ✪ **Rose Hall Great House,** Rose Hall Highway (☎ 809/953-2323), located 9 miles east of Montego Bay along the coast road. The house was built about two centuries ago by John Palmer,

and gained notoriety from the doings of "Infamous Annie" Palmer, wife of the builder's grandnephew, who supposedly dabbled in witchcraft and took slaves as lovers, killing them when they bored her. Annie also was said to have murdered several of her husbands while they slept, and eventually suffered the same fate herself. The house, now privately owned by U.S.-based philanthropists, has been restored. **Annie's Pub** sits on the ground floor.

On a hillside perch 14 miles east of Montego Bay and 7 miles west of Falmouth, **Greenwood Great House,** on the A1 (☎ 809/953-1077), is even more interesting to some than Rose Hall. Erected in the early 19th century, the Georgian-style building was from 1780 to 1800 the residence of Richard Barrett, a relative of Elizabeth Barrett Browning. On display are the family's library, portraits of the family, and rare musical instruments.

If you want a Jamaican doctor bird to perch on your finger or would like to feed small doves and finches from your hand, go to the ✪ **Rocklands Wildlife Station** (☎ 809/952-2009), about a mile outside Anchovy on the road from Montego Bay.

SHOPPING

The same warnings about shopping in Ocho Rios apply to Mo Bay. Still, you can find good duty-free items here, including Swiss watches, Irish crystal, French perfumes, English china, Danish silverware, Portuguese linens, Italian handbags, Scottish cashmeres, Indian silks, and liquors and liqueurs. Appleton's overproof, special, and punch rums are excellent values. Tía Maria and Rumona are the best liqueurs, coffee- and rum-flavored, respectively. Khus Khus is the local perfume. Jamaican arts and crafts are available throughout the resort and at the Crafts Market.

The main shopping areas are at **Montego Freeport,** within easy walking distance of the pier; **City Centre,** where most of the duty-free shops are, aside from at the large hotels; and **Holiday**

Village Shopping Centre, with **Blue Mountain Gems Workshop** (☎ 809/953-2338), where you can take a tour to see the process from raw stone to the finished product available for purchase later.

The **Old Fort Craft Park,** a shopping complex with 180 vendors licensed by the Jamaica Tourist Board, fronts Howard Cooke Boulevard up from Gloucester Avenue on the site of Fort Montego. You'll see wall hangings, hand-woven straw items, and hand-carved wood sculpture, and you can even get your hair braided. Vendors can be quite aggressive, so be prepared for hassle and negotiating. Persistent bargaining on your part will result in substantial discounts.

You can find the best Jamaican handmade souvenirs at the **Crafts Market,** near Harbour Street in downtown Montego Bay, including straw hats and bags, wooden platters, straw baskets, musical instruments, beads, carved objects, and toys. That *jipijapa* hat will come in handy if you're going to be out in the island sun.

Ambiente Art Gallery, 9 Fort St. (☎ 809/952-7919), sells local fine artwork and prints by local artists. Further down the street, **Things Jamaican,** at no. 44 (☎ 809/952-5605), showcases Jamaican artisans, with many carved-wood items as well as hand-woven baskets. You can also buy food, such as Busha Browne's fine Jamaican sauces, and rums and liqueurs. Next door is **Klass Kraft Leather Sandals** (☎ 809/952-5782), which sells sandals (all less than $30) and leather accessories made by Jamaican craftspeople.

You'll easily recognize **Caribatik Island Fabrics,** Rock Wharf on the Luminous Lagoon, 2 miles east of Falmouth on the north coast road (☎ 809/954-3314), by the huge sign painted across the building's side. In the shop are fabrics, scarves, garments, and wall hangings, some patterned after such themes as Jamaica's "doctor bird."

The **Golden Nugget,** 8 St. James Shopping Centre, Gloucester Avenue (☎ 809/952-7707), is a duty-free shop selling watches and jewelry, especially gold chains. The shop also carries leading brand-name cameras and French perfumes.

BEACHES

You may want to skip the public beaches and head instead for the **Rose Hall Beach Club** (☎ 809/953-2323), on the main road 11 miles east of Montego Bay. It sits on a half mile of secluded white-sand beach with crystal-clear water. The club offers a full restaurant, two beach bars, a covered pavilion, an open-air dance area, showers, restrooms, and changing facilities, plus beach volleyball courts, various beach games, and a full water sports program. There is also live entertainment. Adults pay $8, children $5.

Cornwall Beach (☎ 809/952-3463) is a long stretch of white-sand beach with dressing cabanas. A bar and cafeteria offer refreshments. Adults pay $2, children $1.

Doctor's Cave Beach, on Gloucester Avenue across from the Doctor's Cave Beach Hotel (☎ 809/952-2566), helped launch Mo Bay as a resort in the 1940s. Dressing rooms, chairs, umbrellas, and rafts are available. Adults pay $1, children 50¢.

One of Jamaica's premier beaches, **Walter Fletcher Beach** in the heart of Mo Bay (☎ 809/952-5783), is a family favorite with its tranquil waters. There are changing rooms, lifeguards, and a restaurant. Adults pay $2, children $1.

GOLF, RIDING, DIVING, SAILING, RAFTING & TENNIS

GOLF   Wyndham Rose Hall Resort course (☎ 809/953-2650) is an unusual and challenging seaside and mountain course, and one of the world's best. The scenic back nine rises into steep slopes and deep ravines on Mount Zion. Greens fees are $60 for 18 holes, $40 for nine. Mandatory cart rental costs $33 for 18 holes, and the mandatory caddie is another $12 for 18 holes.

The excellent course of **Tryall** (☎ 809/956-5660), 12 miles from Montego Bay, is the site of the Jamaica Classic Annual. For 18 holes, greens fees are $95 year-round.

The **Half Moon,** at Rose Hall (☎ 809/953-2560), features a championship course designed by Robert Trent Jones. For 18 holes, greens fees are $85. Carts cost $25 for 18 holes, and mandatory caddies cost $12.

The **Ironshore Golf and Country Club,** Ironshore, St. James, Montego Bay (☎ 809/953-2800), another well-known 18-hole golf course with a 72 par, is privately owned but open to the public. Greens fees for 18 holes are $51.75.

HORSEBACK RIDING The best program for equestrians is offered at the **Rocky Point Riding Stables,** at the Half Moon Club, Rose Hall, Montego Bay (☎ 809/953-2286). There are about 30 horses and a helpful staff. A 90-minute beach or mountain ride costs $50, while a 2¹/₂-hour combination ride is $70. This latter includes treks along hillside and forest trails and beaches, and ends with a saltwater swim.

TENNIS **Wyndham Rose Hall Resort,** Rose Hall (☎ 809/953-2650), outside Montego Bay, offers six hard-surface courts. Nonresidents must obtain permission from the manager to play.

Half Moon Golf, Tennis, and Beach Club, Rose Hall (☎ 809/953-2211), outside Montego Bay, has the finest tennis courts. The pro shop accepts reservations for the 13 courts. You'll have to purchase a day pass for $40 per person at the front desk, which lets you use the resort's tennis courts, gym, sauna, Jacuzzi, pools, and beach facilities.

Tryall Golf, Tennis, and Beach Club (☎ 809/956-5660), offers nine hard-surface courts. Nonresidents pay $25 per hour.

SCUBA DIVING **Seaworld Resorts Ltd.,** whose main office is at the Cariblue Hotel, Rose Hall Main Road (☎ 809/953-2180), operates scuba-diving as well as deep-sea fishing jaunts, plus water sports such as sailing and windsurfing. There are three PADI-certified dive guides, one dive boat, and all the necessary equipment. Most day dives begin at $35.

SAILING Day cruises are offered aboard the *Calico,* a 55-foot gaff-rigged wooden ketch that sails from Margaritaville on the Montego Bay waterfront. An additional vessel, *Calico B,* carries another 40 passengers per ride. They will transport you to and from the cruise pier for either journey. Departing at 10am and returning at 3pm, the day voyage provides sailing, sunning, and snorkeling (including equipment), plus a Jamaican buffet lunch served on the beach. The daily cruise costs $50 per person. For information and reservations, call Capt. Bryan Langford, **North Coast Cruises Ltd.** (☎ 809/952-5860). They recommend giving three days' notice.

RAFTING Mountain Valley Rafting, 31 Gloucester Ave. (☎ 809/952-0527), offers Great River rafting excursions that depart from the Lethe Plantation, about 10 miles south of Montego Bay. Bamboo rafts are available for $36 for up to two occupants. Trips last about an hour and leave throughout the day. Ask about a taxi pickup at the end of the rafting run. For $45 per person, a half-day trip includes transportation to and from the pier, an hour's rafting, lunch, a garden tour of the Lethe property, and some Jamaican liqueur.

DINING

The **Georgian House,** 2 Orange St. (☎ 809/952-0632), combines grand cuisine and an elegant setting (there's even an art gallery on site). You can sit upstairs or on the garden terrace. Start with Jamaican appetizers such as ackee and bacon. Baked spiny lobster is another specialty (ask that it not be overcooked). When cruise-ship passengers visit for lunch, the menu is primarily Jamaican, becoming continental in the evening.

Set in a coral-stone warehouse 15 miles west of town, ✪ **Norma at the Wharfhouse,** Reading Road (☎ **809/979-2745**), is the finest restaurant in Montego Bay. Menu specialties include grilled deviled crab backs, smoked marlin with papaya sauce, nuggets of lobster in a mild curry sauce, and chateaubriand larded with pâté in a peppercorn sauce. Dessert might be a rum-and-raisin cheesecake or a piña colada mousse. This is the type of food you rarely find in Jamaica. However, it's only open for lunch Thursday through Sunday.

Built on a landfill in the bay, **Pier 1,** Howard Cooke Boulevard (☎ **809/952-2452**), is one of Mo Bay's major dining and entertainment hubs. Fishermen bring fresh lobster, which the chef prepares in a number of ways. You can start with Jamaican soups such as conch chowder or "red pea" (actually red bean). At lunch, their hamburgers are the juiciest in town. The "jerk dishes," however, are better at the Pork Pit (see below). You can drink or dine on the ground floor, open to the sea breezes, but most guests seem to prefer the more formal second floor.

✪ **Pork Pit,** 27 Gloucester Ave. (☎ **809/952-1046**), is the best place to go for famous Jamaican jerk pork and jerk chicken. It's near Walter Fletcher Beach, so many beach buffs come over here for a big lunch. For a filling meal, order half a pound of jerk meat, with a baked yam or baked potato and a bottle of local Red Stripe beer. The reasonably priced menu also includes steamed roast fish.

You ride through the rolling landscape to reach ✪ **Sugar Mill Restaurant,** at the Half Moon Club, Half Moon Golf Course, Rose Hall, along the A1 (☎ **809/953-2228**). The restaurant is set among stone ruins of what used to be a water wheel for a sugar plantation. Lunch can be a relatively simple affair, perhaps an ackee burger with bacon, preceded by Mama's pumpkin soup and followed with a homemade rum-and-raisin ice cream. Smoked north-coast marlin is a specialty,

and the chef makes the island's most elegant Jamaican bouillabaisse.

In a red-brick building dating from 1765, the **Town House,** 16 Church St. (☎ **809/952-2660**), is a tranquil luncheon choice, offering sandwiches and salads and more elaborate fare. Soups are a specialty here, especially the pepperpot or pumpkin. Dishes include the local favorite, red snapper *en papillote* (baked in a paper bag). We're fond of the large rack of barbecued spareribs, with the owners' special Tennessee sauce. The pasta and steak dishes are also good, especially the homemade fettuccine with whole shrimp.

12 Key West ♨ ♨ ♨ ♨ ♨

No other port of call offers such a sweeping choice of fine dining, easy-to-reach attractions, street entertainment, and roguish bars as does this heavy-drinking, fun-loving town at the very end of the fabled Florida Keys. It's America's southernmost city at Mile Marker 0, where U.S. Route 1 begins, but it feels more like a colorful Caribbean outpost. Key West is the last link in a necklace of islands stretching 103 miles from the Florida mainland.

You only have a day, so flee the busy cruise docks and touristy Duval Street for a walk through hidden and more secluded byways such as Olivia or William streets. Or you might want to spend your day being sporty—playing golf or going diving or snorkeling.

COMING ASHORE

Ships dock at Mallory Square, Old Town's most important plaza, or at nearby Truman Annex, a five-minute stroll away. Both are on the Gulf of Mexico side of the island. Virtually everything is at your doorstep, including the two main arteries, Duval Street and Whitehead Street, each filled with shops, bars, restaurants, and the town's most important attractions.

Key West

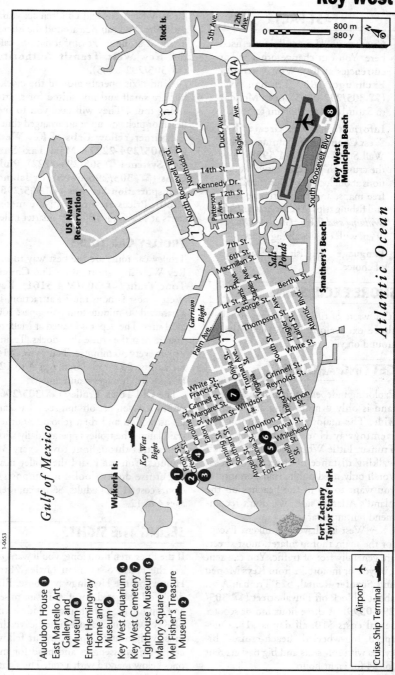

Gulf of Mexico

Atlantic Ocean

US Naval Reservation

Wiskeria Is.

Key West Bight

Garrison Bight

Stock Is.

Salt Ponds

Smather's Beach

Key West Municipal Beach

Fort Zachary Taylor State Park

5th Ave.
12th Ave.
A1A
Duck Ave.
Flagler Ave.
North Roosevelt Blvd.
Northside Dr.
South Roosevelt Blvd.
14th St.
Kennedy Dr.
12th St.
10th St.
Patterson Ave.
7th St.
6th St.
Macmillan St.
2nd Ave.
1st St.
Harris Ave.
George St.
Staples Ave.
Bertha St.
Atlantic Blvd.
Laird St.
Flagler Ave.
Thompson St.
South St.
White St.
Grinnell St.
Reynolds St.
United St.
Vernon St.
Palm Ave.
Olivia St.
Truman Ave.
Virginia
Windsor La.
Simonton St.
Duval St.
Whitehead
Amelia St.
Fort St.
Angela St.
Petronia St.
White St.
Francis St.
Grinnell St.
Margaret St.
Caroline St.
Eaton St.
William St.
Fleming St.
Southard St.
Front St.
Greene St.

0   800 m
     880 y

1-0653

Audubon House ❸
East Martello Art Gallery and Museum ❽
Ernest Hemingway Home and Museum ❻
Key West Aquarium ❹
Key West Cemetery ❼
Lighthouse Museum ❺
Mallory Square ❶
Mel Fisher's Treasure Museum ❷

✈ Airport

⚓ Cruise Ship Terminal

❶ ❷ ❸ ❹ ❺ ❻ ❼ ❽

FAST FACTS

Currency U.S. dollars are used here. You can change other major currencies at **Key West Currency Exchange,** 1007 Truman Ave. (☎ 305/292-0005), open Monday to Saturday from 9:30am to 5pm.

Information The Greater Key West Chamber of Commerce, 402 Wall St. (☎ 305/294-5988), near the cruise-ship docks, answers questions about local activities, distributes free maps, and helps arrange tours and fishing trips. Ask for *Solares Hill's Walking and Biking Guide to Old Key West,* with eight walking tours.

Language English is the language of choice.

SHORE EXCURSIONS

It's a waste of time and money to take a shore excursion. You can easily get around on your own.

GETTING AROUND

Exploring independently is fun, as the island is only 4 miles long and 2 miles wide. The major sights, including the Hemingway House and the Harry S Truman Little White House, are within walking distance of the cruise docks. You'll only need public transportation if you want to go to the beaches on the island's Atlantic side. We don't recommend renting a car.

Key West is a haven for bikers. Except for the main thoroughfares, most streets are generally free of traffic. You can rent a bicycle or motorbike from **Keys Moped and Scooter Rental,** 523 Truman Ave., about a block off Duval Street (☎ 305/294-0399). A three-hour motor scooter rental costs $10; all day is $18. One-speed, big-wheeled "beach-cruiser" bicycles with soft seats and big baskets rent for $4 for eight hours.

The cheapest way to see the island is by bus, which costs only 75¢ for adults, 35¢

for senior citizens and children six years and older. You can ride around the island in about an hour. For information, call the **Key West Transit Authority** (☎ 305/292-8165).

Island taxis operate around the clock, but are small and are not suited for sightseeing tours. They will take you to the beach or pick you up at an arranged time. Call either **Yellow Cabs of Key West** (☎ 305/294-2227), **Maxi-Taxi Sun Cab System** (☎ 305/294-2222), **Pink Cabs** (☎ 305/296-6666), or **Island Transportation Services** (☎ 305/296-1800). Prices are uniform: the meter starts at $1.40, plus 35¢ per quarter mile.

TROLLEY CAR TOURS

Trolley car tours are the best way to see Key West in a short time. The **Conch Tour Train** (☎ 305/294-5161), Key West's most famous tourist attraction, is a narrated 90-minute tour going past 100 local sites. The depot is located at Mallory Square near the cruise-ship docks. Trains depart every 30 minutes. Tours costs $14 for adults, $6 for children ages 4 to 12, and are free for ages 3 and under.

The **Old Town Trolley** (☎ 305/296-6688) lets you get off and see a particular attraction and then reboard another train later. The trolleys operate daily with departures throughout town every 30 minutes. You can board the trolley near the cruise docks (look for signposts). Tours cost $15 for adults, $6 for children ages 4 to 12.

SEEING THE SIGHTS

If the lines aren't too long, you'll want to see the Harry S Truman Little White House and the Hemingway House. But don't feel obligated, for if you want to see and capture the real-life mood and charm of Key West in a short time, leave the most-visited attractions to your fellow cruise-ship passengers and head for the ones below marked with a star. The sights listed below lie within an easy walk of the docks.

The **Audubon House,** 205 Whitehead St. at Greene Street (☎ **305/294-2116**), is dedicated to the 1832 Key West sojourn of the famous naturalist John James Audubon. The ornithologist didn't live in this three-story building, but it's filled with his engravings. The main reason to visit is to see how wealthy sailors lived in Key West in the 19th century. And the lush tropical gardens surrounding the house are worth the price of admission.

Harry S Truman Little White House, 111 Front St. (☎ **305/294-9911**), the president's former vacation home, is part of the 103-acre Truman Annex near the cruise-ship docks. The small house, which takes less than an hour to visit, affords a rare glimpse of a president at play.

There may be long lines at the **Hemingway House,** 907 Whitehead St. (☎ **305/294-1575**), where "Papa" lived with his second wife, Pauline. Built in the Spanish colonial style of native rock hewn from the ground, it's furnished much as the Nobel Prize winner left it. Here, in the studio annex, Hemingway wrote *For Whom the Bell Tolls* and *A Farewell to Arms,* among others. Hemingway had some 50 polydactyl (many-toed) cats, whose descendants still live on the grounds.

Jessie Porter Newton, known as "Miss Jessie" to her friends, was the grande dame of Key West. She invited the celebrities of her day to her house, including Tennessee Williams and her girlhood friend Gloria Swanson, as well as family friend Robert Frost, who stayed in a cottage out back. Today, you can cross her once hallowed ground, look at the antique-filled rooms, and inspect her mementos and her exotic treasures collected by six generations of the Porter family at ✪ **Jessie Porter's Heritage House and Robert Frost Cottage,** 410 Caroline St. (☎ **305/296-3573**).

On the waterfront at Mallory Square, the **Key West Aquarium,** 1 Whitehead St. (☎ **305/296-2051**), in operation since 1932, was the first tourist attraction built in the Florida Keys. The aquarium's special feature is a "touch tank," where you can feel a horseshoe crab, sea squirt, sea urchin, starfish, and, of course, a conch, the town's mascot and symbol. It's worth taking a tour, as the guides are both knowledgeable and entertaining, and you'll get to pet a shark, if that's your idea of a good time.

A visit to a spooky graveyard might not be your idea of a good time, but the ✪ **Key West Cemetery** (☎ **305/292-6718**), 21 prime acres in the heart of the historic district, is the island's foremost offbeat attraction. The main entrance is at Margaret Street and Passover Lane. Stone-encased caskets rest on top of the earth because graves dug into the ground would hit the water table. There's also a touch of humor here: One stone gravestone proclaims "I Told You I Was Sick" and another says, "At Least I Know Where He Is Sleeping Tonight."

Treasure hunter Mel Fisher wears heavy gold necklaces, which he likes to say are worth a king's ransom. He isn't exaggerating. After long and risky dives, Fisher and his associates plucked more than $400 million in gold and silver from the shipwrecked Spanish galleons *Santa Margarita* and *Nuestra Señora de Atocha,* which were lost on hurricane-tossed seas some 350 years ago. Now this extraordinary long-lost Spanish jewelry, doubloons, and silver and gold bullion are displayed at the ✪ **Mel Fisher Maritime Heritage Society Museum,** 200 Greene St. (☎ **305/294-2633**), a true treasure trove near the docks.

✪ **Nancy Forrester's Secret Garden,** 1 Free School Lane, off Simonton between Southard and Fleming streets (☎ **305/294-0015**), is the most lavish and verdant garden in town. Some 130 to 150 species of palms, palmettos, climbing vines, and ground covers are planted here, creating a blanket of lush, tropical magic. It's a 20-minute walk from the docks, near Key West's highest point, Solares Hill. Pick up a sandwich at a deli and picnic at tables in the garden.

Housed in a Civil War fort that's a National Historic Site, **The East Martello Museum and Gallery** (☎ 305/296-3913) is out by the airport, an $18 round-trip taxi ride. You'll see some intriguing nautical exhibits and a great view of the Atlantic Ocean, but we don't think it's worth the time or money.

A SUNSET RITUAL

If your ship leaves late enough, stick around to watch the sunset from Mallory Dock. In Key West, sunset-watching has become a carnival-like, almost pagan celebration. The square, crowded with people, comes alive with entertainment, from a string band to a unicyclist wriggling free of a straitjacket. Cruise ships are banned from Mallory Dock after 5:30pm, so you'll have a clear view.

FLIGHTSEEING

For a bird's-eye view of the Florida Keys and surrounding waters, take a ride with **Island Aeroplane Tours,** 3469 South Roosevelt Blvd., Key West Airport (☎ 305/294-8687). Up to two passengers in an open cockpit biplane can choose from six different tours, ranging from $50 to $200 for two. One tour takes in the south shore, beaches, and resorts, whereas the best tour blankets a vast area of the Florida Keys, including flights over uninhabited islands such as Mud Key. This flight also covers all of Key West and especially Old Town. Flights range from 9 to 55 minutes. It's a $9 one-way taxi fare to reach the airport from the cruise-ship docks.

SHOPPING

The most touristy shops are clustered at the cruise-ship docks, and the most outrageously overpriced merchandise is within a 12-block radius of Old Town. You can find better purchases at stores that lie much farther along Duval Street and on hidden back streets. The stores recommended below are a 15- to 20-minute stroll from the cruise-ship docks.

Bird in Hand, 400 Front St. (☎ 305/296-6324), is the number-one gift store

in Key West. Business is brisk in art objects, crystal paperweights, porcelain sculpture, wind chimes, and souvenirs. Especially appealing are the Indonesian statues and the Austrian Swarovsky crystal. Anything can be shipped.

With a treasure trove of merchandise from all over the world, ۞ **Cavanaugh's,** 520 Front St. (☎ 305/296-3343), stocks the most unusual furnishings and exotic artwork in the Florida Keys. A shopping trip here is like wandering through the souks in the dusty back alleys of the Arab world. The merchandise isn't cheap.

At the small but select **Emeralds International,** 104 Duval St. (☎ 305/294-2060), prices range from $50 to $150,000. Many cruise-ship passengers shop here more modestly for "conch pearls."

۞ **Fast Buck Freddie's,** 500 Duval St., at Fleming Street (☎ 305/294-2007), is a small but eclectic department store carrying fashions, table settings, costumes, chic sportswear, beachwear, linens, and toys.

۞ **Fletcher's,** 1024 Duval St. (☎ 305/294-2032), celebrates the island's bedrock: Key West limestone. You can buy a slice of it here, artfully crafted into lamps, tables, bookends, or soaring columns. The best pieces have fossilized seashells and ancient crustacea embedded within their surface.

۞ **Gingerbread Square Gallery,** 1207 Duval St. (☎ 305/296-8900), is the town's most prestigious art gallery, featuring canvases by John Kiraly, one of Key West's best known artists. The gallery also features ceramics and crystal. You'll find more than 300 Haitian artists represented at the **Haitian Art Company,** 600 Frances St. (☎ 305/296-8932). Their work graphically illustrates the concerns of a changing and troubled nation.

H. T. Chittum and Co., 725 Duval St. (☎ 305/292-9002), has the best selection of informal clothing, a smart ready-to-wear collection from Timberland (including shoes, purses, and backpacks), and clothing from Sportif and Nautica Tommy Bahama. In addition, there's a selection of watches, knives (including dive knives), gift items, hats, belts, leather jackets, and cookbooks, plus some good books on Key West.

✪ **Key West Aloe,** 524 Front St. or 540 Greene St. (☎ **800/445-2563** or 305/295-0775), sells a line of aloe-based sun-block and skin-care products, as well as fragrances based on tropical essences like hibiscus, frangipani, and white ginger. One scent smells like the ocean and is marketed as the perfect cruise cologne.

The locally famous **Key West Hand Print Fashions and Fabrics,** 201 Simonton St. (☎ **800/866-0333** or 305/294-9535), has its silk-screened fabrics popularized by designer Lily Pulitzer. Today, the shop is still committed to its bold, tropical prints.

The **Key West Island Bookstore,** 513 Fleming St. (☎ **305/294-2904**), is well stocked in books on Key West and Hemingway. In the rear is a rare-book section.

You can find coins from sunken wrecks at **Michael,** 400C Duval St. (☎ **305/294-2488**), where they're set into jewelry in a "numismatically correct" fashion—that is, the setting doesn't damage or alter the shape of the coin. Skip the branches of this store near the cruise docks and head for this main store, which has a far superior stock.

Tikal Trading Co., 129 Duval St. (☎ **305/296-4463**), designs and manufactures its own line of women's clothing. They have original floral prints in a 40/60 blend and hand-woven linen clothing without prints. The two lines are made as mother/daughter wear—in other words, you can buy two outfits with similar designs and matching accessories.

Waterfront Market, 201 William St. (☎ **305/294-8418**), is a deli, bakery, seafood market, gourmet shop, and the best venue for hot sauces, beer, and wine. If a cruise-ship passenger wants to compose a picnic for lunch, this is the place, as it sells not only wine but an array of freshly made salads, the most popular of which is fresh curried chicken salad. Sandwiches can be prepared as you want them and while you wait from a wide variety of

breads, Boarshead meats, cheeses, and vegetables.

You'll find interesting pottery at ✪ **Whitehead Street Pottery,** 1011 Whitehead St. (☎ **305/294-5067**), housed in a pre-1890 former Cuban bodega tucked away in an unpretentious residential neighborhood.

BEACHES

Beaches are not Key West's strong point. Most are manmade, often with imported Bahamian or mainland Florida sands. The ones mentioned below are free and open to the public daily from 7am to 11pm. There are few facilities except for locals hawking beach umbrellas, food, and drinks.

Closest to the docks is **Fort Zachary Taylor State Beach,** a 12-minute walk away. The 51-acre artificial beach is adjacent to the ruins of Fort Taylor, once known as Fort Forgotten because it was buried under tons of sand. The beach is fine for sunbathing, picnicking, and snorkeling, but rocks make it difficult to swim. To reach the beach, go through the gates leading into Truman Annex. Near one end of the beach are the raffish Green Parrot Bar and a booze-and-burger joint called Gato Gordo (Fat Cat).

If you want to escape your fellow cruise-ship passengers, consider **Higgs Memorial Beach,** a 25-minute walk from the harbor near the end of White Street. There's lots of sand and picnic tables sheltered from the sun. **Smathers Beach** is the longest (about 1¹/₂ miles) and most isolated beach in town, but it's a $9 one-way taxi ride from the cruise docks and it has few (if any) amenities. The beach borders South Roosevelt Boulevard. Regrettably, there's no shade here.

FISHING, GOLF, DIVING, KAYAKING, SAILING & BOATING

FISHING The 40-footers *Linda D III* and *Linda D IV* (☎ **800/299-9798** or 305/296-9798) offer the best deep-sea fishing. Make arrangements a week or so before you are due in port. Four-hour jaunts, including equipment, cost $375 for the boat or $100 for a chair. You can go fishing daily from 8am to noon.

GOLF The only golf course that's easily accessible lies 6 miles from the cruise docks, near the southern tip of neighboring Stock Island. The **Key West Resort Golf Course,** 6450 E. Junior College Rd. (☎ **305/294-5232**), features a tricky and challenging terrain of coral rock, sand traps, mangrove swamp, and pines. The course is a 20-minute, $12 taxi ride from the dock each way. Greens fees are $48, including use of a motorized cart, for either nine or 18 holes. A full set of golf clubs rents for $21. The pursers of many cruise ships do a brisk business booking tee times at least a day in advance, and in some cases, the cruise line itself will provide transportation from the docks directly to the golf course.

KAYAKING Thanks to ✪ **Florida Keys Back Country Adventures,** 6810 Front St., Stock Island (☎ **305/296-0362**), you can transit the shallow waters of the Keys by kayak. Most cruise-ship passengers opt for the half-day tours, which depart daily between 9am and 10am, last 3¹/₂ hours, and showcase abundant bird life, especially hawks, bald eagles, and ospreys. You'll also see endless fish, stingrays, spiny lobsters, and crustaceans. There's no time for snorkeling during the half-day tour, although you can always dip into the cool waters wherever you come across a clean, sandy bottom.

The kayak tours are great, but they take time and cost money to get to the boats. The company will, however, send a minivan for up to six passengers, at a cost of $20 round-trip, if notified in advance. Otherwise it's a $12 ride by taxi. The half-day tour costs $35 per person. Tours begin and end at the company's headquarters on Stock Island north of Key West.

SCUBA DIVING The resort's largest dive outfitter is **Captain's Corner,** 0 Duval St., opposite the Pier House Hotel a block from the dock (☎ **305/296-8865**). This five-star PADI operation has 11 instructors, a 60-foot dive boat, and a well-trained staff. Most cruise-ship passengers opt for a two-tank dive departing every morning at 9:30am and returning at 1:15pm. The $60 per person cost includes use of equipment and two one-hour dives at two different locations above the teeming reef. To reach the departure point, make a left along the docks, then walk for about a block to the northern tip of Duval Street.

SAILING & BOATING Two of the largest and most crowded of the craft available for tours are a pair of double-hulled vessels run by **Fury Catamarans** (☎ **305/294-8899**). They depart from the Truman Annex, at the western end of Greene Street. A half-day tour devoted to reef snorkeling, priced at $38, will allow a first-hand view of underwater marine life. Morning tours last from 9:30am to 12:30pm, with afternoon sessions from 1 to 4pm.

You'll have a different type of experience aboard the *Reef Chief,* a 65-foot, two-masted wooden schooner built in the 1970s and modeled on a 19th-century Chesapeake Bay boat (☎ **305/292-1345**). The 3¹/₂-hour snorkeling jaunts depart daily at 9am or 10:30am, and cost $25 per participant. The craft moors at the Safe Harbor Marina on Stock Island, a 15-minute, $12 one-way taxi ride from the docks. The shoals you'll visit will be less crowded than the reefs visited by ships berthed at points closer to the cruise docks.

The *Pride of Key West* is a 60-foot catamaran power boat, offering cruises that depart at noon, last two hours, and cost $20 for adults or $10 for children 5 to 12 (ages 4 and under sail free). The boat is wheelchair accessible. Departures are from the foot of Duval Street, two blocks from Mallory Square, close to the cruise-ship docks. Two TV monitors show videos during the cruise, and viewing wells are found on either end of the boat.

DINING

All the restaurants listed below are within an easy 5- to 15-minute walk of the cruise-ship docks. Since you'll be in port only for lunch and will return to the ship by dinner, it isn't necessary to make reservations. Many passengers prefer to have their lunch at one of Key West's legendary bars, and several raw bars near the dock offer seafood, including oysters and clams. But conch is king—served grilled, ground into burgers, made into a chowder, fried in batter as fritters, or served raw in a conch salad. For dessert or a snack, sample a slice of Key lime pie. The pie's unique flavor is achieved from the juice and minced rind of a piquant Key lime that flourishes in the area.

Housed in a sea captain's home built in 1884, ✪ **Bagatelle,** 115 Duval St., at Front Street (☎ **305/296-6609**), is one of Key West's finest restaurants. For lunch, enjoy a daily special or one of the chef's better dishes, such as conch ceviche (thinly sliced raw conch marinated in lime juice and herbs). Keys pasta is served with fresh local seafood, and Jamaican chicken is a spicy but sweet delight. Some of the offerings here are too bland, but most are imaginative, particularly in the use of island spices.

Although it's in a rough neighborhood and housed in a former bordello, ✪ **Blue Heaven,** 729 Thomas St. (☎ **305/296-8666**), has been transformed into one of the best restaurants in town. The chefs get the freshest produce they can find and boost their dishes with herbs and delicately dosed spices. To start, try the carrot and curry soup or zesty barbecue shrimp. The fresh local fish, often grouper or red snapper, is always good, and the hot and spicy jerk chicken is as flavorful as what's served in Jamaica. Vegetarian dishes are also available. Save room for the special Banana Heaven dessert, with Betty's banana bread and flambéed bananas in spicy rum served with homemade vanilla ice cream.

You'll eat the best breakfast in town and get the best value lunches at ✪ **Camille's,** 703 Duval St., between Angela and Petronia streets (☎ **305/296-4811**). It's a hip and unpretentious cafe with downright delectable pancakes, waffles, and French toast and a three-egg omelet that's without competition on Duval Street. For lunch, try one of the homemade soups, perfectly prepared chicken salad, or a sandwich on fresh bread made from the catch of the day. The Key lime pie appears beneath a cloud of meringue sprinkled with caramel.

A $6 taxi ride will bring you back to the golden days of the 1950s at ✪ **El Siboney,** 900 Catherine St. (☎ **305/296-4184**), where you can find such time-tested favorites as ropa vieja (shredded beef), roast pork pungently flavored with garlic and tart sour oranges, and the best crawfish enchilada in town. If you're in a party of at least two, you can order the paella Valenciana. Black beans come with everything, and the starchy Cuban bread is washed down with homemade sangría. This is an aggressively ugly establishment, with plastic-covered tables and a flaming red decor, but that's part of its appeal.

Flamingo Crossing, 1105 Duval St., at Virginia Street (☎ **305/296-6124**), serves 120 varieties of the best ice cream in the Florida Keys. Each luscious scoop is made with natural flavors, often including pure fruit and cream. Cuban coffee, soursop, rum raisin, even frothy guanabana, mango, Key lime, and papaya are just some of the flavors available.

On the waterfront, **Half Shell Raw Bar,** Land's End Marina at the foot of Margaret Street (☎ **305/294-7496**), is Key West's original raw bar, offering fresh fish, oysters, and shrimp direct from its own fish market, served to you at varnished picnic tables and benches enclosed by a shed. In season, try the succulent stone crab claws and tasty Florida lobster. There's also delicious conch chowder, perfectly smoked fish, and a savory "cracked" conch dinner. The famous Gulf shrimp is grilled just right.

At the foot of Duval Street, near the docks, **Harbour View Restaurant** (☎ 305/296-4600) is housed in Key West's premier hotel, the Pier House. It's a good choice on a hot day, as you can order light meals. Try the creamy conch chowder, different since fresh cream is used instead of tomatoes. The fish and chips are better than at almost any pub in London. The best one-dish meal is the Reuben on Cuban bread topped with purple cabbage kraut.

At long last, Key West has a **Hard Rock Café**, 313 Duval St. (☎ 305/293-0230), located three short blocks from where the cruise ships dock. It's the only Hard Rock in the world occupying an antique house, and it also features the largest collection of 1960s rock 'n' roll memorabilia of any Hard Rock in the world. Enjoy a Hard Rock Hurricane, the bartender's special drink, on one of several porches before digging into an array of food perfectly suited to these casual indoor/outdoor lunches. Try the conch chowder, a burger, or a meal-size salad (especially the Oriental version filled with grilled chicken, snow peas, and mandarin oranges).

The legendary ✪ **Pepe's Café and Steak House**, 806 Caroline St., between William and Margaret streets (☎ 305/294-7192), was established in 1909, but moved to its present location on the old commercial waterfront in 1962. Cruise-ship passengers like the "in between" menu served daily from noon to 4:30pm. It includes zesty homemade chili, perfectly baked oysters, fish sandwiches, and Pepe's deservedly fabled steak sandwiches. If you arrive before noon, try the shrimp and mushroom omelet—there's nothing finer. The freshly squeezed screwdriver is the best in town.

The Thai specialties at **Siam House**, 829 Simonton St. (☎ 305/292-0302), are worth the 12-minute walk from the cruise docks. Some say the fiery-hot dishes have been cooled for the American palate, but we think the results are still first class. The best dish is the crispy fish, a whole red snapper fast-fried and served

with a sauce flavored with tamarind, garlic, and red peppers.

The bustling **Turtle Kraals Wildlife Bar and Grill,** Land's End Village at the foot of Margaret Street (☎ 305/294-2640), opens right on the harbor. We prefer the food here to the nearby Half Shell Raw Bar, and we bypass the Southwestern specialties in favor of the fish. You can order tender Florida lobster, spicy conch chowder, or perfectly cooked fresh fish (often dolphin with pineapple salsa or baked stuffed grouper with mango crabmeat stuffing).

Croissants de France Bakery and Café, 816 Duval St. (☎ 305/294-2624), lures with its pretty patio nestled under pink umbrellas. It's one of the best brunch spots on the main drag. Enjoy fluffy croissants with a cappuccino along with freshly squeezed orange juice. Scrambled eggs with mustard sauce is a local favorite. Check out the cozy, intimate **New York Pizza Café,** which lies on a little shopping square at 1075 Duval St. (☎ 305/294-6466). Only 20 customers at a time can be seated. The place is small, but portions are gargantuan, and they serve some of the best lasagna along the street, along with freshly made salads and football-size calzones.

PUB CRAWLING

There's a gritty honky-tonk flavor to Key West, a memory still lingering from its swashbuckling origins. Somehow, bars seem more important to the life here than anywhere else in the Caribbean. Most places recommended below serve fast food to go with their drinks. The food isn't the best on the island, but usually arrives shortly after you order it, which suits most rushed cruise-ship passengers just fine.

Sloppy Joe's, 201 Duval St. (☎ 305/294-5717), is the most touristy bar in Key West, visited by virtually all cruise-ship passengers. It aggressively plays up its association with Hemingway, although when Papa frequented the place it was located on Greene Street, at the site currently occupied by Captain Tony's Saloon (see below). Today, marine flags decorate the ceiling, and its ambience and decor look like a Havana bar from the 1930s. Hemingway T-shirts are hawked here, and, although most patrons come here just to drink, a selection of platters and sandwiches is served in back. The place is often crowded, noisy, and raucous. Live entertainment packs them in from noon to 2am.

Heavily patronized by cruise-ship passengers and occupying the same 1851 building that used to be Sloppy Joe's, **Captain Tony's Saloon,** 428 Green St. (☎ 305/294-1838), is the oldest active bar in Florida, and has it ever grown tacky. Locals have abandoned the bar to others who have decorated it with macho paraphernalia like women's bras and G-string underwear. Country and R&B are the featured music, and the house special is a lethal Pirates' Punch.

The third most popular bar with cruise-ship passengers is **Jimmy Buffett's Margaritaville,** 500 Duval St. (☎ 305/296-3070). His cafe, naturally, is decorated with pictures of the island's biggest pop star. And, yes, it sells T-shirts and Margaritaville memorabilia in a shop off the dining room. Actually, Buffett's "Cheeseburger in Paradise" isn't bad. His margaritas are without competition, but then they'd have to be at his place, wouldn't they?

The popular **Havana Docks Bar and Sunset Deck,** Pier House, 1 Duval St. (☎ 305/296-4600), rivals Sunset Pier Bar and Grill as a vantage point to observe Key West's legendary sunsets. Live local island music toasts the setting sun. It's the type of convivial, open-air bar that many people think exists in the Caribbean, but is really only found in Key West.

When the crowds at Mallory Square get you down, retreat to **Sunset Pier Bar and Grill,** 0 Duval St. (☎ 305/295-7040), behind the Ocean Key House, overlooking the docks. You can see everything but don't have to put up with the hassle. Tropical drinks, including a Sunset Pier margarita, are the bartender's specialties. A jumbo Hebrew National hot dog,

charbroiled on a toasted bun, satisfies as sometimes nothing else can, and you can also order a number of salads, including a veggie pasta, while listening to the live music. Much beer with spicy conch fritters is consumed.

Drinking is a sport at the **Hog's Breath Saloon,** 400 Front St. (☎ **305/296-HOGG**), a watering hole near the cruise docks that has been a Key West tradition since 1976. The place is all laid back and open air. Live entertainment is offered from 1pm to 2am. Raw oysters are still served here, in spite of the health risk, but when they're in season you may prefer the steamed, sweet stone crab claws. There are also sandwiches and a fish plate (usually a nine-ounce piece of dolphin), followed by the only dessert offered, Key lime pie.

If you're desperate to find a bar that doesn't sell T-shirts, yet is within an easy walk of the cruise-ship docks, head for ☺ **Schooner Wharf,** 201 William St. (☎ 305/292-9520). This local dive is rarely discovered by tourists and bills itself as the last funky area of Old Key West. The waterfront bar looks out on charter boats and classic old yachts in the slips. Come here for margaritas, screwdrivers, or whatever else you want to drink. Pizza is the sole food choice. It's the most robust and hard-drinking bar in Key West, and draws a mostly young crowd.

13 Martinique ♊♊

When you arrive at Fort-de-France, Martinique's capital, you would never guess that this is one of the most beautiful islands in the Caribbean. But past the port are miles of white-sand beaches along an irregular coastline.

Martinique is mountainous, especially in the rain-forested northern region where the volcano Mount Pelée rises to a height of 4,656 feet. Hibiscus, poinsettias, bougainvillea, and coconut palms grow in lush profusion, and fruit—breadfruit, mangoes, pineapples, avocados, bananas, papayas, and custard apples—fairly drips from the trees.

COMING ASHORE

The **Maritime Terminal** is in the dreary eastern commercial district of Fort-de-France, about a mile from the commercial center. Many passengers make the usually hot and humid walk to downtown. Taxi drivers will charge $8 or more to make the trip. If you walk, keep to the left after leaving the dock, so you get to Place de la Savane, the heart of Fort-de-France. At the pier you'll find a less-than-helpful tourist information office, a telephone, and a duty-free shop that is best skipped.

Your cruise line may decide to anchor in the Baie des Flamands, where you'll be transported by tender to the waterfront of Fort-de-France. The tourist office is across the street from the landing dock in a building with an Air France logo.

FAST FACTS

Currency   The French franc (Fr) is the legal tender here. Currently, 1 franc is worth 20¢ U.S. (Fr 4.98 = U.S.$1); this is the rate we've used to convert prices in this section. A money-exchange service, **Change Caraibes** (☎ **0596-73-06-16**) is at rue Ernest Deproge 4, open Monday to Friday from 7:30am to noon and 2:30 to 4pm.

Information   The **Office Départmental du Tourisme** is on boulevard Alfassa in Fort-de-France, across the waterfront boulevard from the harbor (☎ **0596-63-79-60**). Open Monday to Friday from 8am to 5pm and on Saturday from 8am to noon.

Languages   French is the official language and is spoken by almost everyone. The local creole patois uses words borrowed from French, English, Spanish, and African languages. English is occasionally spoken in the major hotels, restaurants, and tourist organizations, but don't count on driving around the countryside and asking for directions in English.

SHORE EXCURSIONS

Shore excursions tend to be very limited, but the classic tour is called "The Pompeii of Martinique," one of the Caribbean's most intriguing trips. You're taken through the lush countryside to St-Pierre, where the eruption of Mount Pelée killed 30,000 people in 1902. The 2¹/₂-hour tour costs $50, the four-hour version is $60.

GETTING AROUND

Two types of buses operate on Martinique. Regular buses, called *grand busses,* cost Fr 6 to Fr 10 ($1.20 to $2) to go anywhere within Fort-de-France. The *taxis collectifs,* however, travel beyond the city limits. These privately owned minivans, which bear the sign *TC,* are crowded and uncomfortable. A one-way fare is Fr 35 ($7) from Fort-de-France to Ste-Anne. Taxis collectifs depart from the parking lot of Pointe Simon.

We recommend renting a car if you don't take a shore excursion. Try **Avis,** rue Ernest-Deproge, 4 (☎ **800/331-2112** or **0596-51-11-70**); **Budget,** rue Félix-Eboué, 12 (☎ **800/527-0700** or **0596-63-69-00**); or **Hertz,** rue Ernest-Deproge, 24 (☎ **800/654-3001** or 0596-60-64-64).

Travel by taxi is popular, but expensive. Most cabs aren't metered, so you'll have to agree on a fare before getting in. For a radio taxi, call ☎ **0596-63-63-62.** We suggest renting a taxi for the day with three or four people. Expect to pay Fr 700 to Fr 850 ($140 to $170) and up for a five-hour tour.

The least expensive way to go between quai d'Esnambuc in Fort-de-France and the main tourist zone of Pointe du Bout is by ferry (*vedette*). The one-way fare is Fr 15 ($3). Schedules are printed in the free visitor's guide, *Choubouloute,* distributed by the tourist office.

A smaller ferryboat runs between Fort-de-France and Anse Mitan and

Martinique

Atlantic Ocean

Macouba

Basse-Pointe

Grand Rivière

Leyritz

Le Lorrain

▲▲ Montagne Pelée

N1

Ajoupa-Bouillon

Le Marigot

Le Prêcheur

N1

Le Morne Rouge

Ste-Marie

Tartane

■ Chateau Dubuc

St-Pierre

Morne des Esses

Caravelle Peninsula

Trinité

■ Musée Gaugin

Le Carbet

N3

Gros-Morne

N2

Balata

N4

Bellefontaine

St-Joseph

Case-Pilote

N1

N1

Lamentin

Le François

Fort-de-France

Lamentin
International
Airport

Pointe du Bout ✔

Mt. Vauclin ▲▲

N6

Anse Mitan ✔

N5

Vauclin

Anse à l'Ane ✔

Trois-Ilets

D7

Grande Anse

Anses-d'Arlets

D7

Rivière-Pilote

D37

Le Diamant

Le Marin

✔ Diamant

Ste-Luce

D18A

■ Diamond Rock

Cap Chevalier ✔

Ste-Anne

Petrified Forest ■

Plage des Salines ✔

Caribbean Sea

Airport ✈ Beach ✔ Mountain ▲▲ Cruise Ship Terminal 🚢

Anse-à-l'Ane, across the bay. The boat departs daily at 30-minute intervals from quai d'Esnambuc in Fort-de-France. The 15-minute one-way trip is Fr 15 ($3).

SEEING THE SIGHTS

Once beyond the disappointing port, you'll find **Fort-de-France** to be a mélange of New Orleans and the French Riviera. But overall, Fort-de-France just isn't that great. At the town center lies **La Savane,** a broad garden planted with many palms and mangoes and bordered by shops and cafes. In the middle of this grand square stands a white marble statue of Joséphine, "Napoléon's little Creole." The statue looks toward Trois-Ilets, where she was born.

St. Louis Roman Catholic Cathedral, on rue Victor-Schoelcher, was built in 1875. It's an extraordinary iron building; inside, some of the island's former governors are buried beneath the choir loft.

A statue in front of the Palais de Justice is of the island's second main historical figure, Victor Schoelcher, who worked to free the slaves more than a century ago. The **Bibliothèque Schoelcher,** rue de la Liberté, 21 (☎ 0596-70-26-67), also honors this popular hero.

Guarding the port is **Fort St-Louis,** built in the Vauban style on a rocky promontory. In addition, **Fort Tartenson** and **Fort Desaix** stand on hills overlooking the port.

Facing La Savane, the **Musée Départemental de la Martinique,** rue de la Liberté, 9 (☎ 0596-71-57-05), is the one bastion on Martinique that preserves its pre-Columbian past with relics left from the Arawaks and the Caribs.

Sacré-Coeur de Balata Cathedral, overlooking Fort-de-France at Balata, is a copy of the one in Paris. It's reached by going along route de la Trace (route N3). Balata is 6 miles north of Fort-de-France.

A short taxi ride away on route N3, the **Jardin de Balata** or **Balata Garden** (☎ 0596-64-48-73) is a tropical botanical park set around a Creole house. The

restored house is furnished with antiques and engravings.

AROUND THE ISLAND

Other than St-Pierre, the most idyllic excursion north of Fort-de-France is to **Le Carbet,** where Columbus landed in 1502 and the first French settlers arrived in 1635. The painter Paul Gauguin lived here for four months in 1887. The **Centre d'Art Musée Paul-Gauguin,** Anse Turin (☎ 0596-78-22-66), commemorates the artist's stay.

Pointe du Bout is a narrow peninsula across the bay from Fort-de-France. It's Martinique's best-accessorized resort area, with large hotels, an impressive marina, about a dozen tennis courts, swimming pools, and facilities for horseback riding and water sports. There's also a golf course, some restaurants, a casino, and boutiques. You can get here by ferry.

The **Hotel Plantation de Leyritz,** near Basse-Pointe (☎ 0596-78-53-92), is one of the best restored plantations on Martinique and a good place for lunch. It's sprawled over flat, partially wooded terrain, a half-hour's drive from the nearest beach (Anse à Zerot, in Sainte-Marie). Part of the acreage still functions as a working banana plantation. The resort includes 16 acres of tropical gardens, and at its core is a stone-sided 18th-century Great House. The dining room is in a rum distillery. You can enjoy an authentic Creole lunch for Fr 120 ($24) and up.

TROIS ILETS

Marie-Josèphe-Rose Tascher de la Pagerié was born in the charming little village of Trois Ilets (pronounced *Twaz-ee-lay*) in 1763. As Joséphine, she was to become the wife of Napoléon I and empress of France from 1804 to 1809. To reach her birthplace, take a taxi from the pier through lush countryside 20 miles south of Fort-de-France. In La Pagerié, a small museum (☎ 0596-68-33-06) of mementos relating to Joséphine has been installed in the former estate kitchen (the plantation house was destroyed in a hurricane). Still remaining are the partially restored ruins of the Pagerié sugar mill and the church where she was christened (the latter is in the village itself). A botanical garden, the **Parc des Floralies,** is adjacent to the golf course Golf de l'Impératrice Joséphine.

THE POMPEII OF MARTINIQUE

The focal point for all shore excursions, ✪ **St-Pierre** was until May 7, 1902, the cultural and economic capital of Martinique. That very morning, locals read in their daily newspaper that "Montagne Pelée does not present any more risk to the population than Vesuvius does to the Neapolitans." Then, at 8am, the southwest side of Pelée exploded into fire and lava. At 8:02am, all but one of St-Pierre's 30,000 inhabitants were dead. Only a convict survived, saved by the thick walls of his jail cell.

St-Pierre never recovered its past splendor. Ruins of the church, the theater, and some other buildings can be seen along the coast. High-speed quadrimarans bring visitors by water from Fort-de-France to St-Pierre. Once here, a 50-passenger submarine, operated by the **Campagnie de la Baie de St-Pierre,** 76 rue Victor-Hugo, St-Pierre (☎ **0596-78-28-28**), enables visitors to explore the underwater wrecks of the ships destroyed by the volcano (until 1994 the wrecks had been accessible only to scuba divers). The cost of the submarine exploration is considerable, but worth it to many: Fr 450 ($90) for adults and Fr 225 ($45) for children.

One of the best ways to accumulate an overview of St-Pierre involves riding a rubber-wheeled "train" with an engine and three cars, which departs on tours from the base of the Musée Volcanologique. Tours cost Fr 50 ($10) for adults and Fr 25 ($5) for children. In theory, tours depart about once an hour, but they only leave when there are enough people to justify the trip.

At the **Musée Volcanologique,** rue Victor-Hugo, St-Pierre (☎ **0596-78-15-16**), you can trace the story of what happened to St-Pierre. Included in the

exhibits is a clock that was excavated from the lava—it stopped at the exact moment the volcano erupted.

SHOPPING

Your best buys on Martinique are French luxury imports, such as perfumes, fashions, Vuitton luggage, Lalique crystal, or Limoges dinnerware. Sometimes prices are as much as 30% to 40% below those in the United States. Some luxury goods, including jewelry, are subject to a value-added tax as high as 14%.

If you pay in dollars, store owners will supposedly give you a 20% discount. However, their exchange rates are usually far less favorable than those offered by the local banks, so your real savings will be 5% to 11%. You're better off shopping in the smaller stores, where prices are 8% to 12% less on comparable items, and paying in francs.

The main shopping street in Fort-de-France is **rue Victor-Hugo.** The other two leading shopping streets are **rue Schoelcher** and **rue St-Louis.** However, most boutique-filled shopping streets are **rue Antoine Siger, rue Lamartine,** and **rue Moreau de Jones.** Here you'll find the latest French design fashions.

Facing the tourist office and alongside **quai d'Esnambuc** is an open market featuring local handcrafts and souvenirs. Far more interesting are the vegetables and fruit at the **open-air stalls along rue Isambert.** Gourmet chefs will find all sorts of spices or such goodies as canned pâté or canned quail in the local supermarkets.

Shops on every street sell bolts of the colorful and inexpensive local fabric, madras. So-called haute couture and resort wear are sold in many boutiques dotting downtown Fort-de-France. Set midway between Fort-de-France and the Lamentin airport, **La Galleria,** Route de Lamentin, is the most upscale and elegant shopping complex on Martinique.

Virtually all the jewelry sold at **La Belle Matadore,** Immeuble Vermeil-Marina,

Pointe du Bout (☎ **0596-66-04-88**), derives from models developed during slave days by the *matadores* (prostitutes), midwives, and slaves. The 18-karat gold designs are vivid and bold. Especially popular are the necklaces, brooches, and pendants.

Cadet-Daniel, 72 Rue Antoine-Siger (☎ **0596-71-41-48**), offers the best buys in French china and crystal. Before you buy, though, do some comparison shopping at **Roger Albert,** 7–9 rue Victor-Hugo (☎ **0596-71-71-71**), Martinique's largest emporium of luxury goods. There are five branches, but the one by the waterfront is the busiest. For anyone with a non-French passport, there are discounts of 20%, plus discounts of an additional 20% during seasonal promotions. Even better, value-added tax is not added.

Stop by **La Case á Rhum,** in the Galerie Marchande 5, rue de la Liberté (☎ **0596-73-73-20**), for Martinique rum, considered by aficionados to be the world's finest. Bottles start at $6 and run to $1,000 for a 1924 bottle distilled by the Bally Company in the nearby hamlet of Carbet.

Centre des Métiers d'Art, rue Ernest de Proges s/n (☎ **0596-70-25-01**), is Martinique's best arts-and-crafts store, adjacent to the tourist office and fronting the waterfront. You'll find local handmade artifacts, including bamboo, ceramics, painted fabrics, and patchwork. There are also tapestries made by the store's charming owner.

A small-scale branch of **Galeries Lafayette,** 10 Rue Victor-Schoelcher, near the cathedral (☎ **0596-71-38-66**), discounts merchandise 20% for purchases made with U.S. dollars, traveler's checks, or a credit card.

Paradise Island, 20 rue Ernest Deproges (☎ **0596-63-93-63**), maintains a stylish and upscale collection of T-shirts. Whatever you like will probably be available in about a dozen different colors.

BEACHES

The beaches south of Fort-de-France are of white sand, whereas the northern strands are composed mostly of gray. Idyllic in the south is the 1½-mile **Plage des Salines,** near Ste-Anne, with palm trees and a long stretch of white sand, and the 2½-mile **Diamant,** with the landmark Diamond Rock off-shore. Due to rough seas, swimming on the Atlantic coast is for experts only, except at **Cap Chevalier** and **Presqu'ile de la Caravelle Nature Preserve.**

The clean white-sand beaches of **Pointe du Bout,** site of Martinique's major hotels, were created by developers. The white-sand beaches to the south at Anse Mitan have always been here, however, drawing many snorkelers.

Whereas nudist beaches are not officially sanctioned, topless sunbathing is widely practiced at the big hotels, often around their swimming pools. Public beaches rarely have changing cabins or showers. Resorts charge non-guests to use changing and beach facilities, and request a deposit for towel rentals.

GOLF, HIKING, RIDING, DIVING, SNORKELING & TENNIS

GOLF   Robert Trent Jones designed the 18-hole Golf de l'Impératrice-Joséphine at Trois-Ilets (☎ **0596-68-32-81**), a five-minute, 1-mile taxi ride from Pointe du Bout and about 18 miles from Fort-de-France. Greens fees are Fr 270 ($54) per person for 18 holes.

HIKING   Inexpensive guided excursions are organized year-round by the personnel of the **Parc Naturel Régional de la Martinique,** Excollège Agricole de Tivoli (☎ **0596-64-42-59**). Special trips can be arranged for small groups by contacting them two to three days before your cruise ship arrives.

The **Presqu'ile de la Caravelle Nature Preserve,** a well-protected peninsula, has safe beaches and well-marked trails to the ruins of historic Château Debuc and through tropical wetlands. Sometimes the park organizes serious hiking excursions up Montagne Pelée, into the Gorges de la Falaise, or through the thick coastal rain forest between Grand' Rivière and Le Prêcheur.

HORSEBACK RIDING The premier riding facility is **Ranch Jack,** Morne Habitué, Trois-Ilets (☎ 0596-68-37-69), which offers morning horseback rides at 340 ($68) per person for a 3¹/₂- to 4-hour ride. Call for transportation arrangements to and from the cruise dock.

SCUBA DIVING & SNORKELING Scuba divers come here to explore the Diamond Rock caves and walls and the ships sunk by the 1902 volcanic eruption. Snorkeling equipment is available at dive centers.

Across the bay from Fort-de-France, in the Hotel Méridien, the major scuba center of **Bathy's Club** (☎ 0596-66-00-00) is the best for Pointe du Bout. Depending on demand, daily dive trips leave from the Méridien Hotel's pier. Prices include equipment rental, transportation, guide, and drinks on board. Dives are conducted twice daily, from 8am to noon and 2 to 6pm. Cruise-ship passengers should opt for the morning dives. Dives cost Fr 290 ($58) per person.

TENNIS The large resorts at Pointe du Bout have courts and charge non-guests Fr 50 ($10) per hour. The best are at **Bathy's Club** at the Hotel Méridien (☎ 0596-66-00-00) and the **Golf de l'Impératrice-Joséphine** at Trois-Ilets (☎ 0596-68-32-81).

WATERSKIING & WINDSURFING Water-skiing can be arranged at little kiosks on every beach near the large hotels. Windsurfing equipment and lessons are available at all resort water sports facilities, especially the **Hotel Méridien,**

Pointe du Bout (☎ 0596-66-00-00), where 30-minute lessons cost Fr 60 to Fr 100 ($12 to $20). Board rentals are Fr 100 ($20) per hour.

DINING

In Fort-de-France, **Abri-Cotier,** Pointe-Simon (☎ 0596-63-66-46), is little more than a wood-sided hut with a wide covered veranda. The Creole menu includes a fricassee of shrimp, chicken with curry, rack of lamb, *boudin Creole,* and a brochette of seafood. Flavors are zesty.

Two minutes by taxi north from La Savane will bring you to ✪ **Le Coq Hardi,** 52 Rue Martin-Luther-King, (☎ 0596-71-59-64), the island's premier steakhouse. Juicy steaks and chops are imported from France and grilled over a wood fire. Hearty eaters will appreciate the large portions.

The best restaurants are not in the center of Fort-de-France, but in the suburbs. **La Fontane,** Kilometer 4, Route de Balata (N3) (☎ 0596-64-28-70), is perched high in the hills above the town. Amidst a settling of dowdy antiques you can enjoy such tasty luncheon fare as au gratin of crayfish, a Caribbean version of bouillabaisse, or, perhaps better on a hot day, *bambou de la Fontane,* a flavorful salad with fresh fish, crayfish, tomato, and corn. A 2¹/₂-mile taxi ride north from the cruise ship docks will deliver you here. You should call ahead for a table.

POINTE DU BOUT

Located near the entrance of Pointe du Bout, **Le Poisson d'Or,** L'Anse Mitan (☎ 0596-66-01-80), is easy to find. This inexpensive seafood establishment offers grilled fish, conch, or seafood, scallops sautéed in white wine, poached local fish, and flan—ordinary dishes, yet prepared with flair and served with style. Nearby is **Villa Creole,** L'Anse Mitan (☎ 0596-66-05-53), located in a simple Creole house with a small garden, and lying only a three-minute ride from the big resort hotels of Pointe du Bout. Both set menus and à la carte dishes are served. Here's a chance to sample some real "down-home" Creole fare: accras de morue (beignets of codfish), a local pâté concocted from fresh avocados and pulverized codfish, and red snapper, grilled or in a zesty tomato sauce.

THE NORTH COAST: TWO "MAMA" CHEFS

Like Guadeloupe, Martinique is famous for its female Creole chefs. If you rent a car or take a taxi tour, stop by two of the best Martinique "mamas" on the north coast.

Many visitors prefer to dine at ✪ **Chez Mally Edjam,** Route de la Côte Atlantique at Basse-Pointe, 36 miles north of Fort-de-France (☎ **0596-78-51-18**), instead of at the Leyritz Plantation (see above). Here, grandmotherly Mally Edjam, a local legend, turns out Creole delicacies such as stuffed land crab with a hot seasoning, conch in a tart shell, and a classic *colombo de porc* (the Creole version of pork curry). Equally acclaimed are her lobster vinaigrette and papaya soufflé, which must be ordered in advance.

Directly west of Basse-Pointe, beside the main highway, in a low-slung building painted the peachy-orange of a papaya, **Yva Chez Vava,** Boulevard de Gaulle (☎ **0596-55-72-72**), is a combination private home and restaurant, suffused with a simple country-inn style. Local family recipes are the mainstay here, where à la carte menu items include Creole soup, lobster, sea urchins poached in fish stock, and various *colombos* (curries). Local delicacies include *z'habitants* (crayfish), *vivaneua* (red snapper), *tazard* (kingfish), and *accras de morue* (cod fritters). Reservations are recommended. You can dine all afternoon—that is, until 6pm, at which time you probably should be back on board your ship.

14 Nassau ⚓ ⚓ ⚓ ⚓

Nassau is the capital of The Bahamas, and it has that nation's best shopping, best entertainment, and best beaches. It's big. It's

bold. It's one of the busiest cruise ship ports in the world. It's got the old, it's got the new, there's probably something borrowed here, and there's a whole heckuva lot of blue seas. One million visitors a year make their way onto its shores to enjoy its bounty.

With its adjoining Cable Beach and Paradise Island (linked by bridge to the city), Nassau has luxury resorts set on powdery-soft beaches; all the water sports, golf, and tennis you could want; and so much duty-free shopping that its stores outdraw its museums. Yet historic Nassau hasn't lost its British colonial charm—it just boasts up-to-date tourist facilities to complement them.

Many people come on three- to four-day cruises leaving from Miami, Fort Lauderdale, and Port Canaveral. In recent years, the government has spent millions of dollars increasing its facilities so now 11 cruise ships can pull into dock at one time.

COMING ASHORE

Cruise ships dock near Rawson Square, the very center of the city and its main shopping area. The Straw Market is nearby at Market Plaza. Bay Street, the main shopping artery, is also close at hand, and the Nassau International Bazaar is at the intersection of Woodes Rogers Walk and Charlotte Street.

FAST FACTS

Currency   The legal tender is the Bahamian dollar (B$1), which has a value on par with the U.S. dollar. Both U.S. and Bahamian dollars are accepted on an equal basis throughout The Bahamas. Most large hotels and stores accept traveler's checks.

Information   Stop by the Information Desk at the **Ministry of Tourism,** Bay Street (☎ 242/356-7591). It's open Monday through Friday from 9am to 5:30pm. A smaller information booth is also found at Rawson Square near the dock.

Language   The language of The Bahamas is English.

SHORE EXCURSIONS

Shore excursions in Nassau aren't really necessary, as you can easily get around on your own.

For the best sightseeing value, take one of three separate **guided tours** offered by the Ministry of Tourism, which cost only $2 per person. Tours feature a wide variety of attractions, including the Adastra Gardens, Fort Charlotte, and Fort Fincastle. Each tour lasts approximately 1¹/₂ hours. Call ☎ **242/326-9772** or 242/356-7591 for more information, or else stop by the tourist office on Bay Street.

Many cruise passengers opt to visit **Coral Islands Bahamas,** the country's most popular attraction, but you can go here on your own. This three-hour tour costs $25 and includes a scenic boat ride to the marine park.

On **Seaworld Explorer Glass-Bottom Boat Tour** (☎ **242/356-2548**), which lasts about 1¹/₂ hours and costs $30, you sit in air-conditioned comfort aboard a glass-bottom boat viewing the colorful marine world off New Providence Island.

GETTING AROUND

Unless you rent a horse and carriage, the only way to see Old Nassau is on foot. All the major attractions and the principal stores are within walking distance. You can even walk to Cable Beach or Paradise Island.

The least expensive means of transport is by the medium-size buses called jitneys. The fare is 75¢; exact change is required.

Taxis are practical, at least for longer island trips, and are required to have working meters, so you probably won't be cheated. The official fare is $2 at flag fall and 30¢ for each quarter mile for the first two passengers; additional passengers pay $2. Five-passenger cabs can be hired for $23 to $25 per hour. For a radio taxi, call ☎ **242/323-5111.**

Ferries run from the end of Casuarina Drive on Paradise Island across the harbor to Rawson Square for $2 per person. These "water taxis" operate during the day at 20-minute intervals between Paradise Island and Prince George Wharf. The one-way fare is $2 per person.

The elegant, traditional way to see Nassau is in a horse-drawn surrey, the kind with the fringe on top. Negotiate with the driver and agree on the price before you get in. The average charge for a tour is $5 per person. The maximum load is three adults plus one or two children under the age of 12. The surreys are available daily from 9am to 4:30pm, except when horses are rested—usually from 1 to 3pm from May through October, and from 1 to 2pm from November through April. You'll find the surreys at Rawson Square, off Bay Street.

Motor scooters have become a favorite mode of transportation. For a rental, contact **Ursa Investment,** Prince George Wharf (☎ **242/326-8329**). Mopeds cost $16 per hour or $26 for two hours, $36 for a half day, $46 for a full day, plus $4 for insurance. A $10 deposit is required.

If you want to rent a car, try **Avis** (☎ **800/331-1084** or 242/326-6380), which has a branch at the cruise-ship docks; **Budget** (☎ **800/472-3325** or 242/377-7405); or **Hertz** (☎ **800/654-3001** or 242/393-0871). Good local companies include **Teglo Rent-a-Car** (☎ **242/362-4361**), and **McCartney Rent-a-Car** (☎ **242/328-0486**). Remember to *drive on the left,* British-style.

SEEING THE SIGHTS

It's best to explore historic Nassau on foot. Begin your stroll at **Rawson Square,** home of the Straw Market stalls. We also enjoy the native market on the waterfront, a short walk through the Straw Market. This is where Bahamian fishers unload fish and produce—crates of mangoes, oranges, tomatoes, and limes, plus crimson-lipped conch.

Nassau

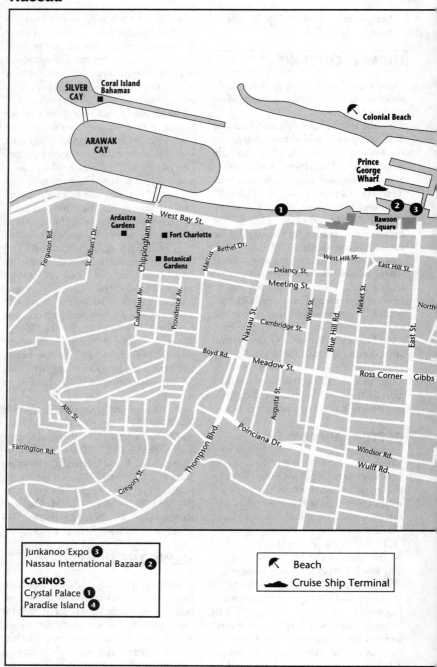

SILVER CAY

Coral Island Bahamas

Colonial Beach

ARAWAK CAY

Prince George Wharf

Ardastra Gardens

Chipplingham Rd.

West Bay St.

Rawson Square

Fort Charlotte

Bethel Dr.

West Hill St.

East Hill St.

Botanical Gardens

Marcus

Ferguson Rd.

St. Alban's Dr.

Delancy St.

Meeting St.

Columbus Av.

Providence Av.

West St.

Blue Hill Rd.

Market St.

East St.

North

Nassau St.

Cambridge St.

Boyd Rd.

Meadow St.

Ross Corner

Gibbs

Alto St.

Augusta St.

Farrington Rd.

Poinciana Dr.

Thompson Blvd.

Windsor Rd.

Gregory St.

Wulff Rd.

Junkanoo Expo ③
Nassau International Bazaar ②

CASINOS
Crystal Palace ①
Paradise Island ④

↖ Beach

⛴ Cruise Ship Terminal

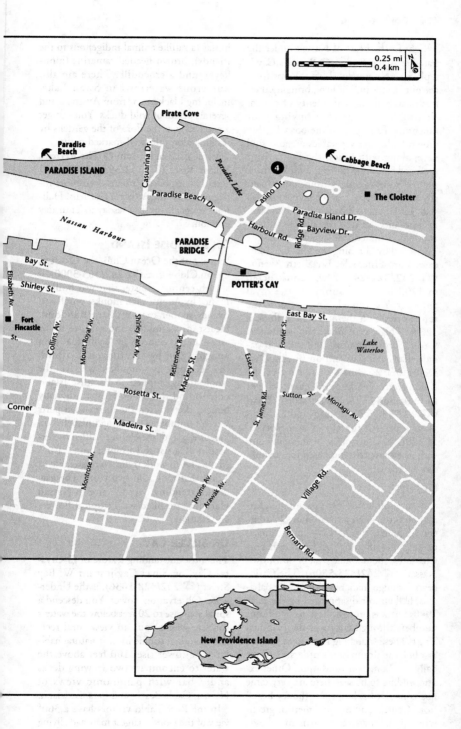

0.25 mi
0.4 km

Pirate Cove

Paradise
Beach

PARADISE ISLAND

Casuarina Dr.

Paradise Lake

Cabbage Beach

The Cloister

Casino Dr.

Paradise Beach Dr.

Paradise Island Dr.

Ridge Rd.

Bayview Dr.

Nassau Harbour

Harbour Rd.

PARADISE
BRIDGE

POTTER'S CAY

Bay St.

Shirley St.

Elizabeth Av.

Fort
Fincastle

St.

Collins Av.

Mount Royal Av.

Shirley Park Av.

Retirement Rd.

Mackey St.

East Bay St.

Fowler St.

Lake
Waterloo

Essex St.

Sutton St.

Montagu Av.

Rosetta St.

Corner

St. James Rd.

Madeira St.

Montrose Av.

Jerome Av.

Arawak Av.

Village Rd.

Bernard Rd.

New Providence Island

Right in the heart of Nassau under the Paradise Island Bridge, ✪ **Potter's Cay** is a place to observe local life. Sloops from the out islands pull in here, bringing their fresh catch along with plenty of conch. You might see the chef buying your lunchtime fish right off the boat. Freshly grown herbs and vegetables are also sold here, along with limes, the Bahamians' preferred seasoning for fish. Tropical fruits such as papaw (papaya), pineapple (usually from Eleuthera), and bananas are also sold. Little stalls sell conch raw, marinated in lime juice, as spicy deep-fried fritters, and in conch salad and conch soup.

Reached by climbing the Queen's Staircase, **Fort Fincastle,** Elizabeth Avenue (☎ 242/322-2442), was constructed in 1793 by Lord Dunmore, the royal governor. You can take an elevator to the top and walk on the observation floor, a 126-foot-high water tower and lighthouse.

You'll probably miss the Junkanoo parade that begins at 2am on Boxing Day, December 26, but you can relive the Bahamian Junkanoo carnival at ✪ **Junkanoo Expo,** Prince George Wharf (☎ 242/356-2731), in the old Customs warehouse. All the glitter and glory of Mardi Gras comes alive in this museum, with its fantasy costumes used for the holiday bacchanal.

GARDENS

A flock of pink flamingos parading in formation is the main attraction in ✪ **Ardastra Gardens,** five acres of lush tropical gardens on Chippingham Road near Fort Charlotte, about a mile west of downtown Nassau (☎ 242/323-5806). The Caribbean flamingo, national bird of The Bahamas, had almost disappeared by the early 1940s but was brought back to significant numbers through efforts of the National Trust. These Marching Flamingos, trained to obey the drillmaster's orders, perform daily at 11am, 2pm, and 4pm. Other exotic wildlife to be seen here are very tame boa constrictors, kinkajous (honey bears) from Central and South America, green-winged macaws, capuchin monkeys,

hutias (a ratlike animal indigenous to the islands), brown-headed tamarins (monkeys), and a crocodile. There are also numerous waterfowl in Swan Lake, including black swans from Australia and several species of wild ducks. You can get a good look at the flora of the gardens by walking along the well-marked paths.

A true oasis in Nassau, ✪ **The Retreat,** Village Road (☎ 242/393-1317), is 11 acres of unspoiled gardens even more intriguing than the Ardastra Gardens. Half-hour tours are given Tuesday to Thursday at noon.

ON PARADISE ISLAND

In front of the Ocean Club, the **Cloister,** Ocean Club Drive (☎ 242/363-3000), is a 14th-century cloister that was built in France by Augustinian monks; purchased by newspaper czar William Randolph Hearst, disassembled, and shipped to his estate at San Simeon in California; then bought again by Huntington Hartford, the A&P grocery stores heir, who had the whole thing shipped to Paradise Island only to find that when Hearst originally bought the cloister, the dismantled parts weren't numbered. Arriving unlabeled on Paradise Island, the cloister baffled the experts until artist and sculptor Jean Castre-Manne set to work trying to reassemble it, a task that took him two years. The gardens, extending over the rise to Nassau Harbour, are filled with tropical flowers and statuary.

ON SILVER CAY

The most outstanding feature of ✪ **Crystal Cay,** on Silver Cay just off W. Bay Street (☎ 242/328-1036), is the Underwater Observation Tower. You descend a spiral staircase to 20 feet below the water's surface, where you can view coral reefs and abundant sea life in their natural habitat. The tower rises 100 feet above the water to encompass two viewing decks and a bar with panoramic views of Nassau, Cable Beach, and Paradise Island.

In the Reef Tank, visitors have a 360° view of the world's largest manmade living reef. Graceful stingrays, endangered sea turtles, and sharks swim in the Shark Tank, which has an overhead viewing deck and a "below-ground" viewing area. It's easy to spend hours in the Marine Gardens Aquarium, a complex of 24 individual saltwater aquariums. Nature trails with lush tropical foliage, waterfalls, exotic trees, and wildlife further enhance this setting. Visitors can get to this marine park via a scenic 10-minute ferry ride from the Prince George Dock.

SUBMARINE SIGHTSEEING

For a fish-eye view of New Providence, take a tour in the air-conditioned *Atlantis* **submarine,** Lyford Cay (☎ 242/327-3740), which offers about seven trips per day, starting at 7:30am. The 2½-hour trip costs $74 for adults, $37 for children. The 7:30am special runs at $59 per adult, $29.50 for children. When you reserve, you can also arrange to have the company van meet you at the cruise dock to take you the 18 miles to Lyford Cay.

GAMBLING THE DAY AWAY

On Cable Beach, the dazzling **Crystal Palace Casino,** W. Bay Street (☎ 242/327-6200), is run by Nassau Marriott Resort. The gaming room features 750 slot machines, along with 51 blackjack tables, 7 craps tables, 9 roulette wheels, a baccarat table, and one big six. An oval-shaped casino bar extends onto the gambling floor; the Casino Lounge, with its bar and bandstand, overlooks the gaming floor.

The ✪ **Paradise Island Casino,** in the Atlantis Resort, Casino Drive, on Paradise Island (☎ 242/363-3000), is a superior casino. For sheer gloss, glitter, and show-biz extravagance, this mammoth 30,000-square-foot casino is the place to go. No visit to The Bahamas would be complete without a promenade through the Bird Cage Walk, an assortment of restaurants, bars, and cabaret facilities. Some 1,000 whirring and clanging slot machines operate 24 hours a day, and there are 60 blackjack tables, 10 roulette wheels, and 12 tables for craps, 3 for baccarat, and 1 for big six.

SHOPPING

In 1992, The Bahamas abolished import duties on 11 categories of luxury goods, including china, crystal, fine linens, jewelry, leather goods, photographic equipment, watches, fragrances, and other merchandise. But before you make a big purchase, check the price. Sometimes you'll find 30% to 50% reductions off stateside prices, but other times you'd do better shopping your hometown discount outlet store.

The principal shopping area is a stretch of **Bay Street,** the main drag, and its arteries. When looking for individual establishments, look for the store signs instead of street numbers.

The **Nassau International Bazaar** consists of some 30 shops in a new arcade, which runs from Bay Street down to the waterfront near the Prince George Wharf.

Prince George Plaza, Bay Street (☎ 242/322-5854), can be crowded with cruise-ship passengers. Many fine shops here sell Gucci and other quality merchandise.

At the **Straw Market,** in Straw Market Plaza on Bay Street, you can watch Bahamian craftspeople weave and pleat straw hats, handbags, dolls, place mats, and other items, including straw shopping bags for you to carry your purchases in. You can order special articles, perhaps bearing your initials, and have fun bargaining to get the stated price reduced.

Bahamas Plait Market, Wulff Road (☎ 242/326-4192), is another good outlet for Bahamian-made products and is far superior to the Straw Market. It's a taxi ride from the cruise docks. You'll find more handmade straw items at **The Plait Lady,** in the Regarno Building, Victoria and Bay streets, across from the Royal Bank (☎ 242/356-5584).

You can get your hair braided in the local style at the government-sponsored

Hairbraider's Centre, an open-air pavilion at Prince George Dock.

Balmain Antiques, a second-floor shop in the Masonic Building on Mason's Boulevard, two doors east of Charlotte Street (☎ 242/323-7421), offers 19th-century etchings, engravings, and maps at reasonable prices. At the corner of Queen and Marlborough streets, **Marlborough Antiques** (☎ 242/328-0502) also sells antique books and maps, engravings, sterling and plate English silver, and unusual table settings. Check out the antique photographs of the Old Bahamas.

Charlotte's Gallery, Charlotte Street (☎ 242/322-6310), only sells Bahamian-produced art. **The Green Lizard,** W. Bay Street (☎ 242/326-4189), specializes in Haitian art but also offers some Bahamian handcrafts, such as handmade wood chimes and hammocks. **Kennedy Gallery,** Parliament Street (☎ 242/325-7832), sells artwork by well-known Bahamian artists, along with pottery and sculpture.

With two branches on Charlotte Street, between Bay and Shirley streets, the **Brass and Leather Shop** (☎ 242/322-3806) offers English brass, handbags, luggage, briefcases, attachés, and personal accessories. You can find some good buys here. There's also a **Fendi,** at Charlotte and Bay streets (☎ 242/322-6300), and a **Gucci,** at Saffrey Square (☎ 242/325-0561).

At **Pipe of Peace,** Bay Street, between Charlotte and Parliament streets (☎ 242/325-2022), you can choose from an amazing collection of Cuban and Jamaican cigars, as well as handcrafts, chocolates, pecans, and name-brand watches.

Tick-Tock, across from the Straw Market (☎ 242/325-7136), offers wooden clocks handcrafted in Germany's Black Forest region, plus Bahamian stamps and coin watches. You also find beautiful Bahamian stamps at **The Bahamas Post Office Philatelic Bureau,** in the General Post Office, at the top of Parliament Street on E. Hill Street (☎ 242/322-3344).

Coin of the Realm, Charlotte Street (☎ 242/322-4497), sells mint and used Bahamian and British postage stamps, Bahamian silver and gold coins, and old and modern paper currency of The Bahamas.

Barry's Limited, Bay and George streets (☎ 242/322-3118), is one of Nassau's more formal and elegant clothing stores. Most of the clothes are for men. **Bonneville Bones,** on the corner of Bay and George streets (☎ 242/328-0804), fronts the best men's store we've found in Nassau. You can find everything here, from the usual T-shirts and designer jeans to elegantly casual clothing and suits.

Cole's of Nassau, Parliament Street (☎ 242/322-8393), offers the most extensive selection of designer fashions for women. For reasonably priced swimwear, stop by **The Girls from Brazil** (☎ 242/323-5966). On the upper floor you'll find casual clothing, plus craft and gift items from Central America. There's a branch on the lower floor of an outlet at Charlotte and Bay streets.

Mademoiselle, Ltd., at Frederick and Bay streets (☎ 242/322-5130), specializes in resort wear, including batik garments. Swimwear, sarongs, jeans, and halter tops are the rage here.

Greenfire Emeralds, on Bay Street (☎ 242/322-2841), is the emerald specialist of Nassau. Exotic gemstones include tanzanite, rhodolite, atatite, and tourmaline. You can also pick up some discounted designer leather bags, Swiss watches, Lalique crystal, and pre-Columbian jewelry.

John Bull, Bay Street near Charlotte Street (☎ 242/322-4253), offers classic selections from Tiffany and Co., cultured pearls from Mikimoto, Greek and Roman coin jewelry, and Spanish gold and silver pieces. The store also features cameras, perfumes, cosmetics, leather goods, and accessories. It's *the* place to buy a Gucci or Cartier watch.

There's a branch of **Little Switzerland** on Bay Street (☎ 242/322-1493), where you can buy top-brand jewelry, watches, china, perfume, crystal, and leather.

The Linen Shop, in the Ironmongery Building, Bay Street (☎ **242/322-4266**), is the best outlet for linens, such as beautifully embroidered bed linens, Irish handkerchiefs, hand-embroidered women's blouses, tablecloths, exquisite children's clothing, and christening gowns.

Cody's Music and Video Center, on the corner of Armstrong and East Bay streets (☎ **242/325-8834**), is the finest record store in The Bahamas, specializing in the contemporary music of The Bahamas and the Caribbean.

The largest cosmetic shop in The Bahamas, **The Beauty Spot,** Bay and Frederick streets (☎ **242/322-5930**), sells duty-free cosmetics. **The Perfume Bar** (☎ **242/322-3785**) has exclusive rights to market Boucheron and Sublime and also stocks the Clarins line. **Lightbourn's,** at Bay and George streets (☎ **242/322-2095**), also carries duty-free fragrances and cosmetics.

If you've fallen under the Junkanoo spell and want to take home some steel drums, go to **Pyfroms,** Bay Street (☎ **242/322-2603**).

BEACHES

Cable Beach, which runs for some 4 miles, is one of the Caribbean's best-equipped beaches, with all sorts of water sports as well as easy access to shops, casino action, bars, and restaurants. You'll need to hunt until you find a spot on the strip that's suitable for you. Waters can alternate between rough and reefy and calm and clear.

Cable Beach is far superior to the meager beach in town, the **Western Esplanade,** which sweeps westward from the British Colonial hotel. This local beach has restrooms, changing facilities, and a snack bar.

Even Cable Beach buffs like **Paradise Beach** on Paradise Island. It's convenient to Nassau—just walk or drive across the bridge or take a boat from the Prince George Wharf. There's a $3 entrance fee for adults, $1 for children, which

entitles you to use of a shower and locker. An extra $10 deposit is required for towels.

Paradise Island has a number of smaller beaches, including **Pirate's Cove Beach** and **Cabbage Beach,** both on the north shore. Bordered by casuarinas, palms, and sea grapes, Cabbage Beach's broad sands stretch for at least 2 miles. It's likely to be crowded with guests of the island's megaresorts. Escapists find something approaching solitude on the northwestern end, accessible only by boat or foot.

GOLF, RIDING, SAILING, TENNIS & WATER SPORTS

GOLF **South Ocean Golf Course,** S.W. Bay Road (☎ **242/362-4391**), is the best course on New Providence Island and one of the best in The Bahamas. (It's a 30-minute drive from Nassau on the southwest edge of the island.) Overlooking the ocean, this 18-hole 6,706-yard, par-72 beauty has some first-rate holes. Greens fees are $45, plus $25 for a golf cart. Call ahead to make sure there's not a golf tournament scheduled for when you want to play.

Cable Beach Golf Course, on W. Bay Street (☎ **242/327-6000**), is a spectacular 18-hole, 7,040-yard, par-72 championship golf course. It's not as challenging as South Ocean, though. Greens fees are $65, and carts can be rented for $60.

Paradise Island Golf Club, operated by the Atlantis Resort (☎ **242/393-3625**), is a superb 18-hole championship course at the east end of Paradise Island. Greens fees are $86 for 18 holes and include use of a shared cart. You'll shoot your ball through such obstacles as a waterpipe, a lion's den, and the twirling blades of a small windmill.

HORSEBACK RIDING On the southwest shore, **Happy Trails Stables,** Coral Harbour (☎ **242/362-1820**), offers a one-hour, 20-minute horseback trail ride for $50 per person. Reservations are required.

SAILING A number of operators feature cruises from the harbors around New Providence Island. **Flying Cloud,** at the Paradise Island West Dock (☎ **242/363-2208**), offers cruises on a 57-foot catamaran that holds up to 55 people. A half-day charter costs $35 per person and includes snorkeling equipment, instructions, and transportation to and from the boat. Sailings depart Monday through Saturday at 9:30am and 2pm.

Majestic Tours Ltd., at Prince George's Dock (☎ **242/322-2606**), has three-hour cruises on two of the biggest catamarans in the Atlantic. They're the most professionally run of the local cruise boats. *Yellow Bird* is suitable for up to 250 passengers, and *Tropic Bird* carries up to 170. The cruises include a one-hour stop on a relatively isolated portion of Paradise Island's Cabbage Beach. The cost is $15 per adult, with children under 12 paying $7.50 on either cruise. Departures are Tuesday, Wednesday, Friday, and Saturday at 1:15pm.

Nassau Cruises Ltd., at the Paradise Island Bridge (☎ **242/363-3577**), maintains a trio of three-deck motorized yachts, all named *Calypso,* which are the most luxurious cruises offered. Their trip to uninhabited Blue Lagoon Island is reason enough to sail with them. Trips depart several days a week. The six-hour day sails, from 10am to 4pm, require advance reservations; they include a buffet lunch and cost $45 per person.

SCUBA DIVING & SNORKELING

Dive operators here cater to snorkelers as well as scuba enthusiasts. **Bahama Divers,** E. Bay Street (☎ **242/393-5644**), offers a half day of snorkeling to offshore reefs for $20 per person and a half-day scuba trip with preliminary pool instruction for beginners at $60. Half-day excursions for certified divers to offshore coral reefs with a depth of 25 feet cost $35, whereas half-day excursions to deeper outlying reefs go for $60. Reservations are required.

Stuart Cove's Dive South Ocean, S.W. Bay Street (☎ **800/879-9832** in the U.S., or 242/362-4171), is about 10 minutes from top dive sites, including the Porpoise Pen Reefs. An introductory scuba program costs $85, with morning two-tank dives priced at $70. Escorted boat snorkeling trips cost $30. A special feature is a series of shark-dive experiences priced at $115. Caribbean reef sharks swim among the guests while the dive master feeds them.

Sea and Ski Ocean Sports, at the Radisson Grand Resort on Paradise Island (☎ **242/363-2011**), offers scuba diving and snorkeling. A one-tank dive, all equipment included, costs $35; a two-tank dive goes for $60. Snorkeling reef trips depart daily at 10am and 2pm and cost $30 with all equipment included.

One way to stay under water without holding your breath is with **Hartley's Undersea Walk,** E. Bay Street (☎ **242/393-8234**), which takes you on a 3½-hour cruise aboard the yacht *Pied Piper.* At one point you (in a group of six) don a breathing helmet and spend about 20 minutes walking along the ocean bottom through a garden of tropical fish, sponges, and other undersea life. Entire families can make this walk, which costs $45 per person. You don't even have to be able to swim. Trips are operated Tuesday to Saturday at 9:30am and 1:30pm. Arrive 30 minutes before departures.

TENNIS Cruise passengers can pay to play at some resorts' courts. The **Radisson Cable Beach Hotel,** W. Bay Street (☎ **242/327-6000**), has 18 courts. Nonguests pay $10 per hour. Other hotels offering tennis courts include **Forte Nassau Beach Hotel,** W. Bay Street, Cable Beach (☎ **242/327-7711**), with six Flexipave lighted courts, and **British Colonial Beach Resort,** 1 Bay St., Nassau (☎ **242/322-3301**), with three hard-surface lighted courts.

Hotels with courts on Paradise Island are **Atlantis** (☎ **242/363-3000**), with nine hard-surface courts; **Pirate's Cove Holiday Inn SunSpree Resort** (☎ **242/326-2101**), with four lighted asphalt courts; and the **Radisson Grand Resort** (☎ **242/363-2011**), with four lighted Har-Tru courts. The **Ocean Club,** Ocean Club Drive (☎ **242/363-3000**), has nine lighted Har-Tru courts.

WATER SPORTS Your best bet is **Sea Sports,** at the Nassau Marriott Resort and Crystal Palace Casino on W. Bay Street (☎ **242/327-6200**). You can rent Hobie cats, Sunfish, Windsurfers, or even a kayak. Prices range from $5 for 30 minutes in a kayak up to $40 for an hour's use of a Hobie Cat. Parasailing costs $40 for five to six minutes. Water-skiing goes for $70 for one hour. A snorkel trip, including gear, costs $25. Many additional activities, such as scuba diving or deep-sea fishing, can also be arranged here.

Sea and Ski Ocean Sports, at the Radisson Grand Resort on Casino Dr. (☎ **242/363-2011**), is the best on Paradise Island. In addition to scuba diving and snorkeling trips, it offers parasailing for $40 to $45, depending on the ride. Windsurfers rent for $20 an hour. Sailors can rent a Sunfish for $20 per hour or a Hobie Cat for $35 per hour.

DINING

You'll get all the conch you can possibly eat on **Arawak Cay,** a small artificial island right in the heart of Nassau, across West Bay Street. The cay was created by the Bahamian government to store large tanks of water, of which New Providence Island often runs out. You don't go here to see the water tanks, however, but to join the locals in sampling their favorite food. The mollusk is cracked before your eyes, and you're given some hot sauce to spice it up. The locals wash it down with their favorite drink: coconut milk laced with gin.

NASSAU

Next to Trinity Church, ✪ **Bahamian Kitchen,** Trinity Place, off Market Street (☎ **242/325-0702**), is the best place in Nassau for good, down-home Bahamian

cookery at modest prices. Specialties include lobster Bahamian style, fried red snapper, conch salad, stewed fish, curried chicken, okra soup, and pea soup and dumplings. Most dishes are served with peas 'n' rice.

Families might want a more down-home eatery like the **Caribe Café,** in the British Colonial Beach Resort, 1 Bay St. (☎ **242/322-3301**). Burgers and grouper sandwiches are the restaurant's main fare. Also served are New York strip steaks, salads, and soups. It's close to the docks, so it will be crowded when a lot of ships are in port.

Reservations are required at ✪ **Graycliff,** W. Hill Street (☎ **242/322-2796**), the only restaurant in The Bahamas deserving of a five-star rating. The remarkable chef uses local Bahamian products and delicacies whenever available and fashions them into spicy and hearty dishes. He takes plump, juicy pheasant and cooks it with pineapple grown on Eleuthera in an award-winning combination. Lobster is his specialty. The Grand Mariner soufflé is worth the trip across town.

We don't want to oversell **Green Shutters Restaurant,** 48 Parliament St. (☎ **242/325-5702**), which is like a transplanted English pub in the tropics. Pub grub favorites are served, as well as Bahamian specialties. Sandwiches at lunch are particularly good and well stuffed.

Poop Deck, Nassau Yacht Haven Marina, E. Bay Street (☎ **242/393-8175**), is a favorite with the yachties and others who find a perch on the second-floor, open-air terrace overlooking the harbor and Paradise Island. At lunch, you can order perfectly seasoned conch chowder or juicy beef burgers. Native grouper fingers served with peas 'n' rice is the Bahamian "soul food" dish. Two tantalizing seafood selections are the broiled crayfish and stuffed deviled crab.

CABLE BEACH

Café Johnny Canoe is set on the less desirable side of the Forte Nassau Beach

Hotel facing W. Bay Street (☎ 242/
327-3373). The menu features those
dishes everybody seems to like: burgers, all
kinds of steaks, seafood, and fried chicken.
The best items on the menu are blackened
grouper and barbecued fish. The outdoor
terrace is often mobbed by college
students.

Adjacent to Forte Nassau Beach Hotel,
the **Rock and Roll Café** (☎ 242/
327-7639) is a Hard Rock Café clone,
celebrating the combination of tropical
weather, loud rock-and-roll music, and all
the paraphernalia that goes with it. You
can dine indoors or out. The menu includes barbecued pork, ribs, stuffed potato
skins, and sandwiches. This is an amusing
place where the cuisine is secondary to
the fun.

PARADISE ISLAND

If you want a break from the gaming
tables, you have only to walk to the far
end of the Paradise Island Casino to find
the coffee shop **Café Casino** (☎ 242/
363-3000). Its menu includes pizza and
well-stuffed sandwiches—corned beef,
pastrami, and Reubens—plus salads. The
cafe also serves full-course meals, but
after sampling one, we decided to stick to
the sandwiches. Go here only for the
convenience.

Located near the beach of the Atlantis,
the most lavish hotel and casino complex
on Paradise Island, **The Cave** (☎ 242/
363-3000) is little more than a burger-
and-salad joint. To reach it, you'll pass
through a simulated rock-sided tunnel illuminated with flaming torches into an
open-air setting with a beach view. The
ice cream is suitably creamy for
midafternoon cool-offs.

In the Atlantis, **Seagrapes Restaurant**
(☎ 242/363-3000) serves buffet
lunches and dinners. This mass-market
eatery caters mainly to families. You can
make a full meal out of the unlimited
salad bar. Don't come here expecting to
find the best food on Paradise Island;
rather, come here to fill up cheaply on
good eats.

15 St. Barthélemy

This little French pocket of posh is a plati-
num Caribbean address. St. Barthélemy
(St. Barts) is sophisticated, chic, and so
very Parisian (yet with a touch of
Normandy). Forget such things as historical sights or ambitious water sports
programs here, and come instead for
white-sand beaches, haute French cuisine,
and relaxation in ultimate comfort.

The island's capital and only town is
Gustavia, named after a Swedish king. Set
in a sheltered harbor, it looks like a little
dollhouse-scale port. About 3,500 people
live on only 8 square miles of island.

COMING ASHORE

The smaller cruise ships anchor right off
Gustavia, and passengers are ferried by
tenders to the center of town. Cruise ships
usually have shaded refreshment stands
ashore for their passengers. It's just a short
walk to the heart of Gustavia's restaurant
and shopping district.

FAST FACTS

Currency   The official monetary
unit is the **French franc (Fr),** but
most stores and restaurants prefer
payment in U.S. dollars. Currently
the exchange rate is Fr 4.98 to U.S.$1
(1 Fr = 20¢ U.S.), but this quotation
should be updated or verified at the
time of your actual visit.

Information   Go to the **Office du
Tourisme** in the Town Hall, quai
du Général-de-Gaulle, in Gustavia
(☎ 0590-27-87-27). Open Monday
through Friday 9am to 5pm.

Language   The official language is
French, but nearly everyone speaks
English as well.

SHORE EXCURSIONS

Many passengers prefer to spend their
time ashore walking around and exploring

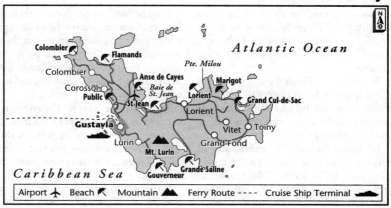

Airport ✈ Beach 🏖 Mountain 🏔 Ferry Route - - - - Cruise Ship Terminal ⛴

Gustavia, which should take no more than two hours. Most cruise ships offer a standard island tour, which takes 1¼ hours and costs about $25. The minibus goes through the center of the port past the village of St-Jean to an overlook in Salinos. On the island's windward side, Grand Fond, you'll notice the different architecture, built to withstand the heavy trade winds. Via the villages of Petit Cul-de-Sac and Toiny, you'll stop at Grand Cul-de-Sac for a view of the lagoon, then have a brief stop at La Savone. You'll be brought back to the ship via Corossol, a tiny fishing village where the locals make straw from lantana palms.

GETTING AROUND

Taxis meet all cruise ships and aren't all that expensive. Call ☎ 0590-27-66-31 for taxi service. The fare is Fr 25 ($5) for rides up to five minutes; each additional three minutes is another Fr 20 ($4).

You can rent open-sided Mini-Mokes and manual-transmission Suzuki Samurais. Try **Budget** (☎ 800/527-0700 or 0590-27-66-30); **Hertz** (☎ 800/654-3001), which operates through a local dealership, Henry's Car Rental; and **Avis** (☎ 800/331-1084 or 0590-27-71-43), whose local name is St. Barts Centre-Auto.

You can rent motorbikes and scooters from **Rent Some Fun,** rue Gambetta in

Gustavia (☎ 0590-27-70-59). The $26 to $34 daily rental fee covers both bike and helmet; a $200 deposit is required.

SHOPPING

You don't pay any duty on St. Barts, so it's a good place to buy liquor and French perfumes. You'll also find good buys on sportswear, crystal, porcelain, watches, and other luxuries. Only trouble is, selections here are limited.

If you're in the market for island crafts, try to find those fine convertible-brim straw hats St. Bartians like to wear. You'll also find some interesting cotton block-printed resort clothes.

Tucked off a courtyard adjacent to one of Gustavia's main streets, **La Boutique,** 8 rue du Général de Gaulle (☎ 0590-27-51-66), sells shirts and blouses decorated with paint. Also available are incredibly elegant beach towels, each a thirsty mass of terry cloth embroidered with gold letters.

Very few shops in the Caribbean are as elegant and upscale as **Le Comptoirdu Cigare,** 6, rue du Général de Gaulle (☎ 0590-27-50-62), which caters exclusively to gentlemen. They carry cigars from Cuba and the Dominican Republic, as well as the Caribbean's most beautiful collection of cigar boxes and humidors. (Remember to smoke those Cuban cigars before you return to the United

States—you won't be able to bring them in with you.) There are also connoisseur-quality rums from Martinique, Cuba, and Haiti, and a worthy collection of silver ornaments.

For women, **Plein Sud,** Galerie du Commerce, St-Jean (☎ **0590-27-98-75**), is the most tasteful and stylish clothing boutique in St. Barts, with prices that are correspondingly high.

Diamond Genesis / Kornérupine, 12 rue du Général de Gaulle/Les Suites du Roi Oskar II (☎ **0590-27-68-11**), stocks ornaments with designs strongly influenced by French and European tastes. One best-seller is an 18-carat gold St. Barts, which sells for around $20. This is one of the few shops on the island where jewelry is handcrafted on the premises. Also for sale are watches by Corumand Jaegar Lecoultre, Brietling, and Tag Heuer.

Maison de Free Mousse, Carré d'Or, quai de la République (☎ **0590-27-63-39**), sells exotic handcrafts. Sharing the same courtyard is **Gianni Versace** (☎ **0590-27-99-30**) and **Polo Ralph Lauren** (☎ **0590-27-90-06**), which together form a chic minimall on the northern edge of Gustavia's harbor front.

Laurent Eiffel, rue du Général de Gaulle (☎ **0590-27-54-02**), remains popular for its well-crafted copies of the trademark shoes, belts, and handbags of Chanel, Hermès, Versace, Gucci, and other leading design houses.

The second floor of **Little Switzerland,** rue de la France (☎ **0590-27-64-66**), is devoted to perfumes and crystal, and the street level is devoted to jewelry and watches. Prices are usually 25 to 30% less than on the North American mainland.

BEACHES

There are 14 white-sand beaches on St. Barts. Few are ever crowded, even during winter, and all are public and free. Nudity is officially prohibited, but topless sunbathing is quite common.

We are fond of St. Barts's secluded beaches. **Gouverneur** on the south is gorgeous and offers some waves, but there's no shade. It can be reached by driving through Gustavia and up to Lurin. Turn at the Sante Fe Bar Restaurant, and head down a narrow road.

Saline, to the east of Gouveneur, is reached by driving up the road from the commercial center in St-Jean. A short walk over the sand dune and you're there. Like Gouveneur, it offers some waves, but no shade.

Marigot, also on the north shore, is narrow but offers good swimming and snorkeling. You can only get to **Colombier** by boat or by taking a rugged goat path from Petite Anse past Flamands, a 30-minute walk. You'll find shade and snorkeling here, so pack a lunch and spend the day.

The most famous beach is **St-Jean,** which is actually two beaches divided by the Eden Rock promontory. It offers water sports, beach restaurants, and a few hotels, as well as some shady areas. **Flamands,** to the west, is a very wide beach with a few small hotels and some areas shaded by lantana palms.

For beaches with hotels, restaurants, and water sports, the **Grand Cul-de-Sac** area on the northeast shore fits the bill. This is a narrow beach protected by a reef. A taxi from the cruise pier will take you here; make arrangements to be picked up at a scheduled time.

TENNIS & WATER SPORTS

TENNIS   Passengers can play at the **Hôtel Manapany Cottages,** Anse des Cayes (☎ **0590-27-66-55**), for Fr 80 ($16) per hour, or on the courts of the **Hôtel Guanahani,** at Grand Cul-de-Sac (☎ **0590-27-66-60**).

WATER SPORTS   Marine Service, quai du Yacht-Club (☎ **0590-27-70-34**), is the island's most complete water sports facility, located on the opposite side of the harbor from the more congested part of Gustavia. Programs include beginners' courses as well as wreck-dives and night-dives for certified divers. A 10-passenger Aquascope is available for a one-hour trip among tropical fish and colorful flora to the 210-foot yacht *Non-stop,* wrecked during Hurricane Hugo in 1989. The rate is Fr 175 ($35) per person. Interesting half-day trips also go to Colombier Beach or Ile Fourchue, a popular rendezvous point for boats. Ile Fourchue is horseshoe-shaped, with a protected anchorage. Its only permanent residents are goats, but a few ruins bear witness to a Breton who lived a Robinson Crusoe–style life here for many years.

A day's excursion to both Ile Fourchue and Colombier costs Fr 480 ($96) per person, with lunch included. A half-day excursion to Colombier goes for Fr 290 ($58) per person, including a French picnic. Trips are daily from 9am to 12:30pm and 1 to 5pm.

Marine Service can also arrange water-skiing between 9am and 1pm or 4:40pm and sundown. Because of the coastline's shape, skiers must remain at least 80 yards from shore on the windward side of the island, and 110 yards off on the leeward side. Stéphan Jouany, the best water-skier on St. Barts, takes out skiers of all proficiency levels. It costs about Fr 200 ($40) per half hour.

For windsurfing, try **St. Barth Wind School,** near the Tom Beach Hotel on Plagede St-Jean (☎ **0590-27-71-22**). Windsurfing costs Fr 100 to Fr 120 ($20 to $24) per hour.

DINING

The most popular gathering place in Gustavia is **Le Select,** rue de la France (☎ **0590-27-86-87**). Named after its more famous granddaddy in the Montparnasse section of Paris, this is a simple place where a game of dominoes might be under way as you walk in. Tables are placed outside on the gravel in an open-air cafe garden near the port. The grill promises a "cheeseburger in Para-

dise," and beer starts at Fr 14 ($2.80). The cafe is a hit with locals. Outsiders are welcomed, but not necessarily embraced.

Established shortly after the 1995 hurricanes, ♦ **La Mandala,** rue Courbet (☎ **0590-27-96-96**), is the most exciting restaurant in Gustavia. It serves Spanish-style tapas, and at lunch it focuses on exotic salads, quiches, and such seafood dishes as jumbo shrimp in ginger sauce or the grilled fresh fish of the day. Main courses are accompanied by local vegetables, such as a gratin of green papaya.

Some villa owners cite **L'Escale,** La Pointe (☎ **0590-27-81-06**), a hip, sometimes raucous, and always irreverent hangout, as their favorite restaurant on the island. It's on the relatively unglamorous south side of Gustavia's harbor. You can either dine lightly and inexpensively here or spend a lot of money. Typical lunch fare includes freshly made salads, pizzas from a wood-burning stove, and pasta dishes. Perennial favorites are steak tartare, fillet of beef pizzaiola, and carpaccio. The chef doesn't try to compete with the grand cuisine of the island's more fabled restaurants, but his food is hearty and full of flavor.

L'Iguane, Carré d'or, quai del la République (☎ **0590-27-88-46**), serves sushi, American breakfasts, and California-style sandwiches and salads. The sushi is served ultrafresh from whatever fishing boat happened to deposit its catch nearby on the day of your arrival.

About a mile east of Gustavia, atop one of the island's highest elevations, sits **Sante Fe Restaurant,** at Morne Lurin (☎ **0590-27-61-04**). This sports bar has carved out a niche for itself with the island's English-speaking clientele and is known for its burgers, cheeseburgers, and fresh-made fries, which are the island's best.

16 St. Croix ⇩⇩⇩

St. Croix now competes with St. Thomas for the Yankee cruise-ship dollar.

Although it gets nowhere near the number of visitors, St. Croix is more tranquil and less congested than its smaller sibling. The major attraction here is Buck Island National Park, a national offshore treasure.

Although large cruise ships moor at Frederiksted, most of the action is in Christiansted. On a coral-bound bay about midway along the north shore, Christiansted has more sights and better restaurants and shopping. The town is being handsomely restored, and the entire harbor-front area is a national historic site.

St. Croix boasts some of the best beaches in the Virgin Islands. The terrain at the island's east end is rocky and arid, whereas the west end is lusher, with a rain forest of mango and mahogany, tree ferns, and dangling lianas. In between are rolling hills and upland pastures dotted with stately towers that once housed grinding mills.

COMING ASHORE

Only cruise ships with fewer than 200 passengers can land directly at the dock at Christiansted. Others moor at a 1,500-foot pier at Frederiksted, a sleepy town that only springs to life when the ships arrive. Both piers have telephones and information centers.

We suggest you spend as little time as possible in Frederiksted and head for the capital of Christiansted, some 17 miles away. You can explore either town by foot.

FAST FACTS

Currency   The U.S. dollar is the coin of the realm.

Information   The **U.S. Virgin Islands Division of Tourism** has offices in Christiansted at 1AB Queen Cross St. (☎ 809/773-0495), and at the Customs House Building, Strand Street in Frederiksted (☎ 809/772-0357). Open Monday through Friday from 9am to 5pm.

Language   English is spoken here.

SHORE EXCURSIONS

Although it's possible to get around St. Croix on your own, the island offers some of the best and most varied shore excursions of any port in the Caribbean.

The premier tour is the four-hour, $40-tour of ✪ **Buck Island National Park,** a tropical underwater wonderland. Transportation is provided from the pier at Frederiksted to Christiansted, where a boat takes passengers over to Buck Island. An experienced guide provides snorkel lessons.

Other options include a four-hour tour that costs $25 per person and explores old Christiansted and visits the botanical gardens, Whim Estate House, the rum distillery, the rain forest, St. Croix Leap mahogany workshop, and the site where Columbus's men, coming ashore to claim the island for Spain, were driven off by a hail of arrows from the local Caribe Indians.

The most economical tours are offered by **Take-a-Hike** (☎ 809/778-6997), which conducts passengers on one-hour walks of the two historic towns of Frederiksted or Christiansted. The Christiansted tour is $5.50 per person; the Frederiksted tour is $6.50.

Most ships can connect you with a three-hour Plantation Hike, as you explore the ruins of an old plantation discovered outside Frederiksted in 1984. The cost runs from $25 to $30 per person.

If you book a round of golf at Carambola as part of an excursion, greens fees are $77 per person in winter, and $47.50 otherwise.

GETTING AROUND

Taxis are unmetered, so agree on the rate before you get in. The **St. Croix Taxicab Association** (☎ 809/778-1088) offers door-to-door service. Taxi tours are a great way to explore the island. For one or two passengers, the cost is about $30 for two hours or $40 for three hours. We don't recommend renting a car.

St. Croix

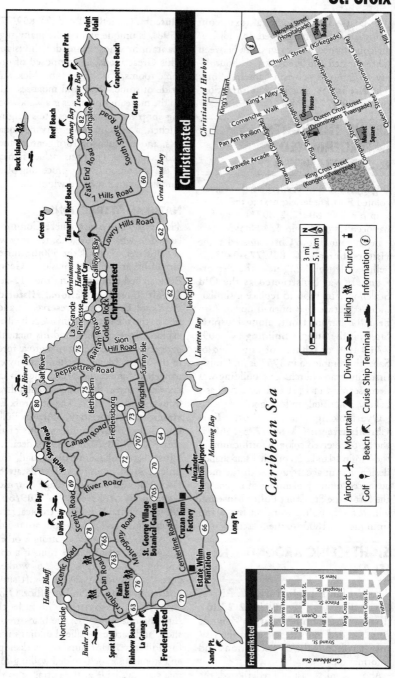

Christiansted (inset)

Christiansted Harbor

Hospital Street (Hospitalgade)
Steeple Building
Church Street (Kirkegade)
King's Wharf
King's Alley
Comanche Walk
Government House
Pan Am Pavilion
Queen Cross Street (Dronningens Tvaergade)
Caravelle Arcade
Strand Street (Strandgade)
King Street (Kongens Gade)
Queen Street (Dronningens Gade)
Compagnietsgade
Company Street (Dronningens Gade)
Queen Cross Street (Compagnietsgade)
Hill Street
Market Square
King Cross Street (Kongens Tvaergade)

Point Udall
Cramer Park
Grapetree Beach
Teague Bay
Chenay Bay
Reef Beach
Southgate
82
Grass Pt.
South Shore Road
East End Road
1 Hills Road
Buck Island
Green Cay
Tamarind Reef Beach
Great Pond Bay
60
Lowry Hills Road
62
Gallows Bay
Christiansted Harbor
Protestant Cay
La Grande Princesse
Golden Rock
Christiansted
62
Longford
Rattan Road
Sion Hill Road
Limetree Bay
75
Salt River Bay
Salt River
Peppertree Road
Sunny Isle
80
75
Bethlehem
Kingshill
Fredensborg
73
Canaan Road
707
64
Manning Bay
72
Alexander Hamilton Airport
North Shore Road
70
69
River Road
705
Cane Bay
Davis Bay
78
765
Mahogany Road
St. George Village Botanical Garden
Cruzan Rum Factory
66
Long Pt.
Hams Bluff
Scenic Road
763
Centerline Road
Northside
Creque Dan Road
76
Rain Forest
Estate Whim Plantation
70
Butler Bay
Sprat Hall
63
Rainbow Beach
La Grange
Frederiksted
Sandy Pt.

Caribbean Sea

Legend

Airport ✈   Mountain ▲   Diving 🤿   Hiking 🚶   Church ✝
Golf ⛳   Beach 🏖   Cruise Ship Terminal ⚓   Information ℹ

N
0   3 mi
0   5.1 km

Frederiksted (inset)

Strand St.
Lagoon St.
Customs House St.
Queen St.
Market St.
Hospital St.
Prince St.
New St.
King St.
Hill St.
King Cross St.
Queen Cross St.
Fisher St.

Caribbean Sea

It costs $20 to take a taxi from Christiansted to Frederiksted. In addition, air-conditioned buses run daily between Christiansted and Frederiksted about every 40 minutes between 6am and 9pm. The fare is 55¢. For more information, call ☎ **809/773-7746.**

SEEING THE SIGHTS IN FREDERIKSTED & CHRISTIANSTED

Begin your tour of **Frederiksted** at russet-colored **Fort Frederick,** next to the cruise-ship pier (☎ **809/772-2021**). The fort has been restored to its 1840 look.

Begin your visit to **Christiansted** at the **visitors' bureau** (☎ **809/773-0495**), a yellow-sided building near the harbor-front. It was constructed as the Old Scalehouse in 1856 to replace a similar, older structure that burned down. Also near the harbor front, along Hospital Street, is the **Steeple Building** (☎ **809/ 773-1460**) or Church of Lord God of Sabaoth, completed in 1753 as St. Croix's first Lutheran church. The building was deconsecrated in 1831 and has served as a bakery, a hospital, and a school.

Overlooking the harbor, **Fort Christiansvaern** (☎ **809/773-1460**) is the best-preserved colonial fortification in the Virgin Islands. Its original star-shaped design was in accordance with the most advanced military planning of its era. At the fort is the **St. Croix Police Museum,** which traces police work on the island from the late 1800s to the present.

SIGHTSEEING AROUND THE ISLAND

The **Cruzan Rum Factory,** W. Airport Road, Rte. 64 (☎ **809/692-2280**), distills the famous Virgin Islands rum. Guided tours depart from the visitors' pavilion; call for reservations and information.

About 2 miles east of Frederiksted, the restored **Estate Whim Plantation Museum,** Centerline Road (☎ **809/772-0598**), is unique among the many sugar plantations whose ruins dot the island. This Great House is composed of only three rooms, with three-foot-thick walls made of stone, coral, and molasses. Also on the museum's premises is a woodworking shop featuring the estate's original kitchen, a museum store, servant's quarters, and a display of 18th-century tools and techniques. The ruins include remains of the plantation's sugar-processing plant, complete with a restored windmill.

NATURAL ATTRACTIONS

The only known site where Columbus landed in what is now U.S. territory was at Salt River. To mark the 500th anniversary of his arrival, then-president George Bush signed a bill creating the 912-acre ✪ **Salt River Bay National Historical Park and Ecological Preserve.** In addition to the site of the original Carib village explored by Columbus and his men, the park contains the largest mangrove forest in the Virgin Islands, sheltering many endangered animals and plants, plus an underwater canyon that attracts scuba divers from around the world. The **St. Croix Environmental Association,** 3 Arawak Building, Gallows Bay, conducts tours of the area. Call ☎ **809/773-1989** for details.

Just north of Centerline Road, four miles east of Frederiksted at Estate St. George, lies **St. George Village Botanical Garden of St. Croix** (☎ **809/692-2874**), a veritable Eden of tropical trees, shrubs, vines, and flowers built around the ruins of a 19th-century sugarcane workers' village. Restoration of the ruins is a continuing project, but two sets of workers' cottages provide space for a gift shop, restrooms, a kitchen, and an office. Other completed restorations include the superintendent's house, the blacksmith's shop, and various smaller buildings used for a library, plant nursery, workshops, and storehouses. Self-guided walking-tour maps are available at the entrance to the Great Hall.

SHOPPING

Americans get a break here, since they can bring home $1,200 worth of merchandise from the U.S. Virgin Islands without paying any duty at all. And liquor here is duty-free.

In Christiansted, you'll find hole-in-the-wall boutiques selling one-of-a-kind merchandise, especially handmade items. Following the hurricanes of 1995, a major waterfront redevelopment included **King's Alley Complex** (☎ 809/778-8135).

There's a branch of **Colombian Emeralds** at 43 Queen Cross St. (☎ 809/773-1928). For convincing look-alikes, stop by **Elegant Illusions Copy Jewelry,** 55 King St. (☎ 809/773-2727), a branch of the successful California chain store that sells amazingly convincing fake jewelry. Next door you'll find the real thing at **King Alley Jewelry** (☎ 809/773-4746), owned by the same company.

For a selection of hip sports clothing, **Caribbean Clothing Co.,** 41 Queens Cross St. (☎ 809/773-5012), carries top name U.S. brands, including Calvin Klein, Guess, Polo, and Dockers. There's also a tasteful selection of quality shoes for both women and men.

If you're seeking unique gold jewelry, head for **Crucian Gold,** 57A Company St. (☎ 809/773-5241), displaying the artistic work of island-born Brian Bishop. He designs the gold jewelry himself, along with less expensive versions in sterling silver.

Folk Art Traders, 1B Queen Cross St. (☎ 809/773-1900), sells local art and folk-art treasures, including carnival masks, pottery, ceramics, batiks, original paintings, and hand-wrought jewelry. For the serious Caribbeanophile, there's nothing like it in the Virgin Islands.

At **Gone Tropical,** 55 Company St. (☎ 809/773-4695), about 60% of the merchandise is created in Indonesia. Prices on new, semi-antique, or antique sofas, beds, chests, tables, mirrors, and decorative carvings are the same (and sometimes

less) than equivalent furniture you might have bought new.

Some of the best accessories for the home are sold at **Green Papaya,** Caravelle Arcade no. 15 (☎ 809/773-8848). The owners have assembled a unique collection of accessories, including picture frames, baskets from Asia, and exotic but tasteful lighting fixtures.

One of the best outlets for duty-free liquor and wine is **Harborside Market and Spirits,** 59 King's Wharf (☎ 809/773-8899), conveniently located in the town center. Woolworth's (see below) also has good prices in duty-free liquor but is hard to reach without a car.

Java Wraps, in the Pan Am Pavilion, Strand Street (☎ 809/773-3770), is known for its resort wear in a kaleidoscope of colors and prints. Also in the Pavilion, **Many Hands** (☎ 809/773-1990) sells only Virgin Islands handcrafts, including West Indian spices and teas, shellwork, stained glass, hand-painted china, pottery, and handmade jewelry.

Discovered in the 1970s, larimar is a pale-blue pectolyte, mined only in the southwestern edge of the Dominican Republic. And at **Larimar,** the Boardwalk/King's Walk (☎ 809/692-9000), you can find the stuff mounted into various gold settings.

A branch of **Little Switzerland,** at 1108 King St. (☎ 809/773-1976), sells luxury goods at a discount.

The Royal Poinciana, 1111 Strand St. (☎ 809/773-9892), is the most interesting gift shop on St. Croix. In what looks like an antique apothecary shop, you'll find such items as hot sauces, seasoning blends for gumbos, island herbal teas, Antillean coffees, and scented soaps, toiletries, lotions, and shampoos.

The **St. Croix Perfume Center,** 53 King St. (☎ 800/225-7031 or 809/773-7604), has the largest duty-free assortment of men's and women's fragrances, usually at a 30% discount, as well as IMAN cosmetics.

Urban Threadz / Tribal Threadz, 52C Company St. (☎ 809/773-2883), carries everything from Bermuda shorts to light-weight summer blazers and men's suits. **Violette Boutique,** in the Caravelle Arcade, 38 Strand St. (☎ **809/773-2148**), carries famous brand names. It also sells many exclusive fragrances and hard-to-find bath lines, as well as cosmetics.

Sonya Ltd., 1 Company St. (☎ **809/778-8605**), is the shop of Sonya Hough, who designs jewelry that local residents won't leave home without. She's most famous for her sterling silver or gold interpretations of the C-clasp bracelet.

The **Woolworth's** in the Sunny Isle Shopping Center, Centerline Road (☎ **809/778-5466**), has the island's largest supply of discounted liquor, including Cruzan rum.

BEACHES

Beaches are the biggest attraction on St. Croix, but getting to them from Christiansted or Frederiksted isn't always easy. Taxi drivers will take you there, but it can be expensive.

In Christiansted, head for the **Hotel on the Cay.** You'll have to take a ferry to this palm-shaded island in the harbor.

Most convenient for passengers arriving at Frederiksted is **Sandy Point,** the largest beach in the U.S. Virgin Islands. Its shallow, calm waters are perfect for swimming. **Cramer Park,** at the island's northeastern end, is a special public park. Lined with sea-grape trees, the beach also has a picnic area, a restaurant, and a bar.

We highly recommend **Davis Bay** and **Cane Bay** as the type of beaches you'd expect to find on a Caribbean island, with palms, white sand, and good swimming and snorkeling. Cane Bay adjoins Route 80 on the north shore. Snorkelers and divers are attracted to this beach, with its rolling waves, coral gardens, and drop-off wall. No reefs guard the approach to Davis Beach, which draws bodysurfers. There are no changing facilities here, however. It's off the South Shore Road (Route 60) in the vicinity of the Carambola Beach Resort.

Windsurfers like **Reef Beach,** which opens onto Teague Bay along Route 82, East End Road, a half-hour ride from Christiansted. On Route 63, a short ride north of Frederiksted, **Rainbow Beach** invites with its white sand and ideal snorkeling conditions. Also on Route 63, **La Grange** is another good beach.

At the **Cormorant Beach Club,** about 5 miles west of Christiansted, some 1,200 feet of white sands are shaded by palm trees. Since a living reef lies just off the shore, snorkeling conditions are ideal. **Grapetree Beach** offers about the same footage of clean white sand on the island's eastern tip (Route 60). Follow the South Shore Road to reach it. Water sports are popular here.

GOLF, RIDING, DIVING, TENNIS & WATER SPORTS

GOLF Robert Trent Jones called the ✪ **Carambola Golf Course,** on the northeast side of St. Croix (☎ **809/778-0797**), the loveliest course he ever designed. Greens fees are $77 per person for a day in winter, $47.50 in summer. Mandatory golf carts cost $12.50 per 18 holes.

The other major course is at the **Buccaneer** (☎ **809/773-2100,** ext. 738), 2 miles east of Christiansted. It's a challenging 6,200-yard, 18-hole course. In winter, greens fees are $25 for 9 holes or $40 for 18 holes, with cart rental going for $14. In the off-season, you play 9 holes for $12 or 18 holes for $20, plus $13 for cart rental.

The **Reef,** at Teague Bay (☎ **809/773-8844**), is a 3,100-yard, 9-hole course charging greens fees of $10 to $14, with carts renting for $5 to $8.

HORSEBACK RIDING Paul and **Jill's Equestrian Stables,** Sprat Hall Plantation (P.O. Box 3251), Route 58 (☎ **809/772-2880**), offers scenic trail rides through the forest, past ruins of abandoned 18th-century plantations and sugar mills, or to the hilltops of St. Croix's western end. A two-hour trail ride costs

$50 per person. Tours usually depart daily in winter at 10am and 4pm. Reserve at least a day in advance.

SCUBA DIVING & SNORKELING Sponge life, the finest black-coral trees in the West Indies, and steep drop-offs near the shoreline have made St. Croix a big dive destination. It's home to the Caribbean's largest living reef, including the fabled north shore wall that begins in 25 to 30 feet of water and drops, sometimes straight down, to 13,200 feet. There are 22 moored sites, which allow dive boats to tie up without damaging the reef.

Favorite scuba-diving sites include the historic **Salt River Canyon,** the coral gardens of **Scotch Banks,** and **Eagle Ray,** named for the rays that cruise along the wall there. **Pavilions** is yet another good dive site, with a virgin coral reef. The major diving target is ✪ **Buck Island,** with underwater visibility of more than 100 feet and a submerged nature trail.

V.I. Divers Ltd., in the Pan Am Pavilion on Christiansted's waterfront (☎ **800/544-5911** or 809/773-6045), is one of the island's best dive operations. A full-service PADI five-star facility, it offers daily two-tank boat dives, guided snorkeling trips to Green Cay, night dives, and a full range of scuba-training programs. Introductory dives are $85 for a two-tank dive, including instruction and equipment. Two-tank boat dives for certified divers are $70. A two-hour guided snorkel tour costs $25; the boat snorkeling trip to Green Cay costs $35.

Dive St. Croix, 59 King's Wharf (☎ **800/523-DIVE** in the U.S., or 809/773-3434), operates the 38-foot dive boat *Reliance.* A resort course is $75, with a two-tank dive going for $70. Scuba trips to Buck Island are offered for $65, and dive packages begin at $190 for six dives.

TENNIS Some authorities rate the tennis at the **Buccaneer,** Route 82 (☎ **809/773-2100,** ext. 736), as the best in the West Indies. Eight courts are open to the public for $12 per person per hour; call to reserve. **Carambola Golf Club,** Kingshill

(☎ **809/778-0797**), has five clay courts open to the public for $25 per hour.

WATER SPORTS The best place for all-around water sports is the **Tradewind Surfing Water Sports Center** (☎ **809/773-7060**), located on a small offshore island in Christiansted Harbor. It's part of the Hotel on the Cay. You can go snorkeling for $12 a day, or have parasailing arranged for $50 a trip. The center also offers Windsurfers, Waverunners, jet skis, and kayaks.

DINING

IN CHRISTIANSTED

Antoine's, 58A King St. (☎ **809/773-0263**), is set directly on King's Wharf, on the second floor of a building overlooking Christiansted's harbor and marina. Many visitors come just for the bar, which dispenses more than 35 different kinds of frozen blender drinks. Antoine's is more of a tradition for breakfast. At lunch you can have a good selection of soups and salads. Some, including the Caribbean fish chowder and the kallaloo soup, have real West Indian flavor. For main dishes there are the usual burgers, sandwiches, and fried shrimp, but you can also enjoy a number of Teutonic dishes, including Wiener schnitzel and bratwurst. The local catch of the day can be ordered as you like it.

Across from Government House, **Camille's Café,** at Queen Cross and 53B Company streets (☎ **809/773-2985**), is your best bet for an inexpensive lunch within the town center. During the day, enjoy a homemade soup, followed by a freshly made salad or one of the sandwiches, which are the best in town. You can also order more substantial fare, such as fresh beef, chicken, and steak. At night (when you're likely to be back on ship) the cafe becomes more of a wine bar, with Mediterranean-style food.

Catherine Plav-Drigger is one of the Caribbean's best chefs, and you'll probably eat your finest lunch in St. Croix at **Indies,** 55–56 Company St. (☎ 809/692-9440). If you want a full and formal midday meal instead of a burger or pizza, this is your place. The beautiful fresh fish and lobster are caught in Caribbean waters, and local seasonal fruits and vegetables are featured. Thai green curry-grilled shrimp with banana, chutney, and scallions has a savory flavor, as does the lobster and corn quesadilla. The pumpkin-ginger soup with coconut and the West Indies–style seafood chowder are excellent. Main courses include a superb grilled wahoo with pepper sauce and grilled scallions and spicy Caribbean chicken with fresh pineapple chutney.

Local fans have followed **Kendricks,** 12 Chandlers Wharf, Gallows Bay (☎ 809/773-9199), the island's toniest restaurant, out to Gallows Bay overlooking Christiansted Harbor. The downstairs dining room is more informal, serving light cafe fare for lunch. However, if you want a more formal lunch, head upstairs, where the dishes are far more elaborate in preparation and texture. Seared scallops and artichoke hearts in a lemon cream sauce is a signature dish, and the roasted, pecan-crusted pork loin with a ginger mayonnaise fairly explodes with flavor.

Tutto Bene, 2 Company St. (☎ 809/773-5229), feels more like a bistro-cantina than a restaurant. The menu depends on simple, hearty, and uncomplicated Italian dishes. At lunch you can enjoy veggie frittatas, a chicken pesto sandwich, or spinach lasagna. A large mahogany bar in back does a brisk business of its own.

IN FREDERIKSTED

Pier 69, 69 King St. (☎ 809/772-0069), has a funky, 1950s living room meets nautical bar kind of ambience. Menu items include predictable salads, sandwiches, and platters, as well as mango coladas or lime lambadas.

At the popular bistro **Le St. Tropez,** Limetree Court, 67 King St. (☎ 809/772-3000), you'll enjoy crepes, quiches, soups, and salads in a sunlit courtyard. Call ahead for a table. The well-prepared

dishes use fresh ingredients, and the daily specials often have a pungent and aromatic Mediterranean flavor.

17 St. Kitts ⚓ ⚓ ⚓

St. Kitts is a delightful and relatively uncrowded stop with beaches, shops, restaurants, and a capital that looks like a Hollywood set for an 18th-century West Indies port. St. Kitts is more active and lively than Nevis, its companion island $2^1/2$ miles across a strait, but it still has a sleepy feel.

For the time being, at least, the bulk of the island's revenue still comes from sugar, not tourists. Cane fields climb the slopes of a volcanic mountain range, and you'll see ruins of old mills and plantation houses as you drive around the island. Any farmer will sell you a huge stalk of cane. To get the nectar-sweet juice, strip off the hard exterior and chew on the tasty reeds. It's best with ice and a little rum.

COMING ASHORE

A new deep-water pier was completed at Basseterre in late 1997, allowing large-scale oceangoing vessels to dock there. Taking a taxi from the dock is the quickest and easiest way to reach town or Brimstone Hill Fort, the island's major attraction. At the docks there are banks of phones that accept AT&T calling cards.

FAST FACTS

Currency The local currency is the **Eastern Caribbean dollar (EC$).** Currently, the exchange rate is about EC$2.70 for U.S.$1. Many shops and restaurants quote prices in U.S. dollars.

Information Local tourist information is dispensed at the **St. Kitts / Nevis Department of Tourism,** Pelican Mall, Bay Road, in Basseterre (☎ 869/465-2620). Open Monday to Friday from 9am to 5pm.

Language English is the language of the island.

SHORE EXCURSIONS

The premier excursion is the Brimstone Hill Tour, a 2½-hour tour that costs $25. This inspiring 17th-century citadel is some 800 feet above sea level, offering a panoramic view of the coastline and the island.

On the Beach Horseback Ride, cruise-ship passengers ride well-trained horses along the beach on the Atlantic coastline. The one-hour trip costs $35. Another active tour is the Catamaran Adventure, a leisurely 45-minute sail along the southern coast of St. Kitts, with a stop in a sheltered cove for snorkeling. The 3½-hour trip costs $45.

GETTING AROUND

Since most taxi drivers are also guides, this is the best means of getting around. Taxis aren't metered, so before heading out you must agree on the price, and ask if the rates quoted are in U.S. dollars or Eastern Caribbean dollars. Taxi drivers will take you on a three-hour tour of the island for about $55. Lunch can also be arranged at one of the local inns. We'd suggest either **Golden Lemon** at Dieppe Bay (☎ **869/ 465-7260**) or **Rawlins Plantation,** Mount Pleasant (☎ **869/465-6221**).

We don't recommend renting a car.

SEEING THE SIGHTS

The capital and chief port, Basseterre, still sports its 18th-century waterfront, white colonial houses with toothpick balconies, and the Circus, the town square, which is actually round. The green Victorian Berkeley Memorial Clock standing in the center of the Circus is one of the most photographed landmarks here. Just like in the old days, country people still come to the marketplace with baskets brimming with just-picked mangoes, guavas, soursop, mammy apples, and wild strawberries and cherries.

The ✪ **Brimstone Hill Fortress** (☎ **869/465-6211**), 9 miles west of Basseterre, is the major stop on any tour. This historic monument, among the largest and best preserved in the Caribbean, is a complex of bastions, barracks, and other structures ingeniously grafted to the top and upper slopes of a steep hill. The fortress dates from 1690, when the British armed the hill to help recapture their Fort Charles below from the French. In 1782 an invading force of 8,000 French troops bombarded the fortress for a month before its small British garrison, supplemented by local militia, surrendered. When the British took the island back the next year, they proceeded to enlarge the fort into "The Gibraltar of the West Indies."

Today, the fortress is the centerpiece of a national park with nature trails and a diverse range of plant and animal life, including green vervet monkeys. It's also a photographer's paradise, with views of mountains, fields, and the Caribbean Sea. On a clear day you can see six neighboring islands. Visitors will enjoy self-directed tours among the many ruined or restored structures, including the barracks rooms at Fort George, which have been turned into an interesting museum. The gift shop sells prints of rare maps and paintings of the Caribbean.

On the northeast coast, **Mount Liamuiga** was dubbed "Mount Misery" long ago, but this dormant volcano sputtered its last gasp around 1692. Today it attracts hikers. A round-trip to the usually cloud-covered peak takes about 4 hours—$2^1/2$ hours going up, $1^1/2$ coming down. The ascent is usually made from the Belmont Estate, on the north end of St. Kitts. The trail winds through a rain forest and travels along deep ravines up to the crater's rim at a cool 2,625 feet. Many hikers climb, or crawl, down a steep, slippery trail to a tiny lake within the volcano's crater, some 400 feet below the rim.

You can reach the rim without a guide, but it's absolutely necessary to have one to go into the crater. **Greg's Safaris** (☎ 869/465-4121) offers guided hikes to the crater for $50 per person (a minimum of four hikers is required). The fee includes breakfast and a picnic at the crater's rim. The same outfit also offers half-day rain-forest explorations, also with a picnic, for $40 per person.

Anyone with a taste for rum will enjoy a trip to the **Sugar Factory,** where raw cane is processed into bulk sugar from February through July. The factory also produces a very light liqueur, CSR, which the locals use in a grapefruit drink they call "Ting." Guests also can visit the **Carib Beer Plant,** an English lager brewery. You don't need a reservation, but check with the tourist information office first to find out if it's open.

SHOPPING

The good buys here are local handcrafts, including goatskin leather items, baskets, and coconut shells. You can also find some good values in clothing and fabrics, especially Sea Island cottons. Prices on some luxury goods can range from 25 to 30% below those on the North American mainland.

For one-stop shopping, head to **Pelican Shopping Mall,** Bay Road, which has banking services, a restaurant, and a philatelic bureau. **Little Switzerland** (☎ 869/465-9859) and some other major retail outlets in the Caribbean have branches here. **The Linen and Gold Shop** (☎ 869/465-9766) has limited gold and silver jewelry, but great tablecloths and napery.

Also check out the offerings along **Liverpool Row,** whose shops have some unusual merchandise. The shops along **Fort Street** also are worth browsing.

In the Circus, **Ashburry's** (☎ 869/465-8175), a branch of a luxury-goods chain based in St. Maarten, sells discounted fragrances, fine porcelain, crystal by Baccarat, handbags, wristwatches, and jewelry. Below the popular Ballahoo Restaurant, **Island Hopper** (☎ **869/465-1640**) is the most complete clothing shop on the island.

In the center of Basseterre, **Cameron Gallery,** 10 N. Independence Sq. (☎ **869/465-1617**), offers Rosey Cameron-Smith watercolors and prints, which capture the true West Indian life. Ms. Cameron also makes greeting cards, postcards, and calendars, and displays the works of some 20 other artists.

A little nugget to discover is **Rosemary Lane Antiques,** 7 Rosemary Lane (☎ **869/465-5450**), housed in an early 19th-century Caribbean building painted purple and white so it'll stand out. The owner, Robert Cramer, has a choice collection of St. Kittian, Caribbean, and international antiques, including furniture, paintings, silver, china, and glass. He'll ship anywhere in the world.

At **The Palms,** in the Palms Arcade (☎ **869/465-2599**), you'll find "island things": handcrafts; larimar, sea opal, and amber jewelry; West Indies spices, teas, and perfumes; tropical clothes by Canadian designer John Warden; and Bali batiks by Kisha.

On Fort Street, **A Slice of the Lemon** (☎ **869/465-2889**) has St. Kitts's largest selection of perfumes, and one room is an outlet for Portmeirion English bone china.

BEACHES

Swimming is best at the twin beaches of **Banana Bay** and **Cockleshell Bay; Conaree Beach,** 3 miles from Basseterre; talcum-powder-fine **Frigate Bay** north of Banana Bay; and **Friar's Bay,** a peninsula beach opening onto both the Atlantic and the Caribbean. The narrow peninsula in the southeast that contains the island's salt ponds boasts the island's best white-sand beaches. All beaches, even those that border hotels, are open to the public, however, you must obtain permission first and pay a fee to use a hotel's beach facilities.

GOLF, TENNIS & WATER SPORTS

GOLF The **Royal St. Kitts Golf Course,** Frigate Bay (☎ **869/465-8339**), is an 18-hole par-72 championship course bounded on the south by the Caribbean Sea and on the north by the Atlantic Ocean. Greens fees are $35 for 18 holes. Cart rentals cost $40 for 18 holes.

TENNIS Call a hotel to see if a court is available. The best are at **Bird Rock Beach Hotel,** 2 miles southwest of Basseterre (☎ **869/465-8914**), and at **Golden Lemon,** Dieppe Bay (☎ **869/465-7260**).

WATER SPORTS From **Pro-Divers,** at Turtle Beach (☎ **869/465-3223**), you can swim, sail, float, paddle, or go on scuba-diving and snorkeling expeditions. A two-tank dive costs $50 with your own equipment, $60 if you rent.

The best diving spots include **Nagshead,** at the south tip of St. Kitts, an excellent shallow-water dive starting at 10 feet and extending to 70 feet. Another good site is **Booby Shoals,** between Cow 'n' Calf Rocks and Booby Island. Booby Shoals has abundant sea life, including nurse sharks, lobster, and stingrays. Dives, ideal for both certified and resort divers, go to depths of 30 feet.

DINING

If you're looking for an unspoiled, casual beach restaurant, you've found it at **The Anchorage** (☎ **869/465-8235**) on the rolling acres of Frigate Bay. After a rum-based drink, you'll be ready for hamburgers or a dozen kinds of sandwiches. Lobster is either broiled or Thermidor. The fresh catch of the day is prepared as you like it, or you can order such standbys as spareribs.

Overlooking the Circus from the sea, the open-air **Ballahoo Restaurant,** on Fort Street (☎ **869/465-4197**), is one of the coolest places in town on a hot afternoon. Blue parrot fish filet is a tasty dish to order here, and the chef also makes zesty chili and baby back ribs. The restaurant is popular with cruise ship passengers, however, and can get crowded.

If you're touring on the northern coast beyond St. Paul's, have lunch at ✪ **The Golden Lemon,** Dieppe Bay (☎ **869/ 465-7260**), a 17th-century house converted into a hotel. The menu, which changes daily, features Creole, continental, and American dishes, made with locally grown produce. Dishes might include baked Cornish hen with ginger, fresh fish, or Creole sirloin steak with a spicy rum sauce.

You can enjoy fine cuisine and panoramic views at the ✪ **Ocean Terrace Inn,** Fortlands (☎ **869/465-2754**). The kitchen does its best preparing real island-style dishes, such as tasty fish cakes accompanied by breaded carrot slices, creamed spinach, a stuffed potato, johnnycakes (Caribbean-style cornmeal dumplings), and a green banana in a lime-butter sauce. If you have a hearty appetite at lunch, you can order lobster in three different ways or else such dishes as Creole-style chicken curry with mango chutney or broiled prime New York strip loin steak.

Set directly on the sands above Turtle Beach, **Turtle Beach Bar and Grill** (☎ **869/469-9086**) is an airy, sun-flooded restaurant. You can spend an hour before your meal swimming or snorkeling beside the offshore reef or relaxing beneath the verandas or shade trees (hammocks are available). Scuba diving, ocean kayaking, windsurfing, and volleyball are possible, and a flotilla of rental sailboats moor nearby. Lunchtime menu specialties are familiar but scrumptious, including stuffed broiled lobster, conch fritters, barbecued swordfish steak, prawn salads, and barbecued honey-mustard spareribs.

18 St. Lucia ⇩⇩⇩⇩

St. Lucia's northwest coast has beautiful white-sand beaches, an interior of relatively unspoiled green-mantled mountains, and two dramatic peaks (the Pitons)

that make it appear more South Pacific than Caribbean. Here you will find gentle valleys, banana plantations, a bubbling volcano, and fishing villages.

Castries, the capital, has grown up around an extinct volcanic crater that's now a large harbor surrounded by hills. Because of devastating fires, the town today has a look of newness, with glass-and-concrete buildings, but there's still an old fashioned Saturday-morning market on Jeremy Street, our favorite site. The country women dress up in traditional cotton headdress to sell their luscious fruits and vegetables. Weather-beaten men sit close by playing *warrie,* a fast game played with pebbles on a carved board.

COMING ASHORE

Most cruise ships arrive at the fairly new pier at Pointe Seraphine, a short taxi ride from the center of Castries. You'll find St. Lucia's best shopping at this pier. Other services include a money exchange, an outlet of the Philatelic Bureau, a small visitor information bureau, and a cable and wireless office that accepts phone cards. Some phones are designated for credit cards, others for AT&T direct-dial access.

If Pointe Seraphine is overcrowded, your ship might dock at Elizabeth II pier, which is a short walk to the center of Castries. Some smaller vessels, such as Seabourn's, anchor off Soufrière and tender you ashore.

FAST FACTS

Currency The official monetary unit is the **Eastern Caribbean dollar (EC$),** which is worth about 37¢ in U.S. currency. Most prices quoted in this section are in U.S. dollars, which are accepted by nearly all hotels, restaurants, and shops.

Information The **St. Lucia Tourist Board** is at Pointe Seraphine in Castries (☎ **758/452-4094**) and is open Monday through Friday from 9am to 5pm.

Cape Moule-à- Chique ❻
Diamond Mineral Baths ❸
Forest Reserve ❼
Frigate Islands ❽
Gros Piton ❺
Morne Fortune ❷
Petit Piton ❹
Pigeon Island National Park ❶

Cariblue Beach
Pigeon Island
Cap Estate
Gros Islet
Anse Lavouette
Rodney Bay
Reduit Beach
Choc Bay
Labrelotte Bay
Grande Anse Bay
Vigie Beach
Vigie Airport
La To
Castries
La Sorcière
Graand Cul de Sac Bay
Fort Charlotte
Marigot Bay
Roseau Bay
Anse-La-Raye
Atlantic Ocean
Canaries
Dennery
Anse Chastanet
Soufrière ❸
La Soufrière ❼
Petit Piton ❹
Fond St. Jacques
Micoud
❺ Gros Piton
Choiseul
Savannes Bay
Hewanorra Airport
Vieux Fort ❻
Maria Islands
❽

0   5 mi
8 km
N

Cruise Ship Terminal
Airport ✈ Beach 🏖 Mountain 🔺

Language English is the official language.

SHORE EXCURSIONS

Shore excursions are the best means of seeing this tropical island. A trip from Castries to the La Soufrière volcano and the Pitons takes you across St. Lucia, with visits to the volcano, the Diamond Baths, and a sulfur spring. The eight-hour trip, which includes lunch, costs $45. Small ships anchoring off La Soufrière offer a two-hour tour for $30 per person. You'll see the same sights mentioned above.

GETTING AROUND

Most taxi drivers have been trained to serve as guides. Their cars are unmetered, but the government fixes tariffs for all standard trips. Be sure to determine if the driver is quoting a rate in U.S. or E.C. dollars.

We don't recommend driving.

SEEING THE SIGHTS

The principal streets of **Castries** are William Peter Boulevard and Bridge Street. A Roman Catholic cathedral stands on Columbus Square, which has a few restored buildings. **Government House** is a late Victorian building.

Beyond Government House lies **Morne Fortune,** which means "Hill of Good Luck." But no one had much luck here, certainly not the French and British that battled for **Fort Charlotte.** You can visit the 18th-century barracks, complete with a military cemetery, a small museum, the Old Powder Magazine, and the "Four Apostles Battery," four grim muzzle-loading cannons. There's a panoramic harbor view and you can see north to Pigeon Island or south to the Pitons. To reach Morne Fortune, head east on Bridge Street.

PIGEON ISLAND NATIONAL LANDMARK

St. Lucia's first national park was originally an island flanked on one side by the Caribbean and on the other by the Atlantic. It is now joined to the mainland by a causeway. On its west coast are two white-sand beaches. There's also a restaurant, Jambe de Bois ("Leg of Wood"), named after a peg-legged pirate who once used the island as a hideout. The Interpretation Centre is equipped with artifacts and a multimedia display of local history.

The Captain's Cellar Olde English Pub sits under the interpretive center. Pigeon Island, only 44 acres in size, got its name from the red-neck pigeon, or ramier, which once made this island home. It is ideal for picnics and nature walks. For more information, call the **St. Lucia National Trust** (☎ 758/452-5005). Take a taxi here, and arrange to be picked up in time to return to the ship.

LA SOUFRIÈRE

This little fishing port is St. Lucia's second-largest settlement and is dominated by the dramatic ❂ **Pitons**, two pointed peaks called Petit Piton and Gros Piton, rising to 2,460 and 2,619 feet, respectively. Formed by lava and once actively volcanic, they are now clothed in green vegetation. Their sheer rise from the sea makes them such a visible landmark that they have become the very symbol of St. Lucia.

Near the town of Soufrière lies the famous "drive-in" volcano, ❂ **Mont Soufrière,** a rocky lunar landscape of bubbling mud and craters seething with fuming sulfur. You walk into an old crater between the sulfur springs and pools hissing steam. The sulfurous fumes are said to have medicinal properties. A local guide is usually waiting beside them; for a fee, he'll point out the blackened waters.

If you do hire a guide, agree, then agree again, on the fee.

Nearby are the ❂ **Diamond Mineral Baths** (☎ 758/452-4759), surrounded by a tropical arboretum. They have an average temperature of 106°F and lie near one of the island's geological attractions: a waterfall that changes colors (from yellow to black to green to gray) several times a day. For EC$5 ($1.85), you can bathe and benefit from the recuperative effects yourself.

SHOPPING

Many stores sell duty-free goods. There are some good but not remarkable buys in bone china, jewelry, perfume, watches, liquor, and crystal. Souvenir items include bags and mats, local pottery, and straw hats.

Bananas are St. Lucia's leading export, so if you're taking a taxi tour, ask to see one of the huge plantations. We suggest the Cul-de-Sac, just north of Marigot Bay; La Caya, in Dennery on the east cost; and the Roseau Estate, south of Marigot Bay.

POINTE SERAPHINE

Built for cruise ship passengers, **Pointe Seraphine** has the island's best collection of shops. You must present your cruise pass when making purchases here. Visitors can take away their purchases, except liquor and tobacco, which will be delivered to their ship.

You'll find a **Benneton** (☎ 758/452-7685), with prices discounted about 20%. **The Land Shop** (☎ 758/452-7488) specializes in elegant handbags, garment bags, briefcases, and shoes discounted at least 25%.

Colombian Emeralds (☎ 758/453-7721) has a more diverse selection of watches and gemstones than its competitor, **Little Switzerland** (☎ 758/451-6799), which sells discounted porcelain, crystal, wristwatches, and jewelry.

The Gallery (☎ 758/451-6116) specializes in Haitian paintings and crafts, including lathe-turned bowls, local souvenirs, hand-carved serving trays, and picture frames.

Images (☎ 758/452-6883) operates two shops. The more interesting one sells a large selection of enameled Indian jewelry. Laboriously handcrafted with exotic swirls, the necklaces, bracelets, earrings, and bangles range in price from $10 to $60. A few steps away, their outlet specializes in perfumes.

ELSEWHERE ON THE ISLAND

Just outside Castries, **Bagshaws,** La Toc (☎ 758/452-2139), is the island's leading hand-printer of silk-screen designs. The birds, butterflies, and flowers of St. Lucia are incorporated into their original designs. The fabrics are made into linens, clothing, beachwear, and T-shirts.

At **Caribelle Batik,** Howelton House, Old Victoria Rd., the Morne (☎ 758/452-3785), a five-minute taxi drive from the pier, you can watch St. Lucian artists creating intricate patterns and colors for batik. You can also purchase batik in cotton, rayon, and silk, made up into casual and beach clothing, wall hangings, and other gifts items.

You can find interesting Caribbean handcrafts and gifts at **Noah's Arkade,** Jeremie St. (☎ 758/452-2523), including local straw place mats and rugs, wall hangings, maracas, handmade salad bowls, shell necklaces, and warrie boards.

St. Lucia native Vincent Joseph Eudovic is a master artist and wood carver who usually carves his imaginative free-form sculptures from local tree roots, such as teak, mahogany, and red cedar. You can reach the ✪ **Eudovic Art Studio,** at Goodlands, Morne Fortune (☎ 758/452-2747), by taxi from the cruise pier. Ask to be taken to his private studio, where you'll see his remarkable work.

BEACHES

Instead of going on a shore excursion, you may want to spend time on one of St. Lucia's famous beaches. We prefer the calmer shores along the western coast, since a rough surf on the windward Atlantic side makes swimming potentially dangerous. All beaches are open to the public, even those along hotel properties, but you must pay to use a hotel's beach equipment.

Leading beaches include **Pigeon Island,** off the northern shore, with white sand and picnic facilities. **Vigie Beach,** north of Castries Harbour, is also quite popular. Its fine sands are often a light beige color. Or you might try the black volcanic sand at **La Toc** in Soufrière.

Just north of Soufrière is that beach connoisseur's delight, the white sands of **Anse Chastanet,** set at the foot of the lush, green mountains. **Reduit Beach,** with its fine brown sand, lies between Choc Bay and Pigeon Point.

GOLF, RIDING, DIVING, TENNIS & WATER SPORTS

GOLF St. Lucia has a nine-hole golf course at the **Cap Estate Golf Club,** at the island's northern end (☎ 758/450-8523). Greens fees are $27 for eighteen holes, $21 for nine. Another nine-hole course is at the **St. Lucia Sandals** resort (☎ 758/452-3081); however, guests of the resort receive preferential booking.

HORSEBACK RIDING North of Castries, you can rent a horse at **Cas-En-Bas and Cap Estate Stables** (call René Trim at 758/450-8273). The cost is $30 for a one-hour ride, $45 for a two-hour ride. Ask about the $55 picnic trip to the island's Atlantic side, which includes a barbecue lunch and drink. Departures are on horseback at 8:30am. Nonriders can be shuttled to the site in a van for half price.

SCUBA DIVING In Soufrière, at the southern end of Anse Chastanet's quarter-mile-long, soft, secluded beach, **Scuba St. Lucia** (☎ 758/459-7000) features great diving and comprehensive facilities. Some spectacular coral reefs, many only 10 to 20 feet below the surface, are a short distance off the beach. A two- to three-hour introductory lesson in shallow water and a reef tour costs $75. Single dives cost $30.

Rosemond Trench Divers, Ltd., at the Marigot Beach Club, Marigot Bay (☎ 758/451-4761), is set adjacent to the waters of the most famous bay in St. Lucia. Divers can go to shallow reefs or to challenging trenches. A resort course that includes a practice dive in sheltered waters and one dive above a reef costs $75. A one-tank dive for certified divers costs $50, including equipment rental.

TENNIS The **St. Lucia Racquet Club,** adjacent to Club St. Lucia (☎ 758/450-0551), has seven courts. Call 24 hours in advance to reserve a court.

WATER SPORTS Except for scuba diving, the best all-around water sports center is **St. Lucian Watersports,** at the Rex St. Lucian Hotel (☎ 758/452-8351). Waterskiing costs $8 for a 10-minute ride. Windsurfers rent for between $12 and $19 an hour; lessons cost $38 per person for a three-hour course. Snorkeling costs $25, including equipment.

DINING

IN CASTRIES

Overlooking Castries Harbour about 1¹/₂ miles east of the commercial center, the elegant **Green Parrot,** Red Tape Lane, Morne Fortune (☎ 758/452-3399), serves St. Lucian specialties. Try the *christophine au gratin* (a Caribbean squash with cheese) or the Creole soup made with callaloo and pumpkin. There are also five kinds of curry with chutney, as well as omelets and sandwiches at lunchtime. The 12-minute walk from downtown is worth it.

With a view of Castries Harbour and the Morne, **Jimmie's,** Vigie Cove Marina (☎ 758/452-5142), is known for its fresh fish and tasty Creole cookery. Fish is the item to order here. For something truly delicious, try octopus Helen, cooked according to an old Lucian recipe.

Constructed in the 19th century as a Great House, **San Antoine,** Morne Fortune (☎ 758/452-4660), has panoramic views of the capital and the water—but

the views are better than the cuisine. You can, however, have a satisfying meal of grilled fish and fresh vegetables.

✪ **The Lime,** in Rodney Bay (☎ 758/452-0761), stands north of Reduit Beach in an area known as Restaurant Row. The Lime continues to keep its prices low and its food good and plentiful. Menu specialties include stuffed crab backs and fish steak Creole. They also serve shrimp, steaks, lamb and pork chops, and roti. Nothing is fancy or nouvelle—just the way savvy local foodies like it. And it's cheaper than the more touristy Capone's nearby.

IN SOUFRIÈRE

A block inland from the waterfront and one floor above street level, **Camilla's,** 7 Bridge St. (☎ 758/459-5379), is a decent Caribbean-style restaurant with simple, unpretentious food. It's the only good place to eat within the village. Opt for Caribbean fish Creole or lobster thermidor instead of the beef dishes. Lunches are considerably less elaborate than dinners. We like dining at the pair of tables on the cantilevered balcony; the inside tables can get a bit steamy since there's no air-conditioning.

If you're near Diamond Falls at lunch time, **The Still** (☎ 758/459-7224) serves authentic St. Lucian specialties. As you drive up the hill less than a mile east of Soufrière you'll see a very old rum distillery set on a platform of thick timbers. The site is a working cocoa, copra, and citrus plantation that has been in the same St. Lucian family for four generations.

19 St. Maarten / St. Martin ↓↓↓

Legend has it that a gin-drinking Dutchman and a wine-guzzling Frenchman walked around the island of St. Martin in 1648 to see how much territory each could earmark for his side in one day. The Frenchman covered the most ground, but the canny Dutchman got the more valuable real estate.

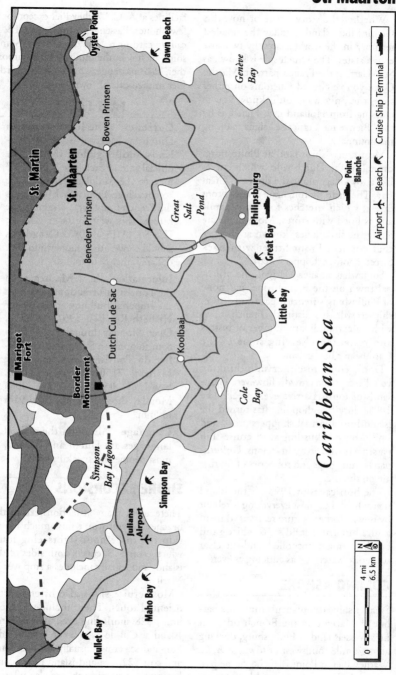

St. Maarten

St. Martin

St. Maarten

Oyster Pond

Dawn Beach

Genève Bay

Boven Prinsen

Beneden Prinsen

Great Salt Pond

Phillipsburg

Point Blanche

Great Bay

Marigot Fort

Border Monument

Dutch Cul de Sac

Koolbaai

Little Bay

Cole Bay

Simpson Bay Lagoon

Juliana Airport

Simpson Bay

Maho Bay

Mullet Bay

Caribbean Sea

Airport ✈   Beach ↖   Cruise Ship Terminal

N

0   4 mi
0   6.5 km

Whether the story's true or not, this Gemini-like island is today the smallest territory in the world shared by two sovereign states. The Dutch side is known as St. Maarten; the French part, St. Martin. Once you've cleared Customs on either side, the only way you'll know you're crossing from Holland into France is by the "Bienvenue Française" signs marking the boundary.

Most cruise ships land at Philipsburg, capital of the Dutch side, which curves like a toy village along the shores of Great Bay. The main thoroughfare is busy Front Street, which stretches for about a mile and is lined with stores. More shops are along the little lanes, known as *steegijes,* that connect Front Street with Back Street, another shoppers' mart.

Somewhat smaller Marigot, the principal town on the French side, has none of Philipsburg's frenzied pace and cruise-ship crowds. It's distinctly French, filled with an extraordinary number of bistros and restaurants serving some of the Caribbean's best cuisine.

Don't come to either side thinking you'll escape the crowds, however. Thousands of tourists arrive every week. The 100% duty-free shopping has turned the island into a virtual shoppers' mall, and Philipsburg is bustling with cruise-ship passengers who arrive in legions. Unfortunately, muggings and robberies of tourists are on the rise.

The hurricanes of 1995 hit the island pretty hard, but most everything is rebuilt by now. Mother Nature rearranged them a bit, but the island's 36 white-sand beaches remain unspoiled, and the clear turquoise waters are as enticing as ever.

COMING ASHORE

Smaller ships can maneuver into the harbor of Marigot on the French side, but most vessels land at Philipsburg, docking about a mile southwest of town, at A. C. Wathey Pier at Point Blanche. Some passengers walk the distance, although taxis await all cruise ships. There are almost no facilities at A. C. Wathey Pier except for a few phones. Passengers can use an AT&T calling card or reverse the charges. Some ships anchor in the mouth of the harbor, then take passengers by tender to Little Pier in the heart of town.

FAST FACTS

Currency   The legal tender in Dutch St. Maarten is the **Netherlands Antilles guilder (NAf).** The official rate of exchange is Naf 1.77 for each U.S.$1 dollar, but dollars are accepted here. French St. Martin uses the **French franc (Fr).** The exchange rate at this writing is Fr 4.98 to U.S.$1 (1 Fr = 20¢). Canadians should convert their money into U.S. dollars rather than francs.

Information   In St. Maarten, go to the **Tourist Information Bureau,** in the Imperial Building at 23 Walter Nisbeth Rd. (☎ **599/5-22337**). Open Monday through Friday from 8am to 5pm. In St. Martin, the **Office du Tourisme** is at the Port de Marigot, 97150 Marigot, St. Martin, F.W.I. (☎ **0590-87-57-21**). Open Monday through Friday from 9am to 5pm.

Language   Although the official languages are Dutch and French, most people also speak English.

SHORE EXCURSIONS

There aren't many attractions except the beaches, so you won't miss much if you skip the three-hour sightseeing tour, which costs $18, covers both sides of the island, and usually includes a stopover in Marigot.

Most cruise ships also offer sports-oriented tours. These include a three-hour, $28 snorkeling excursion to Pinel Island at Cul-de-Sac on the French side. Sun-and-sea cruises usually last two hours and cost $22. Sea-and-island tours, combining the best of both, are also offered, lasting 3 1/2 hours and costing $40.

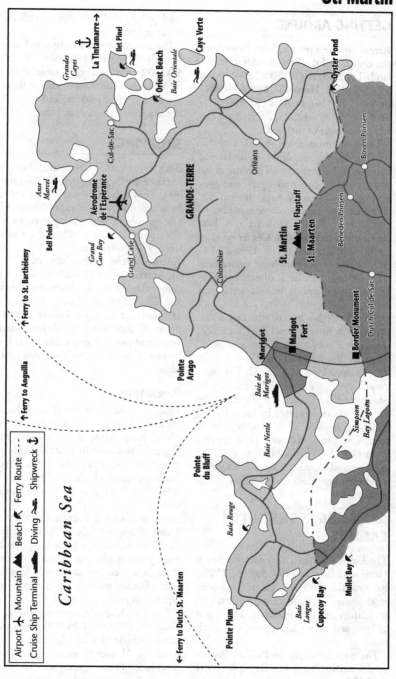

GETTING AROUND

Rental cars are a practical way to see both the Dutch and the French sides of the island. Try **Budget** (☎ **800/527-0700** or 599/5-54030), **Hertz** (☎ **800/654-3001** or 599/5-54314), or **Avis** (☎ **800/331-1084** or 599/5-42322). Drive on the right-hand side of the road.

Taxis are unmetered, but Dutch St. Maarten law requires drivers to list fares to major island destinations. There are minimum fares for two passengers, and each additional passenger pays another $2. Taxis are the most common means of transport on French St. Martin. A **Taxi Service and Information Center** operates at the port of Marigot (☎ **0590-87-56-54**). It also books two-hour sightseeing trips around the island. Always agree on the rate before getting into an unmetered cab.

Buses, though a bit crowded, are a reasonable way to get around the Dutch side. The privately owned and operated minibuses tend to follow specific routes, with fares ranging from $1.15 to $2. The most popular run is from Philipsburg to Marigot on the French side. Buses on the French side are operated by local drivers, with an armada of privately owned minivans and minibuses. One departs from Grand-Case for Marigot every 20 minutes and typically costs $2. There's a departure every hour from Marigot to the Dutch side.

GAMBLING IN THE DUTCH CASINOS

The **Casino Royale,** at the Maho Beach Hotel on Maho Bay (☎ **599/5-52115**), has roulette, blackjack, craps, Caribbean stud-poker, baccarat, minibaccarat, and more than 250 slot machines. They open at 1pm and offer a complimentary snack buffet.

The popular casino at **Pelican Resort and Casino,** Simpson Bay (☎ **599/5-42503**), has craps, roulette, blackjack, stud poker, and 120 slot machines. It opens at 1pm.

The Roman-themed **Coliseum Casino,** on Front Street in Philipsburg (☎ **599/5-32102**), has the highest table limits on St. Maarten: $1,000 maximum. It features blackjack, poker, roulette, and about 200 slot machines. It opens at 11am.

SHOPPING

Both French St. Martin and Dutch St. Maarten are highly touted for their shopping. They're both duty-free ports with no local sales tax. Sometimes you can pick up a bargain here, but many goods, such as electronics, can be purchased for much less in the United States.

Artist **Roland Richardson,** in Orléans, St. Martin (☎ **0590-87-32-24**), welcomes visitors into his home on Tuesday and Thursday from 10am to 5pm to view and purchase his original watercolors and prints of island vistas. A visit here offers a warm and personal way to see life as lived by one of the most sensitive souls on the island.

PHILIPSBURG

Except for the boutiques at resort hotels, the main shopping area is in the center of Philipsburg. Most shops are on Front Street (*Voorstraat* in Dutch), which is closer to the bay, and Back Street (*Achterstraat*), which runs parallel. At small shops, you may be able to bargain over prices.

The lion's head fountain at the **Old Street Shopping Center,** with entrances on Front Street and Back Street, is the most photographed spot on St. Maarten. Built in a West Indian–Dutch style, the center features more than two dozen shops and boutiques.

The **Caribbean Camera Centre,** 79 Front St. (☎ **599/5-25259**), has a wide range of merchandise, plus cameras at a discount. However, we've found better deals in St. Thomas, and you may do better at a discount store back home.

Colombian Emeralds International, Front Street (☎ **599/5-23933**), carries quality unmounted emeralds from Colombia, as well as emerald, gold, diamond, ruby, and sapphire jewelry.

The **Guavaberry Company,** 10 Front St. (☎ **599/5-22965**), sells the island folk liqueur Guavaberry. Sold in square bottles, it's made from rum and gets its unique flavor from rare local berries. The liqueur is aged and has a fruity, woody, almost bittersweet flavor. Stop in for a free taste.

At the local branch of **H. Stern Jewelers,** 68 Front St. (☎ **599/5-23328**), prices can be 25% less than in the United States. We've made some good buys in elegant watches. There's also an outlet of **Little Switzerland** at 42 Front St. (☎ **599/5-23530**).

Arguably the island's most interesting international specialty boutique, **La Romana,** in Royal Palm Plaza, 61 Front St. (☎ **599/5-22181**), offers an excellent selection of the famous La Perla swimwear and beachwear, the La Perla fine lingerie collection, and the latest Fendi bags, luggage, accessories, and perfume. You'll find good bargains here.

Little Europe, 80 Front St. (☎ **599/5-24371**), is an upscale purveyor of all the (supposedly) good things in life—or at least all the ones that will fit in your cabin aboard ship. Prices are relatively inexpensive when compared to boutiques on the North American mainland. Inventory includes porcelain figurines by Hummel, jewelry priced at between $80 and $6,000 per item, and such prestige-name watches as Concorde, Piaget, Corum, and Movado.

The **Shipwreck Shop,** Front Street (☎ **599/5-22962**), isn't quite exactly what its name implies: instead of salvage, you'll find such items as West Indian hammocks, beach towels, baskets, handmade jewelry, T-shirts, postcards, stamps, books, and Caribbean handcrafts.

Yellow House (Casa Amarilla), Wilhelminastraat 1 (☎ **599/5-23438**), sells all kinds of perfumes and luxury items, and also carries discounted luxury gift items.

MARIGOT

Many day-trippers come to Marigot just to look at the very French boutiques and shopping arcades. Because it's a duty-free port, you'll find some of the best shopping in the Caribbean here. There is a wide selection of European merchandise, including crystal, perfumes, jewelry, and fashions, sometimes at 25% to 50% less than in the United States and Canada. There are also fine liqueurs, cognacs, and cigars. Whether you're seeking jewelry, perfume, or St-Tropez bikinis, you'll find it in one of the boutiques along rue de la République and rue de la Liberté in Marigot.

Prices are often quoted in U.S. dollars, and salespeople frequently speak English. U.S. currency, credit cards, and traveler's checks are generally accepted. In addition to their regular hours, some larger shops open on Sunday and holidays if cruise ships are in port.

Harborside in Marigot, there's a frisky **morning market** with vendors selling spices, fruit, shells, and local handcrafts. Mornings are even more alive at **Port La Royale,** the bustling center of everything. Schooners unload produce from the neighboring islands, boats board guests for picnics on deserted beaches, and a brigantine sets out on a sightseeing sail. It's the largest shopping arcade on the French side.

Galerie Périgourdine, another cluster of boutiques, faces the post office. Here you might pick up some designer wear for both men and women.

At the **Gingerbread and Mahogany Gallery,** 4–4 Marina Royale 14 (☎ **0590-87-73-21**), owner Simone Seitre scours Haiti four times a year to secure the best works. You'll also find dozens of charming and inexpensive handcrafts at this little gallery, on a narrow alleyway at the marina next to the Café de Paris.

In Port La Royale, **Havane** (☎ 0590-87-70-39) is the island's leading choice for French designer fashions, and sometimes you get discounts. **Lipstick** (☎ 0590-87-73-24) has the largest assortment of duty-free fragrances and cosmetics. You can also get facials and massages here. There's another branch on rue de la République de Marigot (☎ 0590-87-53-92).

La Romana, Rue de la République (☎ 0590-87-88-16), retails the latest collection of La Perla swimwear, resort wear for day and evening, perfume, and lingerie. Its collection of Fendi bags, luggage, and accessories is one of the largest in the Caribbean.

Maneks, 24 Rue de la République (☎ 0590-87-54-91), has a little bit of everything: video cameras, electronics, household appliances, tobacco products, liquors, gifts, souvenirs, film, watches, T-shirts, sunglasses, pearls from Majorca, and beach accessories, even Cuban cigars.

Well-stocked **Oro de Sol Jewelers,** Rue de la République (☎ 0590-87-56-51), has an imaginative stock that includes gold watches and high-fashion jewelry.

BEACHES

St. Maarten has 36 beautiful white-sand beaches, so it's comparatively easy to find one for yourself.

You can often use the changing facilities at some of the bigger resorts for a small fee. Nudists should head for the French side, although the Dutch side is getting more liberal about such things.

Warning: If it's too secluded, be careful: There have been reports of robberies on some remote beaches. Don't bring valuables to the beach.

THE DUTCH SIDE   On the island's west side, **Mullet Bay Beach** is shaded by palm trees but can get crowded on weekends. Water sports equipment rentals can be arranged on the beach.

Great Bay Beach is preferable if you'd like to stay near Front Street in Philipsburg. This mile-long beach is sandy, but it may not be as clean as some of the more remote beaches. Immediately to the west, at the foot of Fort Amsterdam, **Little Bay Beach** looks like a Caribbean postcard, but it can get overrun with visitors.

Stretching the length of Simpson Bay Village, west of Philipsburg, the white-sand **Simpson Bay Beach** is shaped like a half moon. Water sports equipment rentals are available.

North of the airport, **Maho Bay Beach,** at the Maho Beach Hotel and Casino, is ideal in many ways, if you don't mind the planes passing overhead. Palms provide shade, and food and drink can be purchased at the hotel.

The sands are pearly white at **Oyster Pond Beach,** near the Oyster Pond Hotel northeast of Philipsburg. Bodysurfers like the rolling waves here. In the same vicinity, **Dawn Beach** is noted for the underwater beauty of its offshore reefs.

Cupecoy Bay Beach lies just north of the Dutch-French border. On the island's western side, there is a string of three white-sand beaches set against caves and sandstone cliffs that provide morning shade. The site doesn't have facilities, but is still very popular. One section of the beach is "clothing optional." The 1995 storms, unfortunately, unearthed some rocky parts that sunbathers find uncomfortable.

THE FRENCH SIDE   Top rating on the French side goes to **Baie Longue,** a long, beautiful beach that's rarely crowded. The very expensive deluxe hotel La Samanna opens onto this beachfront. Unfortunately, the 1995 hurricanes created holes offshore, which makes swimming here more hazardous than before. Baie Longue lies to the north of Cupecoy Beach, reached by taking the Lowlands Road. Don't leave any valuables in your car, as many break-ins have been reported.

If you continue north, you reach the approach to **Baie Rouge,** another long and popular stretch of sand and jagged coral.

Snorkelers are drawn to the rock formations at both ends of this beach. There are no changing facilities.

On the island's north side, to the west of Espérance airport, **Grand-Case Beach** is small but select, having recovered from the storm debris left by the 1995 hurricanes.

✪ **Orient Beach** is one of the Caribbean's most famous clothes-optional beaches. A taxi will take you to the **Club Orient Naturist Resort** (☎ 0590-87-33-85), where you can join in the stripped-down fun. Sports equipment is available for rent.

Uninhabited **Pinel Island,** a sandy little islet off the northeast coast, has only about 500 yards of beach, but it's choice. It's set off the coast of Cul-de-Sac in St. Martin. Picnics are possible here, but there are no facilities. You can go on a snorkeling adventure, taking in the beauty of coral reefs inhabited by tropical fish that you can hand feed. The islet is reached by "putt putts," small boats that can be rented on the beach at Cul-de-Sac. It's a memorable way to spend three or four hours in the sun.

GOLF, RIDING, SAILING, DIVING, TENNIS & WATER SPORTS

GOLF The **Mullet Bay Resort** (☎ 599/5-52801, ext. 1851) has a challenging 18-hole course. Greens fees are $105.

HORSEBACK RIDING At **Crazy Acres,** Dr. J. H. Dela Fuente St., Cole Bay (☎ 599/5-42793), riding expeditions end on an isolated beach where horses and riders enjoy a cool postride romp in the water. Two experienced escorts accompany a maximum of six people on the 2¹/₂-hour outings, which begin Monday through Saturday at 9:30am and 2:30pm and cost $50 per person. Riders should wear bathing suits under their riding clothes. Make reservations at least two days in advance.

SAILING A popular pastime is to sign up for a day of picnicking, sailing, snorkeling, and sightseeing aboard one of several sleek sailboats. *Random Wind* operates in conjunction with **Fun in the Sun,** Great Bay Marina (☎ 599/5-70210), on the Dutch side. This 47-foot traditional clipper circumnavigates the island, carrying 15 passengers at $70 apiece.

SCUBA DIVING Scuba diving is excellent around French St. Martin, with reef, wreck, cave, and drift dives going down from 20 to 70 feet. Dive sites include Ilet Pinel for shallow diving; Green Key, a barrier reef; Flat Island for sheltered coves and geologic faults; and Tintamarre, known for its shipwreck. The island's premier dive operation is **Marine Time,** whose offices are in the same building as L'Aventure, Chemin du Port, 97150 Marigot (☎ 0590-87-20-28). It offers morning and afternoon dives in deep and shallow water, to wrecks, and over reefs, at $45 per dive. A resort course for first-time divers costs $75.

On the Dutch side, crystal-clear bays and countless coves make for good snorkeling and scuba diving. Underwater visibility runs from 75 to 125 feet. The biggest attraction for scuba divers is the 1801 British man-of-war, HMS *Proselyte,* which sunk to a watery grave on a reef a mile off the coast.

The best Dutch-side water sports are found at **Pelican Watersports,** Pelican Resort and Casino, Simpson Bay (☎ 599/5-42604). Its PADI-instructed program features very knowledgeable guides. Divers are taken out in custom-built 28- and 35-foot boats. A two-tank dive costs $90. They can also arrange snorkeling trips.

SNORKELING The calm waters ringing the shallow reefs and tiny coves found throughout the island make it a snorkeler's heaven. The waters off the northeastern shores of French St. Martin are protected as a regional underwater nature reserve, **Reserve Sous-Marine Régionale.** The area includes Flat Island (also known as Tintamarre), Pinel Islet, Green Key, and Petite Clef. Snorkeling can be enjoyed individually or on sailing trips. You can rent equipment at almost any hotel on the beach.

One of the best-recommended sites for snorkeling lies on the beachfront of Grand-Case Beach Club, where **Under the Waves** (☎ 0590-87-51-87) launches hour-long snorkeling trips to St. Martin's offshore reefs, costing $25 per person. Reservations are recommended.

TENNIS   In St. Maarten, you'll have to call a hotel and see if courts are free. Try **Maho Beach Hotel and Casino,** Maho Bay (☎ 599/5-52115), and **Oyster Bay Beach Resort,** Oyster Pond (☎ 599/5-22206).

On the French side, tennis buffs can play at most hotels. **Le Méridien L'Habitation,** Anse Marcel (☎ 0590-87-67-00), has six courts; **La Samanna,** Baie Longue (☎ 0590-87-64-00), has three.

WINDSURFING   Winds and waves off most of the island's beaches are relatively unpredictable. The best spots for this activity are the beaches near Grand Case, notably Orient Beach and Coconut Grove Beach. Here, relatively constant winds and reef-protected waters create good windsurfing conditions. To link up with the activity, check with **Bikini Beach Watersports** (☎ 0590-87-43-25).

DINING

PHILIPSBURG

Antoine's, 103 Front St. (☎ 599/5-22964), offers *la belle cuisine* in an atmospheric building by the sea. Its urbane Gallic specialties with Creole overtones are among the island's best. We begin with the chef's savory kettle of fish soup. If featured, opt for the baked red snapper filet delicately flavored with white wine, lemon, shallots, and a butter sauce. Frozen veal and beef are shipped in, thawed out and fashioned into rather delectable dishes, especially the veal scaloppini with a mustard and cream sauce.

Open-air ✪ **Cheri's Café,** 45 Cinnamon Grove Shopping Centre, Maho Beach (☎ 599/5-53361), is the island's hot spot, known for its inexpensive food and live bands. You can get 16-ounce steaks, a simple burger, or grilled fresh fish. The bartender's special is a frozen "Straw Hat," made with vodka, coconut, tequila, pineapple and orange juices, and strawberry liqueur.

Start the day overlooking Simpson Bay with extra-thick French toast made with homemade egg bread at the ✪ **Crocodile Express Café,** at the Pelican Resort & Casino (☎ 599/5-42503, ext. 1127). For lunch and afternoon snacks, hearty deli fare includes well-stuffed sandwiches, grilled local fish, tasty kebabs, and grilled chicken breast West Indian style.

Open to a harbor view, **The Greenhouse,** Bobby's Marina, off Front Street (☎ 599/5-22941), is filled with plants. As you dine, breezes filter through the open-air eatery. Lunches include the catch of the day, a wide selection of burgers, and conch chowder. By no means does this place serve the best food on the island, but it's plentiful and a good value. Some patrons use it merely as a drinking venue.

Near the airport, ✪ **Lynette's,** Simpson Bay Blvd. (☎ 599/5-52865), is the most noteworthy West Indian restaurant in St. Maarten, completely unpretentious and rich in local flavors and charm. The menu is filled with tried-and-true Caribbean staples, including *colombos* (ragouts) of goat and chicken, stuffed crab backs, curried seafood, fillet of snapper with green plantains and Creole sauce or garlic butter. An ideal lunch might be a brimming bowlful of pumpkin soup followed by a main course salad—the one made from herbed lobster is particularly succulent.

IN AND AROUND MARIGOT

Real French people eat at ✪ **La Brasserie de Marigot,** 11 Rue du Général-de-Gaulle (☎ 0590-87-94-43). Lunches include pot-au-feu, choucroûte (sauerkraut garni), blanquette de veau, cassoulet, and even chicken on a spit and steak tartare. If all this sounds too heavy at midday in the West Indies, you can also order lighter fare, such as a salad. You can order interesting terrines here, and wine is sold by the glass, carafe, or bottle. The kitchen also prepares a handful of Caribbean dishes. You'll find the most glamorous "take-out" service on St. Martin here.

La Maison sur le Port, Rue de la République (☎ **0590-87-56-38**), serves French cuisine in elegant surroundings. At lunch, seated on the covered terrace, you can choose from a number of salads, as well as fish and meat courses that include snapper, salmon, and fresh swordfish in a coconut sauce. The place is firmly French, but with some Caribbean twists and flavors.

A flight of wooden stairs leads to a wooden deck above Marigot's seafront, whereon you will find **Le Mini Club,** Rue de la Liberté (☎ **0590-87-50-69**). It's not the best restaurant on the island, but it has many fans because it uses quality ingredients and prepares every dish exceedingly well. Specialties available at lunch include lobster soufflé, fish and vegetable terrines, red snapper with Creole sauce, sweetbreads in puff pastry, and many salads.

The chefs at ✪ **La Vie en Rose,** Boulevard de France at rue de le République (☎ **0590-87-54-42**), turn out the island's best cuisine, and the location is right off the pier, near the tourist information office. Even though the menu is classic French, you can't deny the Caribbeanness of the medallions of lobster in lime sauce or the boneless breast of duck on a bed of raspberry sauce with fried bananas. French visitors seem more willing to pay astronomical prices for these vittles than do Americans. If you don't want to pay the high prices and eat heavy food at lunch, you can patronize the ground floor tearoom and pastry shop, serving a light lunch with wine for about $20.

20   St. Thomas & St. John   ⚓ ⚓ ⚓ ⚓

One of the Caribbean's busiest ports, St. Thomas often hosts more than 10 cruise ships a day during the peak winter season. The most developed of the U.S. Virgin Islands, it has such a large concentration of retail outlets that the territory's somewhat seedy capital, Charlotte Amalie, is now the Caribbean's shopping capital.

In stark contrast to this busy scene, more than half of nearby St. John is preserved within the government-protected Virgin Islands National Park. Ringed by a rocky coastline formed into crescent-shaped bays and white-sand beaches, this smallest of the U.S. Virgin Islands hosts abundant bird life and wildlife. Miles of serpentine hiking trails are dotted with the ruins of 18th-century Danish plantations and provide panoramic views. Although hurricanes battered the area hard in the mid-90s, all shops, restaurants, and attractions should be up and running by the time you read this—unless, of course, another hurricane hits.

Most cruise ships dock in Charlotte Amalie on St. Thomas, but a few anchor directly off St. John. Most offer excursions to St. John, but if yours doesn't, it's easy to get there on your own.

FAST FACTS

Currency   The U.S. dollar is the coin of the realm.

Information   The **U.S. Virgin Islands Division of Tourism** has offices at Tolbod Gade (☎ **809/774-8784**), open Monday through Friday from 8am to 5pm, and Saturday from 8am to noon. There's also a branch office at the Havensight Mall, where you can pick up *St. Thomas This Week,* with maps of St. Thomas and St. John. The St. John Tourist Office (☎ **809/776-6450**) is located near the Battery at Cruz Bay.

Language   It's English.

ST. THOMAS

With a population of some 50,000, tiny St. Thomas isn't exactly a tranquil tropical retreat. The place abounds in shops, bars, restaurants, and resorts.

COMING ASHORE

Most cruise ships anchor at Havensight Mall, 1½ miles from the town center at the eastern end of the Charlotte Amalie harbor. The mall has a tourist information office, restaurants, duty-free shops, a bookstore, a bank, a U.S. postal van, and phones that accept long distance credit cards. We suggest taking a taxi for $5 to the center of Charlotte Amalie; you can walk, but some people have been mugged along the way.

If Havensight Mall is clogged with cruise ships, dockage will be at the Crown Point Marina, to the west of Charlotte Amalie. From here, a taxi into town costs $3.

SHORE EXCURSIONS

Shore excursions here are lackluster, but it's easy to get around on your own.

The typical St. Thomas sightseeing tour may be heavily booked, and it's dull. Far more interesting, especially if you crave the natural environment more than the shopping malls of Charlotte Amalie, is to take the St. John Island Tour, lasting 4 to 4½ hours. Costs, depending on the cruise line, range from $25 to $50. On St. John, an open-air safari bus goes through the national park, allowing time for snorkeling, swimming, and sunbathing.

Shore excursions often feature water adventures, which are much better and more interesting than the sightseeing jaunts. For example, most lines offer a sailing and snorkeling tour which allows you to appreciate the natural beauty of both St. John and St. Thomas. Often you're taken out on a single-hull sailing yacht or a catamaran. Most of these jaunts last 3½ to 4 hours and cost $35 to $45. Scuba adventures last three hours and cost $40 to $75.

GETTING AROUND

Taxis are the chief means of transport. They're unmetered, so agree on a fare with the driver before you get in. Official sightseeing fares are $30 for two passengers for two hours; each additional passenger pays another $12. For 24-hour radio-dispatch service, call ☎ 809/774-7457. Many taxis transport 8 to 12 passengers in vans to multiple destinations.

Comfortable and often air-conditioned **Vitran buses** serve Charlotte Amalie and as far away as Red Hook, jumping-off point for St. John. A one-way ride costs 75¢ within Charlotte Amalie or $1 to outer neighborhoods. For routes, stops, and schedules, call ☎ 809/774-5678.

Less structured and more erratic are **"taxi vans,"** a miniflotilla of privately owned vans or minibuses operated by local entrepreneurs. They make unscheduled stops along major traffic arteries and charge the same fares as the Vitran buses. They tend to be less comfortable, however.

We don't recommend renting a car here.

SEEING THE SIGHTS IN CHARLOTTE AMALIE

The color and charm of a slightly seedy Caribbean waterfront come vividly to life in Charlotte Amalie. Old warehouses once used for storing pirate goods still stand and, for the most part, house today's shops. In fact, the main streets (called "Gades" in honor of their Danish heritage) are now basically a shopping mall and are usually packed with visitors. Sandwiched among these shops are a few historic buildings, most of which can be covered on foot in about two hours. Before starting your tour, stop off in the so-called **Grand Hotel,** near Emancipation Park, which contains shops and a visitor center.

Dating from 1672, **Fort Christian** rises from the harbor to dominate the center of town. Named after the Danish king Christian V, the structure has been everything from a governor's residence to a jail.

St. Thomas

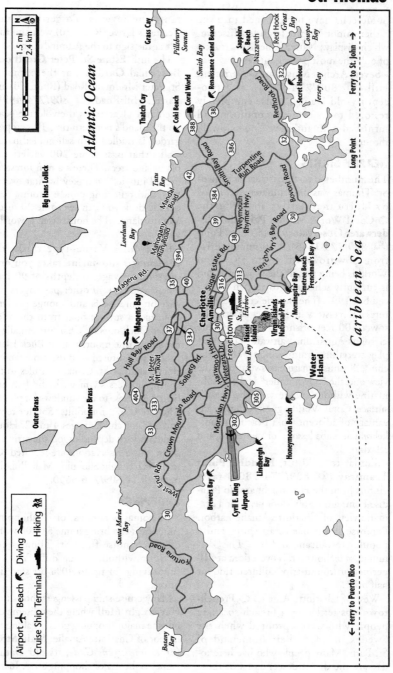

459

Some cells have been turned into the rather minor **Virgin Islands Museum,** which displays Native American artifacts of only the most passing interest.

Seven Arches Museum, Government Hill (☎ **809/774-9295**), is a two-century-old Danish house completely restored to its original condition and furnished with antiques. You can walk through.

NEARBY SIGHTS

The number-one tourist attraction of St. Thomas was unfortunately destroyed by Hurricane Marilyn in 1995: the ✪ **Coral World Marine Park and Underwater Observatory,** 6450 Coki Point (☎ **809/775-1555**), a 20-minute drive from downtown off route 38. Coral World is being rebuilt the way it was and is currently scheduled to reopen in December 1997. The marine complex features a three-story underwater observation tower 100 feet offshore. In the Marine Gardens Aquarium, saltwater tanks display everything from sea horses to sea urchins. A semisubmarine lets you enjoy the view and the "down under" feel of a submarine without ever leaving the ocean's surface. Coral World's guests can take advantage of adjacent Coki Beach for snorkel rental, scuba lessons, or swimming and relaxing.

Similar to a ski lift, **Paradise Point Tramway** (☎ **809/774-9809**) takes visitors from the Havensight area to Paradise Point atop a 697-foot peak for a dramatic view of Charlotte Amalie harbor. Paradise Point has retail shops and a popular restaurant and bar. The 3^1/2-minute ride, however, is overpriced at $10 per person round-trip; children ride for half price.

West of Charlotte Amalie, ✪ **Frenchtown** was settled by a French-speaking people who were uprooted when the Swedes invaded their homeland of St. Barts. Many people who live here today are the direct descendants of those long-ago immigrants. This colorful fishing village contains several interesting restaurants and taverns. To get here, take Veteran's Drive (Route 30) west and turn left at the sign to the Admirals Inn.

The lush **Estate St. Peter Greathouse Botanical Gardens,** at the corner of St. Peter Mountain Road (Route 40) and Barrett Hill Road (☎ **809/774-4999**), decorates 11 acres on the volcanic peaks on the island's northern rim. This tropical garden is riddled with self-guided nature walks that pass some 200 varieties of plants and trees. There's a rain forest, an orchid jungle, a monkey habitat, waterfalls, and reflecting ponds. From a panoramic deck you can see some 20 of the Virgin Islands. The house itself is worth a visit.

For a Jules Verne–type thrill, the ✪ *Atlantis* **submarine** takes you on a one-hour voyage to depths of 90 feet, where you and 30 other passengers will gaze on coral reefs and sponge gardens. You take a surface boat from the West Indies Dock outside Charlotte Amalie to the submarine moorage near Buck Island (not to be confused with the more famous Buck Island at St. Croix, 40 miles to the south). Divers swim with the fish and herd them close to the windows for photos. The fare is $72 for adults, $36 for teens, and $27 for children ages 4 to 12. Hours and days vary depending on the arrival of cruise ships; reservations are required. Go to the Havensight Shopping Mall, Building 6, or call ☎ **809/776-5650.**

SHOPPING

St. Thomas is famous for its shopping. Americans can bring home $1,200 worth of merchandise from St. Thomas and St. John without paying duty. You can find savings of up to 40% off stateside prices.

Many cruise-ship passengers shop at the **Havensight Mall** where they disembark, but the major shopping goes on along the harbor of Charlotte Amalie. **Main Street** (or *Dronningens Gade,* its old Danish name) is the major shopping strip. Just to the north is merchandise-loaded **Back Street,** or *Vimmelskaft.* Many shops are also spread along the **Waterfront Highway** (also called *Kyst Vejen*). Running between these major streets is a series of side streets, walkways, and alleys, all filled with shops. Among these are Tolbod Gade, Raadets Gade, Royal Dane Mall, Palm Passage, Storervaer Gade, and Strand Gade. All the major stores in St. Thomas are located by number on an excellent map in *St. Thomas This Week,* distributed free to all arriving cruise-ship passengers.

If you want to combine a little history with shopping, go into the courtyard of the old **Pissarro Building,** entered through an archway off Main Street. The impressionist painter lived here as a child. On the second floor, the **Camille Pissarro Art Gallery** (☎ 809/774-4621) displays original and fine art from local and regional artists.

Street vendors must ply their trades in a designated area called **Vendors Plaza,** at the corner of Veterans Drive and Tolbod Gade. Hundreds of them converge under oversized parasols Monday through Saturday from 7:30am to 5:30pm and on Sunday if a cruise ship is expected. Food vendors are permitted to sell on sidewalks outside Vendors Plaza.

A. H. Riise Gift and Liquor Stores, 37 Main St. (☎ **800/524-2037** or 809/ 776-2303), is St. Thomas's oldest and largest outlet for luxury items such as jewelry, crystal, china, watches, and perfumes. It also offers the island's widest selection of liquor. Everything is displayed in a 19th-century Danish warehouse that extends from Main Street to the waterfront. The company has a perfume and liquor branch at Havensight Mall.

✪ **Bernard K. Passman,** 38A Main St. (☎ 809/777-4580), is the world's leading sculptor of black coral art and jewelry. Starting in Grand Cayman, he learned to fashion exquisite treasures from this material.

On one side of **Blue Carib Gems and Rocks,** 2 Back St. (☎ 809/774-8525), you can watch the craftspeople fashion raw stones into jewelry by the lost-wax process. Since the items are locally made, they do not count against Americans' $1,200 duty exemption. Incidentally, this establishment also provides emergency eyeglasses repair.

Often called the Tiffany's of the Caribbean, fabulous ✪ **Cardow Jewelers,** 39 Main St. (☎ 809/776-1140), boasts the world's largest selection of fine jewelry. The Treasure Cove section has cases of fine gold jewelry all priced under $200.

In the Havensight Mall, you'll find the best selection of Caribbean handcrafts, but not the best service, at the **Caribbean Marketplace,** Building III (☎ 809/ 776-5400). The store also sells Sunny Caribbee products. At a branch of **Colombian Emeralds International** (☎ 809/774-2442), you buy direct from the source. There's another outlet on Main Street. In Building VI, **Dockside Bookshop** (☎ 809/774-4937), has the island's best selection of books. **H. Stern Jewelers** (☎ 800/524-2024 or 809/ 776-1223) has a mall store as well as three branches on Main Street.

Cosmopolitan, Inc., Drakes Passage and the waterfront (☎ **809/776-2040**), features Bally shoes and handbags and fashionable swimwear. They also offer menswear at discount prices.

You'll smell spices at **Down Island Traders,** Veteran's Drive (☎ **809/ 776-4641**), which stocks spices, teas, seasonings, candies, jellies, jams, and condiments, most made from natural Caribbean products. There are also local cookbooks, silk-screened T-shirts and bags, Haitian metal sculpture, handmade jewelry, Caribbean folk art, and children's gifts.

At **Irmela's Jewel Studio,** in the Old Grand Hotel at the beginning of Main Street (☎ **800/524-2047** or 809/ 774-5875), much of the jewelry is custom-designed by Irmela and handmade at her studio. There's a large selection of cultured pearls, including freshwater Biwa, South Sea, and black Tahitian, as well as unset rubies, sapphires, emeralds, tanzanite, alexandrite, and others.

At A. H. Riise Mall, **The Linen House** (☎ 809/774-1668) has good-value linens, including place mats, decorative tablecloths, and many hand-embroidered goods.

The Leather Shop, 1 Main St. (☎ 809/776-0290), has the best selection from Fendi, Bottega Veneta, De Vecchi, Prima Classe, Furla, and Il Bisonte. Ask how to get to the outlet store on Back Street, where close-outs can net 50% off stateside retail tags.

The branch of **Little Switzerland,** 5 Main St. (☎ 809/776-2010), has an unsurpassed selection of watches. There are several other branches, including one at the Havensight Mall, but this main store has the best selection.

At 33 Main St., ✪ **Royal Caribbean** (☎ 809/776-4110) is a large camera and electronics store and a good source for watches, jewelry, and leather bags.

Billed as the world's largest perfumery, **Tropicana Perfume Shoppes** (☎ 800/233-7948 or 809/774-0010) stands at the beginning of Main Street near the Emancipation Park post office.

When you completely tire of French perfumes and Swiss watches, head for Rothschild Francis Square—or as it's called locally, **Market Square.** Here, under a Victorian tin roof, locals with machetes will slice open a fresh coconut for you so you can drink the milk, and women wearing bandannas will sell akee, cassava, or breadfruit they harvested themselves. Even if you don't buy anything, you still will have had an interesting cultural insight into St. Thomas.

✪ **Jim Tillett Art Gallery and Silk Screen Print Studio,** 4126 Anna's Retreat, Tutu (☎ 809/775-1929), features the gallery and screen-printing studio originally launched by designer Jim Tillett. Once an old Danish farm, this tropical compound now houses arts and crafts studios, galleries, and an outdoor garden restaurant and bar. Take Route 38 east from Charlotte Amalie.

Set near the island's center, **Mountain Top,** Route 33 (☎ 809/774-2400), is a modern shopping mall with about a dozen shops and a panoramic view. There's an aquarium and aviary, a snack bar, and an observation platform that overlooks the island.

BEACHES

St. Thomas has some good beaches, and you can reach them all relatively quickly in a taxi (arrange for the driver to return and pick you up at a designated time). If you're going to St. John, you may want to do your beaching there.

All the beaches are public, but some charge a fee. Guard your belongings from pickpockets and thieves.

THE NORTH SIDE　Magen Bay lies across the mountains 3 miles north of the capital. It's still beautiful, though its reputation has faded since it isn't as well maintained as it should be and is often overcrowded. The entrance fee is $1 per person and $1 per car. Changing facilities are available, and you can rent snorkeling gear and lounge chairs.

Near Coral World, **Coki Beach** is good, but it, too, can get overcrowded. Snorkelers like this beach. An East End bus runs to Smith Bay and lets you off at the gate to Coral World and Coki.

The beautiful **Renaissance Grand Beach Resort** opens onto Smith Bay in the vicinity of Coral World. You will find many water sports available here. The beach lies right off Route 38.

THE SOUTH SIDE　Morningstar lies about 2 miles east of Charlotte Amalie at Marriott's Frenchman's Reef Beach Resort. You can wear your most daring swimwear here and rent sailboats, snorkeling equipment, and lounge chairs.

Limetree Beach lures those who like a serene spread of sand. You can feed hibiscus blossoms to iguanas and rent snorkeling gear and lounge chairs.

Popular **Brewer's Beach,** near the University of the Virgin Islands, can be reached by the public bus marked "Fortuna" heading west from Charlotte Amalie. Near the airport, **Lindberg Beach** has a lifeguard, toilet facilities, and a bath-house, and also lies on the Fortuna bus route.

THE EAST END Small and special, **Secret Harbour** lies near condos whose owners you'll surely meet on the beach. With its white sand and coconut palms, it's almost the definition of Caribbean charm.

Panoramic ✪ **Sapphire Beach** is set against the backdrop of the desirable Sapphire Beach Resort and Marina complex, where you can lunch or order drinks. Windsurfers like this beach, and you can rent snorkeling gear and lounge chairs. A large reef lies close to the shore, and there are good views of offshore cays and St. John. The beach of fine white coral sand opens onto beautiful views of the bay. To reach it, you can take the East End bus from Charlotte Amalie, via Red Hook. Ask to be let off at the entrance to Sapphire Bay.

GOLF, SAILING, DIVING, TENNIS & WINDSURFING

GOLF Beautiful **Mahogany Run,** on the north shore at the Mahogany Run Golf & Tennis Resort, Mahogany Run Road (☎ **800/253-7103** or 809/777-6006), is an 18-hole, par-70 course that rises and drops like a roller coaster. From May through September, greens fees are $55, rising to $75 the rest of the year. Cart fees cost $15 year-round. No cut-offs, tank tops or swimwear are allowed in the clubhouse or on the golf course. It's an $8 taxi ride from the cruise dock.

SAILING You can avoid the crowds by sailing aboard *Fantasy* (☎ **809/775-5652**), which departs from the American Yacht Harbor at Red Hook at 9:30am daily. It sails to St. John and nearby islands, allowing a maximum of six passengers to go swimming, snorkeling, beach combing, or trolling. Snorkel gear with expert instruction is provided, as is a champagne lunch. A full-day trip costs $90 per person. A three-hour, half-day sail, morning or afternoon, costs $55.

SCUBA DIVING & SNORKELING With 30 spectacular reefs just off St. Thomas, the U.S. Virgins are an ideal venue in which to snorkel or dive.

DIVE In!, in the Sapphire Beach Resort and Marina, Smith Bay Road, Route 36 (☎ **809/775-6100**), offers professional instruction, daily beach and boat dives, custom dive packages, and snorkeling trips. An introductory course costs $55. Certified divers can enjoy a two-dive morning trip for $70 or a one-dive afternoon trip for $50.

TENNIS The best tennis is at **Wyndham Sugar Bay Beach Club,** 6500 Estate Smith Bay (☎ **809/777-7100**), which has the Virgin Islands' first stadium tennis court, seating 220, plus six additional Laykold courts that are lit at night.

Four courts are available at **Marriott's Frenchman's Reef Tennis Courts,** Flamboyant Point (☎ **809/776-8500,** ext. 444). Nonresidents are charged $10 per half hour.

WINDSURFING You can windsurf at the major resort hotels and at some public beaches, including Brewers Bay, Morningstar Beach, and Limetree Beach. **Renaissance Grand Beach Resort,** Smith Bay Road, Route 38 (☎ **809/775-1510**) offers windsurfing for $35 per hour.

DINING

In Charlotte Amalie

Beni Iguana (☎ **809/777-8744**), the island's only Japanese restaurant, occupies the sheltered courtyard of an old hotel across from Emancipation Square Park on Veteran's Drive. Perennial favorites include a "surf and surf" roll filled with shrimp and freshwater eel with a teriyaki glaze.

Still relatively undermobbed by cruise-ship passengers, ✪ **Hervé Restaurant and Wine Bar,** Government Hill (☎ **809/777-9703**), is the hot new restaurant of St. Thomas, the domain of Hervé P. Chassin, the island's best and most experienced restaurateur. His menu combines continental, American, and Caribbean influences—and does so in a romantic, historic setting. At lunch, begin with the conch fritters with mango chutney before preceding to the pan-seared Norwegian salmon, the braised lamb shank in red wine, or fresh herb-crusted chicken.

The all-purpose waterfront **Greenhouse,** Veterans Drive (☎ 809/774-7998), is especially popular with tired and shopped-out cruise passengers. The food is not the island's best, but it's satisfying. A breakfast menu segues into daily specialties that are typically American, but include some Jamaican-inspired dishes. A pretty good freshly grilled mahimahi is served here with a Florida Key lime ginger butter and Jamaican jerk. You might also try the barbecued pork ribs.

On the second floor of the International Plaza, the local **Hard Rock Café** (☎ 809/777-5555), carries on the international chain's "Smithsonian of Rock 'n' Roll" theme. Its burgers are the best in town, but most come here for fun and good times, not for the cuisine.

Virgilio's, 18 Dronningens Gade (☎ 809/776-4920), is the best northern Italian restaurant in the Virgin Islands. Lobster ravioli is the best there is. They serve such classic dishes as rack of lamb, except this one is filled with a porcini mushroom stuffing and glazed with a roasted garlic aioli. You can easily walk past the entrance on a narrow alleyway running between Main Street and Back Street.

In Frenchtown

West of town, **Alexander's,** Rue de St. Barthélemy (☎ 809/776-4211), serves Teutonic dishes that may be a bit heavy for the tropics, but are still quite good. There's a heavy emphasis on seafood, including conch schnitzel, plus at least 15 pasta dishes. If you'd like lighter fare at lunch, try either the crepes or the quiches and look for the generally intriguing chef's daily special.

✪ **Craig and Sally's,** 22 Estate Honduras (☎ 809/777-9949), is operated by a husband-wife team who escaped to the Caribbean from the snowbelt. All cuisine is created or inspired by Sally; Craig is the greeter and coordinator. The international cuisine at lunch or dinner includes pasta and seafood, with European and Asian influences. Dishes might include roasted pork with clams, duck sausage with lime sauce and mango-flavored lentils, or grilled swordfish. We especially like the lobster-stuffed, twice-baked potatoes.

On the North Coast

Just east of the Coral World turnoff, cruise-ship passengers flock to ✪ **Eunice's Terrace** for the most authentic cuisine on the island. It's a 20-minute ride from the cruise docks at Havensight, lying at 66–67 Smith Bay, Route 38 (☎ 809/775-3975). The best West Indian restaurant on the island, it specializes in fishburgers at lunch, along with some of the best stuffed sandwiches in St. Thomas. Look for the daily hot specials as well, including "doved" pork or mutton. (Doving involves baking sliced meat while basting with a combination of herb-flavored juices.)

Near the Sub Base

Barnacle Bill's, Crowna Bay Marina, 16 Sub Base (☎ 809/774-7444), serves good food and drink throughout the day and is an intriguing venue if you're interested in boating and mingling with the island's yachting set. Prices are reasonable, and portions are large and well prepared, with lots of burgers, sandwiches, pastas, and freshly made salads being washed down by a considerable amount of drink.

ST. JOHN

Smallest and least populated of the U.S. Virgin Islands, St. John lies about three miles east of St. Thomas, across Pillsbury Sound. The island is 7 miles long and 3 miles wide, with a total land area of some 20 square miles. Since 1956, more than half its land mass, as well as its shoreline waters, have been set aside as the Virgin Islands National Park.

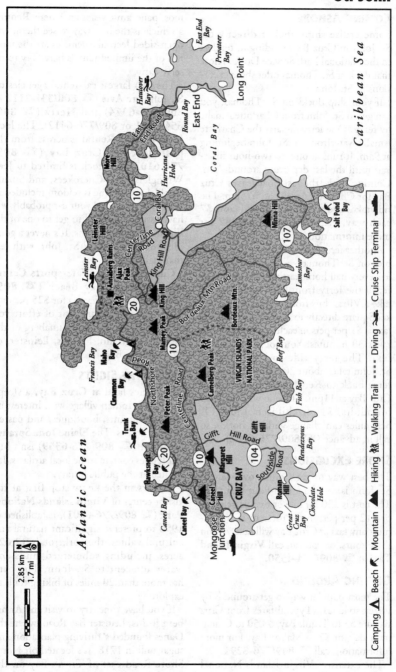

Caribbean Sea

East End Bay

Privateer Bay

Long Point

Hanover Bay

Round Bay

East End Bay

East End

More Hill

East End Road

Coral Bay

Hurricane Hole

Leinster Hill

Leinster Bay

Annaberg Ruins

Ajax Peak

Center line Road

King Hill Road

King Hill

Minna Hill

107

Salt Pond Bay

Lameshur Bay

Bordeaux Mtn. Road

Mamey Peak

Bordeaux Mtn.

10

20

Francis Bay

Maho Bay

Cinnamon Bay

Northshore Road

Camelberg Peak

VIRGIN ISLANDS NATIONAL PARK

Ref Bay

Peter Peak

Centerline Road

Fish Bay

Trunk Bay

Gifft Hill Road

Gifft

Gifft Hill

Rendezvous Bay

10

20

Hawksnest Bay

Margaret Hill

104

Southside Road

Atlantic Ocean

Caneel Bay

Caneel Hill

Ronan Hill

CRUZ BAY

Chocolate Hole

Caneel Bay

Great Cruz Bay

Mongoose Junction

N

2.85 km

1.7 mi

0

△ Camping △ Mountain 🥾 Hiking 🚶 Walking Trail ---- Diving ⚓ Cruise Ship Terminal

🏖 Beach

COMING ASHORE

Some cruise ships anchor directly off St. John in Cruz Bay, sending in tenders to the National Park Service Dock. Those that dock at St. Thomas offer shore excursions to St. John.

If your ship docks on St. Thomas, you can get to St. John from Charlotte Amalie by **ferry.** One ferry departs the Charlotte Amalie waterfront for St. John beginning at 9am. It runs at one- to two-hour intervals until the last departure around 7pm. Coming back, the last boat leaves Cruz Bay for Charlotte Amalie at 5:15pm. The ride takes about 45 minutes and costs $7 each way. Call ☎ **809/776-6282** for more information.

Another ferry leaves from the Red Hook pier on St. Thomas's eastern tip more or less every half hour starting at 6:30am. To reach the ferry from Charlotte Amalie, take a Vitran bus from a point near Market Square directly to Red Hook. The bus fare is $1 per person each way and the trip takes 30 minutes. You could also take a taxi. The ferry ride to Cruz Bay on St. John takes about 20 minutes. The last ferry back to Red Hook departs from Cruz Bay at 11pm. The one-way fare is $3 for adults, $1 for children under 11. Schedules can change without notice, so call in advance (☎ **809/776-6282**).

SHORE EXCURSIONS

The best way to get a quick overview of St. John is to take a two-hour taxi tour. The cost is $30 for one or two passengers, or $12 per person for three or more. Almost any taxi at Cruz Bay will take you on these tours, or you can call **Virgin Island Taxi** at ☎ **809/774-4550.**

GETTING AROUND

The most popular way to get around is by surrey-style taxi. Typical fares from Cruz Bay are $3 to Trunk Bay, $3.50 to Cinnamon Bay, or $7 to Mahoe Bay. For more information, call ☎ **809/776-8294.**

The extensive Virgin Islands National Park has kept the island's roads undeveloped and uncluttered, with some of the most panoramic vistas anywhere. Renting a vehicle is the best way to see them, and open-sided Jeep-like vehicles are the most fun of the limited rentals here. Try to reserve early.

The two largest car-rental agencies on St. John are **Avis** (☎ **800/331-2112** or 809/776-6374) and **Hertz** (☎ **800/654-3001** or 809/776-6412). The local **St. John Car Rental** is across from the post office in Cruz Bay (☎ **809/776-6103**). Its stock is limited to Jeep Wranglers, Jeep Cherokees, and Suzuki Sidekicks. Gasoline is seldom included in the rental price, and your car probably will have just enough fuel to get to one of the island's two gas stations. It's never a good idea to drive around St. John with less than half a tank of gas.

Cinnamon Bay Watersports Center on Cinnamon Bay Beach (☎ **809/776-6330**) rents bicycles for $25 per day. With a moderate amount of effort you can ride to the ruins at Annaberg or the beaches at Maho, Francis, Leinster, or Watermelon Bay.

SEEING THE SIGHTS

The ferries land at **Cruz Bay,** a sleepy little West Indian village with interesting bars, restaurants, boutiques, and pastel-painted houses. The **Elaine Ione Sprauve Museum** (☎ **809/776-6359**) isn't big, but it does contain some local artifacts. It's located at the public library.

Visitors in the know stop first at the visitor center of **Virgin Islands National Park** (☎ **809/776-6201**). Established in 1956 to preserve significant natural and cultural values, the park totals 12,624 acres, including submerged lands and water adjacent to St. John. The park has more than 20 miles of biking trails to explore.

If you have time, try to visit the **Annaberg Ruins,** Leinster Bay Road, where the Danes founded a thriving plantation and sugar mill in 1718. It's located off North Shore Road east of Trunk Bay on the north shore. On certain days of the week, park rangers give guided walks of the area.

SHOPPING

Compared to St. Thomas, there's not a lot of shopping to do on St. John. But the boutiques and shops at Cruz Bay are quite interesting. Most are clustered at **Mongoose Junction,** about a five-minute walk from the ferry dock. **Bamboula** (☎ 809/ 693-8699) has unusual gifts from the Caribbean, Guatemala, Haiti, India, Indonesia, and Central Africa. The store has clothing for both men and women under its own label—hand-batiked soft cottons and rayons. **The Canvas Factory** (☎ 809/776-6196) produces its own rugged and colorful canvas bags. Their products range from sailing hats to handsome luggage to an extensive line of island-made 100% cotton clothing.

The Clothing Studio (☎ 809/ 776-6585) is the Caribbean's oldest hand-painted clothing studio. You can watch talented artists create original designs on fine tropical swimwear, daytime wear, and evening clothes for men, women, and babies.

In the working **Donald Schnell Studio** (☎ 809/776-6420) and its attached gallery, Mr. Schnell and his assistants feature one of the finest collections of handmade pottery, sculpture, and blown glass in the Caribbean. Visitors can watch the staff work daily. The studio is especially noted for its rough-textured coral work. Water fountains are a specialty item, as are house signs. Their coral pottery dinnerware is unique and popular. The studio will ship works all over the world.

Fabric Mill (☎ 809/776-6194) features silk-screened and batik fabrics from around the world. Vibrant rugs and bed, bath, and table linens add the perfect touch to your home. Whimsical soft sculpture, sarongs, scarves, and handbags are also available here.

Also at Mongoose Junction, **R and I Goldsmithing** (☎ 809/776-6548), offers a large selection of island-designed jewelry, three-fourths of which is made locally. Also featured are the works of goldsmiths from outstanding American studios, plus Spanish coins.

As you wait at Cruz Bay for the ferry back to St. Thomas, you can browse through **Wharfside Village,** a complex of courtyards, alleys, and shady patios with a mishmash of boutiques, restaurants, fast-food joints, and bars.

Pusser's of the West Indies (☎ 809/ 693-8489), a link in a famous chain, offers a large collection of classically designed old-world travel and adventure clothing, along with unusual accessories.

A five-minute stroll along the waterfront from Cruz Bay will lead you to **Coconut Coast Studios,** Frank Bay (☎ 809/ 776-6944), the studio of Elaine Estern, one of the best watercolorists on the island. Note cards begin at $8, with unmatted prints priced from $15 to $275.

BEACHES

True beach lovers can't miss the great white sweep of ۞ **Trunk Bay.** But this gorgeous beach will be crowded, and beware of pickpockets lurking about. The beach has lifeguards and offers rentals, such as snorkel gear. Beginning snorkelers are attracted to its underwater trail near the shore. Both taxis and "safari buses" to Trunk Bay meet the ferry as it docks at Cruz Bay.

Caneel Bay, the stomping ground of the rich and famous, has seven beautiful beaches on its 170 acres. The best public beach among them is **Hawksnest Beach,** a little gem of white sand beloved by St. Johnians. The beach is a bit narrow and windy, but beautiful. Close to the road you'll find barbecue grills, and there are also portable toilets on site. Safari buses and taxis from Cruz Bay will take you along North Shore Road.

The campgrounds of **Cinnamon Bay** and **Maho Bay** have their own beaches where forest rangers sometimes have to tell visitors to put their swimming trunks back on. Snorkelers find good reefs here, and changing rooms and showers are available.

Salt Pond Bay is known to locals but often missed by visitors. The bay here is tranquil, but there are no facilities. The Ram Head Trail begins here and winds for a mile to a panoramic belvedere overlooking the bay.

HIKING, DIVING, TENNIS & WATER SPORTS

HIKING   Hiking is the big outdoor activity here, and a network of trails covers the national park. The visitor center at Cruz Bay gives away free trail maps; however, we suggest a tour by Jeep first, just to get your bearings. It's best to set out with someone experienced in the mysteries of the island. Both **Maho Bay** (☎ 809/776-6226) and **Cinnamon Bay** (☎ 809/776-6330) conduct nature walks.

SCUBA DIVING & SNORKELING

Divers can ask about scuba packages at **Low Key Watersports,** Wharfside Village (☎ 800/835-7718 or 809/693-8999). All wreck dives are two-tank/two-location dives. A two-tank dive costs $75. Snorkel tours cost $25 per person, and parasailing goes for $50.

Cruz Bay Watersports, Cruz Bay (☎ 809/776-6234), is a PADI and NAUI five-star diving center operating four custom dive boats daily. Two-tank reef dives with all the dive gear cost $70 to $78. Beginning scuba lessons start at $68.

TENNIS   There are public courts near the fire station at Cruz Bay, available on a first-come, first-served basis.

WATER SPORTS   The **Cinnamon Bay Watersports Center** on Cinnamon Bay Beach (☎ 809/776-6330) offers the best windsurfing. You can rent a board for $15 per hour; a two-hour introductory lesson costs $40. Sit-on-top kayaks are available to paddle to a secluded beach or explore a nearby island with an old Danish ruin. One- and two-person models rent for $10 to $17 per hour. You can also sail away in a 12- or 14-foot Hobie monohull sailboat, which rents for $20 to $30 per hour. Snorkeling equipment rents for $7 from the Watersports Beach Shop.

DINING

The **Caneel Bay Beach Terrace Dining Room,** in the Caneel Bay Hotel (☎ 809/776-6111), is an elegant choice with open-air tables overlooking the beach. The $22 self-service buffet luncheon is one of the best in the Virgin Islands. Although we've found the cuisine here variable over the years, the professional standards remain high.

The Fish Trap, in the Raintree Inn (☎ 809/693-9994), is known for its seafood selection, but it also caters to both the vegetarian crowd and the burger crowd. This is not just another fish and chips joint.

At the **Mongoose Restaurant, Café, and Bar,** Mongoose Junction (☎ 809/693-8677), you can perch at the open-centered bar for a drink and sandwich or sit out on a deck. Lunches include soups, well-stuffed sandwiches, salad platters, burgers, and pastas. The setting, locale, long serving hours, and reasonable prices make this place a winning choice. Be warned: This establishment's Sunday brunch gets mobbed.

The double-decker, air-conditioned **Pusser's** store and pub, at Wharfside Village in Cruz Bay (☎ 809/693-8489), overlooks the harbor near the ferry dock. You can enjoy traditional English fare or jerk tuna loin, or even jerk chicken with a tomato basil sauce over penne. Chicken Tropical is coconut crusted, pan seared, and served up with a rum and banana sauce. Finish with Pusser's famous "mud pie." The food is satisfying, but who can judge how good it is after all that Pusser rum? If you're in your bathing suit and want only a hamburger for lunch, try Pusser's Beach Bar.

Out on the island while touring, plan to have lunch at **Shipwreck Landing,** 34 Freeman's Ground, Route 107, Coral Bay (☎ 809/693-5640), bedecked in tropical plants and palms and lying 8 miles east of Cruz Bay on Salt Pond Beach. Seafood and continental fare are the specialty here. In addition to the usual sandwiches, salads, and burgers, you can opt for more substantial fare, including a pan-seared blackened snapper in Cajun spices.

21   San Juan   ⇩ ⇩ ⇩ ⇩ ⇩

San Juan is the Caribbean's most historical port. Its shopping is topped by St. Thomas and St. Maarten, but overall its historic sights, attractions, gambling, and diversions make it number one in the Caribbean. You'll find some of the best restaurants and hotels in the Caribbean here, and it even has a glitzy beach strip, the Condado.

The Port of San Juan is the busiest ocean terminal in the West Indies. There are about 710 cruise-ship arrivals every year, bringing more than 850,000 passengers.

San Juan is also covered in chapter 8, "Ports of Embarkation."

COMING ASHORE

The harbor where both commercial cargo ships and cruise ships arrive lies outside San Juan Bay, a body of water about 3 miles long and 1 mile wide, and almost completely encircled by land. The dock area, now restored, is an attractive place for strolling, with its plazas, fountains, promenades, and beaches.

From the docks, a spacious walkway connects the piers to the cobblestone streets of Old San Juan, where you can shop, or take a waiting taxi to the beaches of Condado.

SHORE EXCURSIONS

There's no need to bother with organized shore excursions. It's easy enough to get around on your own.

Castillo Watersports and Tours, calle Doncella 27, Punta Las Marias, Santurce (☎ 787/791-6195), offers bus tours. A popular half-day tour travels to El Yunque rain forest. You'll see lush vegetation and waterfalls and stop at an observation tower from which you'll have a view of the entire northeastern coast. The tour departs daily, lasts approximately four hours, and costs $25 per person. A four-hour city tour, which goes for $25 per person,

departs daily and includes a stop at Bacardi's rum factory (with a complimentary rum drink).

For a daytime sea excursion to the area's best islands, beaches, reefs, and snorkeling, contact **Capt. Jack Becker,** Villa Marina Yacht Harbor, Fajardo (☎ **787/860-0861** or 787/385-3509 cell phone). He takes two to six passengers at a time on his sailboat from 10am to 3:30pm for $50 per person.

Puerto Rico's varied and often hard-to-reach natural treasures have been packaged into four ecotours operated by **Tropix Wellness Tours** (☎ **787/268-2173;** fax 787/268-1722). You can explore sea turtles' nesting sites in Culebra, the phosphorescent bay in Vieques, the Rìo Camuy cave system in Camuy, and the dry, desertlike forest in Guánica.

GETTING AROUND

You can cover most of the Old Town on foot or take a free trolley. You can also take buses or taxis to the Condado.

The *Agua Expreso* ferry connects the old town of San Juan with the industrial and residential communities of Hato Rey and Cataño, across the bay. Ferries depart from the San Juan Terminal at the pier in Old San Juan daily. The one-way fare is 75¢ to Hato Rey (until 6:40pm) and 50¢ to Cataño (until 10pm). Rides last about 20 minutes. For more information, call ☎ 787/751-7055.

Taxis, operated by the Public Service Commission, are metered in San Juan—or at least they're supposed to be. The initial charge is $1, plus 10¢ for each thirteenth of a mile and 50¢ for every suitcase. A minimum fare is $3. You can call the PSC (☎ **787/756-1919**) to request information or report any irregularities.

When you tire of walking around Old San Juan, you can board a free trolley. Designated departure points are at the Marina and La Puntilla, but you can get on any place along the route.

The Metropolitan Bus Authority operates buses in the greater San Juan area.

Bus stops are marked by upright metal signs or yellow posts, reading PARADA. A typical fare is 25¢ to 50¢. For route and schedule information, call ☎ 787/ 767-7979.

FAST FACTS

Currency   The U.S. dollar is used here. Canadian currency is accepted by some big hotels.

Information   For advice and maps, contact the **Tourist Information Center** at La Casita, near Pier 1 in Old San Juan (☎ 787/721-2400).

Language   Most people involved in serving the tourist industry speak English, although Spanish is the native tongue.

A WALKING TOUR OF OLD SAN JUAN

The streets are narrow and teeming with traffic, but a walk through Old San Juan (in Spanish, *El Viejo San Juan*) is like a stroll through five centuries of history. In a seven-square-block historic landmark area in the city's westernmost part you'll see many of Puerto Rico's chief historical attractions.

Begin your walk near the post office, at **Plaza de la Marina,** situated at the eastern edge of one of San Juan's showcase promenades: paseo de la Princesa. The paseo sweeps from the cruise piers past La Princesa, around the old city walls beneath the Casa Blanca, and continues to the entrance of 16th-century El Morro fortress.

Walk westward along paseo de la Princesa until you reach **La Princesa,** the gray-and-white building on your right, which for centuries was one of the most feared prisons in the Caribbean. Today it houses a museum and the offices of the Puerto Rico Tourism Company.

Continue walking westward to the base of the heroic fountain near the edge of the sea. Turn to your right and follow the seaside promenade as it parallels the edge of the **City Walls,** even today considered an engineering marvel.

Continue walking between the sea and the base of the city walls until the walkway passes through the walls at the **San Juan Gate,** at calle San Francisco and Recinto del Oeste. This is actually more of a tunnel than a gate. Now that you're inside the once-dreaded fortification, turn immediately right and walk uphill along calle Recinto del Oeste. The wrought-iron gates at the street's end lead to **La Fortaleza** and **Mansion Ejecutiva,** the centuries-old residence of the Puerto Rican governor, located on calle La Fortaleza.

Now retrace your steps along calle Recinto del Oeste, walking first downhill and then uphill for about a block until you reach caleta de las Monjas. Fork left until you see a panoramic view and a contemporary statue marking the center of **Plazuela de la Rogativa.**

Now, continue your stroll westward, passing between a pair of urn-capped gateposts. You'll be walking parallel to the crenulations of the 17th-century city walls. The boulevard will fork. Take the right-hand fork and continue climbing the steeply inclined cobble-covered ramp to its top. Walk westward across the field toward the neoclassical gateway of a fortress that was believed to be impregnable for centuries, the **Castillo de San Felipe del Morro** ("El Morro"). Here, Spanish Puerto Rico struggled to defend itself against the navies of Great Britain, France, and Holland, as well as the hundreds of pirate ships that wreaked havoc throughout the colonial Caribbean. The fortress walls were designed as part of a network of defenses that made San Juan *La Ciudad Murada* (The Walled City).

With El Morro behind you, retrace your steps through the field to the point where you stood when you first sighted it. Walk past the **Antiguo Manicomio Insular,** originally built in 1854 as an insane asylum and now the Puerto Rican Academy of Fine Arts. Walk parallel to its facade, turning right at an unmarked street which passersby might tell you is the Calle de Beneficias. The stately neoclassical

Old San Juan

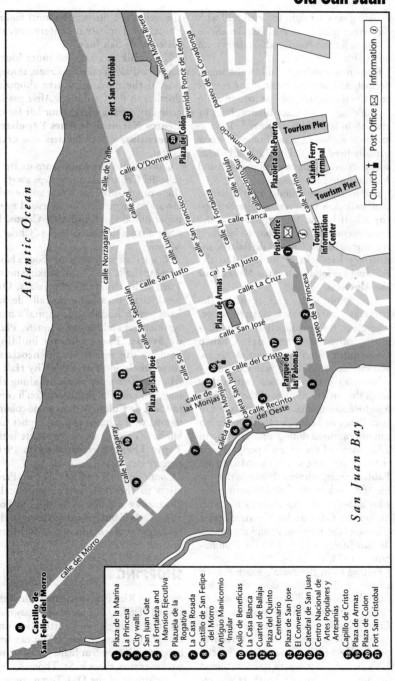

Atlantic Ocean

Fort San Cristóbal

avenida Muñoz Rivera

avenida Ponce de León

paseo de la Covadonga

Plaza de Colón

calle O'Donnell

calle de Valle

calle Sol

calle Norzagaray

calle Luna

calle San Francisco

calle Comercio

calle Tetuán

calle Recinto Sur

Tourism Pier

Plazóleta del Puerto

Cataño Ferry Terminal

Tourism Pier

calle Marina

calle La Fortaleza

calle Tanca

Post Office

Tourist Information Center

calle San Justo

calle San Justo

calle Luna

calle San Sebastián

calle San José

calle Sol

Plaza de Armas

calle La Cruz

paseo de la Princesa

calle de las Monjas

calle San José

calle del Cristo

caleta San Juan

caleta de las Monjas

caleta San Juan

calle Recinto del Oeste

Parque de las Palomas

Plaza de San José

San Juan Bay

calle del Morro

Castillo de San Felipe del Morro

❶ Plaza de la Marina	
❷ La Princesa	
❸ City walls	
❹ San Juan Gate	
❺ La Fortaleza and Mansion Ejecutiva	
❻ Plazuela de la Rogativa	
❼ La Casa Rosada	
❽ Castillo de San Felipe del Morro	
❾ Antiguo Manicomio Insular	
❿ Asilo de Beneficias	
⓫ La Casa Blanca	
⓬ Cuartel de Ballaja	
⓭ Plaza del Quinto Centenario	
⓮ Plaza de San Jose	
⓯ El Convento	
⓰ Catedral de San Juan	
⓱ Centro Nacional de Artes Populares y Artesanias	
⓲ Capillo de Cristo	
⓳ Plaza de Armas	
⓴ Plaza de Colon	
㉑ Fort San Cristobal	

Church ✝ Post Office ⊠ Information ⓘ

471

building on your right (painted buff with fern-green trim) is the **Asilo de Beneficias** ("Home for the Poor"), which dates from the 1840s.

Continue walking uphill to the small, formal, and sloping plaza at the street's top. On the right-hand side, within a trio of buildings, is **La Casa Blanca,** built by the son-in-law of Juan Ponce de León as the great explorer's island home (he never actually lived here). This "White House" today accommodates a small museum and has beautiful gardens.

Exit by the compound's front entrance, and walk downhill, retracing your steps for a half block, heading toward the monumental tangerine-colored building on your right, the **Cuartel de Ballajá,** the military barracks of Ballajá. On the building's second floor is the **Museum of the Americas.**

After your visit, exit through the barracks's narrow back (eastern) door, where you'll immediately spot the dramatic modern **Plaza del Quinto Centenario.** From its lowest elevation, you can see the Old San Juan Cemetery.

Now, walk a short block eastward to reach the ancient borders of the **Plaza de San José,** dominated by a heroic statue of Juan Ponce de León, cast from an English cannon captured during a naval battle in 1797. Around the square's periphery are three important sites: the **Museo de Pablo Casals,** whose exhibits honor the life and work of the Spanish-born cellist who adopted Puerto Rico as his final home; the **Casa de los Contrafuertes** (House of the Buttresses); and the **Iglesia de San José,** established by the Dominicans in 1523.

Exiting from the plaza's southwestern corner, walk downhill along one of the capital's oldest and best-known streets, calle del Cristo (also known as calle Cristo). Two blocks later, at the corner of caleta de las Monjas, is **El Convento,** originally built as a convent in the 17th century, but which has functioned for many decades as a hotel. It was recently restored. Across the street from El Convento lies the island's most famous church and spiritual centerpiece, the **Catedral de San Juan.**

Now walk at least two more blocks southward along calle del Cristo, through one of the most attractive shopping districts in the Caribbean. After passing calle Fortaleza, look on your left for the **Centro Nacional de Artes Populares y Artesanias,** a popular arts and crafts center.

Continue to the southernmost tip of calle del Cristo (just a few steps away) to the wrought-iron gates that surround a chapel no bigger than an oversized newspaper kiosk, the **Capilla de Cristo.** Its silver altar is dedicated to the "Christ of Miracles."

Now retrace your steps for about a block along the calle del Cristo, walking north. Turn right along calle Fortaleza. One block later, turn left onto calle de San José, which leads to the capital's most symmetrical and beautiful square, **Plaza de Armas.** Two important buildings flanking this square are the neoclassic **Intendencia** and San Juan's **City Hall.**

Leave the square eastward along the length of calle San Francisco. You'll come to **Plaza de Colón,** with its stone column topped with a statue of Christopher Columbus. To the side of the square is the **Tapía Theater,** restored to its 19th-century elegance.

Continue to the end of calle San Francisco to the intersection with calle Norzagaray and follow the signs to **Fort San Cristóbal,** built along calle Norzagaray as an adjunct to El Morro fortress.

SHOPPING

As Puerto Rico is a commonwealth of the United States, U.S. citizens don't pay duty on items bought in Puerto Rico and brought back to the States. You can find bargains galore in San Juan; prices are often lower than those in St. Thomas.

The streets of the **Old Town,** such as Calle San Francisco and Calle del Cristo, are the major venues for shopping. Most stores in Old San Juan are closed on Sunday.

You can get good buys on such local handcrafts as *santos* (hand-carved wooden religious figures), needlework, straw work, ceramics, hammocks, *guayabera* shirts for men, papier-mâché fruit and vegetables, and paintings and sculptures by Puerto Rican artists.

The biggest and most up-to-date shopping plaza in the Caribbean Basin is **Plaza Las Americas,** which lies in the financial district of Hato Rey, right off the Las Americas Expressway. The complex has more than 200 shops, most of them upmarket.

For antiques, try **José E. Alegria and Associates,** Calle del Cristo 152–154 (☎ 787/721-8091), opposite the Gran Hotel Convento. Prices are not low, but quality is very high.

Galería Botello, Calle del Cristo 105 (☎ 787/723-2879), is a contemporary Latin American art gallery, a tribute to the late Angel Botello, one of the most outstanding artists on Puerto Rico. His paintings and bronze sculptures are evocative of his colorful background. The gallery also showcases many other outstanding local artists. **Galería Palomas,** 207 Calle de Cristo (☎ 787/724-8904), is also a top art gallery, displaying leading Latin American painters.

Haitian Souvenirs, Calle San Francisco 206 (☎ 787/723-0959), is our favorite store specializing in Haitian art and artifacts. Look for the brightly painted wall hangings crafted from sheets of metal.

Butterfly People, Calle Fortaleza 152 (☎ 787/723-2432), is a gallery and cafe in a handsomely restored building. Mounted butterflies are sold in artful boxes.

Lindissima Shop, Calle Fortaleza 300 (☎ 787/721-0550), is an elegant women's shop, so if you lack an outfit for a special formal night aboard ship, this shop should have what you need.

The prices at the local **London Fog** factory outlet, Calle del Cristo 156 (☎ 787/ 722-4334), are usually so low that a purchase of a raincoat or parka may be well worth the trouble of hauling it home. Items are often marked 50% less than suggested retail price. You'll also find bargains at the **Polo Ralph Lauren Factory Store,** Calle del Cristo 201 (☎ 787/ 722-2136).

Anaiboa, Calle San Francisco 100 (☎ 787/724-0444), sells one-of-a-kind artifacts, such as fine ceramic boxes, hat racks, mirrors, serving trays, and small-scale furniture accented with whimsical drawings of faces, plants, and animals. Most are made in Puerto Rico and sell for as little as $15.

Bared and Sons, Calle Fortaleza 65, at the corner of calle San Justo (☎ 787/ 724-4811), is the main outlet of a chain of upper-bracket jewelry stores. On the floor above the street is a monumental collection of porcelain and crystal where you can find hard-to-get and discontinued patterns from major china manufacturers (priced at around 20% less than at equivalent outlets stateside).

El Artesano, Calle Fortaleza 314 (☎ 787/721-6483), serves as the local outlet for a well-established company in Caracas, Venezuela. You'll find Mexican and Peruvian icons of the Virgin Mary; charming depictions of fish and South American birds in terra-cotta and brass; woven goods; painted cupboards, chests, and boxes; and supremely comfortable mortise-and-tenon leather-covered chairs from Ecuador.

At **Galería Bóveda,** 209 Calle del Cristo (☎ 787/725-0263), the long, narrow space is crammed with exotic jewelry, clothing, wall hangings, and elaborately detailed masks from Thailand, Sri Lanka, Ghana, India, and Thailand.

Olé, Calle Fortaleza 105 (☎ 787/ 724-2445), is the place to buy straw hats from Ecuador, hand-beaten Chilean silver, Christmas ornaments, or Puerto Rican *santos.*

Puerto Rican Arts and Crafts, Calle Fortaleza 204 (☎ 787/725-5596), is a showcase for authentic artifacts, such as papier-mâché carnival masks from the south-coast town of Ponce. Taíno designs inspired by ancient petroglyphs are incorporated into most sterling-silver jewelry. An art gallery in back sells silk-screened serigraphs by local artists.

A favorite with cruise passengers, **Barrachina's,** Calle Fortaleza 104, between Calle del Cristo and Calle San José (☎ 800/515-3582 or 787/725-7912), offers a large selection of jewelry, perfume, and gifts. There's a patio for drinks where you can order a piña colada, which originated here in 1963.

The Gold Ounce, Plaza los Muchachos, 201 Calle Fortaleza (☎ 787/724-3102), is the factory outlet for the Kury Company, Puerto Rico's oldest jewelry factory. Some designs are quite charming, and prices are about 20% discounted.

Local residents consider **Joyeria Riviera,** 205 Calle La Cruz (☎ 787/725-4000), to be the Puerto Rican equivalent of Tiffany's. It's the island's major Rolex distributor and sells other watch brands as well.

200 Fortaleza, Calle Fortaleza 200, at the corner of Calle La Cruz (☎ 787/723-1989), has 14-karat Italian gold chains and bracelets that are measured, fitted, and sold by weight. It also carries Seiko and Citizen watches.

Vergina Gallery, 202 Calle del Cristo (☎ 787/721-0592), is known as an exotic jewelry emporium, showcasing the neo-Byzantine and ancient Greek designs of Zolotos.

Majorca pearls and fine leather garments, bags, shoes and accessories are sold at **Leather and Pearls,** Calle Tanca 252, corner of Calle Tetuan (☎ 787/724-8185), one block from the parking building and post office.

The Linen House, Calle Fortaleza 250 (☎ 787/721-4219), specializes in napery, bed linens, and lace, including embroidered shower curtain liners selling for around $35 each, and lace doilies, bun warmers, place mats, and tablecloths. One corner is devoted to aluminum and pewter serving dishes, crafted in Mexico, which are dishwasher-safe, never tarnish, and are designed in beautiful bold, Spanish-colonial motifs.

CASINOS

Most casinos are open daily from noon to 4pm and again from 8pm to 4am.

You can try your luck at the **Caribe Hilton** (☎ 787/721-0303), one of the better ones, or at the **Condado Beach Trio** (☎ 787/721-6090), **El San Juan Hotel and Casino** (☎ 787/791-1000) at Isla Verde, or **Condado Plaza Hotel and Casino** (☎ 787/721-1000).

The **Radisson Ambassador Plaza Hotel and Casino** (☎ 787/721-7300) is another deluxe hotel noted for its casino action. There's yet another casino at the **Dutch Inn Hotel and Casino,** 55 Condado Ave. (☎ 787/721-0810). A newer casino is at the **Holiday Inn Crowne Plaza Hotel and Casino** (☎ 787/253-2929) on Route 187, and an even newer one is the Stellaris Casino at the **San Juan Marriott Resort** (☎ 787/722-7000).

One of the largest casinos is the **Sands,** at the Sands Hotel & Casino at Isla Verde (☎ 787/791-6100), on Isla Verde Road. This 10,000-square-foot gaming facility offers 207 slot machines, 16 blackjack tables, three dice tables, four roulette wheels, and one minibaccarat table.

BEACHES

Bordering some of the Caribbean's finest resort hotels, the **Condado** and **Isla Verde** beaches are the most frequented in town. Good snorkeling is possible, and both have rental equipment for water sports.

The public beaches on the north shore of San Juan at **Ocean Park** and **Park Barbosa** can be reached by bus from San Juan.

Dorado Beach, Cerromar Beach, and **Palmas del Mar** are the chief centers for those seeking the golf, tennis, and beach life. Some are overcrowded, especially on

Saturday and Sunday, but others are practically deserted.

Beaches on Puerto Rico are open to the public, although you will be charged for parking and for use of *balneario* facilities, such as lockers and showers. Public beaches are closed Mondays; if Monday is a holiday, the beaches are open but close the next day, Tuesday. Beach hours are from 9am to 5pm in winter, 9am to 6pm in the off-season.

Warning: If you find a secluded beach, be careful—all alone, you'll have no way to protect yourself or your valuables if ne'er-do-wells should strike.

BOATING, DIVING, FISHING, GOLF, TENNIS & MORE

BOATING & SAILING   Many marinas have powerboats or sailboats for rent. Try the **San Juan Bay Marina** (☎ 787/721-8062), **Puerto Chico** (☎ 787/863-0834), or **Puerto del Rey** (☎ 787/860-1000), on the east coast in Fajardo.

Deep-Sea Fishing   It's top-notch! You can catch allison tuna, white and blue marlin, sailfish, wahoo, mackerel, and tarpon.

Capt. Mike Benitez has chartered out of San Juan for more than 40 years. **Benitez Fishing Charters** can be contacted at P.O. Box 9066541, Puerto de Tierra, San Juan, PR 00906-6541 (☎ 787/723-2292 until 9pm). Excursions go out aboard the 45-foot air-conditioned *Sea Born.* Half-day fishing excursions for parties of up to six cost $390; full-day excursions go for $690. All equipment is included.

In the waters just off Palmas del Mar, **Capt. Bill Burleson,** P.O. Box 8270, Humacao, PR 00792 (☎ 787/850-7442), operates charters on his fully customized 46-foot sport-fishing boat, *Karolette.* Burleson prefers to take fishing groups to Grappler Banks, 18 nautical miles away. A maximum of six people are taken out at a cost of $450 for four hours, $600 for six hours, and $800 for nine hours. Snorkeling expeditions to Vieques

Island are available for $75 per person for up to five hours, and other half- and full-day snorkeling excursions can be arranged.

GOLF   You'll need a rented car to reach the major courses, which lie within 45 minutes to an hour and a half from San Juan. The **Hyatt Resorts Puerto Rico** at Dorado (☎ 787/796-1234), offers 72 holes of golf, including the 18-hole Robert Trent Jones courses at the Hyatt Regency Cerromar and the Hyatt Dorado Beach, and the par-72 East course at Dorado Beach. Greens fees are $100, including an electric cart.

The **Golf Club,** at Palmas del Mar in Humacao (☎ 787/852-6000, ext. 54), has a par-72, 6,803-yard layout designed by Gary Player. Greens fees are $75 and $90.

Rio Mar Golf Course at Palmer (☎ 787/888-8815), a 45-minute drive from San Juan along Route 187 on the northeast coast, offers 6,145 yards. Greens fees are $75.

SCUBA & SNORKELING   The continental shelf, which surrounds Puerto Rico on three sides, offers an abundance of coral reefs, caves, sea walls, and trenches for scuba and snorkeling.

Open-water reefs off the central coast near Humacao, 45 miles east of San Juan, are visited by migrating whales and manatees. The Great Trench, off the island's south coast, is ideal for experienced sport divers. Mona Island, off the west coast, offers unspoiled reefs at depths averaging 80 feet.

In San Juan, we recommend **Karen Vega's Caribe Aquatic Adventures** (☎ 787/729-2929, ext. 240), with a dive shop in the lobby of the Radisson Normandie Hotel. They offer kayak rentals at $17 per hour, windsurfing, and full-day diving expeditions to various reefs and wrecks.

The **Caribbean School of Aquatics,** 1 Taft St., Suite 10F (☎ 787/728-6606), offers sailing, scuba, and snorkeling trips, as well as boat charters and fishing. A scuba diver pays $99 for a full day and

$25 for a second tank. Snorkelers go along for $79.

SURFING Puerto Rico's northwest beaches attract surfers from around the world, especially from October through February, the best surfing months. The most popular areas are from Isabela around Punta Borinquén to Rincón, with beaches such as Wilderness, Surfers, Crashboat, Los Turbos in Vega Jajja, Pine Grove in Isla Verde, and La Pared in Luquillo. Surfboards are available at many water sports shops. You'll need to drive to these beaches.

TENNIS In San Juan, the **Caribe Hilton** and the **Condado Plaza** have tennis courts. Also in the area is a public court at the old navy base, Isla Grande, in Miramar. You'll find the entrance at avenida Fernández Juncos at bus stop 11.

WINDSURFING The sheltered waters of the Condado Lagoon in San Juan are a favorite spot for windsurfing. Other sites include Ocean Park, Ensenada, Boquerón, Honda Beach, and Culebra. You can arrange for windsurfing at **Karen Vega's Caribe Aquatic Adventures** (☎ 787/729-2929, ext. 240), in the lobby of San Juan's Radisson Normandie Hotel. Rentals cost $25 per hour and lessons are $45.

Along the north shore, windsurfing is excellent at the beachfront of the Hyatt Dorado Beach Hotel, a 22-mile drive east of San Juan. Here the **Lisa Penfield Windsurfing School** (☎ 787/796-1234, ext. 3768, or 787/796-2188) offers one-hour, 15-minute lessons for $60 per person. Board rentals are $45 per hour or $50 per half day.

DINING

In an 18th-century brick-and-stone building across from the Iglesia de San José, ✪ **Amadeus,** Calle San Sebastián 106 (☎ 787/722-8635), gives Caribbean ingredients a nouvelle twist. Appetizers alone are worth the trip, especially chayote and king crab salad with black olives or an eggplant tart filled with spinach, mozza-

rella, and tomato sauce. You can enjoy dishes *de la tierra* (from the land) or *del mar* (from the sea).

✪ **Butterfly People Café,** Calle Fortaleza 152 (☎ 787/723-2432), is on the second floor of a restored mansion. The cuisine is tropical and light European fare such as gazpacho, quiche, or the tantalizing raspberry chiffon pie with fresh raspberry sauce. Everything is made with fresh ingredients. A full bar offers tropical specialties.

Located in a Spanish colonial building with a delightful courtyard dining patio, ✪ **Chef Marisoll,** 202 Calle del Cristo (☎ 787/725-7454), is the province of Marisoll Hernández, the finest female chef in San Juan. We particularly like her cream of exotic wild mushrooms soup and butternut squash soup with crisp ginger. Dishes are imaginative, including curried chicken with papaya and cilantro, or simple, such as the filet of mahimahi in butter sauce served with grilled vegetables.

The **Hard Rock Café,** Calle Recinto Sur 253 (☎ 787/724-7625), is one of the busiest dining spots in old town. Between drinks and burgers, diners look at the collection of rock 'n' roll artifacts.

The oldest restaurant in San Juan, **La Mallorquina,** Calle San Justo 207 (☎ 787/722-3261), has been serving some of the most typical Puerto Rican dishes since 1848, in a three-story building with a glassed-in courtyard. The specialty here is asopao, the famous Puerto Rican rice dish. Chicken with rice is the second most desirable dish.

We like the Puerto Rican fare even better at **La Bombonera,** Calle San Francisco 259 (☎ 787/722-0658), although it doesn't have as fine an ambience as La Mallorquina. Nevertheless, this remains a popular lunchtime rendezvous for the island's literati and for some of the finest San Juan families. Authentic and inexpensive regional dishes are served here in a rather frantic atmosphere.

El Patio de Sam, Calle San Sebastián 102 (☎ 787/723-1149), is a popular gathering spot for American expatriates, newspeople, and shopkeepers and is known for having the best hamburgers in town. For a satisfying lunch, try the black-bean soup followed by the burger platter, and top your meal off with a Key lime tart. Other menu items are not so great.

IN CONDADO

Near the Convention Center, **Ajili Mojili,** Ashford Avenue (☎ 787/725-9195), is the only restaurant devoted exclusively to *la cucina criolla,* the starchy, sometimes greasy century-old cuisine. Dishes include *mofongos* (green plantains stuffed with veal, chicken, shrimp, or pork), *arroz con pollo* (rice with chicken), *lechon asado con maposteado* (roast pork with rice and beans), and *carne mechada* (beef ribeye stuffed with ham). The preferred accompaniment for this hearty island fare is an ice cold bottle of local beer, such as Medalla.

Chart House, 1214 Ashford Ave. (☎ 787/724-0110), attracts hundreds of locals on any night. The food is well prepared, and prime rib is a specialty.

Established by a Galician-born family, **✪ Compostela,** Avenida Condado 106

(☎ 787/724-6088), is one of the island's best restaurants. The chef made his reputation on innovative dishes like roast peppers stuffed with salmon mousse and brochettes of fillet studded with truffles. The shellfish grilled in a brandy sauce is a sure winner. The chef also makes two savory versions of paella. The wine cellar is quite impressive.

On a relatively quiet corner of the Condado, the elegant **✪ Los Faisanes,** Avenida Magdalena 1108 (☎ 787/725-2801), serves dishes influenced by French, Italian, and Spanish cuisine. A winner is the roast duck flavored with cinnamon and guava. There's a fresh, assertive taste to the food, which you can back up with a selection from their good wine cellar.

Near La Concha Hotel, **✪ Ramiro's,** Avenida Magdalena 1106 (☎ 787/721-9049), offers refined cuisine and a touch of Old Spain. You can enjoy "New Creole" cooking, a style pioneered by owner and chef Jesús Ramiro. You might begin with breadfruit "mille feuille," with local crabmeat and avocado, followed by rack of lamb or any fresh fish or meat charcoal-grilled on request.

Sample Daily Calendars & Menus

In your average workaday life you do 1,001 little things every day. You walk the dog, recharge the cel phone, iron your suit, take the kids to the park, recharge the dog, walk the cel phone . . . it's overwhelming, really. That's why you're going on a cruise. Get away from it all for a while. Take it easy.

Or is it? Do you really intend to hole up in a deck chair, slathered with tanning oil, a floppy canvas hat perched on your head and a copy of the latest John Grisham propped on your tan line? Or are you planning to ditch that act as soon as you step aboard, pull out the Armani tux (or your newest Versace dress), and head out to sample the 1,001 excitements available aboard today's cruise ships? We can see you now, leaning beguilingly against the lounge bar. *Hello. Haven't seen you on this ship before . . .*

Whatever your intention, there's a ship out there for you, and plenty where the onboard atmosphere changes depending on the time of day, giving you the broadest possible experience for your cruise buck.

In this section we've reproduced sample daily activity calendars for nearly all the lines we've profiled and listed a representative selection of dinner entrees as well. Understand that this is a *sample:* Each day of your cruise will be different; some of the activities we've listed might not be scheduled during your trip, and many that we haven't listed probably will. Also note that some activities will actually take place more often than it says in these pages. For instance, a movie that we've listed at 2:30pm may also be showing at 6:00, 9:00, and 11:00pm. Our intention here was simply to give you an idea of the kind of activities you might encounter in a typical day aboard a particular line.

A few of the smaller, more individualistic lines—American Canadian Caribbean, Tall Ship Adventures, and Windjammer—don't publish activity calendars at all. On these ships, it's the cruise itself, or the ports of call visited, that draw passengers in; talent shows, Vegas-style entertainment, and vegetable-cutting demonstrations are simply not part of the equation. We've included sample entree lists for Windjammer and Tall Ship Adventures, but American Canadian's bootstrap ethos doesn't even allow this: On their ships, menus are posted on blackboards in the dining rooms during every meal. This in itself should give you some idea of the kind of line ACCL is.

So, delve in. Imagine yourself waking up in your stateroom and reaching down to grab the calendar that's been slipped under your door while you slept. The day stretches out before you like a great, unexplored continent. You've only to step out on deck . . .

DAY IN PORT

6:30am	Early bird coffee
7:30am	Shore Excursion Office opens for last-minute sale of all tours
8am	The pool opens
8am	*Dolphin IV* arrives in Freeport, G.B.I.
8am–8pm	Ping-Pong tables and shuffleboard courts are open
10am	Morning movie
12:30–2:30pm	The sounds of the islands
2pm	Ping-Pong tournament
2pm	Afternoon movie
2:30pm	Line dance—learn a new step. Lots of fun!
2:45pm	Trivia, trivia! Test your knowledge for fun and prizes.
3–4pm	The sounds of the islands
3:30pm	Important disembarkation talk
3:30pm	All aboard! The *Dolphin* sails for Port Canaveral at 4pm.
3:30–8pm	Beauty salon and massage therapy
4pm	Pool games—Fun in the sun with your cruise staff
4:30pm	Horse racing
5pm	Spectacular art auction at sea
5pm	The Casino and gift shop open
5pm	Trapshooting on the high seas
5pm	Tour of the Navigation Bridge
5–6pm	Formal portraits taken
5:30pm	First seating, Captain's Reception
7:30pm	Second seating, Captain's Reception
7:30–8:15pm	The Dolphin Duo entertains
8:45pm	First seating, Grand Farewell showtime. An evening of great entertainment in the Rendezvous Lounge.
9:30pm–1:30am	Dance to the sounds of the Dolphin Duo
10pm	Snowball jackpot bingo
10:30pm	Dance till the wee hours
10:45pm	Second seating, Grand Farewell showtime
11:30pm	The disco is the place to meet
Midnight	A night at the movies

Dining Hours: Breakfast Buffet 7–10am • Breakfast 7am, 8:15am • Buffet Lunch noon–2:30pm • Lunch noon–2pm • Coffee, Tea & Cookies 4–5pm • Dinner 6pm, 8:15pm • Buffet Magnifique midnight–1am

Dress for the Evening: Semiformal (jacket and tie requested)

DINNER ENTREES

Fillet of Tilapia • *sautéed in butter, fresh lemon juice, green peppercorn and lime sauce*

Coq-au-Vin Chambertin • *tender young chicken braised in a robust sauce of red wine with pearl onions*

Veal Schnitzel Modena • *milk-fed veal dusted with Parmigiana, sautéed in butter, glazed with the chef's special sauce and served with fettucini*

Roast Leg of Lamb • *leg of U.S. spring lamb marinated and roasted, served in its own juices*

Tenderloin of Beef Brillat-Savarin • *sliced center-cut of Beef Tenderloin, served with Béarnaise and Bordelaise sauces*

Exotic Vegetable Cannelloni with Roasted Red Pepper Coulis • *broccoli, snow peas, baby corn, mozzarella, and cottage cheese wrapped in a delicate egg crêpe*

DAY AT SEA

7am–8pm	Nautica Spa and Gym open
8am	Slot machines open
8am	Beginners step aerobics
9am	Late seating for breakfast
9am–6pm	Shuffleboard available
9:30–10:30am	Library opens
10am	Ping-Pong tournament
10am–late	Full Casino opens
10:30am–noon	Photo Gallery opens
11am	Horse racing
1pm	Talent show registration
1pm	Ice-carving demonstration
1pm	The slot tournament!
2pm	Dance class
2–2:30pm	Tour of the Bridge
2–5pm	Calypso music
2:30pm	Newlywed and Not-So-Newlywed Game
3pm	Cooking lesson and food carving demonstration
3:30pm	Jackpot bingo
4:30pm	Debarkation briefing by cruise director
4:45–5:45pm	Main seating, "Fun Ship" party—complimentary hors d'oeuvres, cocktail music

7:15–8:15pm	Late seating, "Fun Ship" party—complimentary hors d'oeuvres, cocktail music
8pm	Main seating, jackpot bingo—snowball game
8:30pm	Showtime for main seating—Leonard Miller presents George Piech's "Best of Broadway"
9:30pm–1:30am	Party music with Bobby
9:30pm–1:30am	Rockin' the night away with Scott
9:30pm–1:30am	Visit the spinning piano bar with Brad
9:45pm–1:30am	Great music for listening and dancing with the Starlite Trio
10pm	Late seating, monster bingo
10pm	Disco opens
10:30pm	An Ol' English story
Midnight	Midnight special—in concert, Donna McMillan

Dining Hours: Coffee 6:30am • Breakfast 7:45am • Light Breakfast 8–10am • Salad Bar noon–2:30pm • Sunlovers Luncheon noon–2:30pm • Lunch noon, 1:30pm • Coffee, Tea, Ice Cream & Treats 4:45–5pm • American Dinner 6pm, 8:15pm • Pasta Buffet 12:30–1:30am • Mini Buffet 1:30–2:30am • Coffee, Tea, Bouillion available 24 hours

Dress for the Evening: Casual

DINNER ENTREES—ITALIAN NIGHT

Poached Fillet of Sole • *served over a red bean ratatouille*

Veal Parmigiana • *sautéed and topped with tomato sauce and mozzarella cheese*

Tournedos of Beef Tenderloin • *red wine mushroom sauce*

North Atlantic Cod Meuniere • *pan-fried fillet, lemon butter*

Chicken Cacciatore • *breast of chicken stewed with plum tomatoes, olives, mushrooms, and fresh herbs*

Zucchini and Eggplant Parmigiana • *vegetable entree: buttered noodles*

DAY IN PORT

8:30am	Walk a mile with your sports director
9am	The pools are open
9:30am	Bridge lesson
10am	*Galaxy* is scheduled to dock at the International Pier, Cozumel
10–11:30am	The library is open. Daily quiz is available.

10:30am	Movie Time: *Tin Cup*, starring Kevin Costner
10:30am	Staying aboard? The entertainment staff organizes indoor games.
11am	Computers made easy—A beginner's seminar
11am	Celebrity Social Hour— Coffee talk with the entertainment staff
11:30am–3:30pm	Background music to tan by
2:30–3:30pm	The library is open
3pm	Afternoon bridge play
3:30pm	The "Intra" Net—A basic beginners seminar
3:30pm	Pool Volleyball Challenge with the entertainment staff
3:30pm	Golf lessons with golf pro Arnold
3:30–5pm	Music on deck with the Savoy Melody Makers
4pm	Tea Time. The Verossa Strings bring you a relaxed mood.
4pm	Arts and crafts
4:15pm	Catholic mass
4:30pm	Dance class, ballroom style
4:30pm	Friends of Lois and Bill W. meet
4:30pm	Improve your swing with golf pro Arnold
5pm	Celebrity Lecture Series: Martin Kirschner presents handwriting analysis
5–8:30pm	Happy hour
5pm–1am	Tasty cigars available. Cigar rolling demonstrations.
5:15–6:15pm	Traditional Greek music
6pm	Movie Time: *A Very Brady Sequel*
6:45pm	All aboard, please
7pm	*Galaxy* is scheduled to sail for Montego Bay, Jamaica
7pm	Blue Seas Lotto
7–10pm	Art at Michael's with John Foege, our art expert
7:30–8pm	Savoy Melody Makers play for your musical enjoyment
7:45pm	Casanova's Country Music Jamboree
8pm	Mastermind Team Trivia
8:45pm	Main Seating, Celebrity Showtime: Bob Arno, America's Funniest Pickpocket, and Doug Cameron, Billboard chart-topping instrumentalist
9:45pm–1am	Our musical duo Casanova entertains
9:45pm–1:30am	Hit Music with the Savoy Melody Makers
10pm–late	Spicy disco DJ Scotty plays the beat
10:20pm	The Beijing Acrobats
10:45pm	Late Seating, Celebrity Showtime: Bob Arno and Doug Cameron
11pm–1am	Tex-Mex deck celebration—line dancin'

Dining Hours: Coffee & Tea 6:30–7:30am • Continental Breakfast 6:30–10am • Breakfast Buffet 7–10am • Breakfast 7:30am, 8:45am • Late Breakfast 10–11:30am • Croissants, Danishes & Muffins available 10–noon • Buffet Luncheon noon–2:30pm • Hot Dogs & Hamburgers noon–2:30pm • Pastries 3–5pm • Pizza 3–7pm • Afternoon Tea 4–5pm • Dinner 6pm, 8:30pm • Pizza 10pm–1am • Buffet midnight

Dress for the Evening: Informal (Ladies: informal dress or pants and blouse. Gentlemen: jacket and tie)

DINNER ENTREES

Brochette King Neptune • *grilled sea scallops, shrimp, and assorted fish on a skewer placed on a bed of jasmine rice*

Ziti Alla Gorgonzola • *cooked al dente and served in a creamy gorgonzola sauce with roasted garlic and sliced shiitake*

Tender Young Roasted Chicken • *coated with chicken glace, mustard, and shallots, roasted slowly until crisp and golden, garnished with spring onions and sautéed mushroom caps*

Veal Scaloppine "Celebrity" • *presented with a sweet marsala wine sauce, accompanied by a bundle of fresh vegetables*

Roast Strip Loin of U.S. Choice Beef • *carefully seasoned and served to your preference with country-style potatoes and red wine tarragon sauce*

❖ *CLIPPER*

DAY IN PORT

6am	Departure of the *Nantucket Clipper* en route to Road Town, Tortola
7:30am	Approximate arrival of the *Nantucket Clipper* in Road Town, Tortola
8am	Sage Mountain Park hike
8:30am, 9:30am, 1:45pm, 2:45pm	Departure of Peter Island snorkel excursions
9am, 2pm	Departure of Cane Garden Bay Beach buses
9:30am, 2:15pm	Departure of Tortola Island tours
5:45pm	Lecture Presentation: Naturalist AJ Lippson presents "The Blooms of the Caribbean"
9pm	Enjoy music of the Caribbean performed by local band Splash
9pm	Movie presentation: *Extreme Measures*

Dining Hours: Early-Bird Breakfast 7am • Breakfast 7:45–8:15am • Lunch 12:30pm • Dinner 7:15pm

Dress for the Evening: Casual

DINNER ENTREES

Fresh Broiled Florida Lobster Tail • *stuffed with baby shrimp, blue crab, and fresh herbs, served with drawn butter and fresh lemon*

Boursin Chicken • *boneless skinless chicken breast stuffed with herbed boursin cheese, breaded, baked, and served with sauce veloute*

Fresh Pasta with a Wild Mushroom Cream Sauce

Grilled Mahimahi • *served moist with tropical fruit salsa garnished with lemon and lime*

Vegetable Lasagna • *fresh garden vegetables layered with a low-fat ricotta cheese and fresh lasagna noodles*

Club Med®

DAY IN PORT—ONBOARD SPORTS ACTIVITIES

8:30–9:30am	Fitness instructor available
9am	*Club Med 1* arrives in St. Martin
9am	Relaxation exercises
10am	First tender leaves for shore
10am	Body sculpting
10am–5pm	Waterskiing, sailing, and windsurfing at the Nautical Hall
11am	Meeting for certified scuba divers in the Nautical Hall
11:15am	Departure of scuba diving from the Nautical Hall
11:30am	Water aerobics in the Bahamas swimming pool
2pm	Snorkling departure from the Nautical Hall
5pm	Low-impact aerobics
5–7pm	Fitness instructor available
5:30pm	Stretching flexibility
3am	Last tender leaves from shore

Dining Hours: Full Buffet & Menu Breakfast 7–10:30am • Continental Breakfast 10:30–11:30am • Lunch 12:30–2:30pm • Tea & Pastries 4–5:30pm • Dinner 7:30–9:30pm

Dress for the Evening: Casual

DINNER ENTREES

Emin of Chicken with Curry, Rice, and Exotic Fruits

Rissole of Salt Cod with a Lobster Mousseline

Tagliatelle Pasta with Smoked Salmon

Lamb Fillet with Sage Juice and Celery Flan

Sirloin Steak with Pepper Sauce and Potatoes Alsacian Style

Fillet of Bass with Balsamique Vinegar and Polenta Tassinoise Style

DAY AT SEA

7am	Catholic mass is celebrated with Father Carignan
8am	Interdenominational church service with Pastors Russel and Bauman
9am	Shore excursion briefing and orientation talk
10am	Walk-a-Mile
10am	Brain teasers and crossword puzzles
10am	Horse racing at sea!
10am–1pm	Photo Gallery opens for purchase of pictures
10:15am	Art animation auction at sea
10:30am	Catch the scent: A special perfume seminar
11am	Port and shopping briefing
11:30am	Massage demonstration
Noon–2pm	Out on deck with deck DJ David
1pm	Trapshooting
1pm	Friends of Dr. Bob and Bill and Lois W.
1–4pm	Miller Lite Draft Beer promotion $1.50 at the Pool Bar
2–3pm	The Enchanted Isle Quartet performs for your listening pleasure
2:15pm	"Gem Stone" seminar
2:30pm	Snowball jackpot bingo
2:45pm	Wine and cheese tasting
3pm	Gaming lessons with your Casino staff
3pm	Service club meeting
3–4pm	Shore excursion manager will be available for inquiries
3:15pm	"Afternoon Madness" with your cruise director, Walter
5:15pm	First seating, Captain's welcome aboard cocktail party
7:30pm	Second seating, Captain's welcome aboard cocktail party
7:30–8:15pm	Alan Lee performs in our Intimate Lounge
7:45–8:30pm	Join Donald Lumacad at the piano for your listening pleasure
8:45pm	First seating, the Ray Kennedy Entertainers in "Living in America"
9:30pm	Alan Lee performs in our Intimate Lounge
9:45pm	Music under the stars with deck DJ David
10pm	The Disco opens

| 10:30pm | Late seating, the Ray Kennedy Entertainers in "Living in America" |
| 11:15pm–midnight | Dance with the Enchanted Isle Quartet |

Dining Hours: Breakfast Buffet 7–10am • Breakfast 7:30–9:30am • Lunch noon, 1:30pm • Buffet Lunch noon–2pm • Hamburgers & Hot Dogs noon–1:45pm • Afternoon Snacks 4–4:45pm • Dinner 6pm, 8:15pm • Italian Buffet 11:30pm–12:30am

Dress for the Evening: Formal (jacket and tie requested)

DINNER ENTREES

Ocean Perch Almondine • *sautéed in butter, flavored with lemon and almonds, served with red bliss potatoes*

Pork Chop Milanaise • *lightly breaded with egg and Parmesan cheese, baked to golden brown and served with linguini*

Roasted Spring Chicken with Cilantro Sauce • *served with refried beans and dirty rice*

Beef Roulade, Creole Style • *stuffed with smoked sausage, bell pepper, and serrano chili, with roasted garlic perfumed with wine and fresh thyme, served with mashed potatoes and scallions*

C O S T A ✦ C R U I S E S
Italian Style

DAY IN PORT

7:30am	The *CostaVictoria* is due to dock in St. Thomas, U.S.V.I.
8–9am	Our port lecturer is available for maps and information
9–10am	Host hour: Meet our cruise staff for a friendly chat
10am	Informal cards and games
3:30pm	Dance class with Walter and Judy
4pm	Foozeball with your cruise staff
5pm	Afternoon walkathon
5–6:30pm	Basketball fun!
5:30pm	All on board!
5:30pm	Sailaway celebration
5:30–6:30pm	Sailaway with "Unity"
5:30–6:30pm	Karen and Michelangelo entertain you
6pm	*CostaVictoria* sails to Serena Cay
6pm	Afternoon stretch
7:45pm	It's bingo time!
7:45pm	Honeymooners cocktail party!
8:30pm–midnight	La Festa Italiana, Italian-style entertainment!
8:45pm	Showtime, featuring Richard Ianni
8:45pm–1am	The Italian melodies of Magic Sound

10:15pm	The great *CostaVictoria* pizza-throwing contest
10:45pm	Showtime, featuring Richard Ianni
11pm	The Rockstar Disco opens
11:45pm–1:30am	Enjoy the melodies of Karen and Michelangelo

Dining Hours: Coffee & Croissants 6:30–7am • Breakfast 7:30am, 8:45am • Breakfast Buffet 7–10am • Croissants 10–11:30am • Lunch 11:30am–1:45pm • Lunch Buffet noon–2:30pm • Lunch Grill noon–2:30pm • Afternoon Tea 4–5pm • Pizza 3–8pm, 9:30pm–1am • Dinner 6:15pm, 8:30pm • Ice Cream 10pm–midnight • Late-Night Buffet 8pm–12:30am

Dress for the Evening: Casual

DINNER ENTREES

Lasagna al forno Emiliana • *layers of freshly made pasta filled with a creamy ground beef sauce enhanced by cheese*

Filetto di Cernia al Verde • *grilled fillet of grouper on julienned vegetables with garlic and fresh herbs, served with steamed potatoes*

Pollo alla Cacciatora • *chicken stewed in red wine and tomato sauce with mushrooms, presented with buckwheat polenta*

Scaloppina al Limone con Agrumi • *tender escalope of veal in a refreshing lemon sauce presented with citrus wedges and served with château potatoes*

Melanzane e Zucchine alla Parmigiana • *oven-baked layers of eggplant and zucchini combined with tomato sauce and mozzarella cheese*

CUNARD

DAY IN PORT

8am	Gym Guidance
9am	*Sea Goddess I* anchors off Jost van Dyke, British Virgin Islands
10:30am	Zodiac service to the beach will be established and operate on a continuous basis throughout the day
Noon	"Caviar and Champagne" is served in the surf
12:30pm	BBQ lunch "Sea Goddess Style" is served on the beach
5pm	Last zodiac departs from shore
5pm	Body Toning with Dynabands
5:30pm	Private consultations
6pm	*Sea Goddess I* sails for St. Thomas, U.S. Virgin Islands
7pm	The Main Salon is open for cocktails and dancing
7:30pm	The Captain's Reception, in the Main Salon
10pm	The Main Salon is open for coffee, after-dinner drinks, and dancing

10pm	The Piano Bar is open
10pm	The Casino is open for blackjack
10:30pm	Live music in the Piano Bar

Dining Hours: Early-Risers Coffee 7–8am • À La Carte Breakfast 8–10am • Breakfast 8–11am • Lunch 12:30–2pm • Afternoon Tea 5–6pm • Dinner 8–10pm

Dress for the Evening: Jacket and tie are requested after 7pm.

DINNER ENTREES

Gratinated Fillet of Monkfish served on a Bed of Leaf Spinach

Herb Marinated Veal Scallopini with Sautéed Chanterelles and Risotto "Napoletana"

Grilled Baby Lamb Chops with Mango-Mint Chutney

Fresh Steamed Maine Lobster with Spicy Tomato-Olive Ragout and Wild Rice

Grilled Mignon of Beef Tenderloin "Madagascar" and Pommes Pont Neuf

DAY IN PORT

8am	Pool and whirlpools open
8am	Sports Deck opens—Ping-Pong, basketball, shuffleboard
8am	Walk a Mile with a smile
8am	The *SeaBreeze* arrives in Nassau
8:30am	Tour to Blue Lagoon Island departs
8:45am	City and Ardastra Gardens Tour departs
9am	Cruisercise program
Noon–2:30pm	Islands Sounds with Bahamian Flavor
1:30pm	All Aboard! The *SeaBreeze* sails for San Juan, Puerto Rico at 2pm
2:15pm	Horse racing!
2:30–3pm	Intro to the Gym and its equipment
3pm	Roulette and blackjack lessons
3pm	Snowball jackpot bingo
3pm–2am	Casino open
3:45pm	Art at sea auction
4–5pm	Music on deck—calypso style
5:15pm	Main seating, Captain's Welcome Aboard Reception
7:30pm	Second seating, Captain's Welcome Aboard Reception

7:30–8:15pm	Music for your pleasure
8:30pm	Main seating, Showtime: Musical Revue by SeaBreeze Sensation
9:30pm–midnight	Piano Bar open
9:45pm	Name That Tune for fun and prizes
9:45pm–1:30am	Time to Dance!
10pm–3am	Agitato Disco open
10:30pm	Second seating, Showtime: Musical Revue
10:30pm	Caribbean Karaoke
11:45pm–12:15am	Dance music and romance

Dining Hours: Early-Bird Coffee 6:30am • Buffet Breakfast 6:30–9:30am • Breakfast 7–9am • Lunch noon–2pm • BBQ Grill noon–2:30pm • Coffee, Tea & Cookies 4–5pm • Dinner 6pm, 8:15pm • "Crêpes Flambé" Buffet midnight–1am

Dress for the Evening: Formal

DINNER ENTREES

Penne alla Carbonara • *with double cream, bacon, and Parmesan cheese*

Blanc de Turbot, Sauce Vierge • *supreme of turbot gently broiled, olive-tomato coulis*

Roast Leg of Western Pork • *marinated in tropical juices and spices, served with rice, black beans, and fried plantains*

Fettuccine alla Maggia • *with ham, mushrooms, garlic, and parsley*

Fillet of Baby Cod • *slowly cooked in butter, garnished with diced zucchini and sprinkled with dill*

Herbs Marinated Roast Beef Sandwich • *garnished with pickles, tomato, and matchstick potatoes*

Triple Decker Club Salad • *on a bed of lettuce dressed with beefsteak tomatoes, topped with cooked turkey, slice bacon, and Thousand Island dressing*

Holland America Line
A TRADITION OF EXCELLENCE®

DAY IN PORT

7am	The *Maasdam* is scheduled to anchor at George Town, Grand Cayman
7am–7pm	Fitness instructors are available for assistance
7am–7pm	Thirty-minute workout
7am–9pm	Ocean Spa and Jacuzzis are open
8–8:30am	Walk-a-mile with our fitness instructor
8–9:30am	Port lecturer Donna answers your questions
8:45am	Low-impact aerobics

9am	Larry's Daily Quiz No. 2
9am–6pm	Sports equipment is available
10:30–11am	Lemonade is served on the outside decks
1:30pm	Deck quoits tournament with the cruise staff
2pm	Informal bridge or cards get-together
2pm	Open shuffleboard tournament
3:15pm	Team trivia with the cruise staff
3:30–4pm	Iced tea is served on the outside decks
3:30–4pm	Afternoon tea is served
3:45pm	Open ping-pong with the cruise staff
4–4:30pm	Walk-a-mile with our fitness instructor
4:30pm	Snowball cash bingo
4:30pm	Friends of Bill W.
4:30pm	Volleyball with the cruise staff
4:45pm	Stretch and relax
5:30pm	All aboard! The last tender leaves from the shore!
7:30, 8:30, 9:30, 11:15pm	Art viewing with Max
8:30pm	Showtime in the Rembrandt Lounge
9:45pm	Evening team trivia
10:15pm	Showtime in the Rembrandt Lounge
11:15pm	'50s, '60s, and '70s party night

Dining Hours: Continental Breakfast 6:30–10:30am • Breakfast 7–10am • Lunch 11:30am–2pm • Hamburgers & Hot Dogs 11:30am–5pm • Stir-Fry & Taco Bar 11:30am–2:30pm • Ice Cream 11:30am–2:30pm, 4–5pm, 11:15pm–12:15am • Pizza 4–5pm • Dinner 6pm, 8:15pm • Caribbean Late-Night Snack 11:15pm–12:15am

Dress for the Evening: Elegantly Casual (Ladies: Dress or blouse and slacks. Gentleman: jacket required, tie optional)

DINNER ENTREES

Roasted Prime Rib of Beef • *horseradish cream, broccoli, cauliflower Mornay, and a loaded baked Idaho potato*

Baked Fresh Grouper with Tropical Salsa • *Parisienne potatoes and green beans with red and yellow peppers*

Sautéed Veal Picatta • *thin medaillons of veal in a Parmesan egg batter, rotelle, peas, carrots, topped with artichoke hearts and caper sauce*

Roasted Turkey • *cranberry relish, mashed red jacket potatoes, corn, peas, savory sage chestnut stuffing and pan gravy*

Panfried Sliced Breast of Chicken Romano • *marinated in lemon, garlic, and olive oil, topped with peppers, diced tomatoes, minted rice, and zucchini*

Baked Southwest Manicotti • *with four cheeses, green chilis, corn, and black beans*

DAY IN PORT

8–8:30am	Tai Chi Sunrise
8:30–9:30am	Muscle Works—condition and tone your body into shape!
9–9:30am	Dancin' Beat—time for moving to your favorite tunes!
9–11am	Bookend Library open
9:30am	Hair Demo—learn about braiding and other aspects of hair dressing
10am	Port talk on Key West
10am	Art auction
10–11am	Health Waves—your professional fitness assessment
10:15am	Trapshooting
10:30am	Majesty Madness—the wildest, wackiest fun event this cruise. Don't miss it. Lots of laughs.
10:45am	Ping-Pong tournament
11am	Cocktail demonstration at poolside
11:15am	Important disembarkment talk
11:30am–1:30pm	Caribbean rhythms on deck at the Regal Spa
1pm	*Royal Majesty* arrives in Key West, Florida!
2:30pm	Card players meet in the Queen of Hearts
2:30pm	Scrabble, chess, and backgammon
3–5pm	Bookend Library open
4–4:30pm	Rockin' aerobics
4–6pm	Tea time island beat
4:45–5:30pm	Line dance class
5–8pm	*Royal Majesty* Happy Hour
5:15–6pm	A piano at the Polo Club
5:30–6:30pm	Health Waves—your professional fitness assessment
6:30pm	All Aboard! The *Royal Majesty* sails for Miami, Florida, at 7pm.
6:30–7:15pm	Sailaway Melodies Majesty Style
7–9pm	Formal portraits tonight
7:15–8pm	Farewell to Key West in the Royal Observatory
7:30–8:15pm	A piano at the Polo Club

7:45pm	Enjoy the music of the Royal Court Orchestra in the Palace Theatre
8:30pm	Main seating, Showtime
9:30–10:30pm	Mellow guitar music at the Polo Club
9:30pm–1am	Music for your listening and dancing pleasure
10pm–late	Frame 52 Disco welcomes you
10:30pm–1:30am	Music and entertainment with a panoramic view of the ocean by night. Sing-A-Long Karaoke.
10:45pm	Second seating, Showtime
11pm–11:45pm	Mellow guitar music at the Polo Club
11:45pm–12:45am	Late-night jazz set

Dining Hours: Early-Bird Coffee 6:30am • Buffet Breakfast 7–10am • Breakfast 7:30am, 8:45am • Buffet Lunch noon–2:30pm • Hamburger & Hot Dog BBQ noon–2:30pm • Lunch noon, 1:30pm • Pizza 4–6pm, 11pm–2am • Afternoon Tea 4–5pm • Dinner 6pm, 8:30pm • Oriental Buffet midnight–1am

Dress for the Evening: Semiformal

DINNER ENTREES

Fillet of Tilapia Amandine • *pan-sautéed with roasted almonds and nut-brown butter*

Shrimp Scampi • *plump, juicy shrimp, shelled and sautéed in herb butter, garlic, and a splash of cognac*

Sautéed Choice Calf's Liver with Herbs • *English style, garnished with grilled tomatoes and crisp bacon strips*

Grilled Assorted Vegetables in Corn Crêpes • *mushroom sauce*

Broiled Fillet of Red Snapper Key Largo • *popular delicacy lightly flavored with Key lime and basil*

NORWEGIAN
CRUISE LINE

DAY AT SEA

8:30–9am	Morning stretch with your Sports Afloat staff
8:45–9:45am	The Library is open
9am	Walk a Mile with a Smile with your cruise director's staff
9am	Take the trivia challenge and pick up today's quiz
9am	Cashier's window opens in Casino Royale (slots remain open from last night)
9am	Intermediate Step with your Sports Afloat staff
9am–6pm	Ping-Pong, golf driving, basketball, and shuffleboard equipment available
9:30am	Voice from the Bridge: Captain Olav Søevdsnes' morning address

10am	Make-up boat drill
10am–noon	Morning drink special: Bloody Marys, Screwdrivers, and Mimosas
10:30am	Cooking demonstration with our chef de cuisine
10:30am	Craft Corner with your cruise director's staff
11am–12:45pm	Top Rankin' plays your favorite island tunes
11:30am	Napkin folding—come and learn how to spice up your tables
11:30am–2pm	Connoisseur's Corner: Join your wine steward and talk wine
Noon	Casino Royale opens for your gambling pleasure
12:45pm	Friends of Bill W. meet
12:45pm	Pool games
1pm	Service club meeting: Lions, Kiwanis, etc.
1pm	Vigorous 1-mile walk with cruise director John
1–1:30pm	Fresh fruit smoothie tasting with your bar staff
2pm	Step aerobics with your Sports Afloat staff
2–3pm	Gaming lessons begin: blackjack, dice, and Caribbean stud poker
2:15pm	Port and shopping talk
2:30–5:30pm	Top Rankin' plays your favorite island sounds
2:45pm	Honeymooner's champagne party!
3pm	Giant jackpot bingo
3pm	Perfume seminar: Come sample our "Scentsational" perfumes!
3pm	Belly Buster with your Sports Afloat staff
3–4pm	The Library is open
3:15pm	Art auction extravaganza
3:30pm	Snorkeling demonstration with your Dive-In instructors
3:30pm	Wine tasting
3:45pm	Basketball free throw contest
4:30pm	Bridge play available with your fellow passengers
5–6pm	Enjoy the piano melodies of Katie Guglielmo
5–6pm	Enjoy great music and dancing with Sandy and Lyn
5–6pm	Captain's Welcome Party for main seating
5–6:15pm	Special invitation: professional studio portraits
7–8pm	Captain's Welcome Party for late seating
7–8:45pm	Special invitation: professional studio portraits
7:15–9pm	Sandy and Lyn play all your favorites
7:30–8:30pm	Enjoy Katie Guglielmo at the piano
9pm, 10:30pm	George M.

9:45pm	Enjoy the sounds of Sandy and Lyn
10pm–12:30am	Katie Guglielmo plays your favorite tunes at the piano
10pm–close	DJ Ritchard plays the hits you want to hear
11:15pm	Singles party
11:45pm	Late-night comedy with Max Dolcelli
Midnight–1am	Chocoholic extravaganza

Dining Hours: Continental Breakfast 6:30–10:30am • Breakfast Buffet 7:30–10am • Breakfast 8–10am • Lunch noon, 1:30pm • Sandwich Bar noon–5pm • Ice Cream 2–4:30pm • Dinner 6pm, 8:30pm • Le Bistro Dining 6–10:30pm • Chocoholic Extravaganza midnight–1am • Coffee & Tea available 24 hours

Dress for the Evening: Formal (Ladies: Formal gown or cocktail dress. Gentlemen: Tuxedo or jacket and tie)

DINNER ENTREES

Moroccan Lamb Kebab on Couscous • *grilled ground lamb skewer flavored with Arabian spices*

Sautéed Mahimahi with Lemon-Caper Butter • *complemented with wild rice risotto*

Fillet of Beef Tenderloin "Wellington" • *rich port wine demi-glace and almond-coated pommes Williams*

Manicotti alla Toscana • *pasta tubes filled with spinach and ricotta and baked with sun-dried tomato sauce and provolone cheese*

Grilled Lemon-Pepper Chicken Breast • *with crisp greens and mango-papaya vinaigrette*

Crunchy Caribbean Grouper • *crisp sautéed in a crouton coat and set on a vegetable pot-pourri girdled with tamarind demi-glace*

"Jamaican Jerk" Pork Roast • *fried plantains and traditional rice and beans*

DAY AT SEA

6am–11pm	Exercise Room open
8am	Big Red Boat Golf Academy open. Teaching pro available for lessons.
8am	Walk a mile with your fitness director
8am	Movie: *Phenomenon*
8am–8:30pm	Steiners Beauty and Fitness/Massage Salon open
8am–10pm	Pools and Jacuzzis open
8:30am	Interdenominational service celebrated by Chaplain Draim

9am–noon	Shooting Star Photo Gallery open for photos and videos
9am–1pm	Splashdown/Tour Desk open for snorkeling and shore excursions
9am	Step aerobics with your fitness director
9am	Country line dance class
9am	Trapshooting
9:30am	Putting contest
10am	Legs, tums, and buns workout with your fitness director
10am	Meet your bridge director for lessons and instructions
10–10:30am	Autograph session with the Looney Tunes characters
10am	Lucky Star Casino gaming tables open!
10:30am	Cash bingo!
10:30am	Men's and ladies' table tennis tournament
10:30am	Perfume seminar
10:30am	Friends of Bill W. meet
11am	Trapshooting
11:15am	Comedy spectacular!
11:30am–12:45pm	Learn the art of massage, aromatherapy, nutrition, and how to fight cellulite
11:30am–1pm	Poolside music with "Island Vibes"!
11:30am–1:30pm	Crazy jewelry sale!
Noon	High-noon bingo!
Noon	Movie: *Phenomenon*
Noon–1pm	Slot tournament in Casino
12:45pm	Splashdown sneak preview! Learn how to snorkel.
1pm	Voyages of Discovery: "Pirate's Feud" with the Premier Starliners
1:30pm	Calling all bridge players
1:30pm	Free poker lessons
1:30–2:30pm	Surprise party with our Looney Tune Friends!
1:45pm	Voyages of Discovery presents "The History of the Great Ships"! Followed by a tour of the Navigational Bridge.
2pm	Shuffleboard tournament
2pm	Trapshooting
2pm	Poker game starts
2–3pm	Cards and games available in Pluto's Playhouse
2–3pm	Casino gaming lessons
2:30pm	"Olympics" *Oceanic* Style! Lots of fun and excitement. Chair Volleyball! Pole Jousting! T-Shirt Relay!
2:30pm	International wine-tasting seminar
2:45pm	Voyages of Discovery presents "The Sea"!

3pm	Movie: *Time to Kill*
3–4pm	Surprise party with the Looney Tunes characters!
3–6pm	Foot and ankle massage
3:15pm	Family cash snowball bingo!
3:30–4:45pm	Great art auction at sea!
4pm	Trapshooting
5–6pm	Main seating, Captain's Champagne Reception
6pm	Movie: *Time to Kill*
6pm	Virtual reality—step inside the game
6–8pm	Fitness/wellness evaluations
7–8:15am	Late seating, Captain's Champagne Reception
7:30–8:30pm	Join DJ Jason and dance to Big Band and Ballroom Music
8pm–midnight	Shooting Star Photo Gallery open for photos and videos
8:30pm	Main seating, pre-show music with the "Excalibur Orchestra"
8:15–10pm	Get steamed with "Steamer"! Sit back, relax, and enjoy great music.
9pm	Movie: *The Nutty Professor*
9:15pm	Port Lucaya Talk with your port lecturer, Nikki
9:30pm	Poker game starts.
9:30pm–midnight	Party under the stars with "Island Vibes"!
9:45pm	Family cash bingo!
10–11pm	Join Marilyn Wood for "Name That Tune"!
10pm–1am	Come party with Ray and Carla in the Lucky Star Lounge.
10pm	Karaoke showtime!
10pm	Join DJ Jason! Let's jam to the music, back when it was still rock 'n' roll.
10:15pm	Late seating, pre-show music with the "Excalibur Orchestra"
Midnight	Movie: *The Nutty Professor*

Dining Hours: Early-Risers Coffee & Danish 6–7:30am • Buffet Breakfast 7:30–10:30am • Breakfast 7:30am, 8:45am • Buffet Lunch noon–2pm • Lunch noon, 1:30pm • Ice Cream 2–5pm • Afternoon Tea 4:15–5:15pm • Dinner 6pm, 8:15pm • Late-Night Snacks 9:30–10:30pm • Pizza Time (16oz Draft Beer $2.25) 11:30pm–12:30am • Gala Buffet 12:30–1:30am

Dress for the Evening: Formal (Casual following dinner)

DINNER ENTREES

West Indian Lamb Curry • *with Jamaican dumplings and mango chutney*

Broiled Grouper Filet "Island Style"

Supreme of Chicken St. Lucia • *grilled chicken breast with local herbs and spices, served with rice and beans*

Jamaican Jerked Pork • *roasted loin of pork, marinated with ginger, lime, garlic, and thyme, garnished with marjoram corn, black beans, fried plantains, and tamarind sauce*

The Buccaneer Kebab • *beef tenderloin, shrimp, chicken, mushroom, onions, and bell peppers, grilled on a skewer, served with rice and beans*

Baked Half Caribbean Lobster • *served with lemon butter*

PRINCESS®

DAY AT SEA

8am	Brain-Waves quiz
8am–noon	Princess Links is open
9am	Fine jewelry sale
9–9:20am	Walk-a-mile
9–10am	Men's doubles shuffleboard tournament
9–10am	Ladies' doubles Ping-Pong get-together
9–11am	Tour of the Commanding Bridge
9:30–9:50am	Morning stretch
9:30—10:30am	Snorkeling demonstration
10–10:30am	Talent show sign-up and rehearsal
10–10:30am	Cards and games with the cruise staff
10–10:45am	Morning quiz with the cruise staff
10–10:45am	Hi/Lo aerobics
10–10:45am	Paddle tennis tournament
10–10:45am	Culinary demonstration
10–11am	Fruit and vegetable carving demonstration
10am–noon	The Library is open
10:15am	Captain's Circle scavenger hunt
10:30–11am	Life equipment workout
10:30–11:30am	Scrabble and backgammon tournament
10:45–11am	Minimize your middle
11am–noon	Line dance class
11:15am–noon	Jackpot bingo
11:30am–noon	Singles mingles. Those traveling alone are invited to meet the cruise staff for champagne and introductions.
11:30am–12:15pm	Aerobics circuit
11:30am–2pm	Lunchtime melodies
11:45am–12:15pm	Aquafit
2–2:30pm	Fun in the sun pool games. Crazy aquatic antics with the cruise staff.

2–4pm	Celebrity photo opportunity—an invitation to meet Mr. Gavin McLeod, Captain Stubbing of "The Love Boat"
2–4pm	The Library is open
2–6pm	Prince Links is open
2:30–3:15pm	Water volleyball
2:30–3:15pm	Newlywed and Not-So-Newlywed Game show
2:30–3:30pm	Friends of Dr. Bob and Bill W. meeting
2:30–4pm	Non-host bridge play
3–3:30pm	Collector's seminar—Lladro, the number-one collectible in the world
3:15–4pm	Dice horse racing and horse auction
3:30–4pm	Basketball shoot-out
3:30–4:15pm	Step class
3:30–4:30pm	Outburst: the hilarious and outrageous game hosted by your cruise staff
3:30–4:30pm	Afternoon tea
4–4:45pm	Bonanza bingo
4:30–5pm	Firm and fabulous health and fitness class
5–8:30pm	Early evening music and dancing with Jana and Danny
5:15–5:45pm	Walk-a-mile
5:30–6:30pm	Latin American–style dancing with Yvonne Martin and the Salsa Set
5:30–8pm	Pre-dinner music for your listening pleasure
5:45–6:30pm	Enjoy a pre-dinner dance
7:45–8:30pm	Enjoy a pre-dinner dance
8pm	Evening cards and games
8pm–late	Dance with Bonnie and Slyde
8pm–late	Blackjack, roulette, craps, stud poker, slots in the Casino
8:15pm	Princess Theatre presents "Mystique"—A mysterious undersea adventure
8:15pm	The Vista Lounge presents "Those Happy Days," starring Terry and Theresa.
8:30pm–midnight	Jane Milliken at the piano in the Atrium Lounge
9pm–late	DJ Jazzy Jeff spins the Top 40 sounds
9:15pm–late	Music, hilarity, and a touch of class with Barrington "Barty" Brown
10:15pm	"Mystique"—A mysterious undersea adventure
10:15pm	"Those Happy Days," starring Terry and Theresa
10:30pm	Karaoke
10:30pm	Evening cards and games
11:45pm	Cabaret spotlight starring singer David Pengelli

Dress for the Evening: Casual

DINNER ENTREES

Yellowfin Tuna in a Chunky Tomato Sauce with Oregano • *sautéed fish fillet with braised leeks and saffron rice*

Suprême of Chicken with Riesling • *grilled breast in a fruity white wine sauce and wreath of harvest vegetables*

Tenderloin au Jus • *thinly sliced roasted beef with natural juices, country-fried potatoes, and a bouquet of stir-fried vegetables*

Stir-Fried Chinese Vegetables • *wok-seared carrots, bok choy, snow peas, and baby corn with ginger, soy sauce, and toasted sesame oil*

Gypsy-Style Pork Schnitzel • *seared medallion with a zesty brown sauce accompanied by green peas and buttered noodles*

RADISSON SEVEN SEAS
CRUISES

DAY IN PORT

7:30am	Stretch and walk
8am	Today's trivia and crossword
9am	Fitness at sea—aerobics
9am	Snorkel and scuba instruction in the pool
9:30am	Fitness at sea—gym instruction
10am	Fitness at sea—sit and be fit
11am	Interdenominational worship service will be held in The Club
Noon	The *Radisson Diamond* will arrive in St. Kitts
3–5pm	Hot snacks and afternoon tea are served in The Grill
6:30pm	Captain Lars Österbacka requests the pleasure of your company for his Welcome Aboard Cocktail Party in the Windows Lounge
6:30–7:30pm	Cocktail time with Johnny Johnson at the grand piano
7–9:30pm	Dinner is served in The Grand Dining Room
9:30pm	All Aboard as the *Radisson Diamond* prepares to sail for St. Barts
9:45pm	Dance to the music of the Diamond Five in the Windows Lounge
10:15pm	The Gordeno Connection in Jazz Rock Café
10:30pm	Late-nighters join piano entertainer Johnny Johnson in The Club

| After the Show | Continue dancing to the music of The Diamond Five in the Windows Lounge |
| 11:15pm | Disco with DJ Roger in the Windows Lounge |

Dining Hours: Early-Risers Coffee 6:30–7:30am • Buffet Breakfast 7:30–9:30am • Breakfast 8–10am • Late-Risers Coffee 9:30–11am • Lunch Buffet 11:30am–2pm • Lunch 12:30–2pm • Hot Snacks & Afternoon Tea 3–5pm • Dinner 7–9:30pm

Dress for the Evening: Formal

DINNER ENTREES

Steamed Fillet of Fresh Red Snapper "Shiitake"

Linguini alla Vongole, Clams, Olive Oil, and Parsley

Baked Young Vermont Turkey, Country Stuffing, Giblet Gravy

Veal Cutlet Parmigiana, Tomato and Mozzarella Gratin

Roast Rib Eye Roll, "Au Jus"

DAY AT SEA

8:30am–noon	Eye-opener at the Pool Bar
9–10am	The Library is open
9:15am	Financial lecture with Bennett Zellinger: "Managing Your Money in Today's Market"
9:30am	Morning movie: *Honey Sweet Love,* starring Ben Cross
9:30am	Ping-Pong tournament and shuffleboard open play
10:15am	Vegetable-carving demonstration
10:15am	Horse racing shipboard style
11am	Debarkation talk with your cruise director, Vic Serra
1pm	Passenger talent show sign-up
1–2pm	Music by the pool with Andy Cooney
1:30–2pm	Passengers wishing to visit the Navigation Bridge may do so at this time
2pm	Crazy Legs contest with the cruise staff
2:15pm	Skeetshooting with our staff
2:55pm	Drawing for raffle
3–3:30pm	The Library is open
3pm	Family Feud with the cruise staff
3:45pm	Giant jackpot bonanza bingo
4:30pm	Friends of Bill W. meet in the Library

4:30pm	Afternoon showtime with the magic and illusions of Ronnie Kaye
5–6pm	Cocktail music on deck with Andy Cooney
5:15pm	Passenger talent show
5:30pm	Evening movie: *The Evening Star,* starring Shirley MacLaine
7:30–8:30pm	Join Ariel at the Piano Bar
7:30–8:30pm	Happy hour
7:45pm	Final jackpot bingo
8:45pm	First seating, Showtime: featuring "Night Music" with the Regal Empress Orchestra
9:45pm	Final high-seas horse racing
10pm	Showtime in the Mermaid Lounge with Ewart Williams
10:30pm	Second seating, Showtime: featuring "Night Music"

Dining Hours: Early-Bird Coffee 6:30am • Breakfast 7:30am, 8:45am • Continental Breakfast 8–10am • Buffet Lunch noon–1:30pm • Lunch noon, 1:30pm • Pizza noon–4pm • Ice Cream & Cookies 4–4:45pm • Dinner 6pm, 8:30pm • International Buffet 11:30pm–1:30am

Dress for the Evening: Informal (Please, no shorts in the Dining Room)

ROYAL ⚓ CARIBBEAN.

DAY IN PORT

8am	The *Majesty of the Seas* is due to anchor off George Town, Grand Cayman
8am	Sunrise stretch class
8–10am	Sign up for Saturday's guest talent show
8:30am	Tender tickets are available from the cruise staff commencing at 8:30am in the Blue Skies Lounge
9:15am	Fun fitness (all levels: fun, light, low impact)
10–11am	Daily trivia
10am	Cards and board games available all day
1:30–2:30pm	Sail-away music with "Cruise Control"
2:30pm	Last tender leaves from shoreside
2:30pm	Horse racing at the pool—"The Grand Majesty Derby"
2:45pm	Belly-flop competition
3pm	De-stress clinic
3:15pm–3am	Casino Royale open
3:30–4pm	Preview: Park West art auction at sea

3:30–7pm	Shopping time—Boutiques of the Centrum are now open
3:30pm	Cozumel port and shopping talk
3:45pm	Five-minute makeover
4pm	Ice-carving demonstration
4–5pm	Step aerobics
4–6pm	Auction: Park West art auction at sea
4:15–5:30pm	Bingorama No. 4
4:15–6pm	Music by our steel band, "Cruise Control"
5–5:30pm	Legs, tums, and buns workout
5–5:30pm	Country line dancing
5–6pm	Friends of Bill W. meeting
5:30–8:30pm	Margarita madness!
7:30–8:30pm	Karaoke night
7:45–8:45pm	Join entertainer Clarence Palmer for all your favorite musical requests and fun
9–10pm	Main seating, "Dream Away" with the Wave Revue Singers and Dancers
9pm–1am	Cigar aficionados! Enjoy a quiet moment with good friends, a fine cognac, and a first class cigar
10–11pm	Dance music featuring "Charlie's Swing Band"
10pm–12:30am	Join entertainer Clarence Palmer for all your favorite musical requests and fun
10pm–12:30am	Country-western barn dance with "Pepe"
10:30pm	Stargazing
10:30pm–3am	Dancing to the top discs
10:45–11:45pm	Second seating, "Dream Away" with the Wave Revue Singers and Dancers
11:15pm–12:15am	Dance music featuring "Charlie's Swing Band"
11:30pm–2am	'70s disco inferno
12:30–1:30am	Blue Note jazz

Dining Hours: Early-Bird Coffee 6:30–7am • Breakfast 7–9am • Continental Breakfast 7–10am • Late-Risers Breakfast 7–10am • Luncheon 12:30–2:30pm • Snack Luncheon 2–4pm • Afternoon Snack Service 4–5pm • Dinner 6:15pm, 8:30pm • Italian Galley Buffet 11:45pm–1am • Late-Night Snack 1–6am

Dress for the Evening: Casual or Country and Western

DINNER ENTREES

Pan-Seared Fillet of Halibut • *garnished with sautéed mushrooms and parsley potatoes, served with grilled yellow squash*

Cannelloni with Crabmeat • *served with sautéed fresh vegetables and lobster sauce*

Roasted Pork Loin Scandinavian Style • *natural jus, stuffed with prunes, served with sugar snap peas and parsley potatoes*

Oven-Roasted Crisp Duckling • *served with orange sauce and sugar snap peas with walnuts and croquette potatoes*

Grilled New York Steak • *offered with sugar snap peas, roasted potatoes, and a fresh herb butter*

Indian-Spiced Chickpea and Potato Stew • *served with rice and accompanied by yogurt with minced cucumber, tomato, and cilantro*

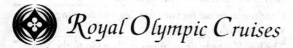

DAY AT SEA

7am	Stretch and tone
7:20am	Deck walk
8am	Catholic liturgy in the Theater
8:30am–12:30pm	The Hospitality Desk opens for information in the Solaris Foyer
8:45am	Sit and be fit
9–10am	The Library is open
9–9:30am	"Today with Carol, Your Cruise Director"
9:30am	Team trivia
9:30am	Video presentation: *Columbus: The Age of Discovery*
9:45–11am	Gym consultations and advice
10:30am	Destinations enhancement lecture: "Historical Role of the Caribbean"
10:30am	Movie presentation: *Witness*
11:30am	Jackpot bingo
11:30am	Bridge lecture
11:45am–12:30pm	Musical cocktails in the Solaris Piano Bar
12:30–1:30pm	Music on deck for your pleasure
1:45pm	Duplicate and rubber play in the Card Room with the Bergs
2pm	Lecture: "The Health Puzzle—Putting the Pieces Together"
2pm	The Hospitality Desk reopens for information
2:30pm	Dance class: "Achey Breaky Revisited"
3pm	Movie presentation: *Legends of the Fall*
3pm	Arts and crafts project: "Magnetic Bookmarks"
3:45pm	"Rhythm and Motion in the Ocean"—upper and lower body toning with rhythmic movements
4–4:30pm	The Library is open

4:30pm	Deck walk
5pm	"Awesome Abdominals with Back Conditioning and Stretching"
6pm	Video presentation: *Columbus: The Age of Discovery*
6:30–7:30pm	Music for dancing in the Solaris Lounge
6:30–7:30pm	Musical happy hour with the Emily Remic Trio
6:45–7:30pm	Billy Dare entertains in the Grill Bar
9–9:45pm	Continuous music for your dancing and listening pleasure with the Starlight Orchestra
10pm	The Ray Kennedy Entertainers in "Just Go to the Movies"
10:30pm	Movie presentation: *Witness*
11pm	Bill Dare begins and goes until the wee hours.
11pm	The Taverna Night Club cranks up with a beat and DJ Apostolis.
11–11:45pm	Continuous music with the Baruelo Trio and the Starlight Orchestra
11pm–midnight	Light night snack buffet

Dining Hours: Early-Risers Coffee & Danish 6:30–7:30am • Breakfast Buffet & À La Carte 7:30–9:30am • Breakfast Buffet 8:30–10am • Hot Bouillion Served 11am • Luncheon 12:30pm • Luncheon Buffet 12:30–2pm • Afternoon Tea 4–5pm • Dinner 7:30 • Light Night Snacks 11pm–midnight

Dress for the Evening: Formal

DINNER ENTREES

Grilled Salmon Fillet, Béarnaise Sauce

Veal Cutlet "Milanese"

Brochette of Chicken and Scallops, Creole Rice

Saffron Risotto, Cottage Cheese

Toasted Almonds and Bean Chutney

Rack of Lamb, Roasted • *with Greek spices*

Souvlakia • *brochette of marinated beef tenderloin*

FIRST-DAY ACTIVITIES

3pm	Embarkation begins. Welcome aboard!
3–10pm	Port talk on St. Barts and Antigua, broadcast on Suite TV channel 7

4:30pm	All ashore who's going ashore! Those sailing should be aboard by this time.
4:30pm	Compulsory lifeboat mustering for all guests
4:45pm	Join the family on deck as Captain Anderssen prepares to depart. Enjoy the music of the Dave Williams Quartet as we sail away.
6:30pm	Enjoy the piano stylings of Jerry Blaine during cocktails
6:45pm	Who's Who! Cruise director welcomes you to the Portofino Bar and introduces our travel manager, cruise consultant, staff managers, and entertainers.
9pm	Join Simo and Debbie for blackjack and slot machine action
9:30pm	Coffee and liqueurs served to the sounds of the Dave Williams Quartet and Jerry Blaine for your listening and dancing pleasure throughout the evening
10:15pm	Musical fun quiz. Jerry and Alan ask the musical questions. Your team could be sipping the prize champagne tonight!

Dining Hours: Dinner 7:30–9:30pm

Dress for the Evening: Casual (jacket for gentlemen) after 6pm

DINNER ENTREES

Fillet of Mahimahi on Herbed Whipped Potatoes, Red Onion Marmalade

Crispy Deep-Fried Squid

Grilled Lemon Chicken on Stir-Fried Vegetables

Baked Garlic-Studded Roast Leg of Lamb "Boulangere"

Mediterranean Eggplant Gratin

DAY IN PORT—TOUR DEPARTURES IN CURAÇAO

8:30–10:30am	Animal Encounter
8:45am	Shoreseeing/Seaquarium/Beach
9am	Curaçao Island/Seaquarium Tour
9:30am	Trolley Tour
12:30pm	Reef Roamer Snorkel Tour

ONBOARD ACTIVITIES

8am	Stretch and relax with your Seawind Crown Dancer
8–8:30am	Seawind Dive Center is open
3–9pm	Steiner Beauty Salon will be open
3:30pm–5:15pm	Sail-away music with "Caribbean Visions"
4pm	Low-impact aerobics
5pm	All aboard!
5:30pm	*Seawind Crown* sails for St. George's, Grenada
6pm	Mandatory lifeboat drill
6:30pm	Friends of Bill W. meet
6:30pm	Casino slots and tables are open
6:30–7:30pm	Music with Caribbean Visions
7–11:30pm	Onboard gift shops open
7:45–8:30pm	Dance to the orchestra
8–11:30pm	Photo Shop opens
8:15–9pm	Happy hour music with "Made in Rio"
8:30pm	Cash bingo!
9:15am	First performance, showtime special: Leroy Schultz (from the world famous Platters)
10:30–11:15pm	Jazz with "Made in Rio"
10:30–11:30pm	Karaoke
11am	Second performance, showtime special: Leroy Schultz (from the world famous Platters)
11:30pm	The Disco opens with our DJ Brian
Midnight	Oriental buffet served
Midnight–1am	Pop, rock, and Latin music with "Made in Rio"
12:15–1am	Oktoberfest! Join the orchestra for a sing-a-long and knees up. Beer drinking festival style with lots of *Ooompa Ooompa Ooompa*.

Dining Hours: Early-Risers Coffee & Danish 6:30–7:30pm • Breakfast 7:30–9:30am • Buffet Breakfast 7:30–10am • Lunch noon, 1:30pm • California Buffet Lunch noon–2pm • Teatime 4–5pm • High Tea (no shorts, please) 4–5pm • Dinner 6:45pm, 9pm • Buffet midnight

Dress for the Evening: Informal

DINNER ENTREES

Lasagna Pomodore • *casserole with layers of semolina pasta, lean beef, and zucchini served with tomato sauce and grated Parmesan cheese*

Broiled Caribbean Grouper Fillet • *served with a cilantro lime butter*

Supreme of Chicken Montego Bay • *marinated grilled chicken breast with fresh thyme*

Jamaican Jerked Pork • *slowly roasted pork loin with authentic seasoning*
Buccaneer Ginger Steak • *sautéed sliced aged kansas beef, onions, and assorted bell peppers in a ginger teriyaki sauce*

STAR CLIPPERS

DAY IN PORT

8–8:30am	Morning fitness on the Tropical Deck
9:45am	Mandatory lifeboat drill for all passengers
10am	The Captain will introduce his officers and staff on the Tropical Deck
10:30am–noon	Sports team hands out snorkeling gear on the Sports Deck
11am	Meeting for certified and noncertified divers in the Library
Noon	"Discover Scuba" theory lesson. If you are interested in trying scuba diving, you should attend this class in the Library.
1pm	*Star Clipper* drops anchor off Hillsborough. A tender service to the island will begin and leave every half hour from the ship.
4pm	"Discover Scuba" practical class in the aft deck pool
4:30pm	Last tender from the beach. Beautiful night sail to Grenada.
5pm	Storytime with Captain Uli on the Sundeck. Information talk on Grenada with Beatrice and Okki.
7–8:30pm	Cocktail hour—Come and join us in the Piano Bar for one of our special early evening cocktails
10pm	Music quiz with Beatrice and Tony in the Piano Bar

Dining Hours: Continental Breakfast 6:30–10am • Buffet Breakfast 8–10am • Luncheon Buffet noon–4pm • Hors d'Oeuvres 5–6pm • Dinner 7:30–9:30pm • Late-Night Snacks 11:30pm–12:30am

Dress for the Evening: Casual

DINNER ENTREES

Fillet of Turbot, Lobster Sauce

Roast Duckling with Grapes and Curaçao Sauce

(Chef's specials are also available each evening)

Tall Ship Adventures doesn't publish daily activity calendars. See the line review in chapter 9 for a description of shipboard life.

DINNER ENTREES

Mahimahi with Scalloped Potatoes and Mixed Veggies

BBQ Chicken and Pork Chops with Rice and Peas

Steak with Oven-Browned Potatoes and Glazed Carrots

Curry Shrimp with White Rice and Peas and Carrots

BBQ Steak/Fish with Cauliflower Cheese Bake and Corn on the Cob

Turkey and Dressing with Mashed Potatoes and Gravy and Mixed Vegetables

Broiled Lobster Tails, Creamed Noodles, and Mixed Veggies

Windjammer Barefoot Cruises doesn't publish daily activity calendars. See the line review in chapter 9 for a description of shipboard life.

DINNER ENTREES

Curried Beef

Grilled Wahoo

Garlic Roast Pork with Guava Sauce

Linguini Bolognese

Prime Ribs

Cornish Game Hens

Coconut Fried Shrimp

DAY IN PORT

6am–midnight	Fitness room and sauna open
7:30am	Sports store is open. Stop by and get your snorkeling gear.
8am	Daily quiz is available at the Reception
8am	*Wind Star* will anchor off Isle des Saintes. Tender service will begin after arrival and run every 30 minutes.
8:15am, 10:30am	Divers meet on Deck 2 aft for your dive
1:30pm–4pm	Sports Platform open. Join Ridlon and Carin for swimming, windsurfing, sailing, water skiing, kayaking, and banana boat rides.
2:30pm	Bridge get-together in the Library
4:30pm	All aboard! The last tender departs from Isle des Saintes.
4:30pm	Meet Ridlon in the lounge for an informal talk on marine conservation
5pm	*Wind Star* sails for Pigeon Island, St. Lucia
6–7pm	Join Stig and Karina in the Casino
6:30–8pm	Cocktails in the lounge with music by Gary and Portia. Join Chef Bill and Chef Helie for caviar and smoked salmon.
7:15pm	Your host Anne will be in the lounge for a briefing on your day tomorrow in Pigeon Island, St. Lucia
9:30pm	Dance to the upbeat sounds of Gary and Portia
9:30pm	Join Stig and Karina in the Casino for blackjack and poker

Dining Hours: Continental Breakfast 6–10am • Breakfast 7:30–9:30am • Lunch 12:30–2pm • Tea 4–5pm • Dinner 7:30–9:15pm

Dress for the Evening: Casual (Please, no shorts, jeans, or tennis shoes in the restaurant.)

DINNER ENTREES

Roasted Duck Breast and Creamy Corn Mash with Green Beans and Ham Hocks

Potato-Crusted Fresh Local Fish with Apple-Braised Leeks and Julienne Fried Green Onions

"Herb and Pepper" Seasoned Prime Rib with Baked Potato and Creamed Horseradish Sauce

Spaghetti Carbonara with Apple-Smoked Bacon and Freshly Grated Parmesan Cheese

Fresh Jerked Flying Fish with a Spicy Remoulade and Chili Yam Fries

Gâteau of Aubergine with a Light Tomato and Tarragon Coulis

Websites

Are you wired? Are you plugged into the Information Super-highway? Do you have a PC perched on your kitchen counter so you can surf while you eat dinner? If so, not only do you really *need* to get away for a while on a nice cruise, but you have the technology to keep up with day-to-day changes at many of the lines we've profiled, via their own handy-dandy Websites. You can check out the fleets, ship itineraries, special promotions, and more, all from the comfort of your own home.

At press time, the lines listed below had established Internet addresses. In addition, we've included a few other interesting and informative sites for your electronic edification.

SITES FROM THE LINES

Carnival	http://www.carnival.com
Celebrity	http://www.celebrity-cruises.com
Clipper	http://www.ecotravel.com/clipper
Commodore	http://www.commodorecruise.com
Cunard	http://www.cunardline.com
Dolphin	http://www.dolphincruise.com
Holland America	http://www.hollandamerica.com
Majesty	http://www.majesty.com
Norwegian	http://www.ncl.com/ncl
Premier	http://www.bigredboat.com
Princess	http://www.princesscruises.com
Regal	http://www.regalcruises.com
Royal Caribbean	http://www.royalcaribbean.com
Royal Olympic	http://www.epirotiki.com
Seawind	http://www.seawindcruises.com
Tall Ship Adventures	http://www.tallshipadventures.com
Windjammer	http://www.windjammer.com
Windstar	http://www.windstarcruises.com

SOME INDEPENDENT SITES

- **ftp://ftp.cdc.gov//pub/ship_inspections/shipscore.txt**
  Twice each year, the CDC (Centers for Disease Control) rates sanitary conditions aboard every vessel that has a foreign itinerary and carries 13 or more passengers. Access this site for the most up-to-date results.

- **AOL Keyword: Cruise Critic**
  Ship reviews, cruise tips, ship recommendations from editor-in-chief Anne Campbell, the latest news and deals, weekly live discussions, and more.

- **http://www.ten-io.com/clia**
  CLIA (Cruise Lines International Association) maintains a Website that lists CLIA-affiliated travel agencies and more.

- **http://www.travelpage.com/cruise/c_news.htm**
  Cruise News lists the latest information direct from the cruise lines. Lots of insider stuff here. Concerned that the ship you want to sail will be sold before you can board? This is the place to get the scoop.

- **http://www.safari.net/~marketc/CruiseShipPage.html**
  Cruise Ship and Cabin Exchange maintains an extremely informative Website that's packed with useful information.

- **http://www.cruisesinc.com**
  Cruises Inc. maintains a Website that lists the latest info on cruise bargains as well as offering "Captain Bob's Cruise Reviews."

- **http://www.fieldingtravel.com/cruiseindex.html**
  Fielding's CruiseFinder Database lists information on every ship under the sun.

Index by Ship

continues

RoyalCaribbean
INTERNATIONAL

A Special Offer for

Frommer's Travelers

This Coupon Entitles You to a

FREE

On Select Ships & Sail Dates

See reverse for restrictions that may apply.
*Redeemable only at Travel Network

For reservations, please call
at 1-888-940-5000 in the U.S.

For reservations, please call  **TRAVEL NETWORK** ®
at 1-888-940-5000 in the U.S.

Terms and conditions

- Offer is not combinable with any existing RCCL promotions/discounts or other discount coupons.
- Upgrades are limited to: INSIDE TO INSIDE CABINS AND OUTSIDE TO OUTSIDE CABINS *Breakthrough Rates* (cruise only or air sea). Upgrades do not apply to Suites and are limited to categories "<u>N through F</u>."
- Rates vary by date and are subject to availability at time of booking.
- Group bookings are NOT eligible & <u>Single</u> and <u>Share</u> guarantees do not apply.
- This offer does not apply to holiday or inaugural sailings.
- Certain restrictions and blackout dates may apply.
- Ships of Norwegian, Liberian Registry.

"The place to go before you go anyplace... globally!" SM

Terms and Conditions

Valid on new bookings only Category 3 and above. Travel must be completed by December 15, 1998. Certain restrictions apply. Not valid with guaranteed promotional rates, group bookings, holiday sailings, Kids Cruise Free promotions, or other offers. Coupon must be submitted with final payment.

Contact Your Local
Professional for More Information.

1-888-940-5000 in the U.S. and
1-905-707-7222 in Canada

☀ TRAVEL NETWORK ®

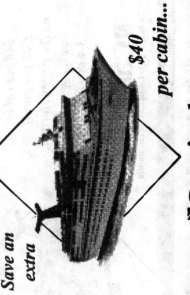

Save an extra

$40
per cabin...

⚓Carnival®
The Most Popular Cruise Line In The World®

Terms and Conditions:

Certificate may be redeemed at any Travel Network® office (call 1-888-940-5000 for the office nearest you), or any other travel agent, and is valid on selected 3, and 4 day Carnival cruises departing between September 1, 1997 and December 15, 1998 Offer valid for bookings made

· Applies to new individual bookings only. Limit one certificate per cabin.
· Not applicable to cruises on Christmas or New Years.
· Offer is capacity controlled and space may be limited on certain cruises. Certain restrictions apply. Specific cruises may be excluded at any time.
· Applies to purchases at the available rates for cabin categories 6 through 12 only.
· Offer is combinable with Carnival's Super Savers discount program
  Not combinable with any other discount or promotional offer.
· Savings for single occupancy bookings is $20 for 3 and 4 day cruises.
· Only original certificates will be accepted. Reproductions will not be accepted.
· Certificate has no cash value and savings amount is expressed in U.S. dollars.
· Certificate must be submitted with deposit payment. Savings amount may not be deducted from deposit amount.
· Ships registered: Panama and Liberia.

Please call Travel Network® in the US at 1-888-940-5000
and in Canada at (905) 7070-7222

TRAVEL NETWORK®

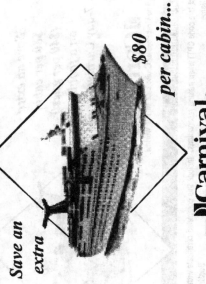

Save an extra

$80

per cabin...

Carnival®
The Most Popular Cruise Line In The World®

Terms and Conditions:

Certificate may be redeemed at any Travel Network® office (call 1-888-940-5000 for the office nearest you), or any other travel agent, and is valid on selected 3, and 4 day Carnival cruises departing between September 1, 1997 and December 15, 1998 Offer valid for bookings made

· Applies to new individual bookings only. Limit one certificate per cabin.
· Not applicable to cruises on the CARNIVAL DESTINY, Christmas or New Years.
· Offer is capacity controlled and space may be limited on certain cruises. Certain restrictions apply. Specific cruises may be excluded at any time.
· Applies to purchases at the available rates for cabin categories 6 through 12 only.
· Offer is combinable with Carnival's Super Savers discount program Not combinable with any other discount or promotional offer.
· Savings for single occupancy bookings is $40 for 7 day cruises.
· Only original certificates will be accepted. Reproductions will not be accepted.
· Certificate has no cash value and savings amount is expressed in U.S. dollars.
· Certificate must be submitted with deposit payment. Savings amount may not be deducted from deposit amount.
· Ships registered: Panama and Liberia.

Please call Travel Network® in the US at 1-888-940-5000 and in Canada at (905) 7070-7222

Terms and Conditoins

Upgrades valid from categories 3-8 and subject to availability Upgrades are not valid from an inside cabin to an outside cabin or to Suites. Cannot be combined with any promotional offer 2 for 1, Sail of the Day, etc.). Not valid for group bookings. Valid on new bookings only. Travel must be completed by December 15, 1998. Coupon must be submitted at time of final payment.

Terms and Conditions

Valid on bookings made on catergories A-I only. Travel must be completed by December 15, 1998. Not valid with guaranteed promotional rates, group bookings, holiday sailings, or combinable with other offers. Certain restrictions apply. Coupon must be submitted with final payment

Terms and Conditions

Offer is applicable to all new bookings on departures for the following programs:

1997-98 Caribbean Program
(excluding Rotterdam 6 & Holiday sailings.)

1997 Fall Panama Canal Program

1997-98 Alaska Cruises & Cruisetours

1997-98 Canada/England Program

1998 Panama Canal Program
(excluding Rotterdam 6 sailings)

Valid now through December 1, 1998

Category exclusions:
WE: S,A,B
RO/NO/NA: A,B
VE/RY/SA/MA: PS, S, A, B

Upgrade is based on availability and capacity control. May be withheld from specific sailings at any time. Offer is not combinable with other upgrade offers applicable to these sailings or cruise night certificates or shipboard credits in excess of $50 per person. Offer is not applicable with tiered rate promotions, 3rd/4th passengers or single share programs. Valid for group sales. Single occupancy rates apply, as published in the most current Holland America Line brochure. Home City Air add-ons available, as published in the most current Holland America Line Brochure.

DLYSQ7/29/1782/U

INSTRUCTIONS FOR REDEMPTION

1. To expedite service, please have your travel dates and times ready for the reservation agent. We suggest you call an airline prior to calling Travel Network so you are aware of current published air fares.

2. Call Travel Network toll free at 1-888-940-5000 in the U.S or 1-905-707-7222 in Canada and advise agent you hold a TRAVEL NETWORK FROMMER GUIDE AIR COUPON.

3. All tickets must be purchased by credit card or cashier's check within 24 hours of receiving air fare. quote.

4. Your Travel Network agent will give you the address to mail the coupon.

TERMS AND CONDITIONS

1. This offer is valid for discounts on published round-trip fares on most airlines. Reservation and ticket purchases must be made through Travel Network. Air Discount coupons are valid for flights originating within the 48 contiguous United States to destinations in the contiguous 48 United States and select cities in Alaska, Hawaii, Europe, Mexico and Caribbean.

2. Travel Network reserves the right to select the airline carrier and to make reservations based on Travel Network's availability outside the stated blackout dates. Reservations require a 14 to 21 day advance purchase and a Saturday night stay to receive a discount. Some airlines may not allow discounts on flights originating from their respective hub cities. The maximum discount allowed is $100.00 per ticket. The maximum discount to Hawaii, Mexico and the Caribbean is $75.00

3. The minimum purchase amount for an airline ticket is $189.00 for discounts to apply. The minimum purchase applies to round-trip ticket, (coach class only) and may not be combined with any other coupon, certificate or voucher, student's fare, child's fare, group fare, senior discount program, frequent flyer award program or airline industry discount program.

4. Discounts are applied to fares before application of any taxes, passenger facility charges, governmental fees, and security charges, if applicable. Once redeemed, your Air Discount coupon cannot be reused and will not be replaced if stolen or lost. This offer is void if coupon is duplicated in any way.

5. Use of Sky Values coupon is not valid where prohibited by law.

6. All tickets issued are non-refundable, non-transferable and subject to change fees.

7. Blackout Dates: 1997: May 23,26; July 2-7; Aug. 29; Sept. 1,2; Nov. 25-30; Dec. 1, 15-31. / 1998: Jan 1-5; Feb. 12-19; Apr. 9-13; May 22-26. Reservations for travel in 1998 cannot be accepted before October 15, 1997. Some discounts may be available during stated blackout dates on some airlines while other unstated blackouts may be in effect during certain holiday periods on some airlines.

8. Travel Network is the final authority on interpretation of these Terms and Conditions.

Call Toll Free in the U.S
1-888-940-5000
and in Canada
1-905-707-7222

WHEREVER YOU TRAVEL, *H*ELP IS NEVER FAR AWAY.

From planning your trip to providing travel assistance along the way, American Express® Travel Service Offices are always there to help.

Caribbean Ports of Call

Mundy Tours (R)
Suite 20, Regent Center 4
Freeport, Bahamas
809/352-4444

Playtours (R)
303 Shirley Street
Nassau, Bahamas
809/322-2931

Boulevard Travel (R)
811 Peacock Plaza
Key West, Florida
305/251-7454

Southerland Tours (R)
Chandlers Wharf Gallows Bay
St. Croix, USVI
809/773-9500

Caribbean Travel Agency, Inc./Tropic Tours (R)
14AB The Guardian Bldg.
St. Thomas, USVI
809/774-1855

Travel

http://www.americanexpress.com/travel

American Express Travel Service Offices are found in central locations throughout the Caribbean.